LIVING WITH COMPUTERS

LIVING WITH COMPUTERS

Patrick G. McKeown
University of Georgia

HBJ

Harcourt Brace Jovanovich, Publishers

San Diego New York Chicago Austin
London Sydney Toronto

DEDICATION

To the memory of my father
Maxwell B. McKeown, 1912–1984.

ISBN: 0-15-551133-5
(IBM) 0-15-551135-1
(Apple) 0-15-551134-3

Library of Congress Catalog Card Number: 85-60872
Printed in the United States of America

Illustrations by Robert Yochum and Cheryl Mayville.

Illustration and picture credits appear on pages 622–25, which constitute a continuation of the copyright page.

PREFACE

Today, society finds itself in an information age, in which the manipulation, storage, and movement of information are extremely important. The keystone of the information age is the computer, a machine that can accomplish many new tasks but at the same time is blamed for many problems. Because the computer is so important in the information age, people must have some degree of computer literacy. The term *computer literacy* means many things to many people, but in this textbook it means a user's understanding of what a computer can and cannot do and his or her ability to make it perform specific tasks.

In *Living with Computers*, the prospective user approaches the computer as a tool—specifically, a mind tool that can extend the capabilities of the user's mind to accomplish many more things than is otherwise humanly possible. As a tool, the computer is used the way that a typewriter, a tape deck, or a camera is used. In each case—computer, typewriter, tape deck, or camera—students need not be experts on the internal mechanism of the tool to be successful users.

An instructional package that makes the student a successful user of computers must have an integrated, flexible approach that blends all the pieces of the total package. The *Living with Computers* package is the result of such an approach. The complete package includes this textbook, a software package, and a comprehensive set of ancillaries—an Instructor's Manual, a Study Guide, a Test Book, and Teaching Transparencies.

The Textbook

Living with Computers is a textbook for the introductory course in computers, which may be called computer literacy, data processing, or introduction to computers. Flexible presentation of the material allows an instructor to choose the chapter sequence that fits his or her specific needs. This choice of sequence is aided by the division of the book into blocks of chapters, with each block covering an essential segment of computing. In addition to this flexible presentation, *Living with Computers* offers the following features:

- Direct link between the text and the HBJ software package.
- Integration of information on personal computers into all chapters.
- Boxed inserts containing historical material, current insights and applications, and the viewpoints of industry leaders.
- A special personal computer buyer's guide.
- Hundreds of full-color photographs and drawings; Study Objectives that open each chapter; a Review of Key Points and a list of Key Terms that summarize chapter contents; and Review Questions that allow students to assess their understanding of the chapter material.

Flexibility

A description of the flexibility of the textbook begins with the two purposes of Block 1, A Short Course in Computer Literacy. First, because this initial block has introductory chapters on hardware, software, computer systems, and the societal implications of computers, it is a self-contained discussion of computer literacy. Block 1 can be read entirely before students progress to any detailed block. Second, Chapters 2–5 in the initial block are each an introduction to a block of chapters later in the book. As soon as Chapter 2, 3, 4, or 5 is covered, students can immediately cover the corresponding block of material, as shown in the diagram on the next page. Instructors can assign the chapters in a detailed block in almost any order.

Block 2, The Details of Hardware—including chapters on the CPU/internal memory, input/output, and secondary storage—may be covered after students read Chapter 2. Block 3, Software Packages, contains chapters on operating systems, word processing and graphics packages, spreadsheet analysis and accounting packages, data

MODULAR APPROACH TO COMPUTER LITERACY

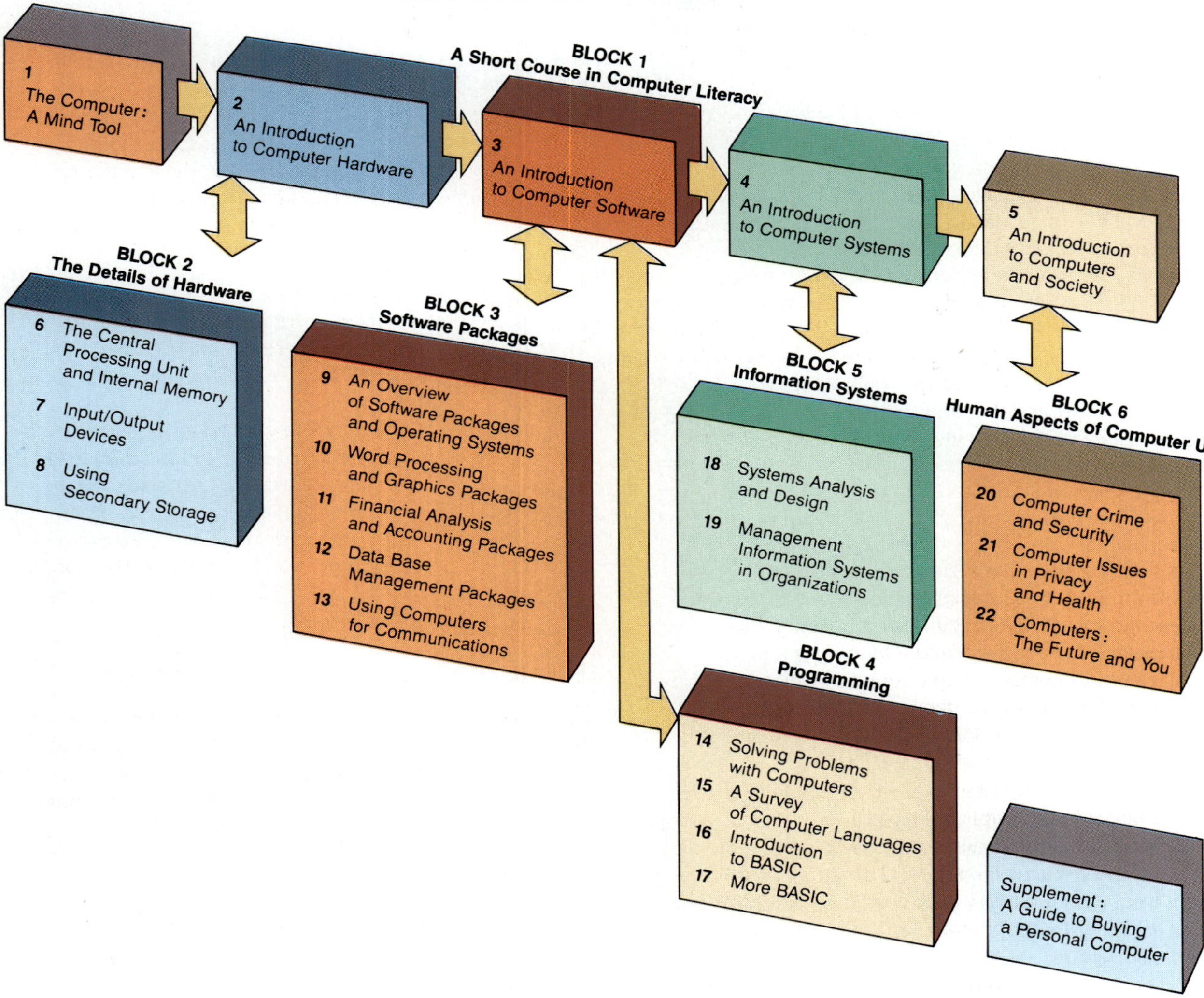

base management packages, and communications software packages. This software package block provides a detailed discussion of the use of computers by nonprogrammers to solve problems or accomplish tasks. Tutorials on the use of the HBJ software package appear after Chapters 10–13 in this block. Block 4, Programming, presents a structured approach to writing computer programs, an overview of popular computer languages, and a two-chapter discussion of the BASIC language. Blocks 3 and 4 may be covered after students read Chapter 3. Block 5, Information Systems, contains a chapter on the systems analysis and design process and a chapter on management information systems. This block may be covered after Chapter 4 is read. Block 6, Human Aspects of Computer Use, includes chapters that cover computer crime and security problems, issues in privacy and health, and the future of computers and computer careers. Block 6 may be covered after students read Chapter 5.

Integration of Software

The software package that accompanies *Living with Computers* was planned, designed, and written concurrently with the textbook and the ancillaries. As a result, the software is completely integrated into the text and ancillaries, which contain sample screens from the software, in-text examples that involve the use of the software, and tutorials on the use of the software. This software package includes word processing, spreadsheet analysis, data base management, graphics, personal budgeting, and telecommunications. Simplicity of use was a major consideration in software development, and prepublication testing has shown that the package is easy for computer novices to use. The software can be used on the IBM PC or the Apple IIe or IIc computers.

Integration of Information about Personal Computers

Because of its ever-increasing availability, the personal computer must play a large role in any computer literacy textbook. In *Living with Computers,* the personal computer is not treated as a special type of computer that is dealt with in a separate chapter. Discussion of the personal computer and its software is integrated throughout the text with the discussion of mainframe computers. Block 3, Software Packages, is especially oriented toward the personal computer because applications software for personal computers is widely available. However, the continuing importance of the large computers is emphasized.

Boxed Inserts

Each chapter of the text contains numerous boxed inserts, which present historical material pertinent to the chapter, insights into computer use, selected computer applications, or views on chapter topics expressed by computer industry leaders.

A unique set of boxed inserts titled Another View presents the opinions of various computer industry leaders. Five such individuals were personally interviewed by the author, and excerpts from these interviews appear as boxed inserts. Interviews from the news media were excerpted for use as boxed inserts or as marginal quotations. The Another View boxes and the marginal quotations give students an insider's view of the computer industry.

The Guide to Buying a Personal Computer

A special Guide to Buying a Personal Computer appears in *Living with Computers* to help students make a personal computer purchase. The buyer's guide, which may be read after the first three chapters, emphasizes the logic behind the personal computer purchase decision rather than particular types of machines or software. The step-by-step procedure presented should help students make appropriate decisions based on their needs, regardless of new technology.

Chapter Components

Each chapter in *Living with Computers* begins with a set of Study Objectives and ends with a Review of Key Points. The Study Objectives are a list of the points that will be covered in the chapter, and the Review of Key Points summarizes the chapter material. The instructor will find both sections useful in preparing lectures, and the student will find them helpful in preparing for examinations. Each chapter is enhanced by full-color photographs and drawings that highlight the text discussion. The Key Terms section at the end of every chapter lists the new terms introduced in each chapter. (A Glossary at the end of the book defines all key terms and notes their chapter location.) A set of Review Questions reflects the major points covered and allows students to assess their mastery of the chapter information.

The Software

A set of six personal computer software programs is available with *Living with Computers.* Planned and designed specifically for this text, the software includes word processing (HBJ: WRITE), graphics (HBJ: GRAPH), spreadsheet analysis (HBJ: PLAN), data base management (HBJ: FILE), personal budgeting (HBJ: BUDGET), and telecommunications (HBJ: TALK).

The HBJ software was designed especially for the person who is new to computers. Although the primary objective was ease of use, the software reflects major concepts and operations of corresponding commercial software. The result is a package that allows a new user to learn about today's popular software packages.

HBJ: WRITE allows the user to create, edit, print, or save a document of up to 150 lines. Longer documents may easily be created by chaining small documents together. The user may view all commands by pressing a single key. The menu-driven HBJ: GRAPH package allows the user to create, view, save, or print a bar graph, a pie chart, a scatter diagram, and a line graph. HBJ: PLAN is a 26 x 26 spreadsheet with commands always available to the user in a command line. All arithmetic operations can be included in formulas, and the resulting spreadsheet can be saved or printed as needed. HBJ: FILE can manage up to 100 records that each contain up to five fields. The records can be sorted, searched, saved, or printed using a menu-driven system. HBJ: BUDGET enables the user to manage his or her personal finances—including setting up a budget, entering transactions, and reconciling checks—all through a menu-driven system. HBJ: TALK is a unique package that simulates the access to an information service. A communications simulator was developed because student users may not have either a modem or a user account available to them. The user obtains experience in dialing an information service, entering a user number and password, and choosing from a menu of options on the information service.

The HBJ software package is an important tool for instructors who are introducing the world of applications software to students. *Living with Computers* contains tutorials on the use of the software, and the Study Guide to accompany *Living with Computers* has more examples showing the use of the programs. The Instructor's Manual to accompany *Living with Computers* also contains suggestions for the instructor on how to use the software package. Finally, Teaching Transparencies contain examples of software use that match those discussed in the tutorials in the text. Students should be able to transfer their experience with the HBJ software directly to most comparable commercial software.

The Ancillaries

The *Living with Computers* package contains a complete set of ancillaries, including an Instructor's Manual, a Study Guide, a Test Book, and more than 100 Teaching Transparencies. The complete package offers an instructor everything needed to teach the computer literacy course.

The Instructor's Manual has the following teaching aids for each chapter in the text: a teaching objective for the instructor, a set of learning objectives for students, a chapter review, a list of teaching suggestions, a list of suggested readings, and answers to the Review Questions at the end of the text chapter. The suggested readings section contains references to current books and articles that pertain to the topics covered in the text. These readings and the teaching suggestions based on the author's experience can be helpful in preparing lectures or developing class projects.

The Study Guide by Robert D. Brown, University of

Georgia, contains many elements that will help students in the introductory computer course. Each chapter of the Study Guide contains a Chapter Review and a series of multiple choice, true-false, matching, and short answer questions for every chapter in the text. The Chapter Review summarizes the material covered in the text chapter, emphasizing the key terms. The questions allow students to test their comprehension of chapter material. The answers to the questions appear at the end of each Study Guide chapter. The Study Guide also offers students information on the use of the software. These tutorials include one or more examples that clearly demonstrate an actual application of the software package.

Prepared by George Bohlen of the University of Dayton, the Test Book contains over 2,000 multiple choice, fill-in, and short answer test items that can be used to prepare quizzes or examinations. The test items cover all important concepts and terminology in the textbook.

The Teaching Transparencies are composed of more than 70 two-color transparencies and 30 four-color transparencies. The transparencies may be used as part of a lecture to demonstrate important concepts, including the use of the HBJ software package.

Acknowledgments

The writing and production of *Living with Computers* was not just the work of one person. It was a team effort that involved many people.

I am very appreciative to several people for the help they afforded me during the writing of this text. I received help on numerous technical aspects of the computer from Dennis Calbos, Mike Ellerson, Roy Green, and Bob Sterns of the University of Georgia computer center. Bob also offered a wealth of historical knowledge. Charles Turner of the College of Business Administration was of great help in preparing the computer programs in Chapter 15. Al Leitch of the University of Alabama was a great aid in the preparation of the systems chapters, and Robert Brown of the University of Georgia made sure the software actually worked as designed.

I wish to express my appreciation to the following reviewers for their careful reading of the manuscript and their thought-provoking comments: George A. Bohlen, University of Dayton; Robert D. Brown, University of Georgia; Nancy Lee Cameron, Corpus Christi State University; William R. Cornette, Southwest Missouri State University; Patricia Fouts, Virginia Polytechnic Institute; Robert S. Fritz, American River College; and Douglas R. Vogel, University of Minnesota. The final product reflects many of their ideas.

I want to thank all the people who were involved in the editing and production of the text. I had almost daily contact with three people who did an outstanding job. Peggy Monahan worked on virtually every editorial and production phase of this project from beginning to end. Johanna Schmid performed many roles on the project, but her particular efforts on the ancillaries have resulted in the final package. The software development was under the direction of Janet Wise, who ensured that the resulting product met our needs. I would also like to thank Ellen Aleksic and Harlan Bleecker for their careful production editing; Lynn Edwards for her expert management of the entire production process; Elizabeth Ely of InfoEdit for her extensive photo research; Eleanor Garner for her help in obtaining reprint permissions; Cynthia Gilham for her work on the software; Susan Holtz for her meticulous coordination of the art program; Linell Maloney for her board work during the dummy process; Pamela Morehouse for her thoughtful page layouts; and Cheryl Solheid for her attractive interior and cover designs. I want to thank the two editors who worked with me on this project. Charles McCormick inspired me to write the book, helped me plan the project, and directed the initial review process. Marlane Agriesti filled in admirably to finish up the reviewing process.

No acknowledgments would be complete without the mention of my wife, Carolyn, who read and edited the first draft of every chapter. She was also the author of the innovative section on the health aspects of computer use. Without her love and support—and that of Ashley and Chris—I could not have completed this project.

Patrick G. McKeown

CONTENTS

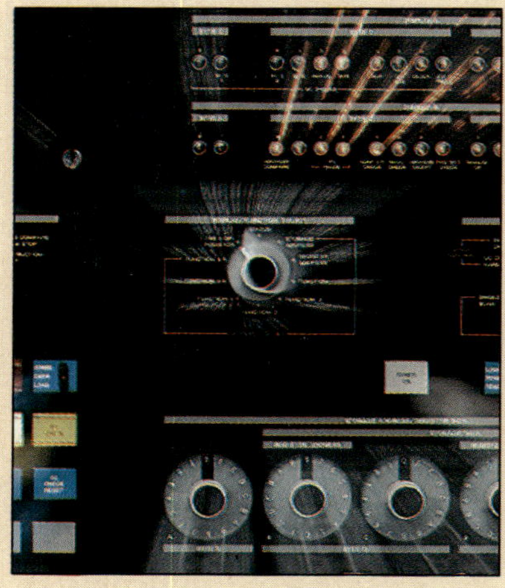

R 口
D 木
F 火
X 造/難
C 金

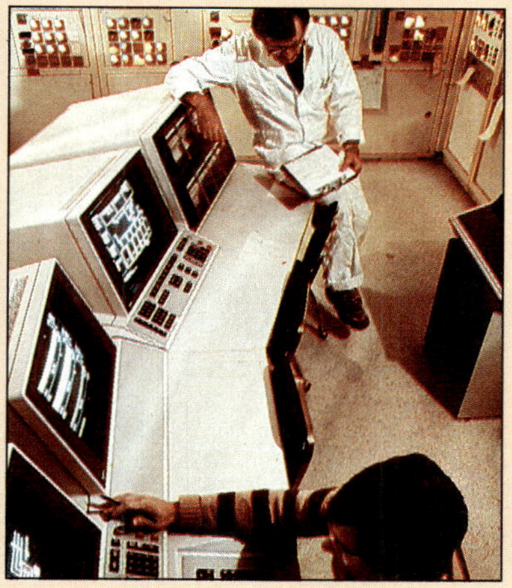

12 Data Base Management Packages 295

13 Using Computers for Communications 325

BLOCK 4 Programming 355

14 Solving Problems with Computers 357

15 A Survey of Computer Languages 385

16 Introduction to BASIC 417

17 More BASIC 441

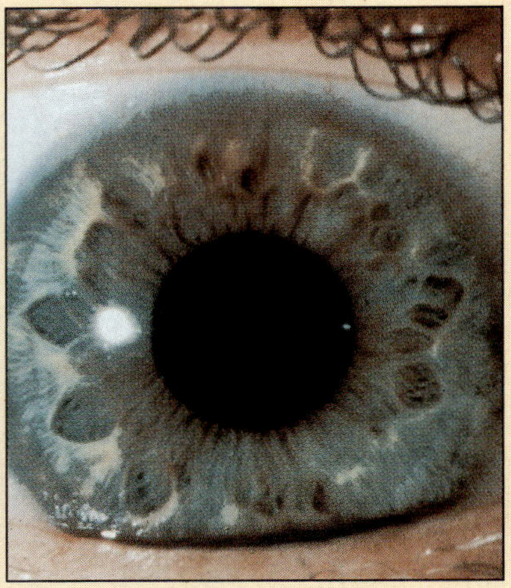

21
Computer Issues in Privacy and Health 555

22
Computers: The Future and You 579

LIVING WITH COMPUTERS

Block 1

A SHORT COURSE IN COMPUTER LITERACY

Block 1 of this text briefly covers the field known as computer literacy. This short course in computer literacy introduces the computer and some computer terminology. Becoming *computer literate* involves not only learning *about* computers but also learning how to *use* computers as a tool to make our jobs easier and to extend the reach of our minds.

Block 1 also serves as a preview of the remaining sections of the book. After Chapter 1, each chapter in this block is a lead-in to another block later in the book. Therefore, after reading this first block of chapters, you can jump right into any other block without reading the intervening blocks. Block 2, The Details of Hardware, continues the discussion of hardware begun in Chapter 2. Block 3, Software Packages, and Block 4, Programming, continue the introductory discussion of software in Chapter 3. Block 5, Information Systems, provides more detail of the initial discussion of systems given in Chapter 4. Block 6, Human Aspects of Computer Use, elaborates on the survey of that topic given in Chapter 5.

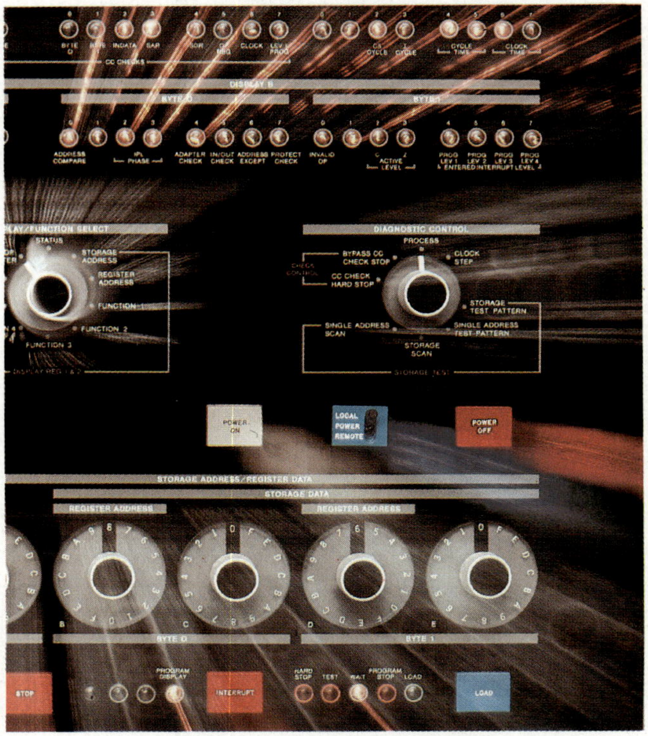

ADDRESS COMPARE
IPL PHASE
ADAPTER CHECK
IN/OUT CHECK
ADDRESS EXCEPT
PROTECT CHECK
INVALID OP
ACTIVE LEVEL
PROG LEV 1
PROG LEV 2
PROG LEV 3
PROG LEV 4
ENTERED INTERRUPT LEVEL
DIAGNOSTIC CONTROL
PROCESS
BYPASS CC CHECK STOP
CLOCK STEP
CC CHECK HARD STOP
STORAGE TEST PATTERN
SINGLE ADDRESS SCAN
SINGLE ADDRESS TEST PATTERN
STORAGE SCAN
STATUS
STORAGE ADDRESS
REGISTER ADDRESS
FUNCTION 1
FUNCTION 2
FUNCTION 3
POWER ON
LOCAL POWER REMOTE
POWER OFF
STORAGE ADDRESS/REGISTER DATA
STORAGE DATA
REGISTER ADDRESS
REGISTER ADDRESS
STOP
INTERRUPT
LOAD

This chapter provides an overview of the role of computers in our lives and discusses the concept of the computer as a **mind tool**—that is, a device that can ease the mind's labor and help the mind extend its creative capabilities. The first section of the chapter explains what a computer is, discusses its possibilities and limitations, and introduces the first words of your new vocabulary of computer terminology. The computer's many uses in today's world and the emergence of the personal computer are then discussed. The various definitions of computer literacy are discussed, along with the importance of computer literacy. After reading this chapter, you should have a good understanding of what a computer can and cannot do, as well as a sound beginning vocabulary of computer terminology.

1

The Computer: A Mind Tool

STUDY OBJECTIVES

After reading this chapter, you should be able to

- Understand the concept of the computer as a mind tool.
- Identify the different types of computers and discuss the components of the computer.
- Appreciate both the possibilities and limitations of a computer.
- Recognize the many ways in which the computer affects your life.
- Explain why computers are now so readily available.
- See how a personal computer may be used in school, home, and business.
- Discuss various definitions of computer literacy.

THE COMPUTER AS A MIND TOOL

In *Megatrends,* his popular book on the direction of Western society, John Naisbitt discusses the many trends that currently affect our lives. One important concept that he presents is the **information society**—that is, a society in which the majority of the workers are involved in the transmittal of information. Naisbitt notes that we have undergone a transition from an agrarian society to an industrial society to the current information society. The tools for such a society have existed for some time. These tools include the adding machine, the typewriter, the file cabinet, the television, and the telephone. The adding machine helps us work with numbers, the typewriter facilitates our work with characters, the file cabinet stores information in an easily retrievable fashion, the television portrays our ideas as pictures, and the telephone allows us to communicate with others instantaneously. However, the key element in the transition from an industrial society to an information society is a "wonder" that performs all these tasks—the computer. The agrarian society depended on the metal plow and wheel, and the industrial society depended on the steam engine. The information society depends on the computer. Because the computer facilitates the work of the mind rather than manual labor, we refer to it as a mind tool—that is, a tool that extends, but does not replace, the human mind.

The key idea behind the computer as a mind tool is that it performs *all* of the operations performed by the adding machine, typewriter, file cabinet, television, and telephone. On a computer, we can manipulate numbers as we do on a calculator (add, subtract, divide, multiply, and so on), we can manipu-

Data processing professionals use such tools as large-screen graphics monitors, terminals, and touch pads.

late letters of the alphabet as we do on a typewriter, and we can have the computer draw pictures based on these manipulations. Any of these symbols may be stored within the computer. Finally, we can communicate with other computer users over a telephone line. If a computer can do all of these things, just exactly how would it be described? Briefly, a **computer** is a machine that stores and manipulates symbols based on a series of user instructions called a program. This ability to execute a list of instructions differentiates the computer from a calculator or other office machines.

In addition to the computer's ability to perform all these tasks, two important characteristics of the computer make it the catalyst that generated the information society. These characteristics are speed and accuracy. The speed of a computer's operations is measured in *nanoseconds*—billionths of a second—and the computer does *exactly* what it is instructed to do. These two characteristics can also lead to problems when the computer is given the wrong instructions. In this case, the computer quickly performs incorrect operations!

Because the computer can perform so many tasks so quickly, some understanding of the principles underlying its operation is necessary. However, it is not necessary to become a computer scientist to use a computer effectively. The computer may be used in the same way that a typewriter or camera is used, without an in-depth understanding of its inner or peripheral operations.

There's a pervasive thought that people have to know *how* computers work to deal with them. It's not so—they need to know *what* computers can do for them and how computers can help them. Once people understand how the computer can be used as a tool to help them, they will indeed use them.

Robert Contino, President of Exxon Office Systems

(As quoted in "Unmasking Some Myths about Computer Literacy," *Modern Office Technologies*, June 1984, p. 118.)

Parts of the Computer

It is useful to understand the important parts of a computer and how they interact to perform its various operations. The two main parts of a computer are the machinery and the human-provided logic. The computer's machinery, or **hardware**, is made up of electronic devices and circuits. The human-provided logic is also called the computer's **software**. The hardware is itself fast and accurate, but hardware can do *nothing* without software. The software, made up of one or more **programs**, is a series of instructions to the computer, and the process of developing the software is **programming**.

Two terms that are often associated with computers are data and information. **Data** are the raw facts that are fed into the computer for processing, and **information** is data that has been processed into a form that is useful to the user. Data can be in the form of numbers, letters of the alphabet, or any other type of symbol, and information is often in the form of tables or reports. Because of this terminology, the operations that the computer performs are often referred to as **data processing**.

An important thing to remember is that *it is not necessary to learn programming to be a computer user*. At one time, this was not true, and every user also had to be a proficient programmer. Now, an increasing amount of commercially available software performs many commonly needed tasks. The **computer package** that contains this commercial software includes an explanation of the software as well as instructions for its use. With computer packages, the computer is now available to everyone, not just to people who take the time to learn programming.

Types of Computers

Computers can be classified in several ways. Here, we classify computers by size, by the type of logic they use, and by purpose.

In terms of size, computers can be broadly classified into three types—mainframes, microcomputers (also called personal computers), and mini-

EARLY ATTEMPTS AT A MIND TOOL

Humans have always tried to make the basic operations of writing and counting easier. This first successful counting device was the Chinese abacus, which is very fast in the hands of an experienced operator. After the Renaissance in Europe, individuals concentrated on building machines that could perform arithmetic operations. In 1614, John Napier of Scotland invented logarithms and the slide rule. In 1643, Blaise Pascal of France created a machine that could add and subtract. In 1673, Gottfried Wilhelm von Leibnitz of Germany developed a calculator that could multiply.

The first attempt at anything that approaches our definition of a computer occurred in 1820 when Englishman Charles Babbage built a machine to make arithmetic computations. His Difference Engine was a special purpose device for calculating the values of polynomials of the form $x^2 + 3x + 20$ to an accuracy of six places. After this success, Babbage tried to develop a much more sophisticated device—the **Analytical Engine**—which would be able to perform any type of arithmetic calculation. The crucial conceptual breakthrough in the Analytical Engine was that it could *store* the series of operations to be made. Babbage was aided by Lady Ada Lovelace, the daughter of the English poet, Lord Byron. Lovelace described Babbage's ideas clearly in written form, supplementing notes on his work with ideas of her own. Unfortunately, the technology of the time was not advanced enough for Babbage to build his machine, which used gears and wheels to carry out the necessary logic. A model that was built later from his plans worked as Babbage claimed it would.

Many of the ideas of Babbage and Lovelace were very advanced. In fact, if the technology had been available to build Babbage's Analytical Engine in 1840, the computer might have been developed 100 years earlier than it was. As an example of their farsighted ideas, consider this quote from Lovelace, which can also be applied to modern computers:

The Analytical Engine has no pretension whatever to originate anything. It can do whatever we know how to order it to perform. It can follow analysis; but it has no way of anticipating any analytical relations or truths. Its province is to assist us in making available what we are already acquainted with.

For her tireless effort on this "grandfather" of the modern computer, Lady Lovelace has been honored by having a computer language, ADA, named after her.

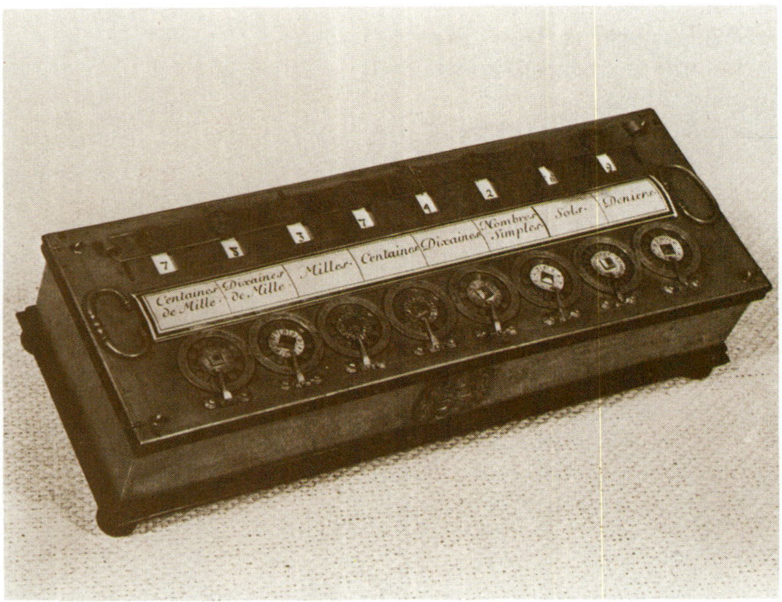

Pascal's adding machine, called the Pascaline, used wheels and gears to add and subtract numbers.

Babbage's Difference Engine was designed to compute mathematical tables.

A mainframe computer (left) can support multiple users and computing activities. A minicomputer (right) can serve many computing needs that do not require the power and speed of a mainframe.

computers. A **mainframe** is a very large and expensive computer (usually costing over $1 million) that requires a special support staff and a special physical environment (for example, an air conditioned area). Mainframes are usually housed in a computer center. Mainframes are generally used in large business, governmental, or academic situations because they can support multiple users (usually in excess of 100 at one time) and multiple functions. **Microcomputers**, or **personal computers**, are small, one-user computers that are relatively inexpensive ($1,000–$5,000) and that do not require a special environment or special knowledge to use them. They fit on a desk top, so they are sometimes referred to as **desk-top computers**. Microcomputers can be programmed or used by one user in a manner very similar to that of mainframes, but they are slower and cannot store nearly as much data as a mainframe. The computer size between a mainframe and a personal computer is the **minicomputer**, which is used mostly by medium-sized businesses and in special academic situations. A minicomputer can support multiple users and often requires a special environment and some support staff, but not on the same level as a mainframe. Currently, the size difference between personal computers and minicomputers is getting hazy as personal computers become more powerful and can support multiple users (so-called *supermicros*). Generally, a computer that fits on a desk or table is a personal computer; otherwise, it is a minicomputer or mainframe. In the remainder of this text, we will refer either to mainframes or personal computers. Minicomputers are included under the broad label of mainframe.

The personal computer, which does not require a specialized knowledge of computing, can be used in almost any environment.

In terms of type of logic used, a computer can be either a digital computer or an analog computer. A **digital computer** uses numbers and is therefore a *counting machine*. An **analog computer** uses physical relationships and is a *measuring machine*. Analog computers are often used to convert physical measurements into values. An example of an analog device is an automobile speedometer, which converts the voltage generated by the automobile's drive shaft (a physical measurement) into miles per hour (a value). Digital computers are far more commonly used; analog computers are used for situations in which physical relationships are involved.

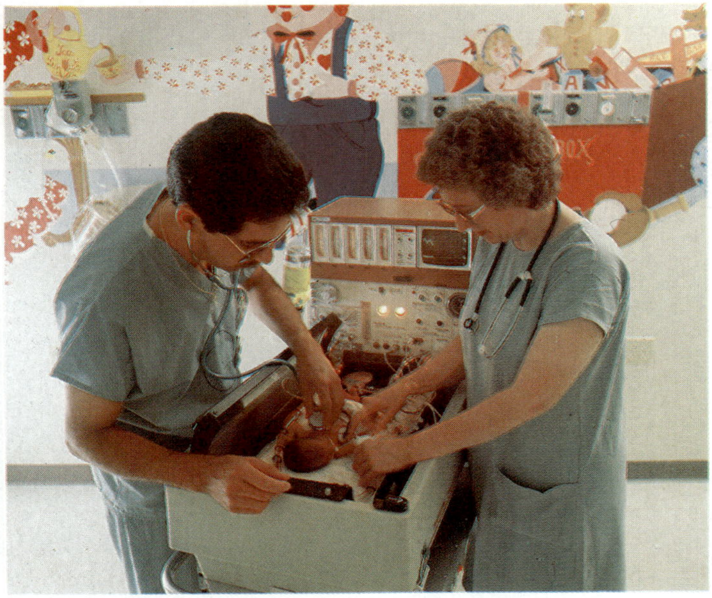

Computers can be classified as analog or digital and as special purpose or general purpose. Fuel pumps (left) utilize analog computers to convert the amount of pumped fuel to a digital value—the price in dollars and cents. Special purpose computers, such as the highly technical equipment used in this neonatal nursery (right), are designed for only one purpose.

In terms of purpose, computers can be classified as special purpose or general purpose. A **special purpose computer** is designed for only one purpose. The computers used for arcade games or for guiding NASA's space shuttles are examples of special purpose computers that cannot be used for other purposes. A **general purpose computer** can be used for many purposes. For example, the same general purpose computer may be used to play games, to handle payroll computations, to use graphics to design buildings, or to solve complex mathematical problems.

In this text, primary attention is given to general purpose digital computers, because most people encounter this type of computer in their work and studies. We also give special attention to the personal computer, because of its growing availability and uses.

COMPUTER-PHOBIA

The increasing use of computers has resulted in a curious side-effect known as **computer-phobia**—the fear of computers. The malady (also known as *cyber-phobia* or *terminal phobia*) occurs in about 30% of students and workers who must contend with the computer for the first time. The symptoms of computerphobia are nervousness, uneasiness, or tension when the affected individual is confronted with a computer. The causes of computerphobia are variously described as fear of change, fear of machines (especially if they can handle the sophisticated tasks that computers do), fear of breaking the computer, frustration with a machine that tends to stop for unknown reasons, fear of job loss, discomfort with the impersonal nature of computers, and an inability to use the keyboard. Several studies have revealed that people who are computerphobes often transfer from a company that is in the process of computerization to a company that has not yet gone through the process. Some people even change professions to avoid using computers. This problem has been blamed on the fact that the current work force is the first to have to come to grips with computers. The problem of computerphobia should disappear when today's kids, who have grown up with computers and video games, move into the work force.

In *2001: A Space Odyssey*, HAL assumed control of the space ship and killed all but one of the human occupants.

Limitations of the Computer

Although the computer is very fast and accurate, it does have definite limitations. A computer *cannot* think and reason. A computer can only do what it is instructed to do by its user. If either the software or the data are incorrect, then the results from the computer are also incorrect. This situation has been described as a **computer error**. However, this term itself is in error, because the problem is not with the computer, but with the instructions it receives from the human using the computer. The acronym GIGO, meaning garbage in, garbage out, also describes this process. When you receive an incorrect bill or are charged an incorrect amount by a computerized checkout system, the machine is not the problem; the problem lies with the human using the computer.

A great deal of research is going on in the field known as **artificial intelligence**, but no design exists for developing a true-to-life version of the famous computer HAL from the movie *2001: A Space Odyssey*. In that story, HAL could reason and eventually took over the space ship. Even in Hal's case, as we learn in the sequel, *2010: The Year We Make Contact,* the problem was caused by humans.

THE COMPUTER IN THE WORLD AROUND US

It is difficult to find an area of business, finance, industry, government, agriculture, education, health care, sports, recreation, or our personal lives that the computer has not influenced. Rarely does a day go by without news of another application of the computer in some new area. In 1982, *Time* magazine selected the computer as its "Machine of the Year," replacing the magazine's usual "Man of the Year." The computer was chosen for this honor because the editors of *Time* perceived it as the biggest newsmaker of that year. In some ways, this was a "coming of age" for the computer and our first acknowledgment of its impact on our lives. The effect of the computer has continued to increase since 1982, as evidenced by the contin-

The naming of the computer as *Time* magazine's Machine of the Year signified the computer's "coming of age."

ued front page articles in newspapers and by stories in magazines and other media. The following list of computer applications is merely an overview. Specific applications are discussed in detail in later chapters.

Business Applications We are familiar with many business uses of computers that affect our everyday lives—such as computerized mailing lists and billings—but many other behind-the-scenes uses of the computer exist in business. The bills and letters we receive are the result of computerized accounting and list-processing systems that enable the business to generate the necessary information to make these mailings. Data processing is also important in many companies for computing the payroll with its many different pay scales and deductions. A not-so-hidden business use of the computer is the point-of-sale (POS) systems in retailing, which are used at checkout counters to speed the process and at the same time automate inventory control (see the boxed insert on page 16). Airlines and national hotel chains depend on large mainframe computers to handle their reservation systems. In the office, the increasing use of computers for word processing and many other clerical chores is called *office automation*.

Finance Applications Banks have been using a computerized check-handling system involving magnetic ink for some time, but recent advances promise a *checkless society* through **electronic funds transfer**. The check-handling system uses magnetic ink character recognition (MICR) to decode those funny-looking numbers printed in magnetic ink at the bottom of a check and to speed the processing of checks. Financial institutions also use computers to process and store the many transactions that they handle each day. The use of computers for electronic funds transfer means that one day we will be able to transfer money and to make purchases from the comfort of our homes. Another development involves the use of a computer element in a credit card to maintain financial records and make purchases without checks or credit card verifications.

Industrial Applications Computers are relied upon heavily to manage the large inventories necessary for manufacturing industries, to help design products and manufacturing processes, and to control the machines that build the products. The management of inventories is important—too much inventory is expensive and too little inventory can shut down the entire manufacturing or supply process. Two areas in which the computer has improved productivity are computer-aided design (CAD) and computer-aided manufacturing (CAM). CAD can be applied to the process of designing faster and more efficient computers. Automated machines called **robots** are commonly used to reduce costs and defects and to increase safety in manufacturing tasks that are either unsafe or boring. These robots are not the walking, talking variety, as in *Star Wars,* but these devices can perform a hot, dirty task—such as welding automobile bodies—time after time without loss of concentration or reduction in efficiency.

Government Applications The defense and space programs are extremely heavy users of computers in government, but numerous other governmental units use the computer. The Internal Revenue Service (IRS) uses computers to compare financial records of businesses and individuals to detect possible tax fraud. The Census Bureau could not complete its count of the U.S. population without the help of the computer. Computers are also

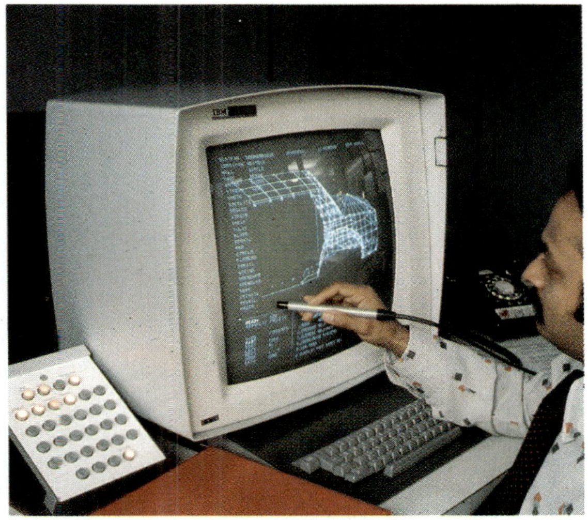

Computers are used in a variety of fields. Clockwise from top left, designers use a computer to design carpet tile patterns. An engineer uses a light pen and CAD to change an automobile design. Computer-produced maps of global weather show pressure patterns and clouds. Robots perform the dirty, dangerous job of welding automobile frames on an assembly line.

used in the various legislative bodies around the country to speed up the processing of legislative acts. The National Oceanic and Atmospheric Administration uses large, high-speed computers to forecast our weather. Law enforcement agencies use computers to fight crime in many ways. For example, a computer analysis of burglary patterns in a suburban area can lead to the arrest of a suspect and the recovery of stolen merchandise.

Agricultural Applications U.S. farmers and ranchers are beginning to use computers to control their herds of dairy cattle, to plan their planting schedules, to handle their accounting problems, to determine the least-cost feed mix to feed their flocks and herds, and to match animals for mating purposes. One Texas rancher uses a personal computer to determine which calves should be sold out of his herd and which ones should be kept for

Research and education benefit from computer use. Scientists (left) use the computer in the greenhouse to monitor the growth of different plants. The computer is often used as a child's learning tool to teach many skills (right).

mating purposes. This decision is made using an analysis of growth statistics. Prior to the personal computer, his handwritten analysis of these statistics took a great deal of time. Now, a personal computer performs the job more efficiently and with greater accuracy.

Educational Applications An area in which the computer is having great impact is education. Computers are used at all levels of education—kindergarten to college—to help students learn and to solve problems. The greatest current uses are computer-aided instruction (CAI), in which the computer acts as a tutor to the student, and computer-managed instruction (CMI), which frees teachers from many administrative chores that distract them from their main purpose, classroom teaching. The number of personal computers in elementary and secondary schools has grown from 100,000 in 1983 to almost 2 million today. At the college level, both mainframes and personal computers are used. Much of the instruction in programming is still on mainframes because of their ability to handle large numbers of users. Personal computers are used to teach the use of various software packages. Some colleges are requiring their students to own and use a personal computer. Retarded, learning disabled, and handicapped students have been taught successfully using the computer. For these special students, the computer is never tired and, when combined with appropriate software, it can be a very interesting teacher.

Using a computerized electrical stimulation and feedback system, paraplegic Nan Davis pedals a modified tricycle built especially for her.

Medical Care Applications A rapidly expanding area of computer use is medicine, for which every day brings a new advance in diagnosis and treatment. Probably the best known computerized diagnostic tool is the CAT scan (for computerized axial tomography), which allows the doctor to obtain a visualization of a cross section of a body part through a series of X-rays that are combined by the computer. As with education, the computer has been extremely useful in the treatment of handicapped individuals. For example, individuals who have lost their speech due to head injuries can now carry on a conversation using a personal computer equipped with a speech synthesizer.

Sports Applications Computers are used to scout opponents and prospective players by analyzing the large amount of data that are available on teams and individual players. The computer has also helped athletes improve their performance by graphically breaking up their body movements. Teams in various sports have used the computer to improve overall team performance by finding weak points to improve or strong points to stress.

Recreation Applications Computers have quickly become an integral part of our recreation with the proliferation of video game arcades across the country. It is almost impossible to go anywhere and not find a game room filled with special purpose computers known as arcade games waiting to digest a player's quarters. Games can be played on both mainframe and personal computers, ranging from the almost ancient Star Trek game available on most mainframes to the newest arcade and detective games available on disk for personal computers. Computers can also be programmed to play such venerable board games as chess, backgammon, or dominoes.

Computers are also becoming a fact of life in other areas of recreation. At the Experimental Prototype Community of Tomorrow (EPCOT) in Walt Disney World near Orlando, Florida, computers run the entire show—from the fountains to the rides to the information service to the animated figures in the shows. EPCOT also includes a special program on the impact of computers.

Personal Life Applications The areas of our personal lives that are affected by the computer are too numerous to cover in one short paragraph. Examples are included throughout this text, ranging from religion, which now has a computerized Bible concordance, to the study of genealogy, which uses programs to track down ancestors, to hobbies, which may require record keeping or control of many operations.

Even our recreational activities are affected by computers. Video games (left) run by specialized computers provide entertainment for millions of children and adults each year. An EPCOT employee (right) uses a touch-sensitive screen to transmit a picture over a two-way video connection to a guest at a remote terminal location in the park.

BAR CODES

A commonly encountered computer application involves bar codes on consumer products. A bar code is a series of black "bars" and white spaces located somewhere on the product. The bar code is converted to a numeric code by an optical reader that picks up the differences between the black bars and the white spaces. This optical reader can be either a "wand" passed over the bar code or a laser device such as that used in grocery stores. A single bar code does not exist for each product, but the Universal Product Code (UPC) is carried by almost every grocery product. The information on the Universal Product (bar) Code is read, converted to a series of digits, and transmitted to the store's computer, where the price is found and sent back to the cash register. At the same time, the store's inventory is reduced by the sale of the product. In this way, the bar code is used for both pricing and inventory. The pricing is updated by store personnel, who enter new prices into the computer. This process of updating prices can cause problems if the incorrect price is entered or a special sale price is not entered. However, this type of checkout error is a human error, not a computer error.

FROM MONSTERS TO MICROS

We know that size is one way of distinguishing among computers, which may be mainframes, minicomputers, and microcomputers. These three size categories also have subcategories. One subset of mainframes includes "supercomputers" or "monsters," which are the biggest and fastest computers in use today. These very large computers are used almost exclusively by universities and government agencies for research projects that require high speed and large storage capacities.

At the other end of the computer size spectrum, the microcomputer category has several subcategories. The supermicros can serve multiple users and may soon replace the minicomputer. Inexpensive micro- or personal computers can be used for many home projects. Middle-sized personal computers are used in business.

The personal computer has received by far the most publicity over the last five years. This is due in part to the phenomenal growth that has occurred in the use of the personal computer since its introduction in 1975. This growth

Today, computers are available in a wide range of sizes. Supercomputers like the CYBER 205 (left) are among the largest and fastest computers currently available. The IBM Personal Computer (right) is extremely popular in homes, schools, and businesses.

The difference between personal computers and mainframe computers may involve more than just size. Nelson Winkless, president of ABQ Communications Corporation and the coauthor of *Robots on Your Doorstep,* has another perspective on the distinction.

ANOTHER VIEW

Nelson Winkless

Before personal computers came among us, we had only institutional computers. They were owned by government agencies, large businesses, and other organizations. The work produced by the institutional computer is looked upon as the work of the organization. The personal computer is looked upon as the implement of the individual. That person uses the computer as if it were a pencil, a pocket calculator, or a telephone. The individual, not the organization, is responsible for the work produced by that personal instrument, even when the individual is operating in an institutional setting. There's no ceremony involved in using the personal computer, no labored allocation of resources, no meetings, no sign-offs (that is, after the initial effort to get the machine). The individual uses the machine as casually as a pad of paper and is fully responsible for what is produced.

SOURCE: Excerpted with permission from Nelson Winkless, "Rover, Fetch a Dozen #9 Ratchets," *Byte Magazine,* January 1984, p. 130.

is expected to continue through the end of the decade, as seen in Figure 1-1. Growth in the use of personal computers is due primarily to the large amount of software that has been developed, which allows an individual to use this mind tool without learning programming. Although software for larger computers is also available for users, it is not always widely publicized or easy to use. A second factor in the phenomenal growth is the owner's instant access to a personal computer. A user might have to wait to obtain access to a mainframe computer **terminal**—a keyboard and video screen. The user often must also have an account with a computer center to pay for the computer time used.

Remember that although the personal computer is the object of so much publicity in the media, it will never replace the larger computers. In fact, the growth in personal computer use is matched by an equivalent growth in the

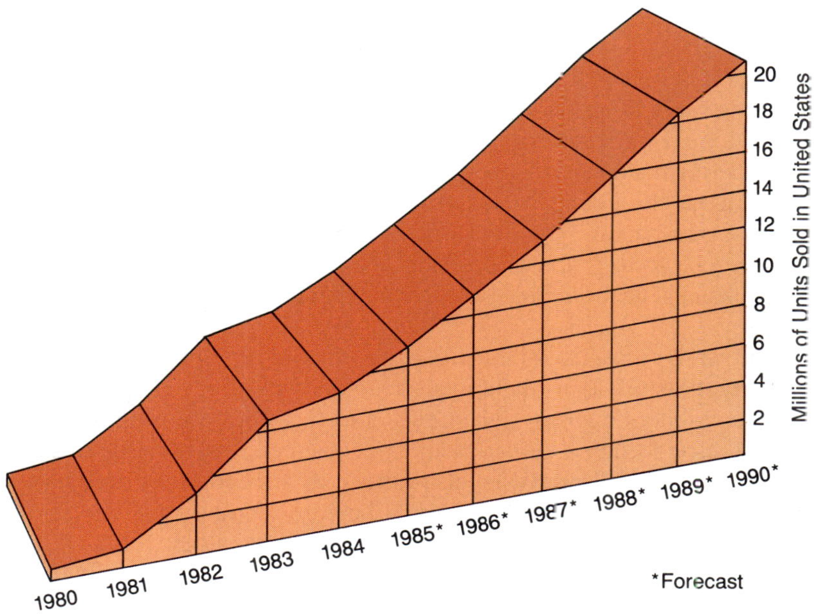

FIGURE 1-1
Growth in the Use of Personal Computers, 1980–1989
(Future Computing, Dallas, TX)

If you want people to use the computer, you have to make it available when they want it. If they have to wait in line, they lose interest.

Richard M. Cyart, President of Carnegie-Mellon University
(As quoted in "The Wired University Is on the Way," *Business Week*, April 26, 1982, p. 68.)

use of mainframe computers. This growth in mainframe use is due to several factors. First, personal computer users are demanding more information. Second, storage capacity is needed beyond that possible on personal computers. Third, the need for the high-speed computing is ongoing. The largest personal computers currently have one million characters of internal memory, but mainframes have several million characters of internal memory. Similarly, personal computers can store millions of characters in secondary storage, but mainframes can store billions of characters. In terms of speed, one study showed that a supercomputer can perform in 1 second the same operation that a personal computer needs almost *21 hours* to perform.

This means that both mainframes and personal computers are here to stay. Mainframes are important for large-capacity storage and for handling the many business, scientific, and engineering problems that require the mainframe's high speed. On the other hand, the use of the personal computer grows as more people and businesses find that they can solve problems and handle their information needs with a small computer. The difference between these two sizes of computers is really just a difference in size. The operating principles for both are the same. Once you are familiar with one, it is very easy to learn to use the other.

COMMON USES OF THE PERSONAL COMPUTER

Because the personal computer is a mind tool that is so easily accessible to so many people, we give special emphasis to its uses. In this section, we focus on the most common uses of the personal computer. These personal computer uses depend on computer packages and not on programming. (Programming the computer is discussed in detail in a later chapter.) Computer packages are an important part of the computer-tool because the user does not need a knowledge of programming. The nine most popular uses of the computer as determined by a recent poll of computer users are shown in Table 1-1.

Table 1-1
POPULAR USES OF COMPUTERS

Use	*Percent of Users*
Video games	61
Computer training	59
Storing data	57
Word processing	53
Education	40
Personal budgeting	38
Business management	29
Graphics	28
Financial analysis	24

(*USA Today* Poll, October 17, 1984, p. 1B)

Home uses include video games, educational applications for children and adults, office work at home, personal budgeting, home business, and word processing.

Although personal computers are important at home, their greatest use in the long run will probably be in the office. Whether linked to a mainframe or used alone, a personal computer allows the manager or information specialist to perform analyses that result in better decisions. The personal computer also speeds the efficient flow of information both within the office and to outside destinations. The six most commonly used business oriented computer packages are word processing, accounting (including personal budgeting), financial analysis, data base management, graphics, and telecommunications.

One of the most useful functions of a personal computer is **word processing**, with its ability to manipulate letters, digits, and punctuation marks to compose letters, papers, documents, and so on. Composing and editing is accomplished using a keyboard and video screen, and then the final result is printed. **Financial analysis**, also known as **spreadsheet analysis**, works with a table of values having rows and columns (called a spreadsheet). The user defines the various relationships among the values in the table. As the user changes a value, the package recomputes all other values to account for

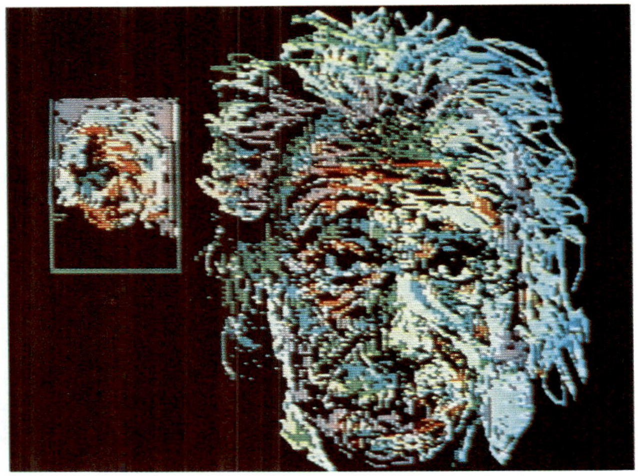

Computer users can choose from a wide range of applications. Families (left) find that the personal computer and printer can be used for both work and play in the home. Most people consider the use of graphics for artistic purposes (right) an exciting application of computers.

the change. This analysis allows the user to ask "What if?" questions about the values in a spreadsheet. **Accounting packages** include programs that allow a business to keep track of its financial affairs, including payroll, money owed to the firm, money owed by the firm, and the firm's current financial position. When used in the home, these packages are referred to as **personal budgeting packages**, which include checkbook accounting and home budget planning. We manage data bases in many situations both at home and at work. **Data base management packages** help manage lists of elements and to find elements that fit some criteria from a collection of data called a **data base**. Keeping track of clients and customers is an important use of data base management packages for businesses. One of the most exciting examples of the computer's manipulation of symbols is the **graphics package** for visual presentation of information or for creation of new and different art forms. This function is important in business because graphics are crucial to presenting information. **Telecommunications packages** allow us to use a personal computer to access informational data bases, to communicate directly with other users, to post messages on an electronic bulletin board, to send mail electronically, and to transact business electronically.

COMPUTER LITERACY—HOW NECESSARY?

One of the most overdefined terms regarding computers is *computer literacy,* which has different meanings in different computer books. Regardless of the number of definitions, it is an extremely important concept that will become even more so as the uses of the computer continue to increase. Computer literacy is now an advantage to those who understand how to use computers. In the not so distant future, computer illiteracy will be a decided disadvantage in dealing with a world of computers.

Computer literacy has been defined variously as being able to write programs for the personal computer, understanding the hardware of the computer, or knowing the many uses of the computer. In this text, the definition of computer literacy coincides with the definition of the computer as a mind tool. **Computer literacy** is *an understanding of what a computer can and*

Computer literacy is a process of making students aware of the collection of tools developed for their particular discipline, and how to use and work with them.

Carter L. Olson, Professor of Pharmaceutical Chemistry, Ohio State University

(As quoted in "Ohio State Eyes 'Computer Literacy': Who Needs It? Who Should Teach It?," *Chronicle of High Education,* January 11, 1984, p. 14.)

cannot do and an ability to make the computer do what is desired. Note that this definition does not automatically assume either an understanding of the electronics that make up the computer's hardware or the ability to write programs. The definition does assume an understanding of a computer's uses and limitations and a knowledge of the software packages needed to accomplish a desired end. However, if the purpose for which you wish to use the computer requires a greater understanding of hardware or programming, then you must increase your knowledge to meet your needs.

Beyond computer literacy, two additional levels of knowledge have been defined. **Computer competence** means an individual can solve sophisticated problems in his or her field of expertise. The computer-competent person is comfortable using the computer and looks for better ways to solve his or her problems. **Computer mastery** refers to the level of knowledge required of an individual who wants to be a success in the computer field.

The importance of computer literacy is a topic of debate almost as widespread as the debate on the definition of computer literacy. Many educators feel that at some time in their academic careers students must become computer literate. Today's student must be prepared to function in a future society in which computers or other automated devices are the rule rather than the exception. This feeling is expressed very well by Dr. John Kemeny, past president of Dartmouth College and co-inventor of BASIC, the most popular computer language for personal computers. According to Kemeny, "In the next three decades, intelligence will be built into most manufactured objects and those who lack even minimal computer literacy will have difficulty functioning in everyday life."[1]

To ensure that students are exposed to computer literacy, many states are enacting statutes requiring high school or junior high school students to take one or more units of computer literacy. Many colleges and universities now require students to take courses in this area. Because the U.S. economic base is shifting toward personal services, information handling, and high technology, workers in many industries must be retrained in computer literacy to prepare them for the changing work place.

By studying this text, you should become computer literate and able to function in a future world. The next four chapters in this introductory block cover hardware, software, computer systems, and computers and society. These four chapters cover the material necessary for you to obtain the knowledge covered in the first half of our definition of computer literacy—that is, knowledge of what a computer can and cannot do.

---

[1]Richard A. Shaffer, "Courses in Computer Literacy Beginning to Draw Bad Marks," *The Wall Street Journal,* September 16, 1983, p. 37.

REVIEW OF KEY POINTS

- A computer is a mind tool that can enable us to ease our mental labors. It is the catalyst that has brought on today's information society.
- A computer is a machine that stores and manipulates symbols quickly and accurately.
- The two parts of a computer are the hardware and the software. Hardware is the electronic part, and software is the set of instructions that direct the computer's activities.
- The activity of developing software is programming, and the resulting software is made up of one or more programs.
- An individual can use a computer without being a programmer by using commercially available software packages.
- Computers can be classified according to size, type of logic used, and purpose.
- The computer has applications in many fields and affects our lives in numerous ways.
- The use of mainframe computers and the use of personal computers are increasing simultaneously; both types of computers are important tools in the information society.
- Computer literacy is an understanding of what a computer can and cannot do and an ability to make the computer do what is desired.

KEY TERMS

accounting packages
analog computer
Analytical Engine
artificial intelligence
bar code
computer
computer competence
computer error
computer literacy
computer mastery
computer package
computerphobia
data
data base
data base management packages
data processing
desk-top computers
digital computer
electronic funds transfer
financial analysis
general purpose computer
graphics package
hardware
information
information society
mainframe
microcomputers
mind tool
minicomputer
personal budgeting packages
personal computers
programming
programs
robots
software
special purpose computer
spreadsheet analysis
telecommunications packages
terminal
word processing

REVIEW QUESTIONS

1. Choose an occupation and discuss the tools needed for that occupation. Which of these tools could be considered mind tools?
2. List some of the ways that symbols can be manipulated.
3. Discuss why the term *computer error* is a misrepresentation.
4. Explain the term *data processing*. Describe the input and output for data processing. Give an example.
5. Classify the computer you are using in terms of size, logic used, and purpose.
6. List some analog devices other than a speedometer.
7. Discuss three applications of computers that affect you on a daily basis.
8. If your school has a mainframe computer center, investigate the requirements for its use. Compare these requirements to those for a personal computer if one is available to you.
9. Which of the six business oriented software packages for personal computers would you most like to learn to use? Explain.
10. List three current or future situations for which you must become computer literate.

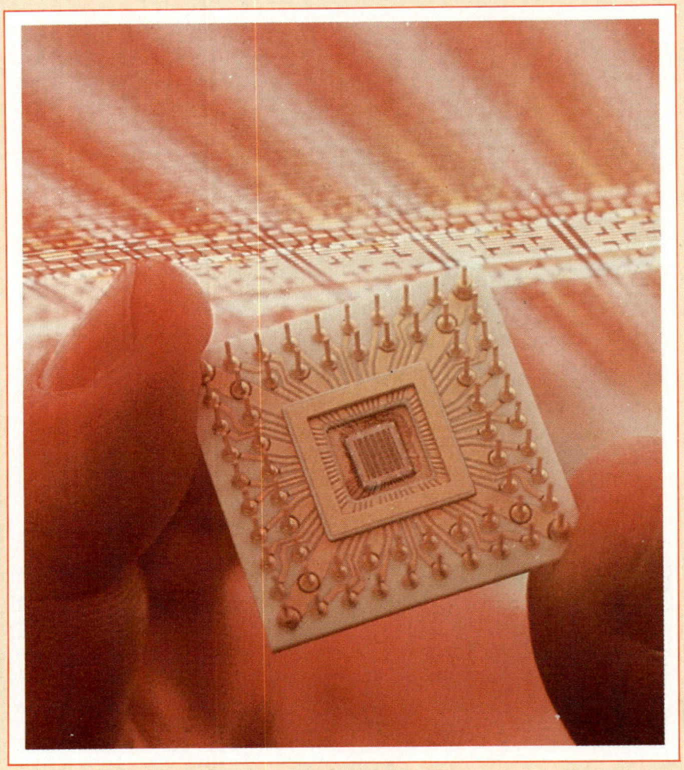

In Chapter 1, we said that the computer has two parts—hardware and software. In this chapter, we discuss the computer's hardware components. More detail and specifics of hardware are addressed in Block 2, The Details of Hardware, for which this chapter is an introduction.

This chapter introduces the various hardware devices that make up a computer. Coverage of this topic includes a look at the components of a conceptual computer and how it works. However, this discussion does not cover the details of the devices that actually carry out the operations. We then discuss some hardware elements and how they combine to "build" a computer. Special attention is given at the end of the chapter to how a computer manipulates and stores symbols.

2

An Introduction to Computer Hardware

STUDY OBJECTIVES

After reading this chapter, you should be able to

- Understand conceptually how a computer works.
- Recognize the four major hardware components of the computer.
- Understand how these four components interact to manipulate and store symbols.
- Put together a personal computer using examples of each computer hardware component.
- Discuss how a computer manipulates and stores symbols in the processing/internal memory unit.
- Include in your vocabulary the most important computer hardware terminology.

A CONCEPTUAL COMPUTER

Computer **hardware** is the electronic part of the computer that stores and manipulates symbols under the direction of the computer software. Because the hardware's operations are electronic, the computer executes programs with speed and accuracy. The speed of many operations within the computer is only limited by the speed of electricity. These operations also obey physical laws that do not change from operation to operation and are therefore accurate. As discussed in Chapter 1, a computer mistake can almost always be traced to a human error, either in the design of the computer or in the software.

To understand how computer hardware is combined to make a machine that stores and manipulates symbols, we first look at a conceptual computer. A **conceptual computer** can demonstrate the major functions of a computer without involving the operational details of the machine. The conceptual computer shown in Figure 2-1 has four major elements—input, processing/internal memory, secondary storage, and output. It also shows the flow of information into, within, and out of the computer.

A computer must be able to **input**, or receive, the symbols to be manipulated and the instructions for manipulating those symbols. The symbols that are manipulated are the **data**, and the instructions for the computer are the **software**, which is discussed in Chapter 3. Input to a computer performs the same function as the input humans receive through eyes, ears, and senses of touch, taste, and smell.

The computer must be able to store the data and instructions internally. Once the data and instructions are stored internally, the computer must be able to perform the manipulations based on the instructions. This storage and manipulation, which occurs in the **processing/internal memory unit**, can involve arithmetic operations (addition, subtraction, and so on), operations on letters of the alphabet, operations that result in pictures (known as *graphics*), or a combination of these. The processing/internal memory unit is comparable to a human brain, which also stores and operates on information.

FIGURE 2-1
The Conceptual Computer

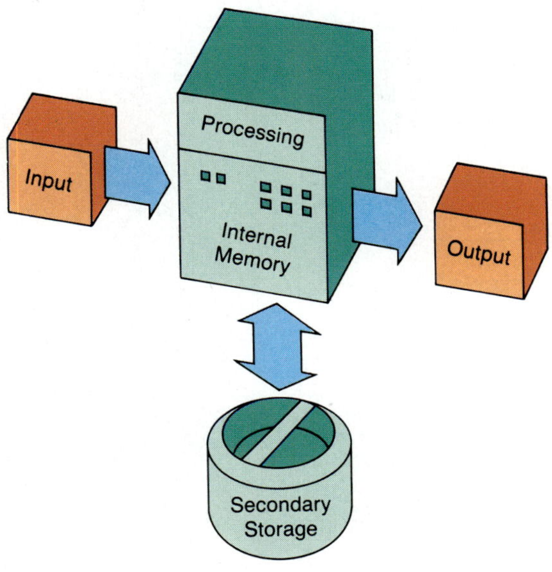

WHO BUILT THE FIRST COMPUTER?

For a machine as important as the computer, it is strange to think that the question of who built the first computer was settled in court. A 1973 lawsuit invalidated early patents on the computer, because the judge decided the wrong persons had received credit for developing the first computer.

The early history of the computer involves three individuals, or groups of individuals, and the machines they built. One pair of individuals were John V. Atanasoff of Iowa State University and his graduate assistant, Clifford Berry, who began work on an electronic computer before World War II and finished a working prototype in 1942. Although there was a great deal of interest in computers that could compute artillery tables during the war, the Atanasoff–Berry Computer, or ABC, did not receive much attention. Iowa State did not even attempt to patent the device, and neither man followed up on this early work. The ABC was eventually forgotten and only a few parts of the original machine remain.

Another important individual in the development of the computer is Howard Aiken. In 1944, Aiken completed the MARK I computer for IBM in cooperation with Harvard University. Even though the MARK I had 760,000 electrical parts connected by 500 miles of wiring, it was not completely electronic, because it used 3,000 electromechanical relays as switches. It was so big that an entire building on Harvard's campus was set aside for it.

The pair of individuals who usually receive the credit for developing a purely electronic computer are J. Presper Eckert, Jr. and John Mauchly. Eckert was working on a government project to build a fast computing device when he visited Atanasoff at Iowa State to learn about the ABC. After his meeting, Eckert and Mauchly built the ENIAC (Electrical Numerical Integrator and Calculator) for the war effort. Unfortunately, it was not finished until 1946, after the war. The ENIAC contained 18,000 vacuum tubes and 80,000 resistors and capacitors, weighed 30 tons, and occupied over 15,000 square feet. It was much faster than the MARK I, because it could multiply two numbers in 0.003 second compared with over 0.05 second for the MARK I. However, ENIAC used so much electricity that the lights in the section of Philadelphia in which it was located supposedly dimmed each time the computer ran. The ENIAC, which ran for nine years, is now on exhibit at the Smithsonian Institution.

An important advance over the ENIAC was the EDVAC (Electronic Discrete Variable Automatic Computer) developed by John Von Neumann. The EDVAC utilized the concept of the stored program, which meant the computer did not have to be rewired for each job as was the ENIAC.

The 1973 court decision named the Atanasoff–Berry team as the builders of the first computer, rather than Eckert and Mauchly. Aiken is best known for getting IBM interested in computers, but the MARK I contributed little to later developments of the computer. Von Neumann is remembered for adding the stored program concept to the computer.

The Atanasoff-Berry Computer (ABC) (top left) was the first electronic computer built, but only a few parts of this computer exist today. J. Presper Eckert, Jr. is shown with the ENIAC computer (top right) that he and John Mauchly jointly designed and built. The MARK I computer (left) was the first computer built by International Business Machines Corporation (IBM).

This microchip contains the central processing unit (CPU), input/output circuitry, read only memory (ROM), and random access memory (RAM).

The person using the equipment is striving to do something significant. I contribute to it by providing a tool.

Seymour R. Cray, founder of Cray Computers
(As quoted in "Supercomputer Power and the PC's Future," *PC Magazine,* May 15, 1984, p. 122.)

Because the internal memory of a computer does not have an unlimited capacity, a storage area is needed outside of the computer to hold the overflow information. This information can be transferred back to the internal memory as needed. This external storage unit is called **secondary storage**. Another reason for having secondary storage is that the computer's internal memory is erased when the power to the computer is turned off. Information in internal memory that must be saved when the power is turned off should be transferred to secondary storage. The file cabinets we use to save large amounts of information are similar to a computer's secondary storage.

Finally, because the results of the manipulations of the data are of no use unless they can be given to the user, the computer has a process called **output**. We humans output the results of our brain's operations in the form of speech, writing, pictures, or body movements.

We have looked at a conceptual computer and have discussed the parts of a computer in general terms. We have also seen how the flow of data into the computer, the flow of information between the computer and secondary storage, and the flow of results out of the computer tie the components of the conceptual computer together. Before we go any further into how a computer works, we should look at the four major parts of a real computer. After reading this section, you should have a clear idea of the main components of a computer.

Input

The many methods of input to a computer range from switches on a computer console to easy-to-use voice input. Other means of input include computer cards, paper tape, the keyboard, optical character readers like those used to read bar codes, touch pads, the light pen, the joystick, the track ball, the touch screen, and a device called a *mouse* that communicates with the computer by its movement over a flat surface. Input to the early mainframes was accomplished through switches on the computer console. This very complex procedure required the user to have a great deal of technical computer knowledge.

A form of input that actually was in use before the computer is the punched card (see the boxed insert on page 28). This form of computer input is familiar from its use in many large-scale data processing operations, such as computerized billing and college registration. A **punched** or **computer card** has a pattern of holes punched in it to represent the numeric digits, the letters of the alphabet, and some punctuation symbols. The process of placing these holes in the card is called **keypunching**, during which a keyboard transmits signals to a punching mechanism that selects the pattern of holes corresponding to the various symbols. The holes are then interpreted by a **card reader**, which converts each set of holes into an electronic signal. This signal is then sent to the computer.

Another fairly old form of input entails punching holes in paper. **Paper tape** works on the same principle as punched cards except that the data are encoded onto a roll of paper approximately 1 inch wide. The tape is then interpreted by a special reader, which converts the holes into signals to the computer in the same way as a card reader.

Today, the most popular input device for computers is the **keyboard**, which sends the appropriate electrical signal to the computer when a key is pressed. Because keyboards have been used on typewriters for a long time, they are familiar to most of us. On a typewriter, the keys transmit a signal to the element that strikes a ribbon, forming a symbol on a sheet of paper. The keyboard has the same function on a computer, except that the symbols are stored in the computer's internal memory and are usually shown on the output video screen rather than on paper.

For game-playing, a popular input device is the **joystick**. Moving the handle and pushing a button on this device sends signals to the computer regarding the movement of figures on the screen. Another device that is often used for arcade games is the track ball, which sends signals to the computer for figure movements that depend on the speed and direction of the ball's spin.

Two devices that only require the user to point to some area of the screen are the light pen and the touch screen. The **light pen** is a device the size of a writing pen with a light in the end of it. The pen is connected to the

This card reader uses punched cards to input data to a mainframe computer or minicomputer.

More than one method of input is available for computers. Joysticks are a necessity for many computer games (left). They can also be used with art software to draw on the screen. A touch pad can be used along with a keyboard for input to a computer (right). It is activated by pressure from a finger or stylus.

THE COMPUTER CARD: DO NOT FOLD, SPINDLE, OR MUTILATE

For many years, the computer card, or punched card, has represented the computer to most people. Bills are received in the form of computer cards, students use them for college registration, and they are still used to input data and instructions to mainframe computers. In a 1950s game show, a great deal of importance was given to a card-sorting device that supposedly selected questions for the contestant in his or her area of expertise.

Actually, the history of the punched card precedes that of the computer. In 1805, a French mechanic named Joseph-Marie Jacquard devised a method of using cards with holes punched in them to control weaving looms. This proved to be a tremendous advance in the weaving industry of the time, because any pattern could be represented by a series of cards. This idea showed that information could be stored on cards by punching holes in them and that an almost infinite number of pattern variations could be saved on the cards.

The next mention of punched cards comes from Charles Babbage, who considered the possibility of using cards to communicate information to his Analytical Engine. In his autobiography, Babbage wrote, "Every set of cards, once made, will, at any future time, reproduce the calculations for which it was first arranged."

Although Babbage envisioned using cards to communicate with his ill-fated Analytical Engine prior to 1850, the first actual use of cards for a data processing problem was for the 1890 U.S. census. An American engineer, Herman Hollerith, approached the Census Bureau about building a machine to process census information that had been punched on cards. It had taken the Census Bureau almost 10 years to complete the 1880 census. At that rate, the 1890 census would not be completed until after the 1900 census began. Obviously, the Census Bureau was excited about a machine that would speed up the counting process. Hollerith's machine used pins that made electrical connections when they encountered a hole in a card. The 1890 census information was processed in less than three years. Hollerith later left the Census Bureau with the machine he had invented and patented. He then formed the company that eventually became a part of International Business Machines Corporation (IBM).

Punched cards are not used as much as they once were. However, their portability and ease of sorting ensure their continued use for years to come.

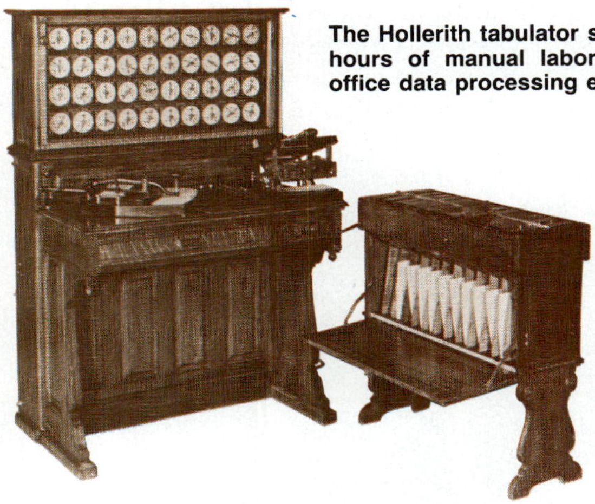

The Hollerith tabulator sorted punched cards, saving hours of manual labor, and led to the development of office data processing equipment.

computer by a cord. When the light pen is pointed at some area of the screen, the computer receives a signal about that area of the screen. As a result of this signal, a program function may be selected, a portion of the screen may be enlarged, or a portion may be deleted. The **touch screen** works in a similar manner, except that the signal is given to the computer by a finger or some other pointer that breaks a pair of vertical and horizontal light beams on the surface of the screen. Touch screens provide information to visitors all over EPCOT at Walt Disney World in Florida. A visitor merely touches one of several colored areas on the screen to receive a message about some feature of EPCOT.

Another input device used with personal computers fits in the palm of the hand. This device, called a **mouse**, controls a **cursor**, a blinking rectangle of light on the screen. The mouse gets its name from its small size and the "tail" that connects it to the computer. Using one, two, or three buttons on the mouse and rolling it over a flat surface, the user can perform various operations when the cursor is located in the desired position.

A **touch pad** input device allows the user to sketch a design. This device is placed on a flat surface, and the user signals the computer by applying pressure to the pad's surface.

Voice recognition input is currently an area in which manufacturers are beginning to offer products with expanded capabilities. When fully developed, voice recognition will make the use of computers easy for almost anyone. This type of input will be especially useful to handicapped persons or those who have trouble with a keyboard.

Processing/Internal Memory

To manipulate and store symbols, the computer must have a "brain" that can perform certain predetermined operations and "remember" information. This "brain" is the processing/internal memory unit of the computer. This element is made up of the following three parts: (1) the arithmetic-logic unit, where actual manipulations are carried out; (2) the control unit, which directs all of these operations; and (3) the internal, or main, memory. The control unit and the arithmetic-logic unit together form the **central processing unit (CPU)** of the computer.

All three units involve the use of an electronic device known as a **microchip**, or simply, a chip. A **chip** is a tiny piece of silicon that packs many thousands of electronic elements onto an area the size of a pea. These elements, called **transistors**, actually carry on the control and logic operations at the rate of close to 1 million operations per second! A combination of transistors and circuits on a chip results in an **integrated circuit**, which is the key to the power and speed of all computers today. (In Chapter 6, we discuss the integrated circuit and its various stages of development since its invention in 1958.) Because the chip is so small, it must be attached to a carrier device to be connected to the computer. The carrier device has wire prongs that plug into the main board, which contains other chips for the CPU, the main memory, and the control of input, output, and secondary storage devices.

The detail of this microchip shows the components and circuitry necessary to perform its many operations.

A CPU chip, or **microprocessor**, contains the control unit and the arithmetic-logic unit. The **control unit** handles the management of the symbol manipulation process, and the **arithmetic-logic unit (ALU)** handles the actual manipulation. A group of high-speed memory devices called **registers** in the ALU hold the piece of data that is being manipulated at any one time. Although registers are very fast, only a few registers can fit on a microprocessor chip. Mainframe computers have several CPU chips, but a personal computer usually has only one CPU chip. Having multiple CPU chips enables the mainframe to run faster and handle the large volume of processing for which it is responsible.

GENERATION UPON GENERATION OF COMPUTERS

The development of computers is usually described as occurring in generations. The first generation, which began with Eckert and Mauchly's ENIAC, is considered to span the period 1946–1959. This generation of computers is characterized by the use of vacuum tubes in the CPU and internal memory units, the first commercial computers, and many fundamental advances in computing. The ENIAC was followed by an improved design called the EDVAC, which incorporated John Von Neumann's stored program concepts. The first commercial computer was the UNIVAC 1 (UNIVersal Automatic Computer), which was sold to the Census Bureau in 1951.

In the second generation of computers, 1959–1964, the vacuum tube was replaced by the transistor. The transistor, a solid-state device, was the major breakthrough that allowed computers to have reasonable size and power. A solid-state device is made of minerals so that it can be instructed to allow or not allow a current flow. Because solid-state devices did not use the hot filament that was in vacuum tubes, the use of transistors reduced the computer's heat output and power requirement. Transistors also increased the reliability of the computer, because they did not burn out the way vacuum tubes did. This breakthrough, in turn, reduced the cost of owning and operating a computer. This period saw tremendous growth in the use of computers by government, business, and industry.

The introduction of the integrated circuit in 1965 was the beginning of the third generation of computers. With this technological advance, an entire circuit board containing transistors and connecting wires could be placed on a single chip. This development meant greater reliability and compactness combined with low cost and power requirements. During this period, IBM controlled the mainframe market with its 360 (later to be 370) series of computers. This series was so well designed and built that the computers are still in heavy use today.

The fourth and current generation of computers began in 1971 with the introduction of the microprocessor—a central processing unit on a chip. This generation includes the introduction of supercomputers. These "monster computers" are in heavy demand for military and meteorological applications that require a high speed of operation. Another important advance of this generation has been the introduction of the personal computer, because the power of the computer has been made available to anybody who wishes to use one.

A possible "fifth generation" of computers has recently been discussed in the media. The Japanese government has a broad-ranging plan to leapfrog American superiority in hardware with a fifth-generation computer that will include parallel processors—several CPUs working in parallel to speed up execution time. No one knows how successful this particular plan will be, but we probably won't have to wait long to find out.

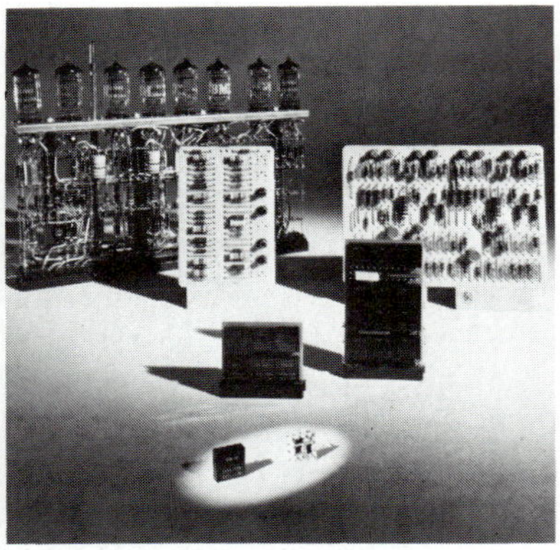

The four generations of computers are exemplified in the photo at right by vacuum tubes, transistorized circuit boards, integrated circuits, and microprocessors. UNIVAC 1 (center), a first generation computer and the first computer available commercially, was used to predict the outcome of the 1952 presidential election. The IBM 360 series of mainframe computers (left) was an extremely popular third generation computer that played a large role in making IBM a dominant force in the computer industry.

Internal memory, also made up of chips, is divided into two major types—random access memory and read only memory. **Random access memory (RAM)** is the section of memory that is available for storing the instructions to the computer and the symbols that are to be manipulated. RAM is the internal memory that is accessible to the user. It is called random access memory because any area of the memory can be accessed with equal ease regardless of when a piece of information is placed in the memory. A shortcoming of RAM is that it is **volatile**—the memory exists only while the computer is turned on or the user is connected to the mainframe. This volatility and the limited capacity of internal memory require that secondary storage be used to save information while the computer is turned off or the user disconnects from the mainframe.

Read only memory (ROM) is the section of memory that is placed in the computer during the manufacturing process and remains there even after the computer is turned off. This type of memory gives the CPU instructions during the startup process before the user has given the computer any instructions. ROM is also useful in managing many of the computer's operations.

SECONDARY STORAGE

Because of the limited amount of internal storage and the volatility of RAM, external or secondary storage is necessary to handle many complex operations and to store data and programs in a form that does not disappear when the power to the computer is turned off or the user disconnects from the mainframe. This secondary, or peripheral, storage is usually in one of two forms—disk or tape.

With either the disk or tape, stored information is accessed by internal memory when the control unit decides that this information is needed by the processing unit. Because the secondary storage unit must locate the information, read it from the disk or tape, and then transfer the information to internal memory, secondary storage is a much slower form of memory than internal memory. However, this slow transfer of information is balanced by the virtually unlimited storage capacity.

Disk Secondary Storage

A **disk** is a thin, record-like piece of metal or plastic that is covered with an iron oxide whose magnetic direction can be arranged to represent symbols. This magnetic arrangement is accomplished by a device known as a **disk drive**, which spins the disk while reading or writing information on it. This process of transferring information to and from the disk is accomplished by the **read/write head**, which rides on or immediately above the disk depending on the type of disk. In a sense, a disk is like a stereo record that is "played" by the disk drive, with two crucial differences. First, signals on the disk are recorded magnetically on concentric **tracks** rather than in a continuous groove on a vinyl record. Second, the computer can record data on a disk in addition to just playing it. Mainframe computers have large **disk packs** made up of 11 disks about the size of a record album. These disk packs usually remain in the disk drive except when a special need requires a transfer. Because disk packs can hold much information, many users can store data on a single disk pack. When a user accesses the mainframe, his or her user number tells the computer where to look on the disk pack for the user's data

Personal computers use **floppy disks** made of plastic and hard disks

These mainframe disk drives are used to store large amounts of data on disk packs. Note that the carrying case for the disk pack is kept on top of the disk drive.

made of metal to store information. Floppy disks, which are made of Mylar plastic and covered with iron oxide are easily moved, but hold only a fraction of the data stored on a hard disk or a mainframe disk pack. For this reason, a user may need many floppies, one for each type of data that is stored. For example, the text of this book was contained on 18 floppy disks. Floppies are available in three sizes—8 inches, 5.25 inches, and 3.5 inches in diameter. Different types of computers use different sizes of floppies. A **hard disk** is a scaled down version of a mainframe disk pack that until recently was not removable from the personal computer. The hard disk rotates at a much faster speed than the floppy and stores a great deal more information.

With mainframe disk packs or personal computer floppy or hard disks, each character can be accessed and read by the disk drive with equal ease. The capability of going directly to any character on a disk is known as **direct access**.

Tape Secondary Storage

Tape that is used for secondary storage can be either reel-to-reel or cassette. Like a disk, tape is covered with iron oxide that is arranged magnetically to store symbols. A tape can easily store millions of characters. However, it is much slower than a disk for transferring information, because the tape must be "played" by the recorder to transfer the data. Another drawback with a tape system is that the information must be accessed in the same order or sequence in which it was placed on the tape. This form of access is known as **sequential access**.

Mainframe computers depend on reel-to-reel tapes to store information not needed immediately. Financial statistics, payroll records, student academic records, and so on are usually stored on tape. When needed, the tape is *mounted* on a **tape drive**, where a read/write head similar to that used on a disk drive transfers information to and from the tape.

Movie makers often use spinning reel-to-reel tape drives to indicate that a computer is working. Of course, reel-to-reel tape is only an external storage device and does not really show what the computer is doing.

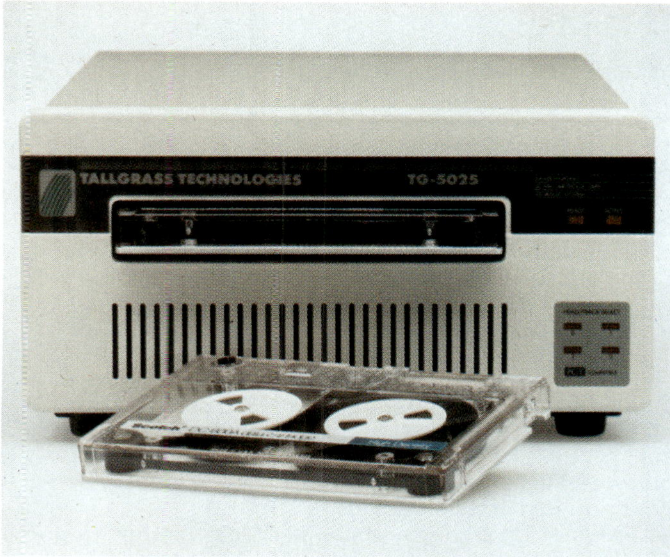

Tape secondary storage takes many forms. The computer operator at left is mounting a tape on the tape drive so a mainframe or minicomputer user can access the data stored on the tape. The tape cartridge (right) is used for backing up a hard disk on a personal computer.

Personal computers primarily use cassette tapes similar to those used for sound recordings. In fact, the same cassette tape that records a hit song can store information that it receives from the computer, and with an adapter and a connector cable, the same recorder can be used to do both. (Getting the two mixed up can lead to strange music and even stranger computer results!) A cassette tape is the least expensive form of secondary storage for personal computers. For this reason, cassette tapes are used for secondary storage for many inexpensive personal computers.

Cartridge and Video Disk Storage

Two forms of read only secondary storage are the cartridge and the video disk. **Cartridges** are often used for games or for educational applications. They also provide information to the computer. However, any new information cannot be placed on this type of secondary storage.

Video disks come in various sizes and types. Shown here, from left to right, are a laser video disk, write-once optical disks in $5\frac{1}{4}$ inch and 12 inch sizes, and a $5\frac{1}{4}$ inch optical read-only memory disk.

FINGERPRINT MATCHING

In television detective stories, a fingerprint is always a crucial clue, because it enables the detective to determine the identity of the suspect. In actual police work, many sets of fingerprints at crime scenes do not result in positive identifications. For example, in the state of Georgia's Crime Information Center, over 7.5 million fingerprint cards must be checked when an unidentified, or *latent,* print comes in. Obviously, it is impossible to check all these fingerprint cards manually. As a result, many latent prints go unmatched. In one year, although 40,000 latent prints from crime scenes were handled, only 952 suspects were identified. As a result of this horrendous matching problem, latent prints can usually only be checked against the fingerprints of suspects in custody.

To develop a faster, more accurate method of matching fingerprints, the state of Georgia and AT&T have combined their resources in an experimental program that uses video disks and computers to take over the matching work. Under AT&T's "Sleuth" system, the fingerprint records would be stored on video disks. When a latent print came in, its characteristics would be entered into the computer, which would compare the characteristics to prints on file.

The importance of this program cannot be understated in terms of its potential for law enforcement. A local sheriff said, "If they can pull it off, it will revolutionize law enforcement. It will be the best thing that has happened to law enforcement since the two-way radio." Thomas McGreevy, head of the Crime Information Center, said that the current turnaround for checking the 1,500 cards that come in each month is 23 to 30 days. Authorities hope the new system can do the same work in 1 or 2 days.

SOURCE: Esther M. Bauer, "Helping Hand Offered on Fingerprints," *Atlanta Journal,* July 3, 1984, p. 6-C.

The **video disk** is the newest form of secondary storage that can hold millions of characters and can be removed from its player. As with the cartridge, this is *currently* a read only device. However, research indicates that read and write video disks may be available before the end of the 1980s.

Output

The two most popular output devices are the printer and the video screen, or monitor. Other names for a monitor are CRT (cathode ray tube) and VDT (video display terminal). The **monitor** is very useful for any computer system for two reasons. First, it shows the user the data or instructions that are input from the keyboard or other input device. A cursor moves on the screen while the data or instructions are input. Second, the monitor is an almost instantaneous outlet for results.

This monochrome monitor is useful for working with text and numerical analyses.

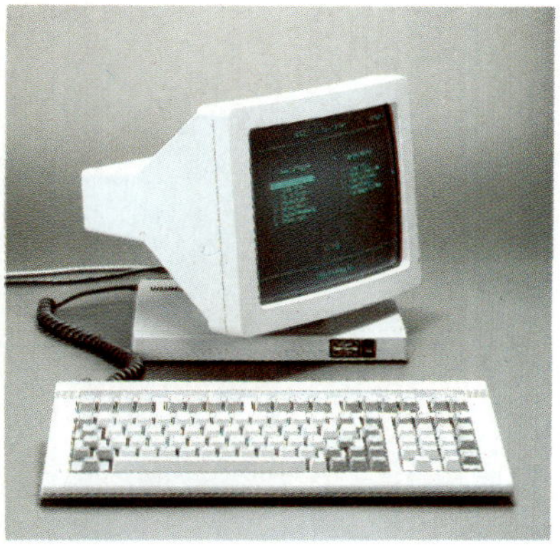

Several varieties of monitors are available. A **monochrome monitor** is the equivalent of black-and-white television, with light symbols on a dark background. Monochrome monitors are acceptable for all applications except those requiring color. **Full color monitors** are very useful for games and graphics. An ordinary television—either black-and-white or color—can be used as a monitor, but the quality of the picture is not as good as with a special purpose monitor, especially for character representation. However, a user may choose this option with an inexpensive personal computer if he or she does not consider high-quality character representation important.

Output to a **printer** yields **hard copy** in the form of a printed page. Such hard copy is useful, because the output to the monitor disappears when additional output appears on the monitor, when the computer is turned off, or when the user disconnects from a mainframe computer. Mainframe users can easily divert the output on the monitor to a line printer at a computer center. A **line printer** is a high-speed printer that can print an entire 132-character line in one motion. For personal computer users, a tremendous variety of printers are available today in all speeds, qualities of print, and price ranges. A full discussion of printers is presented in Chapter 7.

An innovative method of output is the use of synthesized speech to relay results to the user. A fictional example of this type of output is the voice of Kitt, the car on the television series *Knight Rider*. On a more realistic note, speech synthesizers can now generate recognizable speech on some personal computers, and development continues for hardware and software that produce a high quality of recognizable speech.

Secondary storage can also be an input or output device. Results are sent to a disk or tape for storage, or data or instructions are read from disk or tape. Read only secondary storage—such as cartridges or video disks—can be used as an input device to the computer.

Another form of input/output involves computer control of industrial, business, and home processes. The control device receives input as signals from the process that is controlled, such as time, temperature, or moisture content. The computer output signals the control device to respond appropriately. For example, a large shopping mall can use a computer to control its lights, turning them on and off at the appropriate times. Another example is the use of a computer to monitor the temperature and control the heaters in a sports stadium broadcast booth.

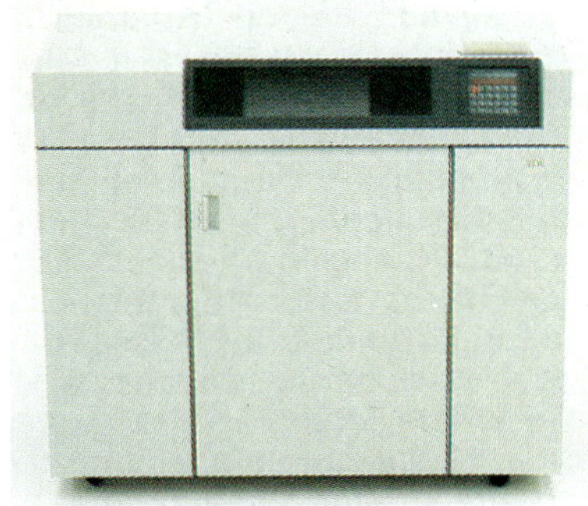

This high-speed printer can print an entire line of text in a single motion—hence, the name, line printer.

Input/Output Telecommunications

A device that facilitates both input and output is the **modem**, which sends information over telephone lines. The modem must be able to convert the electrical signals from the computer that would normally go to an output device into signals that can travel over telephone lines. In other words, the output signal must be modulated before it can be sent over a telephone line, and information received over the telephone line must be demodulated before it can be used for input. The term *modem* is derived because the equipment MOdulates/DEModulates signals. Using a modem a computer terminal or a personal computer can communicate with a mainframe or with other personal computers. Because the computer user can send and receive infor-

The modem at the right hand of this personal computer user is connected directly to a telephone line, allowing telecommunications with other computers.

CONTROLLING YOUR HOME

How would you like to have a computer control the electrical devices in your home, scare off burglars, and water your garden? It may sound futuristic, but it's not! Doug Mosher, a writer living in San Francisco, has used a Radio Shack Color Computer to handle all of these operations since 1982. Mosher purchased a controller that could be attached to his computer and then wrote a clock/date program to manage his household appliances. This program and controller turn on his lights slowly to awaken him, turn on his coffee pot before he rises, and control his lights at night when he is away. This last control might make an observer believe someone is moving from room to room. All of this control is achieved without extra wiring or signaling devices, because the electrical wiring in the house carries the needed signals to the individual devices.

One of Mosher's more interesting uses of the computer is to control his rooftop garden sprinkler system. A set of sensors determines the moisture content of the soil. If the moisture level is below a certain point, then the sprinklers are turned on for a preset length of time.

Other individuals are using the computer to control their homes, too. The only limit to what can be done is apparently the user's imagination.

SOURCE: David Gabel, "How a Computer Can Control Your Home," *Popular Computing,* March 1983, pp. 56–62, 187, 189.

A personal computer can be used to control home appliances. For example, with home appliance control software, a personal computer can be programmed to have this coffee maker brew coffee at a specific time.

mation over telephone lines, the terminal or personal computer acts as both an input and an output device for the mainframe or personal computer. This function is useful for individuals who work at home, use an information service to research some topic, or communicate with other computer users.

A special type of modem is the **acoustical modem**. A telephone handset can be plugged into this type of modem after a desired number has been dialed and the connection made. The acoustical modem then converts signals sent or received over the telephone. **Direct connect modems** have the phone line plugged in directly.

THE COMPLETE COMPUTER

Now that we have considered the four major components of computer hardware in detail, we can put together a basic computer system. By a **system**, we mean all of the items that together produce a working whole. The computer system shown in Figure 2-2 includes terminals (keyboard and monitor) and a card reader for input, a CPU for processing/internal memory, a disk drive with disk pack and a tape drive for secondary storage, and a line printer for output.

A corresponding personal computer system is shown in Figure 2-3. In this case, input is also accomplished with keyboard and monitor. The joystick and mouse are two input devices that are useful for game-playing and drawing on the screen. The processing/internal memory unit includes both RAM and ROM, and secondary storage is a floppy disk drive. The system could also include a hard disk drive. For output, a portable printer is used in addition to the monitor. A modem is also included for communication with a mainframe or with other personal computers.

Although the personal computer system in Figure 2-3 does not represent any particular brand of personal computer, it should give you a general idea of what a personal computer system looks like. With the exception of the processing/internal memory, keyboard, and monitor, the devices in this system are **peripheral devices**. Elementary computing is possible without these devices, but they add much of the power to the computer needed for complex operations.

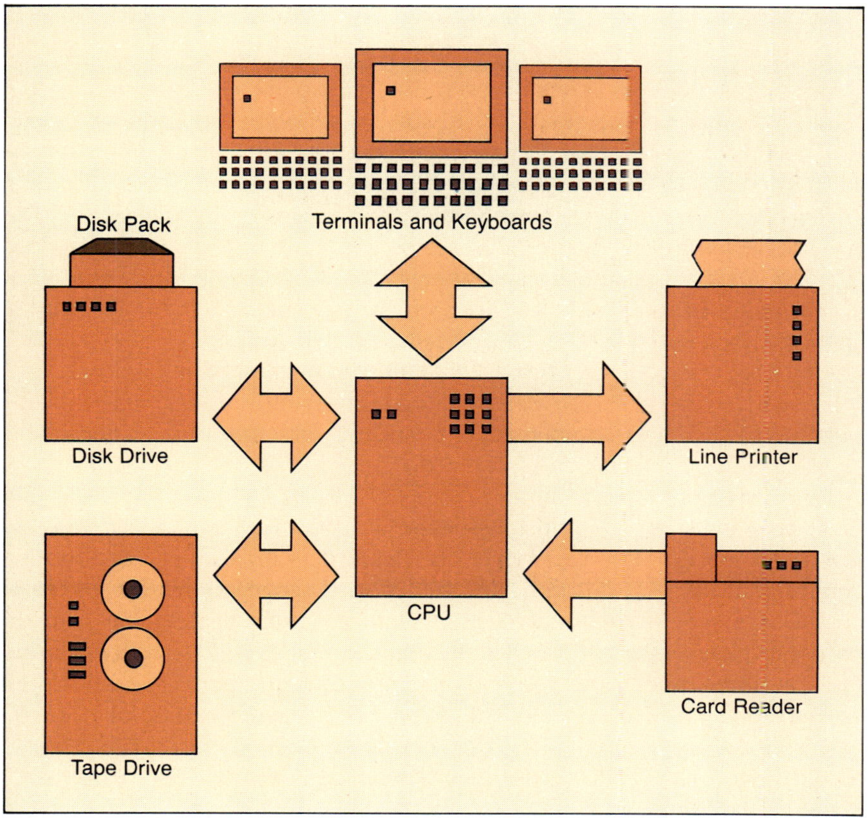

FIGURE 2-2
Mainframe Computer System

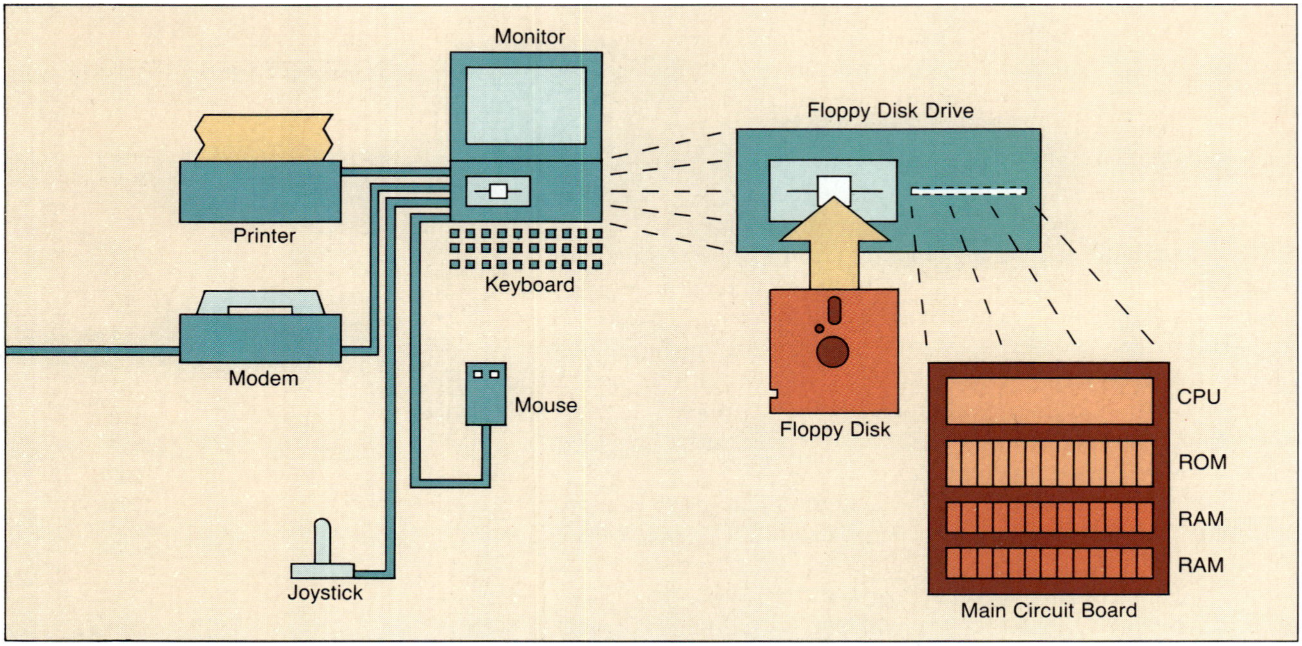

FIGURE 2-3
Personal Computer System

BITS, BYTES, AND BINARY NUMBERS

In this chapter, we have discussed the parts of a computer and have shown how a conceptual computer works. Now we discuss the logic underlying the operation of the central processing unit in somewhat more detail.

We have emphasized that an individual can use a computer without having a complete knowledge of how it works. A good analogy is learning to drive a car without knowing exactly what is happening under the hood. However, because the CPU is the brain of the computer and controls all other units, we must have some understanding of its operations to be knowledgeable computer users. This is like learning enough about your car so that if a mechanic looks under the hood and tells you that you need a new muffler, you know to take your car elsewhere. Another reason for taking a closer look at the logic of the CPU is to understand computer terminology better. Many words associated with computers are connected with this logic, so an understanding of their background is valuable.

Every attempt to automate the drudgery of calculations must solve the problem of representing numerical values in the calculation device. On the abacus, these values are represented by beads on a series of strings. In mechanical calculators, the values are represented by gears and wheels. As a value is input, the wheel turns to a certain position to represent that value. If a second value is added to the first, the wheel turns enough to represent the addition. If the result of the addition is larger than 10, then a second wheel turns to show the tens position, and so on. On a calculator, multiplication is repeated addition, subtraction is the reverse of addition, and division is repeated subtraction. In all cases, the decimal number system (base 10) is used in the calculations.

A mechanical calculator uses a system of gears and wheels. How does a computer that uses only electricity work? This question would be difficult to answer if we used the decimal number system. However, computers do not have 10 fingers, so they do not need to use the base 10 system of counting. The number system used by computers is determined by the key characteristic of electricity—it is either "on" or "off." Mechanical wheels have any number of positions for digits, but electricity can accommodate only two digits, which correspond to the electrical states of on and off. Consequently, the base 2, or **binary number system**, is used for counting in an electronic computer. Table 2-1 shows how the numbers 0–10 are represented in binary.

To represent a number in binary in the computer, we need a series of switches to turn the electricity on and off. Figure 2-4 shows how the computer represents the decimal value of nine internally. The first and fourth switches are "on," causing the first and last light bulbs to glow. Because the second and third switches are "off," those bulbs remain dark. The only difference is in the type of switch used by computers. In one of the first computers, electromechanical relays provided the switching, but they were slow and required constant adjustment. Next, vacuum tubes were used as switches, but they generated a great deal of heat and tended to burn out during calculations. In 1947, the solid-state transistor was developed and could be used as a switch with great speed and low heat and power requirements. Such devices came to be known as *flip-flops,* because their state could be changed—from off to on and back to off—by the application and removal of electrical current. A flip-flop is similar to a switch that would control the light bulbs in Figure 2-4.

Table 2-1
BINARY REPRESENTATIONS OF DECIMAL VALUES

Decimal Value	*Binary Representation*
0	0
1	1
2	10
3	11
4	100
5	101
6	110
7	111
8	1000
9	1001
10	1010

Binary Arithmetic

Counting in the binary number system is like counting in decimal—you simply add one to the previous number. The key difference is that the addition rules are much simpler to remember. In binary, the digit 2 does not exist; therefore, $0 + 0 = 0$; $0 + 1 = 1$ and $1 + 0 = 1$; and $1 + 1 = 0$ with a carry of 1, or 10. Continuing with these rules, $1 + 10 = 11$; $11 + 1 = 100$, because we must carry twice. Addition in binary is easy as long as we follow these rules.

FIGURE 2-4
Representation of the Number Nine Using Light Bulbs

For example, the addition of 2 and 3 in decimal is represented in binary as 10 + 11 = 101.

Multiplication in binary is also very simple, because the multiplication table has only the following four entries: $0 \times 0 = 0$; $0 \times 1 = 0$; $1 \times 0 = 0$; and $1 \times 1 = 1$. The multiplication of 3×3 in decimal is represented in binary as follows:

```
  11
  11
----
  11
 11
----
1001
```

Subtraction and division are simply the reverse of addition and multiplication, respectively.

If arithmetic is so easy in binary, why don't we use it instead of the decimal system? The shortcoming with binary is the same as that with Roman numerals—expressing even moderately large numbers requires many digits. For example, expressing the value 99 requires only two digits in decimal, but it requires seven digits in binary—1100011. Representing large numbers with many digits is a problem for humans, but it causes no problem for computers, which have many switches to handle the necessary positions.

From Bits to Bytes

The basic unit of measure in a computer is a **bit**. The term is a contraction of BInary and digiT. One bit corresponds to one switch in the computer. As discussed earlier, these switches in a modern computer are located on the chips that make up the computer's CPU and internal memory.

Although the computer could use a variable number of bits to represent values of varying size, a standard procedure involves using groups of 8 bits. By working with a group of 8 bits, called a **byte**, the computer can manipulate and transfer information. The actual number of bits that are manipulated and transferred depends on the type of CPU chip used in the computer. Because a byte is made up of 8 bits, the largest number it can represent is 255, or 11111111 in binary. Because 255 is not large enough for any practical calculations, a computer combines bytes to allow representation of larger numbers. The number of bytes that are used depends on the type of computer. Supercomputers use 8 bytes (64 bits), many mainframes use 4 bytes (32 bits), and many personal computers use 2 bytes (16 bits).

Representing Symbols

So far in this section, we have explained how numbers are represented in a computer. We now examine how symbols are represented in the computer.

Representing symbols using bits is easy. We merely choose a pattern of bits to represent a given symbol. Several patterns of bits have been suggested, but the two most commonly used codes are the **EBCDIC** (pronounced eb-see-dick), which is an acronym for **Extended Binary Coded Decimal Interchange Code**, and **ASCII** (pronounced as-key), which is an acronym for **American Standard Code for Information Interchange.** EBCDIC, which uses 8 bits to represent symbols, was developed by IBM for use on their mainframe computers. ASCII is also an 8-bit code that has become the standard code for personal computers. Examples of the EBCDIC and ASCII representation of symbols are shown in Table 2-2.

Table 2-2 EBCDIC AND ASCII REPRESENTATION OF VARIOUS CHARACTERS

Character	*EBCDIC Representation*	*ASCII Representation*
1	11110001	00110001
2	11110010	00110010
3	11110011	00110011
A	11000001	01000001
B	11000010	01000010
Y	11101000	01011001
Z	11101001	01011010
a	10000001	01100001
b	10000010	01100011
y	10101000	01111001
z	10101001	01111010
!	01011010	00100001
;	01011110	00111011

When we set the upper limit of PC-DOS at 640K, we thought nobody would ever need that much memory.

William Gates, Chairman of Microsoft

(As quoted in "Give Me Power," *Infoworld,* April 29, 1985, p. 5.)

These random access memory (RAM) chips each hold 64K bits of memory. A row of nine chips like these is required to store 64 Kbytes of internal memory.

Because each character can be represented by 1 byte in either ASCII or EBCDIC, the terms *byte* and *character* are commonly used interchangeably. For example, in the discussion of the amount of storage available in internal memory or secondary storage, we referred to a certain number of *characters* of storage. This same reference to storage capacity is often given in bytes rather than characters.

Storing Information

Both random access memory (RAM) and read only memory (ROM) use memory chips to store information in binary form. The amounts of RAM and ROM available in a particular computer are measured in **Kbytes** (1 Kbyte = 1,024 bytes). The letter "K" stands for *kilo,* which is Greek for 1,000. Even though 1,024 (which is 2^{10}) does not equal 1,000, the term *Kbyte,* or simply the letter "K," is still used. For example, 64K of memory means $64 \times 1{,}024 = 65{,}536$ bytes of memory. The next measure of memory after a Kbyte is a **megabyte (Mbyte)**, which is 1,024 Kbytes, or approximately 1 million bytes, of storage.

Early personal computers had less than 16K of RAM, but current machines can have over 512K of RAM; 256K is a common amount of memory. Mainframe computers often have well over 1 Mbyte of internal memory available. Less ROM is needed because it is used for a special purpose that is known in advance by the computer designer. The amount of ROM varies from computer to computer. In Chapter 6, we discuss special chips that combine the characteristics of RAM and ROM chips.

REVIEW OF KEY POINTS

- A conceptual computer is composed of input, output, processing/internal memory, and secondary storage units.
- The input unit sends data and instructions to the computer; the keyboard is a common input device for mainframes and personal computers.
- The output unit transmits the results from the computer to the user; the monitor and printer are common output devices.
- The processing/internal memory unit performs the manipulation and storage of symbols within the computer.
- The processing unit, made up of the control unit and the arithmetic-logic unit (ALU), is usually referred to as the central processing unit (CPU).
- Internal memory is made up of random access memory (RAM) and read only memory (ROM).
- Both the CPU and internal memory are built onto silicon chips.
- Secondary storage is needed because RAM is both limited and volatile; tape and disk are common secondary storage devices.
- Communication with another computer is accomplished with a modem.
- The binary number system is used in computers because the computer uses switches to handle logic and memory.
- Using the EBCDIC or ASCII codes, it is possible to represent letters, digits, and symbols in 8 bits (a byte); one character corresponds to 1 byte.
- Memory is measured in Kbytes (1,024 bytes) or Mbytes (1,024 Kbytes).

KEY TERMS

acoustical modem
American Standard Code for Information Interchange (ASCII)
arithmetic-logic unit (ALU)
binary number system
bit
byte
card reader
cartridges
central processing unit (CPU)
chip
conceptual computer
control unit
cursor
data

direct access
direct connect modems
disk
disk drive
disk packs
Extended Binary Coded Decimal Interchange Code (EBCDIC)
floppy disks
full color monitors
hard copy
hard disk
hardware
input
integrated circuit
internal memory
joystick
Kbytes
keyboard
keypunching
light pen
line printer
megabyte (Mbyte)
microchip
microprocessor
modem
monitor
monochrome monitor
mouse
output
paper tape
peripheral devices
printer
processing/internal memory unit
punched (computer) card
random access memory (RAM)
read only memory (ROM)
read/write head
registers
secondary storage
sequential access
software
system
tape
tape drive
touch pad
touch screen
tracks
transistors
video disk
voice recognition
volatile

REVIEW QUESTIONS

1. Explain the analogy between the parts of the computer and the way humans think, act, and keep records.
2. List four items that are commonly used to input data to a computer.
3. List two commonly used output devices for a computer.
4. Differentiate between direct access and sequential access secondary storage devices.
5. Differentiate between RAM and ROM.
6. Why is RAM volatile?
7. Explain the meaning of the term *modem* for input/output computer communications.
8. Discuss a system or process around you that is controlled by a computer.
9. Determine the sum of 6 and 9 using binary addition. Find the product of 6 and 9 in binary.
10. Visit a computer store and determine how much internal memory (RAM and ROM) is available on some of the personal computers available. Ask about the amount of secondary storage on the same machines. Compare these values to those on your local mainframe (if you have one).

ramtek

3

An Introduction to Computer Software

This chapter introduces you to the other half of the computer—the software that directs the operations of the hardware. The chapter discussion stresses the importance of software for the successful use of the computer, addresses the computer languages used in the preparation of software, and comments on a user's decision either to buy software packages or to prepare his or her own software. The three major types of software—systems software, utility software, and applications software—are then discussed. This discussion emphasizes applications software on both mainframes and personal computers. Applications software includes programs for science, engineering, business, home, education, and recreation. The six types of applications software packages for personal computers that have received much media attention—word processing, accounting, financial analysis, data base management, graphics, and telecommunications—are covered in detail. Finally, an overview of programming includes the use of programs by the computer and the process of writing a program.

STUDY OBJECTIVES

After reading this chapter, you should be able to

- Understand the importance of software in the successful use of a computer.
- Discuss how computer languages are used to prepare software.
- Review the three major types of software—systems, utility, and applications software.
- Recognize the use of applications programs in various human endeavors.
- Understand the use of the six most popular business applications software packages for personal computers.
- Understand how a program is written and how it controls the computer.
- Recognize and understand important software terminology.

THE IMPORTANCE OF SOFTWARE

The general term for the instructions given to the computer by the user or the manufacturer is **software**. Any magazine article on the computer and its effect on our lives emphasizes the importance of software. Recent advances in hardware technology are mind-boggling, but without software, the computer is nothing more than a well-constructed combination of silicon chips and electronic circuitry. A computer without software is like a car without a driver or a camera without film. The computer hardware *must* have software to direct it.

In its April 16, 1984 cover story on software, *Time* magazine called software the "wizard in the machine," meaning that software is the real source of those wonderful applications reported in the national media. A *Business Week* article that described software as the "driving force" quoted the president of a commercial software firm as saying, "Hardware is getting less and less distinguished. Software is what's leading the industry."[1] Both articles emphasize that chips and circuitry can be combined in only so many ways to build a

[1] "Software: The New Driving Force," *Business Week,* February 27, 1984, pp. 74–98.

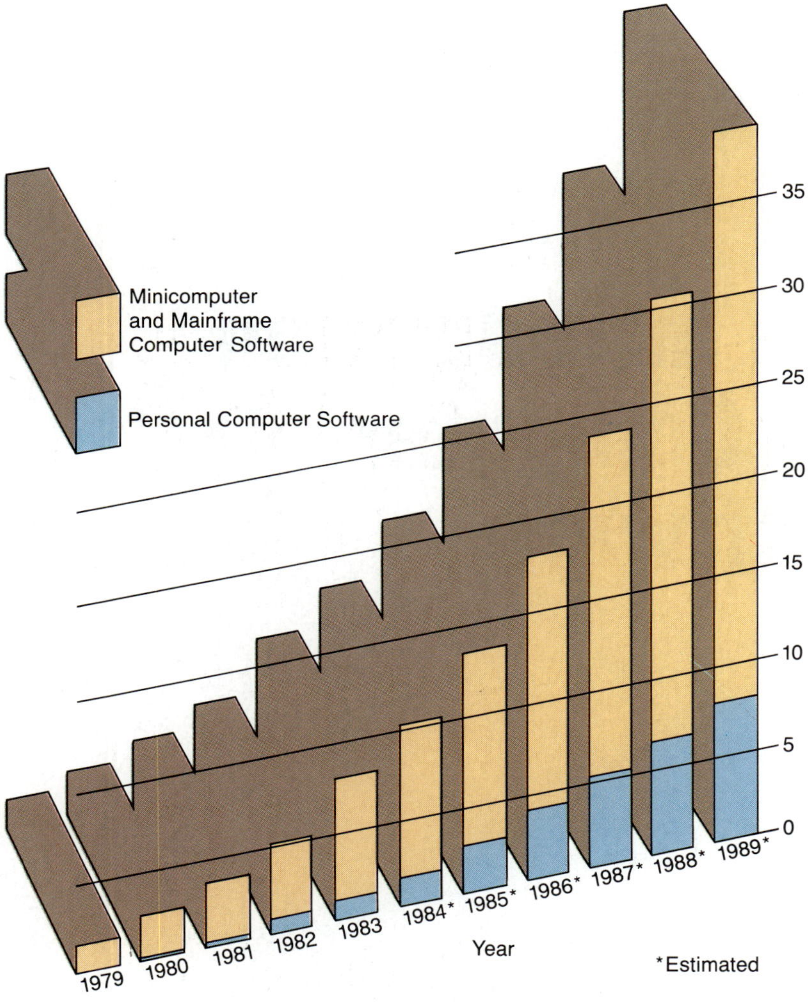

FIGURE 3-1
Growth of Software Sales
(Reprinted from the February 27, 1984 issue of *Business Week* by special permission, © 1984 by McGraw-Hill, Inc.)

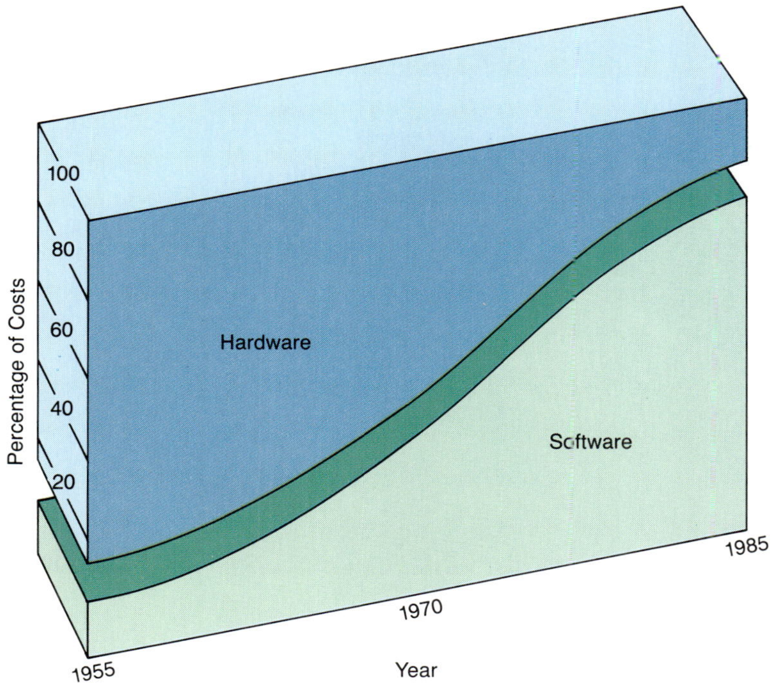

FIGURE 3-2
The Growing Software Gap
(SOURCE: Stanford Research Institute International, Palo Alto, CA)

computer, but software can instruct a computer to perform a virtually unlimited number of activities.

The growth of the software industry has been as dramatic as the increase in personal computer sales. In 1980, total software sales were $2.5 billion. In 1984, software industry sales grew to $10.2 billion, and 1989 sales are projected in excess of $39 billion. Figure 3-1 demonstrates graphically the growth of this industry. Such phenomenal growth has changed the former "cottage industry," in which a one-person company could write one program and make it big. New programs are now marketed with the same Madison Avenue tactics as cars, cereal, and soap. *Billboard* magazine tracks the top 20 personal computer packages in much the same way that it keeps up with top-selling records. Such market research companies as Future Computing and Input also monitor the industry.

Although the cost of hardware has decreased dramatically over the last decade, the cost of software has remained the same or increased. Hardware can be mass produced, but each software package must be individually developed. This relative change in hardware and software costs is referred to as the **software gap**, shown graphically in Figure 3-2.

Programs and Programming

In Chapter 2, we discussed how a computer manipulates and stores symbols by turning switches on and off. To know which switches should be on or off, the computer must have a specific set of instructions. This set of instructions is called a **computer program**, and the process of developing a computer program that controls and directs the computer to perform a desired action is called **programming**. All software, whether built into the machine by the manufacturer, purchased by the user, or developed by the user, is the result of a person's creating the set of instructions for the computer.

The popular Symphony software package from Lotus comes with system disks, utility disks, tutorial disks, and user's manual.

A **software package** consists of one or more programs combined with a set of directions called a **user's manual**. Mainframe software packages, available on a disk pack or tape, are accessed by entering the correct commands from a terminal. Directions for using specific mainframe packages are usually available from a computer center's library. For personal computers, software packages are stored on one or more disks. A bound manual of directions is usually included with the disks, and the combination is often packaged in a box or ring binder.

The computer can only do what it is told by the program. Therefore, the program must tell the computer *everything* about the process that is being programmed. To accomplish this, the programmer uses a step-by-step approach to develop a program. After the program is developed, it is written in a **computer language**. Many computer languages (over 100) can be used to communicate with a computer. Each computer language, like human language, has its own vocabulary and grammatical rules, but all computer languages share a logical approach to communication with the computer. Commonly used languages for programming computers are BASIC, COBOL, FORTRAN, PL/I, Pascal, LOGO, and C.

Would-be computer users who think programming is the computer's only role may not purchase a computer because they do not want to program. However, with the abundance of software packages available, it is not necessary to learn programming to be a successful computer user.

TYPES OF SOFTWARE PACKAGES

An ever-growing number of software packages are available to the computer user. In fact, nobody knows, or can even reasonably estimate, the number of programs that are available. For example, one 1984 estimate stated that between 8,000 and 40,000 programs for mainframes and personal computers existed! Over 1,000 software firms range in size from a large corporation with many products to a small com-

COMPUTER LANGUAGES
Why So Many?

Why do so many computer languages exist? In many cases, a language was developed with a specific purpose in mind, as in the following examples.

FORTRAN (FORmula TRANslator), the first computer language developed, is used for scientific purposes. Developed for business computing, COBOL (COmmon Business Oriented Language) is used in many situations that involve billing and file manipulation. A language that is used for programming the software that manages a computer's operations is C. Bell Laboratories supposedly developed two other languages, A and B, before the language it eventually released. A multi-purpose language developed by IBM for mainframes is PL/I (Programming Language/I).

Several languages were developed as instructional tools. BASIC (Beginner's All-purpose Symbolic Instruction Code) uses some of the vocabulary and grammar of FORTRAN and is a very popular language for personal computers. Pascal, named for French mathematician Blaise Pascal, was developed in 1970 by Niklaus Wirth. Another language that was developed primarily for instructional purposes is LOGO. This language is characterized by a special cursor, called a turtle, which can be moved on the screen by the software to create designs. LOGO has even been used at the kindergarten level to teach beginning computer concepts and programming.

Even a preschool child can learn to control the LOGO Turtle, as shown in the MIT LOGO Laboratory.

pany that specializes in one product. This wide variety of software and software companies can confuse a beginning user.

Three types of software are used in a computer—systems software, utility software, and applications software. All three types of software are usually at work in the computer at the same time, each serving a different purpose.

Systems software is important because it controls the operations of the other two types of software. The most important part of systems software is the operating system that directs the operations of the computer. Each type of mainframe computer has its own proprietary operating system, but several operating systems can be used on different brands of personal computers. Operating systems are discussed in Chapter 9.

Utility software controls the computer's day-to-day "housekeeping" operations. This type of software controls such operations as making copies of information, displaying a list of user information, or allowing different computer languages to be used on a computer. Utility software is usually supplied with the systems software so it is sometimes difficult to distinguish between systems and utility software. For personal computers, the utility software is supplied on the same disk as the systems software.

Science is difficult to learn by lecture. It's easier to learn when you can experiment using the computer. It's not that computers are better than teachers, but students can learn more with a computer around.

Dr. Moira Gunn, spokesperson for Catch on to Computers
(As quoted in "Let Them Eat Cereal," *Infosystems,* December 1983, p. 70.)

FIGURE 3-3
The Onion View of Software

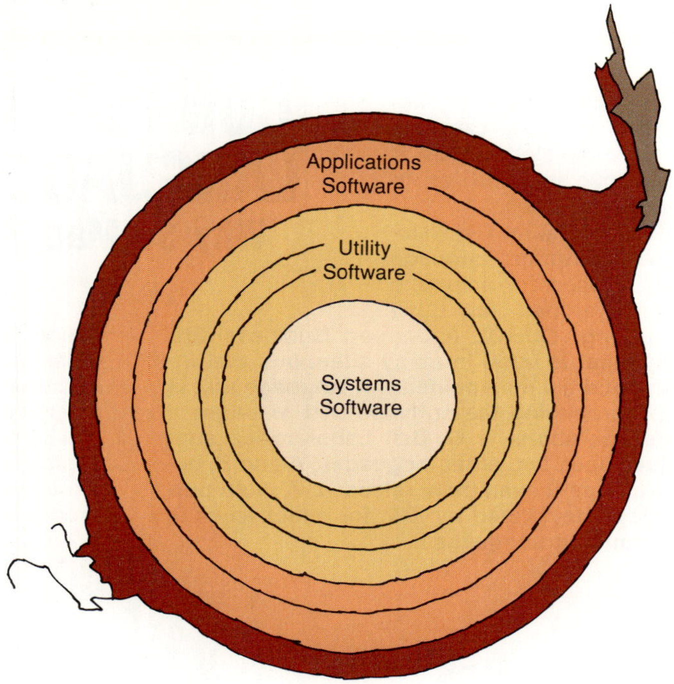

Applications software constitutes the greatest proportion of software used on computers. This software performs the specialized tasks that we hear so much about, including calculating payrolls, guiding space shuttles, word processing, home budgeting, games, and many others.

We can view these three types of software and the way they work concurrently in the computer as the "onion" in Figure 3-3. The outer layer of the onion is applications software, which is evident to the user because it actually performs a desired task. Underneath the applications software is the utility software, which remains invisible to the user until a housekeeping chore—such as copying information—is required. Finally, at the core of the "onion" is the systems software, which is almost completely invisible to the user.

Systems Software

The primary component of systems software is the **operating system**. This software manages the many tasks that are going on concurrently within a computer, including managing the input and output operations and managing the transfer of information between internal memory and secondary storage. On mainframes, the operating system allocates memory to the many individuals who may be using the computer at one time. In this environment, the operating system must also handle the different types of operations that each user requires.

On a personal computer, the operating system must manage the frequent transfer of information between internal memory and secondary storage. Because most personal computers today can use a disk secondary storage system, the term **disk operating system (DOS)** is commonly used to describe a personal computer's operating system. Because different types of personal computers can use the same operating system, some degree of standardization is possible among personal computers through the operating systems. Three commonly used operating systems that are not machine spe-

Multiple users can share the resources of a mainframe computer through interactive terminals such as these.

cific are CP/M (Control Program for Microcomputers), MS-DOS (Microsoft DOS), and UNIX from Bell Laboratories.

Utility Software

Working on a mainframe requires that a user keep track of a library of information that is organized into units called **files**. Files are often modified, copied between disk and tape storage, or combined with language software to write and run programs. These and numerous other operations fall into the utility software category.

A personal computer's DOS also includes the utility software necessary to handle the housekeeping tasks of keeping a user's information straight on his or her disk. As with a mainframe, the information on a disk is organized into files, each of which is given a name by the individual who places it on the disk. Some files may be placed on the disk by the developer of the operating system and others by the user of the computer. Listing a directory of these files is one utility software function.

Applications Software

The largest amount of software available to the computer user is applications software. Applications software has been written for the full gamut of human pursuits; examples are inventory management, resource allocation, production control, religion, astronomy, marriage counseling, contract bridge, horse racing, genealogy, accounting, word processing, and ham radio operation. In fact, it is safe to say that software exists (or will soon exist) for any topic you can imagine! The problem is finding the proper software for a given application. Mainframe computer centers usually have libraries that contain information on applications software, send out literature on new software, and have periodic classes on various types of software. Computer centers also usually have a staff that supports users by answering questions on all types of software.

Applications software is available in a variety of fields. Using specially designed software, a dairy farmer (left) can use a personal computer to measure accurately the feed and lactation of each cow. Using inventory control software and voice input, the operator at right can enter information on receipts and shipments into the computer to update current inventory levels.

To respond to the ever-growing supply of applications software for personal computers, various publications now periodically list available software. *The Whole Earth Software Catalog,* the *PC Clearinghouse Software Directory,* and the *PC Telemart Software Directory* are three popular software publications. The 1984 edition of the *PC Telemart Software Directory* had 1,053 pages of software listings! Various computer magazines also review new personal computer software as it is released.

The use of applications software packages depends on a computer's hardware and operating system. As a result, a package written for one machine or DOS cannot run on another machine or DOS. For example, the wide variety of software that has been written for the Apple series of computers (Apple II, Apple IIe, and so on) does not run on Radio Shack, Commodore, or IBM personal computers, and vice versa. Similarly, applications software written for the CP/M operating system does not run on machines using the MS-DOS operating system. Users must ensure that the software they purchase indeed runs on their machines.

EXAMPLES OF APPLICATIONS SOFTWARE

Applications software for computers can be used in the following five areas: science and engineering problems, businesses, the home, education, and game-playing. In this section, we discuss the types of software packages used in each area.

Science and Engineering Applications

Beginning with the ENIAC, the computer has been used to help with the often complex and tedious calculations involved in science and engineering. Although specific programs must often be written by the user for a particular application, numerous programs have been developed for general use. Examples include linear programming packages for resource allocation and agriculture feed-mix calculations, statistical packages for analyzing large amounts of data in all areas of science, and computer-aided design (CAD) and manufacturing (CAM) packages that increase the effectiveness of these processes. Until recently, these packages were available only for mainframes, but scaled-down versions are now available for personal computers.

Business Applications

For many years, computers were used only in large organizations like business, government, and universities. Not surprisingly, a large amount of software is available for business data processing applications on mainframe computers. Accounting, inventory, project management, list processing, personnel record keeping, and financial analysis are some examples of the data processing applications in large organizations. Sometimes special programs must be written to handle an organization's data processing needs, but in many cases, organizations can use commercially available software packages.

The applications of personal computer business software vary according to the size of the organization. In large organizations, because mainframe computers are necessary to handle the volume of data processing that occurs in this environment, personal computers are used mostly for managerial decision making or for specific applications. Managers often use financial analysis (spreadsheet) packages during the budgeting process to help them consider the result of changes in financial conditions. Small organizations use the personal computer for many of the same functions that large organizations use mainframes. The personal computer is used for word processing in a variety of situations. Personal computer applications in business also exist in farm and ranch management, volunteer organizations, and sports.

Six specific types of business applications software packages for personal computers are commonly used—word processing, accounting (personal budgeting), financial analysis (spreadsheet), data base management, graphics, and telecommunications. The use of these six packages is so widespread in business and in other areas that they are discussed in detail later in this chapter and in Chapters 10–13. These six types of software packages are also available on disk with this text for IBM and Apple computers.

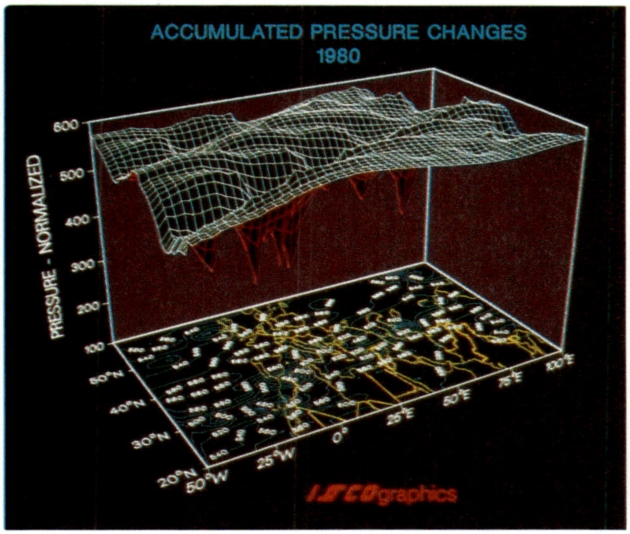

Science and business use applications software to great advantage. Mainframe graphics (left) can dramatically show various types of comparisons in science and engineering. Office systems (right) use computers and software that offer a full range of functions, including word and list processing, networking, and data communications.

Home Applications

Personal computer applications packages written specifically for home use include home management packages and personal financial management packages. Many business applications packages can also be used at home.

Financial analysis (spreadsheet) and accounting (personal budgeting) packages can help plan the yearly household budget and show the effects of expenditures not considered in the initial planning process. Word processing can help with correspondence, and checkbook accounting packages are also available. Other software packages enable a homemaker to save recipes on the computer.

A data base management package can be extremely helpful with a hobby that involves a great deal of record keeping, like bird-watching, stamp or coin collecting, and ham radio operation. Information can be retrieved and sorted in many ways, so the hobbyist can easily find the specific data he or she wants.

Telecommunications packages are widely used in the home. When these packages are combined with a modem and telephone, a user can tie into the mainframe computers at such national networks as The Source and CompuServe to bank, shop, or retrieve information. They can also contact other users by leaving messages on electronic bulletin boards, sending electronic mail, or engaging in a simulated CB (citizens band) conversation (typed on the keyboard, of course). This form of communication is one of the fastest growing uses of the computer.

Educational Packages

The computer has been extremely useful at all levels of education. Mainframe computers have been used at colleges and universities for educational purposes for over 30 years, but the advent of the personal computer has allowed elementary schools, middle schools, high schools, and junior colleges to use computers. A recent study showed that almost every school district in the United States has at least one personal computer for student use, and the number of computers used in schools is expected to grow.

Various studies show that elementary schools tend to use computers for basic skills, whereas middle schools tend to use computers for remedial instruction or for an introduction to the computer as a tool. High schools tend to use computers in vocational education to teach keyboarding skills, word processing, or programming. Colleges use the computer to solve prob-

---

"CHATTING" Via Computer

An interesting facet of telecommunication via a personal computer is the free-wheeling discussion that can take place on either major computer network, The Source or CompuServe. On CompuServe, these discussions, or "chats," take place on 36 simulated CB (citizens band) channels. Armed with a user number and password, CompuServe subscribers can log on by phone and check out each channel's current users. Users have names like CB handles—such as Tar Heel and Bulldog Barry—for identification. After "tuning" into the desired channel, the subscriber can join the conversation simply by typing messages and replying to questions from other users. Subscribers can also use a "private" line for less frenzied communication. Many friendships, and even a few marriages, have resulted between network subscribers who initially knew no more about each other than their respective handles and a mutual interest in computers. We should insert a word of caution: although hourly rates on these computer networks are reasonable—$5–$10 per hour—long-term "chatting" can be expensive!

---

lems and to teach programming in such areas as business, science, and engineering.

With the appropriate software, a computer can be used at least three different ways in the learning process. First, the computer can be a tutor, an approach commonly referred to as **computer-aided instruction (CAI)**. The CAI software often includes programs that provide the student with drill-and-practice routines, learning games, interactive tests, and self-paced learning. Graphics (pictures), sound, and voice emulation often liven up the learning process and reward the student when a correct answer is entered. The use of CAI is especially useful in early grades for teaching math and grammar skills because of the instant response and game-like atmosphere that surrounds the learning. A mainframe educational system called PLATO (see the boxed insert on page 56) provides computer-aided instruction for junior and senior high school students and college students. PLATO has several thousand programs that include everything from language instruction to real estate.

With the second type of educational software, the student can use the computer as a tool rather than as a tutor. For instance, the student may learn keyboarding skills and word processing as an aid to composition because the material is so easily entered and edited to change content and correct errors. The computer is also used as a tool to make tedious calculations and statistical analyses and for record keeping. Some educational software also allows students to run simulated experiments in science class that would not otherwise be possible due to either danger or cost. The military uses this approach to test various defense strategies.

The third type of educational software teaches programming itself. Programming is taught in virtually every college and university and in many elementary, middle, and high schools. Languages commonly taught include LOGO and BASIC at the lower levels and BASIC, Pascal, FORTRAN, and COBOL at the college level. Usually the software used in language instruction allows the student to write, test, and run programs, but occasionally software alerts the student to poor program design.

One exciting use of educational software is in working with learning disabled children. Because these individuals often have very short attention spans, a computer's instant feedback and exciting graphics can help them complete an assignment (see the boxed insert on page 56).

What is missing now and appears to be missing for the future is the development of good software materials . . . for purposes of teaching not only computer literacy, but more importantly, for the purpose of enhancing the teaching of other topics, ranging from expository writing to mathematics.

Joe B. Wyatt, Chancellor of Vanderbilt University

(As quoted in "Nation's Schools Need More Computer Tools," *USA Today*, June 28, 1984, p. 11A.)

The personal computer can make learning an exciting experience for students of all ages, including the very young (center). Many elementary and middle schools (left) use the LOGO computer language to teach programming concepts and logic. High school computer labs (right) are often used to teach programming and the use of software packages.

PLATO
An Education Network

The first large-scale computer network for education was called Programmed Learning and Training Opportunity (PLATO). It was developed at the University of Illinois in the 1960s as a time-sharing system using a mainframe. PLATO's features include Tutor (an early CAI language), touch screens, and high-quality graphics. Currently owned by the Control Data Corporation, PLATO is available on numerous U.S. university campuses and in schools, hospitals, and businesses around the world. PLATO uses special terminals to offer approximately 8,000 lessons in over 60 topics, including astrology, handwriting analysis, physics, finance, aviation, and interplanetary travel.

As a CAI system, PLATO uses the tremendous power and storage of mainframes to allow many different learning formats. It allows individualized instruction for students, insertion of an instructor's test questions, diagnostic testing and placement, and communications between student and instructor. PLATO's flexible structure allows an instructor to tailor material to his or her individual class needs.

PLATO can now be accessed by the home user via a network called Homelink. This network is available for personal computer users via a modem and telephone line. Using this network, a user can access many lessons and some games. A series of team games allows a user to join one of several teams that are fighting for control of the galaxy. Although home use of PLATO is still in its infancy, it offers the home user the same opportunities as those available at large educational institutions.

PLATO can be used for instruction in many different fields—such as helping this pilot train on a new aircraft's controls.

TEACHING DISABLED CHILDREN

An especially gratifying computer application motivates exceptional children to learn by showing them the things they can do on a computer. Dr. Laura Meyers and Dr. Teresa Rosegrant of the Infant Program at the Exceptional Children's Foundation in Los Angeles, California, have combined the ability of the computer to accept text and then to repeat the text via a voice synthesizer to teach handicapped children. One Down's Syndrome child learned 25 new words in his first session on the computer, compared with five words the entire previous year. In another instance, a frustrated and unhappy child, who was in danger of repeating the second grade, was encouraged to write about dirt bikes using the word processor–voice synthesizer combination. The child was later removed from the learning disabled class and sent on to the next grade.

The software and hardware combination used by Meyers and Rosegrant never tells a child what to do. Instead, it builds on what a child can do so that the child no longer feels like a failure. Many children who cannot read or write may be handicapped more by conventional instruction than by organic problems. As Meyers explains, "One way our software is different is that nothing happens unless the child does something. . . . The computer is the child's tool not his teacher."

SOURCE: Paul Trachtman, "Putting Computers into the Hands of Children without Language," *Smithsonian Magazine*, February 1984, pp. 42–51.

Games

Most children are introduced to the computer by a game, either at an arcade or at home with a special game-playing computer or a personal computer. Although computer games seem to be a recent invention, they have actually been around almost as long as the computer itself. Early games included tic-tac-toe, checkers, and Star Trek. The Star Trek game, which is based on the popular 1960s television show, involves the user as the commander of the starship Enterprise in a constant battle with various enemies. The popularity of various mainframe computer games is evidenced by the computer users who break into distant computers to play games. The mainframe games usually do not have the graphics of arcade games, but their power and storage capabilities make the games challenging.

Personal computer games can be either action–graphic games or logic games. These categories are not mutually exclusive, but they do cover most of the games available today. Examples of the action–graphic games include such popular arcade games as Ms. Pac-Man, Zaxxon, Asteroids, and Donkey Kong. Personal computer versions of these games use color graphics, and the player must use a joystick to move figures about on the screen to score points. Most arcade-style games use ROM cartridges and require a computer that can use this type of secondary storage device.

Other action–graphic games can be programmed into the computer and do not require the color graphics or the use of the joystick. These games are not as elaborate as the arcade-style games and they do not require ROM cartridges. Action is accomplished by use of the cursor movement keys or by pressing various other keys. These games are explained in many computer magazines and only require the user to key them into the computer.

Using a specially designed, mouth-controlled joystick and push button, this handicapped youth can play the computer game on an equal footing with his peers.

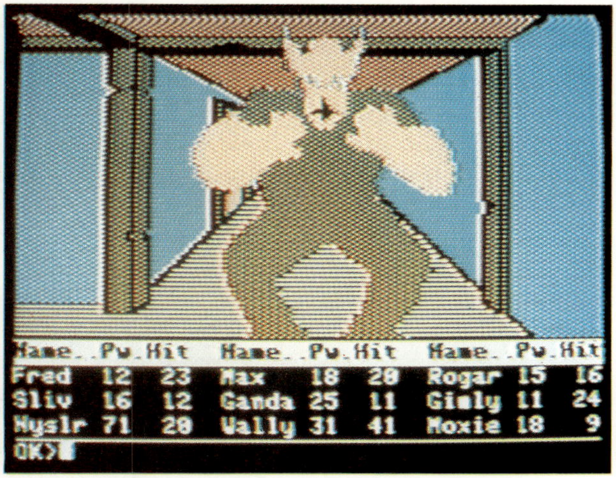

A home computer can draw a family together; at left, different generations find enjoyment in friendly competition in computer games. In the children's computer game at right, each competitor's name and score is displayed at the bottom of the screen.

Logic games include such popular board games as chess, Monopoly, or Scrabble, and many adventure–detective games that require the player to make decisions to score points. A popular series of adventure–detective games is the Zork series. Logic games are not restricted to personal computers, and some are available on mainframe computers. When using the mainframe for these games, finding their location and the commands necessary to access them can be a problem.

PERSONAL COMPUTER APPLICATIONS SOFTWARE

Because applications software has received so much attention in the media, this section discusses the six software packages that are used most often in business, home management, and hobby data collection and retrieval. These six types are word processing, accounting (personal budgeting), financial analysis (spreadsheet), data base management, graphics, and telecommunications. The discussion here briefly describes what each package can do for a user. These packages are discussed in more detail in Chapters 10–13.

Word Processing

One of the most useful functions of a personal computer is the ability to manipulate letters, digits, and punctuation marks to compose correspondence, papers, and documents using **word processing software**. Word processing on a personal computer means composing and editing on the video screen and then printing the final result as desired. Specifically, word processing software sets margins, line spacing, and tabs for the desired page format. When the text is entered from the keyboard, lines "wrap around" the margins and automatically continue to the next line. The user does not have to monitor the margins and "return" the cursor at the appropriate time. Word processing software can insert, delete, and strike over material on the screen; search the document for a particular sequence of characters or misspelled words; center material; paginate automatically; and sometimes even underline, boldface, or italicize material. Word processing software can also electronically "cut" a block of material from the document and "paste" it somewhere else in the current document or in a completely different document.

This textbook was written on a Radio Shack TRS-80 Model III personal computer using the SuperSCRIPSIT word processing package. Using this software, the author could easily key in the rough draft and then make the necessary revisions using the functions just discussed.

Accounting

Accounting software is extremely important for businesses because the accounting function enables the business to keep up-to-date and accurate records of the firm's financial position. Using the output from accounting software, a firm can make better short- and long-term plans. The major accounting functions in a firm include summaries of cash movement (general ledger), a record of money owed the firm (accounts receivable), a record of money owed by the firm to others (accounts payable), computation of salaries and wages along with various deductions (payroll), processing of orders from customers, and monitoring of raw materials and finished goods on hand.

Accounting packages that can handle one or more of these functions for a firm have various levels of specialization, ranging from general packages to industry-specific packages and even to firm-specific packages. An off-the-shelf package may suffice for a firm that is doing business in a standard manner. However, a firm that uses a unique accounting procedure may need special software tailored to its needs.

A family generally does not need full-scale accounting software. However, **personal budgeting software** packages exist that meet the accounting needs of the average family. These packages allow a family to computerize its budget and to record cash inflows and outflows in a manner similar to business accounting packages.

Financial Analysis

Also known as **spreadsheet analysis**, **financial analysis software** works with a table having rows and columns of values, labels, and formulas. The user defines various relationships between the values in the table, which is called a **spreadsheet**. When the user changes a value in the table, the pack-

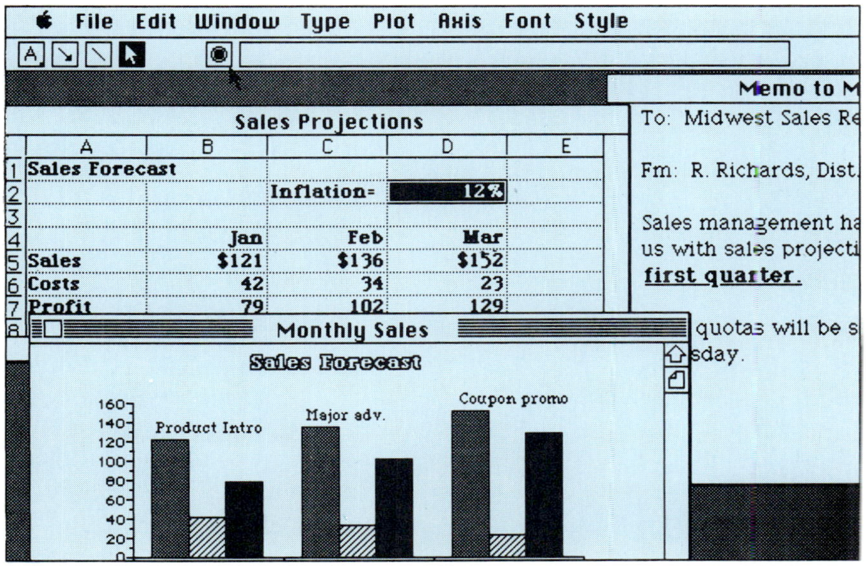

The integrated Jazz software package includes a spreadsheet that can compute monthly sales forecasts. Such forecasts can also reflect inflation rates.

age recomputes the other values to account for the change. This sort of analysis allows the user to ask "What if?" questions about the spreadsheet values. The spreadsheet program is extremely important to the manager who wants to plan for every budgetary situation he or she may face during the next year.

Spreadsheet analysis can be used at home as well. A household budget can be placed on a spreadsheet with the columns representing months of the year and the rows representing income and expense categories. The user can then use the spreadsheet to test various budgetary plans or to track actual income and expenses.

Data Base Management

Work with files often involves finding common elements among files or finding all files that contain one key element. With **data base management software**, a user can choose elements in files that fit some criteria by having the computer perform the actual search through the files. In a sense, this type of package is an "electronic filing clerk." The term **data base** refers to the user's files of information. Data base management packages are important when an individual or firm must manage large volumes of data from which decisions must be made.

The simplest data base management packages allow the user to set up an electronic filing system, which can then be arranged according to any desired characteristic—for example, the alphabet. After the system is in place, any items that match a given criterion can be selected and output from the file. Another important advantage of data base management packages is that a second or third criterion can also be specified, and the elements that match all criteria can then be output.

Data base management packages are a great aid to the hobbyist who wishes to keep complete, accurate records that can be easily accessed. **Integrated software** that combines data base management, spreadsheet analysis, word processing, telecommunications, and graphics software also exists, and it provides powerful data management and decision-making tools. The user can access files, find the answers to various questions about the data, display the results graphically, and write reports—all from the same package.

With this graphics software package on the Apple Macintosh (left), overlaid windows allow the user to see the data and the resulting graph at the same time. The combination of software, personal computer, and printer allows a user to display graphs on the screen and to generate a printed version of the graph.

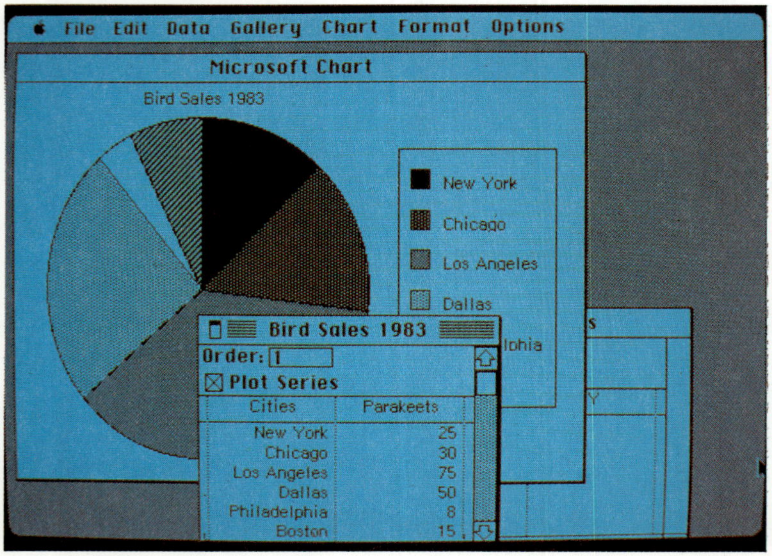

Graphics

One of the most exciting examples of the computer's symbol processing capabilities is the use of **graphics software** packages for visual presentation of information or for creation of new and different art forms. The old saying that "a picture is worth a thousand words" is never more true than when applied to the dynamic graphic portrayal of computer results. The ability to show the information generated by data analysis in a bar or pie chart makes the results more meaningful. However, unlike other software packages that are primarily machine-independent—that is, they have versions that run on most computers—graphics packages depend heavily on the hardware. The quality of the graphics depends on the CPU chip and the monitor used. Some chips can produce very good graphics, whereas others cannot. Some monitors are capable of high-quality color graphics, whereas other monitors can only produce block graphics. However, most new machines can produce high-quality graphics.

Regardless of the hardware being considered, graphics software generally includes the line chart, which simply connects a series of points; the pie chart, which assigns a section of a round pie to a proportional amount of data; the bar chart, which draws a series of horizontal or vertical bars depicting the data; and the scattergram, which plots the points relative to vertical and horizontal axes.

Telecommunications

Telecommunications software combines the computer with a modem and a telephone to communicate with other computers. The modem converts computer signals to telephone signals, and vice versa, and the software manages the transfer of information over the telephone line. The combination of the telecommunications package and modem allows businesses to send and receive information from a centrally located mainframe. Employees who work at home can use telecommunications software to send and receive information from the office computer. National networks can be accessed using the telecommunications package–modem combination to send electronic mail, post messages on an electronic bulletin board, or access national general purpose or special interest data bases.

Most personal computers have a hardware connection known as the **RS-232 port**, into which the cable from a modem is inserted. Some new personal computers have built-in modems that only require the telephone line for a connection.

Telecommunications software packages range from simple packages that merely allow the personal computer to be connected to a modem to sophisticated packages that dial the desired telephone number and handle complex data transfer operations. The choice of telecommunications software depends on the machine and operating system that is used and the amount of money one wishes to spend.

Buying Computer Software

A complete guide to buying all types of software is impossible to state in a paragraph or two, but some general guidelines may be helpful. Purchase guidelines for particular types of software are given in Chapters 10–13, where the various types of software are discussed in detail.

The best general guideline for buying software is the same one that applies to buying a car: Try it before you buy. Determine which software packages appear to fit your needs. Go to an appropriate source, such as a computer store, and try the software on your type of computer. Allow enough time to

Actually trying out software or hardware before buying is an important part of the computer purchase.

Using telecommunications software and a modem, a personal computer user can access such information sources as CompuServe and The Source.

try all of the software operations needed for your particular use. If the software fails to perform as advertised or the store does not let you try out the software, look elsewhere. Remember, a software package that works fine on an Apple II does not work on an IBM PC, TI PC, Tandy 2000, or even an Apple Macintosh. For this reason, the computer hardware and operating system must be matched with the prospective software before buying.

If you have not yet purchased a personal computer, you might want to select the software first, determine which computer runs the software, and then buy the two—hardware and software—as a package. This approach best ensures that you will be happy with both hardware and software.

COMPUTER PROGRAMMING

Sometimes, a software package that fits a particular set of needs is not available. In that case, the computer must be programmed by the user to perform the necessary tasks.

Computer Languages

Programming a computer—that is, giving the computer a sequence of instructions—requires an ability to communicate with the computer. To understand how this communication can take place, we must realize that human language must be translated before the computer can understand it. Recall from Chapter 2 that the computer "thinks" in terms of switches, or bits, so the language of the computer is the binary number system. We also saw the binary equivalents of numbers and symbols. Each instruction the computer performs also has a binary equivalent. The computer's binary language is referred to as **machine language**, a very specific language that details every computer operation as a series of zeros and ones.

Another machine-specific language that is somewhat easier to use than strings of zeros and ones is called **assembly language**. An assembly language has one instruction for each machine language instruction, but it uses words and letters for commands rather than binary numbers. For example, the machine language instruction for a particular computer to subtract one from the current value is

```
00010101
```

The corresponding assembly language command is

```
DEC C ;CURRENT-1 TO CURRENT
```

The remark after the semicolon reminds the programmer of the meaning of the instruction.

A mainframe assembly language is included in most college-level computer science courses. Individuals who can program in this language are in demand by business and industry. Some applications programs for both mainframes and personal computers are written in assembly language because it is usually the most efficient language in terms of computer speed. However, it is a fairly difficult language to learn, and most users do not need to be concerned with either machine language or assembly language. Machine and assembly languages are called **low-level languages**, because they

ANOTHER VIEW

Commodore Grace Hopper

No discussion of programming is complete without the mention of Commodore Grace Hopper of the U.S. Navy. Commodore Hopper, the oldest active duty officer in the navy, has been involved with computers since the MARK I was developed during World War II. She also worked on the successors to the MARK I—the MARK II and MARK III—before joining the Eckert–Mauchly group that built the UNIVAC I commercial computer. Commodore Hopper was also a member of the group that created COBOL and has served on numerous committees for the standardization of software. One of Commodore Hopper's opinions on computer languages is as follows:

One thing I think we should be doing is looking toward more specialized languages. If you go down to any library and go to the shelf that has dictionaries, you'll find one for biology, you'll find one for chemistry, you'll find one for insurance, and you'll find one on taxes—each one of which will contain a specialized area of mathematics and a specialized area of English. I think we ought to have more languages, more subsets to match those.

SOURCE: Corey Sandler, "Keeping up with Grace," *PC Magazine*, December 1983, pp. 199–215.

Commodore Grace Hopper has been an important figure in the development of computer hardware and software since the first computers were built.

are at the computer's level. These types of languages are discussed in more detail in Chapter 15.

Different types of computers have different machine and assembly languages. Because programs written in machine or assembly language must be changed when they are transferred to a new computer, **high-level languages** were developed. These languages combine English words with a specific grammar to give the computer instructions. These languages are generally standardized, so that a program written in a high-level language on one type of computer need *not* be rewritten for a different type of computer.

The most commonly used high-level languages are the ones discussed earlier in this chapter—FORTRAN, PL/I, COBOL, BASIC, C, Pascal, and LOGO. This diversity of high-level languages came about because no one language satisfies every need. Some are business languages, some are teaching languages, and some are scientific languages. Most of these languages have been standardized to some extent. The unfortunate exception to this standardization of high-level languages is BASIC. The original BASIC developed by John Kemeny and Thomas Kurtz is a simple language, but it becomes complex and nonstandard when implemented on modern personal computers. The several different versions of BASIC often require that programs be rewritten when transferred from one computer to another. Kemeny and Kurtz have developed a new version of BASIC, called True BASIC, which they hope will be accepted as an industry standard.

Translation and Execution

If a computer understands only machine language and the programmer writes in a high-level language, how do the two actually communicate? The solution is the same one that the United Nations uses for an English-speaking delegate to understand a Chinese speaker—that is, a translator. In computer terminology, a translator is a program that converts a high-level language like BASIC into the computer's machine language. The CPU actually executes the machine language instructions to arrive at the results. This process is accomplished in one of two ways. First, the translator program, or **interpreter**, converts the high-level language statements into machine language statements. This translation process is performed on each instruction as the program is executed. An interpreter catches the user's grammar or vocabulary errors as the statement is executed. Unfortunately, an interpreter is also slow, because each statement must be interpreted as it is used. If a statement is repeated many times (a common occurrence), the interpretation process must be repeated each time. The interpreter–execution process is illustrated as follows:

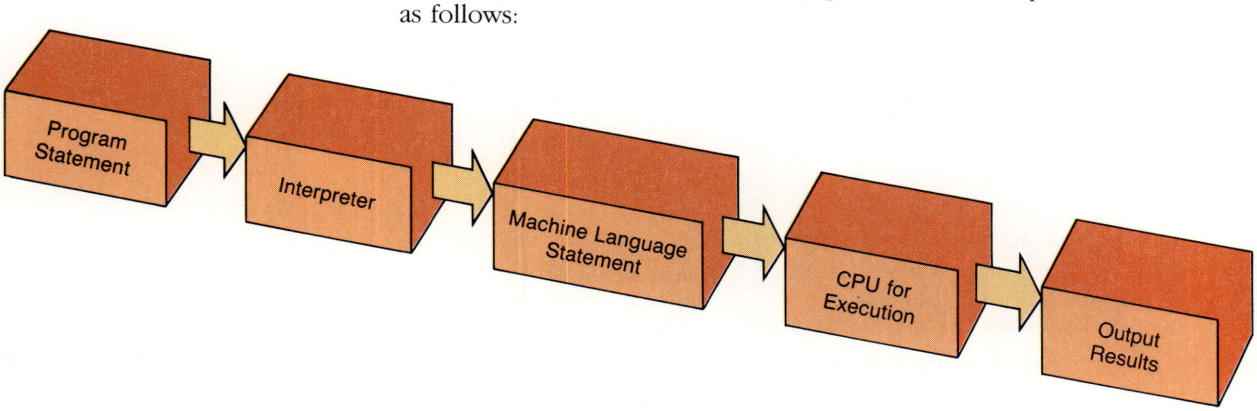

In the second type of conversion, a high-level language is translated into machine language by compilation. This process is accomplished by a translator program called the **compiler**, which converts the high-level language **source program** into a machine language **object program**. Once a correct program is written, it need not be run through the compiler every time it is executed. Instead, the object program can be executed. This results in much faster **execution** times compared with interpreted programs. However, with a compiler, errors in the program are not found until the entire program is input and compiled as a unit. As a result, finding errors, or **bugs**, in the program is more difficult than with an interpreter. Most high-level languages are compiled rather than interpreted. Even a BASIC program can be compiled if desirable.

The compilation and execution of a high-level source program is a two-step process. The first step is as follows:

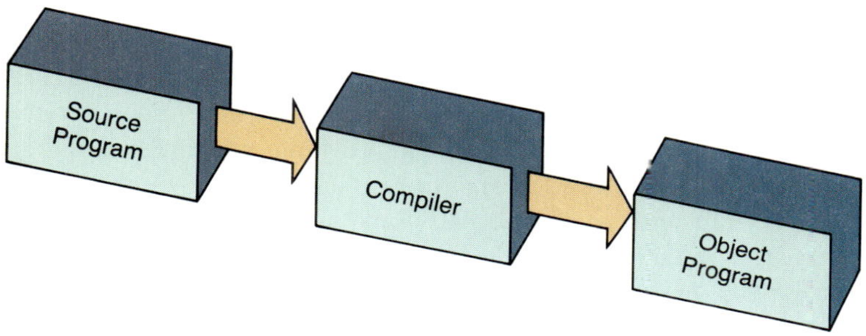

Once the source program is converted into a machine language object program, it is executed as shown below:

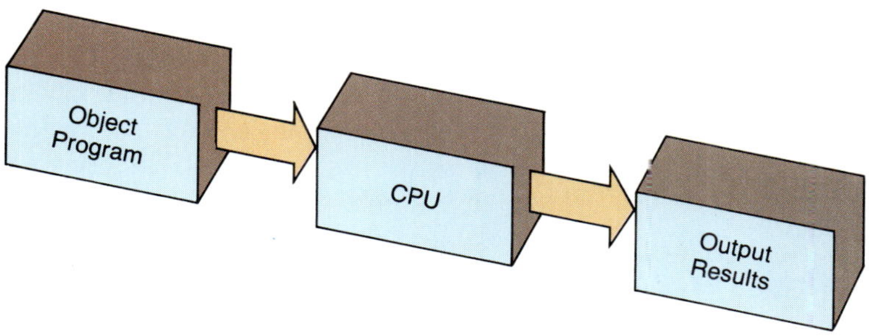

If no program errors are discovered during execution, the results are generated and output to the user.

The Programming Process

Computers are very useful because they can perform arithmetic operations, make comparisons, and manipulate symbols quickly and accurately for large amounts of data. However, before a computer can perform any calculations, make comparisons, or manipulate symbols, a program must be written to instruct the computer on how to perform these operations. The program, written in a computer language, gives the computer the sequence of operations that the programmer wants performed. Writing a program requires an

The First "BUG"

An error in a computer program (and now in many other situations) is called a *bug*. The origin of this term is the result of an event in the life of the MARK II computer. The electromechanical MARK series of computers used relays as switches. The relays were spring-loaded and held open by an electromagnet when the current to the magnet was on. When the current was cut off, the relay closed.

Because of their mechanical nature, the MARK series of machines stopped often due to a failed relay. While Commodore Grace Hopper (see the boxed insert on page 63) worked on the MARK II, one of those failed relays was caused by a misguided moth. The moth was pulled out of the relay and taped into the log book with the notation, "First Actual Debugging." From then on, any problem involving a computer was said to be due to a "bug."

SOURCE: Corey Sandler, "Entomological Etymology: The Birth of Debugging," *PC Magazine*, December 1983, p. 207.

understanding of the problem to be solved and a knowledge of the rules and vocabulary of the particular computer language used.

We can view the process of writing a computer program as one of solving a problem. The problem is developing a sequence of steps using the rules and vocabulary of the computer language to accomplish the desired purpose. The key to the solution is to break the problem up into small pieces rather than approaching it as a whole. Each small piece can then be viewed as a single step in the overall process of solving the problem. This step-by-step solution in computer programming is called the **logic** of the program. Although we can occasionally solve some problems without a logical plan, writing a computer program without a logical plan is almost impossible! All too often, novice programmers learn all the rules and vocabulary of a programming language but still cannot write an effective program. Many times the would-be programmer fails to develop a logical sequence of steps before attempting to write the program. Once a logical plan is developed, it is often fairly easy to write the actual program using the appropriate grammar and vocabulary of the computer language that is used.

Chapter 14 discusses the process of developing a logical plan for writing a computer program. This material applies to any language. Chapters 16 and 17 then discuss programming using BASIC. This language was chosen because it is available on mainframes and personal computers and is easy to learn.

REVIEW OF KEY POINTS

- Computer hardware must have software in the form of a computer program to control its actions.
- All programs are written in a computer language.
- The following three types of software are used in a computer: systems, utility, and applications software. Systems software manages the computer's operations, utility software handles housekeeping chores, and applications software performs the actual tasks.
- Applications software can be used in the following five major areas: science and engineering problems, businesses, the home, education, and game-playing.
- The six most commonly used business packages for personal computers are word processing, accounting (personal budgeting), financial analysis, data base management, graphics, and telecommunications.
- Computer programming can be accomplished using a low-level language, such as assembly language, or a high-level language, such as BASIC, COBOL, FORTRAN, or Pascal.
- A high-level language must be either interpreted or compiled to be executed.
- Programmers must break a problem up into small pieces before attempting to write a program.

KEY TERMS

accounting software
applications software
assembly language
bugs
compiler
computer-aided instruction (CAI)
computer language
computer program
data base
data base management software
disk operating system (DOS)
execution
files
financial analysis software
graphics software
high-level languages
integrated software
interpreter
logic
low-level languages
machine language
object program
operating system
personal budgeting software
programming
RS-232 port
software
software gap
software package
source program
spreadsheet
spreadsheet analysis
systems software
telecommunications software
turtle
user's manual
utility software
word processing software

REVIEW QUESTIONS

1. Discuss the importance of software in the use of a computer.
2. Name the three major types of software that work concurrently in a computer.
3. Find out what operating system is used on the mainframe computer or in the personal computer lab at your school. Determine the utility software operations that are available to users on either system.
4. Determine which computer languages are available at your institution, either on a mainframe or on a personal computer. Which language is best suited to your major? Why?
5. List the five areas of applications software discussed in the text. In which area do you think you would perform most of your computer work?
6. List the six business applications software packages for personal computers discussed in the text. Which package would you like to use? Why?
7. Discuss a situation from your home, school, club, fraternity, or sorority in which a spreadsheet package would be useful to you.
8. Discuss a situation in which a data base management package would be useful to you or to an organization to which you belong.
9. Compare the uses of an interpreter and a compiler in translating a high-level language program into a machine language program.
10. If programming is part of your computer course, find out the computer language and type of translation program you will use.

This introduction to the world of computer systems first defines a system and discusses its components, including input, processing, output, feedback, environment, and boundary. This chapter also discusses subsystems, systems in organizations, the systems approach, and the computer as a system. Computer-based systems, including information systems, are then covered, followed by the various types of management information systems—management support systems, decision support systems, accounting information systems, office information systems, and data manipulation and reporting systems. The chapter concludes with a discussion of systems analysis and design, which is used to assess and solve problems within systems.

4

An Introduction to Computer Systems

STUDY OBJECTIVES

After reading this chapter, you should be able to

- Understand the concept of a system and its components.
- Recognize subsystems, systems in organizations, and the systems approach.
- See that the computer is actually a system made of subsystems.
- Understand the relationship between data processing and computer-based information systems.
- Discuss five types of computer-based information systems that are part of management information systems in organizations.
- Understand systems analysis and design.

A WORLD OF SYSTEMS

The word *system* is used frequently in relation to computers, but it is rarely defined. What is meant by a computer system, a communication system, an information system, and a decision support system? A recent advertisement for American Telephone and Telegraph stated, "The system is the solution," without bothering to explain the slogan. Systems are very important in the world of computers. For that reason, we introduce them here and then cover them in more detail in Block 5.

A **system** is a group of elements (people, machines, cells, and so on) organized for the purpose of achieving a particular goal. Many examples of systems exist in the world, including the human body, the U.S. government, and a computer system. The human body is a system of cells that is organized to support life. The U.S. government is a system of people organized for the well-being of U.S. citizens. A computer system, which is made up of a user, hardware, and software, is organized to solve problems for the user.

A system has the following elements: input, processing, output, feedback, an environment, and a boundary. The relationships among these elements are shown in Figure 4-1.

The **input**, **processing**, and **output** elements of a system have much the same relationships in a system as they do in a computer. Data enter the system as input, which is processed in some way, and then output as information. **Feedback** is a form of output that is sent back to the system's input or processing function, enabling the system to change its operation, if necessary. Feedback can originate from within the system or from the environment. In a sense, feedback monitors the system to ensure that the system achieves its goal. For example, in data processing, feedback informs the system whether the type of output information is appropriate.

Surrounding the system are the **environment** and the **boundary**. These two concepts are often difficult to distinguish from the system itself, because the point at which a system ends and its environment begins can be hazy. The

A complete computer system—user, software, CPU, internal memory, secondary storage, keyboard, monitor, and printer—is shown here.

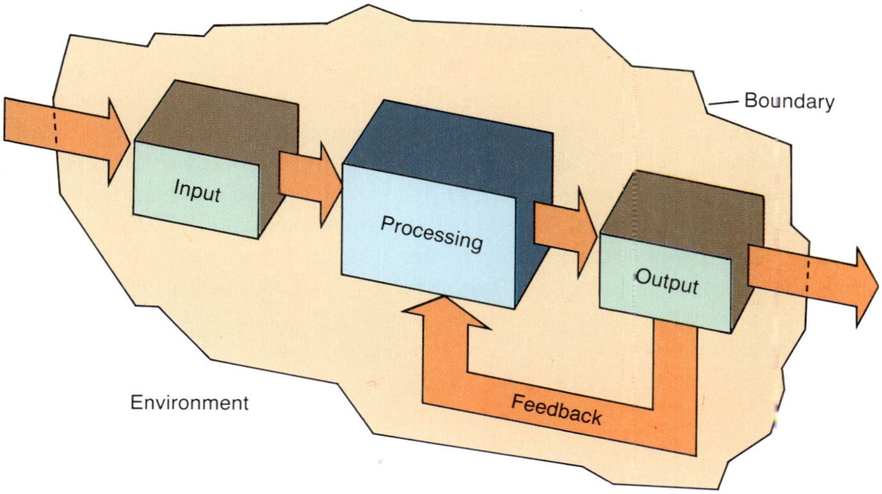

FIGURE 4-1
The Elements of a System

boundary of a human system is the skin, and the environment consists of all outside forces that affect the body. This delineation is not so clear in other situations.

Subsystems

Most systems are made up of one or more **subsystems**, which work as systems on their own and contribute to the whole by handling detailed tasks. In many systems, a specialized subsystem handles input. For example, a keyboard subsystem inputs data to a computer system.

To illustrate the concept of a subsystem, we consider a college student as a system. This student has numerous types of input, processing, output, and feedback occurring at the same time, because she is composed of many physiological and psychological subsystems. However, this illustration concen-

The environment of a student's academic subsystem includes fellow students and computers.

trates on the student's academic subsystem. The input consists of the flow of information to the student in lectures, readings, lab experiments, seminars, and so on. The student's processing element converts this information into an understanding of the subject matter. The student's output is the demonstration of this understanding in exams, term papers, and class discussions. Feedback is made up of the grades on exams and term papers that indicate to the student whether or not her input and processing operations are adequate to achieve a desired grade. If these functions are inadequate, the student must modify her class attendance pattern, her note-taking process, or the study time she allocates to this class. The boundary separates the student from an environment that includes classmates, professors, the library, the computer center, and any other resources involved in the learning process. The complete academic subsystem appears in Figure 4-2.

Subsystems in Organizations

An organization, which can be a club; a business; federal, state, or local government; or a nonprofit group, usually has two primary subsystems. The first subsystem is the **management system**, which has as its goal the management of the organization through planning, organizing, and controlling functions. The second subsystem is the **information system**, which converts data into information that is useful to organization managers and interested outside parties. (Recall that data are raw facts converted by data processing into information and that information is communicated knowledge in a form that is useful to the user.) The information subsystem is extremely important, because information is the lifeblood of any organization. Organizations consider information an asset just as valuable as money or equipment. Because the computer is an important component of an information system, we consider information systems in some detail later in this chapter and in Chapter 19.

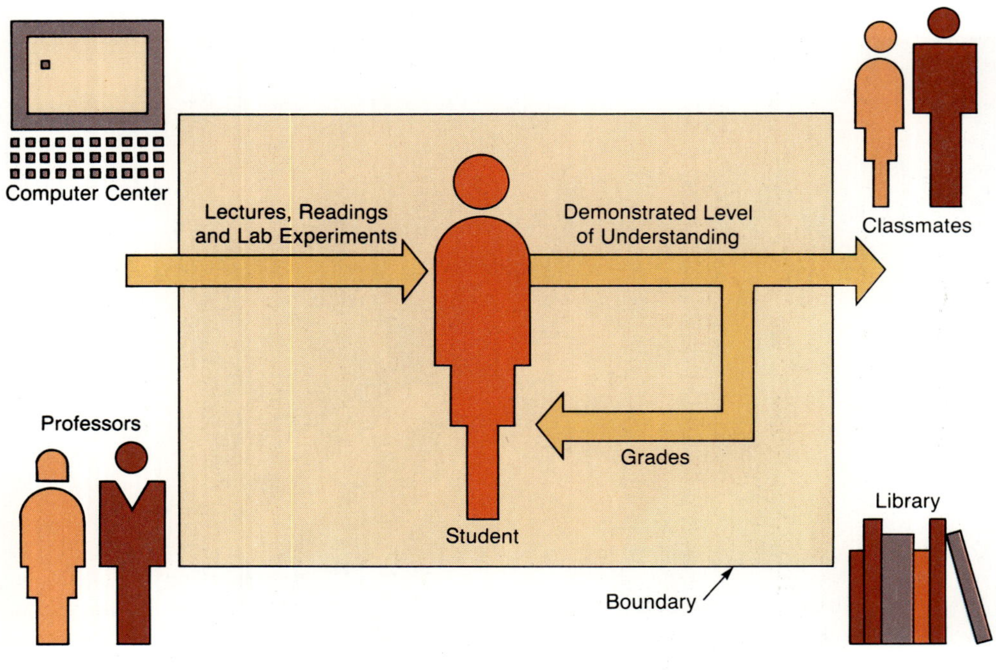

FIGURE 4-2 Academic Subsystem of a Student

The systems approach is needed to avoid suboptimization of the various parts of an assembly operation, such as this one in the electronics industry.

The Systems Approach

The **systems approach** views problems or activities as systems that must be managed. The subsystems or parts must be carefully integrated so that the system as a whole works efficiently.

When the systems approach is not used, each part is viewed as a separate component. Using such an approach to reach an overall goal often leads to difficulties like suboptimization. A **suboptimized system** has some parts that are "too good" for the system as a whole. For example, assume that the design of an assembly line as a system is approached on a component-by-component basis. In a suboptimized system, one section of the assembly line might work at a rate of 10 units per minute, and another section might work at 20 units per minute. The faster section of the line does not improve the system as a whole and actually causes problems because the output from one part of the line does not match the input to the other part. Using the systems approach to design the assembly line would eliminate problems like this,

ANOTHER VIEW
Bertil Nordin

Bertil Nordin is president of Digital Communications Associates (DCA), a computer communications company with over $75 million in annual sales. DCA is active in the personal computer-to-mainframe communications market and in the mainframe-to-mainframe communications market. In an interview, Nordin commented on the importance of the systems approach to marketing and sales.

Due to the nature of the product we sell, our sales people must be able to view the customer's system as a whole so that they can make a "systems-type sale" as opposed to a single product sale. In our business, you're selling more of an intangible—a system. To do this and be successful, it is necessary to have a broad, overall concept of how the customer's business is organized, because when somebody installs one of our network systems, they are not putting in just a single product, they are putting in a system that will change the way they do business.

because the individual parts—the two sections of the assembly line—are viewed as subsystems that must be integrated into one efficient production system. The systems approach is discussed in detail in Chapter 18.

Computer Subsystems

The three major subsystems of a computer are the user, the hardware, and the software. Each subsystem performs a necessary function in the computer's problem-solving process. The user subsystem is the human user who has a problem that he or she wishes to solve. Specific interaction between the user and the computer is discussed in detail in Chapters 20–22. Figure 4-3 shows the breakdown of the computer's subsystems.

The hardware subsystem has four subsystems of its own—input, processing/internal memory, secondary storage, and output. Each subsystem must be integrated with the others to make a computer. For this reason, the term **computer system** is often used to describe the CPU, keyboard, monitor, secondary storage devices, and other peripherals.

The three subsystems of computer software are systems software, utility software, and applications software. The subsystems must be integrated, because without one subsystem, neither of the other two can be used. The key element of these three software subsystems is the operating system, which manages all other software within the computer. The operating system for a mainframe computer is so complex that a group of **systems programmers** are assigned to each mainframe to maintain and update the operating system. When a problem or "bug" is discovered in the operating system, the systems programmers must "take the computer down" (turn it off) to track down and correct the error.

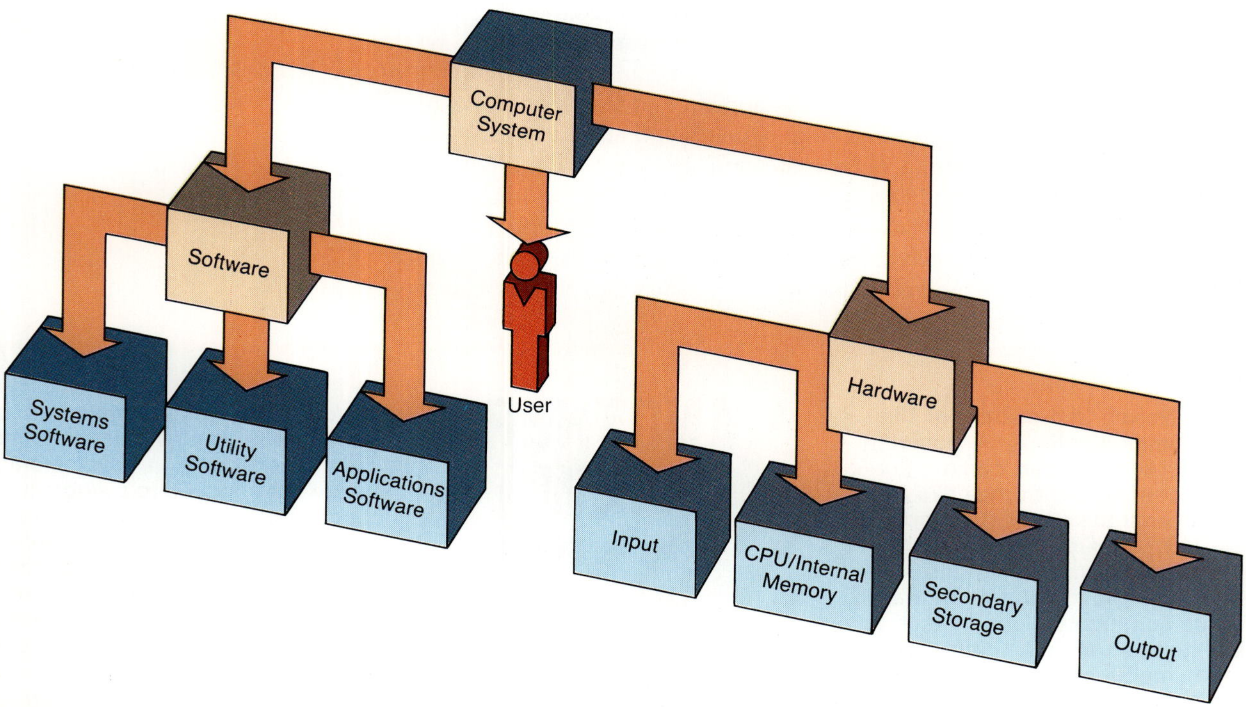

FIGURE 4-3
Computer Subsystems

The operating system on a personal computer is much less complex, because it manages only one user at a time. However, problems can still occur with the operating system. The software manufacturer usually solves such problems by sending registered software owners either a new version of the operating system on a disk or a list of statements to add to the operating system. The group of statements added to the operating system by the software owner is called a **patch**. Different versions of an operating system may be numbered 1.0, 1.25, 2.0, and so on (different manufacturers have different numbering systems), with the original version numbered 1.0 and the latest version given the highest number.

THE BEST DEFENSE

Baseball by Computer

Various football and baseball teams have attempted to use the computer to help coaches and managers make better decisions. The information system installed by the Atlanta Braves should help the team defend against opposing hitters. This system was set up by the Braves' assistant vice-president, Pat Nugent, who said: "We're charting everything—every pitch, every hit ball, every trajectory, how high it's hit, how hard it's hit, who threw it, everything. Down the line, after you get so many games under your belt, when you feel you have enough information, you can start making some serious predictions about probability."

Using this information, the Braves hope to predict where a hitter will most likely hit the ball so fielders can be moved to best defend against the hitter. They also hope to determine some information about each defensive player's "range," that is, how much territory a fielder can cover. This type of information has never been charted before and should help the Braves even more in planning their defense.

The Braves combine software prepared by the Baseball Analysis Company with a Televideo computer system. The Chicago White Sox also use this system. Other professional teams undoubtedly apply this information system technology to their situations.

SOURCE: Jack Wilkinson, "7th-Inning Printout in Braves' Program," *Atlanta Journal,* May 16, 1984, p. 14A.

Atlanta Braves assistant coach Brian Snitker consults a computer printout of team defense statistics before a game.

COMPUTER-BASED INFORMATION SYSTEMS

I think that the personal computer gives those of us in office the ability to have what we call a "house-sign" list—a volunteer list—of the sort that used to be kept on cards, until someone would invariably walk out with all the cards and we'd lose everything. Now it's all stored in computer memory. And data has become virtually theft-proof.

Dianne Feinstein, Mayor of San Francisco

(As quoted in "You Can Automate City Hall," *PC World,* August 1984, p. 298.)

The computer is closely tied to the concept of a system and the use of the systems approach in solving problems or coordinating activities. In fact, the computer is often a key component of an information system that must process a tremendous amount of data. The computer itself is a system with user, hardware, and software subsystems. The systems approach is used to design a computer system, because the various subsystems must be integrated for the computer to work as needed.

The term **data processing** is associated with information systems because data are processed into meaningful information. Data processing, then, is a purely mechanical function. Although data processing is a necessary part of an information system, it does not provide complete reports to management or external users for decision making. For example, raw data may represent a random list of a firm's clients along with last year's sales figures. The computer may arrange or *sort* this list from most sales to least sales as a form of data processing, but the result is still only a list of clients. A truly useful list includes explanatory material about each client—such as the salesperson who handled each account, the total sales to each client, and any other useful information that may explain the sales level. Data processing can handle the sorting, but more information is needed to make the final list useful for managerial decision making or for external users.

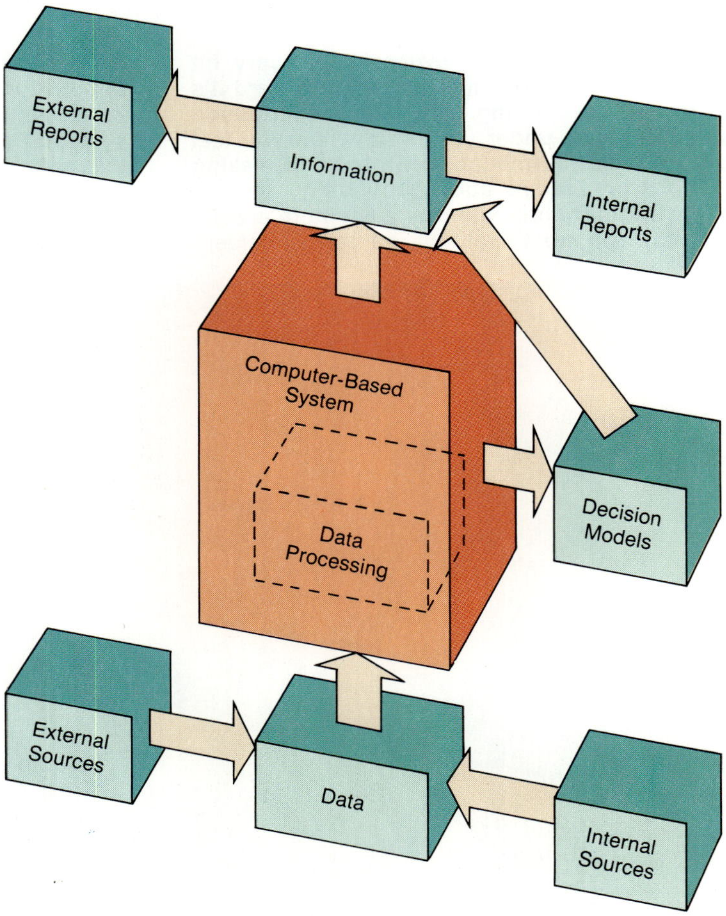

FIGURE 4-4
An Information System
[R.A. Leitch and K.R. Davis, *Accounting Information Systems* (Englewood Cliffs, NJ: Prentice-Hall, Inc., 1983), p. 10. Adapted by permission.]

In Figure 4-4, the data processing function is shown within the computer-based system because this function is an integral part of a computer-based system. Decision models for managerial decision making depend on the output from the computer-based system.

Types of Computer-Based Systems

Computer-based information systems can be classified in at least two different ways. First, we can classify them according to how the data are input. In other words, the system can use on-line processing or batch processing. In **on-line processing**, the user interacts with the mainframe computer system to input the data. On-line systems are necessary when time is a factor or users are competing for resources. A computer system for registering college students for classes must be an on-line system because a student needs to know at registration whether or not his or her schedule has been approved Airline and hotel reservation systems are on-line because in those systems, the same seat or room cannot be sold to two different people.

In **batch processing**, the data from multiple users or time periods are combined and submitted to the computer as a batch. This system is used when the processing is not an immediate concern or a great deal of similar

Computer systems can use batch or on-line processing. Modern batch systems (top right) can handle the huge volume of remittances that a large-scale billing operation must process. With some on-line systems (top left), the user can make airline reservations or check into or out of a hotel. The on-line electronic message system at the 1984 Los Angeles Olympics (bottom) enabled the organizers to overcome the huge geographic obstacle of widely dispersed event locations.

OPSTAR
Student Registration System

One experience that is common to all college and university students is registration. At the University of Georgia, over 22,000 students now use a computerized registration system that makes this chore easier on everyone. OPSTAR (OPtical Scanning and Terminal Assisted Registration) has reduced the number of drop–add transactions by 50% because it allows students to build schedules that are more to their liking. At the same time, because students can check computerized listings of open courses, they can register with greater confidence that their schedules will not be rejected.

In pre-OPSTAR days, students registered for courses and waited several days to learn by mail whether or not their schedules had been accepted, modified, or totally rejected. Because of this delay, 20% of the students did not pay their fees on time. Under the old system, faculty members spent an inordinate amount of time in registration procedures, and postage expenses and clerical costs skyrocketed.

With OPSTAR, the number of students guilty of late payment of fees is less than 10%, faculty time at the registration area is cut in half, and, because students pick up their paper work immediately after registration, postage costs are down 80%. Another benefit is that all information for student data bases can be collected at one time, reducing the number of forms a student must fill out. The student instructional computing system on campus is also tied into OPSTAR. As a result, students are assigned user numbers when they register for a programming course. They need not visit the computer center separately to pick up user numbers.

Students visit the on-line registration system supported by OPSTAR to choose courses for the coming school term. Later, they can pick up a registration form showing whether or not their choices were available.

data must be processed at the same time. A school's grade-reporting system is usually a batch-processing system, because the data and type of processing are the same and the processing is not an immediate concern. Payroll systems are usually batch-processing systems, because they must process the same type of data once during a pay period.

Computer systems are also classified as integrated systems or distributed systems. An **integrated system** has one central storage of data called a data base, which all users can access using terminals. On the other hand, a **distributed system** uses a mainframe computer for storage of data bases and for large-scale processing combined with minicomputers or personal computers. The smaller computers handle much of the data processing at sites that are geographically separate from the mainframe and can access the mainframe data bases.

TYPES OF INFORMATION SYSTEMS

Information systems contribute extensively to the efficient management of any organization. In this section, we discuss the important information system for organizations known as the management information system (MIS). A **management information system (MIS)** can be defined as "an integrated, user–machine system for providing information to support operations, management, and decision-making functions in an organization."[1] Within the MIS, various subsystems carry out specialized information roles. These subsystems may be called different names by different people, but here we define the following five such subsystems: the management support system, the decision support system, the accounting information system, the office information system, and the data manipulation and reporting system. The relationship of these five subsystems to the overall management information system is shown in Figure 4-5.

Regardless of the names and the number of subsystems, they are all part of the management information system. Organizations that are large enough to have a separate computer department may call it the MIS Department, in recognition of its work in supporting management.

Management Support Systems

A key objective of an MIS is to supply the right types and amount of information to each level of a firm's management. At the *operational* management level, the foremen and supervisors need detailed information on the day-to-day operation of the company's production process. These managers must make decisions on such items as keeping records, assigning jobs, checking shipments, and so on, that are based on the rules and patterns set at higher management levels. Because the decision maker can be given a prescribed list of rules to follow to make decisions, decisions at this level are said to be *programmable.* A computerized MIS can greatly aid this decision-making process.

[1]Gordon B. Davis and Margaret H. Olson, *Management Information Systems,* 2nd ed. (New York: McGraw-Hill, 1985), p. 6.

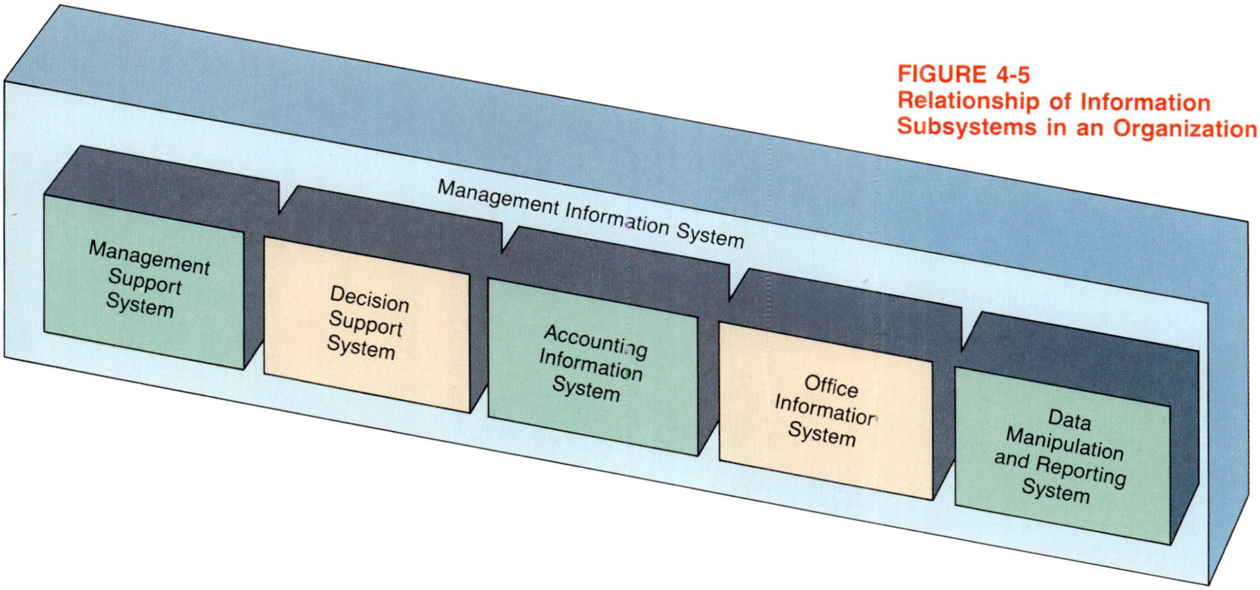

FIGURE 4-5
Relationship of Information Subsystems in an Organization

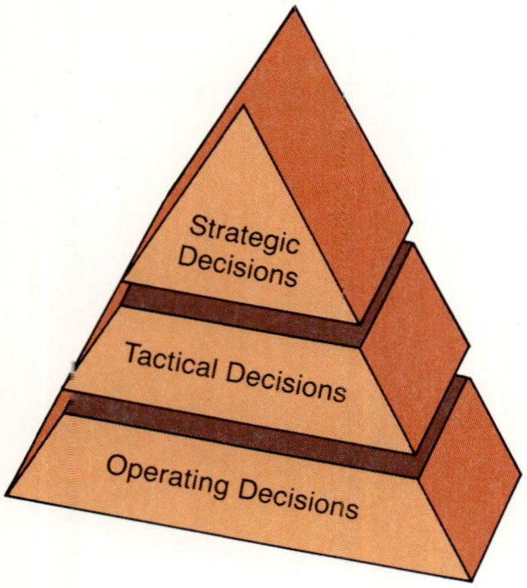

FIGURE 4-6
Levels of Management Decision Making

Middle-level managers need summary reports on the firm's operations to make the *tactical* decisions that implement the *strategic* decisions made at the top level of the company. The decisions at these two upper levels are not as easily programmable as those at the lowest level. The pyramid in Figure 4-6 demonstrates the relative number of people in the organization that make each type of decision.

As shown in Figure 4-6, most organizations have a broad base of day-to-day operational decision makers, fewer tactical decision makers, and only a few strategic decision makers. The flow of decision making is from the top down; each level depends on the level above it for the policy to make its decisions.

Reports are very important to operational managers and some tactical managers in making their decisions. A **management support system (MSS)** provides these reports to those managers. This system is aimed at helping managers make timely and effective decisions. The term *management information system* is often applied to this type of system as well as to the overall information system. However, to avoid confusion, we use MIS to refer to the overall system and MSS to refer to the subsystem that generates reports for managerial use. Because decisions at the tactical and strategic levels cannot be programmed and must depend on intuition and problem solving as well as reports, a computerized MSS can only be an aid to decision making—it cannot specify what the decision should be.

Of the five subsystems of a management information system discussed in this chapter, the management support system is probably the largest. Generating reports for management based on the output from data processing is a very important function of a computerized information system. The remaining four subsystems of the management information system are all closely related to the management support system. They may help make more complex decisions, generate financial and economic information for inclusion in MSS reports, facilitate the actual generation of the reports, or use the information from an MSS to make decisions.

Different levels of management need different kinds of information from a computer system. Operational managers like the factory floor supervisor at left use the computer to make programmed decisions. Middle-level managers (right) use the computer to obtain summary information in various forms to aid them in making tactical decisions.

Top-level managers often use decision support systems to help them think through the unstructured decisions they must make.

Decision Support Systems

To aid the upper levels of decision makers, a **decision support system (DSS)** combines data with models and graphics to answer a decision maker's questions about the data. A decision support system goes further than the management support system to help the decision maker with more complex decisions. A DSS allows a decision maker to ask "What if?" questions about the data by using models to solve problems involving the data. Graphics are an important part of a DSS, because they allow the decision maker to spot trends in the data and to understand the data more easily than by using tables of numbers.

Both the management support system and the decision support system help managers make decisions. However, the degree of structure in the decision dictates how each system is used in the decision-making process. If a decision is highly structured—that is, if it can be made using set policies—then the management support system's reports are sufficient to make the decision. For example, a decision on how many spare parts to keep on hand for production equipment can usually be made based on reports generated by the MSS. On the other hand, if the decision is unstructured—that is, if it cannot be made using clearly defined policies—then the models and graphics supplied by a decision support system must be used. For example, a decision on financing a company's debt might be based on sales forecasts and future interest rates using a DSS.

Accounting Information Systems

An **accounting information system (AIS)** is a subset of a management information system that differs from an MSS or a DSS in the type of information that is processed. An MSS or DSS provides all types of information to managers to help them make better decisions. On the other hand, an accounting information system processes primarily economic and financial data. An accounting information system provides this information for both internal and external users by generating financial information that can be included in the reports from a management support system or the models and graphics of a decision support system.

Two key aspects of an accounting information system are transactions processing and financial reporting. **Transactions processing** converts all monetary transactions (sales, loans, payroll, stocks, bonds, and so on) into an understandable form. **Financial reporting** in an accounting information system includes internal reports to management and external reports to the company's stockholders and other interested parties.

Office Information Systems

An office information system attempts to make the work of so-called *knowledge workers* easier. These workers traditionally have devoted their efforts to collecting, verifying, organizing, storing, retrieving, and transforming information from many sources. An **office information system (OIS)** is a machine or machines combined with a communication system and users to make more efficient the job of obtaining, organizing, storing, retrieving, and preparing needed information. Output from an OIS can be data that have been converted to a form usable by the computer, a report, a proposal or brief, or other forms of information usable by an individual. An OIS is a subset of a management information system that facilitates the smooth flow of information into, within, and out of the office. Without an adequate OIS, the reports generated by the management support system might never be written, and a manager's decisions might never be transmitted to the parties who must carry them out.

Because an office information system is used by individuals to convert field data to a form usable by the computer and to prepare reports, proposals, and so on, it tends to be work station oriented, that is, each worker has a station. A **work station** can be a terminal tied into a mainframe, a minicomputer with several terminals, or a personal computer. Several stand-alone work stations can be tied together for information exchange—a system called a **network**—or for sharing printers or secondary storage units. On the other hand, the MSS, DSS, and AIS are primarily mainframe oriented because they need the tremendous speed and storage capabilities of the larger machines to process data into usable information.

An OIS is also called office automation, because it uses automated procedures to improve office efficiency. Some types of hardware and software that are used to build an OIS are word processing, numerical analyses using spreadsheet packages, graphics, electronic mail, teleconferencing, communications networks, and data base management systems.

Data Manipulation and Reporting Systems

Data Manipulation and reporting systems are oriented toward the individual even more than office information systems. The data manipulation and reporting system allows the individual using a personal computer to manage the information at his or her disposal more easily. A data manipulation and reporting system is a subset of an MIS because it helps the user make decisions based on information provided by other elements of the MIS.

An *integrated* data manipulation and reporting system is needed because the same data may be used by several personal computer software packages, or the output from one package may be needed by another package. In other words, the user must be able to access the same data with different packages or to transfer information between packages. Use of individual packages makes this process difficult because the different packages may be incompati-

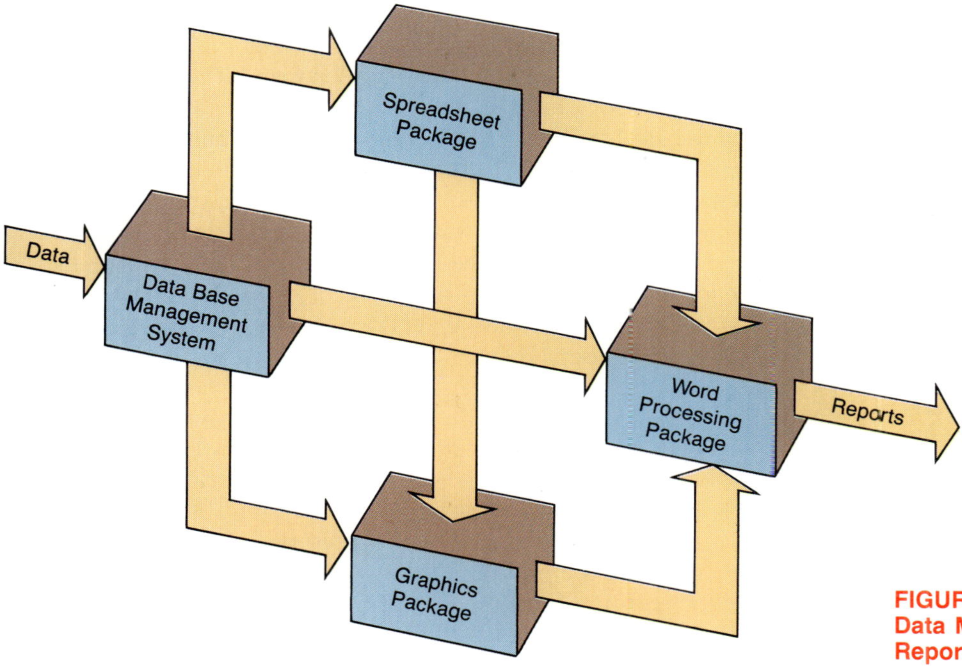

FIGURE 4-7
Data Manipulation and Reporting System

ble. If the individual packages are integrated so that they can all access the same data and information can be passed among them, then the user has complete control over the information.

A data manipulation and reporting system using an integrated package usually consists of a data base management system, a spreadsheet package, a graphics package, and a word processing package. The data base management system organizes and selects the needed data. The spreadsheet package makes analyses and forecasts, and the graphics package compares past, present, and future (forecasted) data. Finally, the word processing package writes reports based on the analyses and comparisons. The integration allows the raw data, spreadsheet analyses, and graphics to be moved directly into the word processing system for inclusion in written reports. Figure 4-7 shows how a data manipulation and reporting system integrates the capabilities of all four packages.

A data manipulation and reporting system can have a dramatic impact on the productivity of personal computer users. Not surprisingly, integrated packages are offered by numerous software companies. Combining a data manipulation and reporting system with an office information system can further increase the productivity of office workers.

SYSTEMS ANALYSIS AND DESIGN

Building a management information system involves the process known as **systems analysis and design**. As the name implies, this process involves developing a system design to meet a new need or to solve a problem in an existing system. Unfortunately, the process is much more complex than this description. In fact, it has spawned an entirely new occupation whose practitioners are known as systems analysts. The **systems analyst** carries out the process to determine the cause of a problem in the current system, suggests solutions to this problem, and then sees that one of these solutions is implemented. The new system can be one that must be programmed or it may be a hardware or software system that can be purchased from an outside vendor. In the former case, the new system must be designed so that the programmer can follow the design to create the software. In the latter case, the analyst must know enough about the various commercial systems to make a recommendation to management.

People can complicate this process. Systems analysis and design should consider the following three groups of people: (1) the users of the system; (2) the programmers or the outside vendors of hardware or software systems who will actually implement the new system; and (3) the managers who must oversee the transition from the old system to the new. Each group views the problem in a different light. Users know they have a problem, but they don't know how to solve it. The programmers or vendors can probably solve the problem, but they are not aware it exists and may not understand the terminology in the users' description of the problem. Management may not know the problem exists or how to solve it, but managers control the money needed to solve the problem. The systems analyst must work with all three groups to rectify the situation. He or she must understand the problem from the users' viewpoint, and the solution methodology of the programmers or vendors. The analyst must also be aware of management's budgetary constraints. In a sense, the systems analyst acts as an intermediary between the users and the programmers or vendors and is also responsible to management. This relationship is shown in Figure 4-8.

Systems analysis and design can be thought of as the following sequence of seven steps, with each step depending on the successful completion of the previous steps:

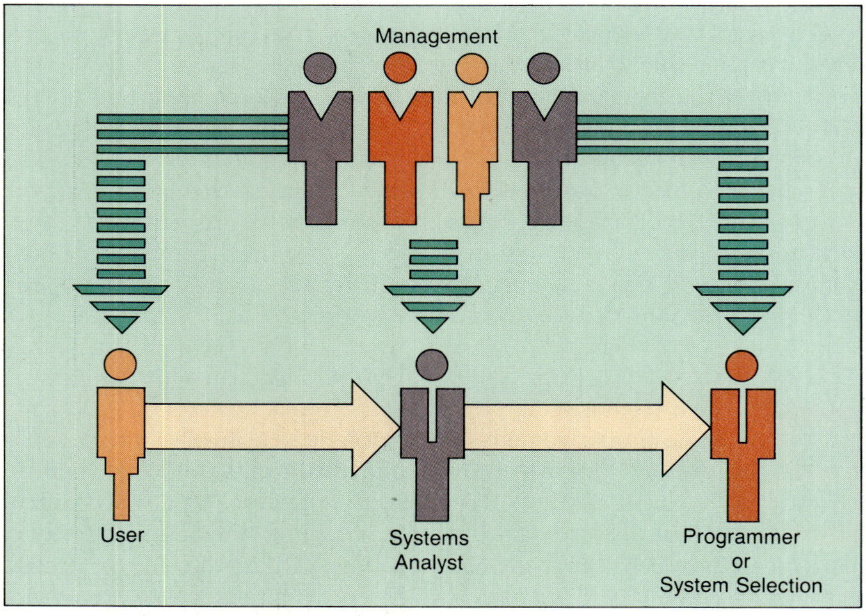

FIGURE 4-8
The Role of the Systems Analyst
[Adapted from: William S. Davis, *Systems Analysis and Design* (Reading, MA: Addison-Wesley, 1983), p. 6.]

A systems analyst must understand a client's needs before he or she can design a system to meet those needs. At right, a systems analyst discusses the secondary storage needs of a project with a computer operator to determine the appropriate storage media to use.

1. Problem definition
2. Feasibility study
3. Analysis
4. System design
5. Detailed design
6. Implementation
7. Maintenance

The key idea behind this seven-step process is the movement from a broad, logical understanding of the problem to a detailed solution of the problem. For example, the construction process for a building starts with an idea and moves to a set of preliminary sketches to preliminary plans to blueprints to the actual construction. In both the construction of a building and systems analysis, the movement is from *logical* to *physical*. This movement is termed a **top-down**, or **structured**, **approach** to systems analysis and design. In the first three steps, the analyst gathers data and moves closer to a detailed understanding of the system in question. In steps 4–6, the analyst and programmers or vendors develop a detailed solution to the problem. In step 7, the solution is in operation, and the system must be maintained on a day-to-day basis. We now consider this seven-step process briefly; Chapter 18 covers this topic in more detail.

Problem Definition

The systems analysis and design process begins with the determination that a problem exists in the current system. Complaints from users of a system may signal that a problem exists, management may find the current system too expensive even though it is working in an acceptable manner, or the output from the system may not match the system's objectives. Once an awareness of the problem exists, the problem definition stage begins.

The first step in problem definition is assigning an analyst to investigate the problem. The analyst meets with management and users to obtain a broad understanding of the problem. Based on these meetings, the analyst prepares a written declaration of his or her understanding of the user's objectives and

In the problem definition stage of systems analysis and design (left), the systems analyst becomes very familiar with the client's problem. During the feasibility study and analysis stages (right), the analyst tries to learn more about the problem and to determine if a solution to the problem exists.

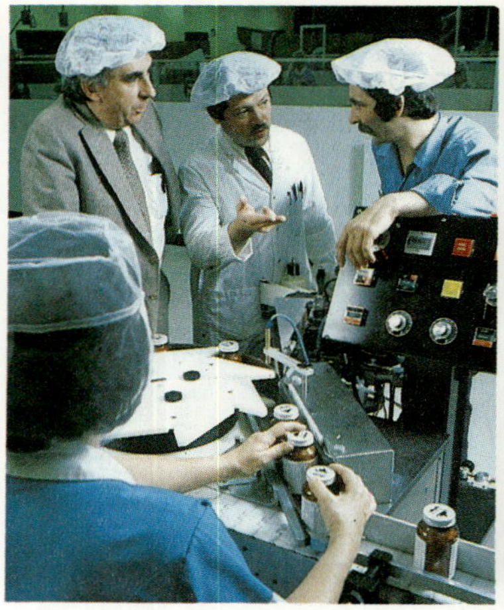

the scope of the problem. The analyst also prepares a preliminary cost–benefit estimate. When users and management agree on the objectives and scope of the problem, the analyst moves to the next step.

Feasibility Study

Now, the analyst can investigate the nature of the problem. A feasibility study is carried out to answer the following questions:

1. Is the problem worth solving?
2. Is a solution to the problem possible?

If the answer to either question is no, then the systems analysis and design process is terminated.

The objective of a feasibility study is not a solution to the problem but a better understanding of the problem. The analyst's understanding of the problem is refined to a point at which he or she understands it almost as well as the user does. The feasibility study can also be considered a "mini" version

ANOTHER VIEW
Frederick P. Brooks

Frederick Brooks was the manager of the team of systems programmers that developed the operating system for the IBM System/360, which was the industry standard from the mid-1960s to the early 1970s. Brooks was also the hardware team's project manager for the same system. A workable operating system, known as OS/360, was the result of many people working for several years. In this book on the problems of managing software development, Brooks made the following comments:

In most projects, the first system built is barely usable. It may be too slow, too big, too awkward to use, or all three. There is no alternative but to start again, smarting but smarter, and build a redesigned version in which these problems are solved. The discard and redesign may be done in one lump, or it may be done piece-by-piece. But all large-system experience shows that it will be done. Where a new system concept or new technology is used, one has to build a system to throw away, for even the best planning is not so omniscient as to get it right the first time.

SOURCE: Frederick P. Brooks, *The Mythical Man Month: Essays on Software Engineering* (Reading, MA: Addison-Wesley, 1975).

of the full systems analysis process. The analyst defines the problem, improves his or her understanding of the problem, develops a logical model that describes the important characteristics of the problem, and then decides whether any solution to the problem exists. The written declaration of his or her understanding of the user's objectives and the scope of the problem prepared by the analyst in the first step is refined, and the cost–benefit estimate is revised. Based on the analyst's report, management decides whether or not to continue with the process.

Analysis

If the feasibility study shows that the problem is worth solving and that an acceptable solution to the problem probably exists, the analysis stage of the process begins. In this stage, the analyst must work closely with the user to develop a logical model of the system. The model is a simplified version of the system, which does not attempt to capture every detail of the system. Instead, the model is used for conceptualizing how the system works and for determining how to solve the problem.

To develop a logical model, the analyst uses such tools as a data flow diagram, a data dictionary, and a rough description of relevant algorithms. A **data flow diagram** is simply a pictorial representation of the flow of data into and out of the system. The data flow diagram at this stage can be fairly elementary, because the analyst does not want a detailed model. A **data dictionary** helps the analyst organize information about the data flowing into the system. For each data element flowing into the system, such information as the name, source, description, and use is recorded in the data dictionary. The relevant **algorithms** are the procedures that can be used to solve the problem. The algorithms are not used at this stage, but their inputs and outputs are noted.

In systems analysis, data collection is an on-going procedure in which the level of detail is greater with each step of the process. In step 1, general data are collected from personal interviews and written descriptions of the system. In step 2, more detailed data are collected from operational reports, interviews with people close to the system's day-to-day operation, and actual data flowing through the system. In the analysis step, the data flow diagram, the data dictionary, and the list of relevant algorithms contain even more detailed data for the analyst to consider.

System Design

After the analysis step, the analyst knows what must be done to solve the problem, but he or she is not sure how to do it. At this point, the systems analyst develops several alternative plans for a new system and presents them to the potential users for comment. Close contact with users is extremely important at this stage to ensure that the new system will solve the current problem without introducing any new problems. At least three alternatives are usually given, including a "bare-bones" system that meets the users' minimum requirements, a "middle of the road" system that satisfies most of the users' needs at a moderate cost, and a high-cost, elaborate system that includes everything the users could ever want in such a system. The users and management now have a decision to make. They can decide that the cost is too high for any further development; they can decide to use one of the analyst's alternatives; or they can ask the analyst to develop another alternative that has characteristics not included in the previous alternatives.

In the system design and detailed design stages, the analyst develops a logical design and then a physical design of the final system.

In the implementation stage, the final product is developed and the system is installed for use by the client.

Detailed Design

If the users and management accept one of the analyst's alternative solutions, the process of detailed design begins, using this alternative as the general strategy. This process should answer the question of exactly how the system should be implemented. During this step, the analyst develops specifications on computer hardware and software that are needed to implement the chosen alternative. If the software can be purchased from a commercial vendor, then the specifications should contain enough information for users to choose a suitable package. On the other hand, if the software will be developed by programmers, the specifications should be detailed enough for the programmers to understand what the program must do. In other words, these specifications show the users what the finished product will look like, and they guide either the actions of the programmers or the selection of commercial software.

Implementation

In this step, all the detailed plans developed in the previous step become a reality. Specified hardware is purchased and installed. The commercial software is also purchased at this step. Both hardware and software should be tested to ensure that the specifications are met. If necessary, program development occurs at this stage. In this case, the testing is extremely important to ensure that the programs are bug-free and satisfy users' needs. The systems analyst is not usually involved in the programming or purchasing phase, but he or she is involved in the development of test plans, the writing of operating and security procedures, and the formal test of all components and procedures.

The implementation process includes installing the computer hardware and software, testing it with actual data, preparing documentation on the use of the new system, training personnel to use the new system, and evaluating the new system to determine whether or not it is performing satisfactorily. A commonly used approach to the implementation process is **parallel conversion**, in which the old and new systems run side by side until it is clear that the new system can handle the required tasks. In **direct conversion**, the old system is discarded and the new system is used immediately. Failure to test a new system adequately before eliminating the old system can affect an organization negatively if problems are found in the new system after the old system has been discarded. Mistakes of this variety have led to the total col-

Over time, the system must be maintained to ensure that it continues to perform as originally designed.

lapse of an information system, dismissal of the persons responsible, and even the failure of a company.

Another problem in the implementation process for a new system involves resistance to change by an organization's personnel. This problem can be avoided to a large extent by involving the personnel in all stages of the analysis, design, and implementation processes and by carefully training personnel on the new system.

Maintenance

Any system, no matter how well it is designed, must be continually modified to handle changes in input, output, or logic requirements. Maintenance is an on-going process that keeps a system up-to-date by making these necessary changes. Maintenance may seem like a minor part of the analysis, design, and implementation processes, but it uses about 70% of a professional programmer's work time. However, if the systems analysis and design process has followed the top-down approach described here, maintenance should be minimal.

REVIEW OF KEY POINTS

- A system is a group of elements organized for the purpose of achieving a particular goal.
- A system is made up of input, processing, output, feedback, an environment, and a boundary.
- Most systems are made up of subsystems.
- Most organizations have two major subsystems—management and information systems.
- The systems approach is a method of solving a problem by viewing it as a system.
- The computer is a system made up of user, hardware, and software subsystems.
- The operating system is an important software subsystem of the computer.
- Computer-based information systems can use batch processing or on-line processing; they can be integrated systems or distributed systems.
- The most important type of information system within an organization is the management information system.
- A management information system commonly has five types of subsystems—management support systems, decision support systems, accounting information systems, office information systems, and data manipulation and reporting systems.
- Organizations commonly have three levels of managerial decision making—operational, tactical, and strategic. Each level needs a different type of information.
- Systems analysis and design is a seven-step process used to solve problems in an existing system by developing a new system.
- The systems analyst, a key figure in the systems analysis and design process, acts as a go-between for users and programmers or vendors.

KEY TERMS

accounting information system (AIS)
algorithms
batch processing
boundary
computer system
data dictionary
data flow diagram
data manipulation and reporting systems
data processing
decision support system (DSS)
direct conversion
distributed system
environment
feedback
financial reporting
information system
input
integrated system
management information system (MIS)
management support system (MSS)
management system
network
office information system (OIS)
on-line processing
output
parallel conversion
patch
processing
suboptimized system
subsystems
system
systems analysis and design
systems analyst
systems approach
systems programmers
top-down (structured) approach
transactions processing
work station

REVIEW QUESTIONS

1. On a system with which you are familiar, point out the input, processing, output, feedback, environment, and boundary.
2. Note any subsystems in the system you selected in Question 1.
3. Discuss the management system and the information system of an organization to which you belong.
4. Discuss the difference between an information system and data processing.
5. Differentiate between on-line processing and batch processing. Give an example of each.
6. What does a systems programmer do? What is a patch?
7. List the five subsystems of a management information system. For the organization you chose in Question 3, discuss these subsystems.
8. List the functions of an office information system.
9. What does a data manipulation and reporting system do for managers?
10. List the seven steps of the systems analysis and design process.

口
廿
F
火
D
木
C
金
X
造/難

In this chapter, we introduce the interaction between people and computers. This discussion first looks at areas in which people come into contact with computers—such as in the work place, classroom, or marketplace. This chapter also discusses the problems of protecting personal privacy in the presence of computerized data banks and the impact of personal computers on the freedom of information. The various types of crimes that involve a computer are then discussed. Finally, the careers that are available to an individual with training or an interest in mainframes, minicomputers, or personal computers are outlined.

5

An Introduction to Computers and Society

STUDY OBJECTIVES

After reading this chapter, you should be able to

- Understand the following four types of interaction between people and computers: (1) situations in which people come into contact with computers; (2) personal privacy problems; (3) computer crime; and (4) computer careers.
- Recognize the types of problems that occur when people interact with the computer in the home, work place, classroom, or marketplace.
- Recognize the dangers to personal privacy that are inherent in the computerization of data banks.
- Discuss various computer crimes, including those that involve software for personal computers.
- List the types of careers involving mainframes, minicomputers, or personal computers, including those that exist in small businesses.

INTERACTIONS BETWEEN PEOPLE AND COMPUTERS

The first four chapters of this book have emphasized the computer half of the computer–user team. Until now, the human half of this team has only been mentioned—such as in computerphobia, software development, and systems analysis and design. However, the interaction between people and computers is so important that we now devote a chapter discussion to how people react to and with computers. The study of the interaction between computers and society includes any interaction between people and computers and the impact of computers on people or organizations. This chapter introduces the computer–user interface, and it also introduces Block 6, which covers this topic in more detail.

This discussion of the interaction between people and computers is divided into the following four sections:

1. Situations in which people have direct contact with computers.
2. The impact of computers on personal privacy.
3. Data security and computer crime.
4. Computer careers, present and future.

The last three topics are discussed in detail in Chapters 20–22 in Block 6.

DIRECT CONTACT WITH COMPUTERS

An individual's contact with a computer can occur in one of the following areas: (1) home, (2) work place, (3) classroom, or (4) marketplace. We now discuss each area of interaction and show how the computer affects people in each case.

The Computer in the Home

Today's increasing personal computer sales mean that the number of families with home computers is also rapidly growing. Recent figures from Dataquest, a Cupertino, California, research firm, show that over 10% of U.S. homes have a computer. Dataquest's projected increase of households owning computers is 18% per year.[1] Of course, the tremendous rise in the use of personal computers at home has increased the interaction between people and computers. For the most part, the personal computer apparently has a positive effect on the entire family. A preliminary study by New York University faculty found that a family that owns a personal computer tends to spend more time together, and watches television less. The children also do more homework using the computer.

Negative effects of computers in the home are attributed to one of two extremes:

1. The purchaser of the computer is the only family member who is interested in it.
2. Other family members are as interested in the computer as the purchaser.

[1] "'88 Computer Sales to Top $80 Billion?" *The Atlanta Journal,* October 4, 1984, p. 10-E.

The computer is fast becoming an important part of our lives in many ways. For example, the high school student at left uses one to complete his homework. Families often find that the computer draws them together. This family computer game (right) involves both joystick and voice input.

In the first case, the computer purchaser is the sole user and may alienate other household members, even cause marital problems, by spending too much time with the computer. On the other hand, if other family members become interested in using the computer, then the allocation of computer time among them causes problems. Either problem is difficult but not impossible to solve. The first problem can be resolved if the purchaser sets aside a specific amount of time to be with his or her family. The second problem can be solved by purchasing a second computer. (A second computer may also be less expensive because it may not need all of the sophisticated functions of the primary computer.)

People who can do their work on a computer at home as well as at their work places have contributed to the development of a new work pattern called **telecommuting**. A worker who telecommutes uses his or her personal computer at home either as a stand-alone computer or as a terminal to

ANOTHER VIEW
Jean Hollands

Jean Hollands is the founder and director of The Good Life Clinic in Mountain View, California, and the author of *The Silicon Syndrome: A Survival Handbook for Couples.* She has studied the Silicon Syndrome, which she defines as any situation in which the presence of a computer can extend the workday to 24 hours. Hollands has found that the over-involvement with work using a computer is primarily a male phenomenon. In an interview, Hollands has stated

Women use the computer as a tool. They use it for the end result. The man in general uses the computer as a companion and a co-worker that's interesting and exciting and stimulating . . . the idea that the machine is rational and logical and programmable is exciting to him . . . . His partner and his children are not programmable, they don't jump when asked to, they're not even rational—you know, there isn't the predictability in a family that there is in a machine.

Hollands has also stated that an individual who is over-involved with computers tends to be "more detached, more reserved, more emotionally quiet" than the average person. "He has very few personal skills in communication. If he was highly skilled in [communication] and could have fun and be joyful and be a good communicator then it would be alright for him to have this distraction [with the computer], but if he isn't, it's going to be a problem for the relationship."

SOURCE: Paul Bonner, "Coping with the Silicon Syndrome," *Personal Computing,* May 1984, p. 82.

Tiny, family-operated businesses will become more possible because computers offer business opportunities that can be pursued at home. By providing an increased degree of self-sufficiency, computers make the electronic cottage industry more feasible.

Dr. Portia Isaacson, President of Future Computing, Inc.

(As quoted in "Portia Isaacson Calculates No Margin for Error," *Peachtree Quarterly,* Summer 1984, p. 92.)

the office mainframe. In either case, the worker can avoid the daily trip to the office. Obvious benefits exist for a person who decides to stay home and work. Transportation costs and commuting time are saved, and child care expenses may be reduced. However, negative effects of telecommuting also exist. First, formal and informal interaction with superiors and co-workers is lost. In numerous situations, workers return to the work place to recover this social contact. Second, family life may be disrupted when the interactions between the worker and his or her family change because the worker is now at home rather than at the work place. This problem requires all family members to work out new ways of interacting.

When the computer is used for work purposes at home, the user may be drawn to the computer at any hour, day or night. Although the flexibility of working odd hours can result in the production of a larger quantity of work, the user may work far more hours than a structured, normal office day would allow. Therefore, the user must structure his or her work situation at home to avoid such a problem.

The Computer in the Work Place

The most obvious evidence of the computer in the work place is the **video display terminal (VDT)**, now a fixture in many offices throughout the United States. The VDT can be either a personal computer or a terminal that is tied into a mainframe or minicomputer. With these terminals, the user can access and manipulate data, display results, and make decisions. As a result, the VDT is considered an important facet of the work place.

Problems have accompanied the use of the VDT, both for the individual and for the organization. Recall from Chapter 1 that a worker may be afflicted with computerphobia, or fear of computers, when forced to work with one. The individual who uses a VDT over a long period of time possibly risks illness associated with the radiation from the screen; eye strain from watching the screen for long periods of time each day; and muscular and joint problems from the rigid posture associated with the use of the keyboard. The study of these problems has resulted in the new science of ergonomics. **Ergonomics** is the study of the relationship between efficiency and comfort

Video display terminals are used in many offices today. The computer can be used for many tasks, including the collection of data from the large number of encyclopedic data banks. The study of ergonomics has resulted in improvements in the design of video display terminals, including the tilting, swiveling monitor with detachable keyboard shown at right.

in a worker's use of machines. Ergonomists study the various body positions of VDT users, the types of keyboards that are used, and other factors involved in the use of a VDT.

The personal computer has introduced a new type of problem for organizations—conflict between corporate managers and the data processing department. Managers often want personal computers at their disposal to help in their decision-making processes. On the other hand, the data processing department does not want to lose control over the organization's computers. To retain control, the data processing department may make the purchase of a personal computer by a manager difficult. For example, data processing may require that only a particular brand of personal computer be used in the organization. As a result, managers cannot select the personal computer and associated software that they feel they need to perform their work.

Unemployment due to the automation of many tasks poses a problem for the organization and the individual alike. Robots have replaced human workers in the automobile, electronics, and supply industries. These robots perform many of the dirtiest and most dangerous or boring jobs in these industries. Some individuals displaced by robots may find other, more responsible positions in the same company. However, tens of thousands of workers may lose their jobs due to automation during the 1980s. In the automobile industry, U.S. companies did not rehire all of their workers after the severe 1981 recession. These companies responded to the competition from Japan by

Robot arms are rapidly replacing human labor for many dirty, dangerous jobs that involve repetition.

attempting to reduce their labor costs through automation. The future holds additional opportunities in many industries for automation using robotics, and the effect on employment is yet to be determined. This loss of jobs to automation is balanced to some extent by the new careers being created in the computer industry, discussed on pages 105–107.

The Computer in the Classroom

The computer has been used in the classroom to teach programming for over 30 years. Today, the introduction of personal computers has greatly expanded the use of computers at all levels of education from kindergarten to college. The use of computers in education has many benefits, but as with any change, resistance or conflict exists over their use. The computerphobia problems that exist in the work place also exist for many students. The phobia occurs most often at the college level in students without any prior experience with a keyboard or a computer. Elementary and secondary school students are so familiar with computers in the form of video games that little resistance to the use of computers occurs in the classroom.

At the organizational level, many colleges and universities are in conflict about what department or departments should teach computer literacy courses. Historically, computer science departments have taught programming and advanced computer classes, and business schools have taught the data processing course. Computer literacy does not seem to fall into either of these areas. Therefore, other departments that have found the personal computer useful have begun to teach applications-oriented courses. For example, a college of education or agriculture may teach a course on how to use the personal computer to solve problems in those areas. Similarly, a school of journalism or forestry and various arts and sciences departments—such as English, political science, or biology—may teach computer literacy courses on the use of personal computers in these areas. The conflict arises when the computer science department and these other colleges, schools, and departments cannot agree on what computer literacy is, who should be teaching it, and how it should be taught. This ongoing controversy will probably not be resolved in the foreseeable future.

Many college computer centers feature interactive terminals that allow students to access a mainframe for activities other than just programming.

EDUCATION
Computer Uses

In a recent report by the American Association of School Administrators, Grayson H. Wheatley, director of graduate research in mathematics education at Purdue University, outlined the following several uses of the computer for education beyond basic instruction in programming:

In science, for the simulation of complex processes and collection and analysis of data from experiments.

In social studies, for access to national data bases for current information and research on special topics.

In mathematics, for problem solving, simulation of functions, and study of the behavior of curves via computer-generated graphics.

In music, for composition of computer-generated music and study of tones and rhythm.

In art, for computer-generated designs.

In architecture, for computer design of structures.

In career guidance, for computer access to career information for all students.

SOURCE: Mike Morris "Classroom Computers Can Go Far Beyond the Basics," *Atlanta Journal and Constitution,* December 2, 1984, p. 6-D.

The Computer in the Marketplace

Interaction between computers and humans in the marketplace occurs constantly. For example, bar codes, banking machines, and computerized billing are encountered on a daily basis. The Universal Product (bar) Code is a pricing and inventory device in grocery stores. The UPC reduces checkout times and inventory costs, but it also causes problems when the wrong price is entered into the store's computer. Use of the bar code also means that consumers cannot always determine prices or make price comparisons by looking at the products.

Another common interaction between computers and people is at the automated teller machines that many banks now offer their customers. The machines are fast and efficient, but they also depersonalize banking. Machines can break down with a customer's access card still inside, and using an automated teller at night increases the risk of robbery.

One of the most frustrating computer-related experiences is trying to straighten out an incorrect bill that was prepared by a computer. Comedians

We encounter the computer in the marketplace every day. Point-of-sale terminals like the grocery store checkout counter at left compute the total customer charges and help maintain an up-to-date inventory. Automatic teller machines (right) are rapidly becoming commonplace, allowing 24-hour banking any day of the week.

have many hilarious routines on the subject, but when it happens to you, it is not funny at all. The problem is usually not the computer, although that is generally the reason given for the problem. People working with the computer usually cause the problem. For example, programming may contain errors, or the data may be improperly entered. Either way, the problem can only be solved if the right *person* is found. Writing letters to the computer cannot fix the situation.

COMPUTERS AND PERSONAL PRIVACY

In George Orwell's *Nineteen Eighty-Four,* Oceania is totally controlled by the Party, which controls information. Although computers are never mentioned in the novel, such complete control of a society would be impossible without computers to collect and store the information needed by the Party. The year 1984 has come and gone, and the United States is not like Oceania. However, some of Orwell's ideas about the collection and storage of data on citizens are now reality. A national data bank that contains the names and records of every U.S. citizen does not currently exist, but many smaller **data banks**, when taken together, come close to forming such a store of national data.

The Social Security Administration keeps data on all individuals who pay taxes into or receive benefits from Social Security. The Internal Revenue Service maintains records on all taxpayers, the Department of Agriculture keeps track of farm incomes, and the Secret Service stores information on threats to the president's life. Currently, at least 20 federal agencies have data banks on U.S. citizens. In 1982, the U.S. Office of Management and

The FBI and other law enforcement agencies can access the National Crime Information Center for information on convicted felons.

Budget reported that the federal government maintains an average of 15 files on each American. The FBI is one of the largest data holders, with criminal records on over 21 million individuals who have run afoul of either federal or state law.

At the state level, in 1982, New York State's Committee on Open Government determined that its state agencies operated over 1,700 data banks on New York citizens. These records include voter registration lists, driver's license holders, car registrations, state income and property tax records, and building permits. State and local police authorities keep records on offenders within their jurisdiction which they are quite willing to share with other law enforcement agencies.

In the private sector, numerous data banks contain data on most Americans alive today. This information can be crucial—for example, the credit bureau records that can often hinder an individual's search for a loan or a job—or seemingly innocent—for example, a magazine subscriber list. Other private data banks include school records, membership lists for unions or other professional organizations, and records of political contributions. Credit card companies keep track of users' payment records, banks retain information on customers' checks, telephone companies record the numbers dialed from particular phones, and insurance companies maintain a large amount of data on customers' driving records, blood pressure rates, and medical histories.

These data banks may be innocent enough individually. However, together they can give a fairly complete, if not altogether accurate, portrayal of any individual's habits, tastes, and even religious and political affiliations. Before computers, collating information on a single individual from several data banks was very difficult. Now, a single key identifier, such as a Social Security number, makes the search easy. The technique of linking two or more individual data banks together to match information is more than a possibility—it has been done. The Selective Service System checks student loan records against its registration records to ensure that each male loan applicant has registered for the draft. The Internal Revenue Service compares reported income figures against data maintained by various business information services to determine if an individual is living beyond his or her reported income. Although matching programs like these are legal, the possibility for abuse exists in the interaction between the data banks, especially when confidentiality is not guaranteed or is waived.

The problem with data banks is compounded if their information is erroneous, either through errors in data collection or in the process of data input. People have been declared dead by some agency computer, even though they are very much alive. A recent attempt to remove ineligible individuals from the rolls of disabled persons receiving Social Security benefits led to many cases of truly disabled people losing their only source of income.

Whether we like it or not, data banks affect personal privacy. Here, we define **privacy** as the control over personal information. Obviously, an individual's inability to control either the input to these data banks or the use of this information is indeed a blow to personal privacy. Since 1970, four federal statutes have been enacted to give the individual more control over the information that goes into these data banks, but continuing technological changes tend to outdate the laws the same year they are passed. The computer and personal privacy is covered in more detail in Chapter 21.

The IRS is perhaps the largest and most sensitive investigative agency around. In many ways more so than the FBI. We're concerned that there may be a massive hemorrhage of information from IRS files to other government agencies.

John Shattuck, legislative director of the American Civil Liberties Union

(As quoted in "Uncle Sam Sniffing Out Tax Cheaters," *USA Today,* February 1, 1984, pp. 1B–2B.)

ANOTHER VIEW

Jerry Pournelle

Jerry Pournelle is a science fact and fiction writer, who contributes to several popular computer magazines. Pournelle's articles often include philosophical and historical commentary as well as technical notes. The following excerpt appeared in his column in *Popular Computing*, "The Micro Revolution":

When Poland invaded itself [in 1982], the first thing the soldiers did was shut down the telephones. Free-flowing communications are anathema to tyrants. If the computer revolution proceeds, closed societies are endangered. When you want to have total control of your population, not only must you keep your people from communicating freely with outsiders, you also have to keep them from communicating with each other.

Closed societies cannot endure widespread use of computers. They have no choice but to keep these machines under strict control. They must suppress the micro revolution.

The result is a dilemma for tyrants. Suppress the microcomputer and lose your technological military power; or embrace it and lose control of the nation. [In my opinion], the microcomputer will do more to make the world an open society than any previous invention.

SOURCE: Jerry Pournelle, "The Mighty Micro," *Popular Computing*, April 1984, pp. 81–86.

Personal Computers and Information Flow

Data banks are maintained by mainframe computers because they require so much internal and external storage. The personal computer is considered the other side of the personal privacy coin. In other words, personal computers are the individual's access to information and means of communication with other users via telecommunications systems. A government cannot control its people without controlling information, and where personal computers are sold freely, information is an uncontrollable entity. Compare the personal computer user who can tap many information sources with Orwell's description of a citizen of Oceania: "Cut off from contact with the outer world, and with the past, the citizen of Oceania is like a man in interstellar space, who has no way of knowing which direction is up and which is down."[2]

DATA SECURITY AND COMPUTER CRIME

The 1983 movie *WarGames* dramatized a fictional breach of data security by showing how a high school student who wanted to play computer games supposedly used a personal computer to access the primary U.S. Defense Department computer, with nearly catastrophic results. Data security and computer crimes are problems facing businesses and the government in light of the increased use of personal computers. These problems existed when individuals used terminals tied into institutional mainframes to steal funds or to destroy data, but the personal computer makes the access much easier. A computer with a telephone connection is probably vulnerable to a breach of security, regardless of the type of system devised to protect it.

Computer crime can be defined as the unauthorized invasion of a computer data file or the theft of money, merchandise, data, or computer time using a computer. Computer crime can take a number of forms, including the following.

---

[2] *Orwell's Nineteen Eighty-Four: Text, Sources, Criticism,* 2nd ed., Irving Howe, ed. (San Diego: Harcourt Brace Jovanovich, 1982), p. 132.

Manipulation of company financial records to steal funds from the company. This type of crime can involve employees of the firm or individuals outside the firm.

Theft of merchandise by manipulating inventory records to hide the loss of the merchandise or by charging it to a fake account or to another customer's account.

Theft of company data. This form of industrial espionage may be the most frequent type of computer crime. Company consumer data, customer lists, or computer programs are common targets for data theft.

Use of the company computer for personal purposes. This includes using the computer to develop personal computer programs or to run a particular program.

Damage to the computer or data storage by angry employees or ex-employees. This category can include physical damage to the hardware, destruction of such secondary storage devices as disks or tape, or damage to the programs that control the computer.

Incursions into the computer programs or files or unauthorized use of the computer for fun or for the challenge. These individuals, who call themselves **hackers**, often work in groups to break into institutional computer systems across the country. The fictional hacker in *WarGames* thought he was dialing into a new game being developed by a computer company. He had programmed his computer to dial all numbers in a certain area code and to record all the numbers that responded with the high-pitched tone of a computer system. Of course, he also had access to the telephone company's computer, so he never received any long distance charges for these calls!

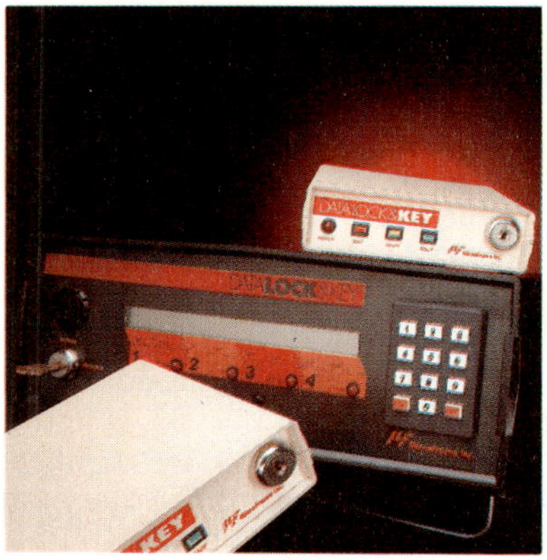

Computer security can range from a simple password scheme to a sophisticated microcomputer—for example, this microcomputer handles security for a mainframe.

When a Department of Defense computer started playing games with a teen-age hacker in the movie *WarGames*, the "games" almost resulted in World War III!

CRIME SPREE

In a recent survey concerning computer crime, the American Bar Association questioned 238 companies and government agencies about their problems with computer crime. Here are some of the results:

25% of the companies reported losses from computer crime.

Individual losses ranged from $2–$10 million annually; total losses for the 238 companies were $145–$730 million.

41% of the companies believe losses in the United States from computer crime exceed $1 billion.

28% of the companies had no system to monitor computer crime.

48% discovered computer crime in the past 12 months.

20% of the companies had not reported the incidents to law enforcement authorities.

39% could not identify the perpetrators.

58% of the companies strongly support a federal criminal law specifically for computer crime.

SOURCE: American Bar Association survey as reported in *USA Today*, June 28, 1984, p. 1B. Copyright 1984 *USA Today*. Reprinted with permission.

Examples of computer crimes show up almost every day in the national media. For example, stock and commodity brokers used computer expertise to cheat their clients out of a combined total of $100 million over a period of years. A sports promoter stole more than $20 million from a California bank through electronic funds transfer. A group of racetrack employees diverted at least $10 million from bettors at a dog track in Florida using the track computers. A group of Milwaukee, Wisconsin high school students called the "414s" (after their telephone area code) used personal computers to access medical and scientific computers. In many cases, these crimes go undetected, unreported, or unpunished because of the complexity of the computers involved.

Until recently, computer crime was difficult to prosecute, because no laws appropriate to such crimes existed. This situation has been rectified to some extent by new laws at the federal and state level. One sticky legal question concerns an incursion into a computer when no harm is done. Is this a crime? Many state laws say yes. Some experts blame lax security measures by the management of institutional and business computers for the ease with which

Many people consider the Flagler Dog Track computer crime case a "pure" computer crime because it involved only computer manipulation.

these crimes can be committed. The most common form of security involves the use of special passwords to keep intruders from using the computer. Unfortunately, easy-to-remember (and easy-to-guess) passwords are often used, and the computer is easily accessed.

Software Piracy

Most of the computer crime discussed so far involves incursions into or theft from institutional or business mainframe computers. A type of computer crime that involves personal computers almost exclusively is **software piracy**. In this case, software on floppy disks is copied and used without payment to the originating company. Some software companies estimate that for every copy of their software that they sell, 20 copies are pirated for use by others. The software industry loses at least $1.5 billion each year to software pirates. Such theft is easy, because users must be able to **backup**, or copy, the software disks as protection against the primary disk being damaged by a power surge or power outage. If software companies make disks that cannot be copied, users will not buy them because the disks cannot be backed up.

Software companies approach this problem in several ways. First, software companies can keep their products from being copied through copy protection. **Copy protection** restricts the user's ability to copy the disk. To meet the need for backups, companies may send backup disks to registered owners of their software. Companies also limit the number of backups that can be made from the original or master disk, or they require that the master disk be used during the package startup process. Although these measures are often adequate security, someone eventually devises ways to get around these protective measures. Ironically, software packages that can break the protective codes are sold openly and may be pirated too! A more detailed discussion of computer crime appears in Chapter 20.

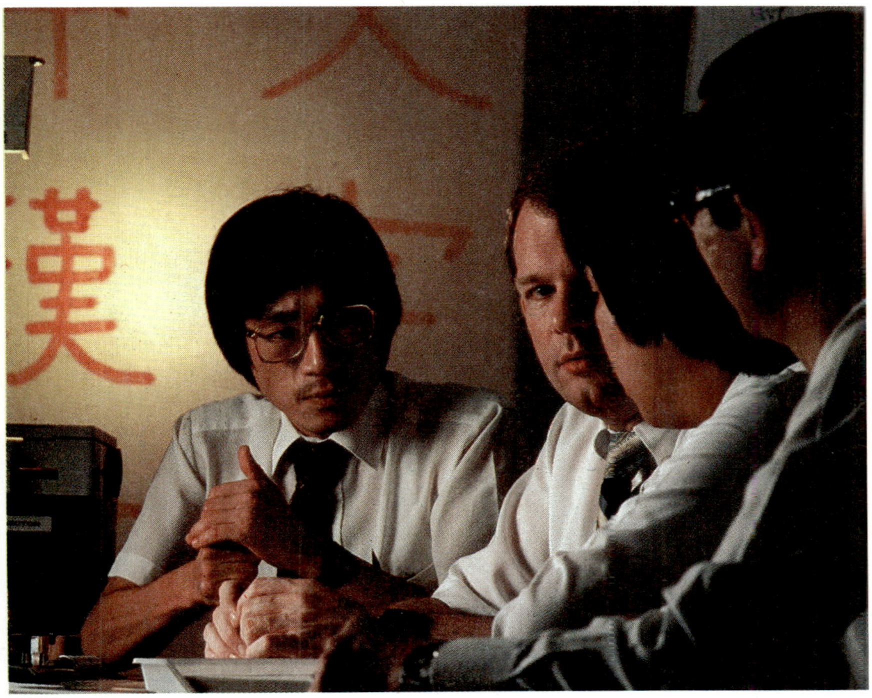

Programming is a career field that has no national or language boundaries. Here, programmers from four countries discuss a computer with multiple language capabilities.

Too many women assume that computers are just beyond them. I always say, "Look, if I can do it, so can you."

Connie Winkler, executive editor of PC Magazine

(As quoted in "She Wants More Women in Computers," *USA Today*, June 7, 1984, p. 3B.)

SUCCESS STORY
Ben Dyer

One well-known success story in the personal computer software world is that of Ben Dyer and Peachtree Software. A 1970 graduate of Georgia Tech with a degree in industrial engineering, Dyer was working for a hardware company when he became involved with a retail computer group in 1977. In 1978, this group expanded its horizons and produced a hardware–software combination called "Clerk." "Clerk" ran a variety of accounting software developed by Dyer's group of programmers. In September 1978, Dyer's company changed its name to Peachtree Software and concentrated on software only. The company's gross sales grew from $500,000 in 1978 to $2.5 million by 1980, when IBM approached Peachtree about writing accounting software for IBM's still secret Personal Computer. This tremendous breakthrough led to Peachtree's acquisition by Management Science America (MSA) in June 1981 for $5.5 million.

Peachtree is still a leader in personal computer software. Peachtree's products include a home accounting package called "Back to Basics" and an educational package called the "Writing Skills System."

What happened to Ben Dyer? He left MSA in 1983 to start a new company that combines personal computers with video disks. In 1985, Dyer and his new company bought Peachtree Software from MSA.

Ben Dyer, founder and chairman of both Peachtree Software and Comsell, Inc., is an example of an entrepreneur who has revolutionized the computer industry.

CAREERS IN COMPUTERS

So far, this chapter has discussed the problems with computers that arise because of the interaction between computers and people. Unemployment caused by automation was one of these problems. On the other side of the coin is the tremendous increase in computer-related occupations that has occurred during this decade. Although many jobs have occurred in the mainframe and minicomputer areas, a great number of jobs have opened up because of the increased use of personal computers. This section contains only an overview of the types of jobs that are open in the computer field. This topic is discussed in detail in Chapter 22.

Jobs that are available in the mainframe and minicomputer areas include such positions as information systems manager, systems analyst, applications programmer, systems programmer, data base specialist or manager, computer operator, and service technician. With the exception of the last two positions, these jobs require some specialized training on the type of system

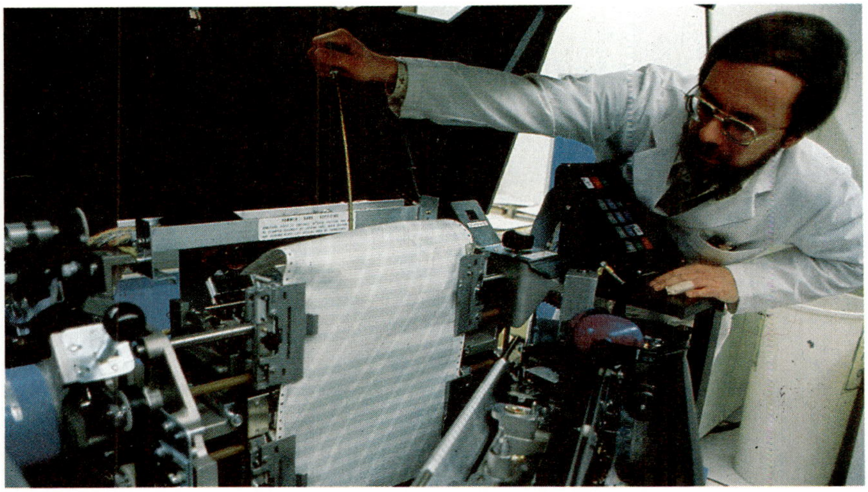

Servicing computers and their peripherals—such as this line printer—is a rapidly growing computer career.

in use, as well as post-secondary education in the general area of computers or data processing. The last two positions usually require extensive knowledge of the computer system in use and training in the specialized occupation.

In the personal computer field, large hardware manufacturers and software companies still need systems and applications programmers. The job field now also includes many small companies that develop one or more products for computers. These products range from a small device that protects the personal computer from power surges or blackouts to specialized software packages. Because producing these products does not require the large investment that mainframe and minicomputer products do, anyone with a new idea and a specialized knowledge of personal computer hardware or software can easily enter this business. Successful companies employ individuals with an interest in and some knowledge of computers as technicians, programmers, and marketing representatives. These positions may not require the formal education that might be required in a mainframe or minicomputer company. The important criterion is a knowledge of the product's

Data processing people tend to be individualists [who] look for working environments where they have a career path that allows for growth.

J. Daniel Couger, Professor of Computer Science, University of Colorado

(As quoted in "'Computer People': Yes, They Really Are Different," *Business Week,* February 20, 1984, p. 67.)

Sales or service positions at a local computer store can give a person interested in computers valuable experience.

COMDEX shows draw software and hardware manufacturers, dealers, and persons interested in computers together at sites around the world.

specialized nature. Some companies that are now worth millions of dollars began when one or two people built a computer or computer-related device in a garage or on a kitchen table. Many small software companies start with one person who writes a specialized program or modifies an existing package. Eventually, the company branches out into other areas of software that require additional programmers and support people.

Another source of employment in the personal computer field is the growing number of retailers who sell computer hardware, software, and supplies. These stores need knowledgeable sales people, service technicians, and programmers to handle the demand for their products. This network of computer dealers is such an important link in the personal computer market that hardware and software companies now get together with dealers at trade shows. COMDEX (COMputer Dealer EXchange) shows are held periodically throughout the year in the United States, Europe, and Japan for over 50,000 exhibitors, dealers, and the media.

An individual who is knowledgeable about personal computers in general or about some phase of personal computers can be a consultant for users and potential users on the merits of one system over another. Persons with a good knowledge of computers and an interest in teaching can train users to get the most out of their personal computer system.

REVIEW OF KEY POINTS

- The interaction between computers and society has many benefits, but has also led to some problems.
- Interaction between people and computers occurs mainly in one of four ways: (1) when people have direct contact with computers; (2) when computers affect personal privacy; (3) when computers are used to commit crimes; and (4) when new careers in computers open up.
- An individual's contact with computers occurs in the following areas: (1) home, (2) work place, (3) classroom, and (4) marketplace.
- The threat to personal privacy from computers exists because computers are efficient at searching for and matching elements from several data banks.
- Personal computers safeguard personal freedom by allowing users to communicate with other users and to have a free interchange of information.
- Computer crime can involve theft of money, merchandise, or data; destruction of hardware, software, or data; or the incursion into a computer "for fun."
- Personal computer software piracy occurs when the software is illegally copied.
- Careers in computers are available for people who know about mainframes, minicomputers, or personal computers. The personal computer career market has many openings in small businesses.

KEY TERMS

backup
computer crime
copy protection
data banks
ergonomics
hackers
software piracy
privacy
telecommuting
video display terminal (VDT)

REVIEW QUESTIONS

1. Name the four types of interaction between society and computers.
2. List the four areas in which people and the computer interact.
3. What is the Silicon Syndrome? How did it get its name?
4. Explain the term *telecommuting*.
5. What is a VDT? Explain the connection between a VDT and ergonomics.
6. Where is computer literacy taught at your university?
7. List the data banks that you think may contain your name. How could data from two or more of these data banks be matched?
8. Why is it sometimes easy for a person to access a mainframe computer illegally?
9. Explain the term *software piracy*. Why is it a problem for both the software company and the personal computer user?
10. Visit a local computer store and determine the types of jobs store employees have. Ask the dealer how he or she became involved with computers.

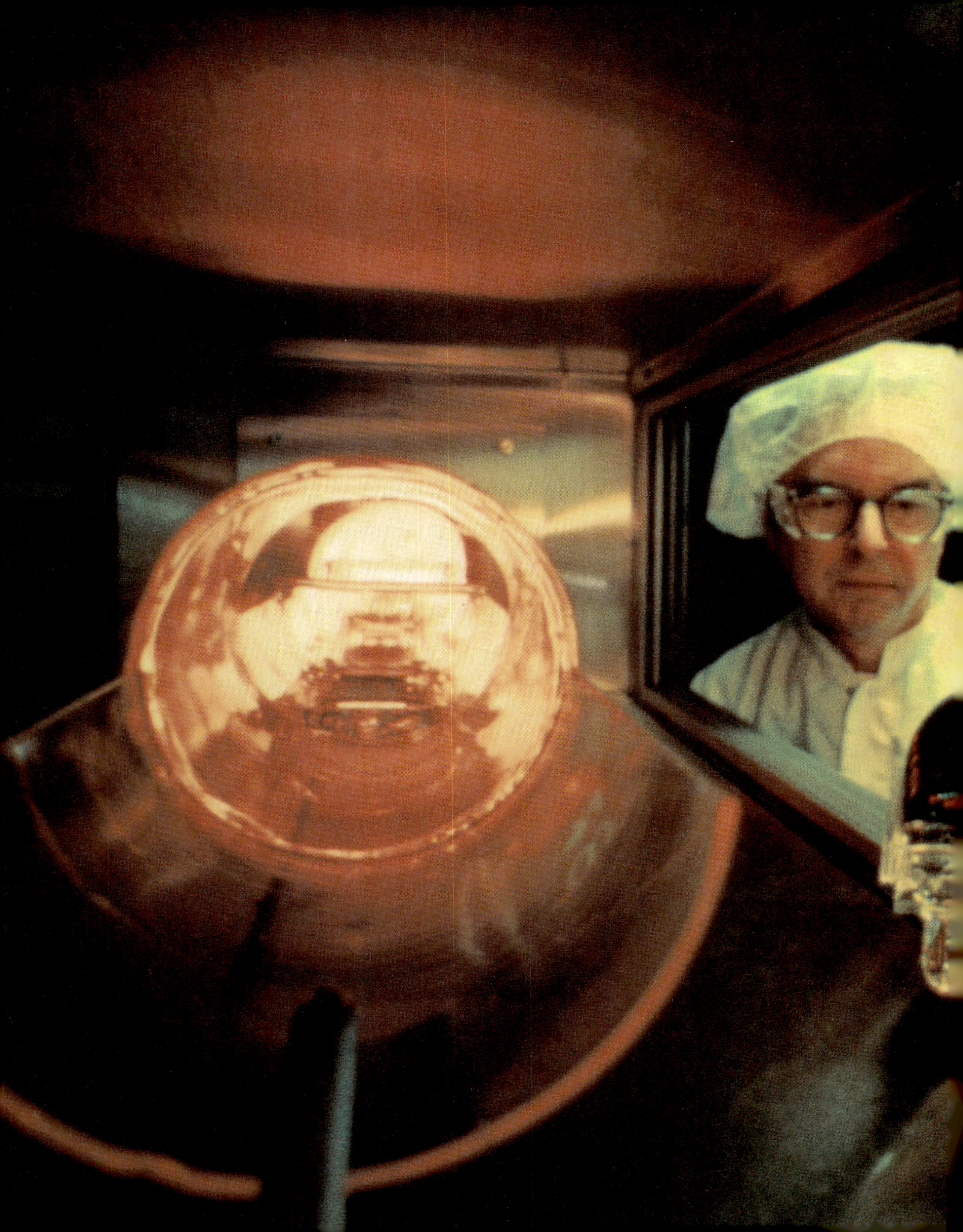

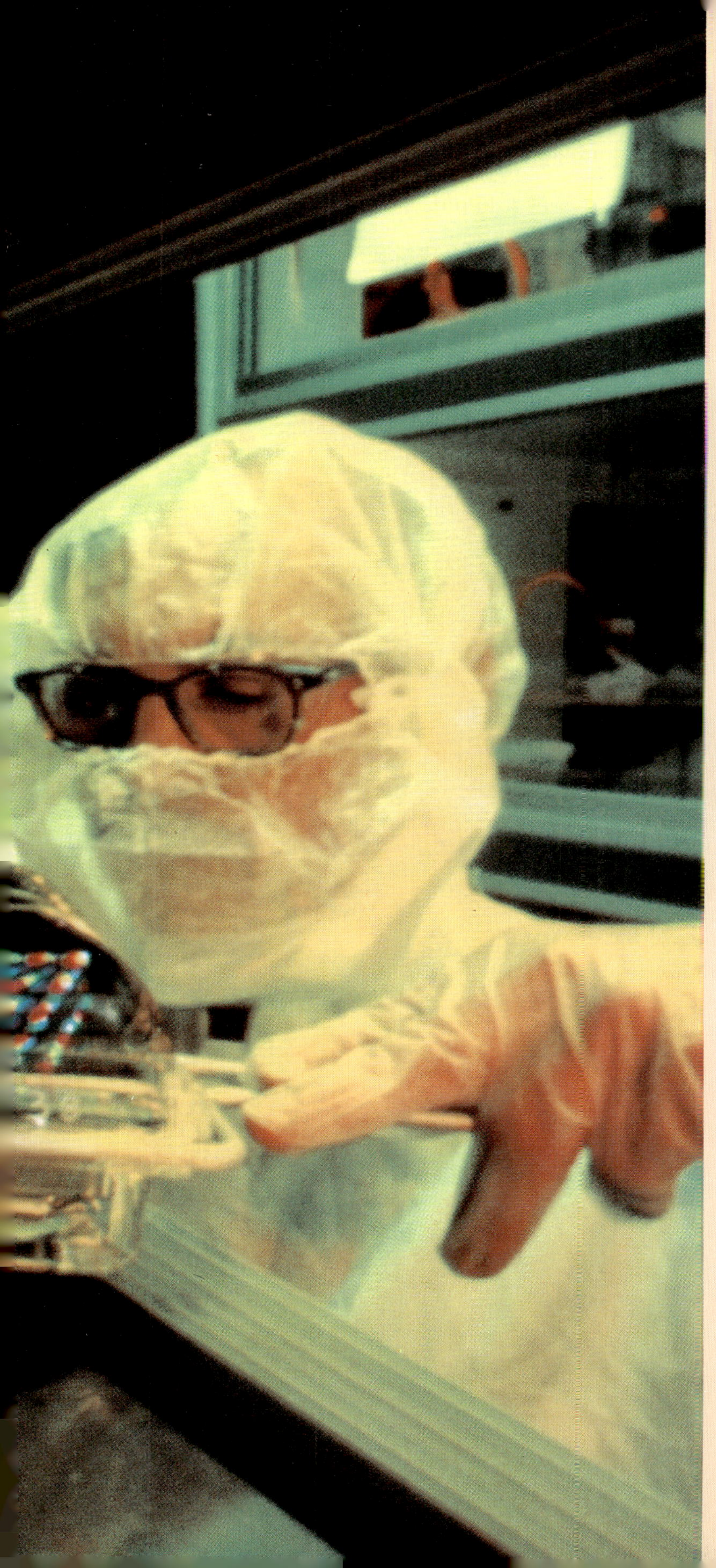

Block 2

THE DETAILS OF HARDWARE

In Block 1, Chapter 2 presented an introduction to hardware. This block of chapters covers the details of hardware. Chapter 6 discusses the central processing unit (CPU) and internal memory. Chapter 7 covers input/output, and Chapter 8 discusses secondary storage in detail. Each chapter reviews the pertinent material covered in Chapter 2 and then enlarges that earlier discussion with detailed coverage. We present material on computers of all sizes, with a special look at personal computers.

This chapter continues the hardware discussion begun in Chapter 2, concentrating on the processing and internal memory functions within the computer. The material begins with a detailed look at the conceptual computer. The parts of the CPU are considered, along with the process of program execution, including a discussion of temporary memory devices in the CPU and how numbers are processed in the CPU. A second look at internal memory includes RAM and ROM as well as other types of memory chips. The internal representation of instructions and data are then considered. Finally, the makeup, construction, and uses of the miniature electronic device known as the chip are considered in words and pictures.

6

The Central Processing Unit and Internal Memory

STUDY OBJECTIVES

After reading this chapter, you should be able to

- Understand the transfer of information into, within, and out of the computer.
- Understand the subdivisions of the CPU and the process of executing a program.
- Discuss registers in the CPU and the concept of a computer word.
- Discuss the concept of a computer word as it relates to computer processing.
- Understand the makeup of RAM, ROM, and other types of memory chips.
- Convert from binary to decimal and from binary to hexadecimal.
- Discuss the construction process for a chip and how chips affect our lives and the development of computers.
- Discuss the robots available today, their problems, and potential.

THE CONCEPTUAL COMPUTER REVISITED

In Chapter 2, we introduced the **conceptual computer** to explain how a computer works. That conceptual computer (page 24) had an input unit, a processing/internal memory unit, a secondary storage unit, and an output unit. The conceptual computer in Figure 6-1 is more detailed than the conceptual computer in Figure 2-1. In Figure 6-1, the computer's **central processing unit** is divided into the **arithmetic-logic unit (ALU)** and the **control unit**. The control unit converts the user's processing instructions into commands to the computer, and the ALU performs the actual processing within the computer. Figure 6-1 also shows the internal memory, input, secondary storage, and output units.

Flows of data, instructions, control, and results into, within, and out of the computer are detailed in Figure 6-1. Data and instructions first go from the input unit into the internal memory unit. This transfer of data and information is labeled "slow," because data must be entered into the input unit and then transferred into the computer.

From the internal memory unit, the instructions are transferred to the control unit, which directs the activities of all other units. The control unit directs the transfer of data to the ALU from the internal memory unit for the actual processing within the ALU. Under control of the control unit, a two-way transfer of data, results, and instructions occurs between the internal memory unit and secondary storage. The results of the processing in the ALU are then

FIGURE 6-1
A Second Look at the Conceptual Computer

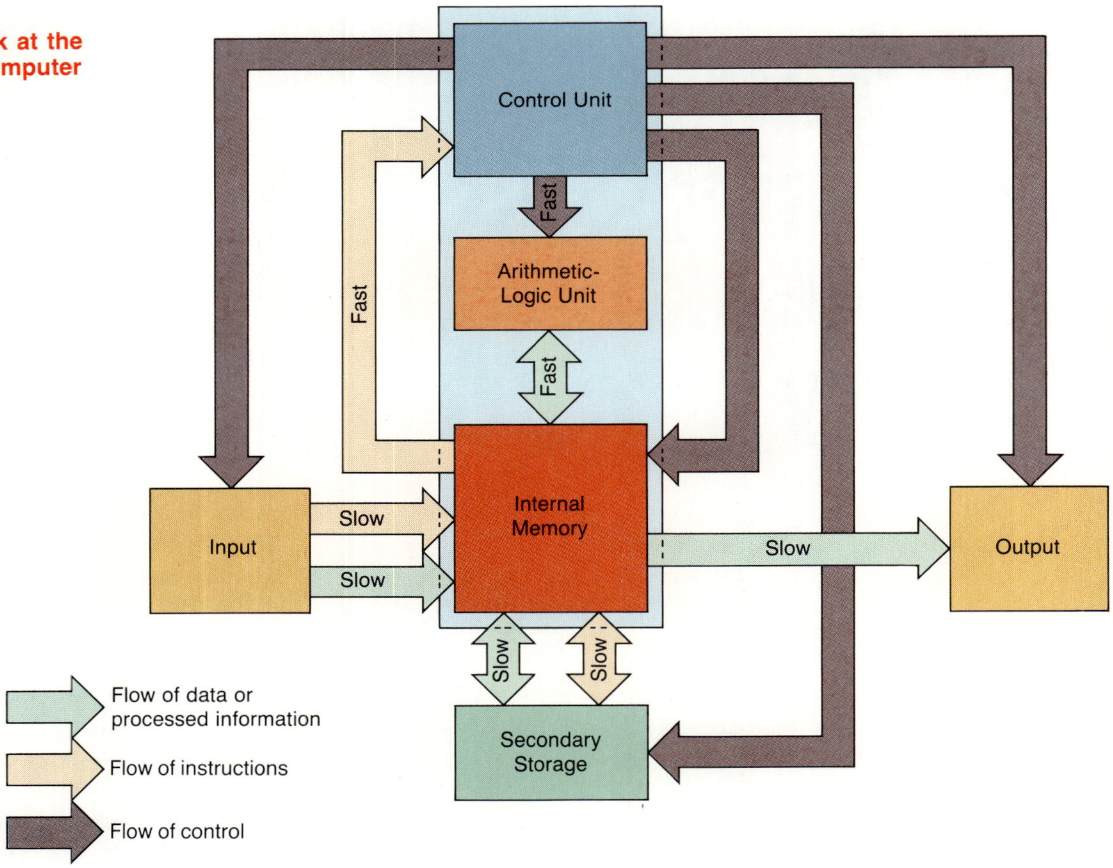

Integrated circuit boards are an important part of computers of all sizes.

sent to the internal memory unit, where they are output under directions of the control unit. The transfers of instructions and data within the CPU and between the CPU and the internal memory unit are considered "fast" because they are either on a chip or between chips. On the other hand, the transfer of instructions, data, and results between the internal memory unit and the secondary storage unit is "slow," along with the flow of results to the output unit, because these flows involve electromechanical devices, such as disk drives. Any flow of control is "fast."

Our discussion of the workings of the conceptual computer applies to both mainframes and personal computers. The differences between the two types of computers involve speed and storage, which depend on the type and number of chips in the CPU and internal memory units.

The microprocessor has brought electronics into a new era. It is altering the structure of our society.

Robert Noyce and Marcian Hoff, Jr.

(From *Fire in the Valley: The Making of the Personal Computer* by Paul Freiberger and Michael Swaine, excerpted in *Popular Computing*, October 1984, p. 103.)

THE CPU UP CLOSE

Within the CPU, the ALU handles *all* of the actual data processing including such arithmetic operations as addition and subtraction as well as logical operations. One logical operation is the comparison of two numbers to determine if they are equal. Only arithmetic and logical operations are performed by the ALU, but these operations can accomplish all necessary computer tasks

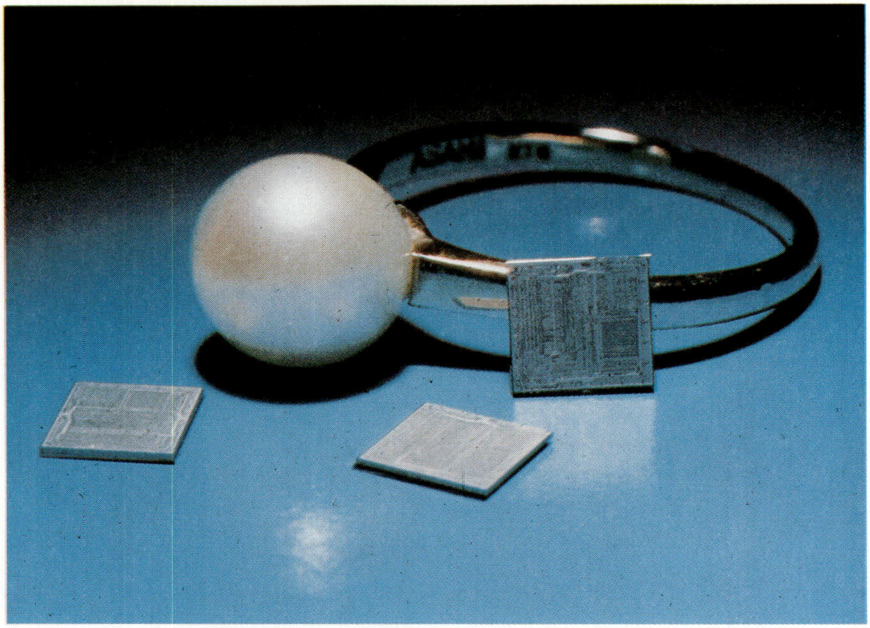

Several varieties of microchip are compared in size with a woman's ring.

The control unit manages the computer's operations, including synchronizing functions, controlling the flow of data into the computer, and providing commands to the ALU. The control unit *fetches, decodes,* and *executes* program instructions that are stored in the internal memory unit. The CPU's control process uses a clock and a system bus. The **clock** sends out electrical pulses at a set rate, which the control unit uses to synchronize its operations. The **system bus** is a communications system that allows the transfer of instructions, data, and control commands among the control unit, the ALU, and the internal memory unit. Figure 6-2 shows how the system bus is related to the control unit, the ALU, and the internal memory unit. Instructions, data, and control commands all flow along the system bus in individual paths called the **address bus**, the **data bus**, and the **control bus**, respectively.

The control unit and ALU combined on a chip are referred to as a **microprocessor**. Personal computers usually have only one such chip to serve a single user. The microprocessor is the key element that distinguishes one computer from another.

Execution of a Program

The control unit and the ALU work together to execute the program instructions that are stored with the data in the internal memory unit. The storage system used in a computer for instructions and data is very much like a series of post office boxes. Each instruction is stored in a particular location defined by an **address**. However, only one instruction or data item can be stored at a given address in memory. Figure 6-3 demonstrates the concept of a computer's storage locations, some of which contain data. The control unit or ALU can fetch the data at any address without destroying the data—a process known as a **nondestructive fetch**.

When the computer is first turned on, the control unit must be able to give initial directions to the other parts of the computer. These instructions are stored in the read only memory (ROM) within the internal memory unit. The

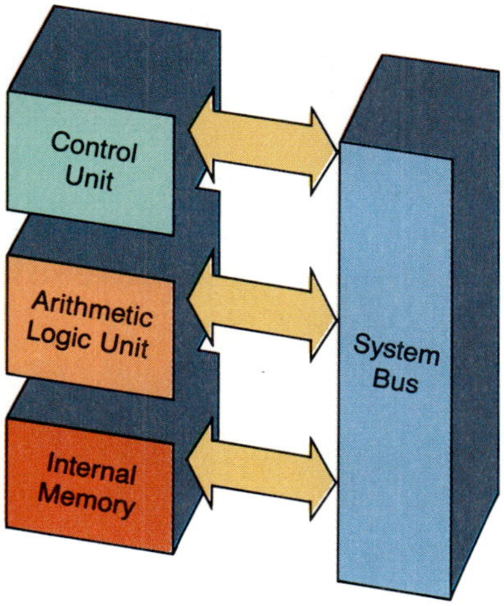

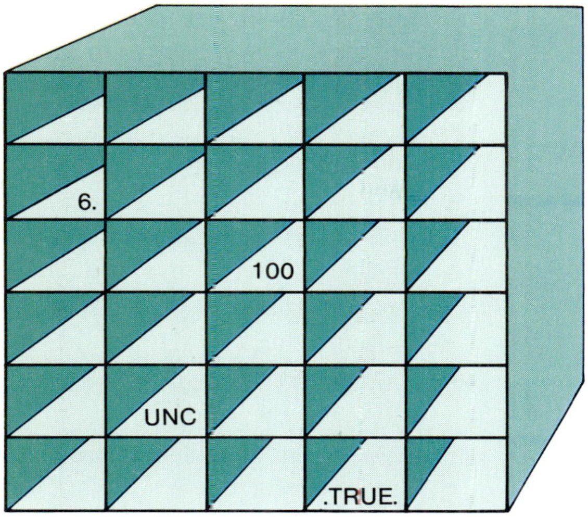

FIGURE 6-2 (left) Computer Units and the System Bus

FIGURE 6-3 (right) Storage Locations within a Computer

ROM is a nonvolatile form of memory that contains permanently stored instructions, which do not disappear when the power to the computer is off. These instructions are sent to the control unit when the computer is turned on. The control unit can then send commands to start the flow of instructions and data from the input unit into the random access memory (RAM) unit. Once in RAM, the instructions are sent to the control unit as required, and the data are sent to the ALU as needed.

Using Registers

Within the CPU is a high-speed type of memory called a register. A **register** is a temporary holding place for a particular instruction, data item, or piece of information. These fast storage areas help the computer perform the actual data processing. Different types of registers exist for the various operations

This Apple Macintosh computer board contains various types of chips, including the CPU, RAM, and ROM chips.

that are executed from program instructions. Often, more than one of some types of registers may be used in a computer. The following types of registers are used:

A storage register is a temporary holding area within the ALU that stores information to be transferred to or from internal storage.

An address register holds the addresses of the data to be transferred from the internal memory unit.

An accumulator register holds the result of any processing that takes place within the ALU.

An instruction register holds an instruction in the control unit before it is decoded.

A program counter register holds the address of the next instruction to be executed.

A general purpose register can be used for any type of operation or storage.

Only one instruction or operation can take place at a time in a register, but that operation can be done extremely quickly. However, the number of registers in a computer is limited, seldom exceeding 20 for the largest mainframe and 9 for a personal computer.

The Fetch, Decode, and Execute Process

To execute a program, the computer must go through the **fetch, decode, and execute process**—in other words, it fetches an instruction, decodes that instruction, and then executes it. This process begins when the control unit receives the address of the first program instruction from the ROM when the computer is powered up. [After the computer is booted (see the boxed insert below), these instructions are provided by RAM, where they have been placed by the programmer or the software.] The control unit fetches the instruction from this address along the data bus, places it in the instruction register, decodes the instruction, and then executes it by sending a command to the ALU along the control bus. A typical instruction might be "move the contents of memory location 1001 to the storage register."

To speed up the process, the control unit tries to store the address of the next instruction that may be needed in the program counter register. If the program encounters a change in the instruction sequence, then the program counter is reset to the new instruction.

"BOOTING"

Booting the computer is a common computer term. It is *not* the act of a frustrated programmer who might be tempted to kick the computer. In fact, "bootstrapping" a computer, which is the proper term, refers to the start-up process necessary for the computer to accept a user's instructions. The origin of the term is the phrase "to pull oneself up by the bootstraps." It also applies to the computer, which loads its first few instructions from ROM without help from the user. Booting a mainframe is a complicated procedure, but it is quite simple for a personal computer. For example, booting the IBM 3081 mainframe can take up to 30 minutes. However, for an IBM PC, the user need only insert the system disk, turn on the computer, and give the date and time.

After the instruction is fetched and decoded by the control unit, a command is sent to the ALU to execute the instruction. If data are needed, the control unit gives a command that the data be fetched from a particular address and placed in an ALU register. Using its registers, the ALU then executes the instruction and, if necessary, sends the results to the internal memory unit. A result that replaces a value determined previously in the program is an example of **destructive replace**. In other words, writing new information into an occupied storage location destroys the old information.

The execution process is shown in Figure 6-4, in which the circled numbers correspond to the following steps in the fetch, decode, and execute process:

1. Fetch instruction from internal memory and store in register.
2. Decode instruction and have data sent to ALU if necessary.
3. Command ALU to carry out decoded instruction using data received.
4. Send results of ALU operation to internal memory.
5. If more instructions remain, go back to step 1; otherwise, terminate execution.

Steps 1 and 2 occur during **Instruction-time (I-time)**, and steps 3–5 occur during **Execution-time (E-time)**.

Computer Words

In a computer, the **bit** is the smallest unit of measure, which shows whether a switch is on or off. A binary value of 1 corresponds to a bit whose switch is on, and a value of 0 corresponds to a bit whose switch is off. The next larger unit of measure in a computer is a **byte**, which is made up of 8 bits and corre-

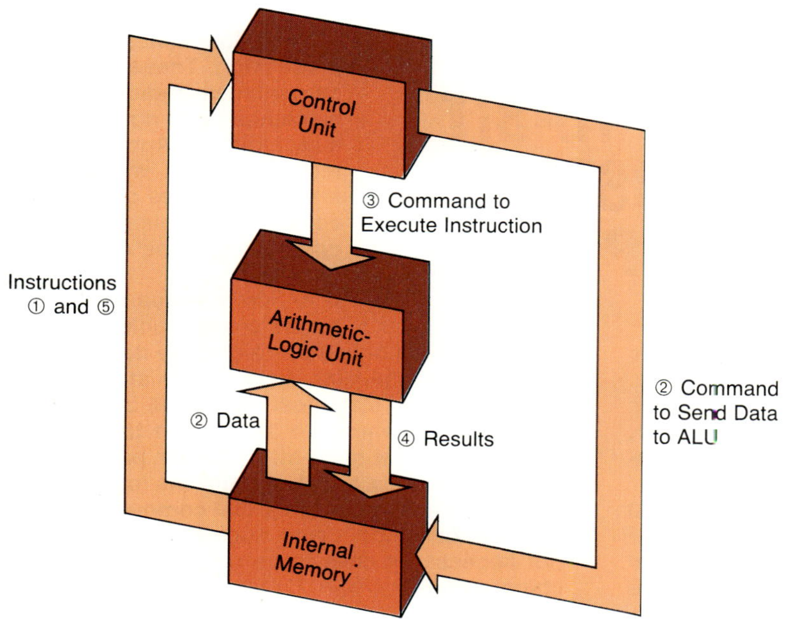

FIGURE 6-4
Execution Process

The STORED PROGRAM of John Von Neumann

In the computer's execution process, the control unit fetches an instruction from the internal memory unit. These instructions are the *program,* which is input along with the data and stored in internal memory. The idea of storing a program and data in internal memory is credited to a true twentieth-century genius, John Von Neumann. For the first computers, each instruction was hooked up by hand prior to solving a problem. This slow process could take many people several days to arrange the electrical connections that represented the program logic. Von Neumann and his associates suggested that a **stored program** could eliminate this laborious process. Today, common operations are built into stored program computers and given an address. The user need only give the computer a list of addresses, and the computer executes in sequence the operations located at those addresses. Without the stored program, computers could not perform their many useful tasks.

John Von Neumann pioneered the use of the stored program concept, which made the computer a general purpose tool.

8-BIT VS. 16-BIT PERSONAL COMPUTERS

A continuing area of controversy in the world of personal computers concerns the advantages of 8-bit versus 16-bit computers. The terms *8-bit* and *16-bit* refer to the word size used in the computer. The first personal computers—such as the Apple II and Radio Shack Model I—were 8-bit computers; that is, they processed data within the CPU 8 bits at a time. They also moved data from internal memory along the data bus (part of the system bus used to transport data) 8 bits at a time. The first 16-bit computer was the 1981 IBM PC, which could process 16 bits of data at a time. Since 1981, companies have developed numerous 16-bit machines similar to the IBM PC.

A 16-bit machine handles computations 2–10 times faster than a comparable 8-bit machine. However, a computer generally performs computational tasks only 15% of the time; 85% of a computer's time is used for such tasks as word processing. These computer use percentages indicate that 8-bit machines are not obsolete. In fact, although Apple has jumped into the 16-bit market with its Macintosh series of computers, it continues to market such 8-bit computers as the Apple IIc portable.

Different types of 16-bit computers are available. For example, the IBM moves only 8 bits along the data bus, but the computer manipulates them 16 bits at a time. On the other hand, the Macintosh moves 16 bits on the data bus but can manipulate 32 bits at a time.

Has the onset of 32-bit machines put 8-bit and 16-bit machines at a disadvantage? As long as software is available for a computer, that computer will perform the role for which it was originally designed. It does not necessarily have to be replaced by a faster machine.

sponds to a single character in storage. The largest unit in computer storage is the computer word. A **computer word** is the number of bits that are processed by the registers in the ALU at one time. Typical word sizes for personal computers are 8 bits (Apple IIe and IIc, TRS-80 Model 4 and Commodore 64) and 16 bits (IBM PC, Tandy 2000, and TI Professional). In other words, the word length for an 8-bit computer is 1 byte and for a 16-bit computer, 2 bytes is the word length. Personal computers that work with 32-bit words will probably be available in the near future, with the Apple Macintosh being a forerunner to these machines.

On mainframes and minicomputers, the word size ranges from 16 bits (the PDP and TI 990 minicomputers) to 32 bits (the IBM 370 series of mainframes) to 60 bits (the Control Data Corporation 7600 series of mainframes). Supercomputers like the CDC CYBER 205 and CRAY 1 use a 64-bit word for their high-speed calculations.

In personal computers, a 1- or 2-byte **fixed length word** is used, but in some mainframes, a variable length word is used. A **variable length word** combines as many bytes as necessary to represent a symbol. Because personal computers can work with bytes as well as words, this differentiation is not significant for personal computer users. Because each byte corresponds to one character, working with strings of bytes or 1 byte is equivalent to working with a string of characters or a single character, respectively. Either way, personal computers can work with any number of bytes.

INTERNAL MEMORY

If the CPU is one-half of the computer's brain, the other half is **internal memory**, also referred to as **main memory**. Here, the list of instructions—the program—is stored along with the data. The two primary types of internal memory are RAM (for **random access memory**) and ROM (for **read only memory**). In **ROM**, information is stored in binary with a permanent series of switches in the chip. In **RAM**, storage is accomplished by the use of "flip-flops," miniature transistors on a chip that act as switches to store the information to binary form. Each bit of information corresponds to one transistor (switch), which is turned on if the bit equals 1 or left off if the bit equals 0.

Computer boards allow a user to increase a personal computer's memory or to enhance its performance and usefulness.

Read Only Memory

Read only memory is a **nonvolatile**, or permanent, **memory** that is built into the computer. The user cannot store information in ROM; information can only be read from ROM. Because ROM is permanent and RAM is not, ROM contains the initial instructions that allow the user's program to begin after the system disk is inserted. Some computers do not even need a system disk because the entire operating system is contained in ROM.

Manufacturing a ROM chip involves a process called **burning in the circuits**, which refers to whether the switches are set on or off. Each switch in a ROM chip is like a miniature fuse, such as those in cars or houses. To turn a switch on, the fuse is "blown" by an electrical current. Once the fuse is blown, it cannot return to the off state and does not require a constant current to be maintained. The instructions on the ROM chip are often referred to as **firmware** to differentiate them from the software instructions that the user places into RAM.

In some computer systems—notably the Apple Macintosh—the ROM contains various instructions for graphics and use of the mouse for input. The ROM in some new portable computers contains word processing and scheduling programs so that secondary storage diskettes are not needed to load the program. The shortcoming of using ROM for other than start-up procedures is that information cannot be written into it. In other words, to change any software application stored in ROM, the entire ROM chip must be changed.

Random Access Memory

The type of memory that is usually associated with a computer is RAM, the memory in which the user stores programs and data. Like ROM, RAM is extremely fast memory, but it is not permanent. Except for a type of RAM called bubble memory, RAM is volatile, and items in RAM disappear when power to the computer is turned off. In RAM, a constant electrical current maintains a transistor's on or off state. When the computer is turned off, the current is removed and the transistor loses the information that was stored there. For this reason, RAM is called **volatile memory**.

RAM chips are used in high-speed mainframe computers to allow multiple users to access the computer concurrently with no noticeable loss of speed.

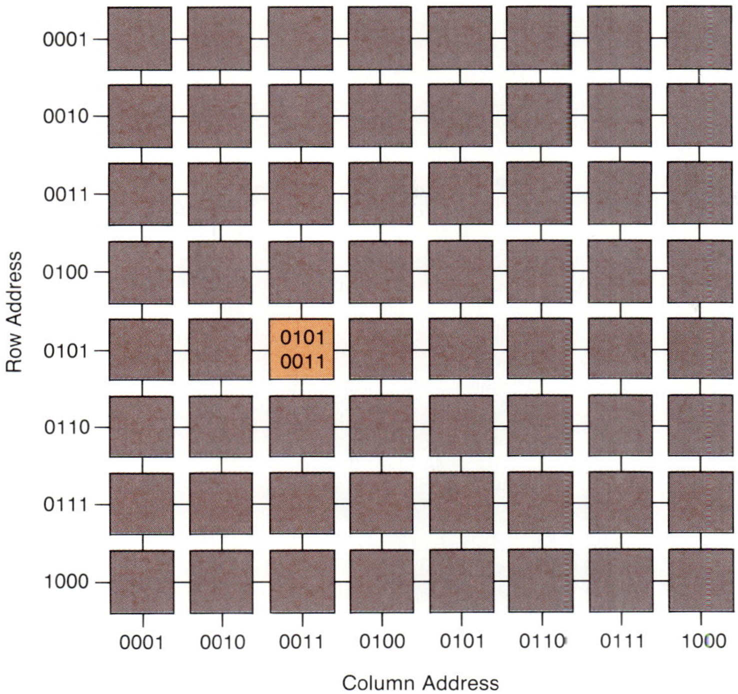

FIGURE 6-5
Addressing Storage Locations

The amount of RAM in a computer system is discussed in terms of Kbytes. One **Kbyte** is equivalent to 1,024 bytes. The actual memory chips used for RAM are measured in Kbits. One **Kbit** is equivalent to 1,024 bits. The first IBM PC's 4K memory chips each contained 4,096 transistors (4 × 1,024), one for each bit stored. Currently, memory chips have either 64 Kbits or 256 Kbits of memory. Soon, over one megabit (1,048,576 bits) of memory will be available on one chip.

The amount of memory on a chip is measured in powers of two (1,024 bits = 2^{10}). Therefore, the memory addresses are also expressed in powers of two. The actual addressing of a memory location from the CPU is beyond the scope of this discussion, but the process of locating 1 bit out of a block of 64 bits is shown in Figure 6-5. In this diagram, the row address and column address are expressed in binary. For example, the bit in row 5 and column 3 would have the address 0101 0011, with the row address shown first and the column address shown second.

Other Types of Memory

RAM and ROM are the two most important types of memory in the computer, but other types of memory chips have many useful purposes. In some cases, these other memory chips attempt to combine the better points of RAM and ROM, and others attempt to avoid the volatility of RAM.

Two memory chips that attempt to have the best of RAM and ROM are **PROM** chips **(programmable read only memory)** and **EPROM** chips **(erasable programmable read only memory)**. The PROM chip is like a ROM chip except that the instructions are not built in at the factory. The chip's user can "burn in" the chip's special instructions. Once the user does this, the chip is like any ROM chip directing applications in the areas of manufacturing, agriculture, or health.

Erasable programmable read only memory (EPROM) chips can be erased with ultraviolet light that is directed through the special window on top of the chip.

CORE
Alias RAM

Another name often used for random access memory is **core**, especially among people who began their computer work on mainframes. The term *core,* part of the history of internal storage, refers to a type of random access memory that was in use prior to microchips.

While the CPU progressed from vacuum tube to transistor to integrated circuit to microchip, memory also went through various stages. The first generation machines primarily used **magnetic drum storage**, with tiny magnetized spots that represented a 1-bit. The drum rotated, and sensing heads determined the pattern of bits that represented the data in memory.

From 1960–1975, the most popular form of memory was **magnetic core**, which was composed of tiny ferromagnetic (magnet-like) donuts or cores strung on a set of wires. Electrical current that was passed through a wire induced magnetism in the core in a clockwise direction for the on state or in a counterclockwise direction for the off state. This process is shown below for one such core.

Computers needed large numbers of the magnetic cores located on core planes. On a core plane, four wires went through each donut to store and retrieve the data. When a particular core was magnetized, two wires each carried one-half the needed current. A sense wire that was passed through the core at an angle determined a core's on or off state. Finally, an inhibit wire ensured that each core returned to its original state after the sensing process. Magnetic core was a nonvolatile form of memory because the presence of a magnetic state did not depend on a constant electrical current. Whereas internal memory using chips can be accessed in billionths of a second, core memory can be accessed in millionths of a second.

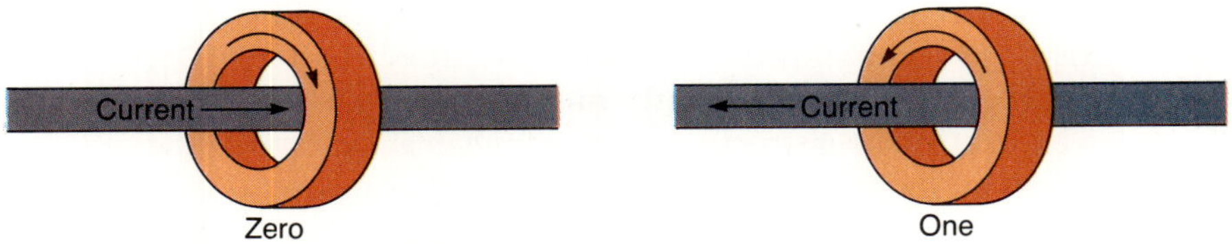

Core Representation of Zero and One

Bubble memory chips are a form of random access memory that does not disappear when the power to the computer is turned off.

The EPROM can be extremely useful in experimental work when the user is uncertain about the instructions that should be placed on the chip. The EPROM chip can be *erased* by exposure to ultraviolet light and then reprogrammed as many times as needed. For example, the instructions on a read only chip that is used to control a piece of farm machinery may be changed several times before the user has full control of the machinery.

All the information stored in RAM is normally lost when the power to the computer is turned off. An unplanned loss of power can be catastrophic. Two different solutions to this problem have been used. In one case, the memory storage device is a thin magnetic film containing a series of bubble-like conditions. This **bubble memory** assigns a 1 to the presence of a "bubble," and a 0 to the absence of a bubble. Inside a tiny package, electromagnetic coils cause magnetic "bubbles" to move around tracks in a tight formation. Bubble memories can deliver a steady 100,000 bits per second to the CPU. Information in this type of memory does not disappear when the power is turned off. High cost has kept bubble memory from being commonly used.

A second solution is the use of batteries to preserve the contents of RAM when the power to the computer is turned off. Some portable computers already use penlight batteries for power. In addition to these main batteries, rechargeable nickel-cadmium batteries provide backup power to the RAM if the penlight batteries fail.

INTERNAL REPRESENTATION OF DATA AND INSTRUCTIONS

Within the computer, the data and instructions are represented in the binary number system as a series of zeros and ones. This form of representation is used because the computer's only two electrical states—on and off—correspond to 1 and 0. Using a string of transistors that act as switches, the computer can represent a number or instruction as a series of on–off states.

MEMORY
How Much Do You Need?

Personal computer manufacturers are offering more and more RAM the way automobile manufacturers offered better and better gas mileage. As a result, it is hard to tell the value of a personal computer purchase. The original personal computers offered small amounts of RAM—only 4K or 16K. As memory chip technology improved and the manufacturing process became cheaper, the amount of a computer's RAM increased to 48K or 64K. Today, 256K or more of RAM is standard in many personal computers. Values of 512K and up are available on enhanced versions like the Fat Mac and the IBM AT. The Fat Mac was introduced to increase the software potential of the original 128K Macintosh, and the IBM AT can store up to 3 Mbytes in RAM. For mainframes, this amount is now well into the millions of bytes of memory.

Although this extra memory is needed to run many software packages, it is of no use in some situations. For example, the BASIC computer language can only access 64K of RAM, regardless of the amount of memory that is available on a particular computer.

So, how much memory is needed? The computer application in use determines the amount of memory that is needed. For programming in BASIC, 64K is adequate. On the other hand, for some of today's sophisticated and highly integrated software, 320K or more of memory may be needed.

Often, the number system the computer understands (binary) must be converted to the form humans understand (decimal), and vice versa. The conversion from binary to decimal is easy if we use the powers of 2 combined with positional notation. Some powers of two are as follows:

$2^0 = 1$	$2^2 = 4$	$2^4 = 16$
$2^1 = 2$	$2^3 = 8$	$2^5 = 32$

We can determine the decimal equivalent of a binary number by computing the product of each binary digit and its corresponding power of 2. For example, let us convert the binary number 110101 to decimal. Multiplying the right-most binary digit by its power of 2 gives us $(1 \times 1) = 1$. Moving from right to left and summing the results of the multiplications, we get the following:

$$1 + (0 \times 2) + (1 \times 4) + (0 \times 8) + (1 \times 16) + (1 \times 32) = 53$$

In this case, 110101 in binary equals 53 in decimal.

A binary number is cumbersome to work with, especially when the number of digits is large. This difficulty led to the use of other number systems to represent binary numbers. The best known system is the hexadecimal, or base 16, number system. Because this system is based on a power of 2, converting the binary number system to the hexadecimal number system is fairly easy. As a result, the hexadecimal number system is used to represent the binary number system in many mainframes and all personal computers.

The **hexadecimal**, or **hex**, **number system** uses the digits 0–9 and the letters A–F to represent numbers. In the conversion from binary to hex, the binary number is divided into groups of four digits, because each hex digit represents four binary digits. Table 6-1 shows the binary digit groups with their corresponding hex digits.

Using Table 6-1, we can convert a binary number to hex by assigning a hex digit to each 4-bit section of the binary number. For example, let us convert

Table 6-1 BINARY EQUIVALENTS OF HEXADECIMAL DIGITS

Binary Digits	*Hexadecimal Digit*	*Binary Digits*	*Hexadecimal Digit*
0000	0	1010	A
0001	1	1011	B
0010	2	1100	C
0011	3	1101	D
0100	4	1110	E
0101	5	1111	F
0110	6		
0111	7		
1000	8		
1001	9		

the binary number 110110100 to hex. The binary number is divided into 4-bit groups, and zeros are added on the left, if necessary, to yield a multiple of 4. In our example, 110110100 can be divided into 4-bit groups of 0001 1011 0100. This corresponds to 1B4 in the hexadecimal number system.

In Chapter 2, we discussed the use of ASCII and EBCDIC to represent characters in binary. As 8-bit codes, both ASCII and EBCDIC use 1 byte to represent each character. As a result, each character can be easily represented by two hex digits. For example, the letter L in ASCII is 01001100 in binary. This binary number converts to 4C in hex, which is a much more compact representation.

Because the amount of memory in a computer is expressed as a power of 2, we can use hex notation to represent memory addresses. Each memory location in Figure 6-5 (page 125) can be represented with two hex digits. For example, the bit in row 5 and column 3 has a binary address of 0101 0011, or 53 in hex. Using this approach, 256 bits can be addressed with 2 hex digits (00 through FF). Similarly, 65,536 (64K) bits can be represented with four hex digits.

The chip is remaking this into a world where information is literally wealth. Without equal skill in using computers to get and employ information, people may divide into "knows" and "know nots" and suffer or prosper accordingly.

Peter Schwartz, former head of Future Studies, SRI International

(As quoted in "The Chip," *National Geographic*, October 1982, p. 448.)

THE AMAZING CHIP

A technological advance that has profoundly affected today's world is the development of the microchip. Originally created so that a transistor could be built into a circuit board, the **chip** first came to prominence when it was used to reduce the size and cost of calculators. The tremendous advances in computer technology can all be traced directly to the use of chips to handle logic and memory operations in all types of computers. The chip is also used in many "computerized" devices in the home, in the work place, in health care, and in agriculture. Consider the following examples:

Automatic microwave ovens, cameras, and television sets use a chip to direct their operations.

Digital watches use chips to keep time, dates, and play games.

CHIP POWERS MUSCLES

In 1982 at age 28, Carmen Scozzari wore heavy braces and was confined to a wheelchair. Scozzari was a victim of a rare disabling disease that had been destroying her body for 22 years. The disease, called *dystonia musculorum deformans,* garbled the nerve messages sent to the muscles, which resulted in severe spasms. Except for her left shoulder and elbow and three fingers of her left hand, Scozzari's body was out of control.

Today, she walks without even a limp and is a research assistant in a department of neurological surgery. What changed Carmen Scozzari's life? An almost miraculous operation was performed by Dr. Joseph M. Waltz at the St. Barnabas Hospital in New York City. During this operation, Waltz implanted four electrodes near Scozzari's spinal cord to stimulate muscles to return them to normal use. The stimulation is controlled by a microprocessor chip that is carried outside the body. The chip communicates with the electrodes by radio signals. These signals speak to the brain, as Waltz puts it, "in a language it can understand" to stop the spasms.

Originally, Scozzari disliked the sensation resulting from the electrodes, but eventually she could reduce the intensity of the signals with a regulation device. Two days after surgery, Scozzari could eat without help, and for the first time in 10 years, she snapped her fingers. After 6 weeks of rehabilitation, she walked out of the hospital and returned to her home in California. A problem with the antenna that receives the signals sent Scozzari back to St. Barnabas for a second operation, which resulted in complete recovery. She now works at St. Barnabas, keeping track of other patients who have undergone this surgery.

SOURCE: Dianne Hales, "A New Life for Carmen," *Family Circle,* February 26, 1985, pp. 16–19, 58–59.

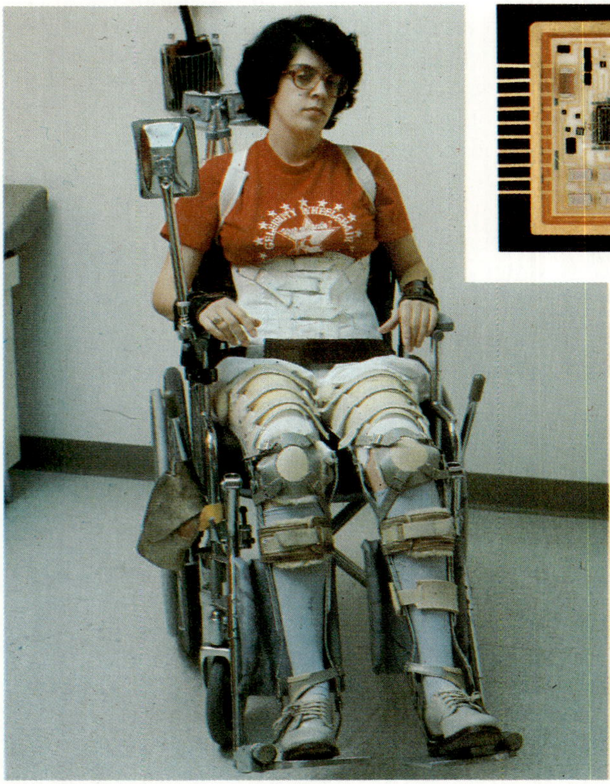

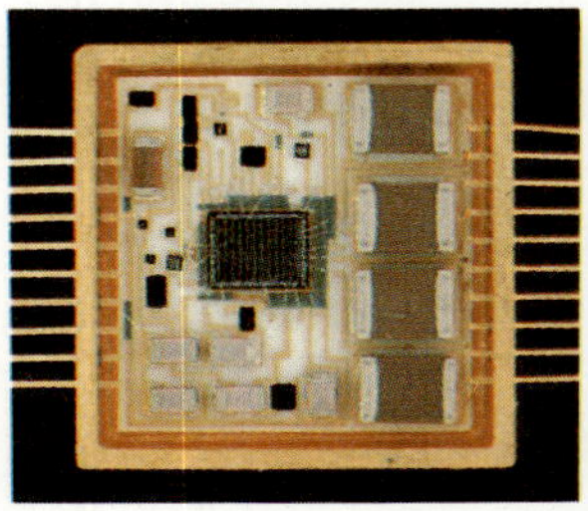

Before a computerized stimulation device was implanted in Carmen Scozzari's spine, she had little control of her muscles and was restricted to a wheelchair.

After the operation, Scozzari could walk. The computerized radio transmitter at her waist controls muscle stimulation. The integrated circuit that allowed her near-miraculous recovery appears in the middle.

The chip controls the operations of a wide range of devices. The computerized chess game (left), which uses a special purpose chip, can play at several levels of expertise. Computer chips also control robot arms that perform many repetitious tasks in modern factories (right).

Arcade games and home video games depend on chips.

Checkout operations at grocery stores use bar code readers that depend on chips to compute costs and print an itemized receipt.

Robots depend on special purpose chips for their "brains" to perform desired operations.

Automobile manufacturers use chips to control car engines by monitoring fuel flow, air–fuel mixture, and timing. Some cars have chips connected to sensors that can be hooked up to a diagnostic computer for service.

Talking devices—including soft drink machines and cars—depend on a speech synthesizer chip to generate conversation.

The growth patterns of cattle are monitored by chips that are placed around the animal's neck.

Chips can control muscles and direct the operations of artificial limbs.

Chips in Computers

This chapter has discussed the use of chips in the CPU and internal memory unit of computers. Chips are also used in many other control situations in the computer, such as in disk control, keyboard control, and video screen control. Chips are used in computers rather than vacuum tubes or magnetic cores for 5 primary reasons:

1. Speed—Because a chip is so small, the distances between connections are almost infinitesimal. Signals can move from one part of the chip to the other very quickly. To understand the chip's effect on computer speed, consider Table 6-2, which shows the increase in the number of operations per second that has occurred since the first electromagnetic relay computer.
2. Size—The chip takes up only a fraction of the space needed by other processing and storage devices. Therefore, computers can be smaller and more useful for individuals.

Manufacturing the Microchip

1 Producing a microchip involves sophisticated chemical and photographic processing. This microprocessor, a highly complex chip, is shown in its dual in-line package.

2 State of the art technology has resulted in a powerful 16-bit microprocessor contained on a single chip.

3 The production of silicon chips begins with the melting down of the raw material shown here. A crystal silicon "seed" is inserted into the molten mass, rotated, and withdrawn.

4 A crystal silicon ingot, 2–6 inches in diameter, is formed from the "seed."

5 The ingot is sawed into wafers, which are then polished.

6 Automatic drafting equipment creates a detailed drawing of the complex circuitry of the chip.

7 The image on the left, magnified 10 times, shows the complex patterns of the wafer at right.

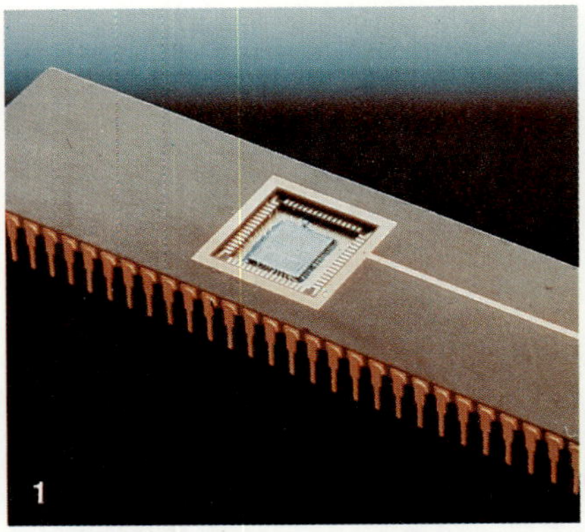

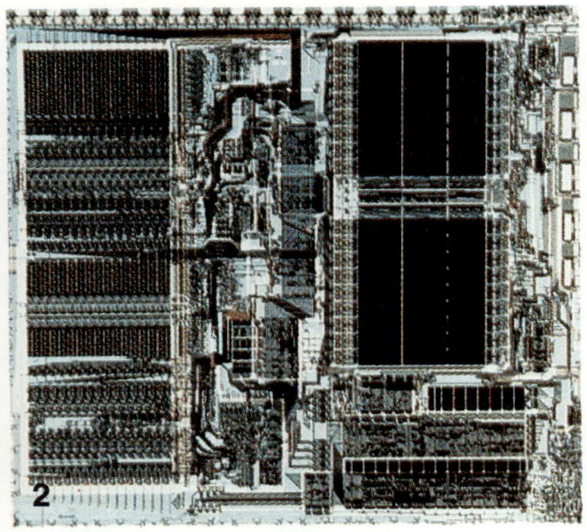

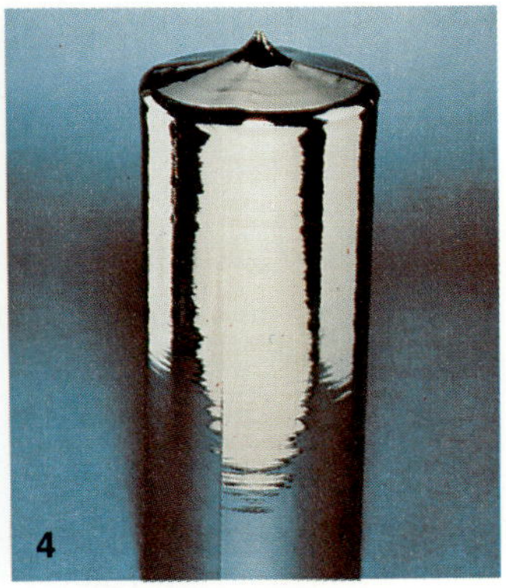

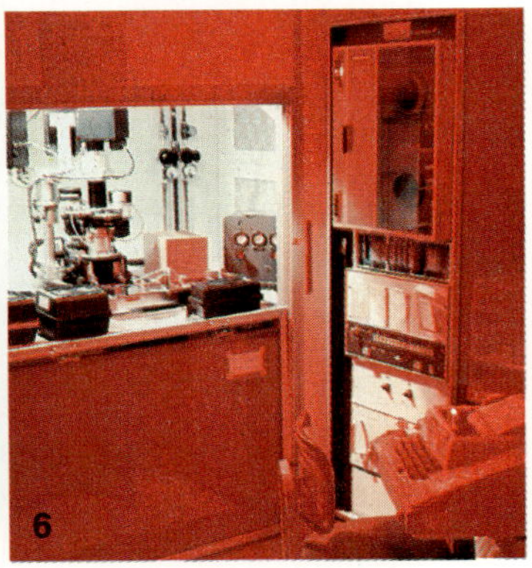

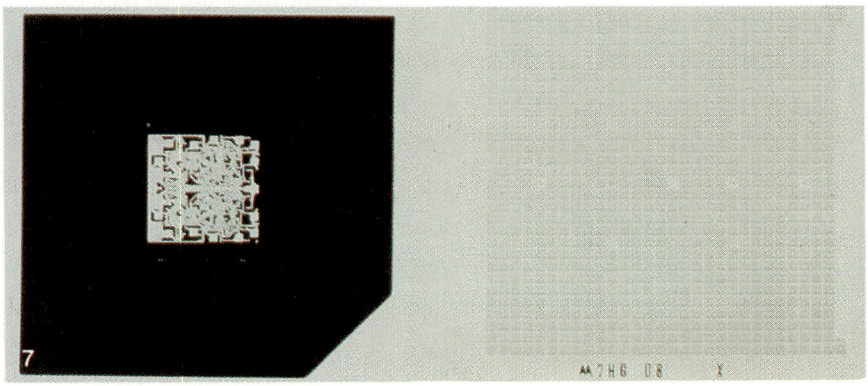

8

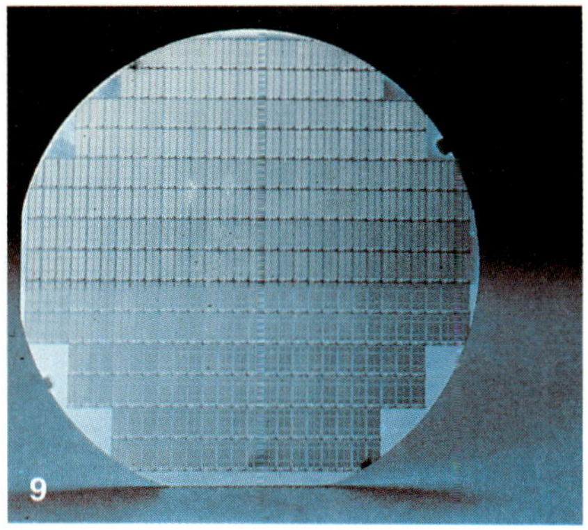

9

10

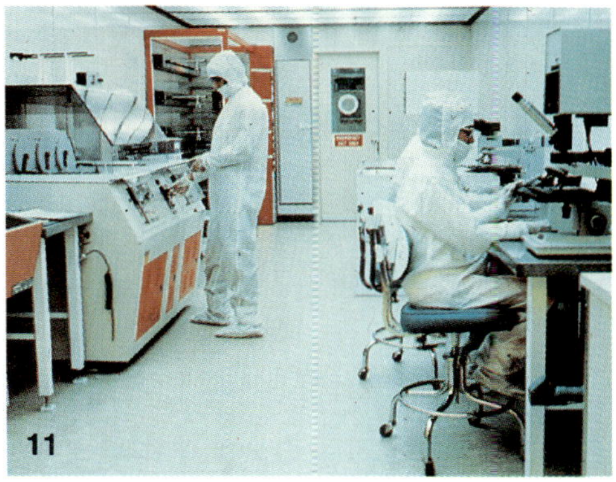

11

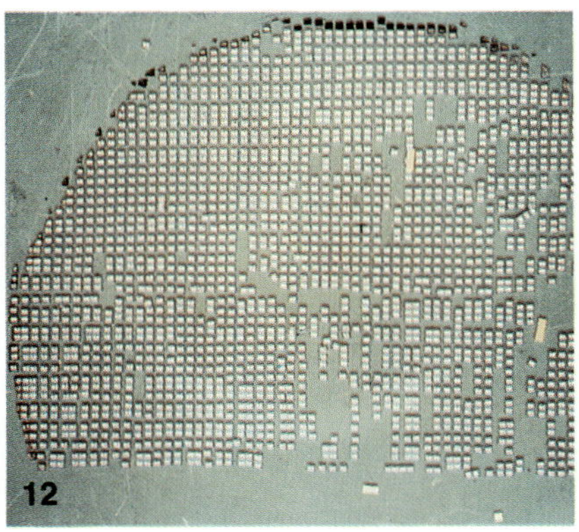

12

13

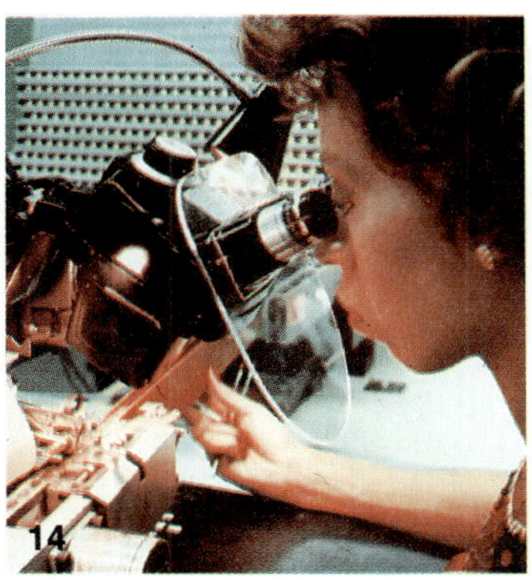

14

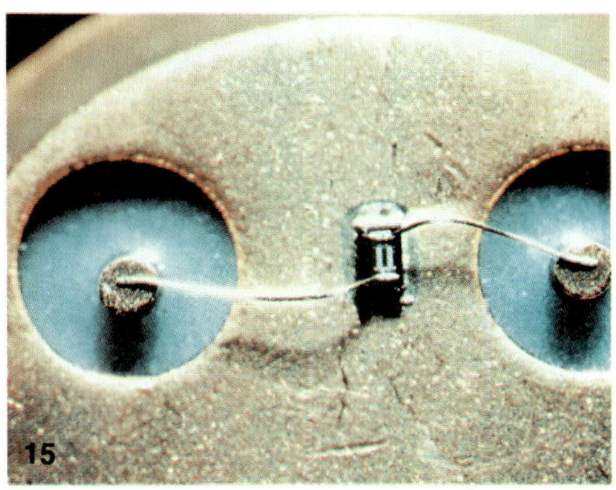

15

8 The step-and-repeat machine prints the circuit patterns in rows and columns on a glass plate, which becomes a mask.

9 The mask's pattern is projected onto the silicon wafer through a layer of photosensitive material. The pattern is printed on the wafer, and the wafer is developed.

10,11 The photosensitive material is removed, and all but the required circuit pattern is etched away by operators.

12 Individual chips in wafers are separated by a diamond saw.

13 Each chip must be inspected before it is placed in a dual in-line package.

14,15 After each chip is wire-bonded to its carrier, it is tested to ensure that it performs as designed.

Table 6-2 COMPARISON OF COMPUTER SPEEDS

Type of Device	*Operations per Second*
Electromagnetic relay	100
Vacuum tube	1,000
Transistor	10,000
Integrated circuit	1,000,000
Very large-scale integration (VLSI)	10,000,000

3. Reduced power requirements—Vacuum tubes required tremendous amounts of electricity and generated large amounts of heat. Consequently, the computer was expensive to use and required a special cooling system. Chips use very little power and generate only small amounts of heat. Personal computers using chips run on normal household electrical current and do not require special cooling requirements.
4. Economic factors—Vacuum tube computers were not only expensive to operate, they were very expensive to build. A great deal of labor was required to wire the early computers and build the magnetic core memory. Mass production of the chip has reduced the cost of computers dramatically.
5. Reliability—Vacuum tubes failed an average of one every 15 minutes. On the other hand, once chips pass stringent quality control requirements at the factory, they rarely fail.

The vacuum tube used in first generation computers is compared in size with the chip used in fourth generation computers. Each chip can perform the duties of thousands of vacuum tubes.

HISTORY OF THE CHIP

In 1959, Jack Kilby of Texas Instruments and Robert Noyce of Fairchild Semiconductor simultaneously developed the first integrated circuit (IC). Noyce and co-worker Gordon Moore left Fairchild in 1968 to form the Intel (for INTegrated ELectronics) Corporation, which is an important part of the chip industry today. The IC was used commercially in the early 1960s, and in 1971, the first true microprocessor chip was developed by the Intel Corporation. This chip was not originally a microprocessor; it was supposed to be one of a family of chips for a programmable calculator built by a Japanese manufacturer. Intel project manager Ted Hoff decided the original multichip approach was too cumbersome and costly, so he came up with an alternative.

Hoff recalls, "Instead of making their device [the programmable calculator] act like a calculator with some programming abilities, I wanted to make it function as a general purpose computer programmed to be a calculator." The key to this idea was placing all logic and arithmetic functions on a single IC so that the chip could be programmed to perform almost any function. This first Intel microprocessor chip was named the Intel 4004. Although the 4004 could only work with 4 bits at a time (compared with today's 16-bit machines), it was revolutionary in design.

The next big step in microprocessors, the 8008 chip, was also developed by Intel. As with the 4004, the 8008 was designed for one purpose and eventually used for another. Original designs called for an 8-bit microprocessor chip that could be used to control a terminal screen. However, even though the 8008 contained 3,300 transistors and could execute 30,000 operations per second, the final product was too slow to control a screen. Intel was left with a chip and no obvious market. Intel stopped work on other microprocessor chips but marketed the 8008 anyway, hoping that it would help to sell Intel's memory chips. To Intel's surprise, the 8008 chip was a sales success. The company revised its plans to develop microprocessor chips and in 1974 developed the forerunner to many of today's chips—the 8080.

The Intel 8080 was the first general purpose microprocessor. It contained 4,500 transistors and could execute 200,000 operations per second. Intel and other companies have developed improved versions of the 8080—including the Motorola 6800, Z80 from Zilog (a company formed by scientists who left Intel), and the Intel 8085. In 1976, Intel released the Intel 8048, the first complete microcomputer on a chip, which contained a CPU, input/output, a clock, RAM, and ROM on a single chip.

Several chips have developed from the original 8080, including the Intel 8088, 80286, and 8087 chips and the Motorola 68000 chip. The Intel 8088 is used in the IBM PC, and the Intel 80286 is an improved version of the 8088 that contains many operations normally handled by other chips, thus speeding up the processing. The Intel 8087 is a **co-processor**, which works with the CPU chip to speed up a particular operation. The Intel 8087, for example, speeds up arithmetic operations, but other types of co-processors exist for such operations as graphics. Another popular chip is the Motorola 68000, which is currently used in the Apple Macintosh and similar machines offered by Commodore and Atari.

SOURCE: Stan Augarten, *State of the Art: A Photographic History of the Integrated Circuit* (New York: Ticknor & Fields, 1983).

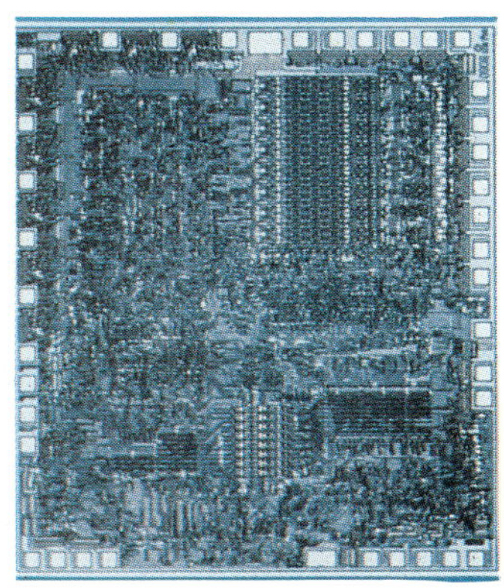

Ted Hoff (left) had the idea for placing all arithmetic and logic functions on a single chip. The Intel 4004 (center) was the first chip used as a microprocessor. The Intel 8080 (right) was the forerunner of the chips used in many personal computers today.

Chip design is heavily dependent on computer-aided design (CAD) to ensure that all functions are included and that all connections are made.

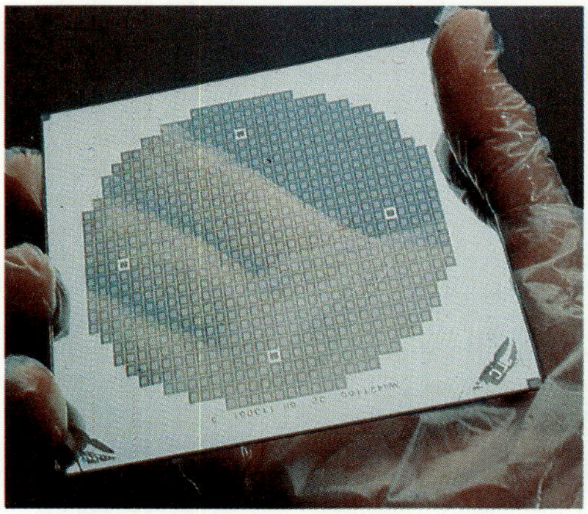

The glass mask at left is used to imprint the chip design on a silicon wafer. The chips at right are in wafer form, before being cut with diamond saws into individual chips.

An engineer views a section of the entire chip design to determine if it meets design requirements.

The chip itself is made of miniature transistors and circuits and is as small as $\frac{1}{8}$ inch on a side. When seen through a microscope, the surface of a chip looks like an aerial view of a modern metropolis with streets running between buildings and plazas. The "streets" in this case are the connecting wires and the "buildings and plazas" are the transistors. Figure 6-6 demonstrates dramatically how small a chip is by comparing it in size with a lady bug. In picture 1, the lady bug is shown sitting on a 3-inch wafer of chips that have not been separated in the production process. In pictures 2–5, the magnification increases. Picture 6 shows that the "wires" on the chip are the same width as the hairs on the lady bug's leg!

The Making of a Chip

The chip is an **integrated circuit (IC)** made up of a "sandwich" of interconnected layers of various elements on a silicon wafer. The first integrated circuits were made in 1959 when a transistor and its associated circuits were etched onto a semiconductor. A **semiconductor** is a mineral—such as germanium or silicon—that conducts electricity only under certain conditions. Since 1959, the integrated circuit has evolved from the one-transistor IC to the current 450,000-transistor chip referred to as very large-scale integration (VLSI). Between these two extremes are small-scale integration (SSI), medium-scale integration (MSI), and large-scale integration (LSI).

Before a chip can be manufactured, it must be designed by a team of engineers. Performed manually, this process could take years of work. Today, the computer can speed up the design process through computer-aided design (CAD). One type of CAD combines standardized sections of a chip to yield a custom design. Another CAD program, called a silicon compiler, can design the chip from scratch based on a description of the required functions.

After the chip is designed, engineers develop a **photomask**, which resembles a photographic negative. The photomask is used to control the process of building the chip's transistors and conductive lines. A tube of silicon that is 3–5 inches in diameter is sliced into wafers, which are processed into many chips. Using the photomask, each silicon wafer is coated with a chemical

FIGURE 6-6
Comparison of Lady Bug to Chip

(Texas Instruments)

called a **resist** to build up each layer of the chip. The desired circuit patterns are then projected onto the resist, which acts as a photographic film recording each layer of the circuit. Next, areas of the wafer are exposed by chemically dissolving sections of the resist. This entire process can be performed as many as 12 times to create the desired circuitry. Between these steps, impurities are implanted in the silicon to create the transistors that control the flow of electricity.

Wafers treated in this fashion are placed in an oven to allow the impurities to sink to the appropriate layer of the chip. The chips are then separated by a diamond saw and tested to determine if each chip performs as designed. Sometimes, less than 50% of a batch of chips are acceptable for use. A "good" chip is then placed in a plastic carrier called a **dual in-line package (DIP),** which protects the tiny chip and is the means by which the chip is connected to a circuit board.

Robotics and the Chip

An exciting use of the chip is in the field of **robotics**, in which machines perform physical work. Currently, robots are used extensively by the automobile industry to perform such boring, dirty, or dangerous tasks as spot welding or hazardous materials handling. The electronics industry also uses robots to build calculators because the same precise task must be performed time after time. The drug industry may use robots to stuff cartons and to screw on bottle caps.

Industrial robots do not resemble *Star Wars'* C3PO at all. Instead, a robot is little more than a mechanical arm that performs a specified set of tasks directed by the instructions built into a ROM chip. Robots have had a tremendous impact on the Japanese automobile industry, which uses them to gain a competitive advantage over the labor-intensive American automobile industry. Approximately 100,000 robots will be needed in 1990; more than 200

Many computer boards are manufactured by robots that place the chips in their sockets. The robots are controlled by a special purpose computer that can be reprogrammed to perform a new sequence of actions.

ROBOT REWARDED

In 1984, the New York City Police Department's Cop of the Month award was presented to a non-human, a first for the NYPD. The winner of the honor was RMI-3, a robot that helped end a 20-hour confrontation between two armed suspects and Elmira, New York, police. When police were unable to contact the two suspects, RMI-3 entered the apartment building to see if the suspects were still alive. RMI-3's mechanical arm opened the apartment door and photographed the interior. When the robot's cameras showed that the two suspects were dead, Elmira police safely entered. SOURCE: John Edwards, "Robot Rewarded," *ONLINE Today*, July 1984, p. 10.

companies worldwide will be building them. The types of operations performed by robots in 1980 and those forecast for 1990, and the percentage of robots used in each operation, are shown in Figure 6-7.

"Smart" robots, or **androids**, have a built-in microprocessor and can move around. Such robots can see the work they do, note imperfections, and take action to solve the problem. Androids are quite different from an industrial robot that does not move and that depends on an external microprocessor for instructions. Two problems are holding up the development of androids—movement and artificial sight. Don't expect to see a robot serving at a cocktail party any time soon. Most androids move only very slowly as they attempt to avoid walls, furniture, and people.

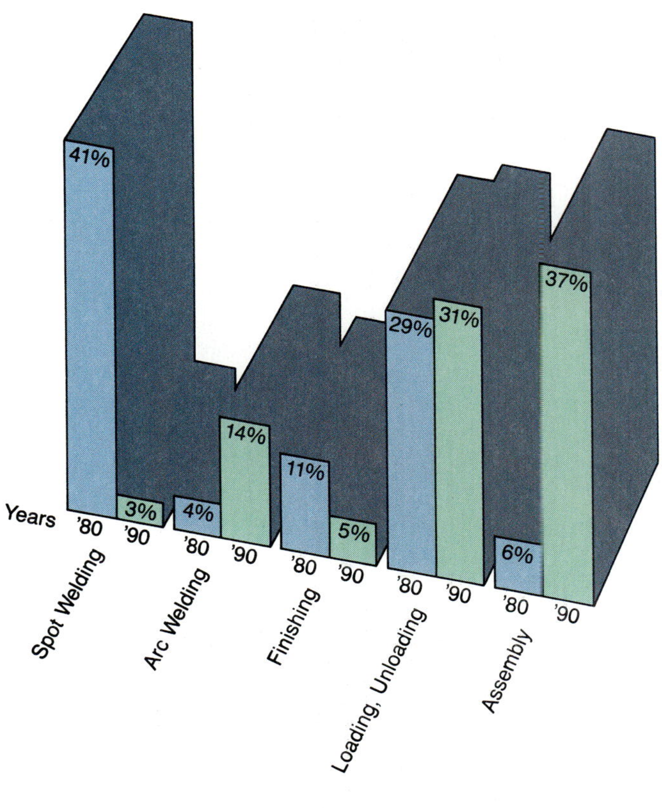

FIGURE 6-7
Uses for Robots

(From "Changing Uses for Robots," *USA Today*, July 3, 1984, p. 3B. © 1984 *USA Today*. Reprinted with permission.)

The Three Laws of Robotics

1. **A robot may not injure a human being, or, through inaction, allow a human being to come to harm.**
2. **A robot must obey orders given it by human beings except where such orders would conflict with the First Law.**
3. **A robot must protect its own existence as long as such protection does not conflict with the First or Second Law.**

Issac Asimov, *I. Robot* (New York: Bantam, 1956), p. 6.

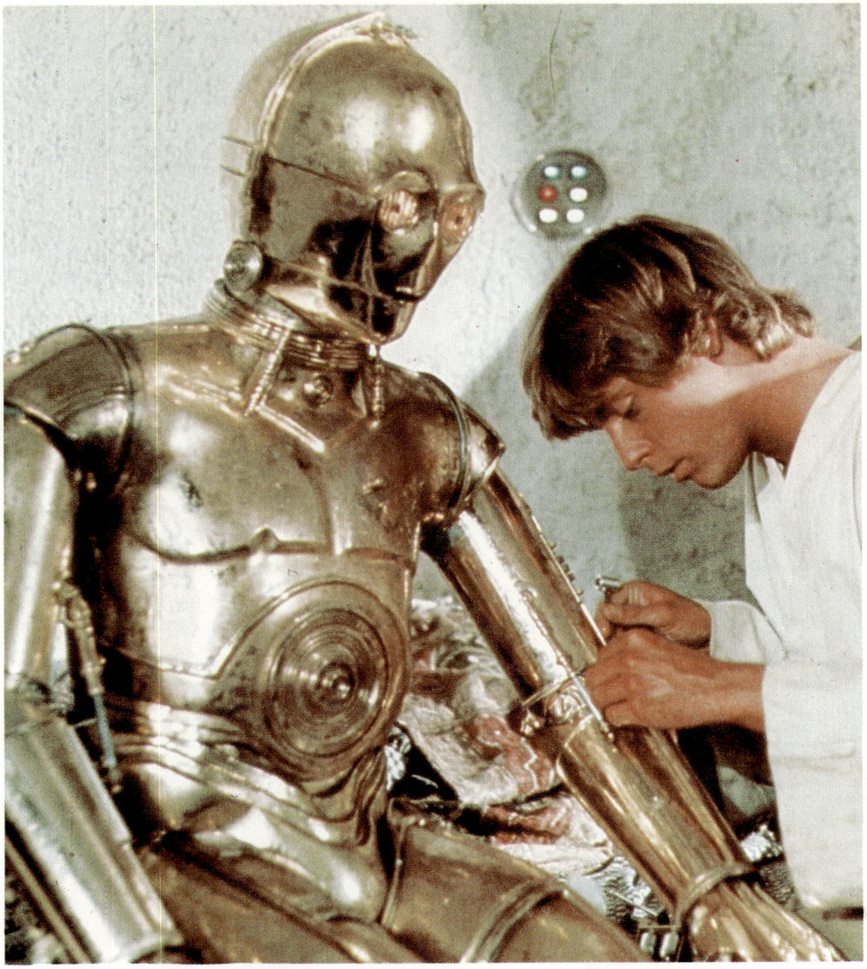

Although movies often portray robots like C3PO in *Star Wars,* in reality, the technology for C3PO does not exist.

REVIEW OF KEY POINTS

- The conceptual computer includes the CPU, internal memory, and the flows of information into, within, and out of the computer.
- The CPU is made up of the control unit, the arithmetic-logic unit (ALU), the clock, and the system bus.
- To execute a program, the control unit must fetch an instruction, decode it, fetch the necessary data, and pass the data to the ALU for execution.
- Both the control unit and the ALU use registers for fast, temporary storage.
- A computer word is the number of bits the CPU can process as one unit.
- Internal memory includes ROM, which is permanent memory burned into a chip, and RAM, which is temporary memory that uses transistors to store information. Except for bubble memory, RAM is volatile; ROM is not.
- Other types of memory chips are PROM (programmable ROM) and EPROM (erasable programmable ROM) chips.
- Current RAM chips can store up to 256 Kbits; future chips may hold over one million bits.
- The hexadecimal number system is used to represent binary numbers for human use.
- A chip is a semiconductor device that uses pure silicon as a base to build a network of transistors and conductive lines.
- Manufacturing a chip involves a process of repeated etchings and the addition of impurities to form the necessary components.
- Robots are devices that use computer brains to perform repetitive tasks in many factories.

KEY TERMS

address
address bus
androids
arithmetic-logic unit (ALU)
bit
booting
bubble memory
burning in the circuits
byte
central processing unit (CPU)
chip
clock
computer word
conceptual computer
control bus
control unit
co-processor
core
data bus
destructive replace
dual in-line package (DIP)
erasable programmable read only memory (EPROM)
Execution-time (E-time)
fetch, decode, and execute process
firmware
fixed length word
hexadecimal number system (hex)
Instruction-time (I-time)
integrated circuit (IC)
internal memory
Kbit
Kbyte
magnetic core
magnetic drum storage
main memory
microprocessor
nondestructive fetch
nonvolatile memory
photomask
programmable read only memory (PROM)
random access memory (RAM)
read only memory (ROM)
register
resist
robotics
semiconductor
stored program
system bus
variable length word
volatile memory

REVIEW QUESTIONS

1. Explain the flow of information within the conceptual computer. Why are some flows considered "fast" and others "slow"?
2. List the components of the central processing unit, explaining the purpose of each.
3. List and give the purpose of three registers in the central processing unit.
4. What is the importance of a computer word? If you or your school has a personal computer, determine the length of the word it uses.
5. How are individual bits accessed in RAM? In Figure 6-5 (page 125), which bit corresponds to location 44?
6. How is ROM different from RAM? How do PROM and EPROM differ from RAM and ROM and from each other?
7. Convert 1101101 in binary into a decimal number.
8. Why do we use the hexadecimal number system? Convert A5B6 into its binary equivalent.
9. Discuss the chip production process. Why are impurities introduced into the silicon?
10. List and discuss the advantages of using the chip rather than vacuum tubes or magnetic cores. Are there any disadvantages?

Expanded coverage of input and output devices begins with a look at how the processes of input and output affect the computer's efficiency. Slow data entry, a problem that particularly plagues mainframe users, is discussed. Commonly used interactive input devices are explained in detail, as well as the problems of voice recognition input devices. The chapter closes with a discussion of output devices for both mainframes and personal computers, particularly monitors and printers.

7

Input/Output Devices

STUDY OBJECTIVES

After reading this chapter, you should be able to

- Understand how input and output processes affect the computer's efficiency.
- Discuss the data entry problem and its possible solutions.
- Recognize data entry devices at the work place or in the marketplace.
- Point out the important elements of keyboards and understand the differences among various types of keyboards.
- Understand the use of a mouse, touch screen, touch pad, and light pen for computer input.
- Explain the differences among various types of monitors.
- Recognize the differences in the output from dot matrix and daisy wheel printers.
- Discuss the various types of nonimpact printers.

THE IMPORTANCE OF INPUT AND OUTPUT

To store and manipulate numbers and symbols, a computer must always be able to receive its instructions and data. Useful storage and manipulation means that the computer must also be able to send processed information back to the user. This process of instructing the computer, feeding it data, and receiving processed information is referred to as **input/output**, or simply **I/O**. Without input and output, the computer cannot receive instructions from the user, receive the data that must be processed into information, or send this information to the user. We begin our discussion of input and output by discussing the problems inherent to entering data into a computer.

THE DATA ENTRY PROBLEM

Because I/O requires human interaction either to input the instructions and data or to receive and interpret the output, it is the *slowest* part of the computer. Input/output is much slower due to its mechanical nature than the blinding speed of transfers between the CPU and internal memory or even the slower transfers to and from secondary storage. For example, a proficient keyboard typist may input instructions and data at the rate of 75 words per minute, or about eight characters per second. The CPU can process 10,000,000 characters per second! The rate at which information is output to a monitor or printer is limited by the speed at which the user can read the material on the screen or by the speed of the electromechanical printer. The fastest printers can print at a rate of 26,000 characters per second, which is still not nearly as fast as the speed with which the CPU operates. When the computer must wait for input or output to be completed before continuing with processing, it is **I/O bound**. A second and just as serious problem with data input involves the errors that are introduced by the person entering the instructions and data.

Slow data input and incorrect data input comprise what is termed the **data entry problem**. The data entry problem is much more common in the use of mainframes and minicomputers for two reasons. First, tremendous quantities of data are processed on these large computers. Second, the time spent entering data directly to a mainframe or minicomputer from a terminal could be used by someone else for actual computing. Because personal computers do not process large amounts of data and because they are usually owned by their users, the data entry problem is not as severe on this smaller computer.

Slow Data Input

Let us consider the first half of the data entry problem—the slow rate at which data can be input. One solution to this problem is to store data as it is input in a storage area, called a **buffer**, within the computer. The buffer frees the CPU from waiting for data and sends the data to the CPU when needed. A second solution to the problem *decouples* the data entry process from the computer. In other words, data entry is **off-line** from a keyboard. Contrast this method with **on-line** or **interactive input**, in which the user interacts directly with the computer.

With off-line input, the data are placed onto some intermediate storage medium using a machine that is not tied to a computer. The data are then transferred to the computer from the storage medium. As a result, the processing is not delayed by the slow rate of data input, and data can be quickly transferred from the storage medium to the computer. Currently, the three

A card reader converts the holes on punched cards into electrical signals, which are then sent to the computer as data or programs.

most popular forms of intermediate storage are punched cards, magnetic tape, and magnetic disk. In each case, a keyboard is used to transfer the data to the intermediate storage medium without using a computer.

Punched Cards The first mainframe users primarily used the **punched card** to decouple the data entry process from the computer. Although the use of punched cards is not as widespread today, many people continue to use them because of their portability. They can be easily boxed up and sent through the mail. Many people use cards because the data coded on the card is also printed at the top of the card.

Data to be stored is keypunched onto a blank card using a **keypunch machine**, which punches a pattern of holes in the card corresponding to each character or digit. This information is transferred to the computer by a **card reader**, which translates the patterns of holes into characters that are sent electronically to the computer as a series of zeros and ones. A **data deck** is a deck of computer cards containing instructions or data. Figure 7-1 shows a punched card with a program instruction on it.

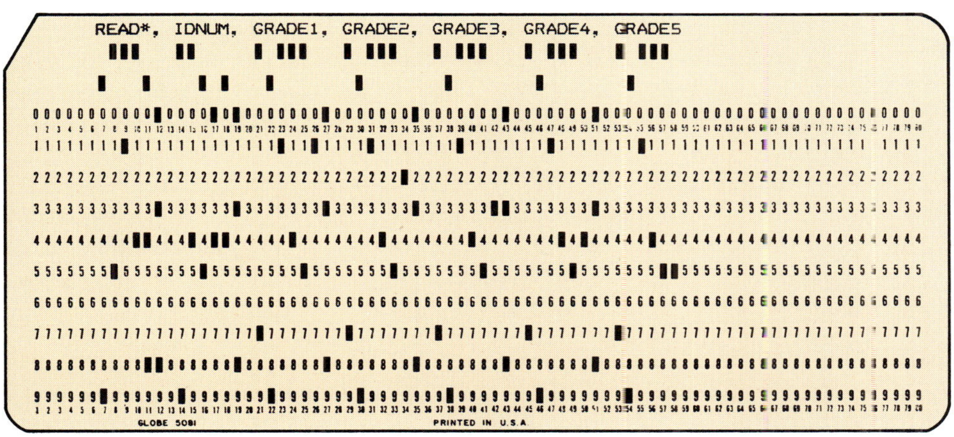

FIGURE 7-1
Punched Card

The Internal Revenue Service uses many data entry operators to enter tax return data to its computers.

A seldom used form of intermediate storage that also uses holes punched in paper is **paper tape**. A roll of paper about 1 inch wide is punched with a pattern of holes which represents the characters of the stored information. Transferring data from paper tape is extremely slow, and the tape is easily torn.

Magnetic Tape The punched card has the disadvantages of being bulky and easily torn. Data decks of punched cards can also be shuffled when dropped. For these reasons, other forms of intermediate storage were developed. A popular form that retains the portability of a punched card but is more durable is **magnetic tape**. The process of entering data onto tape is referred to as **key-to-tape**. Magnetic tape is available as either a reel-to-reel tape or a cassette. Data are coded onto magnetic tape from a keyboard or key-to-tape machine in a manner similar to that for a punched card. Once the information is stored on the tape, the tape can easily be transported as long as it is protected from magnetic fields, which would destroy the information. The information on the tape is transferred to the computer by a **tape drive**, which reads the data on the tape. Magnetic tape is a sequential form of storage; that is, data must be read in the order that they are entered.

Magnetic Disk Magnetic tape's sequential storage is a disadvantage that can be avoided by using a **magnetic disk** to store data. On a magnetic disk, data may be accessed in any order. As with punched cards and magnetic tape, data entry by magnetic disk is most common for mainframes. Data are input to the disk from a keyboard on a **key-to-disk** machine. Often, several magnetic disks are layered together in a **disk pack**. Data on this form of intermediate storage can be transferred to the computer by a **disk drive**, which reads the disk.

A mainframe disk pack is faster and can hold more information than either punched cards or magnetic tape. However, magnetic disk packs are not as easily transported as magnetic tape. Of course, minicomputers and personal computers often use the highly portable floppy disk, but the amount of storage on a floppy disk is much less than that of a disk pack.

Verification

Although the use of intermediate storage solves the problem of slow data entry, the problem of errors introduced during the keying process still exists. **Verification** can solve this problem. In this process, the data entry process is

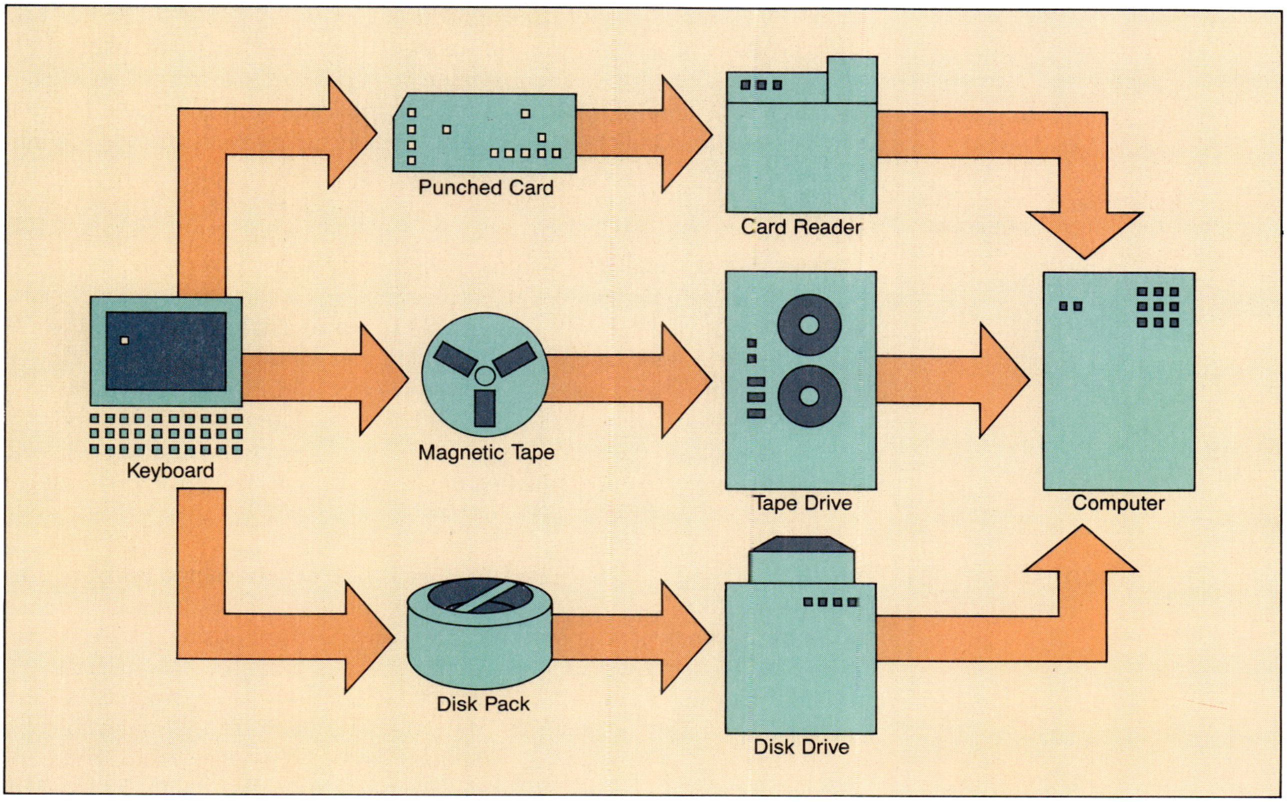

FIGURE 7-2
Use of Intermediate Storage for Data Entry

repeated, and the information being entered is compared with the information already in intermediate storage. If the value input during verification is the same as its corresponding value in storage, then the value is assumed correct. If a difference occurs, the operator can check the value in storage to determine if it is correct. An error on a punched card means the entire card must be punched again. Only the incorrect characters or digits on tape and disk need to be changed.

Once the information on the storage medium is verified, it may be input to the computer with a minimum of delay and errors. The process of using intermediate storage to decouple data entry from the computer is shown in Figure 7-2 for all three types of storage discussed.

OTHER FORMS OF DATA ENTRY

Input of data from a keyboard is by far the most common data entry method. However, several other methods also exist. Other common methods of commercial data entry to mainframes or minicomputers include bar codes, optical character recognition (OCR), and magnetic ink character recognition (MICR). In all three cases, data are entered into the computer using some type of electronic sensor.

Bar Codes

Bar codes are combinations of light and dark bars that are coded to contain product information. The most common bar code is the Universal Product

Type of Product Code → 0

37600 24609

Manufacturer's ID Number

Product or Part Number

FIGURE 7-3
Bar Code Example

Code (UPC) used on all grocery products. Figure 7-3 shows a UPC for one such product. Note that the code has both bars and digits. The bars correspond to the digits, which identify the type of product, the manufacturer, and the particular item. All products made by the same company have different product or part numbers and different manufacturers have different identification numbers.

Other types of bar codes are used for special purposes, but in each case, bars and spaces represent the information to be input. For example, some libraries use bar codes to speed up the book checkout process.

Bar codes can be read by a special laser device at the grocery store checkout counter or by a bar code reader called a **wand**. Each reader device works by bouncing a light beam off a bar code pattern and then measuring the reflected light. This measurement is converted into data that are sent to a computer, where the type of item and price are determined. Price information is sent back to the point of sale. If reproduced with high-quality printing, a bar code may be scanned the first time 99% of the time with an error rate of less than 1 in 10 million.

Optical Character Recognition

Another method of electronic data entry is **optical character recognition (OCR)**. In OCR, a reader is passed over a document to determine which symbols are present. The symbols must be typewritten using a special style (font) of type that the reader can identify. Several large retailers have experimented with this type of data entry at their point-of-sale terminals. A sales clerk passes a wand reader over the price tag attached to the item to relay price and inventory data to the computer. The U.S. Post Office has also experimented with OCR to read ZIP codes that are either typed or hand lettered. Students may have had tests scored by an optical mark reader that picks up black pencil marks on a special answer sheet and sends the data to the computer. Figure 7-4 shows the stylized letters and numbers used by commercial OCR systems.

A nearly error-free OCR system would be the equivalent of a computer that could "see" and read any type of document. This breakthrough would relieve the monotony and strain of transferring information from a document into the computer. However, the current state of the art for an OCR reader is an error rate about 1,000 times higher than a bar code reader. For this reason, many retailers other than grocery stores are using bar codes.

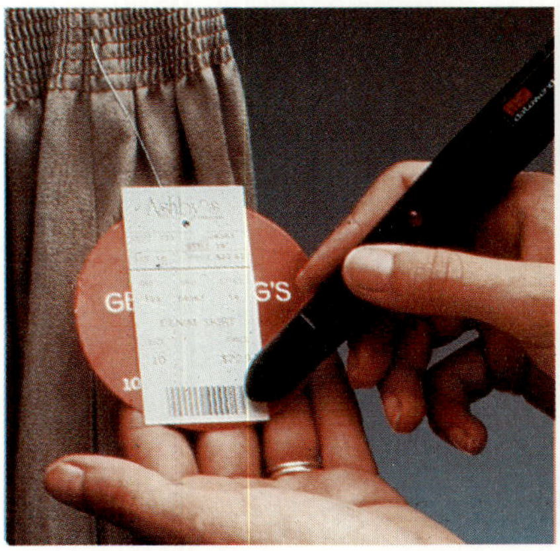

A wand that reads bar codes for inventory control purposes (left) relieves the user from visually checking and recording price and inventory numbers on each tag. The document processing system at right uses MICR or OCR to process documents efficiently.

0 1 2 3 4 5 6 7 8 9
A B C D E F G H I J

FIGURE 7-4
OCR Font

Magnetic Ink Character Recognition

Magnetic ink character recognition (MICR) is used to process bank checks. The bank's identification code, the check writer's account number, and the amount of the check are printed in magnetic ink at the bottom of the check. The check can then be processed by machine and routed to the proper bank. The bank identification number and account number are preprinted on the check, but the amount of the check must be keyed in by a human operator who determines the amount of the check. This step takes time and can introduce errors into the data entry process. A giant breakthrough would combine OCR with MICR to read and print the amount of the check, but this development appears to be some years in the future. Figure 7-5 shows a check with MICR codes.

INTERACTIVE FORMS OF INPUT

So far, this chapter has discussed input devices that are used to solve the data entry problem for mainframes and minicomputers by decoupling the computer from data entry. Now, we cover input devices that are used primarily for interactive input to computers. By *interactive input,* we mean that the user is directly connected to the computer, either with a terminal to a mainframe or minicomputer or with a personal computer. In general, the input devices discussed here work the same for either a terminal or a personal computer. Personal computer input devices just receive more publicity than the devices for larger computers. These devices include the keyboard, the mouse, the touch screen, the touch pad, and the light pen. We also discuss the future of voice recognition and character recognition in data entry.

FIGURE 7-5
Check with MICR

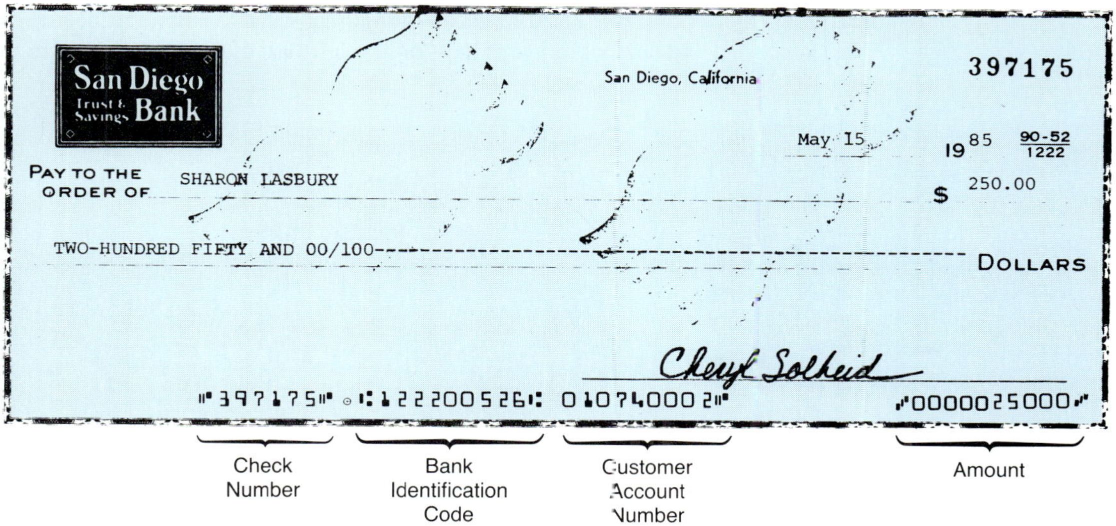

Keyboards

Keyboards have been associated with mainframes and minicomputers for almost as long as computers have been in use. However, the keyboard received little attention until the personal computer became popular. After the IBM PC's expanded keyboard was introduced, the keyboard was considered a competitive feature of a personal computer. The IBM PC also had the first detachable keyboard connected to the computer by a cord. With a detachable keyboard, the user can sit anywhere within 6 feet of the video screen. The advantages of this include physical comfort afforded the user and reduced eyestrain. Now, many mainframe terminals share these same characteristics. Before we discuss various keyboards, we should cover what a keyboard actually does.

The main advantage of the Dvorak keyboard is that lack of fatigue because you can type eight hours a day without getting worn out.

Barbara Blackburn, one-time world record holding typist
(As quoted in "Magic Typing Fingers," *Personal Computing,* January 1985, p. 24.)

Any keyboard, whether for a mainframe terminal or a personal computer, is meant to transmit the symbol (letter, digit, or special character) shown on the key. Various procedures are used to perform this action. Most keyboards transmit information to the computer by sending the ASCII code (01000001 for A, 01000010 for B, and so on) to the computer. Keyboards that transmit ASCII characters directly can send 256 different characters using the full 8-bit code. Of the first 128 characters, some of the first 32 characters are control characters—such as backspace, line feed, and carriage return. These control characters are entered from special keys designated for each particular purpose. The next 96 characters are the upper- and lower-case letters of the alphabet, the 10 numeric digits, and 34 punctuation and special characters. The additional 128 characters are usually used for graphics characters, European letters, or special symbols. The keyboard must be set up specially to send these characters to the computer.

Most personal computer keyboards have 60–100 keys depending on whether they have function keys, special purpose keys, and a numeric keypad. Figure 7-6 shows the keyboards of two popular personal computers—the Apple IIe and the IBM PC. Note the similarities and differences between the two keyboards. They are similar in that the majority of the keys in the center of either keyboard make up the standard typewriter keyboard with which most people are familiar.

The most obvious differences between the two keyboards is that the Apple IIe keyboard has 63 keys, whereas the IBM PC has 83 keys. This difference arises primarily because the IBM PC has a numeric keypad on the right side of the keyboard and a set of function keys on the left side of the keyboard, which

FIGURE 7-6
Keyboards for Apple IIe and IBM PC

Apple IIe Keyboard

IBM PC Keyboard

the Apple IIe does not have. The numeric keypad on the IBM PC directs cursor movement and also gives the user special keys for word processing. Depending on the application used, the function keys allow for the instant entry of common commands and easy selection of options offered by various pieces of software. The two "Apple" keys on the Apple IIe have a similar function in some situations. In addition to these extra keys, the IBM PC also has several other special purpose keys that the Apple IIe does not have. For example, every text key has a different meaning when combined with the ALT key.

KEYBOARDS
QWERTY vs Dvorak

Have you ever wondered why the keys on a standard typewriter keyboard are located as they are? The location does not seem to make any sense, with the "Y" and "T" being so easy to reach and the "C" and "N" not so easy (at least for the author!). The standard keyboard is known as the QWERTY keyboard, named for the first six keys on the upper row. This keyboard was devised during the nineteenth century to *slow down* typists, because their mechanical typewriters jammed when two or more keys were pressed too quickly. The electric typewriter solved the problem of typing too fast, but the QWERTY keyboard was standard by then.

The Dvorak keyboard was invented to increase typing speed with fewer errors. This keyboard (see diagram) places keys in a more logical position, so that the keys that are struck most often are easy to reach. As a result, the Dvorak is 5–25% faster than the QWERTY keyboard with only half the errors. A beginning typist can achieve 40 words per minute in one-tenth the time it takes to learn a QWERTY keyboard.

So why aren't we all using Dvorak keyboards? As with the Metric system in the United States, there is not enough incentive to change. Most people who learned on the QWERTY keyboard do not want to learn a new system. However, many personal computer keyboards can be reprogrammed, and a QWERTY keyboard can become a Dvorak keyboard if the user wishes. The Apple IIc even has a switch that allows the user to change from a QWERTY to a Dvorak keyboard.

SOURCE: Mark Lewyn, "Keyboard, Computers: Fast Duo," *USA Today*, July 5, 1984, p. 3B.

Dvorak Keyboard

The mouse is an easy-to-use input device for computer users of all ages.

It always amazed me that it [the mouse] took so long before it caught on. I always envisioned it would become a way of life with computer users.

Douglas Engelbart, inventor of the mouse
(As quoted in "Mouse Solves Hi-Tech Maze," *USA Today,* May 16, 1984, p. 1B.)

Another difference between the two keyboards is in the placement of the keys that are common to both. For example, note that the cursor movement keys (those with the left, right, up, and down arrows on them) are placed differently on each keyboard. Finally, keys that mean the same thing on both keyboards are labeled differently. For example, the key to delete a character is called DELETE on the Apple IIe and DEL on the IBM PC. Using a different personal computer may require the user to adjust to a new arrangement of keys to perform the same actions.

Having more keys does not necessarily make the IBM PC better than the Apple IIe. That judgment depends on the user and the purpose for which the personal computer is used. The lack of a numeric keypad on the Apple IIe could be a problem for a person used to the IBM PC keyboard. Because the IBM PC keyboard combines the numeric keypad and the cursor movement keys, a user who forgets to shift between the two functions will have problems.

The Mouse

Various studies of managers and executives have found that resistance to computers arises out of an uneasiness with the keyboard. Managers who have not used a keyboard since school (if then) may be anxious about relearning keyboard use. As a result of these studies, manufacturers have developed alternate input devices to make the personal computer less threatening.

A highly publicized alternative input device is the **mouse**. The device is so named because it is about the size of a mouse and has a tail-like cord, which connects it to the computer. When combined with appropriate software, the mouse is a powerful input device that frees the user from dependence on a keyboard. By moving the mouse across a flat surface, the user moves the cursor and selects the various functions for execution by the computer.

The mouse is available in both electromechanical and optical forms. The electromechanical mouse has a ball in the base, which makes contact with two wheels inside the mouse. As the ball moves, so do the wheels, signaling the CPU to move the cursor in the same direction. The optical mouse moves around on a grid. A minicamera records the mouse's position on the grid and transmits the information to the CPU, which then moves the cursor to match the mouse's position on the grid. In either case, one or more buttons on the top of the mouse are pressed to signal the user's commands to the CPU when the cursor is located in the desired position.

Although the mouse is useful in moving the cursor without a keyboard, it is a powerful input device when matched with certain software packages. The software often uses pictures, or **icons**, of the available operations to speed up

DOUG ENGELBART
The "Father" of the Mouse

Many users consider the mouse an exciting input device that enables them to increase their use of the computer. Although Apple has made the mouse popular, the device was not invented by Apple. The mouse was first used with the Xerox Star computer, but it was not as popular as the Apple computers because of its high cost. The mouse is currently offered by Apple for their Macintosh, Apple IIe, and Apple IIc personal computers. Other software companies are now developing hardware and software so that the IBM PC and compatible machines can use a mouse for input.

The origins of the mouse can be found in 1963, when Doug Engelbart published a paper on how to augment human intellect through the computer. Almost 20 years ahead of its time, this paper described such unknown concepts as personal work stations, users communicating with one another in networks, and word processing. Engelbart received a grant to try out his ideas for using the computer. One of his ideas was the mouse.

Engelbart's group devised the mouse to help people use the computer without special training or equipment. The group named the device a *mouse* because of its size and because the cord leading to the computer resembles a tail. The original mouse was made of wood and had a single button for sending commands to the computer. Soon, the number of command buttons was increased to three. The first computer to use the mouse, the Xerox Star, was developed in the early 1970s at the Xerox Palo Alto Research Center (PARC). Another alumnus of PARC later developed the forerunner of the Macintosh—the Lisa—for Apple.

An interesting question of mouse design is how many buttons to use to send commands to the computer once the cursor is located in the proper position. Engelbart's first mouse used three buttons, which he feels strongly is the best number. The Xerox Star used two buttons, and the Apple mouse uses only one button. Because each group feels its number is best, the mouse button design question will probably not be resolved soon.

Today, Doug Engelbart (of Tymshare Corporation) is designing a system that ties the mouse and other devices with a data base to simplify a user's access to information. He did not patent the mouse, so he receives no royalties from the popular device he invented many years ago. He is primarily concerned that people will concentrate only on the mouse and not consider any other methods of augmenting the human intellect.

SOURCE: Steven Levy, "Of Mice and Men," *Popular Computing,* May 1984, pp. 70–78.

Douglas Engelbart—the inventor of the mouse and other tools and techniques that augment the human mind—is shown here with an early version of the mouse.

the selection process. The use of icons is based on the **desk-top metaphor**, which views the computer as a desk equipped with a file cabinet, telephone, scratch pads, wastebasket, and so on. Each item actually appears on the top or side of the screen, and the user can access the related function by selecting an icon with the mouse. For example, on the mouse-driven Apple Macintosh software, the user selects a trash can to delete a file from the work area. Using this system, the user can create, send, file, or discard messages, graphs, charts, and other documents by simply pointing at the appropriate icon. Apple believes so strongly in the desk-top metaphor and mouse that any cursor movement on their Macintosh personal computer must be accomplished via the mouse.

The mouse is an important input device for the individual who is new to computers or who is put off by the keyboard. However, individuals who use computers regularly find that moving a mouse (rather than using a keyboard) can slow down their work and require extra effort.

Other Input Devices

A host of input devices other than the keyboard and the mouse are now available to make a user's data entry job easier. Three important devices are the touch screen, the touch pad, and the light pen. In each case, the computer receives commands or information in a different way.

With a **touch screen**, the user simply touches an area of the screen to give the computer a command. A touch screen has a grid of light beams that crisscross the screen. When a pair of beams are broken, the computer knows what area of the screen is affected.

As with the mouse, the touch screen needs appropriate software for its best work. For example, on the Hewlett-Packard HP-150, the user can choose an operation by pointing at the command on a card file icon. A touch screen software package may show the user various options to create, edit, print, or save a document as tabs on file folders. Users execute the operation by pointing at the appropriate tab. The information center at Disney World's EPCOT Center uses touch screens for visitors to find out about the park's various attractions. EPCOT's touch screens are connected to a minicomputer.

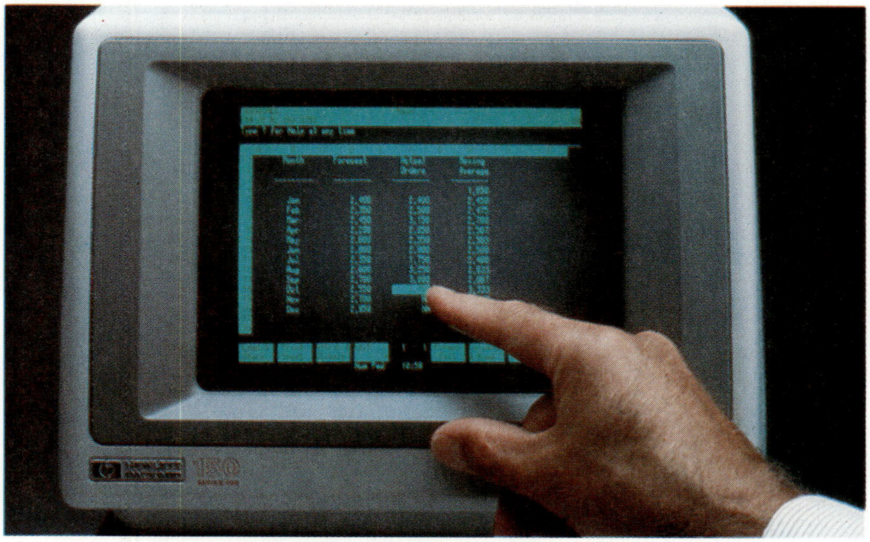

With a touch screen and the appropriate software, a user can choose a function or operation by using a finger or stylus.

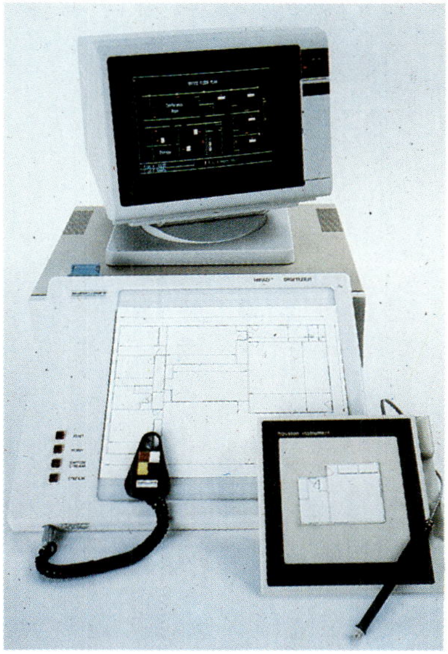

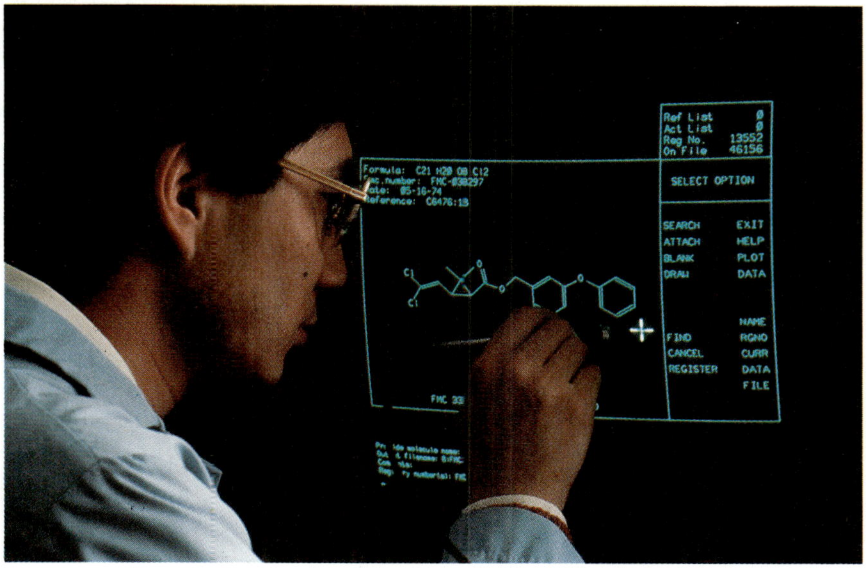

A variety of input devices are available to users. This digitizer pad at left allows the user to transfer drawings and charts from paper to the computer by tracing them with the pointing device. The light pen (right), which is useful for many engineering and scientific applications, allows the user to point at an area of the screen and have that area expand, rotate, or change.

The **touch pad** is a separate pad that the user touches to enter data to the computer. The user selects a command on the screen by touching a section of the pad. The user may also draw graphics by tracing the design on the pad. Pressure on the pad's membrane surface transmits the pattern to the computer, which then shows it on the screen. The translation from touch pad to screen can involve either analog technology or digital technology. In analog technology, the pressure applied to the pad causes two surfaces to make contact. This contact is then translated into a position on the screen. In digital technology, over 10,000 switches make contact whenever the pad is touched. In either case, the appropriate software must be available to translate the signal from the touch pad into useful information to the computer.

Like the other two devices, the **light pen** activates a command at a certain point on the screen. However, the technology is different. The concept of the light pen is based on the fact that every lighted spot on the screen is constantly refreshed. The computer can detect exactly which spot is giving off light when the light pen is pointed at the screen. The light pen has been used with mainframe computers for over 20 years in many engineering applications. In this situation, the user can point the pen at part of a structural design to obtain a more detailed plan or to change the design.

Voice and Character Recognition

In the optimal data input situation, the computer could hear and understand spoken commands and read typed or handwritten data. C3-PO did this with ease in the *Star Wars* movies, but the current generation of computers has a great deal of difficulty with these two tasks. We have already discussed the status of optical character recognition. Although not perfect, OCR is a way for the computer to read information.

Voice recognition input methods are facing significantly greater problems than character recognition input methods. These problems include the large number of words needed by a commercially feasible computer system (2,500–5,000 words); differences in speech patterns among different users or with the same user under different conditions; background noise and the

By working with a set of predetermined commands, this user can control the computer with his voice.

determination of when one word stops and another begins. For example, a computer may not understand the difference between "this guy" and "the sky" because of the similarity in the way they are spoken. Similarly, although we can understand "dyawannagoouttanight?" as "do you want to go out tonight?," a computer would have extreme difficulty in detecting each word and decoding its meaning.

Four types of voice recognition must be considered:

1. One speaker, isolated word.
2. Multiple speakers, isolated word.
3. One speaker, continuous speech.
4. Multiple speakers, continuous speech.

The first case is the easiest and involves teaching the computer to recognize a series of commands such as RUN or EDIT for one user's voice. Products

ANOTHER VIEW
Leland Strange

Leland Strange is the president of Intelligent Systems Corporation, a company that produces products for both the mainframe and personal computer markets. For mainframes, Intelligent Systems produces terminals for interactive input and output. For personal computers, the company produces monitors under the Princeton brand name and enhancements under the Quadram name. In an interview with *Living with Computers,* Strange made the following comments about the future of voice input:

How do you see the future of voice input?

STRANGE: I think voice input will only have a place in a specialty market and not in the office market. There is too much error correction required. It's like the use of bar codes at a grocery checkout counter in that you still cannot check everything out without having to enter some prices by hand. For computers, I do not think that is an acceptable situation. Even anticipating tremendous improvements, there is still going to be that error correction problem to contend with. It may actually become worse as companies try to increase the vocabulary of their systems and the computer has more chances to misunderstand a word. When you have only 200 words, the computer has fewer choices than when the vocabulary goes up to, say, 1,000 words.

allowing a vocabulary of over 100 words are now available in this category. Even toy robots that respond to spoken commands are available for less than $50. In the second case, the computer must recognize a word regardless of who speaks it. This is much more difficult to accomplish than the first case. These personal computers cost much more than standard personal computers ($45,000 compared with less than $1,000), and the vocabulary is severely restricted. In the third case, the computer must distinguish when one word stops and another begins. Although systems are available for this situation, their usefulness is severely restricted. The fourth case is so complex that no systems have been developed for it.

OUTPUT DEVICES

We have said before that the computer's processing is not useful without output. Output is generally available to a user in one of two forms—the video screen or the printed page. Another form of output involves sending commands to other electronic or mechanical devices—such as rocket engines, security devices, or home appliances. An example of this type of output involves the first attempt to launch the space shuttle Discovery on June 25, 1984. When one of the three engines failed to start, an on-board computer stopped the entire mission with 4 seconds remaining until liftoff. The computer recognized a problem and directed its output to the engines, bypassing the human crew and support personnel. Some research is being conducted on audio output but mostly for educational purposes, like the Texas Instruments Speak and Spell or Speak and Math packages. Audio output can also be heard in talking soft drink machines and in cars that warn owners that a door is open. In this section, we concentrate on video and printed output.

When the space shuttle Discovery's on-board computer detected a malfunction seconds before lift-off, the computer aborted the mission and shut down the engines without human intervention.

Video Output

In the early days of computers, output often came from a teletype printer similar to those used in a newsroom. When combined with a keyboard, these devices formed an **interactive link** with the mainframe computer. The user could type commands and receive responses from the computer over the teletype. These devices were very slow, however, and dreadfully loud. Output was also obtained from a modified IBM Selectric typewriter. Although somewhat faster than a teletype and not as loud, the modified Selectric was still not a great output device. Both devices have now been superseded by the video monitor or, simply, the monitor.

The **monitor** is a television-like device on which the output from the computer is shown. A monitor is also called a CRT (for cathode ray tube) or a VDT (for video display terminal). In conjunction with a keyboard, the monitor displays the instructions or data that are input to the computer. This text was composed on a word processor, and the paragraphs appeared on the screen as they were written so they could be read and changed if necessary. Later, the same screen was used as an output device when the text was edited or when the results from a computer program were displayed.

Virtually all computer output can be shown first on a screen if a user desires. On mainframes, a user generally checks the output before "dumping" it to a high-speed printer. On personal computers, the user may view the entire output before having it printed. In either case, the monitor is an important output device that makes using a computer much easier.

The two most common classifications of monitors are made according to size and ability to handle colors. A **monochrome monitor** can display a one-color background on which the symbols are represented in a different color. A **color monitor** can display multiple colors. Most monitor screens range in size from 9 inches up to 19 inches. The smallest monitor screen was

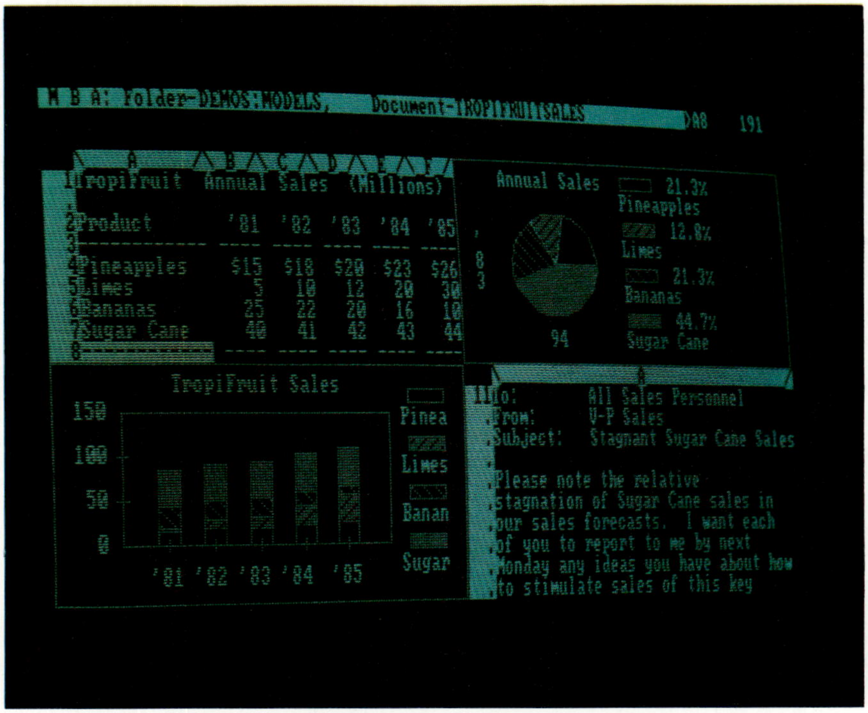

A monochrome monitor provides high-quality reproduction of text and numbers for such functions as word processing, accounting, and spreadsheet analysis.

available with the first portable personal computer built by Osborne. That monitor measured less than 5 inches diagonally! The most popular sizes are 9 inches for portables and 12 inches for desk-top models.

Regardless of size or ability to show color, all monitors work in much the same manner as a television screen. An electron beam that is generated from a device known as an "electron gun" (or cathode ray tube), strikes a phosphorescent compound (phosphor), which coats the inside of the screen. The energy of this collision causes a dot of light to appear on the screen. The electron beam sweeps back and forth across the screen, so when the phosphor starts to fade, it is struck again by the beam and lights up. If the phosphor fades too quickly, it blinks on and off, a condition known as *flicker*. If the phosphor remains lighted too long after it is struck, annoying shadows may appear on the screen. Users can determine the quality of the monitor through **pixel resolution**. The term **pixel** refers to the dots of light on the screen. The more pixels on the screen, the higher the pixel resolution and the resulting quality of the images on the monitor.

High-quality color monitors allow the use of color graphics for many purposes, including business, engineering, and recreation.

The color of the monochrome monitor is determined by the chemistry of the phosphors inside the screen. The characters on the screen may be displayed in white, green, or amber on a black or green background. Monochrome monitors usually accept from the computer a **composite signal**, which includes all information needed to produce a video image on the screen. The monitor decodes the composite signal and converts it into the images on the screen.

Color monitors are available in two forms—composite and RGB (red, green, and blue). In either case, a color monitor has three electron guns rather than one. It also has three color phosphors in each pixel rather than

WHICH COLOR MONITOR FOR YOU?

The best color for the images on a monochrome monitor has been the subject of a continuing discussion. The main concern is the eyestrain that can result from using a monitor for a long period of time. Experts have various theories about which color image is easiest on the eyes.

The first monitors were black and white. Later, monitors using light green characters on a dark green background were introduced. The green screen monitors supposedly relieved the eyestrain caused by the stark white-on-black screen monitors. The latest monochrome monitor uses amber characters on a green background, a combination that is considered to cause the least eyestrain. (Of course, if you are color blind—like the author—it is hard to tell what color the screen is!)

The December 1982 issue of *Personal Computing* reported that studies in Europe determined that white was the *worst* color for the characters on a screen, and that labor unions in Europe subsequently required that amber monitors be used in offices. However, the June 1984 issue of the same magazine stated that *no* tests had ever shown that one monitor color was better than another and that ". . . there are no such mandates [regarding monitor color] from unions or governments [in Europe]." The later article stated, "The color of the phosphor is not what is important—what is important is the lack of flicker, the resolution, and the contrast." The article also cites studies by Professor Marvin Dainoff of Miami University, who stated, "There is no conclusive evidence either way—there are no performance data that suggest green, amber, or white is best." Apparently, the only advice for choosing monitor color is if you like it, then buy it!

SOURCE: David Gabel, "Monitors: The Better to See Your Data With," *Personal Computing*, December 1982, pp. 112–26, 196–97; Lynn Walker, "A Complete Buyer's Guide to Monitors," *Personal Computing*, June 1984, pp. 162–69.

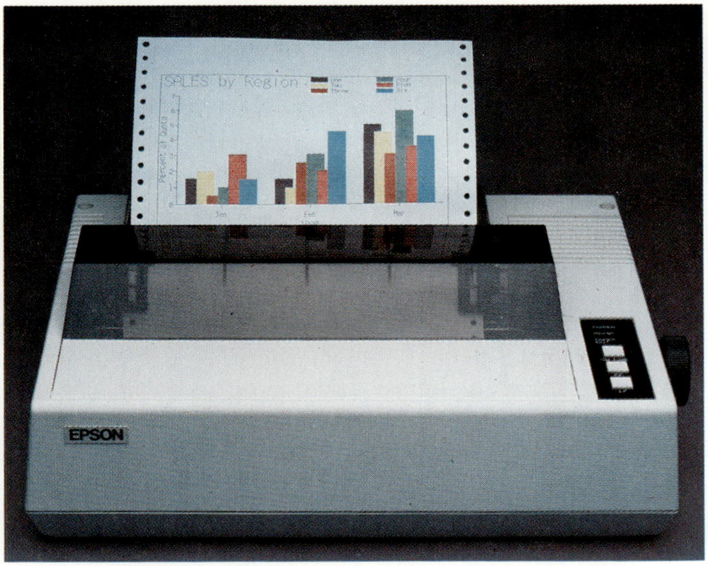

The high-speed line printer at left is needed to keep up with the tremendous computing speeds of mainframe computers. The multi-color dot matrix printer (right) is used more and more with personal computers to provide hard copy of the color graphics generated on the screen.

one. The colors on the screen result from the combination of the three color phosphors. The intensity of the color varies with the strength of the electron beams fired by each gun. In a composite system, the monitor decodes a single signal, which provides the necessary information to generate the picture. The RGB monitor receives three separate signals. The RGB color monitor can generate up to 256 colors, and the composite monitor is usually limited to 8 or 16 colors. The quality of the characters on the RGB monitor screen is superior to that of the composite monitor. However, the RGB monitor also costs nearly twice as much as the composite monitor ($500 versus $300).

Each type of monitor is best suited to a different use. A monochrome monitor is best used for word processing or other work involving text or numbers, because of the high resolution and low cost ($100). The RGB monitor would work for this application, but the cost may be prohibitive. A composite color monitor might not be acceptable, because text material (letters, digits, and so on) tends to be fuzzy. If the monitor primarily displays high-quality color graphics, then the RGB monitor is a must to achieve the necessary level of resolution.

If the monitor is used for entertainment or educational games, a composite monitor or even a television would be acceptable. A television set can only be used for this purpose because the resolution is not good enough to show more than 40 characters per line on the screen. Entering more than 40 characters per line makes the characters fuzzy and difficult to read. Many early personal computers were designed with this 40-character limitation in mind. Now, they require a special adaptation to show the normal 80 characters, regardless of the type of monitor used.

Printers

Output displayed on a screen is extremely useful, but the printed page, or **hard copy**, is necessary in most situations. The teletype and IBM Selectric printers used with the first computers provided hard copy as the only form of output. Today, printers are used in addition to monitors to provide hard copy either for mainframes or for personal computers. We now discuss various types of printers used with mainframes and personal computers.

Printers are broadly classified as either impact printers or nonimpact printers. An **impact printer** uses some type of hammer that strikes a ribbon coated with ink and forces ink onto paper. A typewriter is a manual impact printer. The mechanical hammer on an impact printer tends to be noisy, which can be a problem in some situations. On the other hand, impact printers work without special paper and can print multiple copies using carbon paper or carbonless multiple copy forms. Historically, such impact printers as a chain printer, a band printer, or a drum printer are associated with mainframes. All three are high-speed printers. **Chain printers** are similar to **band printers** in that they both have letters and digits attached to a chain or band, respectively, which then rotates between two pulleys. When the desired symbol is in the proper position on the paper, a series of hammers strike the ribbon and paper to form that symbol. In both cases, changing the typeface (font) is easily accomplished by changing the band or chain. Figure 7-7 shows a chain printer and a band printer.

A **drum printer** is composed of 132 vertical cylinders, each of which has all the necessary characters on the outside. The cylinders rotate independently, so that an entire line of text may be printed at one time by lining up the appropriate characters and striking the ribbon onto the paper with the entire drum. This system can print thousands of lines per minute, which is often necessary for the volume of output from a mainframe or minicomputer. Figure 7-8 shows a drum printer.

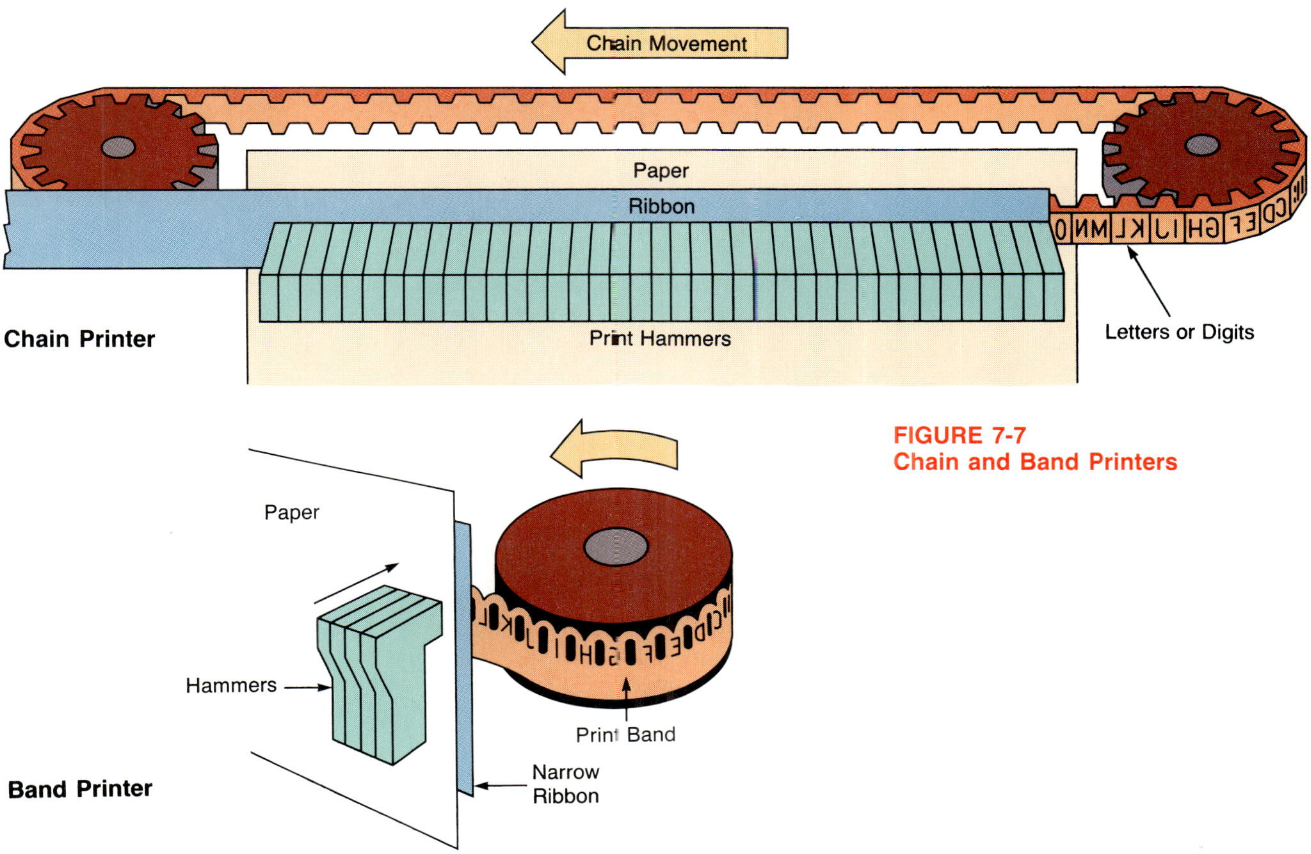

FIGURE 7-7
Chain and Band Printers

FIGURE 7-8
Drum Printer

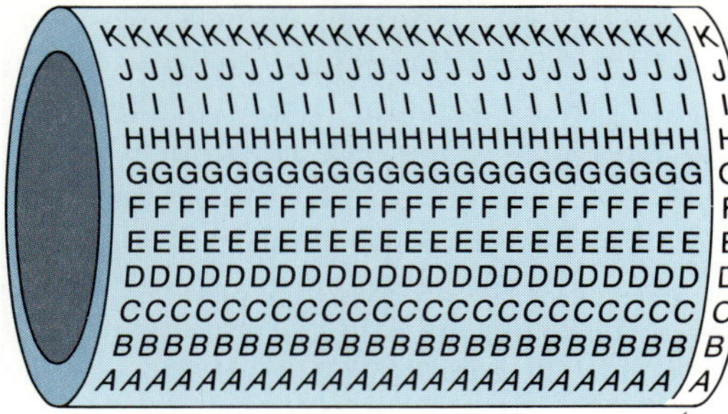

Two types of impact printers are widely used for personal computers—dot matrix printers and daisy wheel printers. A **dot matrix printer** uses a print head with 7–9 rigid vertical wires that form symbols by striking a ribbon to create a matrix, or grid, of dots on the paper. As the print head moves across the paper, the wires strike the ribbon. The vertical line of wires strikes the ribbon 5–9 times per symbol, forming anywhere from a 5×7 to a 9×9 matrix. The more dots in a matrix and the closer the dots are together, the better the quality of the symbol formed. A dot matrix printer is made faster by using **bidirectional printing**. In this process, the printer uses a buffer to store temporarily a line of information. This information is then printed from either side of the printer, that is, forward or backward. Figure 7-9 demonstrates how a dot matrix print head forms a letter.

Dot matrix printers have both advantages and disadvantages for personal computer users. Their advantages include speed (over 100 characters per second), flexibility, and reasonable price (many are available for less than $500). They are flexible because the font may be changed by the software; the print head need not be changed to achieve a different number of characters per inch (10 or 12), to boldface or italicize material, or to underline words. All these functions can be handled by the software directions to the printer. A disadvantage of a dot matrix printer is that the print quality is not high enough to be used for formal correspondence or for most business purposes.

A **daisy wheel printer** uses a wheel of symbols that resembles a daisy. Each "petal" of the daisy wheel has a symbol at the end of it. The wheel spins to the appropriate character and stops, and a hammer strikes the symbol against the ribbon to reproduce the character on the paper. Because the symbols on the wheel are fully formed, the print quality is as good as that found on a typewriter. Such quality is usually referred to as **letter quality**. Disadvantages of this type of printer are the cost (usually over $500) and speed (less than 50 characters per second, even in the most expensive models). The printing mechanism of the daisy wheel printer is shown in Figure 7-10.

Figure 7-11 demonstrates the difference in print quality between medium priced dot matrix and daisy wheel printers. Note that the dots are easy to see in some letters—particularly the "x"—and that overall, the daisy wheel print quality is superior.

To output information from a computer, a printer must be connected to the computer. A special printer cable is plugged into a port in the computer to make this connection. One of two types of signal is sent to the printer by the CPU. In **parallel interface**, all necessary information to print a character

Dot Matrix Print Head
(Printing an "E")

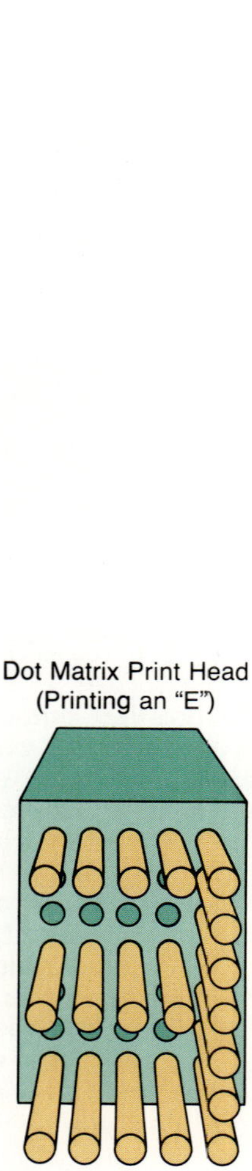

FIGURE 7-9
Dot Matrix Print Mechanism

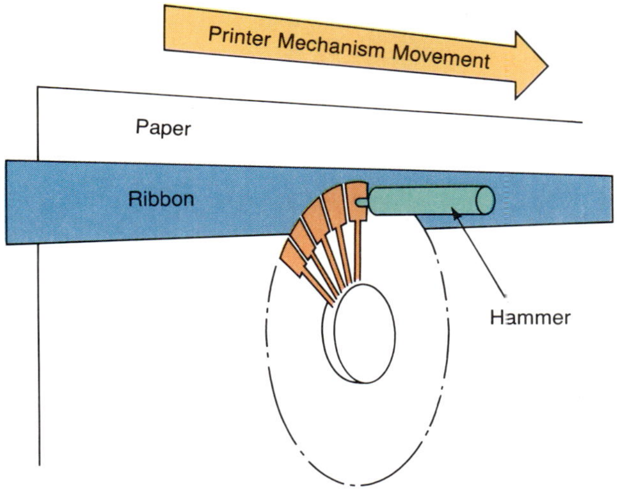

FIGURE 7-10
Daisy Wheel Print Mechanism

is sent to the printer at one time. **Serial interface** means only one bit at a time is sent from the CPU to the printer. A good way to think of these concepts is to imagine a parallel connection as 8 bits marching abreast from the CPU to the printer and a serial connection as the same 8 bits marching single file.

For parallel interface, a wide, flat ribbon cable carries all needed information from the CPU to the printer. An industry standard for a parallel interface is a Centronics parallel interface, named after an early manufacturer of parallel printers. The general trend today is toward parallel printers because of their speed. A serial connection that sends only 1 bit at a time is obviously slower than a parallel connection. However, serial interface is needed when the printer is more than 5 feet from the CPU to avoid losses of information. Most personal computers have outlets for both a serial and a parallel printer cable.

Nonimpact printers use some device other than a hammer to form symbols with ink on the paper. Three popular nonimpact printers are thermal

LETTER QUALITY
What Is It?

Letter quality **is a common term in reference to printers, yet it is seldom defined. Actually, letter quality is the top of a continuum of print quality. The lowest quality of print is referred to as *data processing quality,* produced by one pass of a typical 5 x 7 or 9 x 9 dot matrix printer. In this output, the individual dots are clearly discernible. The next level is *draft quality,* which is simply that—first "draft" quality. Letters are readable, the result of *two* passes of a 5 x 7 or 9 x 9 dot matrix print head. In *correspondence quality* output, the dots blend together and cannot be sorted out. Two passes of a dot matrix printer plus a slight upward movement of the paper achieve this level of output. The highest level of output possible from a dot matrix printer is *near-letter quality,* which requires multiple passes of a dot matrix print head. The resulting output can be mistaken for typewriter output. Finally, *letter quality* is output by a daisy wheel printer, which has fully formed symbols. The print quality is good enough for formal correspondence and business purposes. Dot matrix printers can approach letter quality with multiple passes of the print head, but only a daisy wheel printer yields letter quality.**

SOURCE: Winn L. Rosch, "Defining Print Quality," *PC Magazine,* October 1983, p. 261.

!"#$%&'()*+,-./0123456789:;<=>?@ABCDEFGHIJKLMNOPQRSTUVWXYZ

Dot Matrix Print

!"#$%&'()*+,-./0123456789:;<=>?@ABCDEFGHIJKLMNOPQRSTUVWXYZ

Daisy Wheel Print

FIGURE 7-11
Comparison of Printers

printers, ink jet printers, and laser printers. A **thermal printer** uses a dot matrix type of print head with heated wires. These wires come into contact with a specially treated paper that reacts to the heat to form symbols. Thermal printers are fast and initially inexpensive, but the heat-sensitive paper is expensive and cannot be used for business purposes.

Ink jet printers form dots on paper by spraying the ink from a row of tiny nozzles. Ink jet printers have several advantages over impact dot matrix printers. First, because an ink jet printer has no moving parts and no hammer striking paper, it is quiet. Second, an ink jet printer can achieve speeds of 150–270 characters per second (cps). Finally, because the print head has no moving parts, the mechanism can last an estimated five times longer than impact printers. Disadvantages of ink jet printers are that multiple copies cannot be made, and special paper is sometimes required.

If speed and quality are important but cost is not, then a **laser printer** should be considered. These printers use a laser beam to "write" dots on a drum coated with light-sensitive material. The pattern of dots is then transferred to paper using a toner similar to that used in a copier. A laser printer is essentially a nonimpact dot matrix printer, but it can crowd enough dots into a small space to create high-quality output. A laser printer's speed is measured in *pages per minute* rather than characters per second. For example, one commercial laser printer's speed is advertised at over 40 pages per minute (over 1,000 characters per second). A major disadvantage of laser printers is their cost. A model released in spring 1984 by Hewlett-Packard for personal computers costs well over $3,000. Laser printers are also very useful in mainframe and minicomputer environments for generating near letter quality documents using many different type fonts.

A daisy wheel (left) can provide letter quality print on personal computer printers. It is also easily switched, so the user has access to different fonts and symbols. Parallel printers use a flat ribbon cable to receive an entire character at a time. At right, this cable is connected to a security device to prevent unauthorized use of the printer.

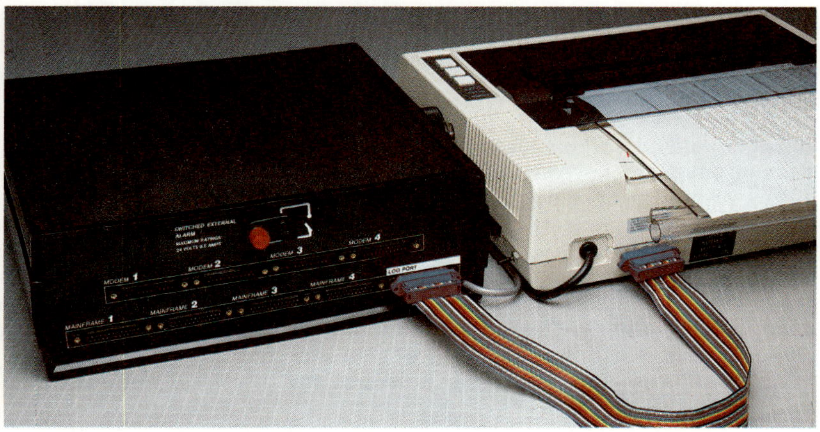

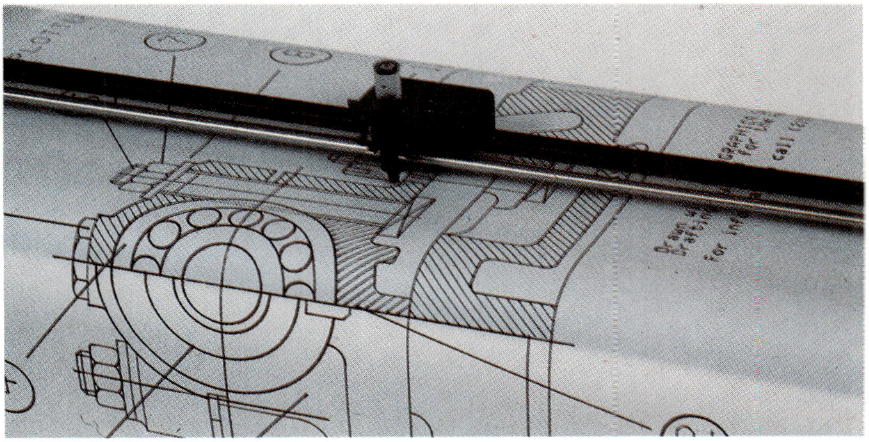

Multiple-pen plotters (top) can provide fine-looking color graphs and charts on a variety of media including paper, transparencies, and vellum. A plotter can also generate high-quality engineering and scientific blueprints (bottom) and drawings based on computer-aided design (CAD) software.

Color Output

The increasing use of color monitors has increased the demand that hard copy output also be in color. Color output can be achieved in one of three ways—dot matrix printers, ink jet printers, and plotters. The color dot matrix printers use the same impact approach as with black and white output, except that a multicolored ribbon provides the color. By moving the ribbon and making multiple passes, the dot matrix printer can produce up to 16 colors.

Ink jet color printers use the same principle as black and white ink jet printers, except that multiple inks are used. Most color ink jet printers use up to seven bright colors, which can be mixed by making multiple passes. A problem with color ink jet printers is the special paper that is required to avoid bleeding of colors.

Plotters have been used for over 20 years to draw graphs and charts. **Plotters** have pens that move across the paper to trace out the pattern of the graph or chart. By using several pens, multicolor graphs and charts can be developed. Plotters can be used on paper, vellum, or transparencies to produce colorful charts and graphs. Although a plotter can be used to reproduce something other than a chart or graph, the drawing of charts and graphs is what the machine does best.

REVIEW OF KEY POINTS

- Input and output are a necessary part of any computer system.
- Data entry is a problem because of the time needed to enter large amounts of data into the computer and because of the errors that can occur in this process.
- One solution to the data entry problem is to decouple the process from the computer, using punched cards, magnetic tape, or magnetic disks as intermediate storage media.
- Bar codes, optical character recognition, and magnetic ink character recognition are methods used commercially to speed data entry.
- Because keyboards tend to differ among personal computers, a user may need some time to become accustomed to a new keyboard.
- The mouse is the most popular alternative input device for personal computers, but touch screens, touch pads, and light pens are also used.
- Touch screens and light pens are also used to input data to mainframes and minicomputers.
- Voice recognition is a form of input that holds great promise for the future if major problems can be solved.
- The two major forms of output for computers are video monitors and the printed page.
- Monitors are available in various sizes and classifications depending on whether they are monochrome or color.
- Widely used impact printers for mainframes include chain, band, or drum printers.
- Popular impact printers for personal computers are dot matrix and daisy wheel printers.
- Nonimpact printers include thermal printers, ink jet printers, laser printers, and plotters—all suitable for personal computers.

KEY TERMS

band printers
bar codes
bidirectional printing
buffer
card reader
chain printers
color monitor
composite signal
daisy wheel printer
data deck
data entry problem
desk-top metaphor
disk drive
disk pack
dot matrix printer
drum printer
hard copy
icons
impact printer
ink jet printers
input/output (I/O)
I/O bound
interactive input
interactive link
keyboards
keypunch machine
key-to-disk
key-to-tape
laser printer
letter quality
light pen
magnetic disk
magnetic ink character recognition (MICR)
magnetic tape
monitor
monochrome monitor
mouse
nonimpact printers
off-line
on-line
optical character recognition (OCR)
paper tape
parallel interface
pixel
pixel resolution
plotters
punched card
serial interface
tape drive
thermal printer
touch pad
touch screen
verification
voice recognition
wand

REVIEW QUESTIONS

1. Discuss the importance of input and output to a computer system. Can you imagine a system without one or the other?
2. Describe the data entry problem. Name two methods for solving this problem.
3. Look at a product that has a UPC bar code and name the company code and the product code.
4. If you have a personal computer at your disposal, determine the characters that can be displayed on the screen using the keyboard. If you are using the school's mainframe, check with your instructor or the computer center on how to answer this question.
5. What are the two types of mouse input devices available as alternative input devices for personal computers?

6. What is the difference between a touch screen and a touch pad? Why is appropriate software important for any type of alternate input device?
7. What are the two major categories of printers? If possible, check with your school's computer center about the type of mainframe printer used and its print rate.
8. What is letter quality print? Is it possible to achieve this quality of print with a dot matrix printer?
9. What are the three types of monitors? List their similarities and differences.
10. What are the three major types of nonimpact printers? If you have more than one type of printer at your disposal, compare the print qualities.

RCA
4
RCA
5

Our discussion of hardware in Chapter 2 mentioned the need for secondary storage. In this chapter, we review secondary storage concepts and then discuss in detail magnetic tapes and disks as secondary storage devices for both mainframes and personal computers. This discussion includes information on the use of floppy and hard disks for personal computers and on the determination of a floppy disk's storage capacity. We then cover the important concept of backup as it applies to both tapes and disks. Finally, the chapter covers other storage devices and techniques, such as video disks and virtual memory.

8

Using Secondary Storage

STUDY OBJECTIVES

After reading this chapter, you should be able to

- Understand fully the importance of secondary storage in the use of mainframes or personal computers.
- Explain how information is stored on a reel-to-reel tape in a mainframe environment.
- Explain how disks store information for mainframes and personal computers.
- Recognize the difference between the storage organization of a disk pack and a floppy disk.
- Recognize the storage capacities of different types of floppy disks.
- Understand the importance of backup for a secondary storage system.
- Explain mass storage, video disks, memory cards, and virtual memory.

SECONDARY STORAGE CONCEPTS AND TERMINOLOGY

Secondary storage is a form of memory that is outside of internal random access memory (RAM). Even on the largest computers, the amount of memory available internally is clearly not enough to satisfy the storage needs of users. A second reason for secondary, or auxiliary, storage is the volatility of RAM. In other words, when the power to the computer is turned off, any information stored in RAM is lost. Various devices store information outside of the computer—such as magnetic tapes, magnetic disks, video disks, and mass storage. Some devices can be written on and read from by the user, whereas others can only be read from. Each device may be available in various forms. For example, magnetic disks may be metallic hard disks or plastic floppy disks.

Some Terminology

It is important to understand how information is organized on a secondary storage device. The terminology describing the storage of information is similar, regardless of which storage device is used. In most cases, the information is stored as a **file**, which is a collection of meaningful information to which the user can attach a name. For example, a list of the names of the members of a college computer club would be considered a file to which we might attach the name MEMBERS.86. The name indicates that this file is the 1986 membership file. Table 8-1 shows a simulated membership file of information that includes the name, phone number, and local address of each club member.

Files can be either program files or data files. A **program file** is the list of instructions, or program statements, for a computer program, whereas a **data** (or text) **file** may contain programs as well as other types of information. The club membership list would be considered a data file, and a computer program that arranged, or sorted, the data alphabetically would be a program file. Each file can be subdivided into **records**. If a file is analogous to a file folder, then records are analogous to the individual items stored in the folder. For example, a file folder might contain membership information forms; these forms are equivalent to records. In Table 8-1, each record contains a club member's name, phone number, and address. If the membership list has 100 names, then the MEMBERS.86 file has 100 records. In a program file, each program statement is a record.

Records are themselves subdivided into **fields**, which are logical subdivisions of the information in a record. The file in Table 8-1 has three fields—a name field, a phone number field, and an address field. Other types of files may have more fields, depending on the types of information they contain.

Table 8-1 1986 COMPUTER CLUB MEMBERSHIP FILE

Name	*Phone Number*	*Address*
Hyatt, Ashley	654-3412	120 Hilltop Dr.
Patrick, Chris	976-7627	P.O. Box 302
Myers, Dale	524-2236	103 Russell Hall
Davis, Carolyn	699-6222	1410 Milledge Ave.

Floppy disks provide secondary storage for personal computers.

For example, an accounts receivable file could have a record for each individual with an outstanding balance. That file may have fields for each individual's account number, name, address, balance due, amount 30 days overdue, amount 60 days overdue, amount 90 days overdue, and comments.

A file placed in secondary storage can be composed of fixed length records or variable length records. The length of a record is defined as the *number of characters* that make up that record. A **fixed length record** has a specified number of spaces set aside for each field, regardless of whether the fields are filled up. For example, if in the MEMBERS.86 file shown in Table 8-1, the first record has a name field of 24 characters, a phone number field of eight characters, four blank spaces, and an address field of 30 characters, the total fixed record length will be 66 characters.

In a file composed of **variable length records**, the user can save storage space by specifying at the beginning of each record exactly how many characters that record will contain. Only the number of positions specified at the beginning of the record are actually stored on the file. For example, if the file in Table 8-1 had variable length records, the first record in MEMBERS.86 would have a length specification of 36 positions (13 for the name, 8 for the phone number, and 15 for the address). All the blanks at the end of the record and between fields have been deleted, and 31 positions less than the fixed length record are used.

The use of fixed length or variable length records is closely tied to how a file is stored on a storage device. On a **direct access file**, each record may be accessed directly, regardless of its relative position on the file or the order in which the records were placed on the file. For a **sequential access file**, the records must be accessed in the *same* order as they were written onto the file. Variable length records are generally associated with sequential access files, and fixed length records are generally associated with direct access files. A sequential access file may be used for variable length records because all records must be accessed in order, and the next record can be immediately accessed when the end of one record is reached.

In direct access files, fixed length records facilitate a record's being accessed directly, regardless of its position on the file. For example, assume each fixed length record on a direct access file is 100 characters long. If record 51 is needed, the computer simply counts 50 × 100 = 5,000 characters to find the end of record 50 (the record prior to record 51). Finding record 51 would be difficult (but not impossible) with variable length records.

SEARCHING FOR "ROOTS"

One storage intensive hobby is *genealogy,* or the study of a person's ancestors. Extra storage may be necessary to trace all the parents, grandparents, great-grandparents, and so on, that make up a family tree. People who can trace their genealogy back several centuries find that keeping names and relationships on index cards is a bulky and cumbersome filing system. For this reason, genealogists are turning to the computer to handle the storage tasks, and the appropriate software makes the job of organizing ancestors much easier.

The Church of Jesus Christ of Latter Day Saints (the Mormons) leads the way in computerizing a list of everyone who has ever lived. Mormons believe that the soul of a dead ancestor of a living church member can be saved if that relationship is known. To find their ancestors, the Mormon Church has saved over 1 billion names on microfilm in several locations. The most impressive storage site is the Granite Mountain Vaults that are 700 feet under the mountains outside Salt Lake City, Utah.

After the Mormons started using computers in the late 1960s, they developed the GIANT (Genealogical Information And Name Tabulation) computer system. Approximately 70 million names have been extracted from the microfilms so far and placed in the computer system. In 1981, local parishes started using small computers to place names on disks that are sent to Salt Lake City's GIANT system.

Amateur genealogists have found the personal computer invaluable in tracking down ancestors. The personal computer stores the information in a compact and easily accessible form. One couple outfitted their mobile home with a personal computer and set off on a cross-country tour to find information on their ancestors. Their mobile home would not have been large enough if they had not used computerized storage.

SOURCE: Rachel Wrege, "The Human Roll Call," *Popular Computing,* December 1982, pp. 48–55.

Storing genealogical data on computers will someday make this manual sort almost unnecessary at the Genealogical Library of the Mormon Church.

Information currently stored on microfilm is rapidly being stored on computers at the Genealogical Library.

MAGNETIC TAPE

A popular form of secondary storage both for mainframes and personal computers is magnetic tape. **Magnetic** (or simply, **mag**) **tape** is a thin Mylar tape from $\frac{1}{2}$ inch to less than $\frac{1}{4}$ inch wide. The tape is coated with ferrous oxide (purified rust), on which information is recorded in binary form by selective magnetization of spots on the tape. Magnetic tape is available in the following three forms:

1. Reel-to-reel tape that resembles the reel-to-reel audio tape used with high-quality recorders
2. Cassette tape similar to that used for audio recordings
3. Cartridge tape, which looks like a cassette but is in a larger plastic case.

Reel-to-reel, cassette, and cartridge tape each has a different transfer rate (speed of data transfer) and storage capacity, summarized in Table 8-2.

A **tape drive**, which is necessary to use any type of magnetic tape, performs two key operations. First, the information is transferred to and from the tape using a **read/write head**, which encodes the magnetic signals on the ferrous oxide tape coating. The tape must be able to move across the read/write head. In cassette and cartridge tape systems, the tape remains entirely within the plastic case. After the plastic case is inserted in the drive mechanism, the tape is moved between the supply and storage reels by a motor in the tape drive. For reel-to-reel systems, a storage reel is part of the tape drive, and the supply reel is removable for storage elsewhere.

Reel-to-reel and cassette are by far the most popular forms of tape storage. The cartridge system is larger and more complex than a cassette, and it uses a different recording system.

Reel-to-Reel Tape

For mainframe and many minicomputer applications, **reel-to-reel magnetic tape** is an extremely useful form of secondary storage. The tape is usually $\frac{1}{2}$ inch wide and is classified by the density and the number of tracks on the tape. The density is measured by the number of **bytes per inch (bpi)** on the tape. Density can range from 800 bpi to 6,250 bpi, but the most common density is 1,600 bpi.

The **tracks** on the tape are parallel magnetic lines that run the length of the tape on which binary information is stored. The most common number of tracks is nine. On some mainframes, information is stored on the tape in EBCDIC (Extended Binary Coded Decimal Interchange Code), an 8-bit code

Table 8-2 COMPARISON OF TAPE STORAGE

Type of Tape	*Transfer Rate*	*Storage Capacity*
Cassette	<1 Kbyte/second	200 Kbytes
Cartridge	6 Kbytes/second	10,000 Kbytes
Reel-to-reel	>100 Kbytes/second	20,000 Kbytes

FIGURE 8-1
Magnetic Tape Section

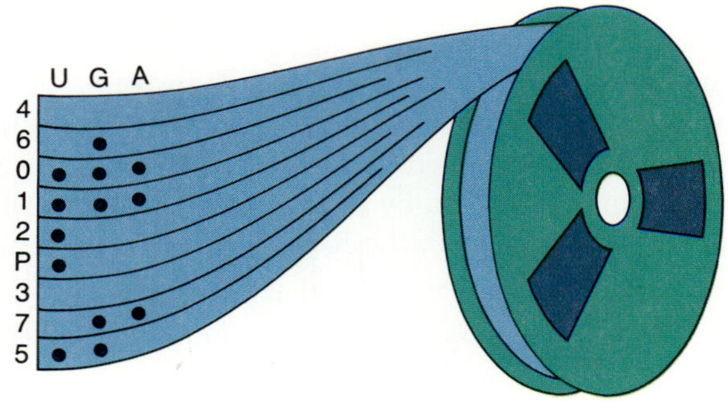

for storing or transferring information in binary form. ASCII (American Standard Code for Information Interchange) is used for other types of mainframes, minicomputers, and personal computers.

The ninth track on a nine-track tape is for a **parity bit**, which is used for error checking. The parity bit is added during the write process to make the number of one-bits across the tape equal to an odd or even number, depending on which standard is used. During the read step, the number of one-bits is checked to make sure they match the parity (odd or even) used. A tape with odd parity means that the total number of one-bits across the tape is always odd. Figure 8-1 shows a section of a nine-track tape with the letters UGA coded on it in EBCDIC. Assuming odd parity is used in this example, a bit is added to the parity track (labeled "P") to make the number of bits in the letter "U" equal an odd number. Because the letters "G" and "A" already have odd numbers of bits, a parity bit is not needed.

Note in Figure 8-1 that the tracks are not numbered sequentially. This ordering places the most commonly used tracks (0, 1, 2, 3, and P) in the middle of the tape and the least used tracks on the outside of the tape. This minimizes wear-and-tear on the tape. Because an entire byte is encoded on the tape in one operation, reel-to-reel tape is a **parallel storage device**.

Individual records on the tape can be blocked or unblocked. **Blocked records** are combined into a physical unit that is then read by the tape drive. A block of records, also called a **physical record**, is the actual amount of tape read by the tape drive at one time. Each block is made up of **logical records**. For example, on a tape that contains a mailing list, each block could have three logical records—each consisting of a name, street address, and city and state. The space between blocks is the **interblock gap (IBG)**. The tape drive starts and stops at each interblock gap.

In **unblocked records**, each physical record corresponds to only one logical record, and logical records are separated by interblock gaps. The read

FIGURE 8-2
Blocked and Unblocked Magnetic Tape Sections

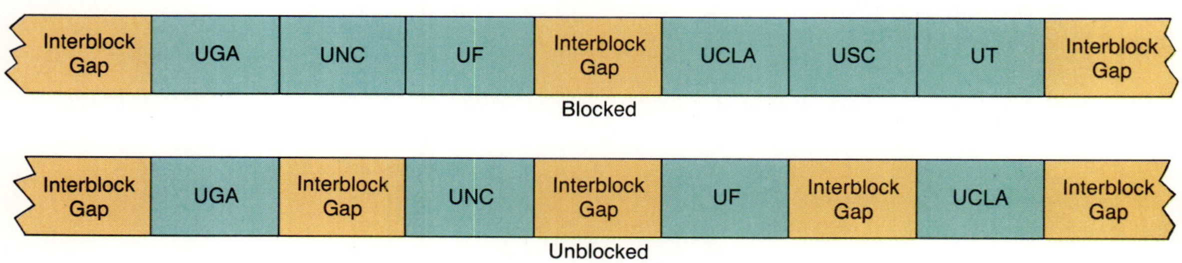

or write process from the tape is slowed down because the tape drive stops more often. Figure 8-2 shows two tapes with the same information. However, one tape is blocked in groups of three logical records, and the other tape is unblocked. Note that the blocked tape can store more information than the unblocked tape in the same space.

On mainframes and minicomputers, reel-to-reel tape is an inexpensive form of storage. A tape 2,400 feet long can hold over 46 million bytes of information at a cost of less than $20.

A user is charged according to the amount of space consumed on the magnetic disk that is used as the primary, or on-line, secondary storage. For this reason, usually only current material is kept on disk and other material is stored on tape. The mainframe user can usually access a file from on-line disk storage in a matter of seconds from a terminal. On the other hand, a request for tape, which is not on-line, usually takes longer, because the tape must be mounted on a tape drive and then transferred to an on-line disk pack.

Reel-to-reel tape can also perform many important operations that require sequential processing—such as payroll or end-of-term grade reporting. In these situations, each name must be processed, either to determine the amount of the payroll check or to record the grades on transcripts. Clearly, tape is an efficient medium for sequential processing.

A final reason for using reel-to-reel tape is that it is an important form of backup. Information in on-line disk pack storage is often copied onto tape to be used if the information on the disk is somehow lost. The topic of backup is discussed in more detail on pages 186–188.

A special reel-to-reel tape drive is needed that can move the tape past the read/write head at speeds up to 125 inches per second. Such high speeds are necessary to handle the large amounts of information stored on tapes. Figure 8-3 (page 174) shows a diagram of a tape drive. The large loops on either side of the read/write mechanism are in vacuum chambers. If the tape ran at normal atmospheric pressure, air resistance to the sudden surges in speed would break the tape.

Most computer centers have a tape library run by a special librarian who manages tape storage. When a computer operator must mount a particular tape on the tape drive, he or she obtains that tape from the librarian.

A computer operator loads a reel of tape onto a tape drive before the tape can be accessed by a computer user.

Tapes are cataloged in a tape library so a particular tape is easily found when a user requests it.

FIGURE 8-3
Reel-to-Reel Tape Drive

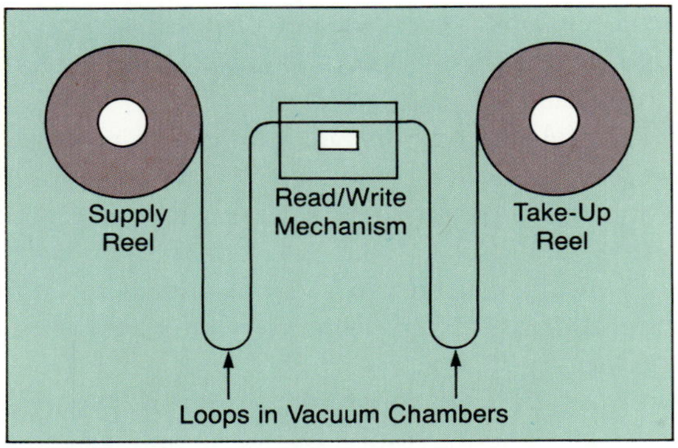

Cassette Tape

Cassette tape is an inexpensive form of secondary storage for personal computers. Only an audio tape, a tape recorder, and a recorder interface on the computer are needed. Because the recorder interface is usually built into the computer, only the tape and recorder must be acquired separately from the computer. The early personal computers used the cassette as secondary storage. Today, some less expensive personal computers still use cassette tape for secondary storage. Cassette tape systems are **serial storage devices**, because information is recorded on the tape one bit at a time. Figure 8-4 shows a schematic diagram of the drive mechanism of a cassette tape.

The obvious advantage of the cassette is its low cost. However, a disadvantage is the fact that cassette tape, like all magnetic tape, is a **sequential access storage device**. Information must be read from the tape in the same order that it was placed there. Users generally want fast, easy access to any information in secondary storage. Searching for a particular file and record using sequential access cassette tape can be a slow and frustrating process.

Another problem with cassette tape as a secondary storage medium is that if multiple files are stored on the same cassette tape, one file cannot be

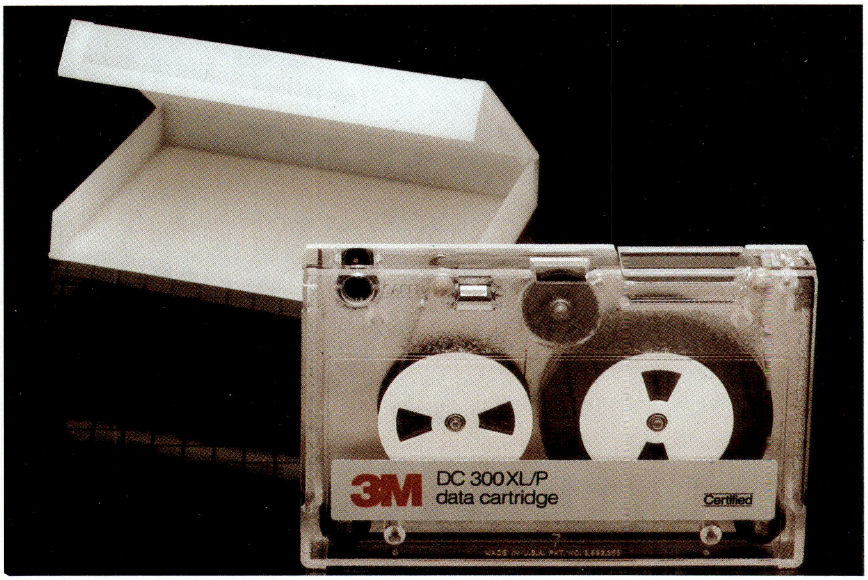

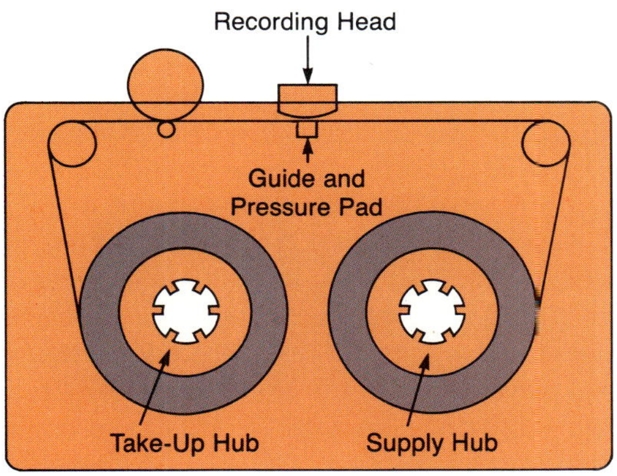

FIGURE 8-4
Drive Mechanism of Cassette Tape

changed without disturbing the other files. Although high-speed cassette tape systems are available with storage and transfer capabilities almost equivalent to magnetic disks, they are not as popular as disks.

Cartridge Tape

Cartridge tape looks like a cassette tape, but it works differently. Whereas a cassette uses audio tones, the magnetic cartridge tape contains an actual bit pattern. Cartridges require a high degree of technology to control tape movement, but they have higher transfer rates and larger storage volumes. Like cassette tapes, cartridge tape systems are serial storage devices, with information placed on the tape one bit at a time.

MAGNETIC DISK

A **magnetic disk** is a metal or plastic disk coated with ferrous oxide. As with magnetic tape, a bit pattern may be magnetically coded onto the ferrous oxide. Because the disk spins like a record in the disk drive, the read/write head can reach any data on

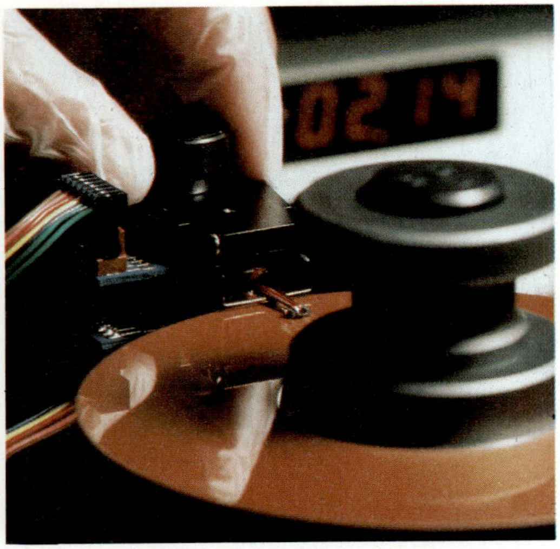

Secondary storage can take many forms. Cartridge tape (left) is a popular method of backup for minicomputers and personal computers. The read/write head tested at right moves across the rapidly spinning disk, magnetically encoding information onto the disk or reading information from the disk.

the disk directly rather than sequentially. For this reason, magnetic disks are **direct access storage devices (DASD)**.

The disk is often compared with a record album. Both are flat platters that are used to transfer information. The read/write head on the disk drive is analogous to the needle on a record player—both can be moved directly to the information that is being transferred. The needle is moved to the desired record "cut," whereas the read/write head is moved to the desired file.

Important differences exist between a disk and a record. First, the information on the disk is stored in magnetic form rather than as grooves in the surface of the record. Second, records always have information on two sides, but disks do not. Third, the record has a continuous groove that spirals from its outside to its center, whereas the disk has concentric tracks. Finally, the needle on a record player can only transfer information *from* the record; the read/write head on a disk drive can write information onto the disk as well as read information from the disk.

Bits are stored serially around each concentric track on a disk. The number of tracks depends on the size of the disk. For example, large metal disks used for mainframes may have 400 tracks and be 14 inches in diameter. A plastic disk for a personal computer may have as few as 40 tracks or be less than 4 inches in diameter. The tracks are numbered from the outside to the inside starting with zero. For example, for a 40-track floppy disk, the tracks are numbered from 0–39. Figure 8-5 shows how the letters "UGA" in EBCDIC form are stored on the outermost track of a disk.

Disk Packs

For mainframes and some minicomputers, **disk packs** composed of up to 11 disks are commonly used. These disks are arranged one above the other with enough space between them for read/write heads to move. Figure 8-6 shows the configuration of a disk pack with the read/write heads. The number of disks in a disk pack is related to the number of read/write heads in the disk drive. Information is written on both sides of each disk, with the exception of the top and bottom surfaces of the disk pack. A disk pack with 11 disks has 20 sides and 10 read/write heads, each of which can transfer information to the sides above and below. Only one read/write head is active at a time, but the

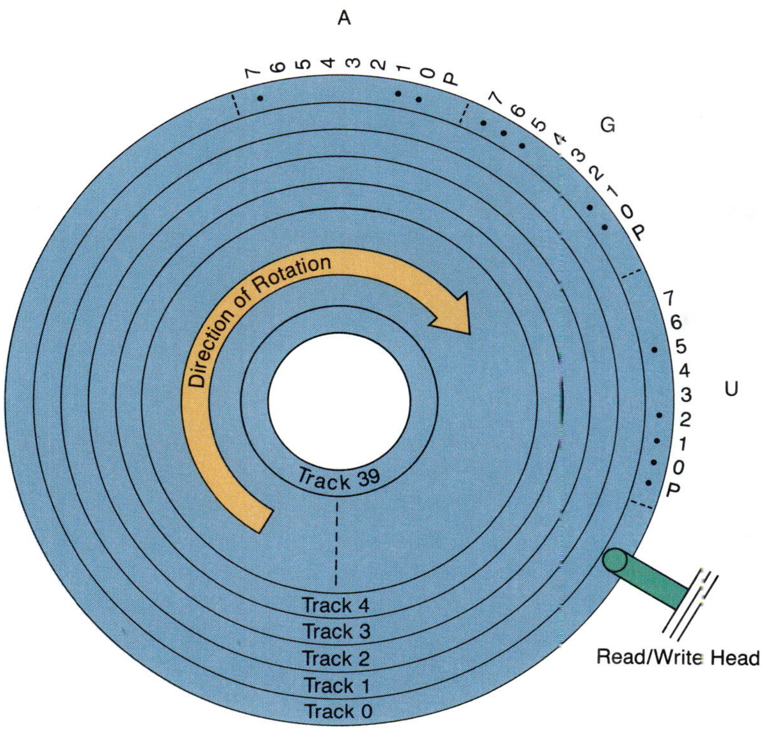

FIGURE 8-5
Disk Storage

transfer of information is so fast that all heads appear to work at once. A disk pack can be transported, but it must be protected by a special container that covers the entire pack. When it is used, the disk pack is placed in the disk drive and the container is removed.

The disks rotate at 3,600 revolutions per minute (140 miles per hour), and the read/write heads "float" (or "fly") above or below the disk on a cushion of air. The distance between the head and the disk is 35–100 micro-inches (0.0000035″ to 0.0000100″). If the head encounters dust or smoke particles, a **head crash** may result. The cushion of air is interrupted and the read/write head makes contact with the disk, digging a furrow in the outer layer and destroying the data stored there. The relative size of dust and smoke particles

If you scaled everything down at mass and velocity, that [read/write] head [of a hard disk] represents a 747 flying at Mach 4 an inch off the ground.

Jim Mahon, Engineering vice-president, Seagate Technologies
(As quoted in "The Amazing Winchester," *Popular Science,* October 1982, pp. 88–90.)

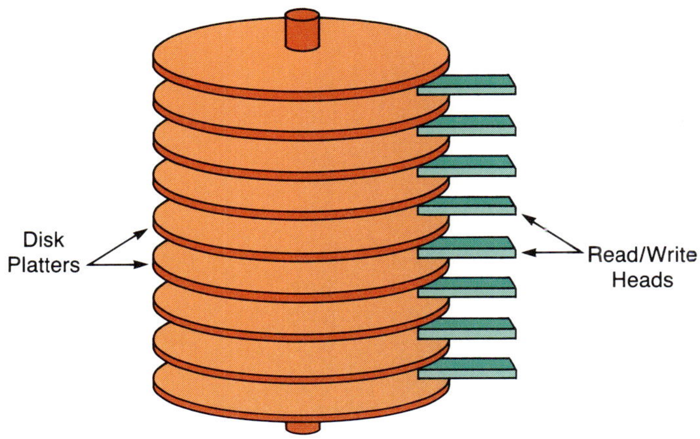

FIGURE 8-6
Configuration of a Disk Pack

Seen here at the factory, a disk pack has several hard disks, each with its own read/write head.

compared with the space between the head and the disk is shown in Figure 8-7. Given the problems that dust and smoke particles can cause for a disk pack, the environment in a computer center is highly regulated, with constant air conditioning and rules prohibiting smoking around the disk drives.

In a disk pack, all tracks with the same track number on all sides of the disks are precisely aligned above one another. All tracks with the same track number make up a vertical **cylinder**. Information that requires more than one track (a common occurrence) is written on other tracks in the *same cylinder* rather than on the same disk. All read/write heads move together, and they are automatically on the same cylinder at any one time. After one head finishes transferring information to a track, another head simply transfers information to the same track on another disk, and the read/write heads

Head crashes are costly in terms of equipment and data. These photographs show the catastrophic effects of a head crash as the head (left) rips the surface—and the data—from the disk (right).

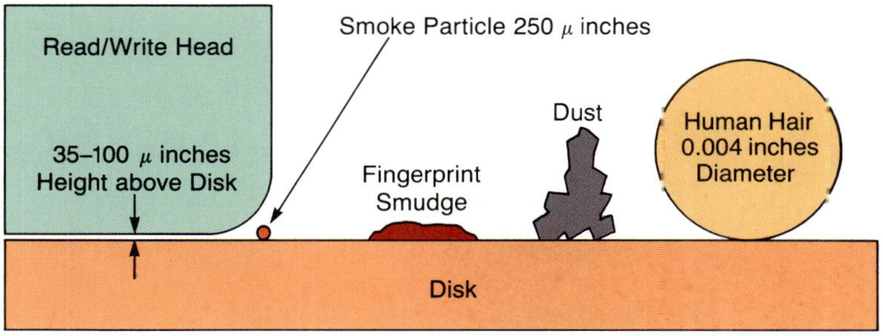

FIGURE 8-7
Separation of Disk and Read/Write Head
(Digital Equipment Corporation)

do not need to move. When all tracks in a cylinder are full, the heads are moved to a new cylinder. The cylinder concept of disk storage is shown in Figure 8-8.

Transfer time to or from a disk comprises the following times:

Seek time, or the time to move the heads to the correct track

Rotational delay time, or the time to wait for the appropriate section of the disk to come under the head

Transmission time, or the actual time to transfer the data

Because seek time is minimized by keeping the heads at the same position, the cylinder approach to storage is quite effective. Figure 8-9 shows the process of reading or writing information from or to a disk.

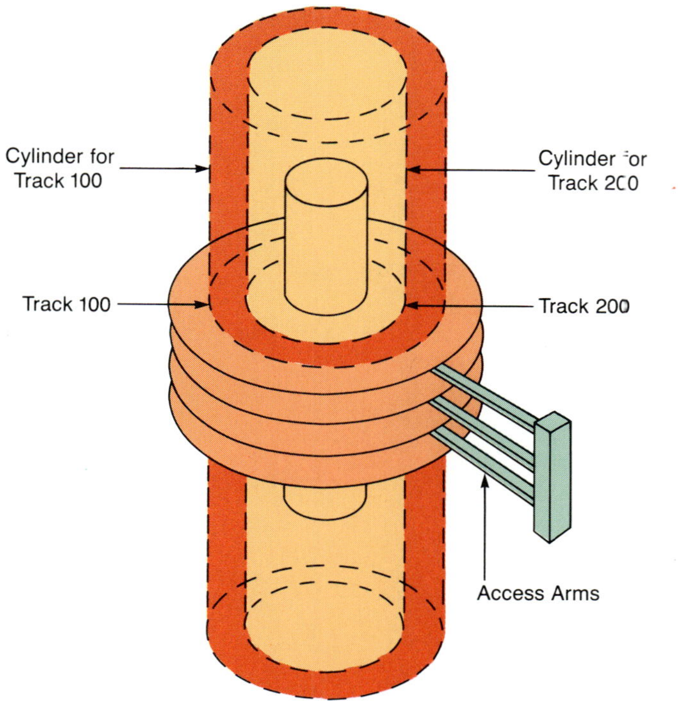

FIGURE 8-8
Cylinder Concept of Disk Storage

FIGURE 8-9
Read/Write Process for a Disk

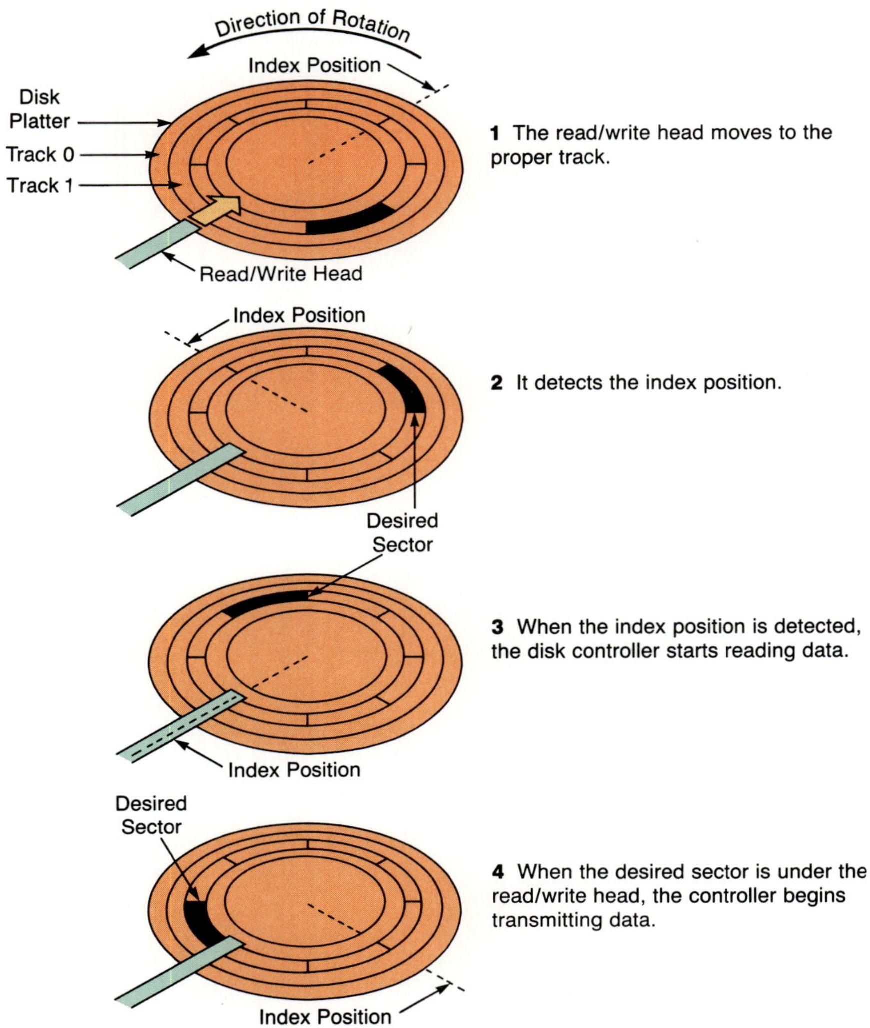

FIGURE 8-10
A Floppy Disk

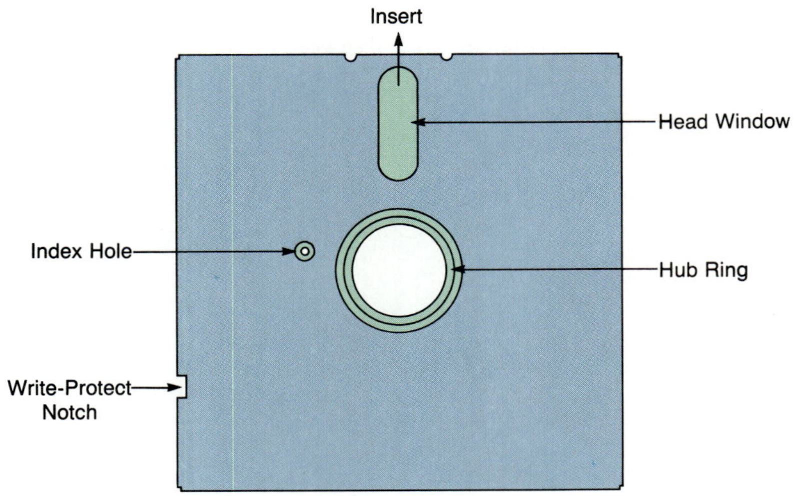

Floppy Disks

For personal computers, the floppy disk is the most common form of secondary storage. A **floppy disk**, also called a **diskette**, is made of Mylar plastic, which is not really "floppy" even though it is flexible. The diskette itself is enclosed in a stiff vinyl jacket, which protects it from dust and dirt. Figure 8-10 shows a typical floppy disk.

The **head window** is the area of the diskette that is in contact with the read/write head. Disk drives for floppy disks can be either single- or double-sided depending on whether they read one side or both. The head actually rubs against the floppy disk rather than flying above it, so the rotation speed of 300 rpm is less than $\frac{1}{10}$ that of a mainframe disk pack. The **hub ring** is where the disk drive clamps onto the diskette and rotates it. This procedure occurs automatically when the diskette is inserted in the disk drive on the personal computer and the drive door is closed. The hole in the vinyl cover of the diskette is the **index hole**, which indicates to the computer where the disk is in its rotation. A second hole is cut in the plastic disk itself. When the

MAGNETIC DRUM

Storage before the Disk

The predecessor of the disk for secondary storage was the magnetic drum, a cylinder whose surface is covered with ferrous oxide like magnetic tapes or disks. The surface of the drum is divided into tracks, each of which has four channels on which spots can be magnetized to represent one bit. In this way, a half-byte, also called a "nybble" (really!), can be coded across each track in a manner similar to that for magnetic tape. In fact, we can think of a magnetic drum as having strips of four-track magnetic tape wound around it, with each strip representing a track on the drum. The magnetic drum has a stationary read/write head for each track on the drum. As the drum spins, the read/write heads transfer data to and from the surface of the drum. The address of information is determined by the track on which it is coded and its position on the track. Because the read/write heads are always in place over each track, a drum has no seek time, but it still has rotational delay time while the head waits for the proper part of the drum to arrive. A schematic diagram of a magnetic drum secondary storage device appears below. Magnetic drums have been almost completely replaced by magnetic disks because of the disk's greater storage capacity and reduced time to find and transfer information.

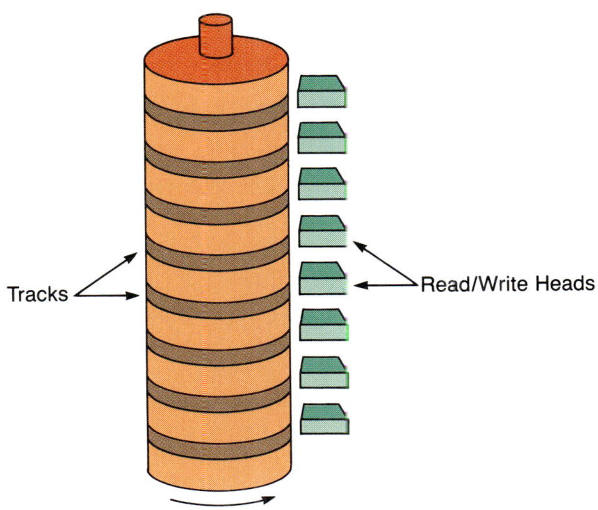

The 8 inch diskette is commonly used on dedicated word processing machines, and the smaller $5\frac{1}{4}$ inch diskette is the most popular size for personal computers.

inner and outer hole match up, a light shines through the combined hole and activates a photoelectric cell under the diskette. When the cell signals the computer about the position of the index hole, the position of the desired information can then be determined. A security device that protects data already on the disk is a **write-protect notch**. When covered by a piece of tape, it does not allow information to be written onto the disk.

Because only one floppy disk is used at a time (rather than a group of platters, as in a disk pack), the cylinder storage system is not appropriate. Instead, the tracks on the disk are divided into **sectors**. Each floppy disk has from 10–16 sectors, and each sector of a track can store between 128 and 512 bytes, depending on the type of personal computer. Typical diskette sectoring is shown in Figure 8-11.

Figure 8-11 shows **soft sectoring**, a sectoring plan that depends on the machine in use and on the particular **disk operating system (DOS)** that manages the disk. Disk operating systems are discussed in more detail in Chapter 9.

The sectoring plan can be built into the disk by the addition of more index holes. Such a disk is said to be **hard sectored**. The choice between hard and soft sectoring depends on the type of computer in use, but most personal computers use soft sectoring.

Before the disk can actually be used, it must be **formatted**. In this process, DOS software records codes on the diskette to identify each track and sector. A directory, or list of the diskette's contents, is recorded in a specific sector and track. The disk controller, which is part of a personal computer's hardware, and the DOS use the directory to find where particular programs and files are stored so that the read/write head can move to the proper position on the disk.

Storage Size Floppy disks come in the following three general sizes: **micro-floppy** (less than 4 inches in diameter), **mini-floppy** ($5\frac{1}{4}$ inches), and **standard floppy** (8 inches). Currently, the mini-floppy is the most popular size, but the micro-floppy is gaining in popularity. Although the size of the

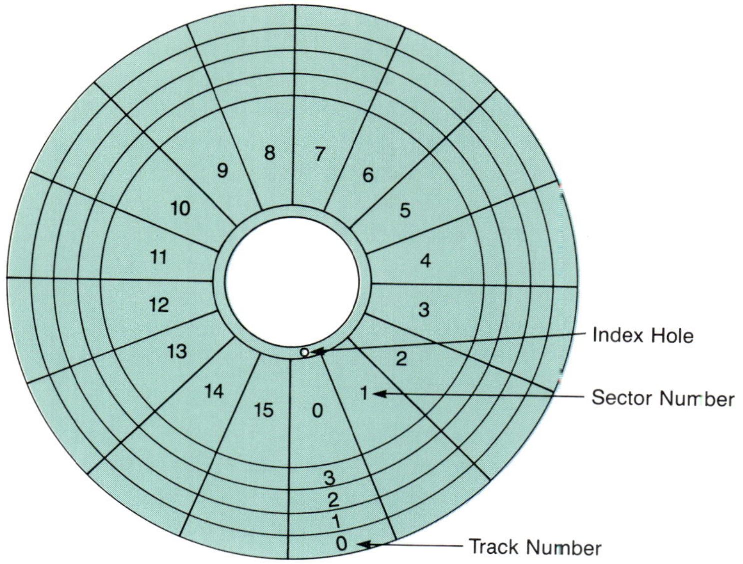

FIGURE 8-11
Diskette Sectoring

diskette is important in determining the amount of information it can store, two other characteristics must be considered—density and whether information is written on one side or both sides of the diskette. The **density** of a diskette, which is based on the number of bits per square inch, can be described in three categories—single density (SD), double density (DD), and quad density (QD). Single- and double-density diskettes store data at a rate of 48 tracks per inch (tpi), but double-density diskettes contain double the number of ferrous oxide particles in the disk coating compared with single-density diskettes. Quad-density diskettes have the same number of ferrous oxide particles as double-density diskettes, but the tpi increases to 96.

FLOPPY DISKS
Care and Handling

Floppy disks are fairly tough storage devices that do not require a great deal of special care. However, you should remember some things about using them. Diskettes are made of Mylar and use a magnetic field to store data. Therefore, a few precautions should be taken.

Don't bend or try to fold the diskette.

Don't store the diskette in extreme temperatures or expose it to direct sunlight.

Store diskettes in a vertical position.

Don't turn the power to the computer off while the diskette is in the disk drive. The directory might be destroyed, or a file might be left without a necessary end-marker.

Don't lay the diskette on the television or on an appliance that creates a magnetic field, because the data will be destroyed.

Don't use magnets to secure diskettes to a bulletin board (don't laugh—this has been done, and with disastrous consequences!).

Avoid touching the disk surface with your fingers.

Clean the head of the disk drive regularly to remove oxide buildup, which can interfere with the operation of the disk drive.

Don't expose the disk to static electricity, which can be caused by a combination of dry air and carpeting, because the data might be destroyed.

SOURCE: Jerry Keith, "Understanding Hard and Floppy Disks," *Peripherals, Etc.*, August 1983, pp. 18–21.

A single-sided (SS) diskette can store data on one side only. Both sides of a double-sided (DS) diskette can be used. The abbreviations for density and number of sides are commonly combined to describe a diskette. For example, SS/SD refers to a single-sided, single-density diskette, and DS/DD refers to a double-sided, double-density diskette. The most commonly used combinations are the SS/DD diskette, which provides 143 Kbytes for the Apple II series, and the DS/DD diskette, which provides 360 Kbytes for the IBM PC and compatibles. In 1984, IBM introduced its PC/AT with disk drives that use high-density diskettes which store up to 1.2 Mbytes of data.

Each storage capacity mentioned above is *unformatted*. In other words, the listed amount of storage does not take into account the storage space used during formatting for directory information. An unformatted 250K disk is often reduced to 230K after it is formatted.

Micro-Floppies The newest innovation in secondary storage for personal computers is the micro-floppy disk. The micro-floppy can be 4 inches in diameter and smaller. The micro-floppy is not really flexible because it is contained within a hard plastic cartridge with an automatic shutter that closes over the disk surface when it is removed from the drive. Micro-floppy density designations can vary from 400 Kbytes to 1 Mbyte.

The micro-floppy can be carried in a shirt pocket or handbag and is protected from the environment by its plastic shell. Its portability and high storage capacity give the micro-floppy some advantages over the standard $5\frac{1}{4}$ inch mini-floppy.

Hard Disks

"There is never enough storage." Personal computer users have said that for at least 10 years! Certainly that statement is true for someone who tries to use a floppy disk for a large-scale business application. Current state of the art in spreadsheets, data base management systems, and integrated systems has pushed floppies to their limits. The increasing complexity of the software requires additional storage space, and larger problems are solved every day using these packages. In many instances, problems that at one time could only be solved on mainframes are now solved on personal computers, but multiple floppies must be used to handle the storage requirements of these sophisticated problems. The user must switch floppies in and out as needed by the package. Obviously, growing storage requirements are a real problem.

To meet this increased need for secondary storage, the hard disk has been developed. The **hard disk**—or "Winchester," as it is also called—is similar to the disk packs used by mainframes. It is metallic rather than plastic and can rotate at the high speeds associated with disk packs.

"WINCHESTER"
The 30-30 Hard Disk

Many theories try to explain why a hard disk is referred to as a "Winchester" hard disk. The most likely reason is in the design of the first IBM hard disk in 1973. The first hard disk had two platters, or disks, each of which held 30 Mbytes. Hence, it was a 30 + 30 Mbyte drive. This storage capacity led designers to refer to the hard disk as a "30-30," which in turn reminded someone of the famous Winchester 30.30 rifle. Eventually, the Winchester nickname was applied to the first hard disk. The name has since been applied to any brand of hard disk.

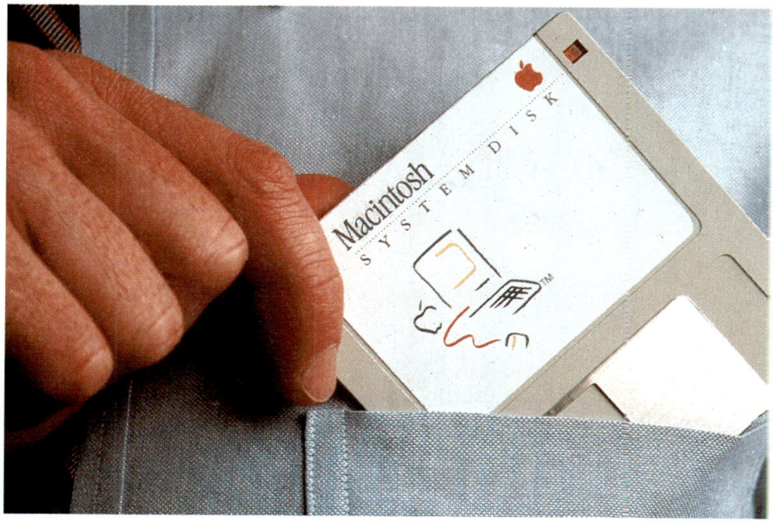

The smallest diskette is the $3\frac{1}{2}$ inch micro-floppy (left), which is becoming popular due to its portability and protective plastic casing. Hard disks—such as the one assembled here at right—can greatly increase the secondary storage capacity of a personal computer.

The differences between a hard disk for a personal computer and a disk pack for a mainframe are size, number of platters, and the manner in which each is enclosed. A hard disk is usually $5\frac{1}{4}$ inches in diameter versus 14 inches for a disk pack, and it has only one or two platters compared with 11 for a disk pack. The hard disk and its drive are usually built into the personal computer with an air filtration and movement system, whereas a disk pack depends on a special drive and a special environment. Because the hard disk and drive are enclosed, they can be used in non-air conditioned environments that would cause a disk pack to crash. Compared with floppy disks, the data or software

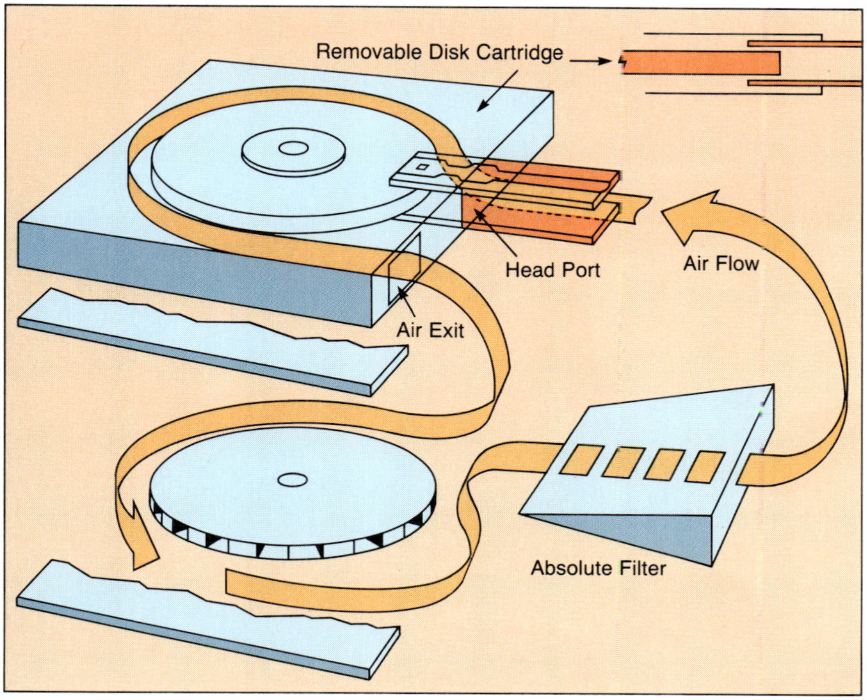

FIGURE 8-12
Air Circulation in a Hard Disk

on hard disks can be accessed 2–10 times faster, and the storage increases from less than 1 Mbyte to 10 (or more) Mbytes.

To rotate at 3,600 rpm, a hard disk must use a flying head and be sealed in a protected environment to keep dust, smoke, and hair out of the drive. Figure 8-12 shows how a hard disk circulates air. For this reason, most hard disk systems are not removable from their drives. Some removable hard disk cartridges are available on the market, but so far, their percentage of the market is quite small.

BACKUPS

In the use of secondary storage, the concept of **backup** is extremely important. Whether magnetic tape or disk is used, some alternate form of storage should be available with a current copy of the material in secondary storage. In a mainframe environment, a tape backup is often made daily of the disk packs that contain user secondary storage. If a tape drive is not available, then a second disk pack may be used. If a backup does not exist and the system disk pack crashes, the data on the disk pack are probably not recoverable (and suicide may seem like a viable alternative!).

Backups of magnetic tape are commonly made and then stored in a different building from the primary tape library. Although a tape does not "crash," it can eventually be unreadable due to everyday wear-and-tear. A backup can help a user avoid the pain and suffering of reading individual files from a worn-out tape.

Backup for Personal Computers

Backup is just as important with a personal computer as it is with a mainframe. The difference is that a computer center does not perform the daily backup procedures. Consequently, the user must make periodic backups for programs. The failure to backup information on a personal computer has the same effect, but on a smaller scale, as the failure to backup a disk or tape on a mainframe. In this section, we discuss backup procedures for personal computers.

Backup for hard disks on personal computers is extremely important because of the large amount of data stored there. Cartridge tape is an increasingly popular form of backup.

TRUE CONFESSION

Failing to Backup a Disk

It's time for a first-hand report on what can happen when the common-sense rule of backing up data at least once a day is not followed. This textbook was written from the keyboard of a personal computer using a word processing package, and each chapter was stored on disk with a second disk used as a backup. However, because of a failure to backup my work at the end of a day, I had to rewrite the first 20 pages of Chapter 2 of this book.

I wrote 13 pages of Chapter 2 late one night, and because I was tired, I decided to backup the material the next day. Naturally, by morning I forgot about backing up the chapter and wrote additional pages for the chapter. After I had completed page 20 of the manuscript, the power in my office went off for less than a second. My trusty computer reacted as if it had been turned off and on again—the contents of the word processing file that held all the Chapter 2 material were dumped. With no backup, I was forced to start over again from scratch! Needless to say, until I finished writing the textbook, I performed backup procedures every night—and several times during the day—after I had written several pages of manuscript.

For secondary storage on cassette tapes, the suggested backup procedure is to save each file on tape in three places. First, the file is written onto the cassette tape for future use. The user sends a command to the computer to send the needed file currently in internal memory to the cassette tape, where it is named and stored. Second, the file is saved on the same cassette tape as the first, but a different name is given to the file to distinguish the *working copy* of the file from the *backup copy* of the file. Third, the file is saved on an entirely different tape using the same name as the backup copy. As a result, if the working copy is unreadable on the cassette tape, the user simply moves to the next file on the same tape, which is the backup copy. If the original cassette containing the working and backup copies is unreadable, the backup copy can be read from the second tape.

For backup using disk secondary storage, most personal computer systems have a procedure for copying the contents of an entire disk to a backup disk. Using this approach, the simplest backup system consists of a working copy of a disk and a backup copy. However, a second backup copy should also be made, because a power surge or blackout could catch both the working copy and the backup copy in the machine at the same time. If a second backup does not exist, the data on both the working copy and the only backup copy could be lost.

In a business setting, a definite policy on backups is needed, including a **backup hierarchy**, in which three or four disks are rotated and the oldest disk becomes the new master disk after each backup. This policy is similar to the use of a second backup, except that the third and fourth backups do not always contain the most recent copy of the material. However, they do provide a margin of safety if both the working copy and the backup copy are lost. A hard (printed) copy of the latest version of the data or program should always be kept in case *all* the disks are lost at the same time. In this case, the information could still be keyed in from the keyboard.

Backing up a hard disk is complicated by the fact that most hard disks cannot be removed from a personal computer. They are sealed inside their drives to keep dust and smoke away from the read/write head. Backing up a hard disk requires a separate recording device. The least expensive method of backing up a hard disk is to use the floppy disk drive that accompanies most hard disk drives on personal computers. This approach works well if only a few files or documents must be copied at each session. However, if many large data or program files are involved, using floppy disks for backup is impractical.

Several new devices are available to meet the need for a backup device for hard disks that does not require the time and effort of floppy disks. One popular backup device is **streaming tape**, which uses a special, high-density recording tape that "streams" by the tape head at high speed as the information on the disk is output in a continuous flow. These streaming tape devices usually come in cartridges that can be swapped in and out of the tape drive. With streaming tape, the contents of a 5-Mbyte hard disk can be copied in about 4 minutes. Another innovative method of backing up a hard disk is to use video tape as a storage medium. The hard disk is connected to a video cassette recorder, and a copy of the data is placed on the video disk. The use of new removable Winchester hard disk cartridges is also increasing.

OTHER SECONDARY STORAGE DEVICES

In addition to magnetic tape and magnetic disk storage, other secondary storage devices are available that use different technology. These devices include mass storage, video disks, and memory cards. Disk storage can also be used to increase apparent internal memory. In this section, we briefly discuss each device or technique.

Mass Storage

A form of secondary storage that combines the high-volume storage capabilities of tape with the speed of disk is commonly referred to as **mass storage**. (This term is also used in place of secondary storage in some situations.) Mass storage, which is used in some mainframe installations, is a cartridge that uses magnetic tape as the storage medium. However, instead of being stored in a tape library, the cartridges are stored in a honeycomb-shaped storage area. Information retrieval is handled by a mechanical device that is directed by the CPU to find and load a given cartridge. The device moves along the honeycomb storage area until the correct storage location is found. The cartridge is then removed from storage, loaded on a special tape drive, and the contents are read into memory. On the IBM 3850 Mass Storage System, this process takes about 10 seconds. Although this procedure takes much longer than retrieval from a disk pack, it is much quicker than retrieval from reel-to-reel tape. Mass storage is also less expensive than disk and takes up much less space than tape.

Video Disks

One of the most exciting recent developments in secondary storage is the **video disk**. Information is stored on this shiny record-sized platter by burning pits into the surface using a laser light beam. The information is then read from the video disk by another laser in a video disk player. A typical video disk can record 108,000 individual video scenes with a much higher quality than a video cassette recorder. These scenes can be pages of a telephone directory; pages from a retail catalog; pictures meant to amuse and inform, such as at Walt Disney World's EPCOT Center; or training devices for soldiers or technicians to learn the operation of a sophisticated weapon or machine. If

Optical disks, shown here during the manufacturing process, can hold as much data as 2,000 floppy disks.

Using video disk technology, the National Gallery of Art can store still frames of 1,645 of its paintings and sculptures.

information is stored in a digital form, a video disk's storage capacity can exceed 1 gigabyte (1 *billion* bytes).

Currently, the primary shortcoming of a video disk is its read-only restriction. Information burned into a video disk cannot be erased, because the pits in the disk's surface cannot be changed. However, video disk makers in Japan indicate that this shortcoming may be rectified with the release of erasable video disks. These new disks use a technology which causes pools of metal to form on the surface of the disk in place of the pits burned into the surface. If this technology can be refined to the point where such storage is economically feasible for consumers, it could mean the availability of almost unlimited secondary storage.

Memory Cards

The smallest form of secondary storage is the **memory card**, a plastic card or key on which information can be stored. The following three forms of memory cards are currently in use:

1. A card containing a microchip that records and outputs financial information.

After a few years, it [optical disk storage] will just explode, and it will be a standard device on every personal computer because you can store such huge amounts of data.

Steve Wozniak, co-founder of Apple Computers

(As quoted in "What's Next? Computer Explosion in Schools," *USA Today,* January 23, 1985, p. 2B.)

2. A card with a special coating on which information can be encoded.
3. A fat key with a nonvolatile semiconductor embedded in it.

The cards and key are used most often for electronic funds transfer (EFT). For example, in Italy, a memory card with a semiconductor memory can pay for phone calls from a pay phone. The consumer buys a memory card that has some amount of credit stored on it. As calls are made using the card, amounts are deducted from the card's credit bank until no more credit exists.

The highest volume of information can be stored on a read-only optical stripe, which could be used to play back information. The optical stripe can store 2 Mbytes of information, compared with semiconductor memory that is limited to 16 Kbytes of information. These storage capacities are small compared with disk storage, but the portability of memory cards is extremely useful.

Virtual Memory

Virtual memory uses a disk drive to give the appearance of increased internal memory. Sections of memory are stored on a high-speed secondary storage device, such as a hard disk. RAM then contains only the section of memory that is actually needed. The section brought into RAM is a "window" to the total memory stored on the disk. The sections of memory in RAM are called **pages**; the memory stored on disk—virtual memory—is divided into the same size pages. When the CPU needs a section of memory, a page is simply swapped between the disk drive and RAM, appearing to create a much larger internal memory.

The CPU accesses virtual memory differently from the way it accesses RAM. The CPU first contacts the **virtual memory controller (VMC)** to determine where the needed information currently resides. If the needed information is in RAM, then the CPU accesses the memory in the normal fashion. Otherwise, the VMC makes the needed page of memory available for the CPU to access. Virtual memory allows mainframe computers to have enough RAM to handle the many users and functions that mainframes support. Some personal computers use virtual memory, but the ease with which RAM is currently increased may make it less desirable on the small computers.

REVIEW OF KEY POINTS

- Secondary storage is necessary because internal memory is both limited in size and volatile.
- The two most popular means of secondary storage are magnetic tape and magnetic disk.
- Magnetic tape is available in three forms—reel-to-reel (used primarily for mainframes), cartridge, and cassette.
- Reel-to-reel and cartridge tapes store information using a magnetized bit pattern on the tape, whereas cassette tapes store information using audio tones.
- Magnetic disks are available as disk packs, floppy disks, or hard disks. Disk packs use multiple disks for storing information from mainframes.
- Floppy disks come in three sizes—standard floppy, mini-floppy, and micro-floppy. Storage amounts of each type of floppy disk depend on size and format.
- When working on a mainframe, minicomputer, or personal computer with either tape or disk, backing up (making an extra copy of) data is very important.
- Mass storage, video disks, and memory cards are three forms of storage that serve different purposes.
- Using disk storage, virtual memory seems to increase internal memory capacity.

KEY TERMS

backup
backup hierarchy
blocked records
bytes per inch (bpi)
cartridge tape
cassette tape
cylinder
data file
density
direct access file
direct access storage devices (DASD)
diskette
disk operating system (DOS)
disk packs
fields
file
fixed length record
floppy disk
formatted
hard disk
hard sectored
head crash
head window
hub ring
index hole
interblock gap (IBG)
logical records
magnetic disk
magnetic (mag) tape
mass storage
memory card
micro-floppy
mini-floppy
pages
parallel storage device
parity bit
physical record
program file
read/write head
records
reel-to-reel magnetic tape
rotational delay time
secondary storage
sectors
seek time
sequential access file
sequential access storage device
serial storage devices
soft sectoring
standard floppy
streaming tape
tape drive
tracks
transmission time
unblocked records
variable length records
video disk
virtual memory
virtual memory controller (VMC)
write-protect notch

REVIEW QUESTIONS

1. Give the two reasons why secondary storage is necessary for either a mainframe or a personal computer.
2. Explain the field-record-file relationship. What is the difference between a sequential access file and a direct access file?
3. Explain the difference between blocked records and unblocked records. How do they relate to physical records and logical records?
4. What does a parity bit do on a nine-track tape? What is the difference between odd and even parity?
5. In addition to physical size and the mechanism that moves the tape past the read/write head, how is reel-to-reel tape different from cassette tape?
6. If each disk of a disk pack has 200 tracks, how many cylinders are on the disk pack?
7. Explain the difference between the cylinder and sector methods of disk storage.
8. What is the difference between a SS/DD disk and a DS/SD disk?
9. Why is backup an important procedure for personal computer users? Do hard disk users need to back up as much as floppy disk users?
10. Explain the difference between a video disk and mass storage.

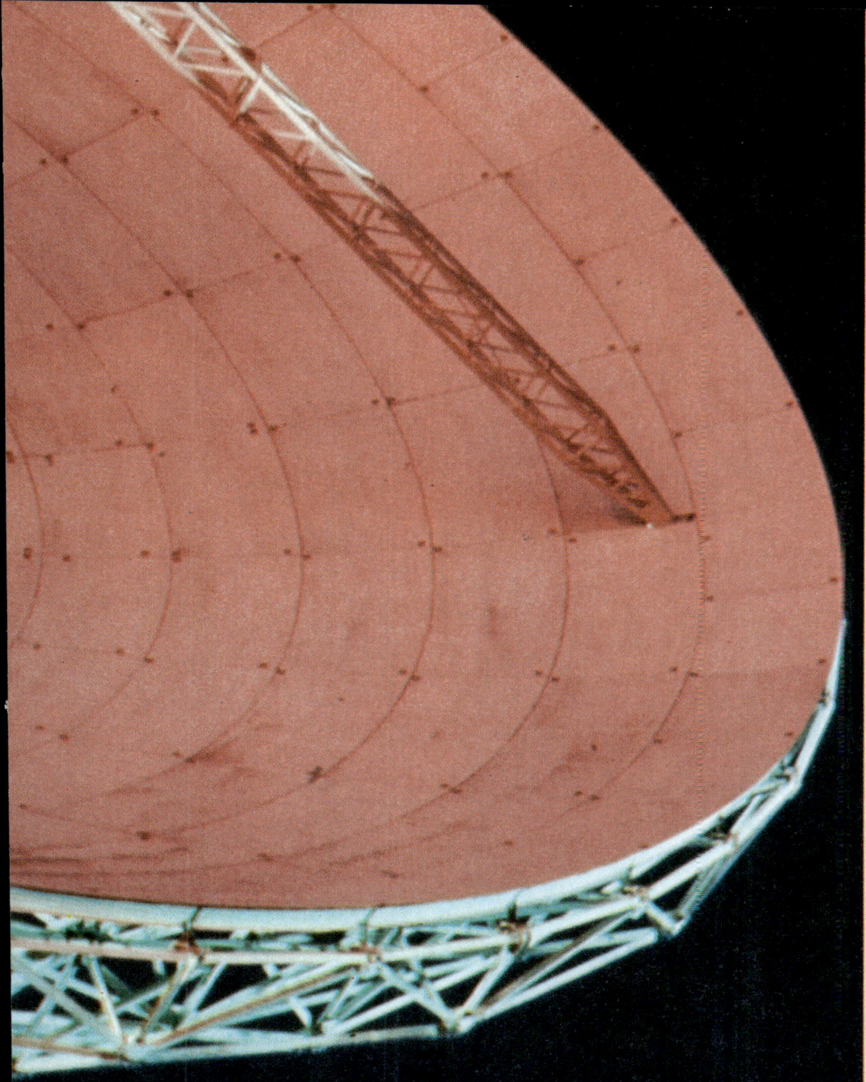

Block 3

SOFTWARE PACKAGES

Chapter 3 introduced the topics of software packages and programming. That discussion included the three types of software used for computers—systems software, utility software, and applications software. Block 3 continues that discussion by covering operating systems and utility software in more detail. We also introduce the particular terminology of software packages, followed by discussions of six important types of software packages for computers.

Chapter 9 introduces software packages and covers both mainframe and personal computer operating systems. Chapters 10–13 cover software packages for word processing, graphics, accounting (both business and personal), financial analysis (spreadsheets), data base management, and telecommunications. Each chapter also presents a tutorial explaining each software package that accompanies this text.

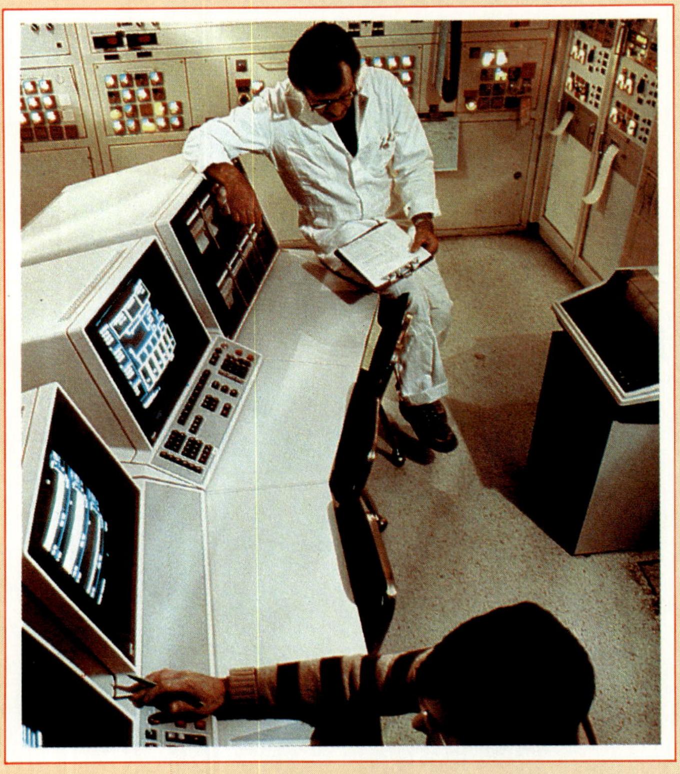

This chapter presents an overview of the types of software packages and their uses on mainframes and personal computers. It includes a discussion of why software packages are important, as well as a presentation of the terminology of software packages. General coverage of operating systems for computers is followed by specific discussions of operating systems for mainframes and personal computers. Each system is discussed in detail, including the hardware that is compatible with each system. The concept of operating systems that run on only one type of computer is covered. Finally, material on the use of integrated packages on personal computers is presented.

9

An Overview of Software Packages and Operating Systems

STUDY OBJECTIVES

After reading this chapter, you should be able to

- Understand the importance of software packages.
- Explain the terminology of software packages and recognize the different types of command structures in those packages.
- Understand the functions of operating systems on all types of computers.
- Recognize differences in operating systems for mainframes and for personal computers.
- Name four commonly used personal computer operating systems and explain their differences.
- Discuss the most popular proprietary operating systems for personal computers.
- Understand the concept of integrated packages and windows.

USING SOFTWARE PACKAGES

During the computer's first 30 years, using a computer almost always meant programming a computer. **Programming** involves writing a series of instructions for the computer to follow in performing some specific task. However, since the late 1970s, the growth of personal computer use has caused a tremendous increase in the use of software packages written to perform specific tasks. (Examples of these packages were highlighted in Chapter 3.) A **software package** includes a commercially prepared program and a written description, called the **documentation** of the program. Software packages have been available for mainframe computers since the early 1960s. The time line in Figure 9-1 shows that mainframe software packages were first introduced in the early 1960s and that personal computer software packages were first introduced in the late 1970s.

Software packages are quite popular, whether for use on mainframes, minicomputers, or personal computers. Why are packages used so often? The answer is very simple. They save time and effort and allow the user to interact with the computer without having to program it. Many situations still call for programming knowledge, but often the problem at hand has already been solved and programmed into a software package. Writing computer programs is a skill that must be learned and then practiced often by a computer user.

FIGURE 9-1
Software Package Time Line

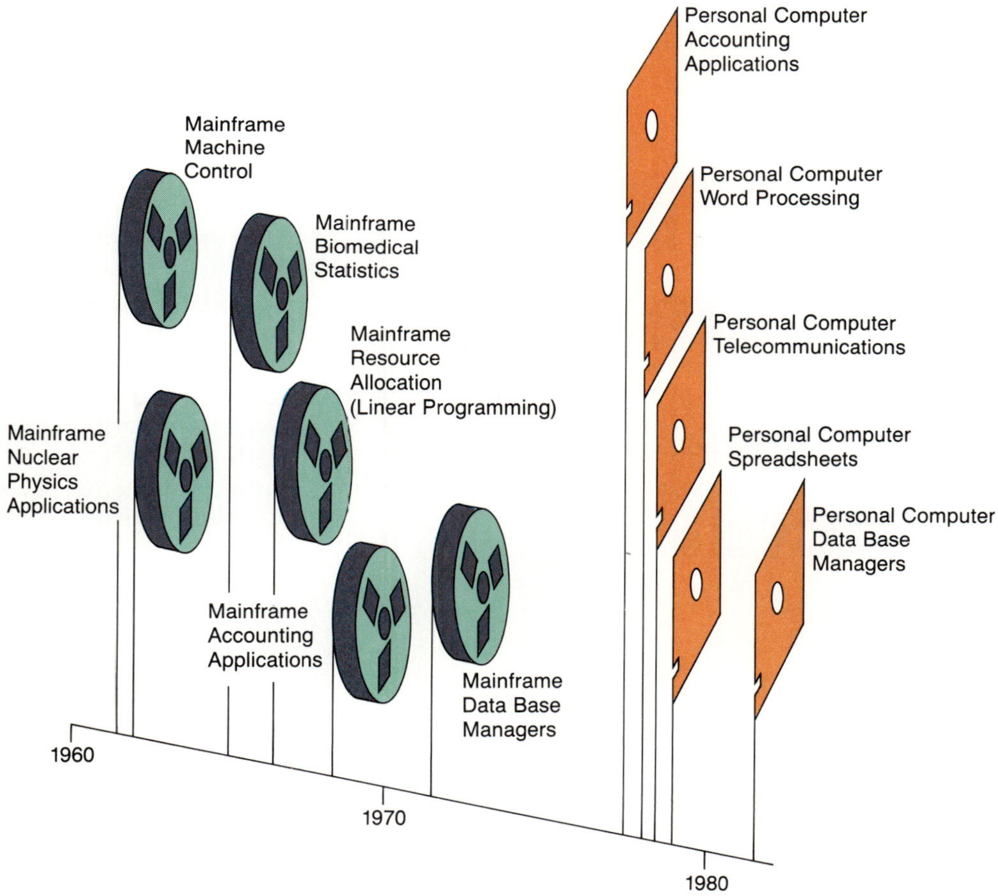

Without software, the computer—either a mainframe or a personal computer—can do nothing.

Even then, a user may not be able to write programs that work as well as the professionally written programs in software packages.

Mainframe Packages Versus Personal Computer Packages

Over the last few years, the media—including newspapers, magazines, and television—have increased their discussions of computer use, especially the use of various software packages for personal computers. Because most personal computer software is sold to individuals, a great deal of media advertising is devoted to personal computer software rather than to mainframe software. This fact does not mean that the use of mainframe software is declining. On the contrary, dollar sales of mainframe software sold mostly to large organizations each year far exceeds that of personal computer software sold to businesses and individuals.

Except for language compilers that allow the same language to be used on different computers and some scientific packages, few generic software packages are available for mainframes. In other words, packages written for one type of machine may or may not run on a different brand of computer. Vendors have developed hardware that makes an Apple personal computer work like an IBM, and vice versa, but the same cannot be said for mainframes. As a result, mainframe software is usually developed only for a particular type of machine. If an organization owns one manufacturer's machine, it can purchase only software for that manufacturer's machine.

Software Package Terminology

The widespread use of computer packages has spawned a new software package terminology. One overused term in reference to computer packages (and to computers in general) is *user friendly*. A **user friendly** package is easy to use. Unfortunately, several packages that are advertised as "user friendly" are really quite difficult to use because of their complexity. Often, sophisticated packages cannot be totally "user friendly," because they are designed to solve complicated problems. The large number of classes available in the use of advanced software packages demonstrates the need for more than a few hours of personal study or classroom instruction to use them.

Software packages can be classified as batch or interactive packages. In a **batch package**, all the data are submitted in a batch at one time. On the other hand, in an **interactive package**, data are entered individually or in groups as the user interacts with the package. Batch packages are used quite often on mainframes to handle problems involving large amounts of data. The data may be input from a data file on disk, tape, or punched card. Resource allocation (that is, linear programming), payroll, and statistics packages are examples of batch packages available for mainframes and personal computers. When the volume of data is not large, an interactive package is useful. For example, the user may wish to change the data or the assumptions underlying the problem being solved while he or she enters the data. Spreadsheet and home accounting packages for personal computers and many instructional packages on mainframes are interactive packages.

Software packages are also classified according to how data and commands are entered. One input method uses a **menu**, which gives the user either a list of commands from which to choose or requests that a particular form of data be entered. A package that uses a menu is **menu driven**. An example of a menu from the software packages that accompany this text is shown in Figure 9-2. In this menu, the user selects the needed package from among the six that are offered. The user enters the number corresponding to the desired package to access that package. This type of selection mechanism—that is, entering a number—is a common method of choosing from a menu.

Batch packages are associated with magnetic tape and punched cards. On a mainframe computer system (left), software programs and data are often stored on tape until requested by a user. Data on punched cards are entered into a computer and processed by the software at one time (right).

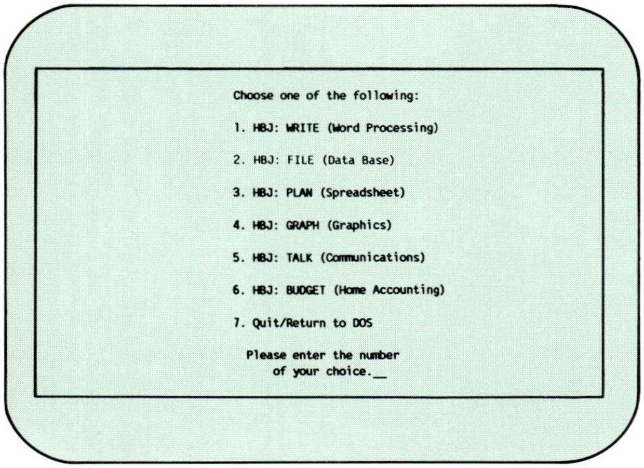

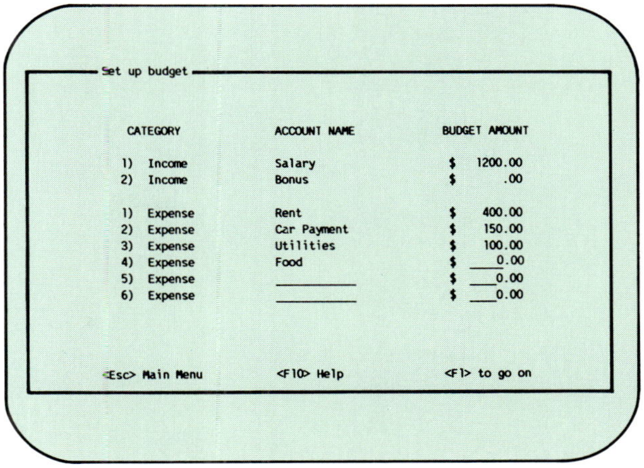

FIGURE 9-2 (left)
Example of Menu Selection

FIGURE 9-3 (right)
Entering Data on a Menu-Driven Package

Another commonly used method to select from a menu is to position the cursor over the selection and press the ENTER key. In Figure 9-2, if the user selects 1, then the word processing package is accessed. Similarly, if 5 is selected, the telecommunications package is accessed.

In many cases, the user not only selects from a menu, but he or she is also asked to enter a file name or specific data. For example, the menu for a home accounting package may request the user to enter the amounts budgeted for various items. Figure 9-3 shows such a menu for the home accounting package—HBJ: BUDGET—that accompanies this book. In the figure, the user has already filled in part of the information, but other data must still be entered.

If a software package is not menu driven, it is probably command driven. A **command-driven** package does not request commands or data. It simply waits for the user to input the appropriate commands or data. Therefore, the user must learn the necessary commands by reading the package documentation. Batch packages are usually command driven, and the instructions for running the package are given in a group along with the data. Interactive packages that do not "lead" the user through the package are also command driven. These packages expect the user to know what command to enter at any point in the package execution. Financial analysis (spreadsheet) packages and data base management packages on personal computers are often command-driven packages. The spreadsheet form shown in Figure 9-4 is part of a command-driven package. The spreadsheet form appears on the screen, and a wide cursor shows where the commands or data should be input. The user either makes an entry in this location or moves the cursor to another location to enter data or a formula.

The advantages and disadvantages of menu-driven packages and command-driven packages seem to trade off; that is, an apparent advantage for one is a disadvantage for the other. The advantage of a menu-driven package is that the user need not learn a series of commands before using the package. The user merely answers a series of questions to implement the package and to input data. However, once the user learns the commands for the package, it is bothersome to wait for the package to present the questions before entering the commands and data. On the other hand, a command-driven program can be difficult for a novice user, because he or she must know the proper commands and the appropriate spot on the screen to enter

We think that there are clearly two identifiable users. The first one is what we call the power user, someone who works with the computer at least several hours a day. The computer literally is an integral tool in the way that person makes a living. There's another class of user, however, we believe says, "I don't need to use a personal computer, but if it really improves my productivity by a factor of 10 to 1, or 100 to 1, and it's not too hard to learn, then I'll buy it."

Fred Gibbons, President of Software Publishing Corporation
(As quoted in "Slippery Pole of Software Success," *Personal Computing,* May 1985, p. 106.)

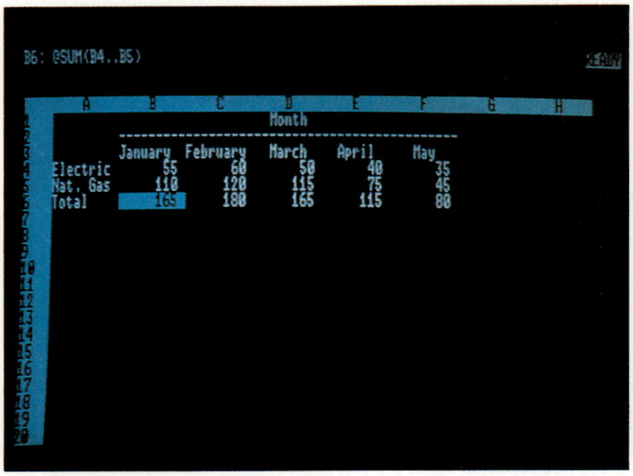

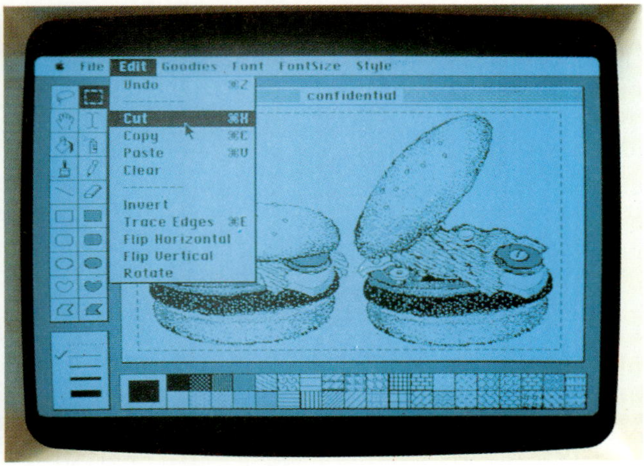

FIGURE 9-4 (left)
Example of Command-Driven Package Spreadsheet

FIGURE 9-5 (right)
A Pull-Down Menu

them. However, once the data format and list of commands for the command-driven package are learned, data or commands are quickly entered.

Sometimes, a software package is both a menu-driven package and a command-driven package. This type of package presents some of the commands that must be used on a menu; other commands are entered by the user. New spreadsheet packages often handle command entry this way. The package may also reduce the amount of menu shown as the user becomes more familiar with the package. As a result, the user can eventually enter commands without waiting for the package to show the options.

A variation of the menu form of command and data entry is available for some computers. The **pull-down menu** uses **icons** or pictures of the functions. With a mouse, the user moves the cursor to the desired function icon and presses a button on the mouse. The box containing the picture of the function expands to present a second menu of more detailed choices from which a selection is made. With a little practice, choices from the menu to enter commands can be made very quickly. Figure 9-5 shows a typical pull-down menu. Another type of menu-driven package is used with a touch screen. The user selects a command by touching the screen. Special software is necessary to make both the pull-down and touch screen menu packages work.

Learning to Use a Package

Learning to use a computer software package can be either a fun or a disastrous experience, depending on several factors. Such factors include the quality of the software, the quality of the instructions that come with the software, and the knowledge of support personnel. If all these factors are good, then learning to use the software should be fairly easy. On the other hand, if one or more of these factors are poor, then the user may expend a great deal of effort to achieve the software's objective. Although we cannot know in advance whether software is bad or good, we can discuss the quality of instruction and support for mainframe and personal computer software.

A mainframe package is actually stored on disk or tape at the computer center. To use the package, the user must first determine the necessary instructions to access the package. An instruction manual is usually available from the documentation library at the computer center. Additional manuals demonstrate the major points of the package with examples or tutorial brochures. The computer center that houses the mainframe computer usually has a **support staff** that can answer questions on the use of a particular package. If the center does not support, or answer questions about, the particular package, someone in the organization has probably used the package and can answer questions for a beginning user.

Personal computer packages are usually available on floppy disks. The user must determine both how to *install* the package and how to use the package once it is installed. Installing a package usually involves following a few directions to ensure that it matches the type of computer in use. To use the package, the user must learn a series of commands much like those for a mainframe package. A description of the package and the necessary commands are found in one or more documentation manuals. The quality of these manuals is an important factor in the selection of a software package. Some packages may include a demonstration disk or a tutorial disk, or both. The **demonstration disk** contains actual examples from the package that

No company today has software that I would call user friendly.

Gary Kildall, inventor of CP/M, Founder and Chairman of Digital Research

(As quoted in "Gary Kildall on Systems, Applications and User Software," *Personal Computing,* December 1982, pp. 39–46).

ANOTHER VIEW

John Imlay

Management Science America (MSA) is the largest independent developer of software for mainframe computers and for the microcomputer-to-mainframe linkage. Founded in 1961, MSA employs over 2,000 people worldwide. John Imlay is the Chairman of MSA and, as a past president of the Association of Data Processing Service Organizations (ADAPSO), is a spokesman for the computer industry. Imlay and MSA were among the first to develop the concept of an applications computer package that is usable in more than one situation or location. In an interview, Imlay talked about software.

How do you see software fitting into the entire computer market?

IMLAY: To understand the importance of software, you have to remember that it used to be that you bought a computer first and then bought software. Now, a computer user first selects the applications for a computer, then selects the software that best suits those applications, and only then does he or she purchase a computer that will run that software. For this reason, the software people are the driving force in the computer market and are at the leading edge of computer developments.

People are coming to understand that computing power itself is becoming a commodity, and the keys to this commodity are companies such as MSA that are developing applications software that provides results. The attitudes toward the computer are themselves changing. At one time, the computer was viewed as a service to handle the payroll or inventory. Now, people are realizing that it is becoming the competitive edge that makes a company successful.

John Imlay is the chairman of Management Science America, the largest independent developer of software for mainframe computers.

the user can study or modify while learning about the package. A **tutorial disk** provides the user with an on-disk step-by-step tutorial on the use of the package. The presence of either a demonstration disk or a tutorial disk in a software package usually helps make the package easy to learn.

Many software companies offer users a toll-free number to call with questions. The presence of such a number is a further aid to using the package.

THE OPERATING SYSTEM

People have described the computer's operating system as a "traffic cop," "office manager," "nervous system," and the "computer–user interface." The **operating system** is actually a collection of software programs that manages the tasks that are going on concurrently in a mainframe, a minicomputer, or a personal computer. For example, the operating system monitors the keyboard to determine when a key is pressed to provide input to the computer. It also manages the video screen and printer to provide output from the computer. The operating system also controls the transfer of data back and forth between secondary storage and internal memory. The operating system of a mainframe or minicomputer is responsible for tasks that do not exist on a personal computer. A mainframe or minicomputer operating system manages many hardware sites and terminals and ensures that users have the proper identification to access the computer. A mainframe operating system also handles the allocation of resources to multiple users. Finally, the operating system for any size computer controls the execution of application programs.

Personal computer operating systems usually support only one user at a time.

The operating system for a mainframe differs from a personal computer operating system primarily in the number of users and the complexity of the peripheral devices. Mainframes usually are multi-user machines, whereas most personal computers are single-user machines. (However, a few multiple-user personal computer systems are now available.) Mainframes must manage a large number of disk and tape drives, input devices, and printers, but a personal computer system usually has only one or two disk drives and a printer. Because of these differences, mainframe operating systems are extremely large programs that require a staff of systems programmers to maintain them. Personal computer operating systems are less complex and should operate without any day-to-day maintenance.

Mainframe operating systems are *proprietary;* that is, they only work on one variety of machine. *Generic* personal computer operating systems run on different types of personal computers. Some personal computers can even run multiple operating systems to take advantage of a larger variety of software. Proprietary operating systems for personal computers still exist, but the trend is toward the use of generic systems.

Functions of the Operating System

In Chapter 3, we depicted the operating system as the core of an onion, with layers of utility software and applications software. The operating system is the core of the "onion" because it is the least visible form of computer software. It can require many commands, but it does not require data. The only visible output from an operating system is the error message shown on the screen when an error occurs. Although invisible, the operating system is crucial to the operation of the computer.

The functions of the operating system can be summarized as follows:

- Provides an interface between the user and the computer.
- Schedules an efficient use of the CPU and eliminates the need for human intervention.
- Manages data and files, making them available as needed, and provides security to multiple users.
- Executes other computer programs.
- Manages peripheral devices such as printers, disk drives, and tape drives.

IT ALL BEGAN WITH VISICALC

The introduction of the VisiCalc software package was a momentous event in the history of the personal computer. Finally, the public knew that the personal computer could indeed be a "mind tool" that made work easier. VisiCalc users were relieved of the drudgery of recalculating by hand the many values in budgeting and forecasting tables because the software performed the calculations. For example, in a yearly budget prepared in tabular form, called a spreadsheet, with months across the top and categories down the side, various row and column values were calculated by hand. VisiCalc allowed a user to enter the values once, tell the package what formulas to use to make the calculations, and then let the computer do the work. If one value changed, the entire spreadsheet did *not* have to be recalculated by hand; rather, the user entered the changed value and VisiCalc made the necessary recalculations. This idea was so revolutionary that 200,000 copies of VisiCalc were sold in its first two years on the market. Because VisiCalc was initially available only on the Apple II computer, it is also credited with selling approximately 20,000 of these machines.

The history of VisiCalc is a classic story of one person trying to make a task easier. In 1978, Dan Bricklin was an MBA student at Harvard. Harvard's MBA program is taught using the case method, which involves using spreadsheets. Bricklin decided that spreadsheet calculations could be computerized. Even though a Harvard professor told him the idea would never work, Bricklin enlisted the aid of MIT student Bob Frankston to program the project. They named the finished product VisiCalc for VISIble CALCulator. Another Harvard MBA student, Dan Fylstra, marketed the finished product.

VisiCalc could be considered the "grandfather" of spreadsheets compared with today's new and more powerful spreadsheets. However, the package still does the job for which it was designed. FlashCalc, an advanced version of VisiCalc, is now available, along with related graphing and filing packages. This is one grandfather that continues to work just fine!

J4 (V) +I4*(1+C3) CA 82

	A	B	F	G	H	I	J
1							
2		January	May	June	July	August	September
3							
4	San Juan	33	94.2513	122.52669	159.28470	207.07011	269.19114
5	Santa Fe	563	1607.9843	2090.3796	2717.4935	3532.7415	4592.5640
6	Puerto Rico	234	1314.144	1576.9728	2050.0646	3075.0970	4920.1551
7	Burbank	6	33.696	40.4352	52.56576	78.84864	126.15782
8	Milpitas	3	16.848	20.2176	26.28288	39.42432	63.078912
9	Inglewood	3	16.848	20.2176	26.28288	39.42432	63.078912
10	Menlo Park	234	1314.144	1576.9728	2050.0646	3075.0970	4920.1551
11	Minsk	34	190.944	229.1328	297.87264	446.80896	714.89434
12	Vancouver	52	292.032	350.4384	455.56992	683.35488	1093.3678
13	Des Moines	24	134.784	161.7408	210.26304	315.39456	504.63130
14	Rapid City	67	376.272	451.5264	586.98432	880.47648	1408.7624
15	Boise	22	123.552	148.2624	192.74112	289.11168	462.57869
16	Regina	687	3858.192	4629.8304	6018.7795	9028.1693	14445.071
17	Smith Falls	44	247.104	296.5248	385.48224	578.22336	925.15738
18	Tappahannock	12	67.392	80.8704	105.13152	157.69728	252.31565
19	Harrisburg	44	247.104	296.5248	385.48224	578.22336	925.15738
20	Braintree	21	117.936	141.5232	183.98016	275.97024	441.55238

One VisiCalc grandchild is FlashCalc, which has one of the largest spreadsheet templates available.

MAINFRAME OPERATING SYSTEMS

The operating system for a mainframe computer must be able to run multiple jobs concurrently. Here, *concurrently* does not mean *simultaneously,* because the CPU can only work with one set of instructions at a time. Concurrent means that the computer has multiple activities in process at one time, but it alternates among them. From the box on the history of operating systems (p. 205), we know that the first computers could execute jobs only one at a time. Later machines could overlap jobs, and today, they can run jobs concurrently. The effect of this change is seen in Figure 9-6.

In Figure 9-6, CPU1, CPU2, and so on, each designate the job that the CPU is working on at any one time, and I/O-1, I/O-2, and so on, each designate the job that is at the input/output stage at each point in time. For example, with serial execution of jobs, job 1 is input, goes to the CPU, and is then output. After job 1 is output, job 2 is input and the process starts over. For overlapping jobs, job 1 is input, goes to the CPU, and is then output. While job 1 is in the CPU, job 2 is input, and more jobs are executed in a given time period than with serial processing. In the concurrent job execution diagram, the same job may appear in the CPU more than once because it may take multiple accesses to the CPU to finish the job. However, many more jobs can be executed in the same time period than with either serial or overlapping processing.

When a computer runs concurrent jobs, it must manage numerous activities, including accessing disk drives, tape drives, high-speed line printers, user terminals, and centralized and remote batch job entry sites. Because the disk and tape drives are used for secondary storage, they are accessed as needed by the CPU and internal memory. The line printers are used for printed output. The user terminals allow user interaction with the computer, with input coming from a keyboard and output going to a video screen. Because multiple terminals interact with the computer at the same time, the computer must have some way of handling all of the terminals concurrently.

FIGURE 9-6
Serial, Overlapping, and Concurrent Execution of Jobs

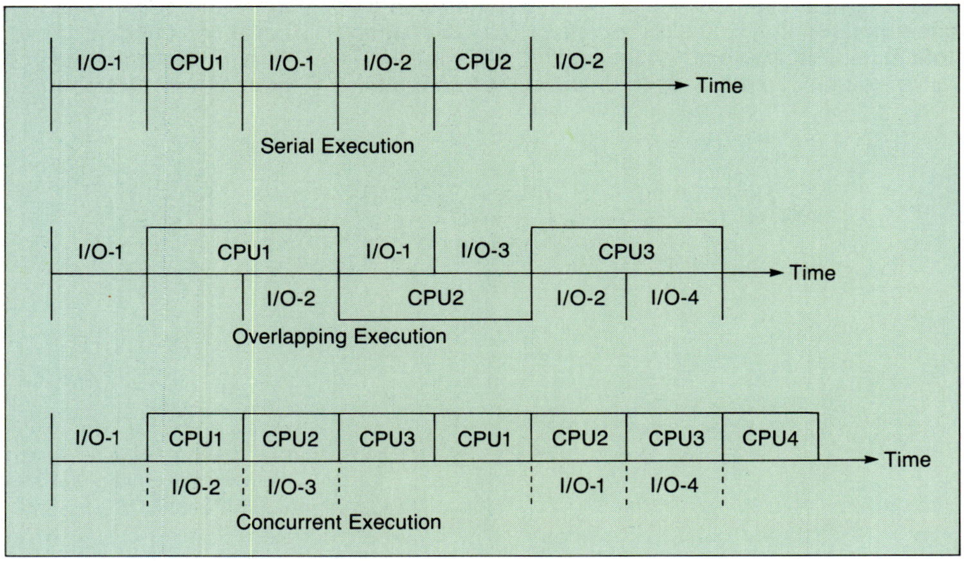

The operating system handles terminals through a procedure known as time sharing. In a **time-sharing system**, a computer gives each active terminal a fraction of a second (usually around 0.002 second) of CPU time. During this time, a portion of a program entered at the terminal is executed. Another terminal is then given its **time-slice**. Because the CPU returns to each terminal three or four times per second and because a great deal of work can be accomplished in a short period of time by modern mainframe CPUs, the user is usually not aware of any delay.

Another method of entering jobs is the **batch mode**, in which an entire job is entered at one time from a card reader, disk drive, or tape drive. Each job is assigned a priority and placed in a queue, or waiting line, to be executed. Multiple batch entry sites are called **remote job entry (RJE)** sites. These sites are *remote* because they are separate from the main computer center, handling job entry through cards or tape. Each RJE site also has a line printer to accept printed output. The CPU can execute several batch jobs concurrently with the jobs entered from the interactive terminals by allocating time-slices to the batch jobs. The Control Data Corporation CYBER 750 mainframe for the University System of Georgia supports over 250 interactive

OPERATING SYSTEMS
A Short History

Before 1960, computers could execute, or "run," only one job at a time. A job included the program and its pertinent data, which were entered into the computer using punched cards, paper tape, or magnetic tape. When one job was completed, a new job could be loaded and run. This process wasted time, because the CPU was idle while each job was entered and the output printed. To avoid wasting CPU time, operating systems were written to allow overlapping and concurrent execution of jobs. Overlapping jobs meant that one job was input, a second was executed, and a third was output, all at the same time. Concurrent jobs were run two or more at a time, because the CPU shared its time between multiple jobs. In other words, the CPU would run a section of one job, then a section of another job, and so on, until the CPU had rotated to all jobs. When one job was completed, a new job would enter the rotation. The CPU was never idle, and it completed a greater number of jobs. These two approaches dramatically increased the amount of work that could be performed by the computer.

The first operating systems were written by computer users, not by computer companies. Because computer companies initially considered themselves hardware vendors only, they were not involved in writing software. However, when companies decided that a particular operating system could enhance computer sales, the user-designed systems were purchased and developed. The first operating system that allowed multiple users and concurrent jobs was the Master Control Program for the Burroughs 5500 series of machines in 1964–1965. This development was followed by the operating system for the IBM 360 series of machines, which, with the addition of virtual memory in 1976 (see p. 209) and other later enhancements, has remained in use since 1966 for IBM mainframes.

The Burroughs 5500 series of computers was the first to accommodate multiple users and concurrent job execution.

terminals and over 30 RJE sites scattered across the state of Georgia. Figure 9-7 shows the various types of devices and terminals that can be handled by a mainframe CPU.

How Does the Operating System Do It?

The operating system for a mainframe obviously spends a large portion of its time supervising the many input, output, and secondary storage devices that are linked to it. The major unit of the operating system is the **supervisor program**. This program remains in internal memory at all times and manages the loading of other parts of the operating system into internal memory as needed. It also supervises the loading of applications programs into internal memory. For example, if the computer is to run a FORTRAN program, the supervisor loads the FORTRAN translator, or **compiler**, into internal memory and then links the compiler and the program together. With only the supervisor program in internal memory while other operating system programs are loaded as needed, the internal memory unit is not overloaded.

The operating system manages the process in which a program written in a high-level language is compiled from a **source code** into an **object code**, which is then executed. In addition to converting the source code into an

FIGURE 9-7
Devices Operating from a Mainframe

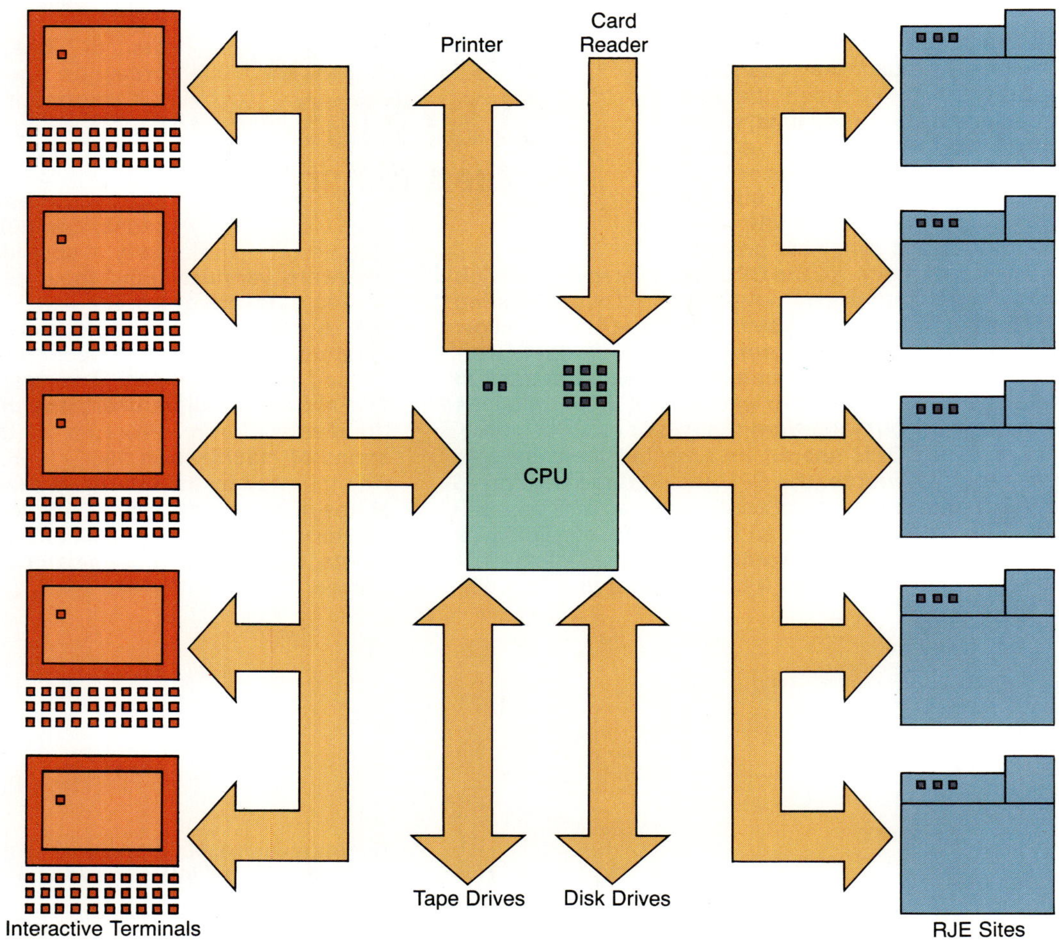

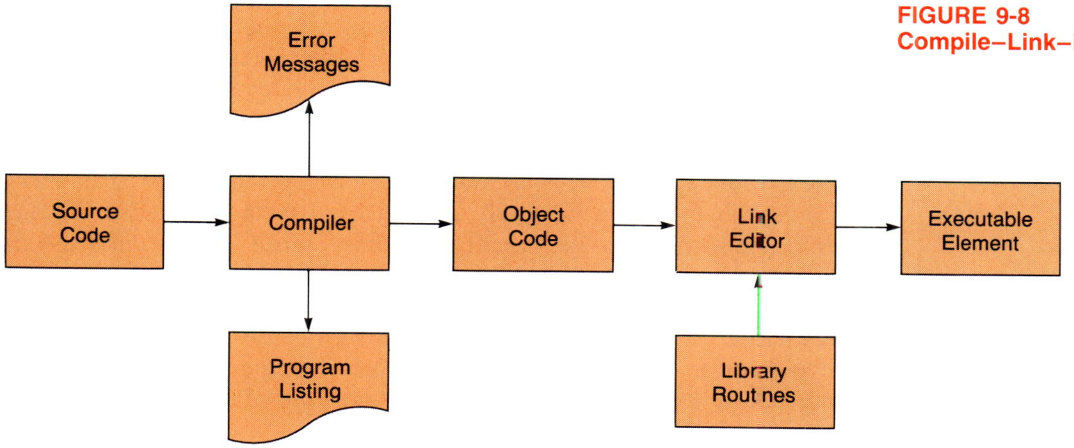

FIGURE 9-8
Compile–Link–Execute Process

object code, the operating system handles all of the linkages necessary for the program to run. The linkage process is handled by a **link editor** program, which links with the object code all of the small programs that are stored as library routines. An example of a library routine is that of finding a square root. The compile–link–execute process is shown in Figure 9-8.

A series of commands from the user tells the operating system what must be done. On mainframes, these commands are often combined to form what is called **job control language (JCL)**. JCL is like a high-level language, because it uses English terms. However, it merely communicates with the operating system; it does not solve a problem. Figure 9-9 shows the necessary JCL to compile and run a FORTRAN program on an IBM mainframe.

FIGURE 9-9
JCL to Compile and Execute a FORTRAN Program

```
                              Maximum Time
           User ID#           = 30 seconds       128K RAM Needed
//JOB      CO9PAT     TIME = (,30),REGION = 128K  <------ Job Line
//PASSWORD = ASHLEY  <------ Password
//EXEC FORTCLG  <------ Compile and Link/FORTRAN Program

                             File Name of Program
//FORT.SYSIN DD DSN = CO9PAT(LWCPROG),DISP = SHR
                                               ------ Shows Location of Program
//GO.SYSIN  <------ Execute FORTRAN Program

                  Data File Name
//DD DSN = CO9PAT(LWCDATA),DISP = SHR  <------ Shows Location of Data for Program
//  <------ End of JCL
```

Channels, Buffers, and Preprocessors

To relieve the CPU from activities other than processing data, channels, buffers, and preprocessors are used on mainframes. These hardware devices speed data processing by isolating the CPU from the relatively slow input/output process. A **channel** can be either a small computer separate from the CPU or a special section of the CPU. In either case, it controls the input/output process without direction from the CPU. A **buffer** is a section of memory separate from the internal memory unit which acts as an intermediate storage area for input or output. The data that is input at human or mechanical speeds are stored in an *input buffer* before being transferred to internal memory at electronic speeds. Similarly, an *output buffer* stores processed information sent there at electronic speeds by the internal memory unit before sending the information on to the much slower printer. In either case, the CPU is not slowed down by the input/output process because of the buffer. Finally, a *front-end processor,* or **preprocessor**, is a small computer that controls the terminals and RJEs to relieve the CPU from this responsibility. Figure 9-10 depicts the relationship of channels, buffers, and preprocessors to the CPU.

System Interrupts and Virtual Memory

In addition to the use of channels, buffers, and preprocessors to isolate the CPU from input/output tasks, two other techniques speed the processing of high-priority jobs and seemingly increase internal memory. These two techniques are system interrupts and virtual memory. When the CPU runs multiple jobs concurrently, it often must use a **system interrupt** to stop the processing of one job to run a higher priority job. Priority is assigned by the CPU based on the length or source of the job. For example, a long job may be interrupted to run a short job, or an applications job may be interrupted to run a systems job to fix a problem with the operating system. With a system

FIGURE 9-10
Relationship of Channels, Buffers, and Preprocessors to the CPU

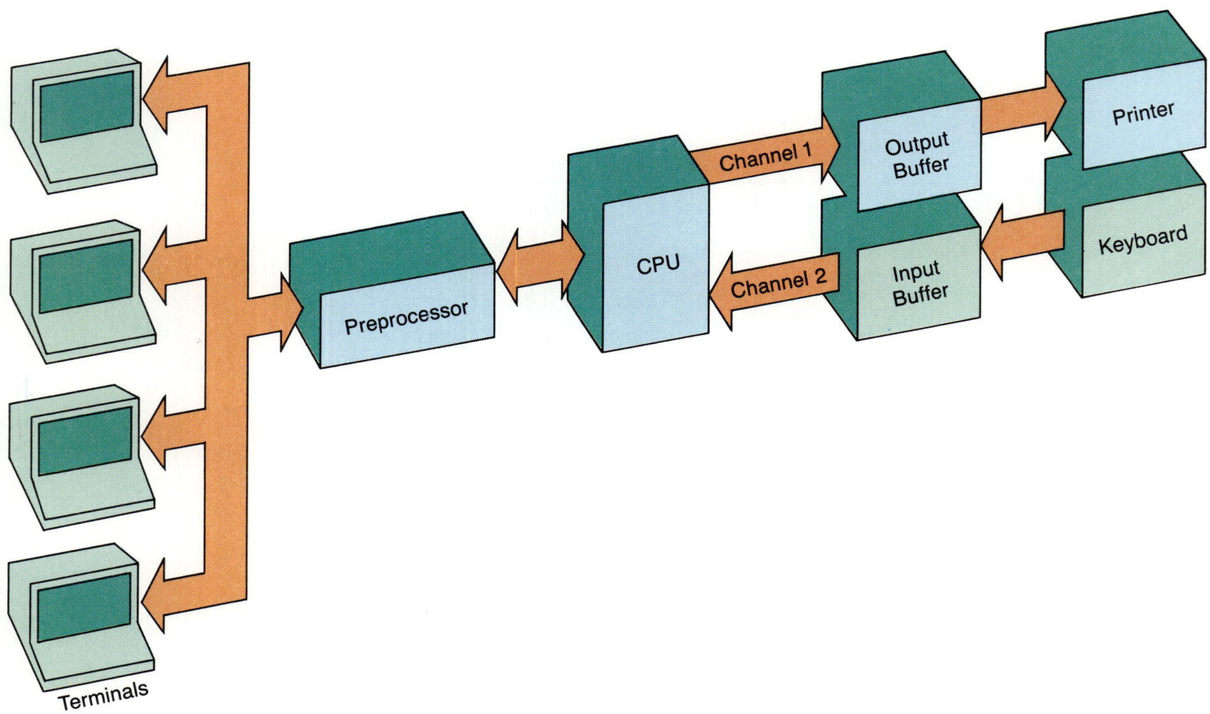

interrupt, the processing of one job is suspended, and internal memory is partitioned into sections. This action separates data and instructions for the interrupted job from those of the higher priority job. This same partitioning technique is utilized when time-slices are used to run multiple jobs.

Virtual memory is a technique used to increase the apparent memory of a computer. The concept of virtual memory began with mainframe computers in the mid-1970s. In this procedure, the internal memory is divided into pages, or sections, which match equal-sized sections of memory on disk. The internal memory is exchanged, or *swapped,* with the disk or virtual memory when needed. As long as the processing only needs data or instructions that are currently in internal memory, it proceeds as usual. However, when the needed information is on disk, a page is swapped into main memory. The CPU tries to "think" ahead to determine which pages from virtual memory will be needed next. As a result, the apparent memory is greater than the actual internal memory without great loss of processing speed. Virtual memory is used in most mainframes in existence today and greatly enhances the ability of these machines to run multiple jobs at high speeds.

Software systems will have to use graphics and memory to be competitive.

Gary Kildall

(As quoted in "Gary Kildall on Systems, Applications and User Software," *Personal Computing,* December 1982, pp. 39–46).

PERSONAL COMPUTER OPERATING SYSTEMS

Operating systems for personal computers share the same characteristics as mainframe operating systems, except that personal computer operating systems are primarily generic, single-user, single-task systems. (Some exceptions to these general features are discussed later in this section.) Table 9-1 compares mainframe and personal computer operating systems.

Let us consider personal computer operating systems in general. A personal computer operating system performs the following three important functions for the user:

1. *The operating system controls the hardware.* The keyboard, video screen, secondary storage, communications modem, printer, and any other hardware devices are all under the control of the operating system. Because of the operating system, new peripheral devices—such as a hard disk—can be easily added without the user having to learn several new commands.
2. *The operating system interprets the user's commands.* When the user types in a command like COPY, the **command interpreter** determines what these keystrokes mean and sends a message to

Table 9-1 COMPARISON OF OPERATING SYSTEM FEATURES

Feature	*Mainframe*	*Personal Computer*
Machine use	Proprietary	Generic
Number of users	Multiple	Single
Number of tasks	Multiple (concurrent)	Single
Support	Systems programmers	User

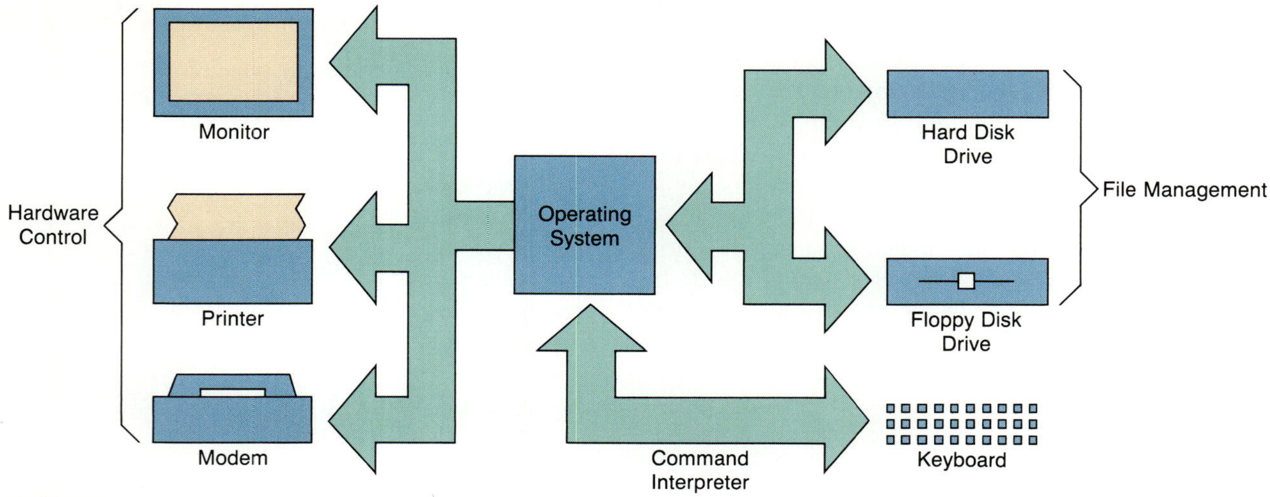

FIGURE 9-11
Functions of a Personal Computer Operating System

the appropriate utility or applications program to carry out the command. If an error exists in spelling or information, an error message is returned to the user. When the requested procedure is completed, the operating system looks for new instructions from the keyboard (or other input devices).

3. *The operating system maintains a file system on secondary storage.* Because the personal computer is heavily dependent on its secondary storage, it must be able to save and retrieve files from secondary storage.

These three operations of a personal computer operating system are demonstrated in Figure 9-11.

Because most personal computers use disks for secondary storage, the name **disk operating system (DOS)** usually describes the operating system of a personal computer. The DOS file system has a unique name for each file, which is supplied by the user and is used for future retrievals. The list of the files on a disk is known as the **disk directory**. Figure 9-12 shows a disk directory for a commonly used DOS.

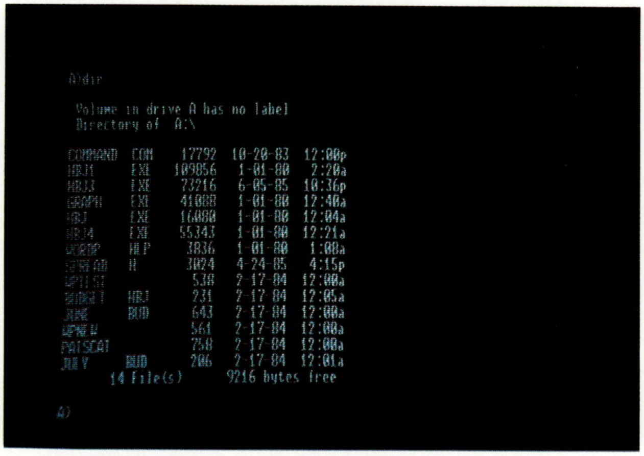

FIGURE 9-12
Disk Directory

Generic Operating Systems

An operating system is important to the computer because *everything* that runs on the computer depends on it for instructions. For this reason, the capabilities of a computer depend largely on the capabilities of its operating system. Different personal computers that use the same DOS can run the same applications software. This situation is very different from a mainframe environment, in which operating systems tend to be machine specific. The use of a single DOS to run the same applications software on different personal computers has led to the development of **generic operating systems**. Four generic disk operating systems are commonly used, and several other systems also exist. The four generally used systems are CP/M (Control Program for Microcomputers) from Digital Research, MS-DOS (Microsoft DOS) from Microsoft, UNIX from AT&T, and UCSD p-system (University of California, San Diego pseudo-system) from SofTech Microsystems, Inc. Only the UCSD p-system has versions that run on all types of personal computers. These generic systems are broadly characterized by

1. The number of users that the operating system supports.
2. The type of CPU chip on which the operating system runs.

The single-user system is by far the most dominant in the personal computer market. An 8-bit or 16-bit CPU chip is commonly used. Table 9-2 classifies the four major types of personal computer operating systems by number of users and by type of CPU chip (8- or 16-bit).

An important thing to remember about operating systems in general is that many commands normally associated with the operating system are utility commands. For example, the command to copy a file from one disk to another is a utility command. However, because utility software is closely related to systems software, both are included in the discussion of operating systems.

CP/M

The first commonly used generic operating system for 8-bit personal computers was CP/M, which runs on machines using the Intel 8080 and 8085 chips and the Zilog Z80 chip. CP/M has two parts—**resident commands** that are kept in RAM and **disk commands** that are stored on disk. When the operating system disk (usually referred to as the system disk) is placed in a disk drive and the machine is booted up, the resident commands are placed in RAM. The resident commands can be accessed immediately by the CPU even

Table 9-2 COMPARISON OF OPERATING SYSTEMS

Operating System	*Number of Users*	*Type of CPU Chip*
CP/M	Single	8-bit
MS-DOS	Single	16-bit
UNIX	Multiple	16-bit
UCSD p-system	Multiple	8- or 16-bit

in the absence of the system disk, but the disk commands must be read from the system disk. Through a judicious choice of resident commands and disk utilities, CP/M offers a powerful operating system to a knowledgeable user.

CP/M is a command-driven system that requires the user to have a knowledge of its commands. A new user must study the CP/M system before attempting to use it. Digital Research offers a 16-bit version of CP/M called CP/M-86.

CP/M, MS-DOS, UNIX, AND THE P-SYSTEM

Short Histories

CP/M In the early 1970s, Gary Kildall, a consultant for semiconductor manufacturer, Intel, was developing compilers to convert high-level languages into machine languages. While working on languages for desk-top computers, Kildall decided he needed an operating system to run these languages. He developed CP/M and offered it to Intel, which decided there was no need for a disk operating system. Kildall received requests for the CP/M anyway, so in 1974 he and his wife formed a company to market the product. CP/M allowed users to develop a program for an operating system rather than a machine. The first operating system for small computers, CP/M has had over 15,000 programs written for it.

MS-DOS Shortly after Intel first offered the 16-bit 8086 chip in 1979, a small hardware firm called Seattle Computer Products devised an operating system for an 8086 product under development. Called the QDOS (Quick and Dirty Operating System), this operating system was as compatible as possible with CP/M. The operating system was renamed 86-DOS and licensed to Microsoft, which was developing 16-bit software. Microsoft eventually bought the system, renamed it MS-DOS, and later licensed it to IBM as PC-DOS.

UNIX The oldest of the four systems, UNIX was developed in 1970 by Bell Labs (now AT&T) for use on minicomputers. Although AT&T holds the copyright on UNIX, it has since been licensed to other companies—such as Radio Shack and Microsoft—and sold for 16-bit computers under the name Xenix.

UCSD P-System The University of California, San Diego developed the p-system using a computer language called Pascal. Pascal was invented in 1970 by a computer scientist named Niklaus Wirth. Wirth developed the idea of using a p-code so that Pascal would not be a machine dependent language. A group of computer scientists at the University of California, San Diego incorporated this idea in the p-system operating system.

Gary Kildall, the chairman and founder of Digital Research, invented CP/M.

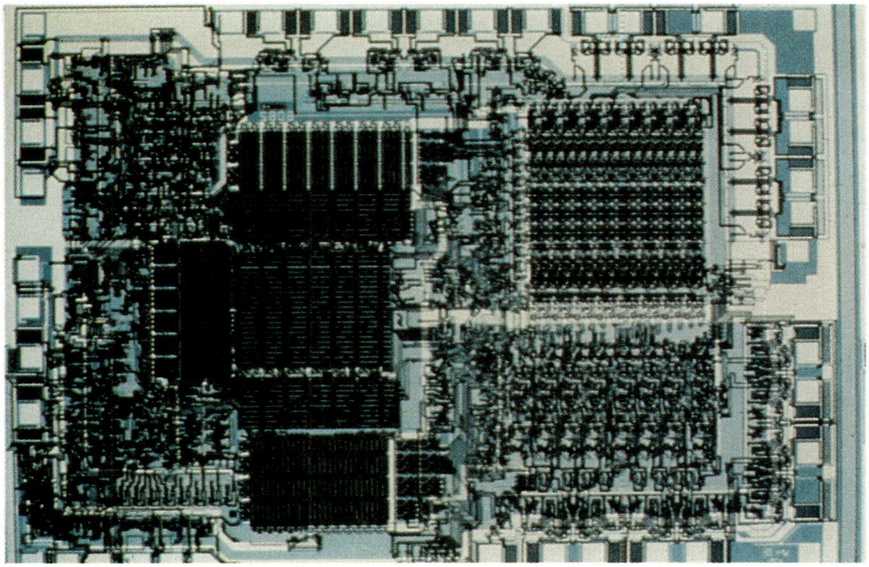

CP/M runs on the Intel 8085 chip.

MS-DOS

What CP/M did for portability in 8-bit machines, MS-DOS did for 16-bit machines. MS-DOS was first used as PC-DOS by the IBM PC. IBM's choice of MS-DOS as the operating system for the company's entry into the personal computer market immediately stamped MS-DOS as an industry standard operating system for 16-bit computers. Currently, over 100 types of computers use the MS-DOS operating system. Reportedly over 80% of all applications software developed today is for MS-DOS. As more companies introduce competitors to the IBM PC, the number of computers using MS-DOS grows and the number of applications programs approaches the number available for CP/M.

MS-DOS is similar to CP/M. Both systems are command driven and require the user to know much about the system. Both systems use the same prompt to request a command from the user. As with CP/M, MS-DOS uses resident, or internal, commands and disk, or external, commands. The external commands tend to use up more memory, or they are not used as often as the internal commands. For applications programs that are used often, the internal commands can be placed on the applications software disk, and the user can bypass the system disk when booting up the program. Table 9-3 shows

CP/M was really developed to provide an environment for running compilers.

Gary Kildall

(As quoted in "Gary Kildall on Systems, Applications and User Software," *Personal Computing,* December 1982, pp. 39–46).

Table 9-3 EXAMPLES OF MS-DOS COMMANDS

Command	*Action*	*Example*	*Location*
COPY	Copies one or more files to a new disk or location	COPY A:TEST B:TEST	Internal
DIR	Displays a directory of the user's files	DIR A:	Internal
DISKCOPY	Copies disk in drive A to disk in drive B	DISKCOPY	External
FORMAT	Initializes a disk	FORMAT B:	External

I think you'll find that UNIX will be the key glue in starting to tie these things [multiple tasking and multiple types of machines] together.

Jack Scanlon, Vice-President, AT&T Technologies Computer Systems Division

(As quoted in "Major Leaguers Join the Fray over Operating Systems," *Business Week,* April 16, 1984, pp. 120–22.)

some MS-DOS commands, the resulting actions, and whether each command is internal or external. (In each case, the A: or B: refers to the A disk drive or B disk drive, respectively.)

With new versions of MS-DOS, a user can set up a hierarchial directory, which divides a long list of files into several short lists, each of which may be given a name. A hierarchical directory is particularly useful for file storage on hard disks. For example, assume an author has five books stored on a single hard disk, and each book has at least 10 chapters. If each chapter corresponds to one file, then over 50 files relate to books. A hierarchical directory made up of five subdirectories would allow the author to use one subdirectory for each book. The author could then go to the subdirectory corresponding to a particular book to find a desired chapter, rather than looking through a long directory that contains chapters of all of the author's books.

UNIX

Both CP/M and MS-DOS are single-user, single-task operating systems, which are used on a majority of today's personal computers. A multiple-user, multiple-task operating system that is gaining favor for large personal computers is UNIX from AT&T. UNIX was originally developed for minicomputers, but it has since been adapted to personal computers. Because this complex operating system is written in a combination of high-level language (C) and assembly language, only the assembly language portion must be rewritten to convert the UNIX program to a new computer.

UNIX is not especially easy for a beginner to use, but its "kernel" and "shell" structure, shown in Figure 9-13, helps the beginner somewhat. The kernel contains the operating system commands, and the shell contains the commands that the user sees. User friendly commands can be added to the shell without affecting operating system commands. As a result, a user would

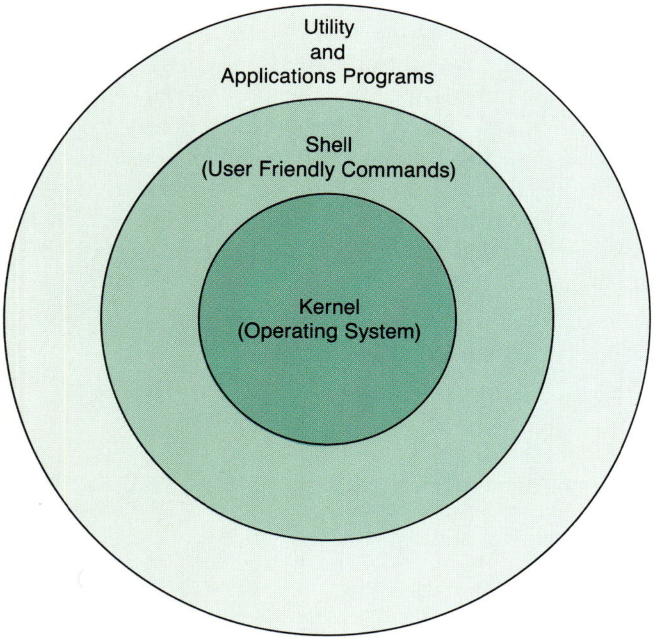

FIGURE 9-13
The Structure of UNIX

(Curtis Sanford and David Walden, "Developing Programs with UNIX," *Mini-Micro Systems,* May 1983, p. 279.)

not have to know the commands that reside in the kernel. Outside the shell are the utility and applications programs associated with UNIX.

UNIX is a complete system that offers hierarchical file structures and the ability to send data from one file to another through a system called piping. It also has over 200 utility programs that can perform almost any task a user could desire.

UCSD P-System

In terms of operating system portability, the p-system ranks at the top of the list. In theory, any p-system applications program can be shifted to almost any other machine regardless of the chip used. The portability of the p-system is the result of the unique method used to implement this operating system. Like UNIX, the p-system is written in a high-level language—in this case, Pascal. However, unlike UNIX, the p-system is not translated directly into the computer's machine language. Instead, an intermediate translation is made into **p-code** (pseudocode). A machine specific piece of software called a **p-machine emulator** then translates the p-code into the machine language. The p-code is always the same, but each p-machine emulator is different. Figure 9-14 demonstrates how this process works for three types of personal computer chips—the 6502 (Apple), 8088 (IBM PC), and 68000 (Sage and Macintosh).

Using the p-machine emulator system, the applications software is never seen directly by the hardware. The hardware–software interface occurs between the CPU and the p-machine emulator. In addition to the p-machine emulator, a new input/output system must be written for each machine.

The p-system is often considered the most user friendly of the four operat-

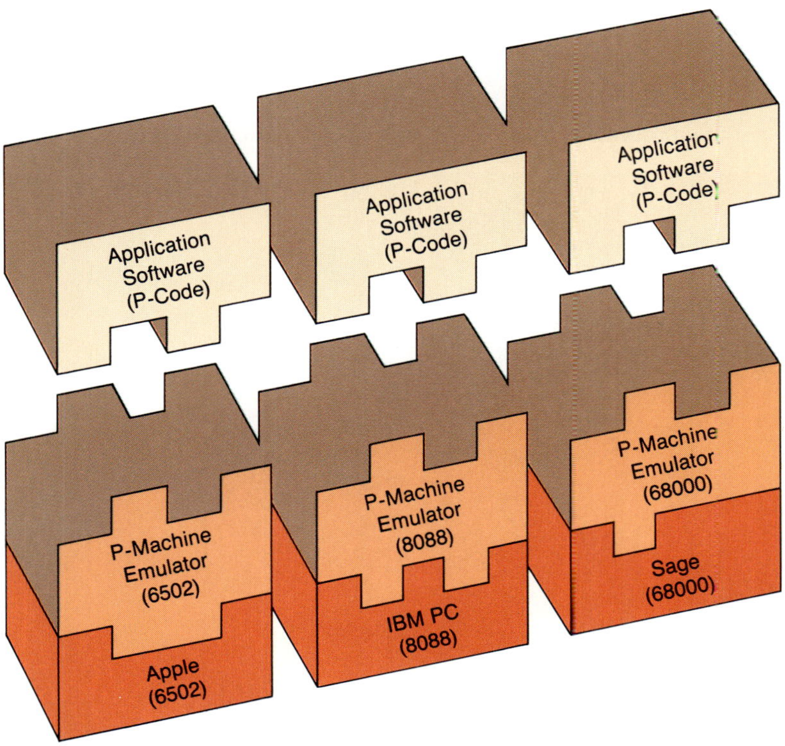

FIGURE 9-14
Use of P-Machine Emulator

(Gary Legg and Roy Friedman, "Microcomputer Operating Systems Compete in Portability and Performance," *Mini-Micro Systems*, January 1984, p. 235.)

ing systems discussed here because it is menu driven. Using the menus, the user can give most commands with single keystrokes. Once a command is given, submenus are presented, if necessary, to allow the user to select a more detailed command.

Proprietary Systems

Two large manufacturers of personal computers, Apple and Tandy, use **proprietary operating systems** in some of their products. For its Apple II series, Apple uses the 6502 chip, which is incompatible with CP/M. Hardware modifications are available to rectify this problem, but most Apple owners use Apple DOS (or its more recent version, ProDOS). Similarly, although Tandy uses the Z80 chip in its popular Models I, III, and 4 computers, the

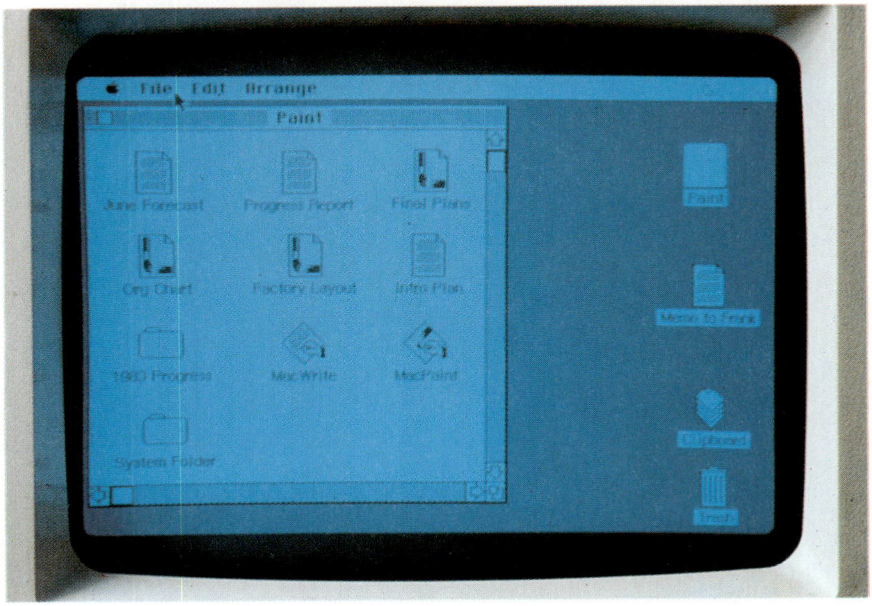

Both Apple and Tandy use proprietary operating systems in their personal computers. The TRS-80 Model 4 (top) runs under a proprietary operating system called TRSDOS. The Macintosh operating system (bottom) uses icons to guide users as to which operation to choose.

internal design of the computers makes them incompatible with CP/M. These machines use the TRSDOS (Tandy Radio Shack DOS) series of operating systems.

Apple DOS and TRSDOS, both aimed at the home user, are fairly easy to use compared with CP/M and MS-DOS, which were seemingly written with the computer in mind rather than the user. Other personal computers that use proprietary operating systems include the Commodore series and the Radio Shack Color Computer series.

The newest and possibly the most exciting proprietary operating system in use is the Macintosh operating system. This system uses icons, a mouse, and pull-down menus to select commands. The user can concentrate on the job itself rather than on how to do the job. In the 1970s, the Palo Alto Research Center (PARC), which was involved in the development of the mouse, worked on this approach to the computer for Xerox. PARC personnel were concerned with finding ways to structure the computer so that the user need not be an expert on a given machine. Apple adapted PARC's work to make the operating system on the Macintosh very user friendly. A Macintosh user need only select the icon corresponding to the task to be performed (for example, a trash can is the icon for deleting a file), move the mouse to place the cursor over the trash can, and click the mouse button. Next, a pull-down submenu exposes an expanded list of commands. The user positions the cursor over the appropriate command in the submenu, presses the button again, and finishes the task. This proprietary operating system is so easy to use that many popular applications packages have been rewritten to run on the Macintosh. Mouse–icon systems are also under development for packages that run with MS-DOS.

WINDOWS AND INTEGRATED SYSTEMS

Today's personal computers can perform a variety of tasks—such as word processing, graphics, spreadsheets, data base management, accounting, and communications. Users often need to move easily back and forth between packages. For example, a user may be writing a report with a word processing package and need a table from a spreadsheet package or a bar chart from a graphics package. The table or chart may be physically cut out and pasted into the word processing document. However, a better solution is to have the computer shift the table or chart from the spreadsheet or graphics package into the word processing document. This transfer can be cumbersome if the user must shift disks in and out of the disk drive to handle it. Integrated packages make working with multiple packages easy. An **integrated package** contains some or all of the most commonly used packages and a procedure that accesses these various packages.

Three different types of integrated packages are available—multiple-function programs, integrated operating environments, and data base application environments. Multiple-function programs offer a variety of applications within one program, so the user must only learn one program. Examples of multiple-function programs include 1-2-3 and Symphony from Lotus and Framework. Integrated operating environments allow several programs to run simultaneously and share information. Several companies offer packages with this type of integration, including Microsoft, Digital Research, and IBM. Finally, a data base application environment has individual applications programs that all access a single data base. Examples of this type of integration include Data Base Manager II and Condor.

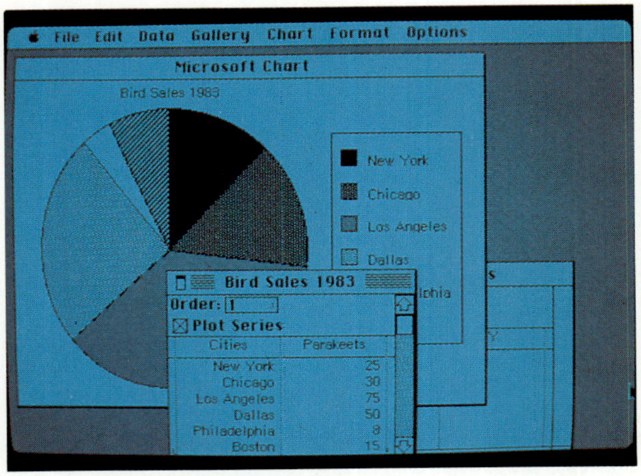

Overlaid Windows

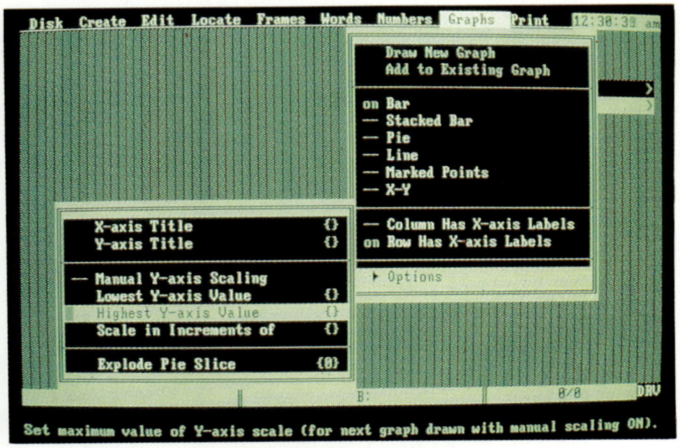

Tiled Windows

FIGURE 9-15
Overlaid and Tiled Windows

The use of multiple packages and the ability to transfer information between packages are often tied together by a concept known as *windows.* A **window** is a section of the monitor screen that is set aside by the package to display a portion of output. Windows are used with integrated packages to show output from packages that are running concurrently on the computer. Depending on the type of package used, windows can be overlaid or tiled. With **overlaid windows**, the current task is shown in a window that appears to be on top of the other windows. In effect, you are looking at the top sheet of several sheets of paper, but sections of the other sheets are showing. With **tiled windows**, each window is shown completely in a separate section of the screen. Figure 9-15 shows overlaid and tiled windows.

Windows are important in the use of integrated packages because they show the current status of each package and aid in shifting information from one function of the package to another function. For example, with an integrated package, a user can begin writing a report, decide to include a graph, open a window on the graphics part of the integrated package, design the graph, and then shift the results of the window into the report. With some packages, a change in one part of the package is immediately made known to all other elements of the package. For example, if the results of a spreadsheet are included in a graph and the values of the spreadsheet change, the graph changes to reflect these changes.

A great deal of software development work is now spent in developing integrated packages. Users are demanding the ability to access all major package functions from one package, and software companies are responding to this need.

REVIEW OF KEY POINTS

- Software packages are quite popular for use on all types of computers.
- Packages are classified as menu driven or command driven according to how user commands are entered.
- Packages are classified as batch or interactive, depending on the type of input.
- Operating systems are a necessary form of software for all types of computers.
- An operating system performs various important functions that allow the user to execute utility and applications programs.
- Mainframe operating systems must manage time-sharing and batch systems of data input using a supervisor program that calls in other parts of the operating system.
- Channels, buffers, and preprocessors are hardware devices that help to isolate the CPU from the input/output functions.
- Most personal computer operating systems are aimed at single users performing single tasks.
- Personal computer operating systems control the hardware, interpret the user's commands, and maintain a file system on secondary storage.
- Generic operating systems can run many different computers, but proprietary systems only run one type of machine.
- The most used generic operating systems for personal computers are CP/M, MS-DOS, UNIX, and the p-system.
- Multiple packages or functions can be run on integrated packages using windows to view two or more outputs simultaneously.

KEY TERMS

batch mode
batch package
buffer
channel
command driven
command interpreter
compiler
demonstration disk
disk commands
disk directory
disk operating system (DOS)
documentation
generic operating systems
icons
integrated package
interactive package
job control language (JCL)
link editor
menu
menu driven
object code
operating system
overlaid windows
p-code
p-machine emulator
preprocessor
programming
proprietary operating systems
pull-down menu
remote job entry (RJE)
resident commands
software package
source code
supervisor program
support staff
system interrupt
tiled windows
time-sharing system
time-slice
tutorial disk
user friendly
virtual memory
window

REVIEW QUESTIONS

1. Explain why computer packages make the power of computers available to many more people.
2. What is the difference between a menu-driven package and a command-driven package? A batch package and an interactive package? Discuss the advantages and disadvantages of each.
3. What is a pull-down menu? Why is it described as user friendly?
4. Name the functions of an operating system.
5. What is the difference between time-sharing and batch mode for a mainframe? Visit your school's computer center and ask to see both in action.
6. What is the difference between generic and proprietary operating systems? Which system does a mainframe use and why?
7. Name the four most commonly used generic operating systems for personal computers. If you have a personal computer at your disposal, determine what type of operating system it has.
8. How are CP/M and MS-DOS the same? How do they differ?
9. Why do Apple and Tandy have proprietary operating systems in their products?
10. What is a computer window? How are windows used with integrated packages?

Chapter 1 stated that the computer works with symbols in addition to processing numeric data. This chapter discusses computer software packages for processing words and pictures, commonly known as word processing and graphics packages, respectively. With a word processing package, the user can enter text to create a document, edit the document to reach a final version, and format the document to achieve a particular printed form. A word processing package also allows additional changes to be made with ease. Graphics packages work with pictures to present ideas. Four types of graphics packages are discussed in this chapter—analysis graphics; presentation graphics; computer-aided design; and graphics editors, or "paint packages," for developing computer art. The importance of hardware in selecting and using graphics packages is also covered.

10

Word Processing and Graphics Packages

STUDY OBJECTIVES

After reading this chapter, you should be able to

- Understand how the key operations of a word processor make this type of computer package superior to a typewriter.
- Distinguish between the replace, insert, and command modes for word processing packages.
- Understand how a document is formatted and printed.
- Understand how graphics work on a computer.
- Discuss the four types of graphics packages that are commonly used on computers.
- Explain the importance of hardware in selecting and using a graphics package.
- Recognize the key points in selecting a word processing or a graphics package for a personal computer.

WORKING WITH CHARACTERS AND SYMBOLS

We have described computers as **symbol processors** capable of storing and manipulating symbols. When numbers are manipulated—that is, added, divided, and so on—the process is termed **data processing**. Data processing is an extremely important part of computer use, but manipulating characters and pictures is a growing aspect of computer use. Word processing is probably the number one use of personal computers. However, generating pictures using graphics is fast becoming one of the most exciting uses of computers. Computer graphics are used for games; animation and special effects in movies; analysis of business, scientific, and engineering data; presentation of ideas to groups; design of industrial and electronic equipment; and artistic purposes. Through word processing and graphics, the computer facilitates the communication of ideas from the user to other people.

With word processing, a user can quickly and easily convert his or her ideas into words that appear on the monitor screen. Those words may then be edited to correct mistakes and modify ideas. The margins, tab stops, vertical spacing, and number of characters per inch are selected by the user to put the document in a desired form. Once formatted, the document may be printed. If the document needs additional changes after printing, it is easily called back to the screen for correcting. This capability of quick revision clearly gives a word processing package a big advantage over a typewriter.

Arcade games that use graphics have delighted and entertained us in game rooms and on home computers. Such science fiction movies as *Star Wars* could not be produced without high-speed mainframe computers to generate the special effects. The animation in the movie *TRON* was entirely generated on computer. Graphics are also used to analyze and understand numerical data. For example, a user can prepare a slide presentation in much less time than would otherwise be possible. Computer-generated slide presentations can carry far more color and impact than hand-drawn presentations. Specialized graphics packages can speed up the design process for engineers and architects. Frequently used designs are stored and may be combined to develop a new product or building. Finally, artists use the computer to combine colors and shapes in ways that were not possible before, making computer art a significant use of graphics.

The personal computer is a powerful and important machine for one simple reason: When I am using it, it is an extension of what I think about and the way I express my ideas.

Fred Gibbons, President of Software Publishing Corporation

(As quoted in "Fred Gibbons on Inflated Software Costs and Hardware Incompatibility," *Personal Computing,* March 1983, p. 43.)

Two popular commercial word processing software packages are WordPerfect (left) and WordStar (right).

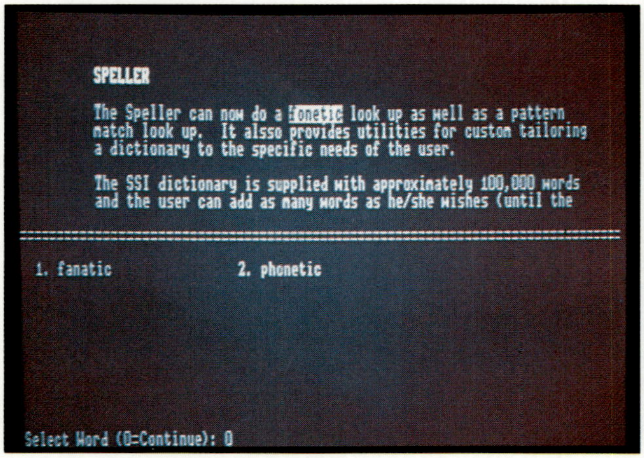

Combining text and graphics has enabled business persons, engineers, and others to develop in one afternoon what would take a typist and art department several days to prepare. This combination of words and pictures makes computers more useful than ever.

No specific word processing packages are discussed in this chapter. Instead, the key ideas and functions that are common to all word processing packages are presented. The discussion of graphics packages covers how graphics work and what types of graphics packages are available. Tutorials appear at the end of the chapter on the word processing and graphics packages—HBJ: WRITE and HBJ: GRAPH—that are available with this text.

WORD PROCESSING PACKAGES

Before the personal computer, specialized minicomputers were used for word processing. These **dedicated word processors** supported several work stations with a printer. The word processing packages on these machines were similar to the packages now available for personal computers. The dedicated word processors are slowly being replaced by personal computer **word processing packages** that perform essentially the same operations for a lower cost

The four key operations of a word processing package are as follows:

Enter the text from a keyboard.

Edit (modify) the text.

Format (control the form of) the text.

Print the text.

All word processing packages offer these operations. Differences among packages involve the ease of use and the volume of work that can be handled. Therefore, the choice of a word processing package depends on the user's needs.

These operations have three modes—replace, insert, and command. When the word processor is in the **replace mode**, any text that is entered replaces existing material, beginning with the cursor's current position. The **cursor** is the blinking light-colored square or rectangle that signals the current position on the screen. When the screen is empty, the text "replaces" the empty area on the screen. The **insert mode** is used to insert the text after the cursor, and any existing text is pushed to the right. Finally, **command mode** is used to enter commands. For example, deleting material and printing a document is done in the command mode. A command is often entered using a **control key** plus some other key. The exact sequence of keystrokes to enter a command depends on the computer and the word processing package. All three modes are used in the text-entry and editing operations whereas the formatting and printing operations use only the command mode

The definition of word processing has been very narrowly conceived. We believe the use of that phrase today is for inputting and editing, but there's activity that precedes that and succeeds that in a logical progression.

Glen Haney, President of Micropro International Corporation

(As quoted in "Micropro to Launch New Low-End Package," *Infoworld,* April 29, 1985, p. 35.)

Entering Text

Of the four operations listed above, the text-entry operation differs the least from the use of a typewriter. For either a word processor or a typewriter, the text is entered from a keyboard. However, a word processor does much more than a typewriter. For entering text (typing the document), the word proces-

These specially designed word processing terminals are used for typesetting books at a composition house.

sor has a useful function called word wrap. With **word wrap**, the user simply enters text and lets the computer determine how many words fit on the current line. When the computer decides that a word does not fit on a line, it is moved to the next line. For example, the following line is too long for the margins (denoted by the dotted lines):

```
This line is too long, so the last word is shifted.
```

Therefore, the last word is shifted to the next line, as follows:

```
This line is too long, so the last word is
shifted.
```

Word wrap is a real advantage for typists, who usually have to worry about typing past the right margin. The typist only needs to use the ENTER key at the end of each paragraph.

With a word processing package, the left margin is always left-justified; that is, the text always lines up on the left. However, the right margin depends on whether or not the user requests **justification** from the software. When the user requests right justification, the software adds extra spaces in the line to make the right margins line up. Consider the two sections of the Gettysburg Address in Figure 10-1. The example on the left is unjustified, and the example on the right is justified.

Four score and seven years ago, our forefathers brought forth on this continent a new nation, conceived in liberty, and dedicated to the proposition that all men are created equal. We are now engaged in a great civil war testing whether that nation, or any nation so conceived, can long endure.

Four score and seven years ago, our forefathers brought forth on this continent a new nation, conceived in liberty, and dedicated to the proposition that all men are created equal. We are now engaged in a great civil war testing whether that nation, or any nation so conceived, can long endure.

FIGURE 10-1
Comparison of Unjustified and Justified Text

Another function that is available on many word processors for the text-entry stage is centering. **Centering** allows the user to center a line of text. The cursor is placed on the line to be centered, and the centering command is given. The line the cursor is on is then centered. For example, compare the following line before and after centering:

```
Final Report for Computer Science 101

        Final Report for Computer Science 101
```

Editing Text

The ability to edit (modify) text easily is an important and useful characteristic of a word processing package. **Text editing** in its simplest form means inserting and deleting characters from existing text. With most word processors, editing means much more than this. For example, blocks of text can be moved to other points in a document or to an entirely different document. The editing function on a word processor also allows the user to search for a string of characters or even to replace that string with another string.

Performing any editing operation requires **cursor control**, because any insertion, deletion, block movement, or search requires that the user move the cursor to a particular point in the document. If the desired line of text is currently on the screen, the cursor is moved by a series of **cursor movement keys** (with the arrows on them) or by a control sequence involving the CONTROL key and letter keys on the keyboard. This movement can be horizontal (left or right) or vertical (up or down). If the desired line of text is not on the screen, then the user must scroll through the text, up or down, to a

LINE EDITORS
Forerunners of Word Processors

The idea of using a computer to enter and then edit text did not begin with the personal computer. These functions have been available on mainframes for at least 20 years. The programs for entering and editing text are known as line editors. Line editors work with only one line of text at a time. Using a line editor, a command may be given to go to a particular line number, change any part of that line, delete the line, replace the line with another, or insert other lines. When the text that is entered and edited is made up of program instructions, the line editor is usually satisfactory for making changes. However, when the text that is entered continues from one line to the next, a line editor is not nearly as useful as a word processor with the word wrap feature. Similarly, editing is easier with a word processor that can access any word or character on the screen. With full-screen editing, any character on the screen can be reached and changed using the cursor movement keys.

Using this combination of standard size and large screen monitors, a newspaper editor can edit and make up a full page of a newspaper before it is typeset and printed.

different **video page**, which is the amount of material that can be seen at one time on the screen. **Scrolling** usually involves the up or down arrow keys or specialized keys such as the Pg Up (Page Up) key. To understand better the insertion, deletion, text block movement, and search functions in editing, let us consider each function separately. When possible, examples of each function are given.

Insertion Character insertion is performed in the insert mode. The insert mode is usually activated by first positioning the cursor where the insertion should be made and then pressing the INS key or entering a control sequence, such as CTRL I. When the insert mode is activated, any characters that are entered push the existing text to the right. This continues until another control sequence signals the computer to exit the insert mode. Depending on the type of word processing package and the computer, exiting the insert mode may be accomplished by pressing the INS key again or by another key sequence. As an example of inserting material, consider the following familiar line of text:

```
Now is the time for all persons to come to
the aid of the party.
```

Note that the word "good" has been deleted. To insert this word, the cursor is moved to the "p" in persons, the insert command is given, the word "good" is entered, and the command to exit the insert mode is given. The result of this sequence is as follows:

```
Now is the time for all goodpersons to come to
the aid of the party.
```

Because the space after the word "good" was not entered by the user, "good" and "persons" run together. Failure to add necessary spaces during the insert mode is a common error. Going back into the insert mode and adding the necessary space yields the following:

```
Now is the time for all good persons to come to
the aid of the party.
```

A word processing package can do many things, but it *cannot* determine where spaces should and should not go. A space is treated just like any other character that must be entered by the user.

Deletion To delete material, the user positions the cursor over the character to be deleted and gives the delete command. In most word processors, the delete process repeats until the delete command keys are released. For example, assume the delete command is given by pressing the DEL key or other sequence, such as CTRL D. If we wish to remove the word "all" from our example, the cursor is positioned over the "a" and the DEL key is pressed and held down while all three letters *plus* the space after the word are deleted on the screen. The resulting line of text is as follows:

```
Now is the time for good persons to come to the
aid of the party.
```

Although insertion and deletion are considered part of the editing process, both procedures are often used during the text-entry process to modify text as it is entered. The edit operation can be used to correct errors or to add or delete text anytime during text entry.

A large amount of material can be deleted simply by holding down the delete command keys. However, it is easier to perform a block-action command to accomplish this task with a large section of text. In a **block-action command**, a block of text is first defined. The cursor is positioned at the beginning of the block and the block-define command is given. The same procedure is performed at the end of the block of text. After a block is defined in this way, a series of actions can be performed on the block, including the deletion of the entire block. The sentence used in the previous examples could be removed by defining it as a block and giving the appropriate block-delete command.

Text Block Movement Text block movement is another block-action command. This process is also called **cut-and-paste**, because a block-action move is the same as cutting out a block of material from a manuscript and pasting it down somewhere else in the manuscript. For example, a user might decide that a particular paragraph should be located somewhere else in a document. Using block-move commands, the paragraph could be lifted from its current location and shifted to the new spot. A block of text can also be copied to other locations in the document or to entirely different documents. A block of text used in many locations is referred to as **boiler plate material**, because it can be used over and over again. The boiler plate is copied to those other locations with a block-action command.

Search Most word processors can search for the occurrence of a word or some sequence of characters. In this operation, the user defines the desired

WORD PROCESSOR
A Communications Device

Usually word processing is thought of as an intermediate step in the process of turning ideas into written documents. Word processing can be used as a communications medium as well. One example of this use of word processing involved Dr. John Fisk of the State University of New York at Albany. A well-known scholar in the area of production management, Dr. Fisk was involved in a major automobile accident on December 3, 1983, and received severe head injuries. As a result of these injuries, he was in a coma for several months. Gradually, his awareness returned, and he could use a pointer and letter board to communicate.

After almost a year, Dr. Fisk regained many of his functions, but because speech is among the last functions to return after such injuries, he still could not talk. To improve communications with Fisk beyond the pointer and letter board, his wife, Bernadine, decided to use a personal computer with word processing. Because Dr. Fisk used a computer keyboard often before his accident, Bernadine hoped he would regain his ability to use the keyboard, too. She purchased a lap-sized personal computer with a built-in word processor. Using this computer, Fisk could type messages, store them, and then replay them for his wife at her convenience. In this instance, the computer and word processor *were* the communication media, not just an intermediate stage.

word, enters the command mode, and then enters the appropriate command to initiate the search. When the defined word is found, the computer positions the cursor over the word and waits for user action. An extension of this process is the **search and replace** operation, in which the user defines both the object of the search and a replacement word. A search and replace operation is commonly used to find misspelled words in a document and to replace them with the correct words. For example, if a user suspects that the word "compiler" has been spelled "compilor" throughout a document, the search and replace operation could be used to correct this error. The object of the search is the word "compilor," and the replacement word is "compiler."

Some word processors can perform a **wildcard search**, which locates a word when only part of the word is known. For example, assume both "in-

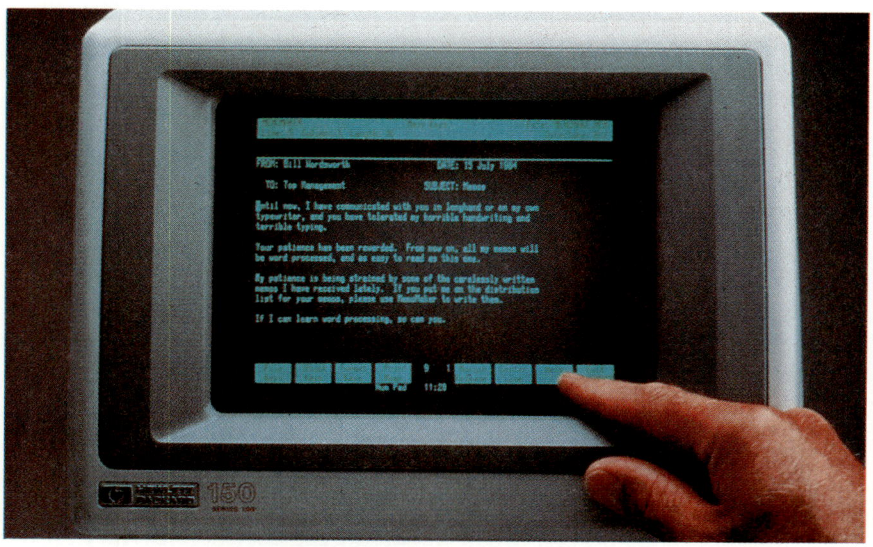

Using a touch screen with a word processing package enables the user to edit and format a document quickly.

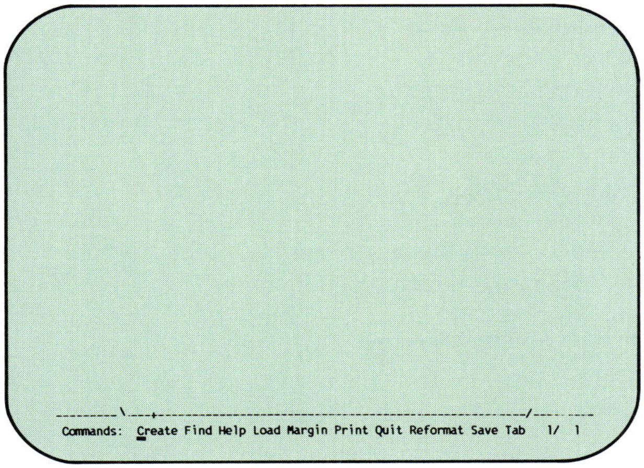

FIGURE 10-2
Example Ruler Line

sure" and "ensure" are used in a document and the user wishes to search for both words. The user substitutes a special character, such as "?," for the first letter. The computer would then search for "?nsure" to find all occurrences of both "insure" and "ensure."

The insertion, deletion, block movement or copy, and search and replace operations make the editing function a useful part of word processing. Editing really sets a word processor apart from a typewriter.

Formatting the Document

Before a document is printed, it must be formatted, or placed in a particular form. **Formatting** includes setting margins, tab stops, vertical spacing (single, double, or some other spacing), number of lines per page, and number of characters per inch. How formatting is accomplished and when it occurs in the document preparation process depends on the particular word processor. In some cases, formatting occurs before any text is entered. With other packages, the text is entered on an 80-column line and then formatted after the text-entry and editing processes. Formatting most commonly occurs *before* text entry.

When the document is initially entered some formatting values are also entered. For example, a user might define the vertical spacing as double spacing with 56 lines per page. The number of characters per inch for horizontal spacing might be defined as 10 or 12 characters per inch, the standard typewriter pica and elite fonts, respectively.

Once the format is defined, the user probably faces a blank screen except for a **ruler line** at the top or bottom of the screen. A ruler line from HBJ: WRITE appears in Figure 10-2. On this particular ruler line, the slash (/) and backslash (\) denote the left and right margins, respectively, and the plus symbol (+) denotes the position of the tab. This ruler line uses 10 characters per inch, with margins at 1 inch and 7½ inches. A single tab is set ½ inch from the left margin for the paragraph indent.

Saving and Printing the Document

Once a document has been formatted, it should be ready for saving and printing. Saving a document simply involves giving it a name—say, CHAPTER 10—and giving a command to store it on disk. Printing the document requires an additional form of software known as a printer driver.

A **printer driver** converts the special characters inserted in the document by the word processing software for underscores, boldface, subscripts, and so on, into signals that the printer can understand and use. Each printer needs its own driver, so word processing software usually includes a driver for the most popular types of printers. When printing a document, the user tells the word processing package which printer is in use so the appropriate driver is used.

It is often useful for a word processor to create **boldface type**, underlining, superscripts (2^{10}), or subscripts (S_1). The presence of these functions on a printed document depends on both the word processor and the printer in use. For example, the word processor may support underlining, but if the printer does not have this capability, the printed copy will not contain underlined words. The reverse situation is also true. To print these functions, the user incorporates **imbedded print codes**, which turn each function on and off. Some word processors display these codes on the screen, but for others, the material actually appears boldfaced or underlined on the screen.

Other Operations

Various word processors have other features in addition to text entry, editing, formatting, and printing. Popular features include proofreading, mail-merge, importing files, and a print spooler. These features, which are often purchased separately from the word processing package, require additional disks and drives to be implemented. **Proofreading** checks the spelling in a document through the use of an electronic dictionary. The words in the document are compared with the words in the dictionary, which is usually on a separate disk and contains the most commonly used words. When a word in the document does not match a word in the dictionary, the proofreader marks it for investigation by the user. After the entire document is checked, the user can look at each word that has been marked by the proofreader. Often, the marked words are personal names or technical terms not in the dictionary. However, many words that are actually misspelled can be found and corrected.

The **mail-merge** function allows a word processor to prepare form letters. The form letter is prepared like any other document, except that the inside address and salutation are blank. The names and addresses are then entered into another file. A user's command causes the two files to merge so that each letter has a name and address when it is printed.

With the **importing files** function, the user can incorporate information from other, possibly non-word processing, files within a document. This function is extremely useful for incorporating information in a financial package

This IBM compatible keyboard has special word processing keys—such as Insert, Delete, and Print—in addition to the function keys.

(financial analysis or accounting, for example) into a word processing document. For example, a table of values can be imported directly from the financial package rather than entered again from the keyboard.

Finally, a **print spooler** is software that enables the user to print one document while he or she works on another document This software directs the CPU to print the document during the slices of time between keystrokes. Even the fastest typist is much slower than the CPU, so time gaps always exist, during which the CPU can print the document. This feature is useful when several documents (letters, reports, and so on) are prepared at the same time.

Function and Special Keys

On many personal computers, special keys exist only for word processing. These keys have commands such as INS, DEL, PgDn, and PgUp. These keys correspond, respectively, to entering or exiting the insert mode, giving the delete command, scrolling to the next video page, and scrolling back to the previous page.

In addition to these special keys, some personal computers also have **function keys** down one side of the keyboard or above it. These keys, which

OTHER USES FOR A WORD PROCESSOR

Word processing packages have other uses in addition to preparing documents. Three areas in which such uses have been found are education, file processing, and the preparation of nondocuments.

Learning to print using a pencil is usually considered a difficult skill that kindergarten or first grade students must accomplish. After they have learned to print, students must then learn an entirely different set of skills for script handwriting. To communicate ideas, students must not only be able to organize thoughts, they must also be able to write in a legible fashion. For children who cannot learn to write or for physically or neurologically handicapped adults, the inability to use a pen or pencil for expression has stood in the way of written communication. Fortunately, the word processor can solve many of these problems.

As an example of the possible use of the word processor in education, consider the case of a sixth grade girl who could write only at the second grade level. Using a computer with word processing, the girl wrote a letter to her aunt. Her success in composing a two-line letter gave her the confidence to try other writing projects, including short stories, then longer stories, and finally poems. Two years later, one of her poems was published in a national student magazine. Needless to say, her self-esteem had grown enormously.

In any area of research, information must usually be filed as it is found. Before computers, information was filed on index cards, which were then arranged by subject before the final report was written. Today, data base management packages are available for personal computers, but they may be too expensive or may not fit the particular research needs. A word processor can be an electronic index file. A series of index titles is entered, and the search function of the word processor then locates the appropriate title when information is recorded. The information is then entered after the appropriate title. New titles are easily added if needed. The block-move function (cut-and-paste) can then be used to arrange the material in any order to yield an outline for the final report.

Because the word processor is an effective full-screen editor, it can be used to create nondocuments. A nondocument can be a file of commands for the operating system, a computer program, or a data file. In all three cases, the word processor facilitates the creation, editing, and printing of the nondocument material. For example, a user could write a Pascal program using the word processor. Once written, the program could be converted from word processing format into standard ASCII format and then run. If any errors occurred, the program could be converted back into word processing format, edited, converted into ASCII, and run again.

SOURCE: Daniel Watt, "Word Processors and Writing," *Popular Computing,* June 1982, pp. 124–26; Dara Pearlman, "Managing Data with a Word Processor," *Popular Computing,* February 1984, pp. 160–61.

are labeled F1, F2, F3, and so on, have different functions for different word processing packages and different computers. However, they usually perform such actions as boldfacing, underlining, and so on. Facilitating the use of function keys, plastic templates that lay on the keyboard are available for the popular word processing packages and personal computers. These templates describe the use of each function key for a particular package. Because not all computers have function keys, some word processing packages do not always depend on them, but make their use optional.

WORD PROCESSING ON A MAINFRAME

Word processing on mainframes can be a very useful function in some situations. Word processing on a mainframe is oriented toward creating very long or very complex documents that require footnotes, indices, and tables of contents. For example, a mainframe word processor called SCRIPT can be used to write doctoral dissertations, master's theses, and reports. A mainframe word processor can set up the document for typesetting, which is then handled by a laser printer. In this case, the document can go directly from the screen to the printer to the bindery.

An important difference exists between mainframe and personal computer word processors. Personal computer word processing packages have editing and formatting in one package, but mainframe word processing packages—such as SCRIPT—are primarily formatters that must be combined with a separate full-screen editor. This difference means that with a mainframe word processing package, the document does not appear on the screen in the same form that it is printed. On the other hand, "what you see is what you get" on most personal computer word processors.

SELECTING A WORD PROCESSOR

Word processors are available in many different forms and price ranges. Selecting an appropriate package requires a decision on the use of the package, the type of computer in use, and the price. Frequency of use is important and can be divided into three broad categories—occasional (less than once a week), often (at least once a week), and heavy (every day). Another consideration is document length—short (less than 10 pages), intermediate (11–30 pages), and long (more than 30 pages). An occasional user who writes short documents (letters, book reports, or perhaps a term paper) does not need a very sophisticated and expensive word processing package. Instead, the occasional user might consider a less sophisticated, inexpensive package that can create those letters and book reports. On the other hand, a user who writes a book or dissertation may need a sophisticated package to handle any complex operations.

Remember that not all packages run on all machines. For this reason, it is important to select a word processing package that runs on the user's hardware. Some word processors are developed for specific machines, so it may be useful to purchase a word processing package when the hardware is purchased.

Table 10-1 COMPUTER MAGAZINES

Magazine	*Computer Orientation*
A+	Apple
Byte	General interest
Creative Computing	General interest
80 Micro	Radio Shack
MacWorld	Apple Macintosh
PC	IBM and compatibles
PC World	IBM and compatibles
Personal Computing	General interest
Popular Computing	General interest

So what graphics offers us is an opportunity for particular user disciplines to move throughout the applications in the discipline without ever learning a new vocabulary.

John Rowley, President of Digital Research

(As quoted in "John Rowley on the New Graphic Interfaces," *Personal Computing,* February 1985, pp. 88–94.)

When selecting a word processor or any other personal computer software, it is extremely important to try the package out before purchasing it. A user should be able to sit down with the software at his or her type of computer and try any sample application. Several computer magazines review software and hardware for computer users. Some magazines are directed toward a particular type of computer, whereas others are general interest computer magazines. Table 10-1 lists some popular computer magazines and the type of computer toward which each magazine is directed, if any. Virtually every piece of software available on the market has been or will be reviewed in at least one of these magazines. These reviews can help a potential buyer determine whether a particular package could possibly fit his or her needs.

Various software surveys keep track of the top-selling packages. These surveys, which appear weekly and monthly in newspapers and computer magazines, are useful in determining the most popular software. However, software shouldn't be selected on the basis of its popularity. A popular software package may not suit every user's needs.

GRAPHICS PACKAGES

Word processing packages communicate ideas via words. **Graphics packages** communicate ideas via pictures, which are designed by the computer software to present material in a form that is either easier to understand or easier to work with. Graphics packages can also be used for artistic purposes to produce dramatic and beautiful pictures.

Four types of graphics packages are currently in use on mainframes and personal computers—analysis graphics, presentation graphics, computer-aided design (CAD), and graphics editors. **Analysis graphics** analyze data to determine if patterns exist or to gain a better understanding of the data. The results of an analysis graphics package, primarily charts and diagrams, are generally not used for presentations. When the impact on the audience is important, presentation graphics are used. **Presentation graphics** are usually full color pictures, sometimes three-dimensional, that portray an idea vividly to an audience. If graphics are used to design a building or an elec-

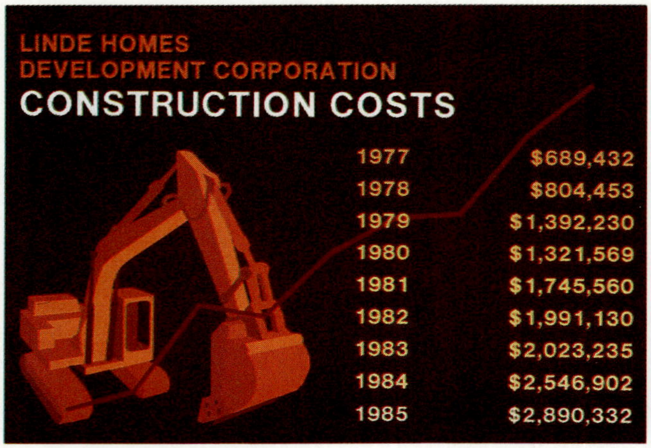

Pictures, graphs, and text can be combined by the computer to generate eye-catching presentation graphics (left). At right, CAD is used to design computer chips by combining a mouse, a keyboard, and a special monitor with appropriate software.

tronic or mechanical device, then **computer-aided design (CAD)** is needed. Using CAD, an engineer, architect, or draftsperson can greatly reduce the time necessary to develop a blueprint for an electronic or structural design. Finally, if the computer is used for artistic purposes, then a **graphics editor**, (or a **paint package**), is needed. Using such a package, the user may pick a type of "brush," choose colors from a "palette," and then use the cursor to draw on the screen.

We discuss each type of graphics package in some detail, including the type of computer—personal computer or mainframe—that is used most often for each package. However, first we cover how graphics are created and the importance of hardware in graphics.

Understanding Graphics

To understand how graphics work, look at a picture in a newspaper. This *half-tone* picture is made up of black dots on a white background. The black areas are completely covered with dots, and the grey areas are a mixture of dots and white background. Graphics on a computer screen work exactly like the half-tone picture in a newspaper, except that the background is usually dark and the dots are light. Each dot corresponds to a **pixel**, or picture element, on the screen which is either turned on or off. The letters of the alphabet, digits, punctuation marks, and graphics symbols are all formed this way. Figure 10-3 demonstrates how the letter A and a rectangle can be portrayed on the screen using pixels.

If the dots can be controlled individually, the package has **bit-mapped graphics**. In this type of graphics, the on–off condition of each pixel corresponds to the on–off condition of a bit in internal memory. The number of dots on a screen determines the **resolution** of the screen. A medium resolution screen has at least 300 dots horizontally and 200 dots vertically. Some high resolution monitors have over 1,024 horizontal dots and 1,024 vertical dots. High resolution is important when the user attempts to draw such figures as a circle or a triangle on the screen. Without high resolution, a circle does not look circular and a triangle has a "stair-step" appearance.

Block graphics result if the dots on the screen can only be controlled as a group. Each block corresponds to an ASCII character. Figure 10-4 shows the block graphic characters corresponding to ASCII positions 176–223. These

Computer-generated graphics can solve many business communications needs. But corporate users must understand the capabilities and limitations of a system before it is installed—not after they get a request for a chart the system cannot produce.

Robert Corr, Marketing Director for General Motors Information Systems and Communications Activity

(As quoted in "More Than Pretty Pictures," *PC Magazine,* January 8, 1985, p. 91.)

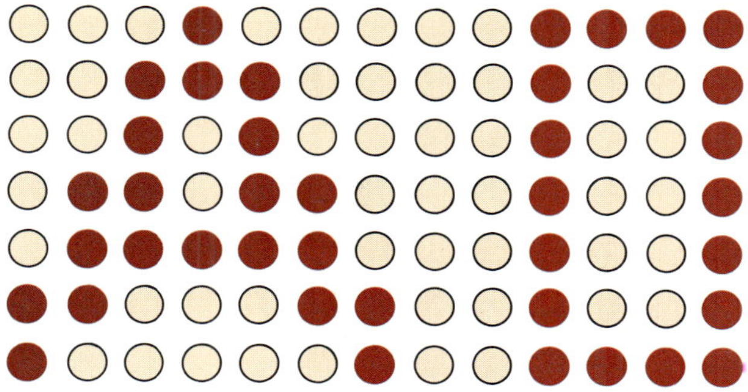

FIGURE 10-3
Pixel Representation

block graphics include lines and solid figures that can be combined using a programming language such as BASIC to portray various types of charts and diagrams. For example, a vertical bar of any size may be constructed using the block graphic characters 219 and 220. Some versions of BASIC also offer special commands—such as COLOR (to change the screen color), PAINT, DRAW, and CIRCLE—to generate graphics pictures on the screen.

The Hardware Connection

Of the software packages commonly used on either mainframes or personal computers, graphics packages are most dependent upon hardware. With mainframes, the central processing unit must be set up to generate graphics, *and* the user must have a special graphics terminal to display the resulting pictures. For personal computers, certain chips are suited to displaying graphics. For example, the 6502 chip used by the Apple II series of computers supports high-quality graphics, whereas the Z80 chip used on CP/M machines and other computers can only support block graphics.

Cost is not an indicator of the quality of the graphics that a computer can support. Some inexpensive computers can support high-quality color graphics using a standard color television. On the other hand, some larger computers for businesses can only portray block graphics. These higher-priced computers need a special color/graphics board to support the same quality graphics as less expensive computers. For this reason, it is very important to match graphics software with the graphics capabilities of a particular computer.

FIGURE 10-4
Block Graphic Characters

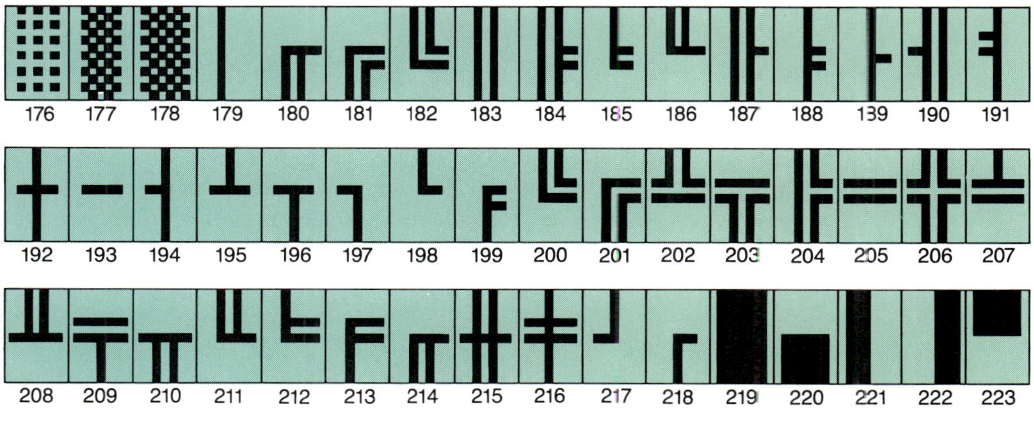

Presentation graphics in two dimensions make good use of colors to show different sales levels.

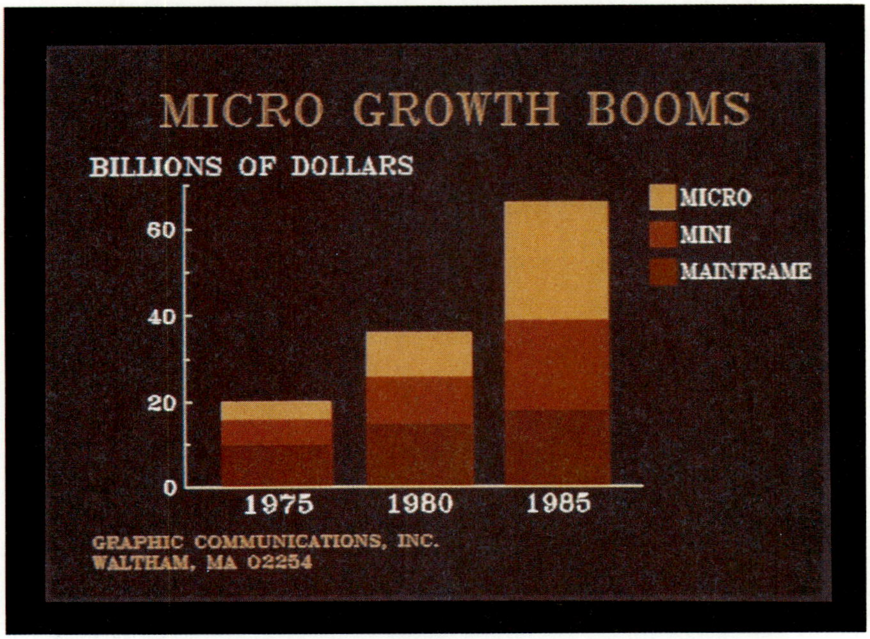

A CLOSER LOOK AT GRAPHICS PACKAGES

All four types of graphics packages mentioned earlier are available for mainframes and personal computers, but some packages are better on one type of computer than the other. For example, mainframe computers tend to be better at computer-aided design and presentation graphics packages because of the need for additional computer speed and storage. On the other hand, analysis graphics and paint packages are used more often on personal computers because of the instant access and complete control of the central processing unit.

Analysis Graphics

Analysis graphics help a decision maker understand or analyze data. Because the computer can handle large amounts of numerical data and the human mind can conceptualize pictures better than numbers, analysis graphics help a user understand numerical data. Thousands of pages of numerical data can be presented in a single picture to reveal relationships that might otherwise go unnoticed. The combined use of color, three-dimensional representations, and motion can reveal the effects of changes in data over time in a way that would otherwise not be possible.

On mainframes, analysis graphics can represent such diverse physical relationships as the amount of light coming from a distant galaxy, the effect of a steam pipe breaking within a nuclear power plant, and the reconstruction of a tornado to reveal unexpected down drafts. This scientific or engineering use of analysis graphics often requires a supercomputer to handle the mass of data and calculations that must be made to represent the relationships as a picture.

On personal computers, analysis graphics are used mostly in business. Analysis graphics, or business graphics, can result in pictorial representations of the budgeting and forecasting processes. Personal computers are often used for this type of graphics because of the immediate access and the reduced level of computation and storage required.

In this sequence, a CAD simulation of a rear-end car crash (middle) is compared with the actual crash (top).

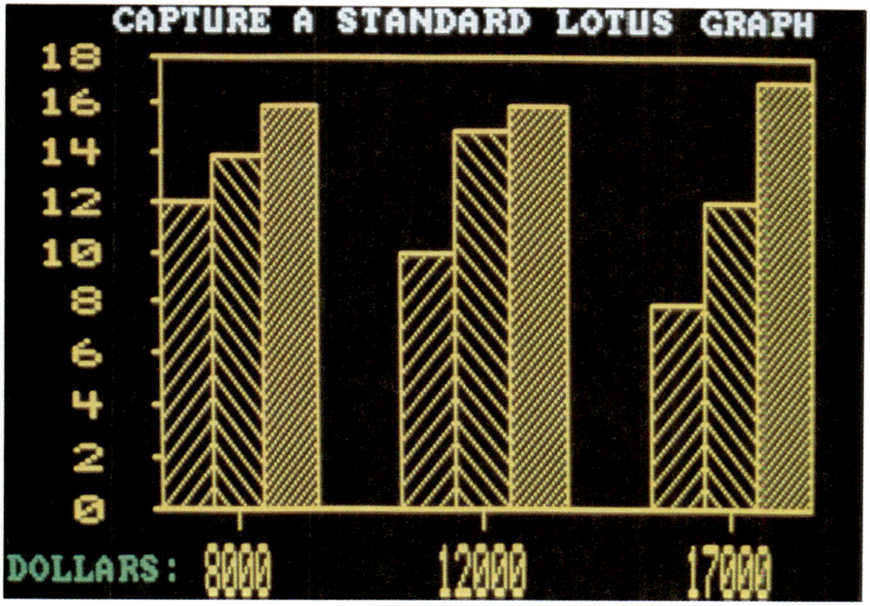

Analysis graphics often use bar charts to compare different sets of values.

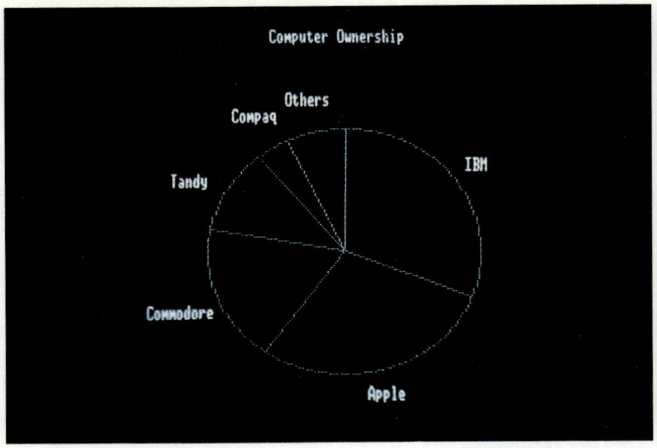

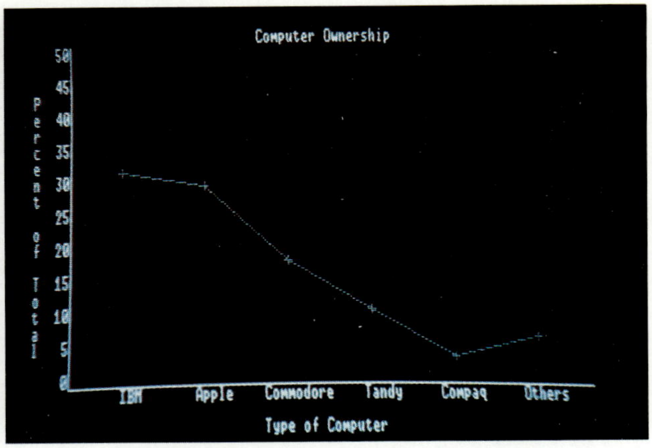

FIGURE 10-5
Examples of Analysis Graphics

Business graphics on a personal computer usually include bar charts, pie charts, scatter diagrams, and line charts. A **bar chart** shows relative differences between categories of data using vertical or horizontal bars. The length or height of the bar represents some quantity. A **pie chart** demonstrates the manner in which some quantity (budget, income, and so on) is proportionately divided by showing those divisions as pieces of a pie. A **scatter diagram** uses some symbol, usually an asterisk or plus sign, to show the relationships among values on the horizontal and vertical axes. Finally, a **line chart** connects the points in a scatter diagram with lines. The incline or decline of each line segment demonstrates the change in values on the vertical axis for each unit change on the horizontal axis. Figure 10-5 shows an example of a pie chart and a line chart generated by HBJ: GRAPH, part of the software available with this text.

Input to an analysis graphics package can be menu driven. The user answers a series of questions about the type of graph to be drawn and the data that are represented in the graph. Another method of input for generating analysis graphics is a spreadsheet. In several integrated packages, the data are taken from the spreadsheet after the calculations are made and converted into various types of graphs. Figure 10-6 shows a Lotus 1-2-3 spreadsheet and the corresponding bar chart.

FIGURE 10-6
Lotus 1-2-3 Spreadsheet and Bar Chart

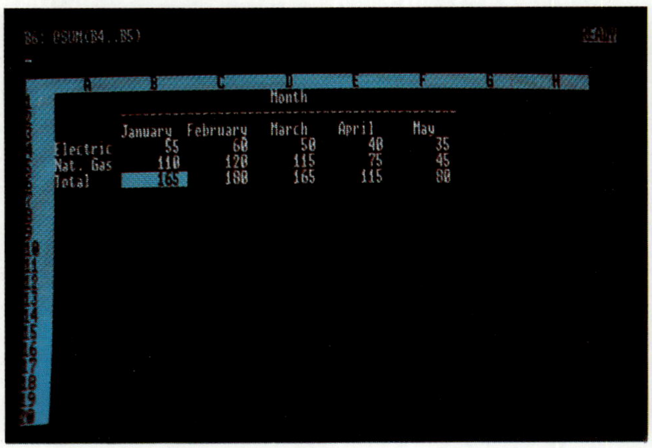

	Month				
	January	February	March	April	May
Electric	55	60	50	40	35
Nat. Gas	110	120	115	75	45
Total	165	180	165	115	80

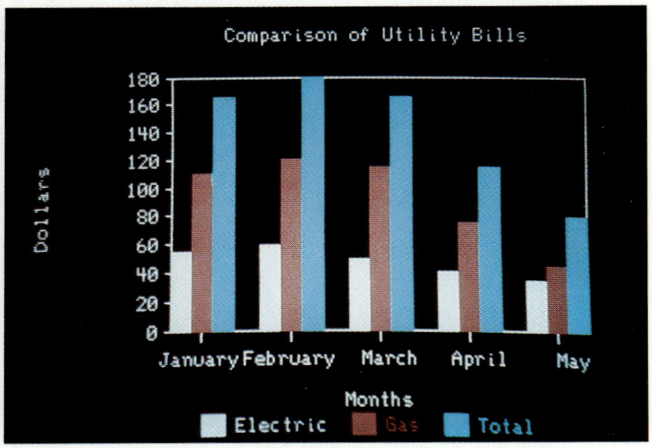

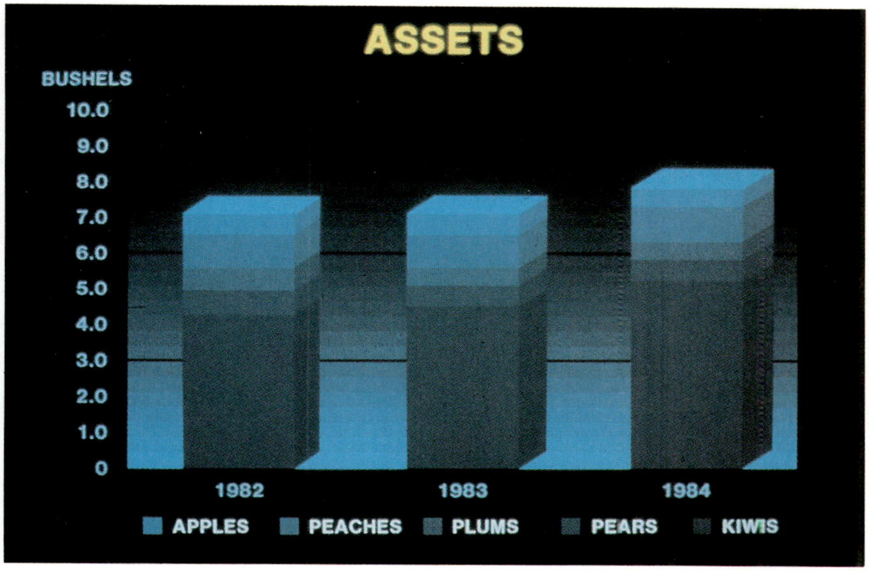

Three-dimensional graphics yield a presentation that clearly shows the difference in production among various products.

Presentation Graphics

Analysis graphics help the user understand data, but presentation graphics present results to others. As a result, presentation graphics must have a "professional" look to deliver their message with "punch." The actual graphs used in presentation graphics may include those used in analysis graphics, but they are much more elaborate and use more colors to emphasize key points in the graph. Three-dimensional graphs are used to compare more than two variables or to add depth to a picture. Personal computers can generate adequate presentation graphics, and the quality is constantly improving. However, they are not good as the presentation graphics generated by a mainframe. The increased computational speed and power of the mainframe allows it to generate more sophisticated graphs than those generated by a personal computer. Figure 10-7 demonstrates the difference between presentation graphics on a personal computer and those on a mainframe.

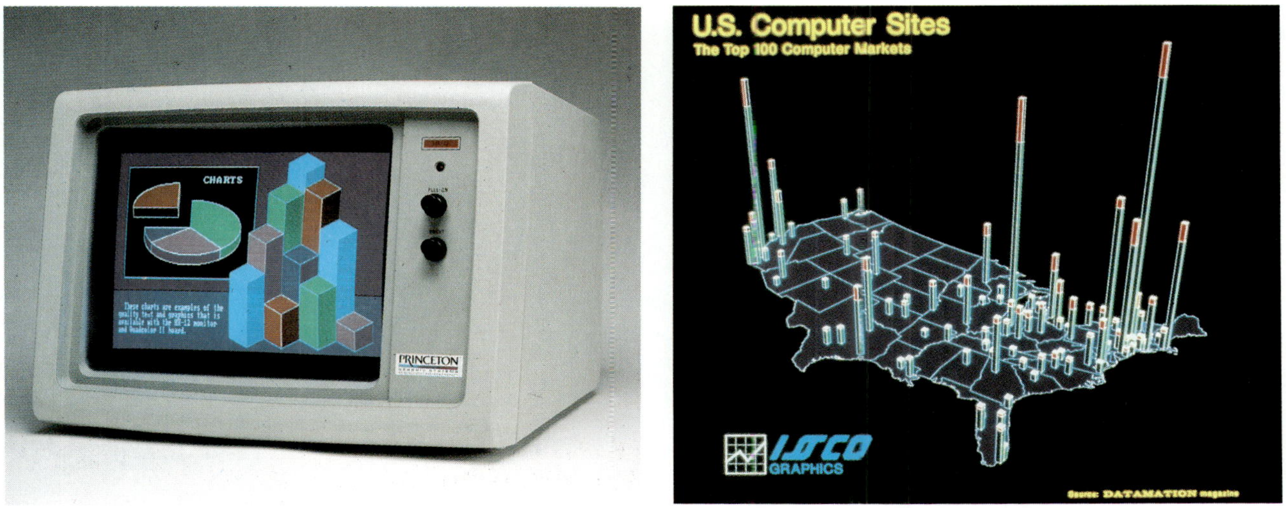

FIGURE 10-7
Comparison of Personal Computer (left) and Mainframe (right) Presentation Graphics

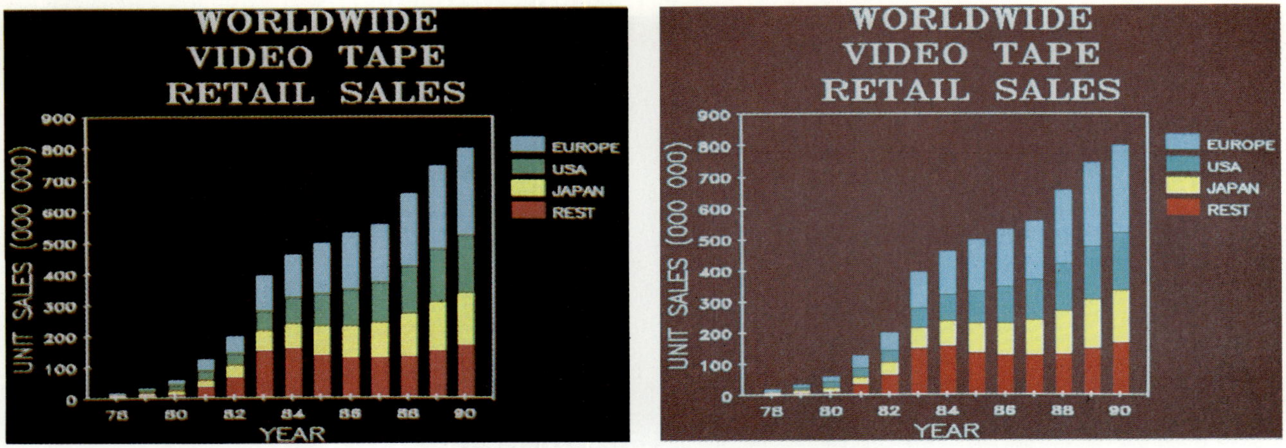

The Polaroid Palette can be used to make color slides or instant prints from either a monochrome or color monitor in any set of colors chosen by the user.

Although a dot matrix printer is sufficient for hard copy of analysis graphics, it is necessary to use a plotter or a color ink jet printer or to make 35mm slides to obtain hard copy of presentation graphics. A plotter uses multicolored pens that move across paper, transparencies, vellum, or other media to produce a copy of the graphics that appear on the screen. A color ink jet printer uses different colored inks that are "shot" at the page to form the multicolored graph. Producing 35mm slides can be done by simply taking a picture of the screen using a camera mounted on a tripod and a shutter-speed setting of less than 1/60 second. The slow setting is necessary because the screen is refreshed 60 times per second, and anything faster would miss all or part of the picture.

Computer-Aided Design

CAD (for computer-aided design) has been used on mainframes and minicomputers since the 1960s for design of airplanes, automobiles, semiconductor chips, and so on. With CAD, an engineer or designer can look at a particu-

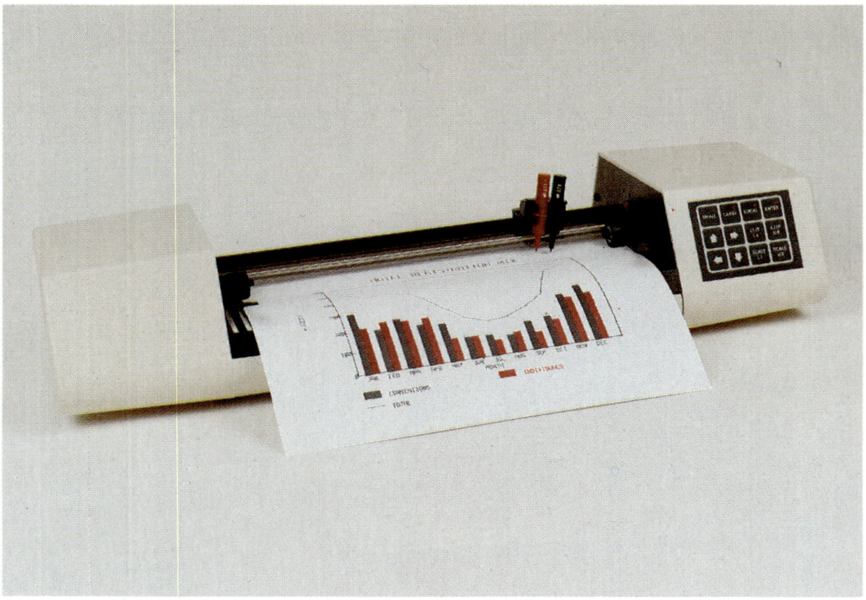

This two-pen plotter reproduces charts and graphs on many different media, including paper, vellum, and transparencies.

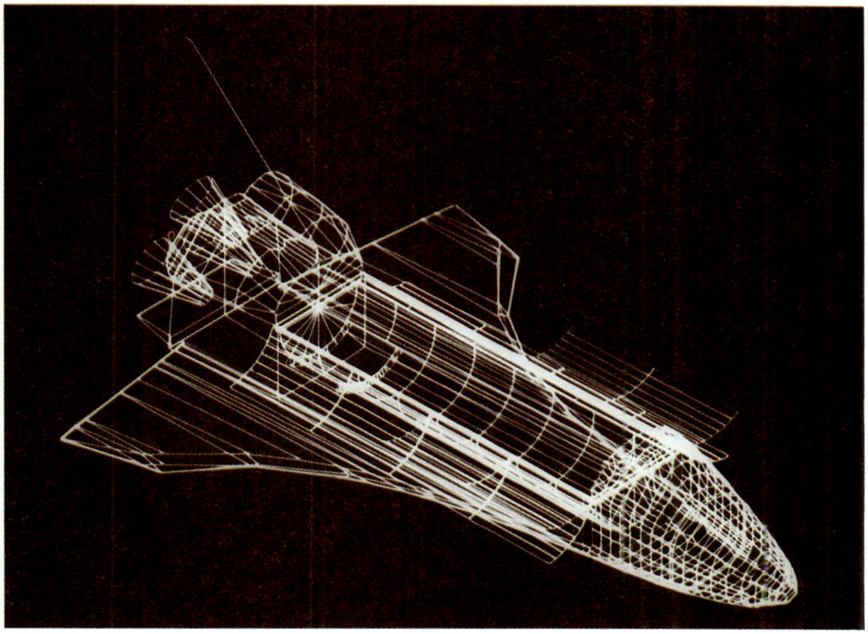

CAD graphics can be used to design machine parts, computers, and space shuttles.

lar design in detail from many angles. Frequently, a designer points a light pen at a specific part of the design that he or she wants enlarged or rotated. Special large screens allow the designer to see every detail of the object in design.

Using a CAD package, a designer or an architect can do a number of tasks faster and easier than with a drawing board. New designs may be created by drawing with a stylus, or **puck**, onto a digitizer tablet, or designs previously stored in internal memory may be adapted for a new design. A joystick or

CAD AT QUADRAM

Quadram Corporation is one of the many computer company success stories of the 1980s. Quadram has annual sales of over $100 million in the computer field, but the company does not build computers. Instead, Quadram produces "enhancements" for personal computers. Enhancements are components that can be added to a computer to allow it to do more work faster and more easily.

Most of Quadram's enhancements involve the design and production of computer boards. A **computer board** is a hard plastic-like board that is approximately $\frac{1}{8}$ inch thick and usually measures about 4 inches × 13 inches. Various electronic components (transistors, capacitors, chips, and so on) are soldered into holes that are drilled in the board. These components are connected by a printed circuit on the back of the board. Such boards as the **mother board**—the main board in the computer—or the **memory board** come with the computer. However, other boards can be added to the computer in one of several "slots." These additional boards can enhance the operations of the computer by adding color and graphics, extra memory, game-playing capabilities, or special purpose chips.

At Quadram, CAD is an important part of the design of a new board. The engineer must ensure that all of the needed connections are made and that no unwanted connections are made. CAD allows the engineer to design the board and show the computer the desired connections. The computer then tries to find a path for each connection. If the path is found, the desired connection, denoted by a yellow line on the screen, disappears. When all such yellow lines have disappeared, the computer has verified all the engineer's desired paths and the board can be built and tested.

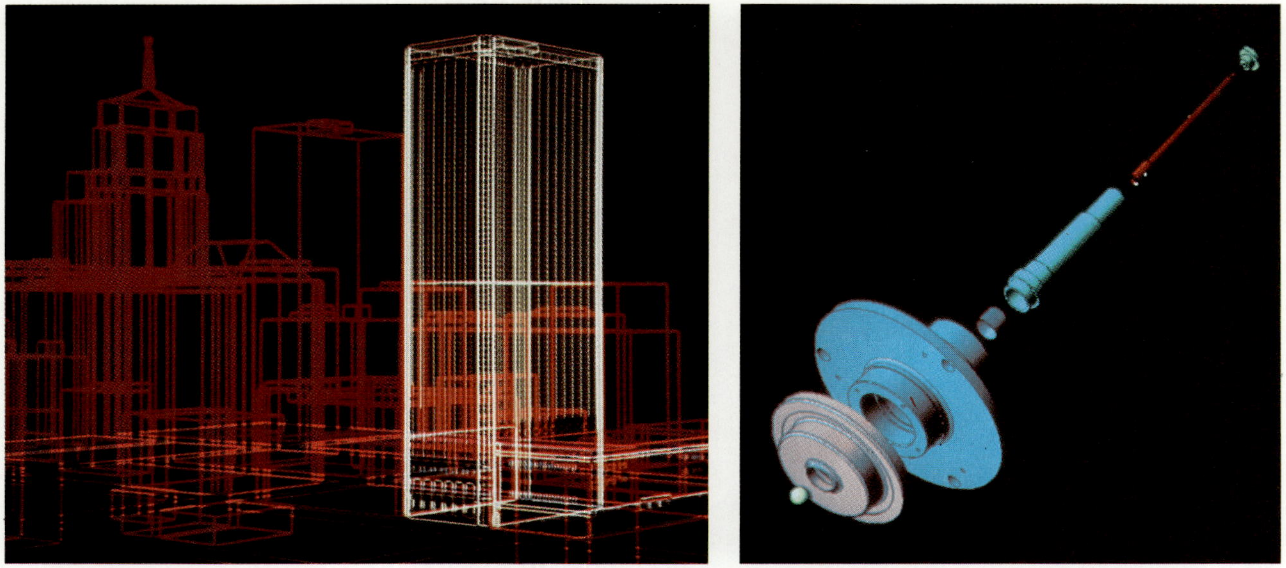

FIGURE 10-8
CAD Drawings

mouse can also be used to create a design on the screen or to make menu selections by moving the cursor. Figure 10-8 shows the use of CAD in engineering designs.

Most CAD packages are used in a mainframe environment, but such packages are being developed for use on personal computers. As the computing power and storage capacity of these small computers increase, the number and variety of CAD programs for them will also increase.

Graphics Editors

A graphics editor, or paint package, allows the user to manipulate pixels to produce freehand drawings or a combination of freehand and library drawings of various shapes. Library drawings are various geometric shapes (circles, squares, and so on) that are stored in internal memory. With a graphics editor, the user controls the screen through the cursor, and, depending on the type of graphics available with the hardware, pictures may be drawn or "painted." If the hardware supports only block graphics on a monochrome monitor, then the pictures may be coarse and uninteresting. However, if the hardware supports bit-mapped graphics on a color monitor, the results can be amazing. Some mainframe computers can now generate pictures that look like oil paintings.

Personal computers are generally used to draw or paint directly on the screen with a controller like a joystick or touch pad, because the user has almost complete control of the CPU. Using a personal computer and one of several paint packages on the market today, the user can obtain immediate results on the screen. Because most mainframes work in a time-sharing environment, a lag may occur between the action and the result on the screen.

The paint package that really triggered the expansion in this field was MacPaint for the Apple Macintosh. Although the graphics are only in black and white, the MacPaint results are startling. Other manufacturers have followed MacPaint's lead. Now, paint packages in color are available for most computers that can support bit-mapped graphics. Figure 10-9 shows the results of a paint package.

FIGURE 10-9
Paint Package Results

Using Mindset, an IBM compatible graphics personal computer, a user can generate plans for a home carpentry project (left) or an artistic design (above).

Using pull-down menus and a mouse, a user can select from the color, texture, and pattern icons surrounding the working area to generate a picture.

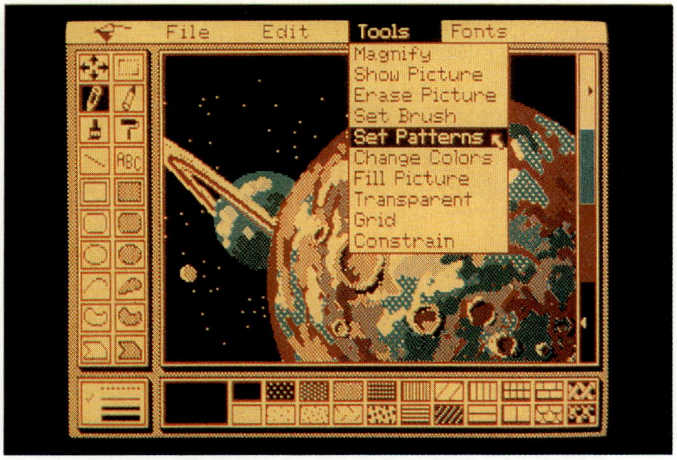

SELECTING A GRAPHICS PACKAGE FOR A PERSONAL COMPUTER

Because graphics packages for personal computers are hardware dependent, a prospective buyer must be sure that the package under consideration indeed runs on the available hardware. Package selection is not usually a problem for an Apple IIe or IIc, because these machines support high-quality graphics on a monitor or television screen. The same is true of such inexpensive computers as the VIC-20, Commodore 64, or Radio Shack Color Computer. However, special precautions must be taken with the IBM PC and compatibles to ensure that the graphics software runs on the computer. Very little graphics software exists for the "standard" IBM PC, so a color/graphics board must be added to the computer along with a monitor other than the IBM monochrome monitor.

Because of the hardware incompatibility problem with graphics software, a user should test a package thoroughly before buying it. When considering the purchase of a paint package, the buyer should determine which device performs the actual drawing. On some packages, this device is a mouse, whereas other packages use a joystick or touch pad. Without the correct input device, the paint package is useless.

REVIEW OF KEY POINTS

- Word processing and graphics packages are used to communicate the user's ideas to other people.
- Word processing is composed of text entry, editing, formatting, and printing.
- The three modes of operation for a word processor are the replace mode, the insert mode, and the command mode.
- Editing text means inserting, deleting, or moving material in a document.
- Formatting a document consists of setting margins, tab stops, vertical spacing, number of lines per page, and number of characters per inch.
- Printing consists of converting the electronic form of the document to hard copy; this function requires printer driver software.
- Graphics packages use the monitor's picture elements, or pixels, to display pictures on the screen.
- The four types of graphics packages are analysis graphics, presentation graphics, computer-aided design (CAD), and graphics editors.
- Analysis graphics are used to analyze data for the user, and presentation graphics are used to present material to someone else.
- CAD facilitates and improves the design process, and graphics editors are used to design art using a computer.

KEY TERMS

analysis graphics
bar chart
bit-mapped graphics
block-action command
block graphics
boiler plate material
centering
command mode
computer-aided design (CAD)
computer board
control key
cursor
cursor control
cursor movement keys
cut-and-paste
data processing
dedicated word processors
formatting
full-screen editing
function keys
graphics editor
graphics packages
imbedded print codes
importing files
insert mode
justification
line chart
line editors
mail-merge
memory board
mother board
nondocument
paint package
pie chart
pixel
presentation graphics
printer driver
print spooler
proofreading
puck
replace mode
resolution
ruler line
scatter diagram
scrolling
search and replace
symbol processors
text editing
video page
wildcard search
word processing packages
word wrap

REVIEW QUESTIONS

1. How are word processing and graphics packages similar? How are they dissimilar?
2. What are the four operations of a word processor? How do these operations compare with those on a mainframe line editor?
3. Name a word processor's three modes of operation. Explain how each mode is used in each word processor operation in question 2.
4. What does *cut-and-paste* mean in a word processing package? Explain the block-delete command.
5. How are mainframe word processing packages different from personal computer word processing packages?
6. How are graphics depicted on the screen? What is a pixel?
7. What is the hardware connection for graphics packages? If you have a personal computer at your disposal, explain what type of graphics it displays.
8. Name the four types of graphics packages. Which type do you think you would use in school? If your school has a mainframe, which types of graphics packages does it support?
9. What types of charts and graphs are used most often for analysis graphics and presentation graphics? When is a mainframe graphics package more appropriate than a personal computer package?
10. What word processing and graphics software packages does your local computer store carry for the personal computer at your disposal? Which package(s) would you purchase and why?

Hands On
GETTING STARTED

A set of six software packages is available with *Living with Computers* to enhance your learning experience. This set of packages includes the popular types of personal computer software—word processing (HBJ: WRITE), graphics (HBJ: GRAPH), spreadsheet analysis (HBJ: PLAN), personal budgeting (HBJ: BUDGET), data base management (HBJ: FILE), and communications (HBJ: TALK). Each package can be accessed from either Apple or IBM disks that may be supplied with this textbook. Before we discuss how to access these packages, we should consider the two types of computers for which the packages are available and the preparation of the data disks that receive the files generated by the HBJ software packages.

The IBM PC and the Apple II Series

HBJ software packages are available for two types of computers—the IBM PC and the Apple IIe/c series of computers. The IBM PC includes the IBM PC, XT, and Portable; the Apple IIe/c series includes the Apple IIe and Apple IIc.

In our discussion of data disk preparation and accessing the HBJ main menu, we will refer to the disk drives on each type of computer. For the IBM PC, these drives are referred to as drive A and drive B. Drive A is usually located on the left. For the Apple II series, the disk drives are referred to as drive 1 and drive 2 (abbreviated d1 and d2, respectively). Drive 1 is usually located on top when the drives are stacked one above the other.

Preparing a Data Disk

Before using any HBJ software package (or any other software package), you must prepare a data disk to store the files generated by the package, because these files are not stored on the HBJ disk itself. The major difference in this process between the IBM PC and the Apple computers lies in the commands needed for the disk preparation process. A data disk should be prepared only *once*. If the disk is prepared again after information is stored on it, the information on the disk is lost.

To prepare a data disk on the IBM PC, you should insert the DOS system disk in drive A and turn the computer on using the switch at the back of the computer. The computer then accesses the DOS disk and requests the date and time. You may enter the date and time and press the Enter key, or you may simply press the Enter key for each value. (If the computer does not ask for the date and time, then it probably has a clock/calendar board that automatically supplies these values.) In any case, the A-prompt (A>) is displayed on the screen next, and the computer is ready to prepare, or format, a data disk. Simply insert a blank, double-sided, double-density floppy disk (available at any computer store) in drive B, type the following:

```
FORMAT B:
```

and press the Enter key (the key with the ↵ symbol, the word Enter or Return, or something similar) when instructed to do so. (We will refer to it as the Enter key.) When the computer asks whether you wish to format another disk, type an "n" for no if you do not wish to format another disk. If you do want to format another disk, answer "y" and insert a new disk in drive B.

To prepare a data disk on an Apple computer, insert the DOS disk in drive 1 and turn the computer on using the switch located at the rear of the computer. When the prompt appears, insert a single-sided, double-density data disk in drive 2, type the following command:

```
INIT name,d2
```

and press the Enter key. In this situation, *name* is any combination of eight characters or less, and d2 refers to drive 2. For example,

```
INIT DATADISK,d2
```

prepares the blank data disk in drive 2 to receive files generated by any HBJ software package. At this point, the DOS disk in drive 1 and the data disk in drive 2 should be removed and the computer turned off.

Accessing the HBJ Main Menu

To access any HBJ software package, you should first *boot* the computer and then access the HBJ main menu. For either the IBM PC or the Apple computers, booting the computer involves simply inserting the disks and turning on the computer. However, the order for inserting the disks in the IBM PC is different from that in the Apple II series.

To boot the IBM PC, first insert the DOS disk in drive A and turn on the computer. When the A-prompt (A⟩) appears, remove the DOS disk from drive A and replace it with the IBM version of the HBJ disk. The data disk prepared earlier is then inserted in drive B. Type the command "HBJ" at the A-prompt, as follows:

```
A>HBJ
```

When the main menu appears, choose the package you want by entering the appropriate number.

To boot an Apple computer, simply insert the Apple version of the HBJ disk in drive 1 and the data disk in drive 2 and turn on the computer. The Apple version of the HBJ disk includes DOS 3.3. To access the main menu, type "HBJ" and press the Enter Key.

Loading DOS on the IBM Disk

If you own a version of DOS for the IBM PC, you can load DOS on the HBJ system disk. Simply insert your DOS disk in drive A and the HBJ system disk in drive B. When you type the command

```
A>B:ONLOAD2
```

DOS is copied onto your HBJ system disk. After this procedure, you may boot an IBM computer by inserting the HBJ system disk in drive A and turning on the computer.

Choosing from the Menu

When the main menu appears on the screen, as shown in Figure A-1, you can access any package by choosing the appropriate number between 1 and 6. Enter the number 7 to exit from the main menu. You need not press the Enter key after entering the number. All menus require only a single keystroke to make a selection. Instructions for each package are given in tutorials at the end of this supplement and of the next three chapters. Further instructions and examples are given in the Study Guide to accompany *Living with Computers*.

Defaults and Completion Aids

In all six software packages, you will be requested to supply information by choosing from a menu, answering a yes/no question, or filling out a completion aid. When a menu is presented, simply enter the number corresponding to your choice. You need *not* press Enter when choosing from any HBJ menu. However, you must press Enter when answering a yes/no question or filling out a completion aid.

In each HBJ software package, you may be asked to answer yes/no questions. When yes/no questions are posed, the cursor appears under either "y" for yes or "n" for no. If you press the Enter key without changing the cursor's position, you have implemented the *default answer*. If you do not wish to accept the default answer, simply type in the first letter of the acceptable answer and press Enter.

When the computer requests more than a simple yes or no answer, a completion aid is provided. A *completion aid* is a series of underlines that shows the maximum length of an acceptable answer. When information is required, the cursor appears at the beginning of the completion aid. The information that is entered replaces the underlines in the completion aid. When the completion aid is filled in, press the Enter key to implement the information. Until the Enter key is pressed, you can change this information by using the arrow and Delete keys.

FIGURE A-1
HBJ Main Menu

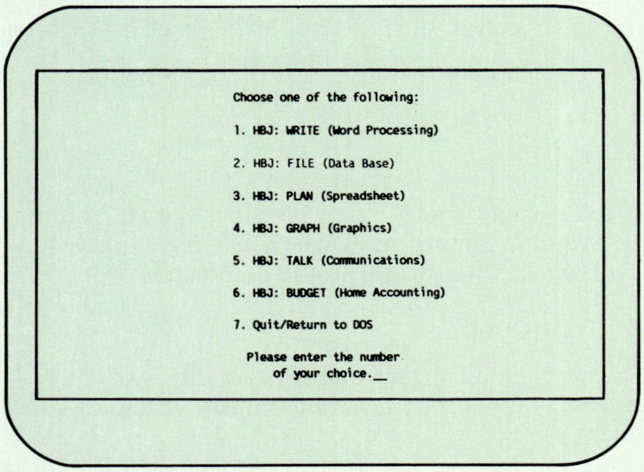

File Names

When information that is generated by a software package is stored for later use, it must be saved on the data diskette that was prepared earlier. The information on the data diskette is easily saved by the use of completion aids. When information from the HBJ software is saved, the completion aid shows 14 positions for a file name. However, file names can only be eight characters long, unless special circumstances exist—such as having only one disk drive, having a hard disk, or needing to use an extension to the file name. When a file name is entered and the Enter key is pressed, the information is automatically stored under that file name on the data diskette in drive B for the IBM PC or in drive 2 for the Apple IIe/c.

To save a file on a diskette in a one-disk drive system, you must specify the drive by name. For example, to save a file on a diskette in drive A of an IBM PC, type

```
A:SOMEFILE
```

For an Apple system with one drive, type

```
SOMEFILE, D1
```

Any information that is stored on the data diskette can be retrieved later by giving the appropriate file name and loading the file into internal memory. The data diskette must be in the appropriate disk drive for the file to be accessed.

Using the Different Keyboards

Because IBM and Apple II keyboards are different in their makeup, we should explain how each keyboard handles different commands. In our discussion, the ⟨⟩ symbols signify the use of a particular key on either keyboard. For example, ⟨F1⟩ indicates that the F1 key is used, and ⟨Ctrl⟩ refers to the Control key. The IBM keyboard has function keys (F1, F2, and so on) and the Apple does not. Therefore, when a package calls for an IBM function key, we show the Apple equivalent in parentheses in our discussion. For example, if ⟨F10⟩ on the IBM keyboard is pressed for on-screen help, we follow this instruction with (or ⟨Ctrl⟩⟨i⟩), indicating that the Control key and "i" should be pressed at the same time for on-screen help on an Apple computer.

The two computers have the same cursor movement keys—the up, down, left, and right arrows. When pressed, these keys move the cursor in the direction of the arrow on the key pressed. If held down, these keys repeat, moving the cursor several positions in the indicated direction.

Error Messages and the Esc Key

When an inappropriate key is pressed or an unacceptable answer is given, an error message appears on the screen, giving you the opportunity to correct your answer. If your command is incorrect, you can cancel it by pressing the Esc (Escape) key. In general, ⟨Esc⟩ can be used to "back out" of any command or menu choice. When in doubt, press ⟨Esc⟩.

Hands on

HBJ: WRITE

As we discussed in Chapter 10, a word processing software package allows you to enter, edit, and print text using a computer keyboard, screen, and printer. The text entry process involves typing the text from the keyboard, and the editing process allows you to make changes, additions, and deletions to the text to arrive at a final document. This final document may then be printed.

Word Processing

Most word processing packages are command driven; that is, you must learn a series of commands to prepare the screen for data entry, to perform text editing, and to print the document. HBJ: WRITE is menu driven for ease of use through a *command line* that appears when you press the Esc key. The last line of the screen normally contains the following message

```
Type text or press <Esc> for commands
```

The command line appears when ⟨Esc⟩ is pressed, and you select a command by entering the first letter of the desired command or moving the cursor to the appropriate command with the left and right arrow keys. If you enter the first letter of the command, you need not press ⟨Enter⟩ to activate the command. On the other hand, if you select the command by moving the cursor, you must press ⟨Enter⟩ to activate the command. A command can be aborted at any time by pressing ⟨Esc⟩.

In addition to the command line, the software includes a *ruler line*, which shows the margins and tabs, and a *column/line counter*, which shows the current location of the cursor. The ruler line appears on the next to last line on the screen, and the column/line counter and command line are on the last line of the screen. Figure 10-2 (page 229) shows the ruler line, column/line counter, and command line for HBJ: WRITE before any text is entered.

HBJ: WRITE supports *word wrap*, so you need not press ⟨Enter⟩ when the text you are entering reaches the right margin. The software automatically moves the next word to the next line. However, HBJ: WRITE does *not* support word "unwrap"—that is, it does not move text up from a previous line during deletion, and it does not rewrap lines during insertion in the middle of a line. These two limitations are handled by a *reformatting* command that reorganizes a paragraph to account for an addition or deletion.

HBJ: WRITE limits the document size to 150 lines. Single-spaced documents are printed at 50 lines per page; double-spaced documents have 25 lines per page. Documents may be up to six double-spaced (three single-spaced) pages long, and they may be chained together by printing them one after the other. You can also save one document and then either load an existing document or create a new document from within HBJ: WRITE without exiting the package and starting again.

Using the Keys

In addition to the standard letter, number, and punctuation keys used in preparing text, ⟨Esc⟩ accesses the command line. The cursor can be moved around on the screen with the arrow keys. Four other actions are implemented on different keys on the IBM and Apple computers. Table WRITE–1 shows these four actions and the IBM and Apple keys that activate them. The backspace key (delete left) is active on the IBM. On the Apple, the effect of a backspace key is obtained using the left arrow key plus the delete key. When the strikeover mode is activated by the Ins key for the IBM (or ⟨Ctrl⟩⟨o⟩), the cursor changes from an underline to a large block. The cursor change indicates that any characters entered will replace the current characters rather than push them to the right, as in the insert mode. Pressing the strikeover key sequence again changes the cursor back to an insert mode underline.

Table WRITE–1
ACTION KEYS

Action	*IBM*
Strike-over mode	⟨Ins⟩
Delete character	⟨Del⟩
Top of document	⟨Home⟩
End of document	⟨End⟩

Action	*Apple IIe/c*
Strike-over mode	⟨Ctrl⟩⟨o⟩
Delete character	⟨Delete⟩
Top of document	⟨Ctrl⟩⟨t⟩
End of document	⟨Ctrl⟩⟨e⟩

Getting Started

To use HBJ: WRITE, you must first boot the computer, access the HBJ main menu, and select option 1. Once you have selected this option, the ruler line, the column/line counter, and the command message appear on the screen. The ruler line has default margins of 1 and 80 and default tabs of 8, 16, 24, 32, 40, 48, 56, 64, and 72. The column/line counter is set to 1/1 to denote that the cursor is initially at the first column of the first line.

You probably will want to change the default margins and tabs to something standard for creating letters, memos, papers, and so on. To change the margins, press ⟨Esc⟩ to view the command line and then select Margin. The current margins are shown with the cursor on the value for the left margin. To change these values, simply type a new value for the left and/or right margin, pressing ⟨Enter⟩ after each new margin value. You can change both margins before returning to the text screen. The margins may be changed during text entry, but these changes only affect text that is subsequently entered. This function can be very useful for indenting long quotations.

Changing the tabs is similar to changing the margins—that is, you press ⟨Esc⟩ and select Tab. At this point, the current tab settings are shown with the cursor on the first one. New tab settings are entered simply by typing over the old ones or by entering new values. The space bar can be used to wipe out the old values, or the left and right arrow keys can be used to move to a particular value that you wish to change. The Del key (or ⟨Delete⟩) can also be used to delete current tab settings. Press ⟨Enter⟩, and the new ruler line is shown with the new tab settings. Figure WRITE–1 shows a new ruler line with margins of 10 and 70 and tab settings of 15, 20, and 50.

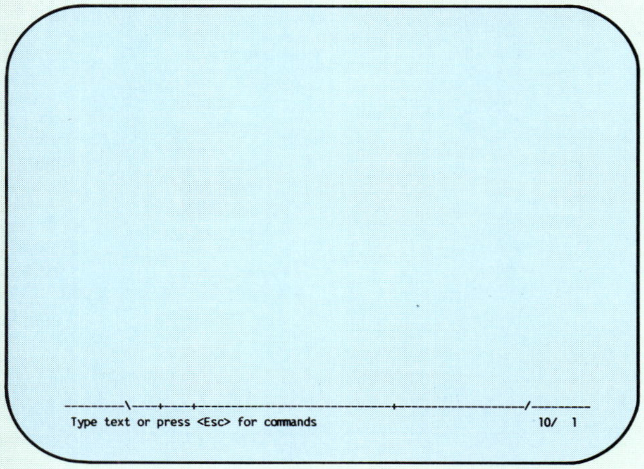

FIGURE WRITE–1
HBJ: WRITE Ruler Line

Working with Text

With the margins and tabs set to your needs, you can enter text simply by typing. As you type, note that the column/line counter changes to account for the current cursor location. To move the cursor to the first tab setting, simply press the Tab key. Pressing it again moves the cursor to the second setting and so on. To create a blank line, simply press ⟨Enter⟩ for each blank line needed. The cursor may be moved anywhere within existing text by means of the cursor keys.

Editing Text

After text is entered, it may be *edited* by inserting new text, replacing existing text, or deleting existing text. To insert text within existing material, move the cursor to the location of the desired insert, and type the new text. After inserting all of the new text, remember to press ⟨Esc⟩ and select Reformat to reorganize the paragraph.

To replace existing text, place the cursor over the text to be replaced and change to the strikeover mode by pressing ⟨Ins⟩ (or ⟨Ctrl⟩⟨o⟩). The cursor changes from an underline to a block, and any new text is typed over the existing text. To return to the insert mode, press ⟨Ins⟩ (or ⟨Ctrl⟩⟨o⟩) again, and the cursor becomes an underline.

Existing text can be deleted through the use of ⟨Del⟩ (or ⟨Delete⟩), which deletes the character under the cursor. If the Del key is held down, the line of text is pulled to the left underneath the cursor and deleted. You cannot delete text past that on the current line without moving to a new line or reorganizing the paragraph using the Reformat command. If you attempt to delete past the end of the current line, the message

```
Can't delete
```

appears on the message line. Figure WRITE–2 shows the effect of deleting text before and after the use of the Reformat command.

FIGURE WRITE–2
Original Document (left)
Deletion of Text before (right)
the Reformat Command

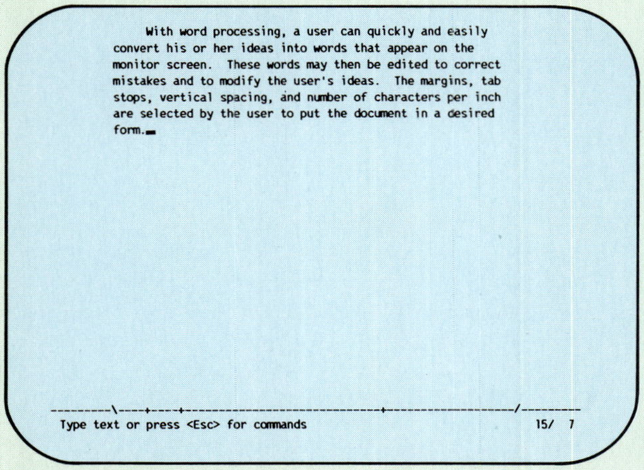

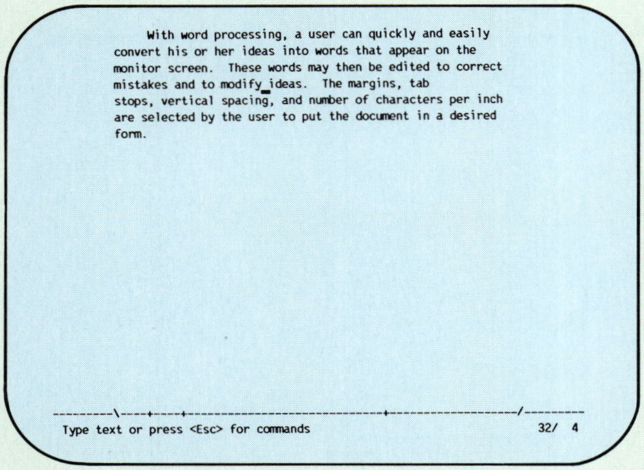

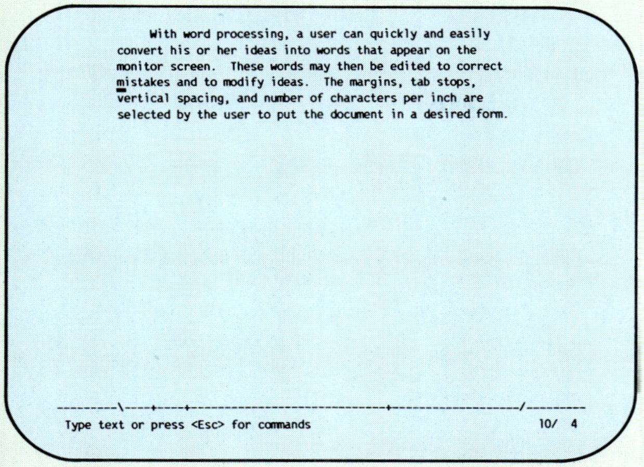

FIGURE WRITE–2 (continued) Deletion of Text after the Reformat Command

Printing or Saving a Document

After you have entered your document, turn your printer on and use the Print command to output the document to your printer by pressing ⟨Esc⟩ and selecting Print. You will then be asked if you wish the document double-spaced. If you answer "y," then the resulting document will contain 25 lines per page. Otherwise, it will contain 50 lines per page.

The document may also be saved by pressing ⟨Esc⟩ and selecting Save. Be sure your data disk is inserted in drive B; the document is saved to that disk. You must assign a file name (eight characters or less) to the document. Figure WRITE–3 shows a document that is saved.

Loading or Creating a Document

You may retrieve an existing document (one that was previously saved) by pressing ⟨Esc⟩ and selecting the Load command. At this point, if a document displayed on the screen has not been saved, the software will ask if that

FIGURE WRITE–3 (left) Saving a Document

FIGURE WRITE–4 (right) HBJ: WRITE Help Screen

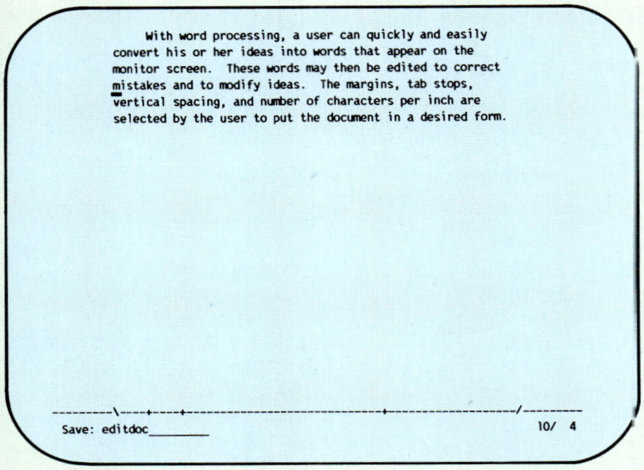

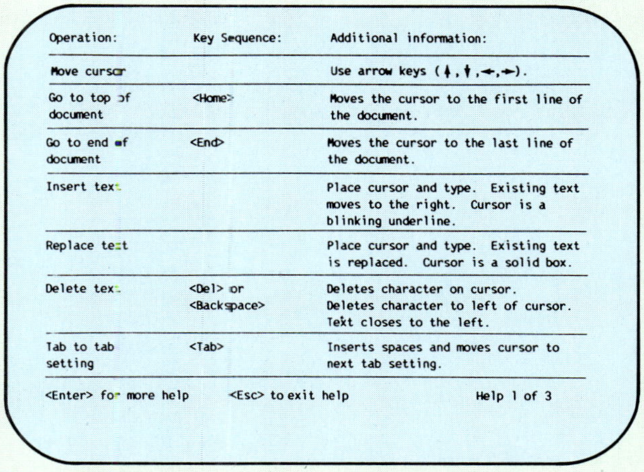

document can be erased. If you answer "y," then you must give the file name of the document to be retrieved. If the document exists, it is displayed on the screen. Otherwise, an error message is displayed.

At any point during the use of HBJ: WRITE, you may choose to work on a new document through the Create command. This command clears the screen and erases the current document. If you need the current document, be sure to save it before you use the Create command.

The Create command is useful for *chaining* text together. If your document is longer than three single-spaced pages, you may save the first three pages, use the Create command, and begin the next three pages of the document. This procedure may be repeated as many times as needed. Remember to give each three-page section of the document a different file name—DOC1, DOC2, and so on. The document can be printed by sequentially loading each section using the Load command and then the Print command.

Finding a String of Characters

To search for a particular word or string of characters within your document, use the Find command. When this command is selected, you are asked for the character string to be found. You should enter the exact characters that you want to find, including spaces or special characters. When the character string is first found, the cursor is placed on the first character of the word or string. Additional occurrences can be found by pressing the space bar. In each case, the cursor is placed on the first character of the string.

Exiting the Document and Obtaining Help

If at any point during the use of HBJ: WRITE you need help with the package, press ⟨Esc⟩ and select Help. You will be shown the commands that are available to you. Figure WRITE–4 shows the first help screen in HBJ: WRITE.

To exit HBJ: WRITE, save your document, press ⟨Esc⟩, and select Quit. At this point, you will be returned to the main menu.

Command Summary

Table WRITE–2 contains the commands available with HBJ: WRITE. Note that you need not press ⟨Enter⟩ when a command is selected, but you must press ⟨Enter⟩ when additional information is included with the command.

Table WRITE–2 SUMMARY OF HBJ: WRITE COMMANDS

Command	*Key Sequence*	*Additional Information*
Find a string	⟨Esc⟩⟨f⟩	String to be found
On-screen help	⟨Esc⟩⟨h⟩	
Create a new document	⟨Esc⟩⟨c⟩	Ok to lose changes? (y/n)
Load a document	⟨Esc⟩⟨l⟩	File name of document
Save a document	⟨Esc⟩⟨s⟩	File name of document
Set margins	⟨Esc⟩⟨m⟩	Location of left and right margins
Set tabs	⟨Esc⟩⟨t⟩	Tab locations
Reformat a paragraph	⟨Esc⟩⟨r⟩	
Print a document	⟨Esc⟩⟨p⟩	Double spacing? (y/n)
Exit program	⟨Esc⟩⟨q⟩	Ok to lose changes? (y/n)
Terminate a command	⟨Esc⟩	

Hands On

HBJ: GRAPH

With HBJ: GRAPH, you can construct pie charts, bar graphs, line graphs, and scatter diagrams by entering labels and data. HBJ: GRAPH, which is completely menu driven, has menus from which to choose options and completion aids to be filled out. On-screen help is available for all menus by pressing ⟨F10⟩ (or ⟨Ctrl⟩⟨i⟩).

To use HBJ: GRAPH, boot the HBJ system disk and choose option 4. Insert a prepared data disk in drive B (drive 2 for an Apple computer). This data disk is used to store the graph data for future use.

Graphs can be created and displayed using a nongraphics (monochrome) system. For best results, HBJ: GRAPH should be run on a system with graphics capability.

Getting Started

The HBJ: GRAPH main menu, shown in Figure GRAPH–1, is the first thing you see. This menu shows four options. You can select options from this menu to create a new graph, to load data from the data file for a previously created graph, to delete data for a previously created graph, or to exit HBJ: GRAPH.

If you select options 2 or 3 from the main menu, you must enter a file name of eight letters or less. If graph data are loaded from the data disk (option 2), then the file name you enter is the file from which the data are retrieved. If graph data are deleted (option 3), then the file name you enter is the file that is erased. You should remember that once a file is erased, that file (and the data stored on it) cannot be recalled.

Pressing ⟨Esc⟩ from the file name completion screen returns you to the HBJ: GRAPH main menu. If you select option 4 from the main menu, you return to the HBJ main menu.

Creating a New Graph

If you select option 1—that is, create a new graph—then you see a second menu from which you can select one of the following types of graph: pie

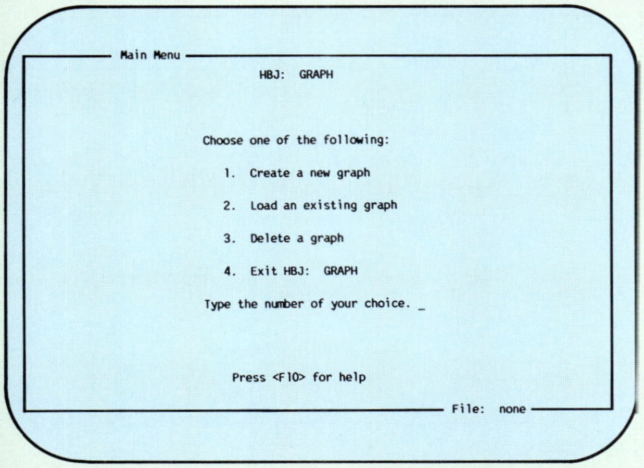

FIGURE GRAPH–1
HBJ: GRAPH
Main Menu

chart, bar graph, line graph, or scatter diagram. Enter the number corresponding to the type of graph you want—that is, 1 for pie chart, 2 for bar graph, 3 for line graph, or 4 for scatter diagram. Figure GRAPH–2 shows this graph selection menu.

After you select the type of graph you want to create, a *graph design screen* appears for that graph. This screen allows you to design the graph by filling out completion aids for the name of the graph, the number of categories, and the names of the horizontal and vertical axes (if applicable). Move the cursor to each completion aid by pressing ⟨Enter⟩. When all the information has been entered, you move to a *data entry screen* by pressing ⟨F1⟩ (or ⟨Ctrl⟩⟨f⟩). Press ⟨F10⟩ (or ⟨Ctrl⟩⟨i⟩) for help. You may quit this option by pressing ⟨Esc⟩.

The data entry screen shows you the type of graph generated, the name given to that graph, the number of categories selected, and the names of the horizontal and vertical axes (if applicable). The screen then allows you to enter labels and data values by using completion aids. One set of completion aids exists for each category. All completion aids must be filled out and ⟨Enter⟩ pressed each time before the graph can be generated.

Once these data are entered, you have several alternatives: return to the previous screen by pressing ⟨F1⟩ (⟨Ctrl⟩⟨f⟩); display the graph by pressing ⟨F3⟩ (⟨Ctrl⟩⟨v⟩); print the graph by pressing ⟨F4⟩ (⟨Ctrl⟩⟨p⟩); save the data under the desired file name by pressing ⟨F5⟩ (⟨Ctrl⟩⟨s⟩); obtain help by pressing ⟨F10⟩ (⟨Ctrl⟩⟨i⟩); or quit the option by pressing ⟨Esc⟩. You must save the graph data *before* attempting to print the graph.

Creating a Pie Chart

After you enter a "1" at the graph selection menu, you must enter the name of the pie chart (up to 20 characters in length) and the number of categories (to a maximum of 12). After you enter this design information and press ⟨F1⟩, a data entry screen for the pie chart appears. This screen requests a label and a numeric value for each category. The numeric values for the categories *must*

FIGURE GRAPH–2
Graph Selection Menu

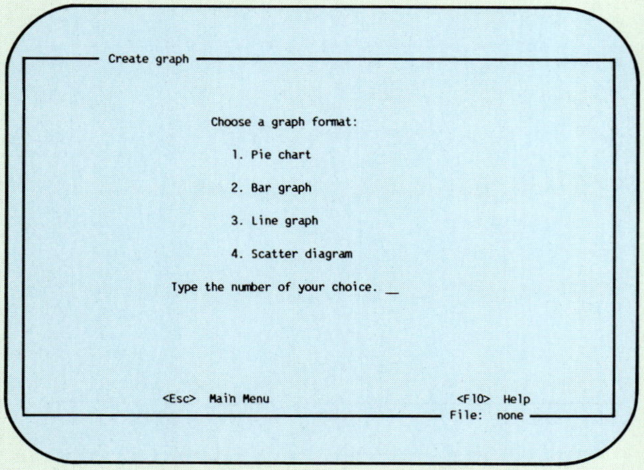

be integer values (*no* decimal portion) that sum to 100. Press ⟨Enter⟩ after entering each label or data value. Figure GRAPH–3 shows a design screen, a data entry screen, and the pie chart for the results of a hypothetical survey of computer owners. The chart's six categories are IBM, Apple, Commodore, Tandy, Compaq, and Others. The values for these categories are, respectively, 31%, 29%, 18%, 11%, 4%, and 7%. We use these data to demonstrate the other graphs available in HBJ: GRAPH.

Press ⟨F3⟩ (or ⟨Ctrl⟩⟨v⟩) to display the graph. Press any key to return to the data entry screen. After returning to the data entry screen, you may change the design screen information or the data and redisplay the graph without starting over again.

Creating a Bar Graph

If you enter a "2" at the graph selection menu, your design process for a bar graph involves entering the name of the graph, the number of categories

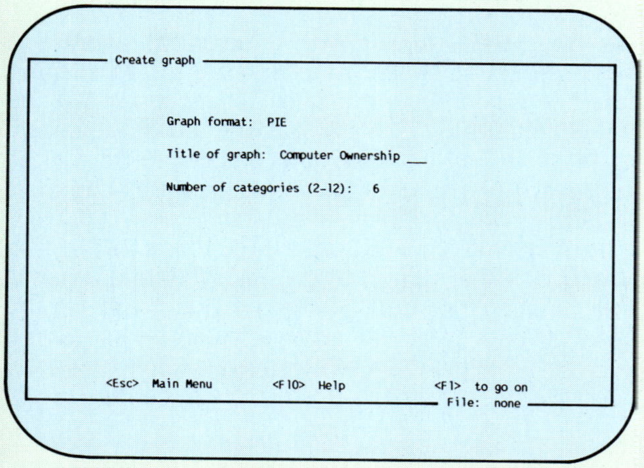

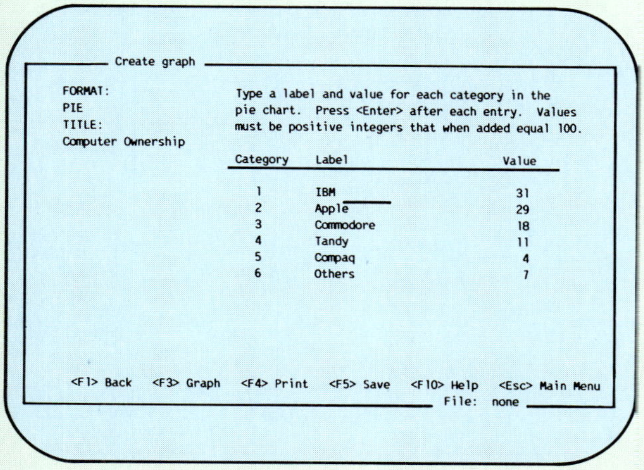

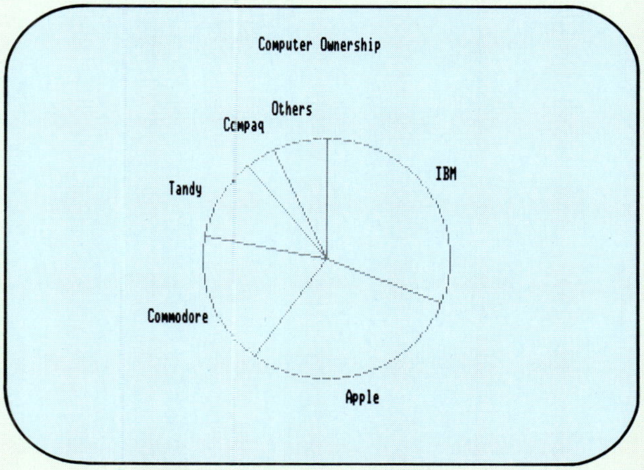

FIGURE GRAPH–3
Creating a Pie Chart
Design Screen (top)
Data Entry Screen (bottom left)
Final Pie Chart (bottom right)

(2–12), the name of the x (horizontal) axis (up to 20 characters in length), and the name of the y (vertical) axis. The design screen for the bar graph is similar to the one shown in Figure GRAPH–3 for the pie chart. In the computer survey example, the label for the x axis is Type, the label for the y axis is Percentage, and six categories of information are graphed.

After the bar graph is designed, press ⟨F1⟩ (or ⟨Ctrl⟩⟨f⟩) to call up the data entry screen. This screen shows the name of the bar graph, the names of the x and y axes, and the completion aids for the labels and values. The values must be integers between 0 and 100. Press ⟨Enter⟩ after entering each label and value. The names and values in the bar graph are the same as those used for the pie chart. The data entry screen for the bar graph is similar to that for the pie chart shown in Figure GRAPH–3.

Figure GRAPH–4 shows the bar graph for the computer survey data displayed previously as a pie chart. The labels and the x axis title are shown across the x axis, and the numeric range and the y axis title are shown down the y axis on the left.

Creating a Line Graph

After you select "3" from the graph selection menu, the software presents design and data entry screens that are similar to those used for the pie and bar charts. The title of the line graph, the number of categories (2–12), the name of the x axis, and the name of the y axis are all entered in the design screen. Press ⟨F1⟩ (or⟨Ctrl⟩⟨f⟩) after all information is entered to call up the data entry screen, which displays the names of the graph, the x axis, and the y axis, along with the completion aids for entering the data.

Completion aids for the x axis labels and values are shown in the data entry screen for each category. Press ⟨Enter⟩ after each label and value is entered to save these values. Figure GRAPH–5 shows a line graph for the computer survey data previously displayed as a pie chart and a bar graph.

FIGURE GRAPH–4
The Bar Graph

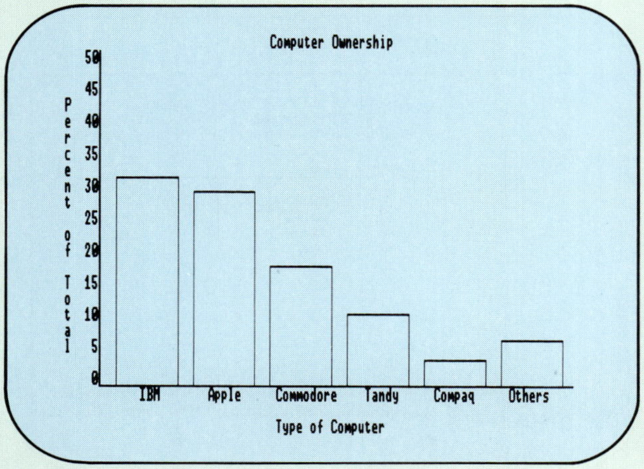

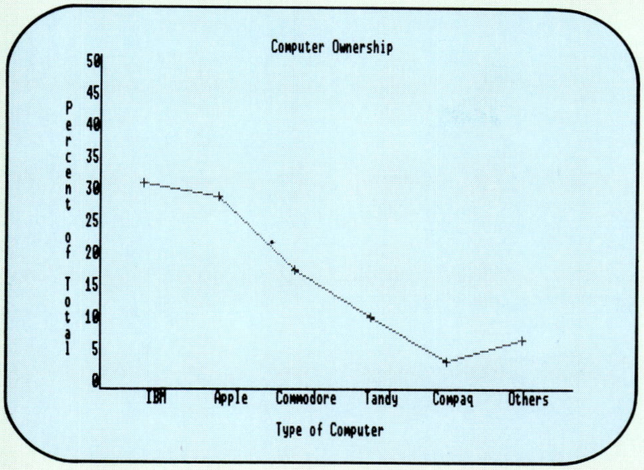

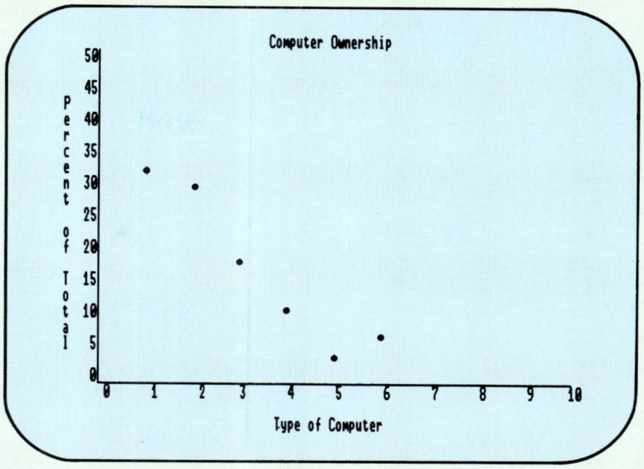

FIGURE GRAPH–5 (left)
The Line Graph

FIGURE GRAPH–6 (right)
The Scatter Diagram

Creating a Scatter Diagram

Entering a "4" for the graph selection menu produces design and data entry screens that are similar to those used for the previous graphs. The design screen requests the name of the graph, the number of points shown on the scatter diagram (2–36), the name of the *x* axis, and the name of the *y* axis. Press ⟨F1⟩ (or⟨Ctrl⟩⟨f⟩) after all the information is entered, and the software displays the data entry screen for the scatter diagram.

The data entry screen for the scatter diagram is a little different from those used for the previous three graphs. You must enter an *x* and *y* (horizontal and vertical) numerical coordinate for each point on the scatter diagram. Both values must be positive integers between 0 and 100. After entering coordinates for all the points in the scatter diagram, you have the six alternatives mentioned earlier on page 256. Figure GRAPH–6 shows the computer survey data in a scatter diagram.

Saving and Printing a Graph

You can save a graph from any data entry screen by pressing ⟨F5⟩ (or ⟨Ctrl⟩⟨s⟩). The graph data are saved under the file name you are requested to enter (8 characters or less). A graph must be saved before it can be printed.

A graph may be printed by pressing ⟨F4⟩ (or ⟨Ctrl⟩⟨p⟩). The printer must be connected to the computer and turned on before you attempt to print the graph. With an Apple system, the graph may be printed using an Imagewriter or Epson compatible printer. With an IBM system, an Epson compatible printer can be used.

Exiting HBJ: GRAPH

If you press ⟨Esc⟩ in any graph design screen or data entry screen, you return to the main menu for HBJ: GRAPH. At this point, you may select option 4 to exit the package.

Because financial matters are so important to individuals and companies, numerous software packages manage and analyze financial information. These packages can be broadly divided into two types—financial analysis packages and accounting packages. Financial analysis packages, or spreadsheets, allow a user to work with data in a tabular format. Spreadsheets also allow the user to ask "What if?" questions about data. Accounting packages are available for businesses and for individuals. Personal budgeting packages include functions for managing investments, tax preparation, and managing personal finances. Business accounting packages, which track a firm's financial status, include such modules as a general ledger, accounts receivable, accounts payable, payroll, order processing, and inventory control.

11 Financial Analysis and Accounting Packages

STUDY OBJECTIVES

After reading this chapter, you should be able to

- Recognize financial software packages for computers.
- Explain how a spreadsheet works and the types of entries used in a spreadsheet.
- Understand how a spreadsheet can be used to plan budgets and make forecasts.
- Discuss the various types of packages that are available for managing personal finances.
- Explain personal budgeting packages and how they may be used to track an individual's finances.
- Understand the purpose of business accounting software packages and the modules that compose a business accounting package.

INTRODUCTION TO FINANCIAL PACKAGES

People put just about anything on a spreadsheet. Any application that you can do with paper, pencil, and a calculator you should be able to do better with a spreadsheet.

Tod Riedel, President of First Micro

(As quoted in "Building Simple Spreadsheets," *Personal Computing*, January 1985, pp. 61–67.)

Shortly after the first commercial computers were available, large corporations and institutions discovered that a computer could easily keep track of company finances. Because a computer stores numerical data and quickly adds and subtracts those numbers, tracking finances was a natural application of computers. Initially, only large companies could afford mainframe computers. However, with the increased availability of minicomputers and personal computers, more small companies and individuals have financial management by computer.

Financial management consists of several functions, including budgeting, forecasting, inventory control, break-even analysis, investment analysis, and accounting. **Budgeting** compares anticipated expenses with anticipated income. **Forecasting** uses currently available information to predict future occurrences. **Inventory control** keeps track of raw materials, goods in process, finished goods, and other supplies needed by the company. **Break-even analysis** calculates the number of units of a given product that must be produced and sold before a profit is realized. **Investment analysis** seeks to determine the best use for available cash, and **accounting** encompasses a host of activities that track the financial health of a company or individual.

Financial management software for mainframes and minicomputers is available for institutions and companies that process large amounts of data. For small companies and individuals, a large number of financial management software packages can be run on all varieties of computers. Software for all computer sizes is necessary because of the differences in users' needs. A personal computer could not handle the payroll for a large university, state government agency, or automotive assembly plant. A mainframe or large minicomputer is needed for this function. On the other hand, a small, family-run store with a few part-time employees can use a personal computer with a hard disk to handle its inventory control and accounting needs very easily. The individual who wishes to keep track of finances and tax records can use almost any personal computer with a disk drive to perform this function.

Using personal budgeting software, a family can better track finances and plan for future expenditures.

Financial management software packages for mainframes are often extremely expensive to purchase (over $50,000) and involve much interaction between the company and the software supplier. Therefore, we concentrate here on the software that is available for personal computers. Three broad categories of financial management software exist—financial analysis or spreadsheet packages, personal financial management packages, and business accounting packages.

A financial analysis, or spreadsheet, package can be used for most of the functions listed earlier, but its greatest applications are in the areas of budgeting and forecasting. With a spreadsheet package, an entire budget or sales forecast can be set up, and the effects of changes to one or more of the anticipated values can be determined. A tutorial on HBJ: PLAN, the spreadsheet package that is available with this text, follows this chapter.

Personal financial management packages can help an individual keep track of finances. The three major operations of this type of software are personal accounting (classifying and summarizing all financial transactions), investment analysis, and tax planning. Each operation is discussed later in this chapter, and a tutorial explaining HBJ: BUDGET, the budgeting software that is available with this text, appears at the end of this chapter.

A business accounting package may have several modules that handle most of the functions listed above. However, the package is usually used for tracking the firm's financial health. This package includes a general ledger, accounts receivable, accounts payable, payroll, order processing, and inventory control.

FINANCIAL ANALYSIS PACKAGES

The explosion in the use of personal computer software packages can be traced directly to the 1979 introduction of VisiCalc, the first financial analysis package. Since that time, numerous packages containing many variations and improvements on VisiCalc have been released, for example, Lotus 1-2-3, SuperCalc^3, VisiCalc IV, and Multiplan. Regardless of the package, the general concept of using a table of numbers to represent budgets, sales forecasts, and so on, is the same. The term **spreadsheet** originated with the accountant's pad that had printed row and column lines. Budget or sales forecast figures were entered in pencil on the spreadsheet, and when one value was changed, all other values had to be recalculated by hand. Before explaining computer spreadsheet packages, let us consider a manual spreadsheet in more detail in the following budgeting example.

Jill Bradley, a recent college graduate, begins work in July with a local computer store as a salesperson/consultant. Jill has determined that her monthly take home salary will be $1,200 after deductions for federal and state taxes, Social Security, and health insurance. Jill can also receive a bonus of $100 if her sales are above $10,000 for a month, but she cannot depend on this extra income. Because her new job is in a large city away from her hometown, Jill must pay $400 a month to rent an apartment near her office. She has also bought a car that carries a monthly payment of $150. These expenses are **fixed expenses**, which do not change from month to month.

Financial management software is an important facet of the total personal computer software market.

Table 11-1 JILL BRADLEY'S BUDGET IN TABULAR FORM

	Month			
Item	*July*	*August*	*September*	*Total*
Salary (S)	$1,200	$1,200	$1,200	$3,600
Rent (R)	400	400	400	1,200
Car payment (C)	150	150	150	450
Utilities* (U)	100	100	100	300
Food* (F)	150	150	150	450
Gas* (G)	50	50	50	150
Expenses* (E = R + C + U + F + G)	850	850	850	2,550
Miscellaneous* (M = S − E)	350	350	350	1,050
Entertainment* (0.2 × M)	70	70	70	210
Clothing* (0.2 × M)	70	70	70	210
Savings* (0.6 × M)	210	210	210	630

Jill also has **variable expenses** for food, utilities (electricity and telephone), entertainment, clothing, and fuel for her car. Jill estimates the following monthly expenses: food, $150; utilities, $100; and gas for the car, $50. She also wants to save as much as possible over the next three months to purchase a video cassette recorder (VCR). The cost of the VCR is $500, the minimum that Jill must save in three months. The amount left from Jill's salary after expenses will be budgeted as follows: 20% to entertainment, 20% to clothes, and 60% to savings. This sounds complicated in text form, but it is very easy to see in tabular form in Table 11-1.

When a spreadsheet like VisiCalc is combined with a touch screen (shown here) or with voice input, "What if?" questions are quickly answered.

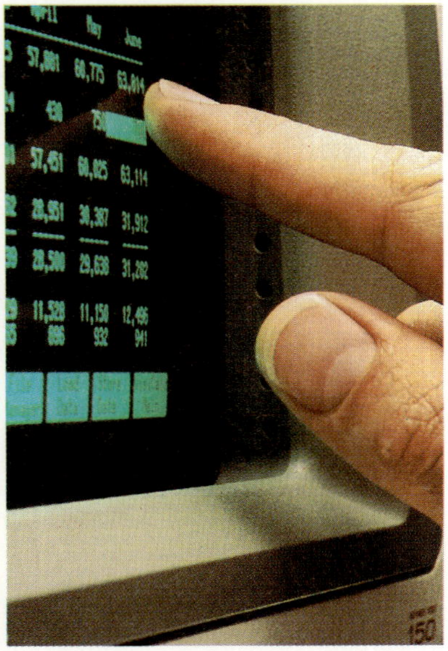

In Table 11-1, letters are assigned to the various quantities to show the relationships among the various values. Estimated values (for example, utilities) are marked by an asterisk (*), because these values are subject to change. Note also that Jill's total savings for the three months starting with July is $630. If Jill can follow this budget, she will have sufficient savings to buy the VCR.

Let us ask some "What if?" questions to determine how changes affect Jill's anticipated values. For example, what if the monthly utility bills are higher than expected (a very common occurrence) by 25%?. Total utility bills are $125 instead of $100, and the expense value (E) increases by $25 per month. This increase causes a corresponding drop in the amount available for entertainment, clothing, and savings. Recalculating all these values yields the revised budget shown in Table 11-2. The revised information in Table 11-2 shows that Jill can still expect to have enough savings to buy the VCR after three months.

What if food expenses are greater than expected, and a heat wave during this period drives up the cost of utilities even more? On the other hand, what would be the effect of Jill's receiving that $100 bonus some month? How would the budget be affected if Jill spent more on entertainment and clothing? These types of "What if?" questions can be checked with this spreadsheet.

Table 11-2 REVISED BUDGET

Item	Month			Total
	July	August	September	
Salary (S)	$1,200	$1,200	$1,200	$3,600
Rent (R)	400	400	400	1,200
Car payment (C)	150	150	150	450
Utilities* (U)	125	125	125	375
Food* (F)	150	150	150	450
Gas* (G)	50	50	50	150
Expenses* (E = R + C + U + F + G)	875	875	875	2,625
Miscellaneous* (M = S − E)	325	325	325	975
Entertainment* (0.2 × M)	65	65	65	195
Clothing* (0.2 × M)	65	65	65	195
Savings* (0.6 × M)	195	195	195	585

However, calculating table values with pencil and paper is tedious, especially if the number of months is extended to include an entire year or the number of expense categories increases.

Before the VisiCalc software package existed, a manager in a large company assigned the task of manipulating a spreadsheet with paper and pencil to a staff member. A busy manager could not take the time required to work with a spreadsheet manually. Small firms could not afford to have someone perform this type of manipulation because of the time and effort involved. With the advent of the electronic spreadsheet, any manager in any firm can personally do this manipulation quickly and easily. Because the manager is involved in this process, firms can hope for better planning, forecasting, and management.

Setting Up an Electronic Spreadsheet

An **electronic spreadsheet** on a computer works conceptually like a manual spreadsheet. However, once the values and relationships among the values (called formulas) are entered, the computer manipulates the values by performing a recalculation of all values when one value changes.

Before we discuss electronic spreadsheets in detail, let us look at some spreadsheet terminology. A spreadsheet is made up of horizontal **rows** and vertical **columns**. The intersection of a row and a column is a **cell**. One of the following three entities can be inserted into a cell: a label made of letters and digits; a numeric value; or a formula that shows the relationships among cells containing values. A **label** is any combination of letters and numbers that describes the contents of a row or column. Labels are not used in any sort of calculation. The months at the top of each column and the items listed at the left of each row in Table 11-1 are labels. **Values** are numbers, either positive or negative, with or without a decimal. They may be placed in any cell and then used in other calculations. The original values for salary, rent, car payment, and so on, in Table 11-1 are examples of values. **Formulas** are combinations of values in the spreadsheet with other constants that define the relationships among those spreadsheet values.

Formulas are an important part of a spreadsheet. A formula entered into a cell is a combination of cell identifiers and arithmetic symbols. In spreadsheet formulas, a plus sign (+) represents addition, a minus sign (−) represents subtraction, an asterisk (*) represents multiplication, a slash (/) represents division, and a caret (^) means raising a number to a power. The user can change the values in some cells and the computer automatically recalculates the values in the cells that contain formulas. For example, if the C8 cell is the sum of the C3, C4, C5, C6, and C7 cells, then the formula C3 + C4 + C5 + C6 + C7 would be entered in the C8 cell.

Using this notation, we can set up Jill Bradley's budget in electronic spreadsheet form using HBJ: PLAN. In Figure 11-1, the row numbers and column letters are shown in the form in which they would appear on the screen. The values for the blank cells depend on formulas to be input later.

The labels in Figure 11-1 are shortened to a maximum of nine characters. Label length is a function of the column width, which can be changed either for the entire spreadsheet or for individual columns depending on the software package in use. On most spreadsheets, a user can make global or local changes to such characteristics as cell width. A **global change** changes all cell widths, and a **local change** changes only a designated group of cells.

In Figure 11-1, the cell containing August rent would be identified as C3, where 3 is the number of the Rent row and C is the letter for the August column. Note that row 1 is used for column headings and column A is used for the item names. Using the same approach to identify the remaining cells, the formula for August expenses would be C3 + C4 + C5 + C6 + C7. If this formula is entered in the C8 (Expenses—August) cell, then the values in the cells that appear in the formula are used to calculate the value in the C8 cell.

To enter labels, values, and formulas, a special cursor called a **cell pointer** is moved into the cell in which the entry is to be made. This special cursor is the width of the cell and usually is in **reverse video**. In other words, dark letters appear on a light cursor, the reverse of the normal dark background and light letters. The entry does not actually appear in the cell when it is entered. Instead, it appears on an **edit line** above or below the

FIGURE 11-1 (left) Partial Electronic Spreadsheet for Jill Bradley's Budget

FIGURE 11-2 (right) Electronic Spreadsheet for Jill Bradley's Budget

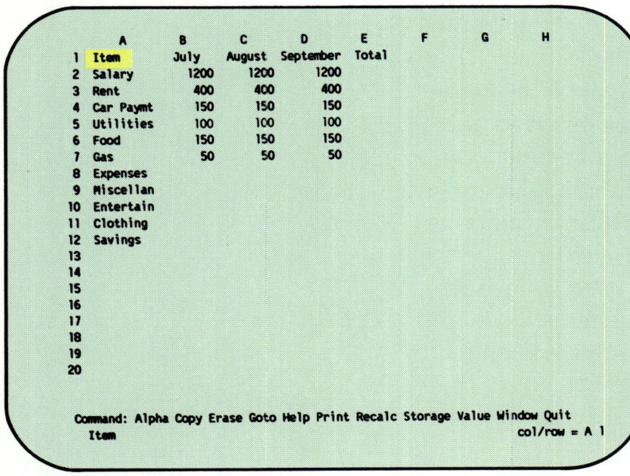

	A	B	C	D	E	F	G	H
1	Item	July	August	September	Total			
2	Salary	1200	1200	1200				
3	Rent	400	400	400				
4	Car Paymt	150	150	150				
5	Utilities	100	100	100				
6	Food	150	150	150				
7	Gas	50	50	50				
8	Expenses							
9	Miscellan							
10	Entertain							
11	Clothing							
12	Savings							
13								
14								
15								
16								
17								
18								
19								
20								

Command: Alpha Copy Erase Goto Help Print Recalc Storage Value Window Quit
Item col/row = A 1

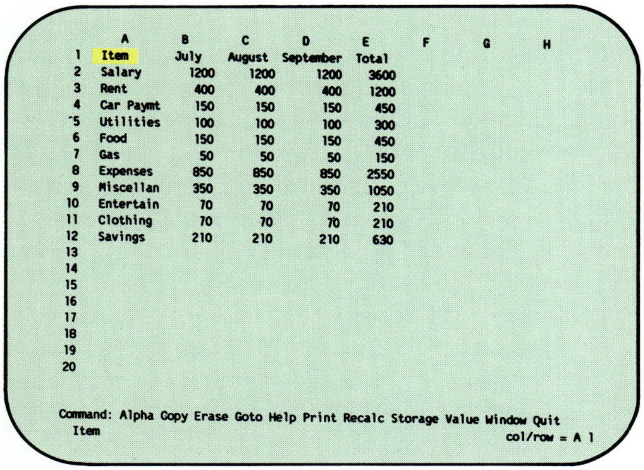

	A	B	C	D	E	F	G	H
1	Item	July	August	September	Total			
2	Salary	1200	1200	1200	3600			
3	Rent	400	400	400	1200			
4	Car Paymt	150	150	150	450			
5	Utilities	100	100	100	300			
6	Food	150	150	150	450			
7	Gas	50	50	50	150			
8	Expenses	850	850	850	2550			
9	Miscellan	350	350	350	1050			
10	Entertain	70	70	70	210			
11	Clothing	70	70	70	210			
12	Savings	210	210	210	630			
13								
14								
15								
16								
17								
18								
19								
20								

Command: Alpha Copy Erase Goto Help Print Recalc Storage Value Window Quit
Item col/row = A 1

spreadsheet during the entry process and then in the cell after the ENTER key is pressed. An individual label or value appears in the cell as entered, but only the result of a formula appears in the cell.

The formulas that are used to fill in the July column's blank cells in the spreadsheet in Figure 11-1 are shown in Table 11-3. The formulas for the corresponding August and September cells substitute C and D for B in each formula for the July cells. Each total column cell is the sum of each row's values. For example, the total Rent row, cell E3, equals B3 + C3 + D3. The formulas for other rows are the same except for the row number. After inserting each formula in the appropriate cell, the initial spreadsheet is obtained. However, only the results of the formulas, *not* the formulas themselves, appear in the appropriate cells. The Jill Bradley spreadsheet after the addition of formulas is shown in Figure 11-2, which is the same as the manual spreadsheet in Table 11-1, except Figure 11-2 has column and row identifiers.

Table 11-3
JULY CELL FORMULAS

Cell	*Formula*
B8	B3 + B4 + B5 + B6 + B7
B9	B2 − B8
B10	0.2*B9
B11	0.2*B9
B12	0.6*B9

Working with an Electronic Spreadsheet

Making spreadsheet changes by hand is tedious, but changes in an electronic spreadsheet are easy to make. Assume that Jill Bradley's utilities expenses for the first two months are $150 per month rather than $100. Monthly food costs for July and September are $200 rather than $150. To make these changes, the user simply moves the cursor to the four cells that are affected (B5, C5, B6, and D6) and changes the values in these cells. The HBJ: PLAN spreadsheet revised for these changes is shown in Figure 11-3.

Testing various assumptions on an electronic spreadsheet is very easy. Using a spreadsheet, Jill can test the effects of changes in her original estimated expense figures. In Figure 11-3, the amount available in her savings after three months is barely enough to purchase the VCR. In many business situations, managers may want to test various assumptions while developing an annual budget or forecasting the coming year's income.

Common Spreadsheet Features

Although commercial spreadsheet packages all differ in their ease of use and scope, most spreadsheets share a group of features. To understand the power of spreadsheets, we should discuss each feature briefly. Spreadsheets usually have the capabilities listed on the following page:

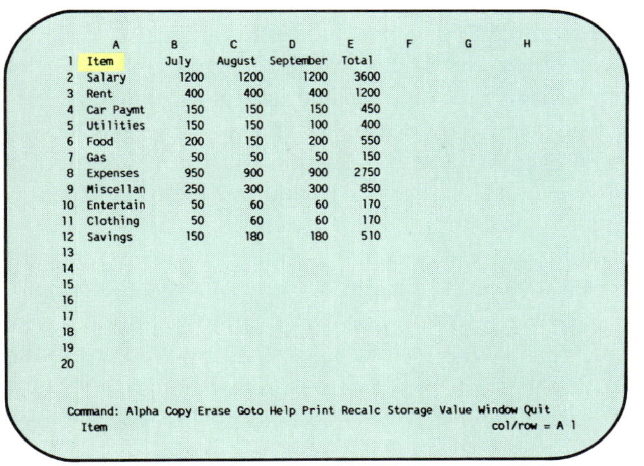

	A	B	C	D	E	F	G	H
1	Item	July	August	September	Total			
2	Salary	1200	1200	1200	3600			
3	Rent	400	400	400	1200			
4	Car Paymt	150	150	150	450			
5	Utilities	150	150	100	400			
6	Food	200	150	200	550			
7	Gas	50	50	50	150			
8	Expenses	950	900	900	2750			
9	Miscellan	250	300	300	850			
10	Entertain	50	60	60	170			
11	Clothing	50	60	60	170			
12	Savings	150	180	180	510			
13								
14								
15								
16								
17								
18								
19								
20								

Command: Alpha Copy Erase Goto Help Print Recalc Storage Value Window Quit
Item col/row = A 1

FIGURE 11-3
Modified Electronic Spreadsheet for Jill Bradley's Budget

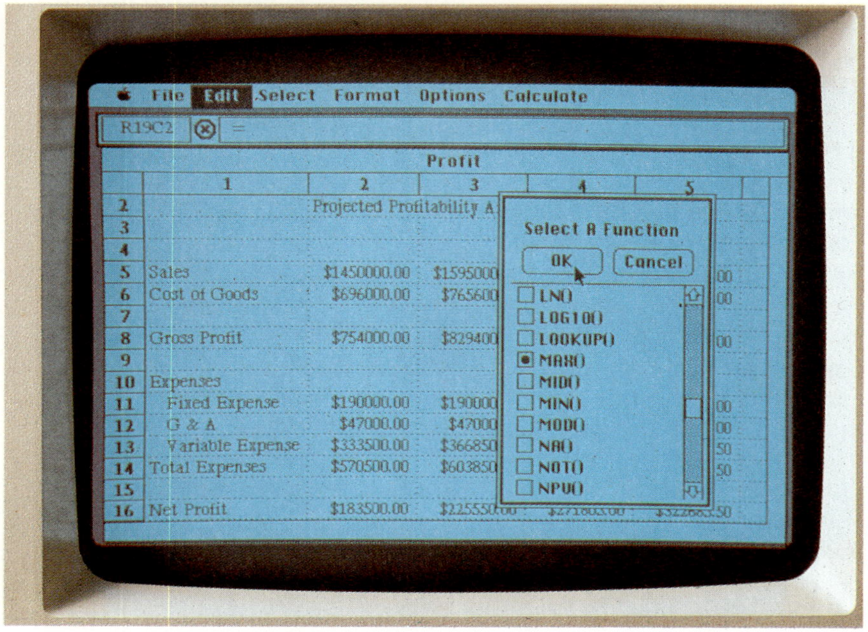

Using a spreadsheet with a pull-down menu and icons often leads to a shorter learning period and greater satisfaction for the user.

Copy the contents of one cell into another.

Move the contents of one cell to another.

Insert or delete a row or a column.

Format the rows and columns.

Print a spreadsheet.

Save a spreadsheet to a disk or load one from a disk.

Use windows that allow the user to look at two parts of a big spreadsheet.

Include functions that perform specialized operations.

When an entry in one cell of a spreadsheet is to be the same as that in another cell, the *copy* or *replicate* command may be used to make the value or formula the same in both cells. When a formula is involved, a relative copy of it can be made. A **relative copy** uses the same formula structure in the new cell, but changes the formula to match the location of the new cell. For Jill Bradley's budget spreadsheet, the values in each row were summed to generate a Total column. Each formula is the same except for the row number. The relative copy of the first row formula—that is, B2 + C2 + D2—would be inserted into each cell of the last column but the row numbers would change. *Moving* the contents of one cell to another is similar to copying, except that the original cell is empty after the move.

If Jill Bradley wanted to know how much she could save in two months rather than three, she could *delete* the September column and the spreadsheet would recalculate all values based on only the first two months. The September component of any formula would be given a value of zero in the spreadsheet calculations. Similarly, if Jill decided to wait another month for the VCR, she could *insert* a column for October after September and then use the copy command to enter the correct values and formulas.

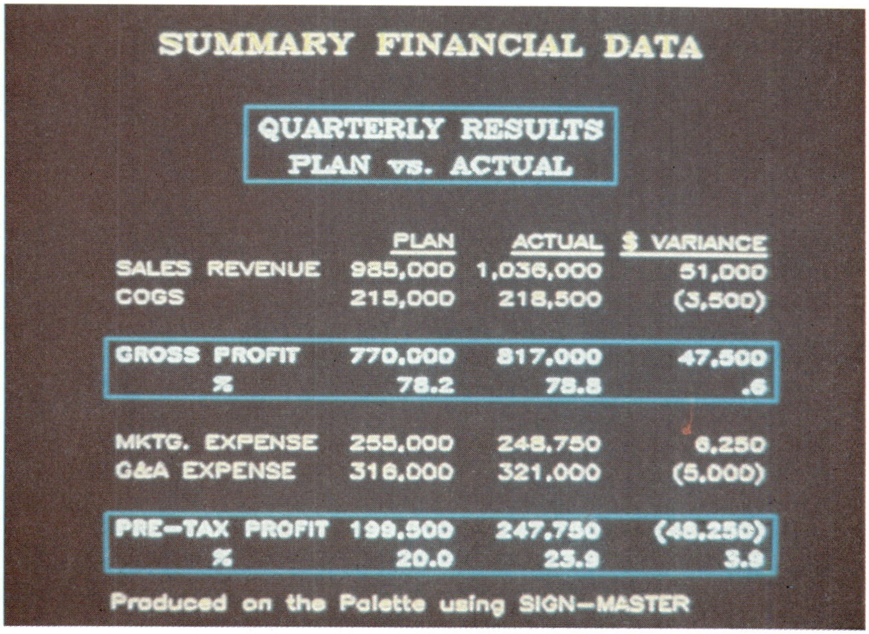

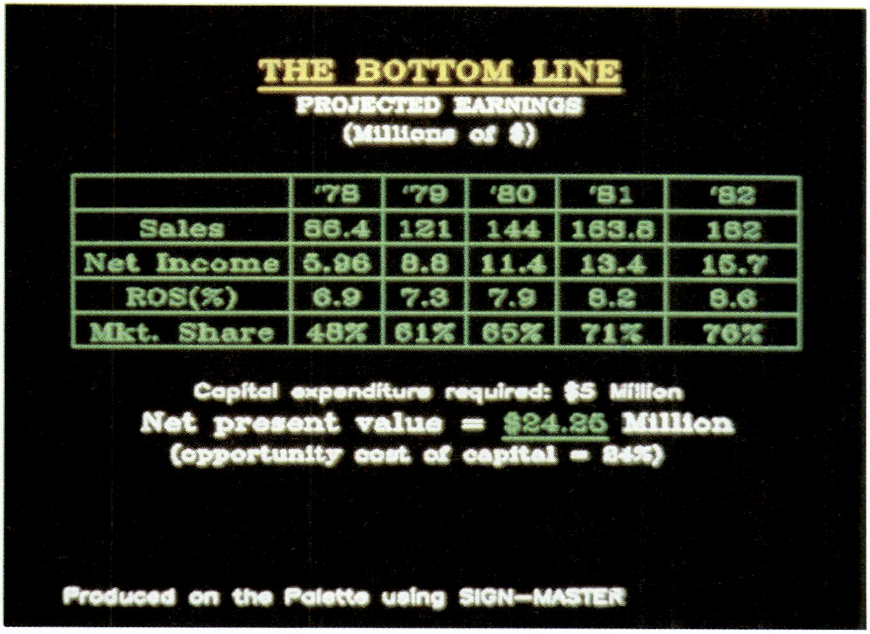

Financial (spreadsheet) analysis enables decision makers to study data from different viewpoints and to test various assumptions.

To make the spreadsheet appear a certain way, a user can *format* the spreadsheet. Formatting can move all values as far to the left or right as possible in a cell for a pleasing appearance. It can also be used to add commas in large numbers, to place negative values in parentheses, or to treat all numeric entries as dollar amounts with two places to the right of the decimal point. On some spreadsheets, individual column widths can be changed, whereas other packages force all columns to have the same width.

Once a spreadsheet has tested various assumptions and is formatted to a desired form, some or all of the spreadsheet can be printed. The part of the

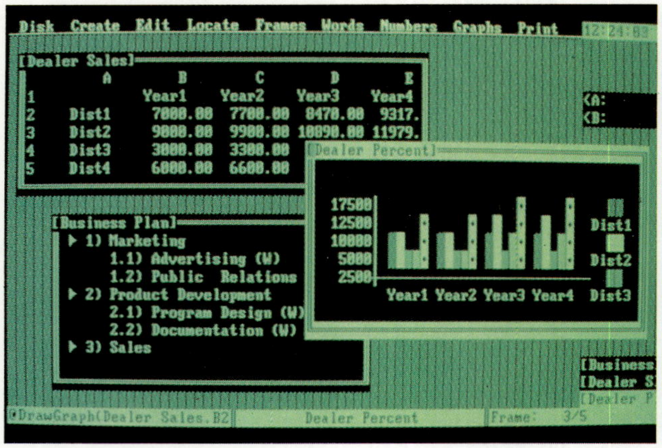

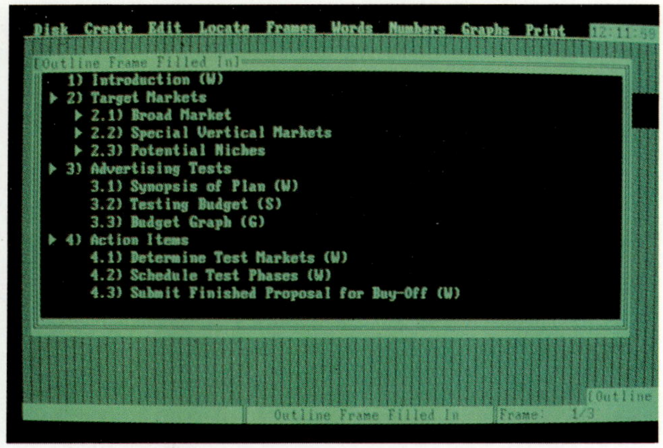

Windows allow an integrated package to show graphics, text, and spreadsheet analysis all at the same time.

spreadsheet that is printed depends on the commands given. A user can have as little as one cell printed, or the entire spreadsheet can be printed.

It may be necessary or useful to *save* a spreadsheet to a disk for future reference. For example, if an incomplete spreadsheet is saved, the user can *load* the spreadsheet at some later point and begin work again. A spreadsheet template may also be saved on disk. A **template** is a skeleton spreadsheet that matches a particular application. For example, the labels and formulas from Jill Bradley's budget could be used as a template. When new values are input for salary, rent, and so on, the template provides the formulas needed to calculate the values for the blank cells.

When a spreadsheet's rows and columns cannot all appear on the screen at one time (the number of rows and columns differ from package to package and machine to machine), the **window** feature of the spreadsheet is useful. In this situation, the user can see two different parts of a spreadsheet at the same time. *Windowing* can be vertical, which shows two sets of columns. It can also be horizontal, which shows two sets of rows. As an example of the use of windowing, assume that Jill Bradley's budget spreadsheet is extended.

SPREADSHEETS FOR WORD PROCESSING

Because a spreadsheet accepts characters as labels, it can be used for text entry. A spreadsheet format can be used for short documents and for special documents that do not fit easily into the normal word processing format. For example, the sales department at Apple Computer uses a spreadsheet package to generate a special demonstration and training document that must have three columns on 11 inch paper. Word processing packages could not set up the column forms using more than the normal 80 columns. With the word processing package, when a character was deleted in one column, the material in all columns shifted over at least one position. In some cases, material moved into another column. However, using the original VisiCalc package, the Apple sales department could set up the three columns easily and enter data in each one as needed. The only problem was that all the cells in VisiCalc must be the same width. To solve this restriction, multiple cells were used so that some columns could be wider than others. As a result, the sales department could work with three text columns of different widths. On today's Lotus 1-2-3 or Advanced VisiCalc packages, cell widths may be changed individually.

SOURCE: David Gabel, "Stretching Your Software," *Personal Computing,* May 1983, pp. 80–83.

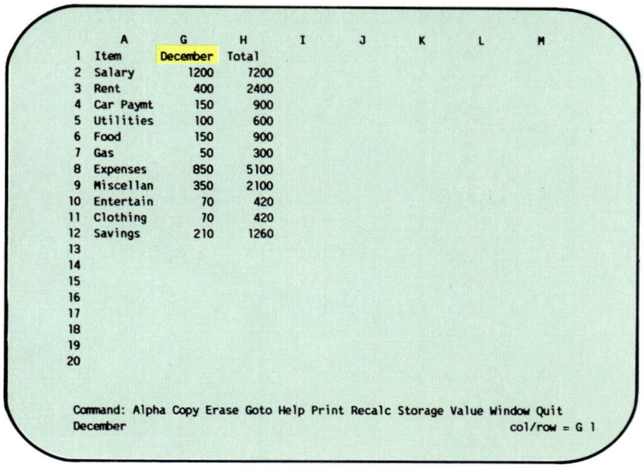

FIGURE 11-4
Budget Spreadsheet with Windows

With a spreadsheet this large, **horizontal scrolling** moves the columns off the screen on the left as more columns are viewed on the right. When this occurs, the row labels are no longer visible, and the values in the right-hand columns are not easily identified. With windowing, the user can see the labels in the left-hand window and the monthly columns in the right-hand window on the screen at the same time. Figure 11-4 shows the result of using windows with an extended Jill Bradley budget spreadsheet in HBJ: PLAN. In Figure 11-4, the left window contains the row labels, and the right window contains the December data and totals.

Finally, to help the user make many common calculations—such as finding sums and averages—a spreadsheet has a set of functions. Each spreadsheet package has its own set of functions, but the most common **functions** are SUM, AVERAGE, ABS (for absolute value), and a series of mathematical and trigonometric functions. For example, assume we want to find the total of Jill Bradley's savings after three months. Rather than placing the formula B12 + C12 + D12 in the E12 cell, the function B12:D12 can be used on HBJ: PLAN instead. The colon (:) shows that the function should sum everything in row 12 between columns B and D. Another useful operation is the GO TO command, which directs the cursor either to a particular cell or to enter data in a given cell.

The supplement at the end of this chapter contains a tutorial for the spreadsheet software package that is available with this text. This spreadsheet package, called HBJ: PLAN, provides the basic operations for budgeting and planning.

Purchasing a Financial Analysis Package

Before looking for a spreadsheet package that fits your needs, you should be aware of the three "generations" of spreadsheets available today. The first generation of packages includes VisiCalc and the many other "calcs" that are similar to it. These "calc" packages have various names, but they usually have the same features as the original VisiCalc spreadsheet package. A second generation of spreadsheet packages took one of two approaches to differentiate themselves from VisiCalc. These packages either had improved versions of the spreadsheet or they combined improved spreadsheets with such other functions as data base management and graphics. Finally, third generation spreadsheet packages integrate spreadsheets, word processing, data base

As a follow-up to the best-selling Lotus 1-2-3, Symphony combines word processing and communications software with spreadsheet analysis, graphics, and data base management software.

management, graphics, and telecommunications. These packages are integrated in such a way that two or more functions can be accessed at the same time using multiple windows.

The prices of first generation packages have decreased as second and third generation packages have become available. In some cases, the first generation packages are available for less than \$100, compared with over \$200 several years ago. The second and third generation packages are more expensive, with list prices ranging from \$250 for an improved spreadsheet to almost \$500 for a package that combines spreadsheet, data base manager, and graphics capabilities. Integrated packages that include word processing, telecommunications, and multifunction windows have list prices well over \$600. Once again, the choice depends on the user's needs and how much is needed in each package. If only a spreadsheet is needed, the user would be wise to

FREEWARE
"Free" Software

Freeware is a form of software that is available at a much lower cost than commercial software. Public domain software, which is not copyrighted, is supplied by user's groups or by individuals. Copying such software is not illegal. Other forms of freeware are available from the developers. User groups share public domain software with their members. Software libraries usually rent public domain software for a fee, which allows the user to make copies of the packages needed. Finally, an individual may send a user a "free" package, which he or she has developed, but then ask for a "donation" to defray costs. The best freeware information is found in the classified advertisement section of a computer magazine. It can be an inexpensive way to acquire very useful software.

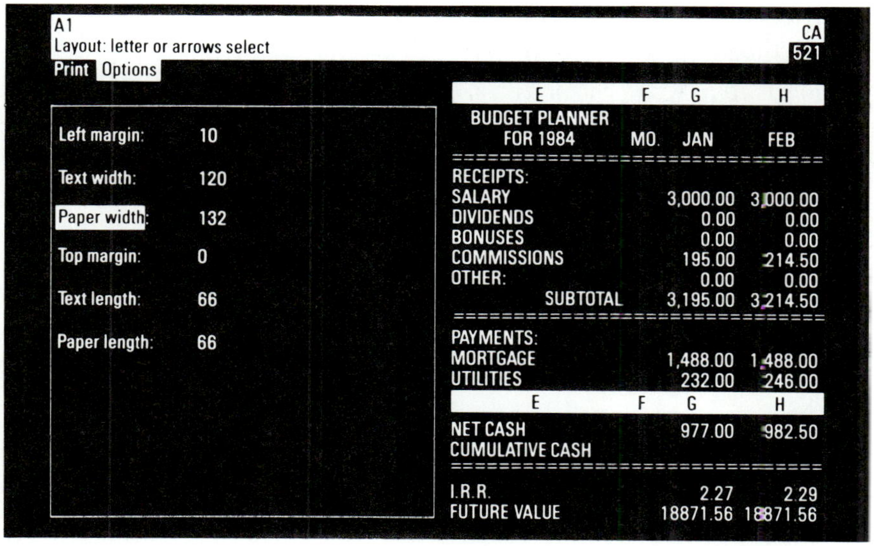

The FlashCalc software package offers one of the largest spreadsheets on the market. Windows allow the user to compare different parts of the spreadsheet.

compare prices and features of the first and second generation spreadsheets. If additional features are needed, then the user must decide how many features to add and how much money to spend. Numerous articles and reviews describe combined and integrated packages. A computer salesperson should be only too happy to show these packages to you. Decisions should be based on the reviews, the sales representative's demonstration, and your pocketbook.

PERSONAL FINANCIAL MANAGEMENT PACKAGES

Personal financial management is a popular use for a personal computer. Studies have shown that close to 50% of all personal computer owners use their computers for some sort of financial management. Personal financial management packages fall into three major categories—personal budgeting (accounting), tax planning and preparation, and investment analysis. **Personal budgeting packages** allow a user to perform a number of tasks on a computer, including the following:

- Assign checks to various expense classifications and keep a running total of each budgeted amount.
- Record checks as they are written and then use the computer to do a bank reconciliation (comparing the checkbook balance to the bank balance).
- Track tax-deductible expenses as they occur and sum them at the end of the tax year.
- Provide a calculation of net worth.
- Keep an inventory of home furnishings and valuables.

Tax planning and preparation packages may be used to keep tax records throughout the year and determine the effects of financial decisions as

Tax-planning software allows an accountant to manage a client's tax affairs within the limits of the complex U.S. tax code.

they are made throughout the year. At year-end, a tax package can help in the preparation of state and local income tax returns. Such packages can be useful if the user knows the tax laws well and is in a financial situation that could benefit from careful tax planning. However, annual software updates are needed because the government constantly modifies the tax code.

Investment analysis packages may be stand-alone packages or they may be tied into a national data bank that updates the information in the package. Portfolio management and security analysis are two basic types of investment analysis software. Portfolio management software is primarily a stand-alone package that helps the investor manage a list of stocks, bonds, mutual funds, treasury bills, and so on. Such packages can also determine the effect of selling a stock by calculating the gain or loss and the resulting tax effect. Security analysis software is usually tied into a national data base that updates the prices of a selected list of securities to aid the investor in making investment decisions.

Although the tax preparation and investment analysis software are designed for a specific group of users, the personal budgeting software can be used by almost anyone. In fact, the personal budgeting software package available with this text, HBJ: BUDGET, allows a user to track monthly expenditures using a computer.

Personal Budgeting Software

Double-entry bookkeeping is the standard form of accounting for most businesses. Most individuals use a single entry for each expenditure. This system is called single-entry bookkeeping, checkbook accounting, or cash-basis accounting. For each expenditure, an individual records a check number, the person or business to whom the check is written, and the amount of the check. Amounts and sources of deposits are also entered. The checkbook contains a running balance, which shows the current level of cash in the bank account. At the end of each month, the individual compares the balance shown in the checkbook with the balance provided by a bank statement. The bank balance must first be corrected by subtracting checks and adding deposits that have not cleared.

Numerous software packages reduce the time and effort involved in personal budgeting. Such packages have the following similarities:

- A user can set up a budget with some number of accounts.
- Each check that is written is entered with a number or name that matches an account in the budget.
- A running total of all expenditures in each account is kept.
- At the end of the month, the actual expenditures in each account are compared with the budgeted amounts.
- At the end of the month, the software can be used to reconcile the check returns.

Most such personal budgeting packages use completion screens to prompt the user for needed information. A **completion screen** has questions to answer and places to enter category names and amounts. Usually, these packages ask the user to define income and expense categories and to enter budgeted amounts. Figure 11-5 shows a completion screen from HBJ: BUDGET, in which Jill Bradley has set up two income categories—salary and bonus—and six expense categories—rent, car payment, utilities, food, gasoline, and miscellaneous. For each type of income and expense category, Jill enters the budgeted amount. Note that Jill has entered her salary as $1,200, but she has entered a budgeted bonus of $0, because she cannot count on that income. She has also entered the budgeted amounts for each expense category, which are compared against the actual income and expenditures at the end of the month.

A **transaction screen** prompts the user to enter the actual income and expenses. This screen may request such information as the check number (or other code), the date, a description of the transaction, whether it is an income or expense transaction, the amount, and the category from the budget screen in which this transaction falls. Figure 11-6 shows a transaction screen from HBJ: BUDGET for Jill Bradley's budget. The transaction screen shows that she

FIGURE 11-5 (left)
Jill Bradley's Budget Screen

FIGURE 11-6 (right)
Transaction Screen

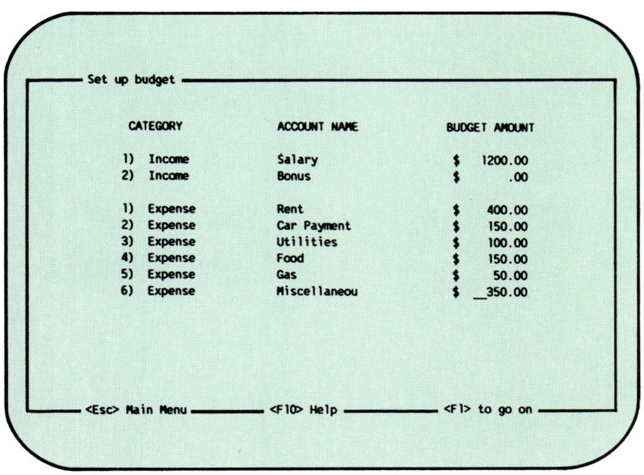

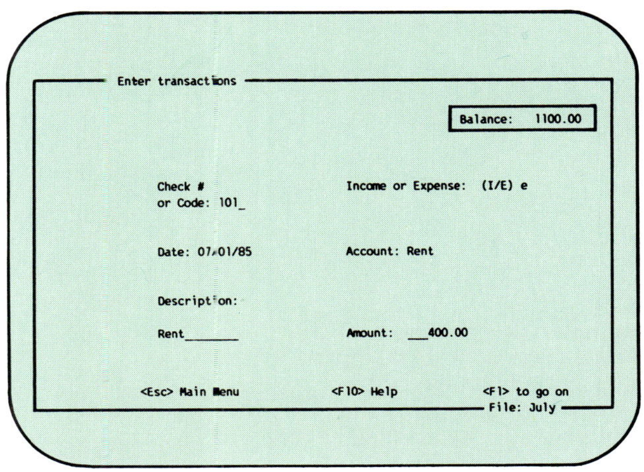

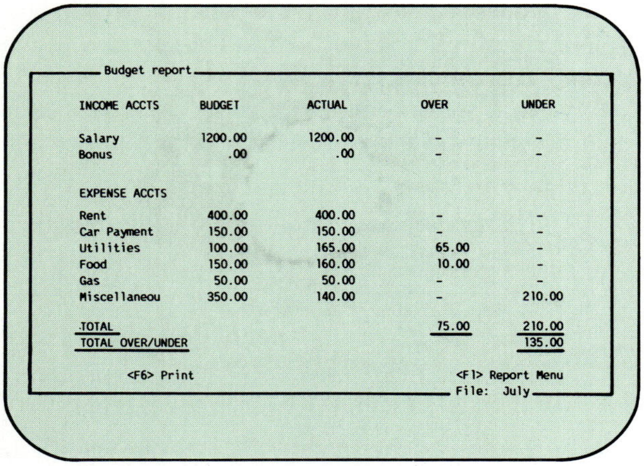

Budget report

INCOME ACCTS	BUDGET	ACTUAL	OVER	UNDER
Salary	1200.00	1200.00	-	-
Bonus	.00	.00	-	-
EXPENSE ACCTS				
Rent	400.00	400.00	-	-
Car Payment	150.00	150.00	-	-
Utilities	100.00	165.00	65.00	-
Food	150.00	160.00	10.00	-
Gas	50.00	50.00	-	-
Miscellaneou	350.00	140.00	-	210.00
TOTAL			75.00	210.00
TOTAL OVER/UNDER				135.00

<F6> Print <F1> Report Menu

File: July

FIGURE 11-7
Jill Bradley's Income and Expense Summary

has bought $75 worth of food. Note that the balance in the upper left-hand corner of the screen is $1,100. Jill started her budget with a $1,500 loan from her parents, and she has already paid $400 rent. This balance drops to $1,025 when the food transaction is completed.

Another characteristic of personal budgeting packages is that they show a monthly income and expense summary that compares actual amounts with budgeted amounts. Figure 11-7 shows Jill Bradley's summary from the HBJ: BUDGET package. This package shows income and expense accounts, budgeted amounts, and the amount that the actual income or expense was *over* or *under* the budgeted amount. Jill Bradley's actual utility costs were $165, which was $65 over the budgeted amount. Total monthly expenses were $1,065, which is $75 more than the total budgeted amount. As a result, Jill's savings for the month are $135 rather than $210.

Personal budgeting packages can help an individual or even a small business keep track of finances. In addition to the screens shown here, personal

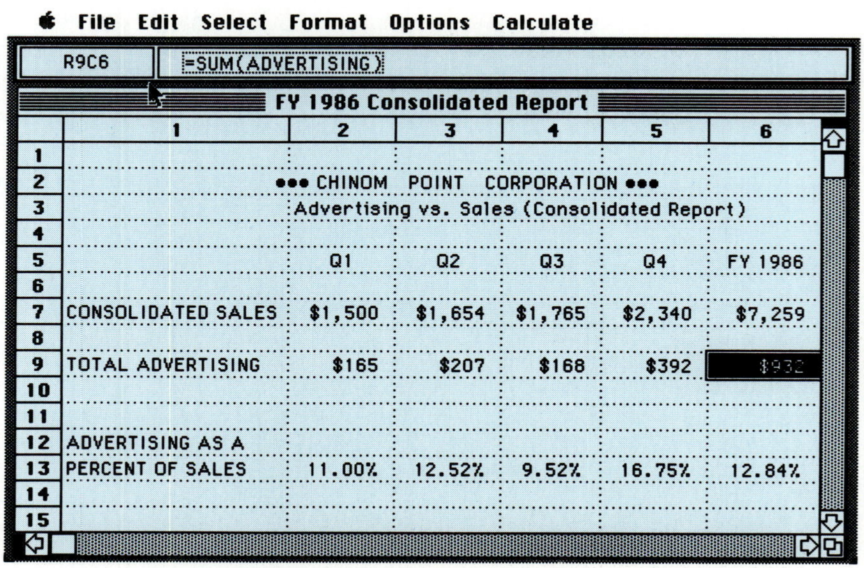

File Edit Select Format Options Calculate

R9C6 =SUM(ADVERTISING)

FY 1986 Consolidated Report

	1	2	3	4	5	6
1						
2		••• CHINOM POINT CORPORATION •••				
3		Advertising vs. Sales (Consolidated Report)				
4						
5		Q1	Q2	Q3	Q4	FY 1986
6						
7	CONSOLIDATED SALES	$1,500	$1,654	$1,765	$2,340	$7,259
8						
9	TOTAL ADVERTISING	$165	$207	$168	$392	$932
10						
11						
12	ADVERTISING AS A					
13	PERCENT OF SALES	11.00%	12.52%	9.52%	16.75%	12.84%
14						
15						

Multiplan by Microsoft for the Apple Macintosh is designed to take full advantage of the windowing, graphics, and mouse-input capabilities of this popular computer.

SELECTING PERSONAL BUDGETING SOFTWARE

The purchase of a personal budgeting software package should occur only *after* a consumer has considered and satisfactorily answered the following questions:

1. **Is it easy to set up the accounts? A package that is difficult to set up can signal problems with other activities.**
2. **Is it flexible enough? A package with pre-established budget categories may be easy to use, but may not allow the addition of needed new categories.**
3. **Is its capacity sufficient? If the package restricts the user to 25 checks per month, and the user normally writes over 50 checks, the package is not useful.**
4. **Is it easy to use? A package may do everything that is desired, but if it is difficult to use, it will cause more problems than it solves.**
5. **Can the package search for and report transactions in a desired manner? If not, it may not help a user who needs specific information.**
6. **Can transactions be edited? If not, an incorrect entry may be difficult to correct.**
7. **Does the package interface with a tax program? This facility can make income tax computations much easier.**

SOURCE: "Finding the Right Personal Finance Program," *Personal Computing*, October 1983, p. 102. Reprinted with permission from *Personal Computing*, October 1983, p. 102, Copyright 1983, Hayden Publishing Company.

budgeting packages may generate reports involving bank reconciliations, assets, liabilities, credit cards, and summary reports.

Selecting a Personal Budgeting Package

As with business accounting, personal budgeting can often be handled with a spreadsheet if the user is proficient in setting up and using a spreadsheet. For other users, a personal budgeting package like the one we have shown has distinct advantages over a spreadsheet. For example, the personal budgeting package is menu driven, has data entry screens that do not accept incorrect data, has the necessary formulas built into the program, and generates easy to understand reports. Some personal budgeting packages only reconcile a checkbook; others are more sophisticated than the example package shown here. Usually, the cost of the package corresponds to the number of features offered. A user can do comparison shopping before going to the computer store by reading various reviews of such packages in magazines. A user should also take some financial records to the computer store and try to enter them into the package. If the user's budgeting system and the system used by the software package do not match, the package should not be purchased.

In spite of the many advantages of the financial analysis package, it will probably *not* save enough money or time to offset the cost of a computer and printer just to do personal budgeting. If a computer and printer are already available, then a package such as this can be very helpful and will probably more than offset its cost over a year.

BUSINESS ACCOUNTING PACKAGES

Tracking the inflow and outflow of money is crucial to the management of a business of any size. This tracking operation is referred to as accounting. The recent high interest rates and the increasing complexity of the tax laws have emphasized the importance of the accounting function to businesses. Because of the importance of accounting and the large amounts of data involved, large corporations and institutions

Financial analysis software is a must for farmers who want to manage the business side of their farms adequately.

have used mainframe computers to handle this function for over 20 years. When minicomputers and personal computers were developed, accounting packages were among the first packages made for these smaller computers. Today, many commercial accounting packages are available for standard accounting systems. Many small software companies start out by developing packages for special situations in which a company could not use a standard package.

Six major operations exist within business accounting—general ledger, accounts receivable, accounts payable, payroll, order processing, and inventory control. Each operation is usually developed as a module. A **module** is a separate program that performs a specific task and shares data with the other modules to lead to an integrated system. Let us take a closer look at each accounting operation.

The **general ledger** is the record that contains all the firm's financial transactions. The term **double-entry bookkeeping** originated here, because each transaction must be recorded twice; once as a **credit** to some account and once as a **debit** to some account. For example, the purchase of a delivery truck for $1,000 is recorded in two accounts. The asset account is debited for $1,000, and the cash account is credited for the same amount. All business accounting software packages have some form of general ledger module.

The **accounts receivable** module of a business accounting software package keeps track of money owed to a firm and when payments are due. Some packages generate sales reports on sales volume and print reminders that can be sent to past due accounts. The software also ages the various accounts from current status to past due to uncollectible. Most firms must track credit accounts, so all business accounting software packages have some form of accounts receivable module. This module accounts for all money that is owed to the firm. Figure 11-8 shows an accounts receivable summary from a typical business accounting software package.

The **accounts payable** module of a business accounting software package monitors the money owed by the firm to its suppliers. Because creditors may give some form of discount if bills are paid before the due date, an accounts payable module can save money as well as ensure that all bills are paid. An accounts payable module can also print checks to suppliers and generate reports on amounts paid to each supplier. As with the general ledger and accounts receivable modules, the accounts payable module is found in all business accounting software packages.

To speed payment of employee wages, a **payroll** module is commonly included in business accounting software packages. This module computes employees' gross wages due from regular time work, overtime, and tips. It then determines the deductions from the wages for taxes, Social Security, health insurance, union dues, and so on. After subtracting the deductions from the gross wages, the payroll package can then print a check for each employee. At the end of each tax year, a payroll package can also generate the W-2 forms for employees based on the total wages for the year.

The **order processing** module is important to a retail or wholesale operation by making sure that customers' orders are filled in a timely manner. Using this module, orders can be received, entered, and managed. Once the order is entered, the module can print an order confirmation for the customer and the packing slip used to select the ordered goods. If out-of-stock goods are input, the module generates an order to replace these items. If standing orders exist, the order processing module prints a reminder that these orders should be filled.

Along with order processing, the inventory control module manages the flow of goods into, within, and out of the firm. Inventory is the storage of raw materials, work in process, and finished goods. An inventory module keeps track of the numbers of items that are kept in inventory at any one time. It is not unusual for even a small company to have over $100,000 tied up in inventory. Therefore, the inventory module can be a key element in the management of a firm's resources.

I think opportunities in the financial software arena are phenomenal, and I would include accounting in that. When you look at the number of personal computers and microprocessors that are going into the marketplace by the leading suppliers, remember that each of those things has got to have software on it.

David R. Fernald, President of BPI

(As quoted in "BPI President: Accounting Market Is Phenomenal," *Infoworld,* May 6, 1985, p. 39.)

FIGURE 11-8 (left)
Accounts Receivable Summary

PAGE 1

ACCOUNTS RECEIVABLE SUMMARY
Scott's TV & Stereo
PERIOD: 02/01/85 TO 02/28/85

ACCT. NUM.	DESCRIPTION	JOURNAL	DEBIT	CREDIT
4000	Sales - TV & Stereo	SALES JOURNAL		9734.99
4010	Sales - Records & Tapes	SALES JOURNAL		4321.77
4020	Sales - Misc. Hardware	SALES JOURNAL		4288.65
4030	Sales - Service & Repair	SALES JOURNAL		650.00
2400	Sales Tax Payable	SALES JOURNAL		1019.06
4200	FINANCE CHARGE REVENUE	SALES JOURNAL		134.25
1100	ACCOUNTS RECEIVABLE	SALES JOURNAL	20148.72	
1000	CASH IN BANK	PAYMENTS JOURNAL	16397.33	
1100	ACCOUNTS RECEIVABLE	PAYMENTS JOURNAL		16397.33
		TOTALS	36546.05	36546.05

FIGURE 11-9 (right)
Accounts Receivable Entry Screen

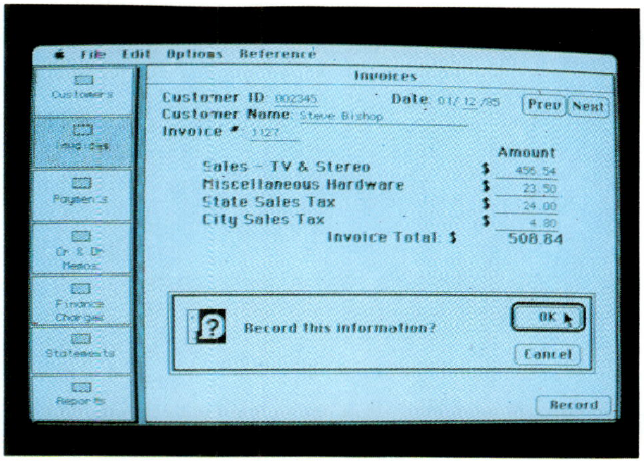

PAYROLL PACKAGES

An accounting software package can be a great help to a business in handling payroll. A payroll package on a personal computer can save significant amounts of time and money. For example, a package can save money because the payroll need not be sent to an outside service, and the number of people involved in computing the payroll and writing the checks is reduced. Time is saved because the payroll operations can be completed in less than half a day instead of a week. In-house control of the payroll process can also give the company greater flexibility to write checks for travel and other expenses without delay.

Payroll programs must be able to handle any type of pay, including straight salary, hourly wages, commissions, and tips. They must also ensure that each employee is paid the correct amount, taking into account myriad deductions, including FICA; federal, state, and local withholding taxes; health insurance; and union dues. The package should also generate all the reports that are associated with payroll. These reports include W-2 forms (annual taxes withheld), checks and check stubs, a check register, and a payroll register detailing all the information associated with payroll. Because the payroll function is closely scrutinized by employees, mistakes are obvious in this accounting package module. For this reason, the payroll module must handle these operations correctly.

SOURCE: Edgar Coudal, "Put a Program on the Payroll," *Business Computer Systems,* March 1983, pp. 101–105.

Selecting and Using a Business Accounting Package

Why does a company use a specialized accounting package rather than a spreadsheet? Although a spreadsheet is a flexible financial tool that can be used for a wide range of applications, accounting packages also have a wide range of uses. The answer to the question depends on the size of the firm and the consistency of the applications. If the firm is small or the applications vary a great deal, then a spreadsheet probably should be chosen. On the other hand, accounting packages are a necessity for most firms, because the same operation is carried out many times. Such repetition on a spreadsheet would be very tedious.

Another advantage of accounting packages is that they are usually *menu driven,* and spreadsheets are generally *command driven.* A menu-driven package is easier to use because a user need only answer the questions shown on the screen. Many packages have an **error trapping** mechanism that keeps a user from entering an incorrect type of data. For example, if the package requests an employee's name and the user tries to enter the number of hours worked, the package would flash an error message and refuse to accept the input. Figure 11-9 shows an example of the questions that might be asked by an accounts receivable module of a business accounting package.

Business accounting software packages are very complex because they perform so many tasks. Users should read the documentation carefully before proceeding because one step may affect the next. Due to the complexity of the accounting packages and of the accounting function in a firm, a great deal of thought must be given to the selection of a package. The package should match the firm's accounting system. If a firm's accounting system does not match a standard software package, the firm has two choices—have an accounting package written to match the company's accounting system or change the accounting system to match an available software package. Having a software package specifically developed for an existing system can be a time-consuming and expensive process with no guarantee that an acceptable package will result. On the other hand, changing the accounting system to match an existing package may seem like a radical solution. However, the user is guaranteed a computerized accounting system that works as expected.

REVIEW OF KEY POINTS

- Software packages involving finances are very popular programs for personal computers.
- The following three types of packages can be used to manage or analyze finances: financial analysis (spreadsheets), personal financial management packages, and business accounting packages.
- A financial analysis, or spreadsheet, package allows a user to analyze relationships among values by using a table of numbers.
- Spreadsheets are commonly used to work with budgets and forecasts.
- Spreadsheet entries are made up of labels, values, and formulas.
- Once a spreadsheet is set up using labels, values, and formulas, a user can ask "What if?" questions by changing any value to determine the resulting changes in other values.
- Personal financial management packages include personal budgeting, investment analysis, and tax planning and preparation.
- Personal budgeting packages help individuals track their expenditures and compare them with a budget.
- Investment analysis packages help individuals analyze and manage investments in various types of securities.
- Tax planning and preparation packages can help individuals plan their tax strategies and prepare income tax returns.
- Business accounting software packages are designed to keep track of a company's finances.
- Most business accounting packages include modules for general ledger, accounts receivable, accounts payable, payroll, order processing, and inventory control.

KEY TERMS

accounting
accounts payable
accounts receivable
break-even analysis
budgeting
cell
cell pointer
columns
completion screen
credit
debit
double-entry bookkeeping
edit line
electronic spreadsheet
error trapping
fixed expenses
forecasting
formulas
freeware
functions
general ledger
global change
horizontal scrolling
inventory control
investment analysis
investment analysis packages
label
local change
module
order processing
payroll
personal budgeting packages
relative copy
reverse video
rows
spreadsheet
tax planning and preparation packages
template
transaction screen
values
variable expenses
window

REVIEW QUESTIONS

1. Why is a financial analysis package also referred to as a *spreadsheet*?
2. What are the three ingredients in a spreadsheet? How do they relate to one another?
3. How can a spreadsheet be used to ask "What if?" questions about a budget or forecast?
4. What is a *cell* in a spreadsheet? How is cell location denoted?
5. Why are cell locations rather than values used in formulas?
6. What is *windowing* in a spreadsheet? Why is it useful?
7. Under what circumstances could a spreadsheet be used instead of a business accounting package? Instead of a personal budgeting package?
8. What problem can occur in the use of a tax planning and preparation software package?
9. Explain the terms *over* and *under* in a personal budgeting package income and expense summary.
10. What is the accounts receivable module in a business accounting software package? What is the order processing module?

Hands On

HBJ: PLAN

With an electronic spreadsheet package, you can manipulate a table of labels, values, and formulas to determine how changes affect the values. HBJ: PLAN, the electronic spreadsheet package that is available with this text, is an easy-to-use package that incorporates the major characteristics of commercial spreadsheets. Most commercial spreadsheet packages are completely command driven; that is, you must know the commands to give and the data to enter. HBJ: PLAN is a combination command- and menu-driven package. Although the user must select a command from the command list, the entry that is expected by the spreadsheet package is specified by a prompt or a completion aid. You need not memorize commands or types of data. Simply select a command and answer the resulting prompt or completion aid.

Getting Started

To use HBJ: PLAN, select option 3 from the HBJ main menu (do *not* press ⟨Enter⟩). A blank spreadsheet appears on the monitor screen, along with the command prompt line and message/status line. The blank spreadsheet includes row numbers (1–20) and column headings (A–H) for a total of 160 cells on the screen. A total of 26 rows and 26 columns in the spreadsheet are available for your use. Cells in HBJ: PLAN are denoted by a letter–number combination. For example, the upper left-hand corner cell is A1, and the lower right-hand corner cell shown on the initial spreadsheet template is H20. Because each cell is nine characters wide, a maximum of nine letters or digits can be entered in a cell.

The *command/prompt line* always has a list of commands from which you may choose, a prompt, or a completion aid related to your chosen command. Choose a command by entering the first letter of the command—"A" for Alpha (text input), "C" for Copy, and so on. (You need not press ⟨Enter⟩ when selecting a command.)

After you choose a command, a prompt or completion aid appears. A *prompt* requests a single-letter answer, often either "y" for yes or "n" for no. A *completion aid* requests more information—such as a file name, a formula, or a value. In either case, press ⟨Enter⟩ to complete the prompt or completion aid. Table PLAN–1 shows the commands that are available with HBJ: PLAN.

The *message/status line* shows either a message or the current location of the cell pointer. The *cell pointer* is the large light-colored rectangle that completely fills cell A1 of the spreadsheet when it first appears on the screen. You can move the cell pointer from cell to cell vertically or horizontally using the arrow keys.

In the initial spreadsheet screen, the command/prompt line contains the commands that may be used with this package. The message/status line shows the current location of the cell pointer—cell A1. If cell A1 contained anything, the contents would also appear on this line. If you make a mistake in entering a command or answering a prompt, an error message appears on the message/status line. Move the cell pointer around the spreadsheet using the arrow keys and note the change in the location as shown in the message/status line.

Because the screen only shows a portion of the spreadsheet at a time, moving the cell pointer to the right of column H results in horizontal scroll-

Table PLAN–1 SUMMARY OF HBJ: PLAN COMMANDS

Command	*Effect*
Alpha	Allows input of character (non-numeric data)
Copy	Copies contents of source cell to destination cell
Erase	Clears spreadsheet of its current contents
GoTo	Moves cell pointer to a designated cell
Help	Provides on-screen help
Print	Prints current spreadsheet
Recalc	Recalculates spreadsheet after changes
Storage	Saves current spreadsheet to data disk or loads a previously saved spreadsheet from data disk
Value	Allows input of numeric value or formula
Window	Creates a window composed of the first column and any other column
Quit	Exits HBJ: PLAN

ing. In other words, the columns on the screen change Similarly, moving the cell pointer below row 20 results in vertical scrolling, in which new rows appear on the screen.

Entering a Command

To enter a command in the spreadsheet, place the cell pointer on the appropriate cell and press the key corresponding to the first letter of the command. If you enter a letter other than the first letter of the commands listed on the command/prompt line, you receive an error message. To cancel a command at any point until the final prompt is answered, press the Esc key.

The Alpha Command

To enter a label of letters and digits in a cell, use the Alpha command. Move the spreadsheet cell pointer to the desired cell and press the A key. Once the Alpha command is given, the command list is replaced by a prompt with a completion aid, as follows:

```
Type text to be entered: _________
```

The text replaces the underlines as it is entered. The cursor can be moved back and forth using the space bar, backspace, or right and left arrow keys. After you enter the text, press ⟨Enter⟩ and the text appears in the cell. Figure PLAN–1 shows the entry of the label "Item" in cell A1 *before* ⟨Enter⟩ is pressed. After ⟨Enter⟩ is pressed, the label appears in cell A1. The contents of the cell are also displayed on the message/status line.

The Value Command

To enter a numeric value or formula, use the Value command. When you enter this command, the following prompt appears:

FIGURE PLAN–1
Entering a Label with the Alpha Command

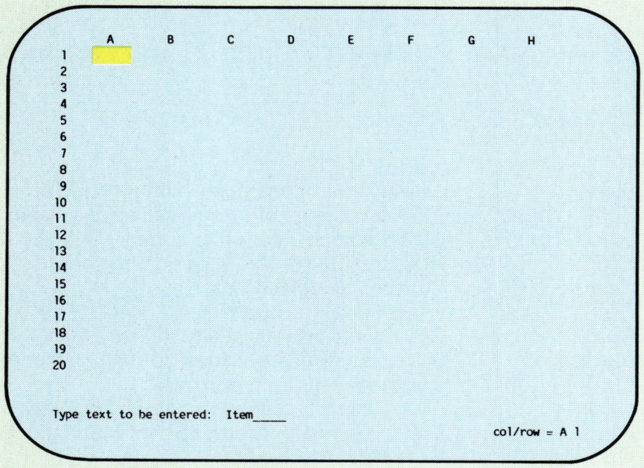


```
Do you want to enter a number or formula? (n/f)_
```

If you answer "n," then the following completion aid is displayed:

```
Type number to be entered: _________
```

The number can have only nine places including the sign and decimal, if needed. Numbers that are stored may have only two digits to the right of the decimal. If you enter a character other than 0–9, a plus sign, a minus sign, or a decimal point, an error message is displayed. As an example of the entry of a number, consider the entry of Jill Bradley's salary in the spreadsheet example (p. 264) after all labels are entered. The answer to the completion aid is shown before ⟨Enter⟩ is pressed in Figure PLAN–2. All of Bradley's expenses are entered in the spreadsheet in the same manner.

If you answer the initial Value prompt with "f," then the following completion aid requesting a formula is displayed:

FIGURE PLAN–2
Entering a Number with the Value Command

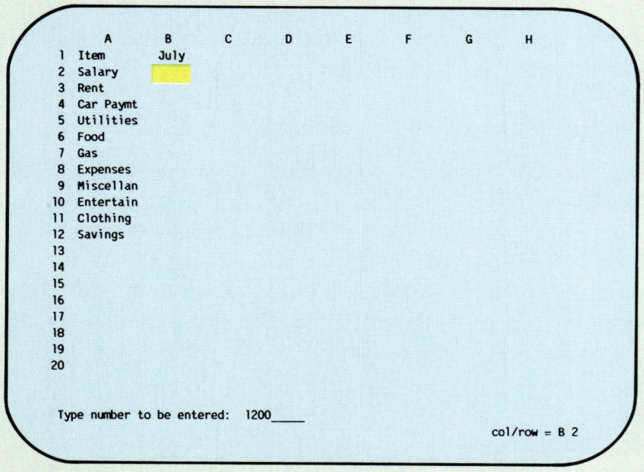

```
Type the formula to be entered:
--------------------------
```

The formula can contain numbers, cell names, and the arithmetic operators—that is, ^ (exponentiation), ~ (square root), + (addition), − (subtraction), * (multiplication), / (division), and the special symbol ":" for summing a series of values in a row or column. For example, the following formula

```
100*C6 + C1/C2
```

multiplies the contents of cell C6 by 100, divides the contents of cell C1 by the contents of cell C2, and then sums the two results. If any ambiguity exists about the order of operations, parentheses can be used to group operations.

As an example of the summation operation, consider summing all the contents of the second column from the second row to the sixth row. The formula to do this is B2:B6, where B refers to the second column and 2 and 6 refer to the second and sixth rows.

To subtract Bradley's total expenses from her salary to find the miscellaneous amount in the spreadsheet, we enter the formula after all numeric values are entered. The answer to this prompt is shown in Figure PLAN–3. If an invalid formula is entered, an error message is displayed in the message/status line.

The Recalculate Command

After all labels, values, and formulas are entered, use the Recalculate command. Until this command is entered, all cells calculated by formulas contain question marks.

A formula's computational results are displayed in the appropriate cell, but the formula for that cell is displayed on the message/status line. You need not answer any prompts or fill in any completion aids. However, if a formula cannot be carried out or the result of a formula does not fit into a cell, an error message is generated. You must find the cause of the error, change the value or formula, and use the Recalculate command again.

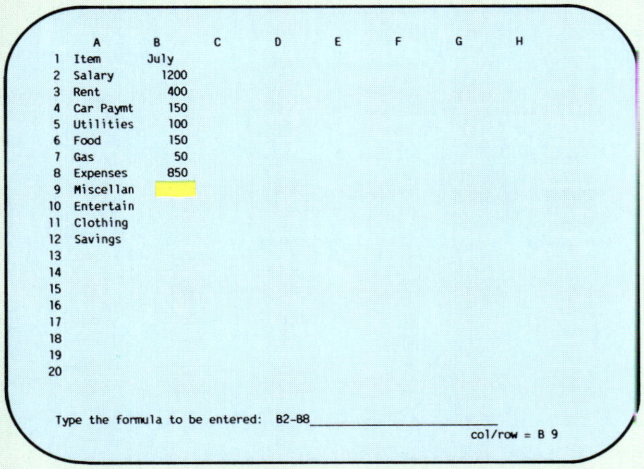

FIGURE PLAN–3
Entering a Formula with the Value Command

When a value or formula is changed, the Recalculate command is used to compute the new cell values. Figure PLAN–4 shows how changing Jill's salary to $1,300 affects the other values in the spreadsheet. The change in her salary is made using the Value command, but the computation of other affected values in the spreadsheet is carried out through the Recalculate command.

The Copy Command

Use the Copy command to copy the contents of one cell to another cell. When the C key is pressed, the following prompt appears:

```
Move cell pointer to source cell and press <Enter>
```

The cell pointer should be moved to the cell *from which* the information is copied. After the cell pointer is moved to the source cell and ⟨Enter⟩ is pressed, another prompt is given, as follows:

```
Move cell pointer to destination cell and press <Enter>
```

This prompt is answered the same way as the first. As an example of the use of the Copy command, try copying the salary value for the first month in the spreadsheet in Figure PLAN–3 into the corresponding cell for the second month. In this case, the source cell is B2 and the destination cell is C2.

If the destination cell has something in it, the following prompt appears:

```
Cell is occupied, Okay to change it? (y/n) y
```

Answer this prompt by pressing ⟨Enter⟩ to accept the default answer "yes" or by pressing "n" followed by ⟨Enter⟩ to stop the copy.

When a formula is copied, HBJ: PLAN uses a relative copy. A *relative copy* copies a source cell formula involving a single row or column to a destination cell in another row or column and *changes* the row or column reference in the formula to match the new row or column. For example, assume the source cell is B8, which contains the formula B3:B7 (sum rows 3–7 in the second column). If we copy this formula to destination cell C8, the resulting

FIGURE PLAN–4
Jill Bradley's Budget before (left) and after (right) the Recalculate Command

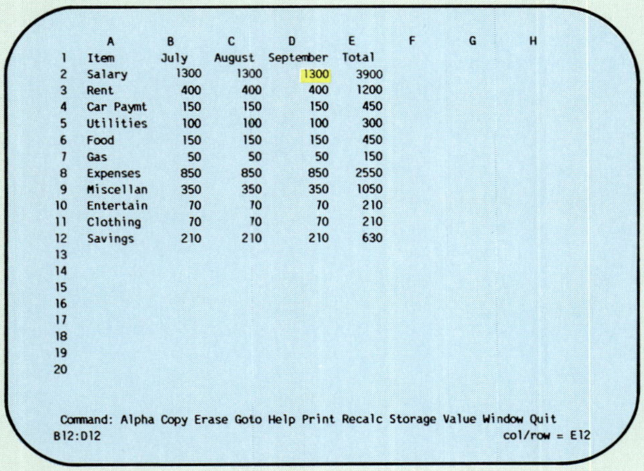

	A	B	C	D	E	F	G	H
1	Item	July	August	September	Total			
2	Salary	1300	1300	1300	3900			
3	Rent	400	400	400	1200			
4	Car Paymt	150	150	150	450			
5	Utilities	100	100	100	300			
6	Food	150	150	150	450			
7	Gas	50	50	50	150			
8	Expenses	850	850	850	2550			
9	Miscellan	350	350	350	1050			
10	Entertain	70	70	70	210			
11	Clothing	70	70	70	210			
12	Savings	210	210	210	630			
13								
14								
15								
16								
17								
18								
19								
20								

Command: Alpha Copy Erase Goto Help Print Recalc Storage Value Window Quit
B12:D12 col/row = E12

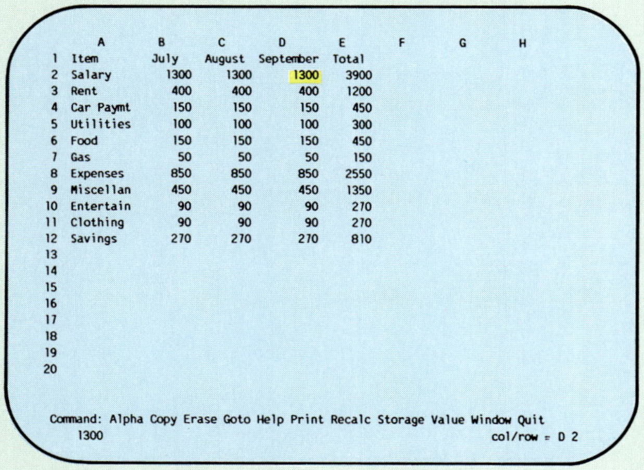

	A	B	C	D	E	F	G	H
1	Item	July	August	September	Total			
2	Salary	1300	1300	1300	3900			
3	Rent	400	400	400	1200			
4	Car Paymt	150	150	150	450			
5	Utilities	100	100	100	300			
6	Food	150	150	150	450			
7	Gas	50	50	50	150			
8	Expenses	850	850	850	2550			
9	Miscellan	450	450	450	1350			
10	Entertain	90	90	90	270			
11	Clothing	90	90	90	270			
12	Savings	270	270	270	810			
13								
14								
15								
16								
17								
18								
19								
20								

Command: Alpha Copy Erase Goto Help Print Recalc Storage Value Window Quit
1300 col/row = D 2

formula C3:C7 is copied. The column reference in the formula is changed to match the column of the destination cell.

The GoTo Command

You may use the GoTo command instead of the arrow keys to move the cell pointer to another cell. After the G key is pressed, a completion aid requests the new cell pointer location, as follows:

```
Type new cell pointer location: ___
```

When you enter the name of the new cell in the space denoted by the underlines, the cell pointer moves to the new cell. If an incorrect cell name is given, an error message appears.

The Print Command

To output the spreadsheet to a printer, you may use the Print command. When you enter this command, a prompt asks whether the column headings and row numbers should be included with the output. If you answer yes, the column headings (A–Z) and row numbers (1–26) are included; otherwise the spreadsheet output does not include them. Eight columns of 26 rows are printed per page. The printer must be connected to the computer and turned on before the Print command is used. If the printer is not connected or turned on, an error message appears on the message/status line.

The Storage Command

To save a spreadsheet to disk for future use or to recall a spreadsheet from disk, use the Storage command. When this command is given, the following prompt asks whether to recall (load) a spreadsheet or to save a spreadsheet:

```
Do you want to save or load a spreadsheet? (s/l) s
```

To save a spreadsheet, press ⟨Enter⟩. To load a spreadsheet, press ⟨L⟩ and then ⟨Enter⟩. If you want to save an existing spreadsheet, a completion aid requests the name of the spreadsheet, as follows:

```
Save spreadsheet as: _______________
```

If an invalid file name is given or the disk does not have enough room for the spreadsheet, an error message appears. In Figure PLAN-5, the spreadsheet for Jill Bradley's budget is saved under the name BRADLEY.

After you indicate that you want to load a spreadsheet, the following completion aid requests the name of the file containing the spreadsheet:

```
Load spreadsheet called: _______________
```

If a spreadsheet is loaded over a current spreadsheet, a prompt confirms the action. An error message appears if an invalid file name is entered or if the file does not exist.

FIGURE PLAN–5
Jill Bradley's Budget

	A	B	C	D	E	F	G	H
1	Item	July	August	September	Total			
2	Salary	1300	1300	1300	3900			
3	Rent	400	400	400	1200			
4	Car Paymt	150	150	150	450			
5	Utilities	100	100	100	300			
6	Food	150	150	150	450			
7	Gas	50	50	50	150			
8	Expenses	850	850	850	2550			
9	Miscellan	450	450	450	1350			
10	Entertain	90	90	90	270			
11	Clothing	90	90	90	270			
12	Savings	270	270	270	810			
13								
14								
15								
16								
17								
18								
19								
20								

```
Save spreadsheet as:  BRADLEY_______
   1300                                          col/row = D 2
```

The Window Command

Because the spreadsheet extends beyond the width of the screen, the Window command can show the first column, which often contains labels, together with columns that do not normally appear on the screen. When the Window command is entered, the following prompt is displayed:

```
Window starts at column:_
```

At this point, you enter a letter between B and Z that represents the column to be shown *next* to the first column. The spreadsheet is replotted so that the column entered at the prompt appears next to the first column.

To undo the window, select the Window command and enter "B" as the column to appear next to the first column.

The Erase, Help, and Quit Commands

To clear the spreadsheet, use the Erase command. After this command is given, a prompt requests verification. If you answer yes to the prompt, a message states that the spreadsheet is being erased.

To obtain on-screen help, you may use the Help command. This command results in an on-screen list of the commands and their effects.

The Quit command exits HBJ: PLAN and returns you to the HBJ main menu. A prompt requests verification that you are exiting the spreadsheet software. If the spreadsheet has not been saved, you are also asked whether to lose the information.

Hands On

HBJ: BUDGET

HBJ: BUDGET is a personal financial record-keeping package with which you can set up a budget, enter transactions that are compared with a budget, generate a report on the budget and the transactions, and reconcile checks against a bank statement. To access the menu-driven HBJ: BUDGET package, you must boot the computer, access the HBJ main menu from the HBJ system disk, and choose option 6 from that menu.

Getting Started

The HBJ: BUDGET main menu has the following five choices:

1. Set up a monthly budget.
2. Enter transactions.
3. Reconcile transactions.
4. Budget and summary reports.
5. Exit HBJ: BUDGET.

Setting up a Monthly Budget

Option 1 gives you a choice of creating a new budget or editing an existing budget. If you choose to create a new budget, any existing budget values are destroyed. If you choose to edit a budget, then a budget must exist to be edited. In either case, you are presented with a screen that allows you either to fill out information for a new budget or to edit an existing budget.

You create a new budget by filling in the completion aids that appear after you press ⟨Enter⟩. To edit an existing budget, press ⟨Enter⟩ repeatedly or use the up and down arrow keys to reach the desired line of data, and use the left and right arrow keys to position the cursor so that existing information can either be typed over or deleted. Press ⟨Esc⟩ to return to the main menu; press ⟨F10⟩ (or ⟨Ctrl⟩⟨i⟩) for on-screen help.

When a new budget is created or new expense or income categories are added to an existing budget, an account name and budget amount must be given for each income and expense category defined in the budget menu. Completion aids are presented for each item, and ⟨Enter⟩ is pressed after each completion aid is filled in. Press ⟨F1⟩ (or ⟨Ctrl⟩⟨f⟩) when all information has been entered or changed. Figure BUDGET-1 shows a new budget with the account names and amounts filled in.

An existing budget to be edited is presented for you to change the account names and amounts. If you want the number of income and expense categories reduced, then the software presents all existing income and expense categories for possible deletion. Enter a "y" (for yes) or "n" (for no) for each category in the DELETE? column of this screen. If you do not wish to delete *any* categories, press ⟨F1⟩ (or ⟨Ctrl⟩⟨f⟩) to go on with a default answer of no to all questions. Figure BUDGET-2 shows the screen used to delete income or expense categories.

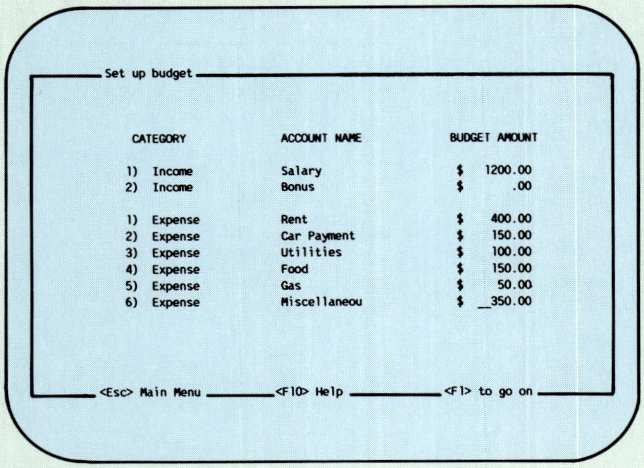

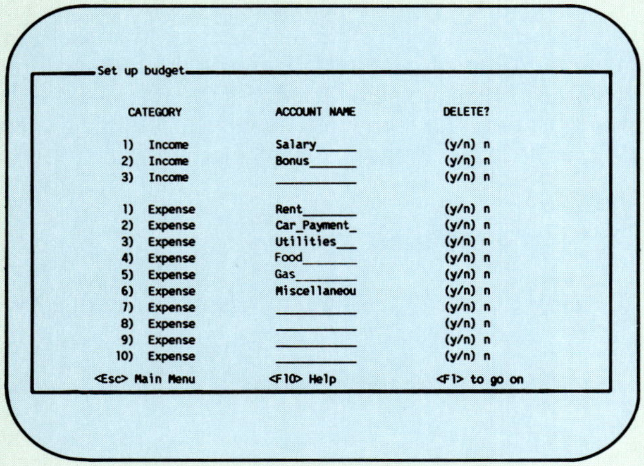

FIGURE BUDGET-1 (left)
Creating a New Budget

FIGURE BUDGET-2 (right)
Editing a Budget

Finally, the information in the newly created or edited budget must be saved. The software asks whether the information should be saved. After this decision, you return to the HBJ: BUDGET main menu.

Entering Transactions

After a budget is created, the transactions that pertain to that budget can be entered. Select option 2 from the main menu, and enter transactions. If no budget exists, you receive an error message and control returns to the main menu. Otherwise, the following transactions menu appears:

1. Begin a new month.
2. Add transactions to existing month.
3. Change existing transactions.
4. Print transactions.
5. Return to main menu.

If you select alternative 1, you are requested to enter the name of the month (the file name under which the group of transactions is stored) and a beginning bank balance. Next, a screen for entering transaction data appears. This screen has completion aids for a check number or code, a date, a description, the amount of the transaction and whether it is an expense or income transaction, and the account name. Each completion aid appears after information is entered into the previous aid and ⟨Enter⟩ is pressed.

For an expense transaction, you should enter a check number or other expense code of your choosing (ATM for automatic teller machine, CC for credit card, and so on) in the first completion aid. For an income transaction, enter a code (such as D for deposit) to denote that money is added to the checking account.

Enter the date with two digits each for the month, the day, and the year. The description should be a word or abbreviation that describes the type of expense or the source of income. For example, Gas can describe the purchase of gasoline for an automobile, and Salary might describe the source of a deposit.

Enter "I" (for income) or "E" (for expense) to inform the package that the entry is an income transaction or an expense transaction. After ⟨Enter⟩ is pressed for the type of transaction, the screen shows the list of your budget accounts, from which you may select by moving the cursor with the up and down arrow keys. After you position the cursor over the desired account, press ⟨Enter⟩ to select that account. A completion aid then requests the amount of the transaction (which should be less than $99999.99). Figure BUDGET-3 shows the final screen after all completion aids are filled in for the rent expense account. In these figures, note that the initial $1,500 budget balance is reduced to $1,100 to reflect the rent expense of $400. When all transaction data are complete, press ⟨F1⟩ (or ⟨Ctrl⟩⟨f⟩) to continue.

When all transactions are entered, terminate the transaction input process by answering "n" to the following prompt:

```
Would you like to add another transaction? (y/n) y
```

You return to the main menu, from which you may terminate the package or choose another option.

If you select alternative 2 from the transaction menu, then you can add another transaction to a month in an existing transaction file. A list of months for which transactions already exist appears. Move the cursor to the desired month and press ⟨Enter⟩. At this point, you can enter data for a transaction the same way that you entered data for the initial transactions using a screen similar to that shown in Figure BUDGET-3.

FIGURE BUDGET-3
Entering a New Transaction

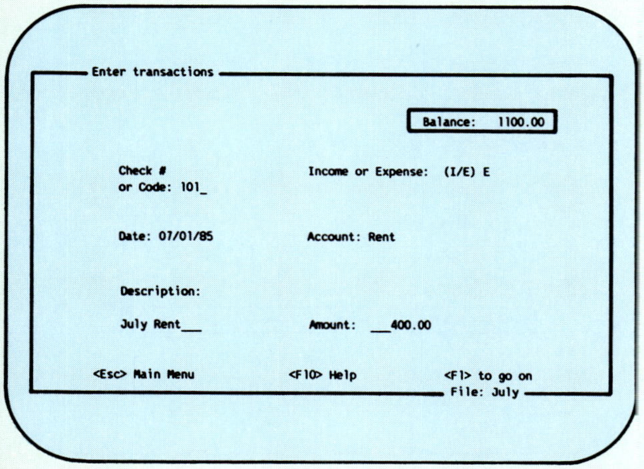

If you choose alternative 3 from the transactions menu, then you can correct a transaction that was entered previously. Select a month from the list of months for which transactions exist. After you select a month, the first transaction for that month appears on the screen. If you wish to edit this transaction, use the arrow keys to move to the field you wish to change and replace the entry by striking over it. Press ⟨F1⟩ (or ⟨Ctrl⟩⟨f⟩) to move to the next transaction. If you do not wish to edit the first transaction, use ⟨F1⟩ (or ⟨Ctrl⟩⟨f⟩) to move to subsequent transactions until you find the transaction you wish to edit. When all transactions have been viewed and the editing is completed, you may save the data and return to the main menu.

Selecting alternative 4 from the transactions menu causes all transactions for a given month to be printed (be sure the printer is turned on). Finally, alternative 5 returns control to the main menu.

Reconciling Transactions

Main menu option 3 of HBJ: BUDGET can reconcile your checks against your bank statement. After you select a month, a list of all transactions appears on the screen with a column labeled CLEARED? and a yes or no completion aid. If the transaction appears on your bank statement, enter "y" for yes; otherwise, enter "n" for no and press ⟨Enter⟩ after each answer. After this question is answered for all transactions, press ⟨F1⟩ (or ⟨Ctrl⟩⟨f⟩) to go on to the next screen. Figure BUDGET-4 shows the screen used to determine whether or not transactions have cleared.

The transaction summary screen has completion aids that allow the entry of the statement balance, previously uncleared checks that remain uncleared, and additional items not shown in your checkbook—that is, bank service charges and interest earned on the account. Figure BUDGET-5 shows the transaction summary screen after all completion aids are answered and a balance is computed. The ending balance should match that in your checkbook. Print this report by pressing ⟨F6⟩ (or ⟨Ctrl⟩⟨p⟩). Press ⟨Esc⟩ to return to the main menu.

FIGURE BUDGET-4 (left) Indicating Cleared Transactions

FIGURE BUDGET-5 (right) Transaction Summary Screen

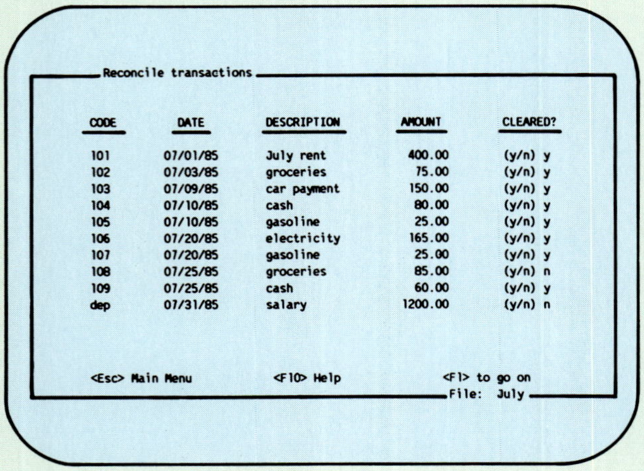

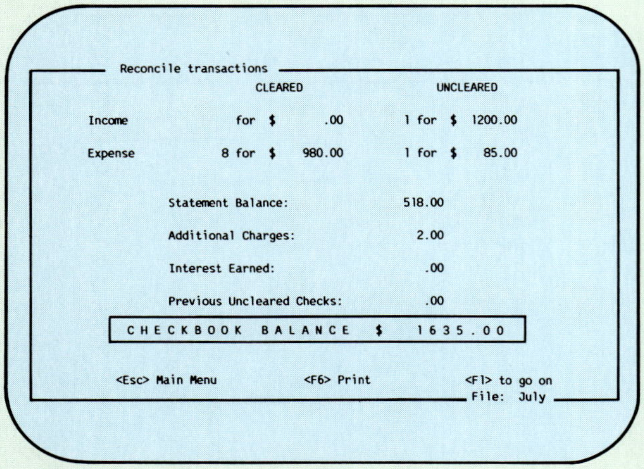

Budget report

INCOME ACCTS	BUDGET	ACTUAL	OVER	UNDER
Salary	1200.00	1200.00	-	-
Bonus	.00	.00	-	-
EXPENSE ACCTS				
Rent	400.00	400.00	-	-
Car Payment	150.00	150.00	-	-
Utilities	100.00	165.00	65.00	-
Food	150.00	160.00	10.00	-
Gas	50.00	50.00	-	-
Miscellaneou	350.00	140.00	-	210.00
TOTAL			75.00	210.00
TOTAL OVER/UNDER				135.00

<F6> Print <F1> Report Menu

File: July

FIGURE BUDGET-6
Budget Report

Budget and Summary Reports

If you select option 4 from the HBJ: BUDGET main menu, reports comparing transactions with the budget are generated. To view these reports, select a month. Two types of reports for the chosen month are available from a report menu—a budget report or an income/expense summary. The budget report compares budgeted amounts with the actual income and expense amounts for every account. Figure BUDGET-6 shows an example of such a budget report. Print a copy of this report by pressing ⟨F6⟩ (or ⟨Ctrl⟩⟨p⟩).

The income/expense summary shows the beginning balance, total income, total expenses, and ending balance. Print this report by pressing ⟨F6⟩ (or ⟨Ctrl⟩⟨p⟩). After completing either report, you can return to the report menu by pressing ⟨F1⟩ (or ⟨Ctrl⟩⟨f⟩). Select alternative 3 to return to the HBJ: BUDGET main menu.

Exiting HBJ: BUDGET

If option 5 is selected from the HBJ: BUDGET main menu, the package is exited back to the HBJ main menu.

12

Data Base Management Packages

Because the management of large amounts of information is crucial in many situations, the use of a data base is extremely important. This chapter presents general concepts and terminology of data bases. Different types of data base management software packages are discussed, including file processing, relational data base, and network/hierarchical packages. The file processing packages work with only one file at a time, but the relational data base packages can manage multiple files. File processing and relational data base packages are commonly used on personal computers. Network/hierarchical packages, which are used predominately on mainframe computers, handle data differently from the first two types. To demonstrate the operations of a data base package, an example data base situation is discussed. Finally, suggestions for selecting data base management packages for personal computers are given.

STUDY OBJECTIVES

After reading this chapter, you should be able to

- Understand the concepts and terminology of managing data bases.
- Understand how data base management packages store information, manipulate the information, and then output some or all of that information.
- Discuss the three primary types of data base management packages—file processing, relational data base, and network/hierarchical packages.
- Understand how a file processing package handles fields and records on a single file to manipulate and output information.
- Discuss how a relational data base management package operates.
- Explain network/hierarchical data base systems on mainframes.
- Describe the criteria for selecting a data base management package for a personal computer.

INTRODUCTION TO DATA BASE CONCEPTS

The term data base is often used today in many contexts. A **data base** is simply a collection of information. Examples of data bases are all around us. Phone books, dictionaries, encyclopedias, stock quotes in the newspapers, and lists of baseball batting averages are all data bases. Cooks have used data bases for years by storing recipes on cards, and students develop data bases of information to write term papers. Simply stated, if you have a collection of information, then you have a data base.

Computerized searches for books and articles by author, title, or subject can now be conducted in many libraries, such as the National Library of Medicine.

What does an individual do with a data base? Data bases may be used to access particular pieces of information, for example, choosing one recipe from the group of recipes stored in the card box. The information in a data base can also be manipulated into another form, such as rearranging a mailing list by ZIP Code. The information in a data base can be output as summaries, or reports can be generated based on the collected information.

Before computers, data base information was stored in lists, on index cards, in file folders, and so on. In many cases, data bases are still stored in this manner. Working with a nonelectronic data base is usually tedious because it involves a great deal of paper or card shuffling to derive any summary information or reports. The computer can be used to do the same work much quicker and with less effort. By using programs developed specifically for storing and manipulating information in the form of a data base, a user may access a particular data item, manipulate the data base into another form, or even isolate parts of the data base for special attention. A summary report may be output based on the contents of the data base.

The programs that allow a user to work with an electronic data base are called **data base management packages**, which have built-in functions that make this work easy. All data base management packages can perform the following three basic operations:

1. Storing and retrieving information.
2. Manipulating and rearranging information.
3. Generating reports.

In Chapter 10, we discussed the use of word processing packages to store, manipulate, and output text, and in Chapter 11, we discussed how spreadsheet packages can be used to perform the same operations on numbers. Data base management packages can be used to perform these same operations on any type of data that are stored as a *list* or *table*.

Problems with Individual Data Bases

When organizations began using data bases, each department or unit of the organization often set up its own data base. For example, a college or university could have one data base for the registrar's office with applications and admissions data, another data base for the housing office to handle room requests, and still a third data base for the financial aid office with information on scholarships and loans. Each data base worked for the particular department, but having separate data bases caused some severe problems.

First, the data that were stored in each individual data base included much of the same information. In our example, all three departmental data bases probably included information on many of the same students, including name, home address, Social Security number, and so on. This repetition of data caused **data redundancy**. Such redundancy was costly in terms of the money required to collect and process the data for computer storage and in terms of computer storage itself. With separate data bases, each department also wrote its own software to match the data that it stored. As a result, the data from one department could not be used with another department's software. This dependency between software and data storage is called **data dependence**.

When each department in an organization had its own data base and software, any change in the data had to be changed in *all* data bases. For example, a student's change of address had to be entered in all three data bases mentioned above. If the change was not made in all the data bases, severe problems of **data integrity** resulted for the users of the data base and the person referred to by the incorrect data. Finally, having separate data bases meant slow response time for the user who wished to generate a report utilizing data from two or more separate data bases. In our example, if a college administrator wished to write a report on the number of students who were accepted who also requested financial aid and on-campus housing, the process of collecting and collating the necessary data from all three sources could be quite slow.

To resolve the problems caused by separate data bases within an organization, the concept of the integrated data base was developed. In an **integrated data base**, all information used by the separate units is gathered in a single data base that can be accessed by all users. Each user may not need all of the information, but any information that is needed is found in the integrated data base. Of course, an integrated data base has some drawbacks because of its size, sophistication, and the fact that its use requires agreement and planning among all participating units. However, an integrated data base can mean more effective data base management for an organization.

One of the most popular data base management systems is pfs: file by Software Publishing Corporation.

Data Base Management Software

The first software for managing a data base on a computer was developed for mainframes and minicomputers. These **data base management systems (DBMS)** required the user to write computer programs to give the DBMS instructions. Consequently, the user had to be a programmer before he or she could use the data base. Computer science programs at colleges and universities usually include a course in mainframe or minicomputer data base management systems for students who have already had at least one course in programming.

On the other hand, data base management software for personal computers is usually menu or command driven, like the software for word processing, spreadsheets, accounting, or graphics. Personal computer data base management software is usually easier to use and requires less preparation on the user's part than the software on mainframes and minicomputers. On the other hand, mainframe data base software manages much greater quantities of data for more users than the personal computer software.

Data base management packages for personal computers are among the most popular types of software available today. These packages may be simple file processing packages that allow the user to store, manipulate, and output single lists, or they may be very sophisticated packages that can work

A DEFENSIVE DATA BASE

The 1980–1983 University of Georgia Bulldogs football team had the best regular season record in the country at 41 wins, 2 losses, and 1 tie. Superior athletes and excellent coaching certainly had a great deal to do with this record, but a defensive data base was also a contributing factor. The data base was developed by the defensive coach, Bill Lewis, for use on a mainframe.

Coaches generate information for the data base by watching an opponent's game films and, for each offensive play, recording the opponent's position on the field, the line formation, whether it was a running or a passing play, and the result of the play. For a running play, the data include the player who ran the ball, the "hole" (position on the line of scrimmage) to which the play was directed, and the blocking patterns. For a passing play, the data include information on the pass routes and the receiver.

Using this data base and the software that was written to generate reports from it, Bulldog defensive coaches can anticipate an opponent's plays. For example, what play does the opponent run most often on third down and three yards to go between its own 20-yard line and midfield? With the answer to this question and other similar questions, coaches can develop a defensive game plan that prepares the team for the most likely play under any given situation.

with multiple lists simultaneously. A popular one-file package, pfs: file, is easy to use, whereas dBase II is a sophisticated, multifile package that has sold over 200,000 copies since its introduction in 1981.

DATA BASE TERMINOLOGY, STRUCTURE, AND OPERATIONS

Before we see how a data base management package allows the user to work with a collection of information, we should understand the underlying terminology. In Chapter 8, we discussed the concepts of files, records, and fields as they apply to the storage of information on secondary storage devices. In that context, a **field** was a single fact or piece of information—such as a name, Social Security number, or profit value. A **record** was a collection of fields, and a **file** was a collection of records that have the same fields. This terminology also describes the contents of a data base, which is usually stored on disk.

As an example of files, records, and fields, consider the data for individuals seeking admission to a Masters of Business Administration program. The application data for each individual form a *record,* and the records for all applicants form a *file.* A file may contain the records for each entering class. Together, this information forms the MBA data base.

Each record in this data base may be made up of numerous fields, including the following:

1. Name
2. Social Security number
3. Undergraduate cumulative grade point average
4. Graduate Management Admission Test (GMAT) score
5. Names of colleges and universities attended
6. Names of persons who write letters of recommendation (minimum of two)

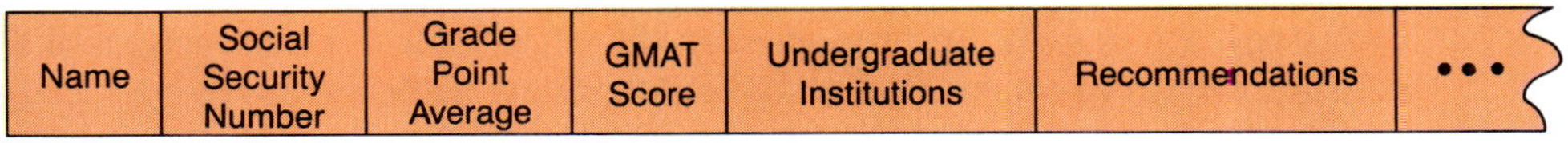

FIGURE 12-1
MBA Application Record

If the admissions office sets up a record for each applicant using this information, then there would be at least one field for each item—that is, the record would contain a name field, a Social Security number field, and so on. Item 5 could have multiple fields, because a student may have transferred during his or her undergraduate schooling. Item 6 should have at least two fields. This record is demonstrated in Figure 12-1.

Each applicant in the file may or may not have an entry in each field, but a space for an entry always exists. For example, if an applicant only attended one school, then the second college or university field is empty. If the GMAT score has not arrived, this field is empty. A specified number of positions is set aside for an entry in each field. This number of positions, referred to as the **field width**, differs from field to field.

To avoid redundancy, the structure of the MBA data base must be planned so that information is not repeated. This planning is done using a **schema**, which shows the relationships among various data base elements. Figure 12-2 shows a schema for the MBA data base.

In Figure 12-2, blocks represent each field in the MBA data base, and arrows represent the relationships among the blocks. A single arrow denotes a *one-to-one* relationship between fields, and a double arrow denotes a *many-to-one* relationship among fields. In the MBA data base, a one-to-one relationship exists between an applicant's name and Social Security number. On the other hand, a many-to-one relationship exists among recommenda-

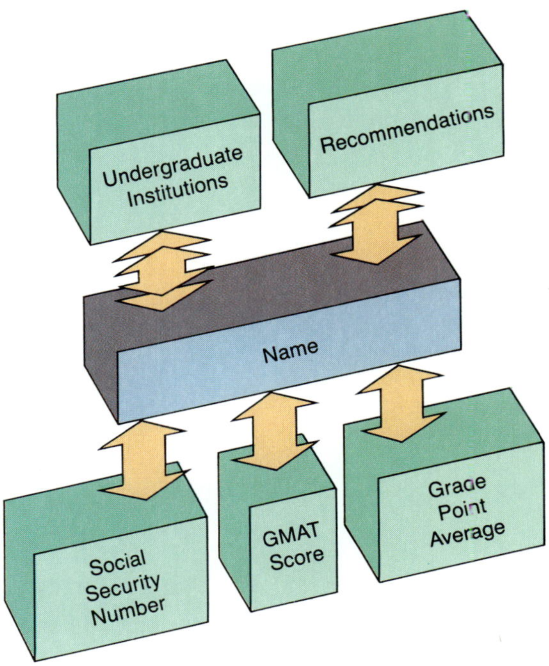

FIGURE 12-2
Schema for MBA Data Base

tions and the student because each student has several recommendations. Finally, a *many-to-many* relationship exists among applicants and undergraduate schools. A student could have attended more than one undergraduate school, and many students could have attended the same undergraduate school. With this schema, a separate file of undergraduate schools can be set up and linked to the file of applicants. A frequently attended undergraduate school need only be listed once in the separate file rather than many times in the main MBA applicant file.

Data Base Storage Techniques

Three methods of physically storing data base information are commonly used—sequential access, direct access, and indexed sequential access. **Sequential access** means that the records are physically stored in the same order that they are accessed. Records stored sequentially must be accessed one after the other; the user cannot skip around among the records. Sequential access storage is usually associated with magnetic tape, which is a sequential access storage medium. Because of its inflexibility, sequential access is seldom used for data base storage when the data base must be accessed frequently for information retrieval. Sequential access is often used to produce reports for which every record must be processed.

In **direct access** storage, a magnetic disk stores the information so that any record can be accessed as needed. The computer must have an **address** of each record to locate it on the disk. One method of finding a record's address is to start with the primary key. The **primary key** is one field (or a combination of fields) that uniquely identifies a record from all other records. In the MBA record in Figure 12-1, the Social Security number is a primary key, because it is unique for each applicant. Applicants' last names or colleges attended may or may not be unique, so they cannot be used as primary keys. However, they may be used as **secondary keys** if, for example, an individual wanted a printout of all students who attended UCLA.

Once a primary key is identified, the hashing process may occur. In **hash-**

For large or highly sophisticated data bases, a mainframe computer is necessary for storage and retrieval.

ing, the primary key is converted by a formula to a relative address for the record. The **relative address** gives a record's position relative to all other records. The computer's operating system converts this relative address to an **absolute address**, which it uses to find the record on the disk. The difference between relative address and absolute address is similar to the difference between a description of where someone lives and his or her address. A description of "the fourth house on the right from the end of the street" is a relative address, and 130 Pinehill Road is an absolute address.

A popular hashing scheme for a numeric primary key is the **division/remainder procedure**. In this procedure, the primary key number is divided by some smaller number and the remainder is a relative address. For example, if a primary key number of 266647055 is divided by 100,000, the remainder is a relative address of 47055. Although two records may end up with the same relative address, procedures exist for resolving these *collisions*. Other hashing schemes handle key fields made of letters and symbols.

The final method of storing and retrieving records on secondary storage is the **indexed sequential access method (ISAM)**. This method combines direct and sequential access methods using disk storage. Storage using ISAM is similar to the method used in telephone books for storing names, addresses, and phone numbers. In a telephone book, a primary key may be the full name and address, because this information is normally unique. Showing at the top of the page the names of the first and last persons on each page allows a user to go directly to the page that contains the desired name and begin a sequential search. The same procedure is used with ISAM on a computer disk, except that the primary key field is used to locate the area on the disk where the sequential search begins.

ISAM works well as long as a large number of additions and deletions are not made. Deletions are not actually removed from the disk; they are simply marked for removal when the entire disk is rewritten at a later time. Additions to the disk are simply added onto the end of the records already present in the appropriate area. When this area is filled, an **overflow area** is used to store the new records. If a record cannot be retrieved from the appropriate search area, the user must perform a sequential search of the overflow area.

A data base is a neat way of keeping data in one place and accessing it in a number of ways with programs.

Fred Gibbons, President of Software Publishing Corporation

(As quoted in "How to Buy Data Base Software," *Personal Computing,* February 1984, pp. 116–25, 206, 209.)

Sorting and Indexing

An important term often used in reference to a data base is sort. To **sort** a data base means to arrange the information in some specific order. The order of the list can be based on the alphabet or on some numbering system, depending on what is selected by the user. The resulting list is in either ascending or descending order. When the MBA data base is listed alphabetically, it is sorted in ascending order based on the alphabet. Sorting is usually not done physically—that is, the records are not rearranged on the disk. Instead, sorting is handled via **indexing**, which is a system of keeping track of record locations using record numbers. A **record number** refers to the physical position of a record in a list.

As an example of using an index, consider records made up of the name, Social Security number, undergraduate grade point average (UGPA), and Graduate Management Admission Test (GMAT) score fields in our MBA applicant data base. Several applicants' records from this data base are shown in Table 12-1. An alphabetical ordering of these records would be expressed by record number—that is, 3-7-4-2-1-6-5. This alphabetical indexing is shown in a separate column in Table 12-1.

Table 12-1 INDEXED RECORDS FROM MBA DATA BASE

Record	*Alphabetical Index*	*Name*	*Social Security Number*	*UGPA*	*GMAT*
1	5	McCormick, Charles	999-89-1234	4.00	690
2	4	Hyatt, Ashley	999-80-2269	3.10	500
3	1	Boat, Rhoda	999-21-9876	2.95	480
4	3	Fields, Samuel	999-09-0744	2.90	490
5	7	Quay, May	999-99-1532	2.50	650
6	6	Monk, Chip	999-13-4321	3.65	570
7	2	Deplant, Susan	999-40-2772	4.00	600

If a record is added to or deleted from the data base, the index is quickly and easily changed. For example, assume Ben E. Factor's application is added to the data base. His information is record 8, and the alphabetical index is changed to reflect the new record. The alphabetical order of the MBA data base is now 3-7-8-4-2-1-6-5. The new data base is shown in Table 12-2.

Common Operations

All data base management packages have a file management function and a report generator. The **file manager** controls the actual creation of a file and various utility functions. Utility functions include such operations as searching a file for records with desired characteristics and, if desired, changing one or more fields; copying one file to another file; and merging two files. For example, the file manager is used to name the file, give each field a name, enter information, and manipulate the information as desired.

The **report generator** outputs the information in the order it was input or in a sorted order with appropriate headings. The report generator can also output only the records that match a desired characteristic. For example, the report generator can be used to output the first three fields of a file for all records that meet some criteria.

Table 12-2 INDEXING AFTER ADDITION OF RECORD

Record	*Alphabetical Index*	*Name*	*Social Security Number*	*UGPA*	*GMAT*
1	6	McCormick, Charles	999-89-1234	4.00	690
2	5	Hyatt, Ashley	999-80-2269	3.10	500
3	1	Boat, Rhoda	999-21-9876	2.95	480
4	4	Fields, Samuel	999-09-0744	2.90	490
5	8	Quay, May	999-99-1532	2.50	650
6	7	Monk, Chip	999-13-4321	3.65	570
7	2	Deplant, Susan	999-40-2772	4.00	600
8	3	Factor, Ben E.	999-04-3043	3.75	490

A personal computer and data base software help catalog the contents of a wine cellar and record and organize wine tasting results.

The operations of a data base management package usually include, but are not limited to the following:

Setting up a data entry screen to use in entering the information onto the file.

Entering the information to create the data base.

Listing the information in some specified order.

Searching for a particular record on the data base.

Listing all records on the data base that have some special characteristic.

Creating a new field by combining two or more existing fields.

A **data entry screen** is a special set of user requests for data that are displayed on a monitor. Different data base packages have different types of data entry screens. The user may develop data entry screens to fit his or her data. Figure 12-3 shows a data entry screen from HBJ: FILE, the software package that accompanies this text.

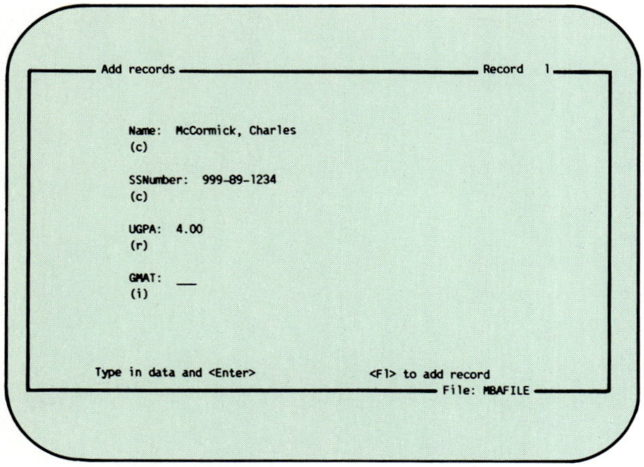

FIGURE 12-3
Data Entry Screen from HBJ: FILE

With a data entry screen, a user can simply answer questions and enter the needed data. An appropriate user command will then generate reports containing desired information. For example, a command to list the MBA applicants in alphabetical order would result in the output shown in Figure 12-4.

To illustrate how a data base manager searches for one or more records, we can instruct the computer to look for applicants with a GMAT score greater than or equal to 500. The output would only include the applicants who meet this criterion. This report, sorted alphabetically, is shown in Figure 12-5.

Many data base managers can perform very complex searches. For example, the program could search for all applicants whose GMAT scores are greater than 600 *and* whose undergraduate grade point averages are greater than 3.5. A list of the applicants who meet these compound criteria is shown in Figure 12-6.

FIGURE 12-4
Alphabetical Listing of MBA Applicant Data Base

Name	SS Number	UGPA	GMAT
Boat, Rhoda	999-21-9876	2.95	480
Deplant, Susan	999-40-2772	4.00	600
Factor, Ben E.	999-04-3043	3.75	490
Fields, Samuel	999-09-0744	2.90	490
Hyatt, Ashley	999-80-2269	3.10	500
McCormick, Charles	999-89-1234	4.00	690
Monk, Chip	999-13-4321	3.65	570
Quay, May	999-99-1532	2.50	650

FIGURE 12-5
Records from MBA Applicant Data Base with GMAT Scores Greater Than or Equal to 500

Name	SS Number	UGPA	GMAT
Deplant, Susan	999-40-2772	4.00	600
Hyatt, Ashley	999-80-2269	3.10	500
McCormick, Charles	999-89-1234	4.00	690
Monk, Chip	999-13-4321	3.65	570
Quay, May	999-99-1532	2.50	650

Name	SS Number	UGPA	GMAT
Deplant, Susan	999-40-2772	4.00	600
McCormick, Charles	999-89-1234	4.00	690

FIGURE 12-6
MBA Applicants with GMAT Scores Greater Than 600 and UGPA Greater Than 3.5

Name	SS Number	UGPA	GMAT	CSCORE
Boat, Rhoda	999-21-9876	2.95	480	1,070.00
Deplant, Susan	999-40-2772	4.00	600	1,400.00
Factor, Ben E.	999-04-3043	3.75	490	1,240.00
Fields, Samuel	999-09-0744	2.90	490	1,070.00
Hyatt, Ashley	999-80-2269	3.10	500	1,120.00
McCormick, Charles	999-89-1234	4.00	690	1,490.00
Monk, Chip	999-13-4321	3.65	570	1,300.00
Quay, May	999-99-1532	2.50	650	1,150.00

FIGURE 12-7
List of MBA Applicants with CSCORE Column

The report generator can also help to compute a new column. This new column is formed by arithmetically combining two or more columns of values or by modifying a single column. In the case of the MBA data base, the GMAT score could be combined with the undergraduate grade point average. This combination, called CSCORE (for combined score), equals 200 × UGPA + GMAT. Applicant Charles McCormick's CSCORE value is 200 × 4.00 + 690 = 1,490. In Figure 12-7, we show the same output as in Figure 12-4 with the addition of a CSCORE column. A search can be performed on a CSCORE column just as it can on any other column to generate a report.

TYPES OF DATA BASE MANAGEMENT PACKAGES

Three types of data base management packages are available—file processing packages, relational data base packages, and network/hierarchical packages. Each package is distinguished by its level of complexity, the number of files it can work with at one time, and the manner in which it handles data. A **file processing package** is aimed at the user who only needs to work with one file at a time to produce various types of reports. On the other hand, **relational data base packages** are complete data base management systems that allow the user to work with multiple files simultaneously. Finally, **network/hierarchical data base packages** allow mainframe computers to work with multiple files and multiple users. File processing packages and relational data base management packages are used primarily on personal computers, whereas network/hierarchical data base packages are used on mainframes.

File processing packages tend to be easier to install and use than relational data base packages, which are, in turn, easier to install and use than network/hierarchical data base packages. On the other hand, the network/hierarchical packages manage far more data than the personal computer packages.

File Processing Packages

Most organizations, regardless of size, have some form of record keeping. These records may be nothing more than lists of the members or employees of the organization. In large organizations, the records may contain great

BUSINESS DATA BASE SOFTWARE

Data base software may be used many ways to increase the profits for small and large businesses. Data base software fits naturally into the daily operations of almost any firm. Mailing lists, employee lists, and inventory lists are all generated by data base management software.

Before choosing a business data base manager, a user must assess his or her current record-keeping system and decide exactly what information is needed. Next, a data base package that fits these needs must be chosen. Finally, the data must be initially entered into the software. As examples of how data base software can be useful to small businesses, consider the following two situations.

The Professionals Computer Management Consultants, Inc. is an employment agency that specializes in placing computer professionals. Initially, the company manually organized a mailing list of over 2,000 clients according to geographic location. Because this project was unwieldy, agency partner Robert C. Parker used a DB Master software package on an Apple II to do the job. The result was a data base list of all clients. The data base package was so successful in keeping track of clients that Parker expanded the data base to include a resume file. Using this resume file, the agency could extract a one-page resume of any client that appeared to fit an employer's needs. This alphabetical file saved tremendous amounts of time. Currently, Parker uses an advanced version of DB Master on an IBM PC to work with a 3,000-resume file to place contract programmers with major corporations' mainframe computers.

International Aviation Development Corporation specializes in purchasing airplane parts from all over the world for its clients. International Aviation had problems storing and accessing the forms and paperwork necessary to monitor the parts it was procuring for its clients. The corporation's offices regularly had overstuffed file cabinets and paper strewn everywhere. Receipts and purchase orders were often lost. To resolve this problem, the company installed the dBase II data base management system on an IBM PC with a hard disk. With the new system, workers could look at one report that contained numerous facts on many different airplane parts. Even more important, the dBase II system enabled the company to organize its shipments more easily. An order that used to be processed in one day now takes 12–14 minutes to process!

When asked what makes a successful business data base system, Robert Parker suggested that the prospective user should identify the most needed use for the data base and then select the package that best fits that need.

SOURCE: Thomas Maremaa, "Getting Down to Business," *Popular Computing,* June 1984, pp. 111–12, 198.

International Aviation Development Corporation combines an IBM PC using a hard disk with dBase II to keep track of numerous facts on many different airplane parts.

Database software applications are used in business, industry, education, and science.

detail about employees and the products or services provided by the organization. Prior to computers, these records were kept on cards, on paper lists, or in folders in file cabinets. When information was needed from these records, an individual went through the cards, lists, or folders manually to collect the information.

Today's file processors are essentially electronic forms of these record-keeping systems, but they allow the user to go through a file quickly and easily. These software packages work with one file made up of many records to organize information and to generate reports containing needed information. Popular examples of file processing packages include pfs: file, Please, and Friday!. The data base package available with this text is a file processing package.

File processing packages are often menu driven, leading the user through a step-by-step process to set up data entry screens, to enter data, and to request reports. A file processing package can accept multiple fields for numerous records to set up a file, sort those records depending on a designated field, search through the file for records that meet certain criteria, or even compute additional fields based on the input fields. Finally, the file processing package can print all of the records, sorted or unsorted, or it can print only those records that are found in the search process. Such commands as

Someday, people all over the world will be able to tie their families together electronically.

Joanna Posey, publisher of **Genealogical Computer Pioneer**

(As quoted in "Database Managers Come Home," *Popular Computing,* June 1984, pp. 117–22.)

USING DATA BASE MANAGEMENT PACKAGES AT HOME

Individuals use data base packages to handle their record-keeping needs, just as businesses do. Hobbies that involve collecting things—for example, stamps, coins, and baseball cards—are popular among adults and children. Once a hobbyist's collection grows beyond that which is easily viewed at one time, records must be kept on the elements in the collection. These records are the data base that describes the collection. For years, data bases for collections were kept in shoe boxes, loose-leaf binders, or bundles of folders. With the advent of personal computers, collectors can manage the mass of information that is involved with a large collection by using data base packages.

In bird-watching, a data base management package enables a bird-watcher to manage the list of birds he or she has seen. The data can easily be sorted alphabetically by the popular name of the bird, the scientific name of the bird, the geographic region where the bird was sighted, or the year in which the sighting was made.

A data base management package can also be a great aid in genealogy. The software package can store the various names and relationships of ancestors and uncover hidden patterns in family history that may go unnoticed if the information is stored on cards or paper.

A personal computer data base management package can help some people perform their volunteer roles in an organization. Such tasks may include handling membership rolls for an organization; managing registrations for such events as marathons, dog or horse shows, kayak or canoe races, and swim or track meets; and overseeing fund-raising campaigns. A data base management package enables the user to find and print any information from the files that is useful to the organization. For example, in a swim meet, each swimmer's time for a given event can be sent directly from the electronic touch pad at the end of the pool to the computer, where it is combined with the swimmer's name in the data base. The package can then be used to determine the swimmers in a certain event who have achieved specific time standards that qualify them for meets with a higher level of competition. This process is much faster than manually copying each swimmer's time onto a card, physically sorting the cards by event, and then determining which swimmers have achieved the standard that qualifies them for higher level meets.

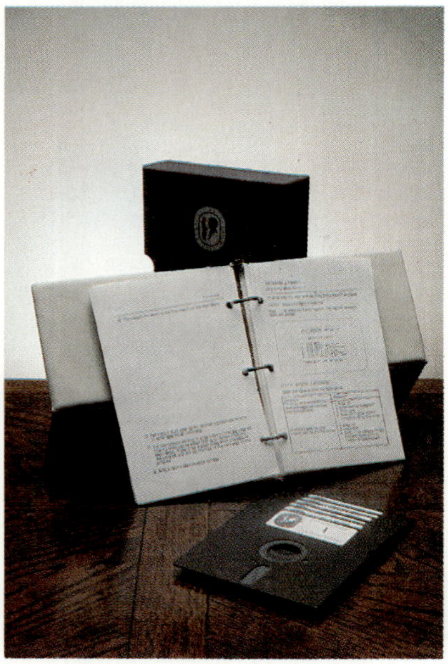

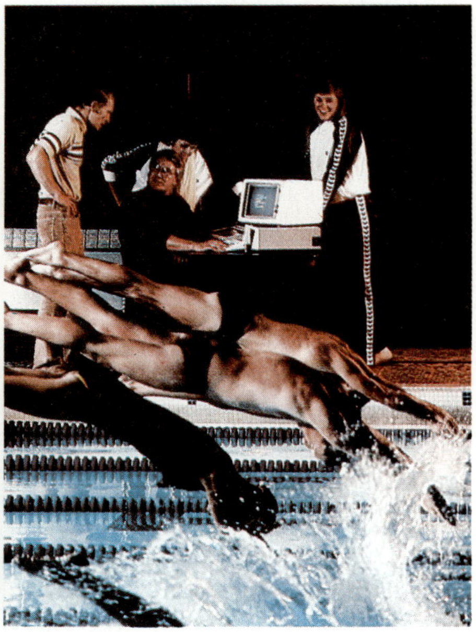

Specialized genealogical research software (left and middle) was developed by the Church of Jesus Christ of Latter Day Saints.

By combining a personal computer and data base software with electronic timing, much of the paperwork at a swim meet (right) can be eliminated.

Before making purchases, many horse breeders use Bloodstock Research, an on-line data base service, to research the bloodlines and race records of approximately 1 million thoroughbred horses.

DESIGN FILE, ADD, COPY, SEARCH/SORT, PRINT, and DELETE are commonly used to, respectively, set up a screen, enter data, copy data from one part of a file to another, search for a given record or records, sort the records, print a report, and delete a record or records.

A negative point about file processing packages is that they are not *true* data base managers because they can only work with one file at a time. A true data base package is often made up of several interrelated files from which data must be correlated to generate a needed report. Only relational or network/hierarchical data base packages can handle multiple files.

Relational Data Base Packages

File processing packages are easy to use and can satisfy many data base management package users. However, a large group of users need the additional power and flexibility of a relational data base package. The main difference between file processing and relational data base packages is that file processing packages work with only one file and relational data base packages can work with multiple files. With a relational data base package, information on various files can be combined to develop comprehensive reports. For example, a personnel file can be combined with a payroll file to generate a report that shows each employee's length of service, number of dependents, and salary. Before this report could be generated with a file processing package, the two files would have to be merged. Merging files with a large number of records can be a slow and tedious process with a file processing package. Therefore, a relational data base package is preferred.

To understand why file processing and relational data base packages differ in the number of files that can be managed, we should look at how they differ in the way they handle information. A file processing package manages data as a *list of records*. A file processing package cannot combine data from two or more lists. As a result, a file processing package cannot set up a new file to handle additional information in the data base. To see why this might be necessary, consider again our MBA applicant data base.

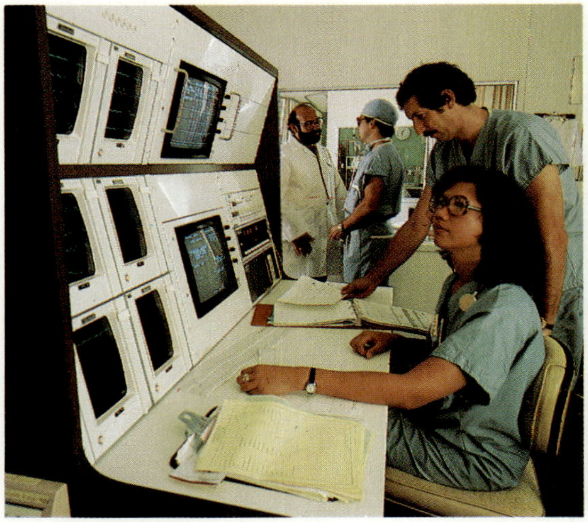

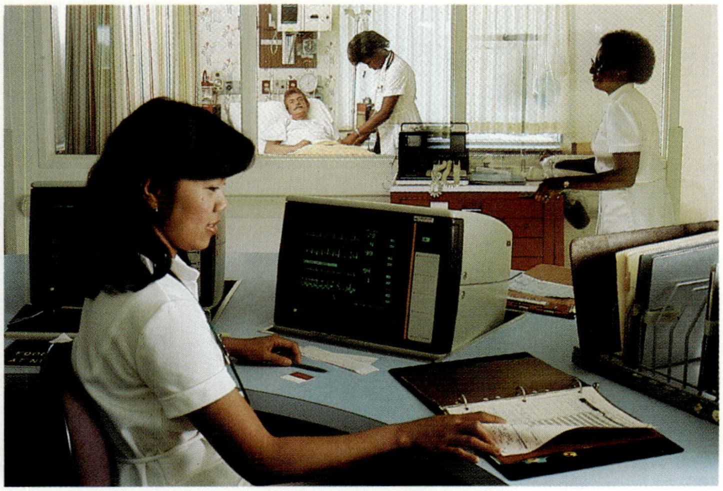

Placing medical records in a data base improves doctors' diagnoses and the quality of patient care.

In our initial discussion of the records on the MBA data base (p. 299), space was set aside for two letters of recommendation, the minimum required by the admissions office. What if an applicant has three or more recommendations sent to the admissions office? Entering the additional recommendations on a file processing package would require a new file design. All records on the current file would be copied to the new file, and the extra recommendations would be added to the appropriate applicants' records. Space must be set aside in *every* record for third and fourth recommendations even though only a few applicants may actually submit them. Because storage space on disk files is not inexhaustible, setting aside space that is seldom used is not a good idea.

A relational data base package avoids this space problem by treating a data base as a *table* with rows and columns rather than a list. The rows in the table correspond to the records in the file, and the columns correspond to the fields in the data base. Eight records in the MBA applicants data base are shown again in Figure 12-8.

Note that the horizontal and vertical lines in Figure 12-8 show the row and column nature of the relational data base. The word *relational* refers to the

FIGURE 12-8
MBA Applicant Data Base

Name	SS Number	UGPA	GMAT
Monk, Chip	999-13-4321	3.65	570
Boat, Rhoda	999-21-9876	2.95	480
McCormick, Charles	999-89-1234	4.00	690
Quay, May	999-99-1532	2.50	650
Factor, Ben E.	999-04-3043	3.75	490
Fields, Samuel	999-09-0744	2.90	490
Deplant, Susan	999-40-2772	4.00	600
Hyatt, Ashley	999-80-2269	3.10	500

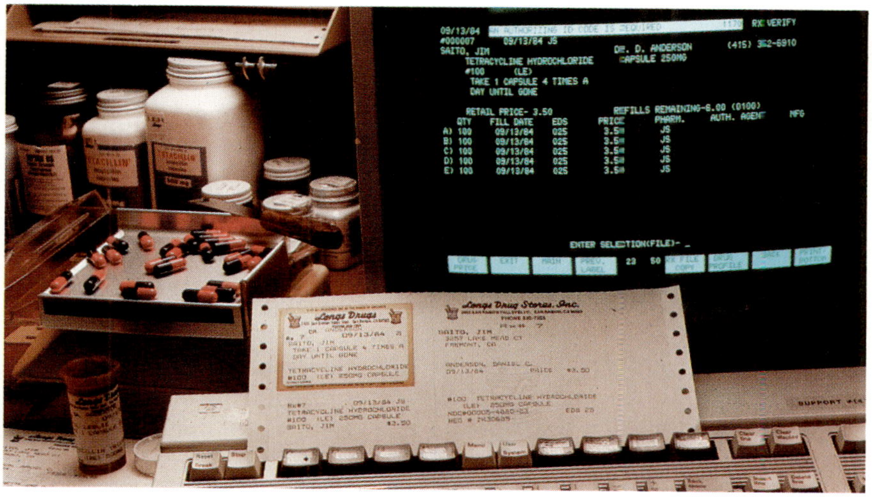

A data base system in a local pharmacy helps the pharmacist improve customer service and monitor possible harmful drug interactions.

software's ability to relate the table in Figure 12-8 to other tables that contain the recommendations. These other tables are new files that have *one field* in common with the MBA data base, in this case, Social Security number. Figure 12-9 shows a second table made up of the Social Security number and the first two recommendations. Note that only the records with recommendations are listed in this figure. Another row is added if more than one recommendation is received for any student. Empty fields are not entered in a relational table. The Social Security number relates each recommendation to the appropriate applicant.

To find a particular individual's required recommendations, the relational data base package must go through a two-step process. First, the individual's name must be found in Figure 12-8 using a search procedure. When the desired record is found, the Social Security number is noted. Using the Social Security number, the file manager goes to the second table to find the corresponding recommendations. For example, if the admissions department wishes to know who has written a recommendation for an applicant, his or her name is entered into the MBA relational data base package. The file manager function in the package finds that name and the corresponding Social Security number. Using the Social Security number, the file manager would then find the needed recommendations in the second table.

REQUIRED RECOMMENDATIONS

SS Number	Recommendation
999-13-4321	Mr. Ben Dyer
999-89-1234	Dr. Andrew Seila
999-89-1234	Dr. Ronald Armstrong
999-04-3043	Dr. Ann Scott
999-40-2772	Dr. Chris Patrick
999-40-2772	Dr. Roscoe Davis
999-80-2269	Dr. Ralph Steuer
999-80-2269	Dr. Dana Marshall

FIGURE 12-9
Required Recommendations Table

With a relational data base, any number of items can be connected if they have something in common.

***Adam Green, author of* The dBase II User's Guide**

(As quoted in "The Relational Data Bases That Take on the 'Big' Jobs," *Personal Computing*, May 1984, p. 146.)

If an unknown number of additional recommendations might be sent in for an applicant, the user could set up a third table. The same field that related the second table to the first need not be used to relate the third table to the first. However, this procedure is convenient. In our example, we again use the Social Security number to relate the third table to the first. Because not all applicants will have extra recommendations sent in, the new table will have records for only those applicants with three or four recommendations. (This approach saves space; the file processor approach requires a third and fourth recommendation field for *every* applicant.) If more than four recommendations are sent in, a new table is easily set up to handle them. As with the second table, it could be related to the main table by the applicants' Social Security numbers, as shown in Figure 12-10.

A relational data base package is more flexible than a file processing package because the user does not have to consider all possible fields before setting up the data base. Instead, a user can start with a basic set of fields in one table. As needed, tables with additional fields can be set up that relate to the main table through a primary key.

A relational data base package is more powerful than a file processing data base management package because of its wide range of commands which can be used to manipulate and output the information. For dBase II, the most popular relational data base package, commands such as CREATE, EDIT, MODIFY, USE, and DELETE are available to the user to work with the information stored in the data base. Most of these commands resemble verbs, and like verbs, they can be modified with clauses that narrow down the scope of the command verb's actions or that further specify the desired action. Table 12-3 shows some important dBase II commands and their actions.

Taken together, the commands in dBase II and other relational data base packages are actually a programming language that allows the user to develop a *logical procedure* to perform some task. For this reason, the language used in these packages is referred to as a **procedural language**. On the other hand, a **nonprocedural language** refers to the language used in menu-driven file processing packages. It requires the user to answer questions on the menu and to fill in blanks with data rather than to develop a logical procedure.

An important operation in the use of a relational data base is that of joining two tables. This action generates a new file that contains all records in one file that are referred to by another file. For example, a complete file of MBA applicant information could be generated by joining the file that contains name, Social Security number, grade point average, and GMAT score with all records in the recommendation file having the required two recommendations. Because the process of joining two files usually requires much disk

FIGURE 12-10
Extra Recommendation Table

```
EXTRA RECOMMENDATIONS

SS Number          Recommendation
-----------        ---------------

999-89-1234        Dr. Robert Brown
999-80-2269        Dr. James Cope
999-80-2269        Ms. Carol Calbos
```

Table 12-3 COMMANDS USED IN dBASE II

Command	*Operation*
CREATE	Used to set up the data base and to enter data
USE	Instructs system to use a particular data base
APPEND	Instructs the system to add records
EDIT	Used to revise a previously entered record
MODIFY	Changes the structure of an empty data base
LIST	Used to display records on the screen
BROWSE	Used to look through a set of records
GO TO	Instructs the system to move to a particular record
NEXT	Used with another command to restrict action
DELETE	Used to delete records

activity, it is often a slow procedure on personal computers unless a hard disk is used for secondary storage.

Network/Hierarchical Data Base Packages

Network/hierarchical data base management packages are used extensively on mainframes and minicomputers based on the standards set by a computer industry group called CODASYL (Conference on Data Systems Languages). Examples of network/hierarchical data base systems include IMS and Ramis.

The physical makeup of network/hierarchical systems is very different from file processing or relational data base packages, whose key elements are files, records, and fields. Network/hierarchical systems have records and fields, but the file has no meaning in this system. Each field has an *owner,* that is, a particular set of which it is a member. For example, a white wine could be "owned" by a brand, which in turn is "owned" by a location of the grape used in the production of the wine. Figure 12-11 demonstrates the hierarchical structure of such a data base.

The advantages of a network/hierarchical package are as follows:

Data base software on mainframe computers helps stock brokers on the New York Stock Exchange manage the tremendous number of transactions that take place each trading day.

FIGURE 12-11
Structure of a Network/Hierarchical Data Base

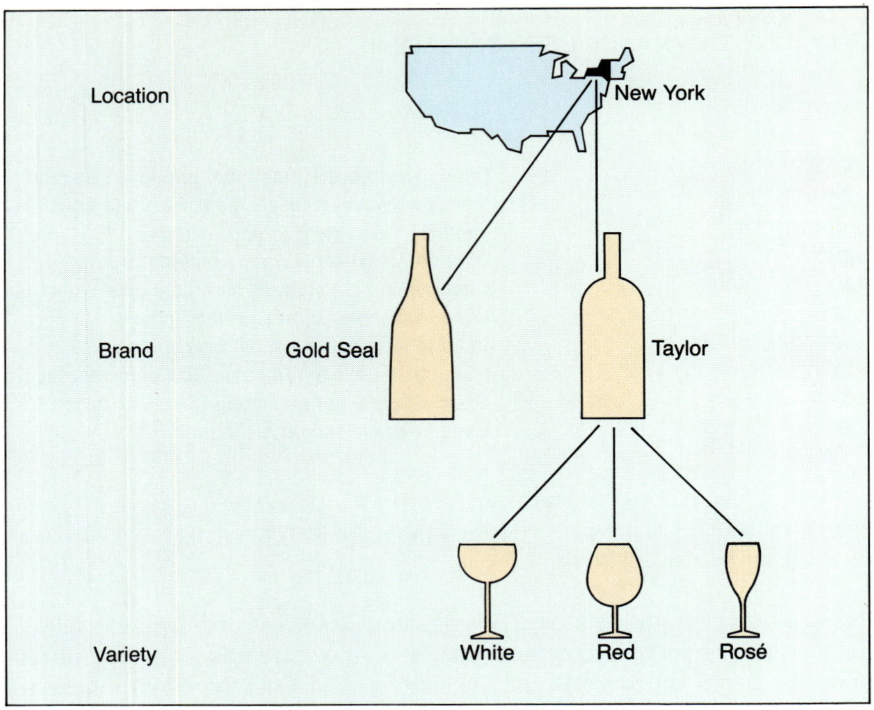

It avoids repetition of information and can handle large amounts of information.

It can interrelate individual data bases through the data base management system.

It can handle "ad hoc" or "spur of the moment" requests more easily than highly structured data base packages.

It tends to be program and hardware independent.

It allows data linkages so that the system can be built one piece at a time.

It has built-in data recovery and backup systems.

The major disadvantages of a network/hierarchical package is that the user must have a knowledge of programming to install and use the package. This programming knowledge can include a high-level language such as Pascal or COBOL, or it can include a specialized language for the particular package known as a **query language**. Figure 12-12 shows an example of a query language command from a system known as OQL (for On-line Query Language). This set of statements requests a list of all MBA applicants with GMAT scores greater than or equal to 500.

FIGURE 12-12
Example of Query Language

```
DNAME MBA
LIST NAME SSNUM UGPA GMAT
WHERE GMAT GE 500
END; START
```

dBASE II MANAGES THE METS

During the 1984 baseball season, Dave Johnson, the manager of the New York Mets, had an unusual advantage over the competition. This advantage was an IBM-XT personal computer, which ran an application of dBase II to help Johnson plan the best lineup for each game. Johnson, who has an undergraduate degree in mathematics, has long been interested in using computers to help determine the best lineup for a particular circumstance. He firmly believes that baseball is a game of statistics and percentages and that the computer is the best thing around to play percentages and aid a manager in decision making.

While Johnson played for the Baltimore Orioles in the early 1970s, he researched this concept at night on an IBM 370 at a local brewery owned by the owner of the club. He wrote a program in FORTRAN (a programming language) to simulate a baseball game using various lineups. When he became the manager of a minor league team, he applied some of his ideas using the IBM-XT and won two straight league championships.

When Johnson became manager of the Mets, he used the approach he had used in the minor leagues. First, he developed a dBase II program that would generate the needed reports on how the Mets hitters did against opposing pitchers and how the Mets pitchers had performed against other teams. Next, he entered nine years of data to set up the data base. After each game, the data base was updated with that day's results. Then, before the next game, Johnson could determine how his hitters and pitchers had done against that opposition and thereby decide on a lineup based on the most up-to-date information.

SOURCE: Martin Porter, "The PC Goes to Bat," *PC Magazine*, May 29, 1984, pp. 209–13.

Dave Johnson, manager of the New York Mets, uses his IBM PC/XT and dBase II to develop his game strategy.

SELECTING A DATA BASE MANAGEMENT PACKAGE FOR A PERSONAL COMPUTER

Data base management packages for personal computers are more difficult to select than the four types of packages we have discussed so far (word processing, graphics, spreadsheet, and personal accounting) because two distinct types of packages are available for managing a data base. The prospective user must give a great deal of thought to *exactly* what the package should do. The user should know the amount of data involved, the number of fields needed, the size of the fields, and the kind of reports required.

If the prospective user plans to work with only one file at a time and he or she can clearly define information needs, then a file processing package is probably adequate. With this package, the user can usually work with as many records as necessary, but the number of fields and positions available on each record is limited. Another consideration in selecting a package is the user's

DEVELOPING A DATA BASE

1. **Understand the data needs. A data base management package cannot be used without knowing what information is needed from the package. To determine the data needs, the user must understand how a particular operation is performed manually. Then, the user must determine how a data base package can perform this operation.**
2. **Specify the output requirements. All the operations required of a data base management package may not be known ahead of time. However, the user does know that certain reports will be needed on a continuing basis. The structure of these reports should be determined.**
3. **Specify the input requirements. The input requirements are set by the output requirements determined in step 2. To obtain specific output, the system must have appropriate input.**
4. **Determine the file structure. This step involves determining if one file is sufficient or if multiple files are needed. Multiple files must be linked by a data item that is common to all files in the data base (the key field).**
5. **Design forms. These input/output forms are determined by the file structure and output requirements specified earlier.**
6. **Test. Use dummy data to test the data base structure before using real data. The user must be prepared to change things at any point to derive the needed data base structure using the chosen package.**

SOURCE: David Gabel, "Starting from Scratch with a Data Base," *Personal Computing,* March 1984, pp. 105–13, 178–79. Reprinted with permission from *Personal Computing,* March 1984, pp. 105–13, 178–79, copyright 1984, Hayden Publishing Company.

I view the computer system as composed of three components—the hardware, . . . the data, . . . and the data manager.

Philip Ingebo, President of Condor Computer Systems
(As quoted in "How to Buy Data Base Software," *Personal Computing,* February 1984, pp. 116–25, 206, 209.)

background. A computer novice without the resources to hire a consultant or programmer to work with the new data base management package should probably purchase an easy-to-use, menu-driven file processing package.

When large, complicated data bases are involved and the exact structure of the data will not be known until the development process is well established, a relational data base package is probably the answer. These packages have both the power and flexibility to serve the requirements of almost any user. However, the user must learn the command language and develop the necessary logic to write manipulation and output procedures. The user can always hire someone to set up the initial data base system and write the necessary procedures, but this can be an expensive process. A file processing package can be used for a standard type of data base problem, but a relational data base package can be used to develop custom applications, because it is made up of a file manager/report generator *and* a programming language.

Once the broad category of package needed is determined, sample data must be tried out on the package. The following questions about the package must also be answered:

1. How can the data entry screens be set up?
2. How much effort is involved in the actual input process?
3. What is involved in manipulating the information to answer various questions?
4. Are reports easily generated? Do they contain the needed information in a form that is readily usable?

If two packages are similar, then the price should be considered.

REVIEW OF KEY POINTS

- A data base is a collection of information.
- Data base packages manipulate and output information in the form of reports.
- A data base is made up of information in the form of files, records, and fields.
- The three major types of data base packages are file processing packages, relational data base packages, and network/hierarchical packages.
- All data base packages have a file manager and a report generator.
- Common operations of a data base package include sorting records, searching for a particular record, listing a group of records, and generating a report based on information in the files.
- File processing packages can work with only one file at a time.
- Relational data base packages can work with multiple files simultaneously.
- Network/hierarchical data base systems, which are used on mainframes and minicomputers, are usually program-driven packages.
- Selecting a data base package requires a great deal of planning to match a user's needs and knowledge to the appropriate package.

KEY TERMS

absolute address
address
data base
data base management packages
data base management systems (DBMS)
data dependence
data entry screen
data integrity
data redundancy
direct access
division/remainder procedure
field
field width
file
file manager
file processing package
hashing
indexed sequential access method (ISAM)
indexing
integrated data base
network/hierarchical data base packages
nonprocedural language
overflow area
primary key
procedural language
query language
record
record number
relational data base packages
relative address
report generator
schema
secondary keys
sequential access
sort

REVIEW QUESTIONS

1. Define *data base*.
2. What are the elements of a data base? How are they ordered?
3. What is a data base management package? Name the three operations that data base management packages perform.
4. Define the *primary key*. Why is the primary key important in a data base management package?
5. What is the difference between sequential access and direct access? Which process uses indexing?
6. How do file processing packages differ from relational data base packages?
7. What type of data base package would you choose to set up a membership list for a student organization? Why?
8. In a data base management package, what is the difference between the file manager and the report generator?
9. Why is the concept of a table important in a relational data base package? Why is a relational data base package more flexible and powerful than a file processing package?
10. What are the advantages of a network/hierarchical data base package?

Hands On
HBJ: FILE

As we discussed in Chapter 12, a data base management package allows you to work with data in the form of *records* made up of *fields*. In a manual index card system, a record is comparable to an index card; a field is similar to an item of data on the index card. After you define the structure of the data base by choosing the number and types of fields, records can be added to the data base. Later, more records can be added or existing records can be deleted. Records added to the data base can be rearranged, or *sorted*, depending on the values in a particular field. The data may also be searched for records that fit some criterion. At any point in the process, the user may print the sorted records or the records that are found in the search.

Data Base Management

HBJ: FILE is a menu driven data base management package that requires you to select from a menu and fill in blanks with the information that makes up the data base. Various options from a main menu can be chosen to create a data base, to add records to an existing data base, to delete records from a data base, to search for or sort specific records, to print the records, or to exit the package. Each main menu option has screens for entering data or submenus from which selections are made.

Using the Keys

In addition to letters and numbers, other keys are important in HBJ: FILE, including the arrow keys, the Enter key, and the F1 and F10 keys for the IBM PC (or the ⟨Ctrl⟩⟨f⟩ and ⟨Ctrl⟩⟨i⟩ key sequences for Apple computers). The arrow keys move the cursor to different options on some menus. The Enter key is used to choose from a menu or after each data item is entered.

To save the information after an entire screen is filled, use ⟨F1⟩ (or ⟨Ctrl⟩⟨f⟩). Until ⟨F1⟩ is pressed, any entry on the screen can be changed. Finally, press ⟨F10⟩ (or ⟨Ctrl⟩⟨i⟩) to obtain help when it is available in the package. The Esc key returns you to a previous menu without saving any changes or data entries.

Getting Started

To use HBJ: FILE, you must first boot the computer and access the HBJ main menu. Select option 2 from the HBJ main menu. (Remember that you need not press ⟨Enter⟩ to make this selection.) The HBJ: FILE main menu now appears on the screen, as shown in Figure FILE–1.

Figure FILE–1 contains the following six options:

1. Set up the data base.
2. Add records to the data base.
3. Delete records from the data base.

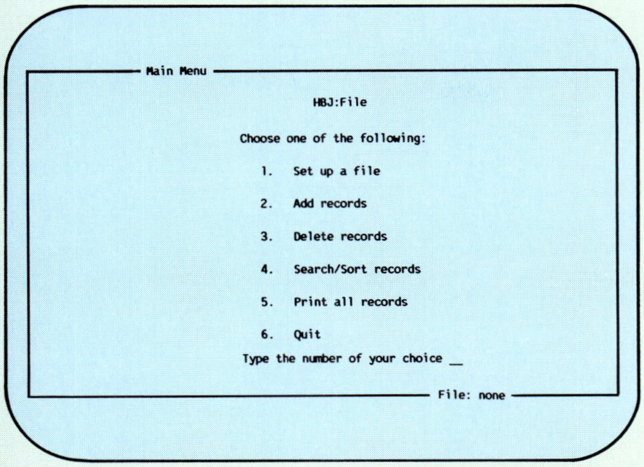

FIGURE FILE–1
HBJ: FILE Main Menu

4. Search or sort records.
5. Print all records.
6. Exit from HBJ: FILE.

The message "File: none" appears at the bottom of the screen. This message indicates that you have not yet created or loaded a file to store your data. To create a data base, select option 1 by entering a "1" (you need *not* press ⟨Enter⟩ to activate this or any other option from any menu).

You must give the file on which your data base will be stored a name (eight characters or less) by filling in the completion aid shown on the screen and pressing ⟨Enter⟩. A new screen now shows the new file name. If you already have a file with this name, you are asked if the information in the existing file can be lost.

The creation of the data base structure begins when the program requests the maximum number of records to be entered. Because you cannot make the file any bigger once you create it, you should allow enough room for all needed records (up to 100). After you enter the number of records, the software asks for the number of fields in each record (up to five). Press ⟨Enter⟩ to move the cursor to the next completion aid, and press ⟨F1⟩ (or ⟨Ctrl⟩⟨f⟩) to save all of the information that is entered. Figure FILE–2 shows the screen for a file named MBAFILE, which corresponds to the example in Figure 12–3 (page 304). This file has up to 50 records, with 4 fields per record.

Setting Up the Data Base Structure

The next screen allows you to create the data base structure by giving each field a name (up to 15 characters long) and a type (i for integer, r for real, or c for character). Remember, name a field by its overall category—such as

FIGURE FILE–2
Creating MBAFILE

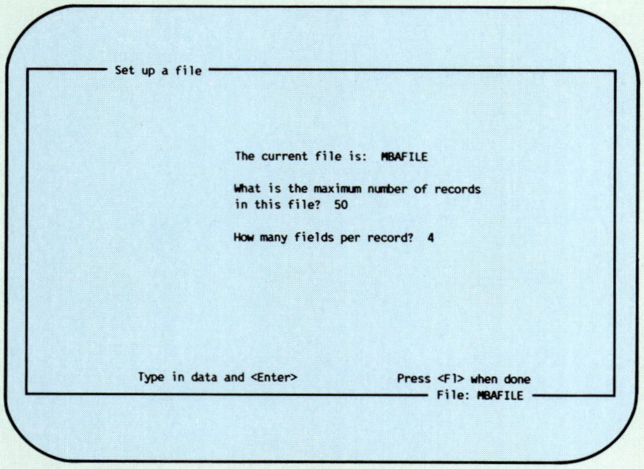

Address—not by its contents—for example, 112 Flower Lane. An *integer* field may have up to 10 digits with *no* decimal point. A *real* field may have up to seven digits, including two digits to the right of the decimal point. Finally, a *character* field may have up to 20 letters, digits, or punctuation marks. You may only enter the type of data that matches the type of field—that is, integers are entered in an integer field. Press ⟨Enter⟩ after each field is named and typed and ⟨F1⟩ (or ⟨Ctrl⟩⟨f⟩) to save the information on all fields. Figure FILE–3 shows the information for the four fields in MBAFILE. A Name field has 15 characters, an SSnumber field has 11 characters, a UGPA (undergraduate grade point average) is real with three digits (*not* counting the decimal), and a GMAT (Graduate Management Admission Test) score field is an integer with three digits.

After filling out this screen and saving the information, you are asked if the structure is correct. If it is incorrect, you may return to the previous screen

FIGURE FILE–3
Defining the MBAFILE Fields

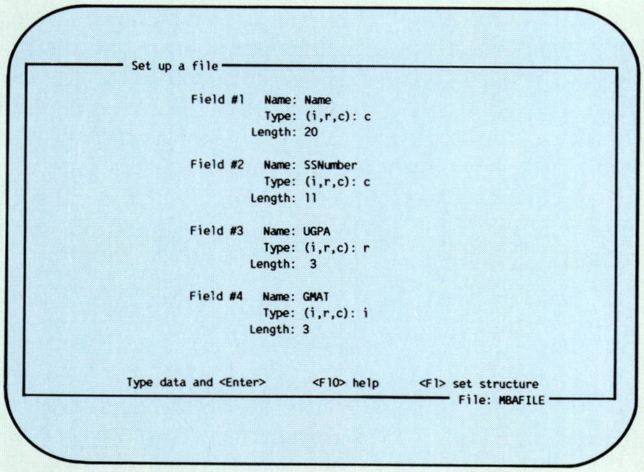

and make corrections. When the structure is correct, you are asked if you wish to add records to this data base. If you answer "y" and press ⟨Enter⟩, you may enter records into the data base. If you answer "n" followed by ⟨Enter⟩, you return to the main menu.

Working with the Data Base

After the data base is created, you can add records, delete records, search and display records that fit some criteria, sort and display records according to any field, or print records. The software always asks what file you are using. It automatically shows the name of the file that was just created or selected. If you want to work with another data base file, you must supply the file name of another existing data base file.

Adding Records

You can add records to the data base immediately after it is created or later by selecting option 2 from the HBJ: FILE main menu. A *data entry screen*, which consists of the field name and a space for entering the data, handles the addition of records. Figure FILE–4 shows the data entry screen for a record in the MBA data base. The four fields are listed with their names and spaces for the data entry. Note that when a real number is entered—such as for the UGPA—the decimal is *not* entered. After all data are entered, pressing ⟨F1⟩ (or ⟨Ctrl⟩⟨f⟩) adds this record to the data base. You are then asked if you wish to add another record. This process continues until all records are added. You need *not* add all records at one time. The data base can be saved to disk, and additional records may be added later. For the remainder of this discussion, we assume that all the records shown in Figure 12–4 (page 304) have been added to the data base.

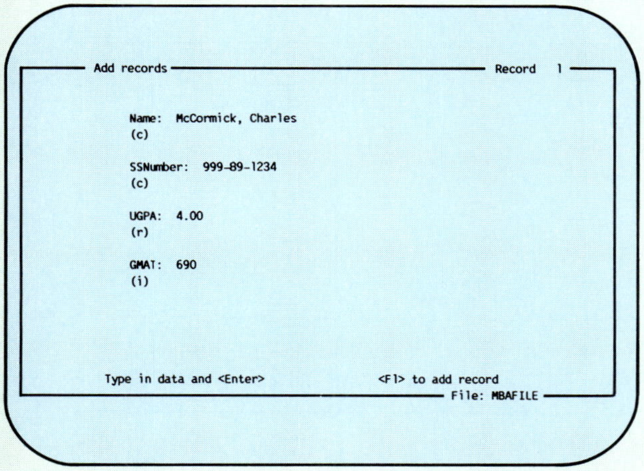

FIGURE FILE–4
The Data Entry Screen

Deleting Records

If you want to delete one or more records from the data base, select option 3 from the HBJ: FILE main menu. The *delete screen*, used for deleting records, consists of the field names, a space for a condition (= , >, or <), and a space for a data item. To delete a record with a field that matches some condition, move the cursor to the appropriate field, place a condition in the first space, and insert a valid data entry in the second space. For example, if we wish to delete a record from the MBA data base because the applicant decided to attend another school, we use the delete option. The delete screen shown in Figure FILE–5 is for applicant Ashley Hyatt, whose Social Security number is 999–80–2269. Because more than one applicant may be named Ashley Hyatt, we delete a record with SSnumber = 999–80–2269. Once the condition is entered, press ⟨F1⟩ (or ⟨Ctrl⟩⟨f⟩). We could also delete records of all applicants with GMAT scores less than 500 by entering <500 for the GMAT field. You should note that when the delete command is used, only one condition may be entered for a given delete screen.

Searching Records

To find all records in the data base that fit some criterion, select option 4 from the HBJ: FILE main menu. A sub-menu asks whether you wish to search or sort. If you select search, the search screen appears. Similar to the delete screen, the *search screen* lists fields with a space for a condition and a data entry. When these spaces are filled in for a particular field, the records that match the desired criterion are arranged according to the first field and output one at a time. Press any key to display the next record.

Assume we wish to find all applicants in the MBA data base with UGPA greater than 3.00. The appropriate search screen is shown in Figure FILE–6. After the search criterion is defined, we begin the search by pressing ⟨F1⟩ (or

FIGURE FILE–5 (left)
The Delete Screen

FIGURE FILE–6 (right)
The Search Screen

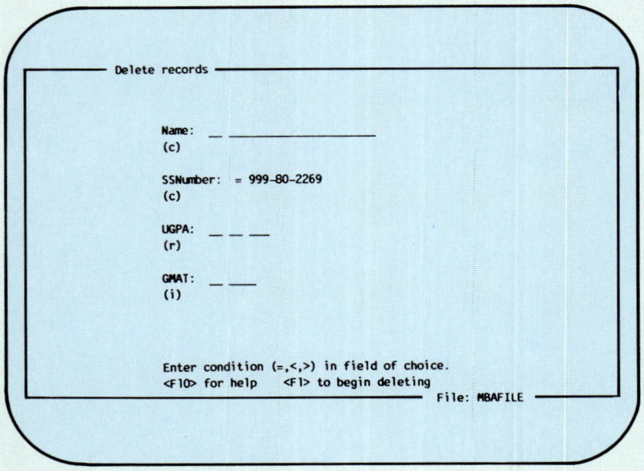

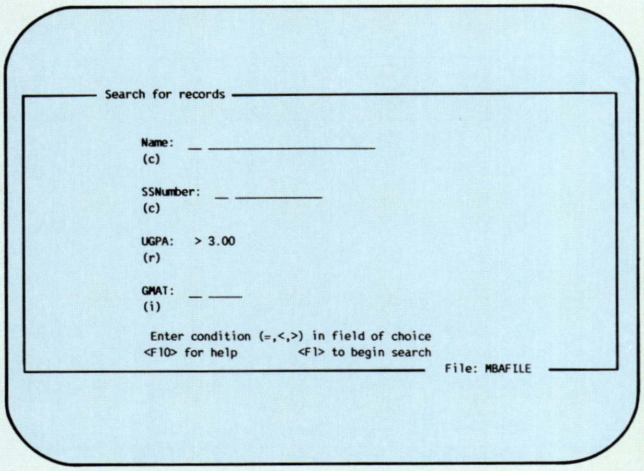

⟨Ctrl⟩⟨f⟩). All records that meet this criterion are sorted according to the Name field and are then either displayed on the screen or printed.

Sorting Records

If you select option 4 from the HBJ: FILE main menu to sort the data base, a sort screen appears. The *sort screen* consists of the field names, with the first field name highlighted. The up and down arrow keys can then be used to move the highlighting, and therefore change the field on which the sort is based. For the MBA data base, Name is the initial sort field, but we could also sort the records based on SSnumber, UGPA, or GMAT by moving the highlighting down. Figure FILE–7 shows the sort screen for sorting according to the GMAT field. The sort is initiated by pressing ⟨F1⟩ (or ⟨Ctrl⟩⟨f⟩).

After the records are sorted in ascending order, they can be displayed on the screen or printed, depending on the sub-menu selection. Another sub-menu selection can be made to begin a new search or sort or to return to the main menu.

Printing Records

To print the records in the order of their entry, select option 5 from the HBJ: FILE main menu. Remember, the printer *must* be turned on before you attempt to print a list of records. The records will be output five to the page.

Exiting the Package

You can exit the package at any time by selecting option 5 from the HBJ: FILE main menu. The data base is saved on the data disk, so you can use it later as needed.

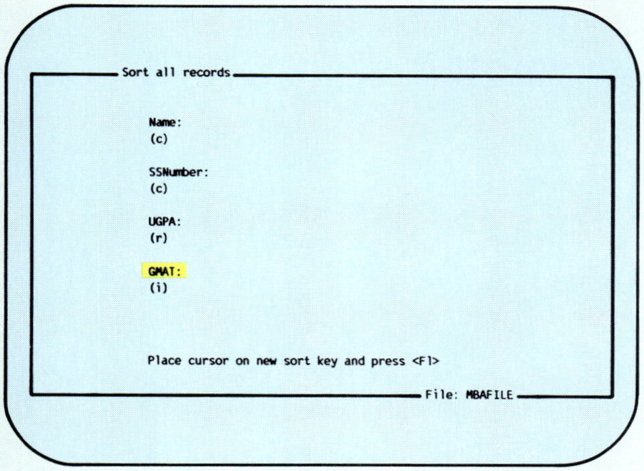

FIGURE FILE–7
The Sort Screen

A computer's two-way communication with other computers and data bases is called telecommunications. Telecommunications by computer can make our work easier and our lives more enjoyable. Exciting telecommunications applications are discussed in the first part of the chapter. Technical details of the subject appear later in the chapter. The chapter discussion of mainframe telecommunications includes computer networks and distributed data processing. Personal computer telecommunications involve users interacting with national information services and other users, sending mail via telephone lines, shopping for goods and services, and using the computer to work at home. Communications hardware and software are also discussed, along with important terms related to telecommunications. Finally, guidelines for selecting communications hardware and software for a personal computer are given. A short tutorial on the use of HBJ: TALK, the software package that is available with the text, appears at the end of the chapter.

13

Using Computers for Communications

STUDY OBJECTIVES

After reading this chapter, you should be able to

- Understand the many opportunities that telecommunications offer users of personal and mainframe computers.
- Discuss computer networks and distributed data processing for mainframe computers.
- Understand how a personal computer can be used to obtain information from national data bases and information services.
- Explain how electronic bulletin boards and electronic mail operate.
- Understand the term *videotex* and its relation to the purchase of goods and services via computer.
- Explain how a modem and communications software enable a computer to telecommunicate.
- Select communications software and a modem for a personal computer.

INTRODUCTION TO TELECOMMUNICATIONS

We have already defined a computer as a machine that electronically manipulates and stores symbols. When combined with a communications link, a modem, and the appropriate communications software, a computer can be an effective communications tool. This equipment combination allows **telecommunications**. With telecommunications capabilities, the computer can communicate with other users, mainframes and personal computers, data bases, and an increasing number of commercial services. Telecommunications has been described in various national media as the wave of the future in computers. Today, a communications company *must* be into computers, and a computer company must be into communications. Research is currently under way to determine how the many different types of personal computers can "talk" to one another. The first company that successfully handles the telecommunications problems among different types of small computers and between personal computers and mainframes will almost certainly guarantee its future success.

Telecommunications is a powerful tool because it is two-way and because of the variety of information that can be transmitted using a computer with a communications link. These links include telegraph and telephone lines, microwave relays, coaxial cables, fiber optics, and so on. The telephone allows two-way audio communications, but pictures cannot be transmitted by phone. On the other hand, television can transmit pictures, but only in one direction. Telecommunications between computers means two-way communication of all types of information through words, data, and graphics. Computers can exchange financial and scientific data, processing results, messages, pictures, software, and product information. Through telecommunications, computer users can also obtain from large data bases information on articles in newspapers, magazines, journals, and encyclopedias.

Computers transmit data over a variety of communications links. A microwave tower (left) is very important in telecommunications for transmitting data and voices. Fiber optic cables (right) hold great promise for increased transmission speed and capacity over that currently available through copper cables.

ANOTHER VIEW

Dennis Hayes

Hayes Microcomputer Products, Inc. is an acknowledged leader in the production of telecommunications products. Nearly 70% of the modems sold today are made by Hayes. The president and founder of the corporation is Dennis Hayes, a physics graduate of Georgia Tech. Hayes started the company in 1977 on his dining room table. Today, the company's annual sales exceed $100 million. The following is an excerpt from an interview with Dennis Hayes.

What role do you see for telecommunications in the world today?

HAYES: It boils down to people-to-people and people-to-information. With computer systems like Dialog or Nexis, you're able to store vast amounts of information and have almost instantaneous access to it. I think the thing we'll see happening more and more is that in addition to that storage aspect, machine intelligence will evolve so that the machine becomes more of a partner in getting work done. It will become a stronger and stronger tool in accomplishing knowledge-work or information-work types of jobs. In so doing, it will free humans to pursue more creative or meaningful endeavors.

There is so much information that you're not going to want to duplicate and store in different locations, but you will be able to access it through communications. The other thing is that communications is causing the world to shrink further. We are, in a very real sense, Spaceship Earth, and communications is going to help us manage that.

The first telecommunications occurred when mainframe users accessed the computer to write and run programs using terminals instead of using cards. This was the beginning of time-sharing by many users of large computers. Soon, a computer terminal was used for other purposes. Informational data bases were accessed, and the mainframe was a storage area for sending messages between users.

Today, mainframe telecommunications involves sharing information among multiple computers in networks and using small computers geographically separate from a mainframe to engage in distributed data processing (DDP). Mainframes are also host computers for telecommunications with personal computers for data processing, programming, information services, and message transmittal. Personal computers can communicate with mainframes or other personal computers. In fact, personal computers can be formed into a special local area network in an office.

A telecommunications software package, HBJ: TALK, is available with this text. HBJ: TALK simulates telecommunications with a data base. Therefore, the package does not require a modem, telephone, or host computer.

COMPUTER NETWORKS AND DDP

Two or more computers linked via some communications medium form a **network**. This network can be two large mainframes that share information almost constantly, or it can be several large computers, each of which has numerous terminals tied into it. An educational system with branch campuses that each have a computer tied into a central or **host computer** is an example of a computer network. With this arrangement, a user can access any computer in the network, depending on his or her processing needs. Even a single computer with multiple terminals forms a network. Other examples of computer networks include the following:

Computer networks can offer several types of services. The Electronic Mall (left) is only one of many telecommunication services offered to subscribers by CompuServe and The Source. When a company needs to send mail electronically, the digital facsimile transceiver at right can send a business document anywhere in the world in less than 30 seconds.

Information networks—like CompuServe or The Source—that serve many users.

Banking networks in which one bank card can be used at most automatic teller machines in a given area.

Message networks that allow users to send mail electronically.

U.S. Department of Defense computer networks that allow users in numerous universities and research centers to send results and data to one another.

Airline, car rental, and hotel reservation networks that enable travelers to make reservations from anywhere in the country.

Corporate computer networks that transfer the results of data processing to other corporate locations.

Types of Networks

Two common forms of computer networks are the star network and the ring network. A **star network** has one central host computer to which many smaller computers or terminals are linked. The **ring network** links multiple computers in a circle or ring. No one computer is the host in the ring network, and information is shared by sending it around the network. Figure 13-1 shows diagrams of the star and ring networks. Star and ring networks can be combined in many ways. For example, a series of host computers may be connected in a ring configuration, and each host may have a series of smaller computers or terminals linked to it in a star configuration.

Distributed Data Processing

In the 1960s, the first mainframe computers were considered big enough to handle any processing needs. However, even the biggest and most powerful computer was overwhelmed by the increasing requests for processing. This high demand for processing led to the development of distributed data processing. **Distributed data processing (DDP)** is the use of small computers that are usually geographically separated from the central mainframe to handle part of the processing load.

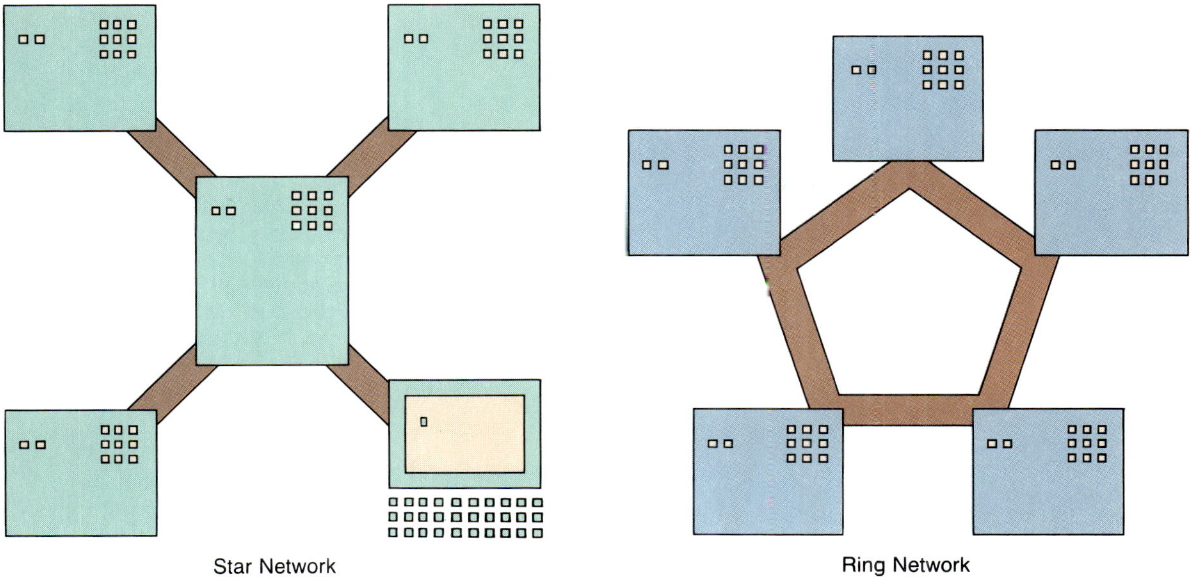

FIGURE 13-1
Star and Ring Networks

How does DDP work? Assume that a manufacturing firm has one central administrative office and several plants located in different parts of the country. A mainframe in the administrative office handles data processing that involves the firm as a whole. Minicomputers at each manufacturing plant handle the processing for that site. The minicomputers are connected to the mainframe via high-speed telephone **leased lines**, which are leased from a telephone company. Using these telephone lines, the computers can send data back and forth at high speed (close to 1,000 characters per second is now normal). As a result, the minicomputers can obtain information from the mainframe, and, if necessary, transfer the results of their processing back to the mainframe. The mainframe stores the company's primary data base, and the minicomputers have smaller local data bases, or **distributed data bases**, which are separate from the primary data base. The minicomputers can also access the primary data base for needed information.

Using DDP has certain obvious advantages. Minicomputer users experience quicker response time and easier access, and the mainframe's processing load is reduced. With DDP, local users can customize software to fit their individual needs and develop their own management information systems. At the same time, they can interface with the central computer. These advantages often result in lower costs for the organization.

On the other hand, problems with using DDP include lack of data security over the telephone lines, inconsistency between the software and hardware at the local sites and that at the central computer, and less technical support at the local sites than at the central site. The hardware inconsistency problem is aggravated when users attempt to interface personal computers with the central computer or the local minicomputers. Users often find that their personal computers cannot "talk" to the mainframe or transfer data without additional hardware. As a result, the selection of a personal computer may depend on its ability to communicate with mainframes and with other personal computers.

The recent advances of on-line systems rank as the most important development in information dissemination since the invention of the library.

John Page, Vice-president of corporate research and development at Software Publishing Corporation
(As quoted in "Lighting the Fuse," *PC Magazine,* October 16, 1984, p. 93.)

"LOGGING ON"

When a user accesses a host computer, he or she must go through a procedure known as "logging on," which identifies the user to the computer. Usually, this process involves the following three steps:

1. Contacting the host computer by phone.
2. Entering the user's identification number.
3. Entering the user's password from the keyboard.

When contact is made with the computer, the user hears a high-pitched tone over the telephone. This **carrier tone** carries the information between the user's computer and the host computer.

If the user enters an incorrect identification number or password, the host computer will not allow the user access. If the identification number and password are correct, then the user is **on-line** and may continue the access.

TELECOMMUNICATIONS WITH THE PERSONAL COMPUTER

With the combination of personal computer and telephone, increasing numbers of people can conduct many activities without leaving home. Tasks that once required a trip to the library, the store, the post office, or the work place can now be accomplished with a computer at home. More information data bases can be accessed by home computers every day. Using telecommunications to search for material is much faster than a manual search.

An individual need not be a computer expert to use telecommunications. If a user knows how to turn on the computer and insert the appropriate disk, he or she can use telecommunications simply by answering on-screen questions or selecting options. For this reason, telecommunications will contrib-

Using a personal computer, a telephone, special software, and the computer at her bank, this personal computer owner can pay her bills directly from her home.

This menu and subsequent sub-menus allow a subscriber of this telecommunication service to use his or her personal computer to browse through and purchase various products and services without leaving the comfort of home.

ute to the tremendous growth in computer use in the coming years and give the largest number of people service and pleasure.

Telecommunications uses with the personal computer fall into five broad categories—information sources, interaction with other users, electronic mail, business services, and telecommuting. Each category is covered separately, along with suggestions for accessing each type of activity. In most cases, the user communicates with a host computer from a personal computer or terminal. The host computer can be a mainframe, a minicomputer, or another personal computer, depending on the application.

If a large number of people access the host computer, a mainframe or large minicomputer is needed, but a personal computer can be used for communications involving a small number of users. National data bases and information services use several mainframes to handle up to 500 users at one time, but a local bulletin board may be run by a personal computer equipped to accept messages from one caller at a time.

CompuServe and The Source

Before we discuss the five individual types of telecommunications, we should consider two large information networks that offer services in all five categories. A user can subscribe to CompuServe or The Source by paying an initial fee for the necessary access information. This information includes a **user number**, which identifies the user for billing and electronic mail addressing purposes, and a **password**, which ensures that only the user can access the information service with the given user number. The user is charged an hourly fee for the time he or she is connected to the service.

To handle the many requests for information, user interaction, user communication, work uses, and business services, both networks use several mainframe computers. The Source has *nine* mainframe computers and 19 hard disk drives with a total secondary storage capacity of over 6 *gigabytes* (6 *billion bytes*)! CompuServe has similar facilities to handle its subscribers. As we discuss each use of telecommunications, we will describe how CompuServe and The Source are used for each purpose.

Information Sources

Commercial information data bases have been available since 1972. The early data bases were accessed via terminals that were found only at academic institutions and large corporations. These terminals looked like today's per-

TELECOMMUNICATIONS APPLICATIONS

The various applications of telecommunications are increasing each day as new data bases and services are available. The following five applications appeared in *USA Today* from May to August of 1984.

Need financial information? Call the "Ask Mr. Fed" financial service offered by CompuServe. Callers can enter questions on any financial topic from their keyboard and then wait for Mr. Fed to answer. Ten economists answer the questions on a rotating basis.

Need a letter, picture, contract, or other document sent to you from across the country *today*? Use ZAP mail from Federal Express to obtain a computer-generated facsimile of the document in two hours. ZAP mail is a form of *electronic mail*.

Need a job? The Computer Job Bank in Honolulu publishes an up-to-date list of jobs that are related to computers. This information is available to CompuServe subscribers who can then send a cover letter and resume to The Computer Job Bank via CompuServe's form of electronic mail.

Want to rally public support for or against an issue? Use a local bulletin board to make other computer users aware of it. David Hughes of Colorado Springs, Colorado, used this approach to spread the word on a proposed local ordinance. Hughes was the lone dissenter at one board meeting, but the bulletin board brought over 200 people to the next meeting.

Want to know the news before the networks? Subscribe to The Source and access the current news section. Users who were logged onto The Source on July 11, 1984 at 11:23 P.M. found out before anyone else that Walter Mondale had picked Geraldine Ferraro as his running mate for the 1984 presidential election.

The use of data bases by personal computer owners is approximately at zero today, relative to where it's going.

Roger K. Summit, President of Dialog Information Services, a division of Lockheed Corporation

(As quoted in "A New Shortcut to Electronic Libraries," *Business Week,* May 28, 1984, p. 106b.)

sonal computers. However, because the terminals did not have disk drives or a CPU, they could only be used to enter data and instructions to a mainframe and to receive output from the mainframe. Now, a personal computer equipped with a modem and communications software can access these information sources. Generally, four types of information sources are available to users via telecommunications—information utilities, news and business information services, encyclopedic data bases, and specialized networks. The host computer is either a mainframe or a large minicomputer, because of the storage capacity and speed necessary to search the data bases for a particular piece of information.

This fisheye view of CompuServe's computer facility shows the multiple mainframe computers and secondary storage equipment necessary to support this information service.

Table 13-1 INFORMATION SERVICES OF COMPUSERVE AND THE SOURCE

Category of Information	*CompuServe*	*The Source*
Wire service	Associated Press (AP)	United Press International (UPI)
Newspapers	Ten different newspapers	*The New York Times*
Business and finance	Standard and Poor's	BIZDEX (a business index)
Stock quotes	MicroQuote and QuickQuote	UPI Unistox service
Magazines	Summary articles from three popular magazines	Abstracts from 30 magazines
Airline schedules	Official Airline Guide	Airsched
Medical	Medical Advice data base	Health Tex
General information	Academic American Encyclopedia	Information on Demand

Information Utilities CompuServe and The Source are major sources of information for their subscribers. The variety of information services available on both CompuServe and The Source is suggested in Table 13-1, which lists some of the services available on these two networks. This list includes only general services in each category.

News and Business Information Services Table 13-1 lists news and business information services for both CompuServe and The Source. In fact, both operations offer commodity reports, news letters, reports on various subjects, and miscellaneous information. In addition to these two operations, the Dow Jones News/Retrieval Service (DJNS) specializes in news and business and financial information. The DJNS currently offers these comprehensive services to over 250,000 subscribers. In the news area, DJNS draws reports from *The Wall Street Journal, Barrons,* and United Press International.

In the business and financial information area, DJNS offers stock and bond information, reports on domestic and foreign companies, economic forecasts, Securities and Exchange Commission reports, and forecasts on earnings per share for over 2,400 companies. Subscribers can also access an encyclopedia and use a keyword that characterizes a topic to search for articles in either *The Wall Street Journal* or *Barrons.*

Using a modem (shown in the foreground) in conjunction with a personal computer and telephone line, a user can research almost any topic in an encyclopedic data base without leaving home or work.

Encyclopedic Data Bases With encyclopedic data bases, a user can specify a subject and then receive a bibliographic list of all available references to this subject. The bibliography is based on a search through the many data bases that are stored in each service. Based on these bibliographic listings, a user can then obtain summaries of the articles. A user may either order photocopies of desired articles or find one or more of the articles that were located by the search in the local library.

The Big Three encyclopedic data bases are DIALOG, ORBIT, and BRS (Bibliographic Reference Service). The largest of the three, DIALOG, has nearly 200 data bases with over 60 *million* records that can be searched for a given subject. All three services constantly upgrade and add to their data bases. Some information overlap among the services does occur because each service does not actually create the data bases. Outside companies collect and

Table 13-2 EXAMPLES OF DATA BASES IN ENCYCLOPEDIC NETWORKS

General knowledge encyclopedia
Directory of items available in mail order catalogs
List of books in print
Index of articles from over 370 magazines
Index of magazine articles on personal computers
Directory of yellow page listings from 4,800 telephone directories
List of all commercially available software
Daily index of over 2,000 news stories
Employment registry
Index of all large advertisements that appear in 148 magazines
List of all entries in *Chemical Abstracts*
Index of engineering articles that appear in over 3,500 journals
List of many federal government activities
Index of doctoral dissertations

(SOURCE: Alfred Glossbrenner, *The Complete Handbook of Personal Computer Communications* (New York: St. Martins Press, 1983), pp. 152–55.)

compile the information to sell to the data base services. Examples of the data bases available on these services are given in Table 13-2.

Specialized Networks The number of specialized networks that are available to users through telecommunications seems to increase every day. These networks offer information to special groups of users. In many cases, these users could not obtain this specialized information through their own resources. These networks are really specialized versions of the encyclopedic data bases discussed earlier. Each network or data base has different billing and log on procedures. Table 13-3 gives examples of some specialized networks.

Interaction with Other Users

Just as the personal computer allows users to obtain information from mainframe computer data banks and information networks, it may also be used to interact directly with other users. This interaction can occur through either a bulletin board service or a teleconference.

Bulletin Board Service If a computer is combined with one or more telephone lines, a modem, and some type of communications software, users can call in and "post" messages on an **electronic bulletin board**. Both CompuServe and The Source have national bulletin board facilities, and well over 1,000 local bulletin boards are available around the country. Each local bulletin board has a **system operator (sysop)** who invests a great deal of time, effort, and money to ensure that the bulletin board runs smoothly and meets users' needs.

To access a bulletin board, a user needs a personal computer, a modem, a telephone, communications software, and the telephone number of the bulletin board. When contact is made with the bulletin board, a menu-driven program asks whether the user wishes to leave a message or read messages. These services are *free* unless the call itself is long distance. Contacting an electronic bulletin board can be an interesting and rewarding experience for a very low cost.

Table 13-3 EXAMPLES OF SPECIALIZED NETWORKS

Specialized Network Name	Nature of Information
MEDAB	Information on the Middle East
The Information Bank	Abstracts from newspapers and magazines
NEXIS	Full text of articles from newspapers, magazines, and wire services
Medline	Articles in medical journals since 1966
RTECS	Toxicological measurement of 47,000 chemicals
Bioethicsline	Citations to articles involving science and ethics
Lexis	Full text of legal decisions, statutes, and so on
Energynet	Information on 3,000 energy-related organizations
Compustat	Publicly available data on U.S. and foreign companies
Exceptional Child Educational Resources	Provides citations and abstracts on education of handicapped and gifted children
SSIE	Descriptions of 160,000 on-going and completed research projects
Horse	Breeding and race information on over 1 million thoroughbred horses in North America
Coffeeline	References to articles and books on coffee

(SOURCE: Gerald Lanson, "Information Please," *Science 82,* pp. 38–41.)

Users often exchange public domain software on national and local bulletin boards. Public domain software is not copyrighted and therefore can be copied without breaking copyright laws. It may be software that a computer user has written and wishes to share with other users or "freeware" that is distributed by its author for a "donation." To exchange software (or other information), the user must have a personal computer with a disk drive and communications software with which the public domain software can be **downloaded** and saved on disk. Software that is sent from a disk to the host computer is **uploaded**. A terminal cannot be used to exchange software because it has no secondary storage and CPU.

Teleconferencing Because CompuServe and The Source can serve multiple users simultaneously with their mainframe host computers, these net-

Using teleconferencing with special microphones and video equipment, geographically separated parties can confer "face-to-face."

MEDLINE

Treating Patients with Computer Advice

Dr. Rodney Bryant of Woodbury, Tennessee, had a problem. His two-year-old patient had convulsions, high fever, and an abnormal heart rate. Phenobarbital is the usual prescription for older patients, but Bryant did not know how the drug would affect a two-year-old child. Because Woodbury is not a metropolitan area with a large medical center, Bryant could not consult with colleagues who had more advanced training. However, he could use the Medline data base available through DIALOG for accurate and almost instantaneous information on how to treat his young patient. Bryant used his personal computer to sign onto DIALOG. By giving the keywords "epilepsy and infant," Bryant requested all references to epilepsy and infants. He then narrowed his search by using the words "seizure," "convulsions," and "phenobarbital." The search produced an article titled "The Long-term Effect of Phenobarbital on Cognitive Functions in Children with Feveral Convulsions." Out of 40 million medical references, this was the exact article Bryant needed to determine that his patient could be treated with phenobarbital with no long-term effects. All this information was available to Bryant without his ever leaving his office!

SOURCE: Craig Zarley, "Dialing into Data Bases," *Personal Computing*, December 1983, p. 135.

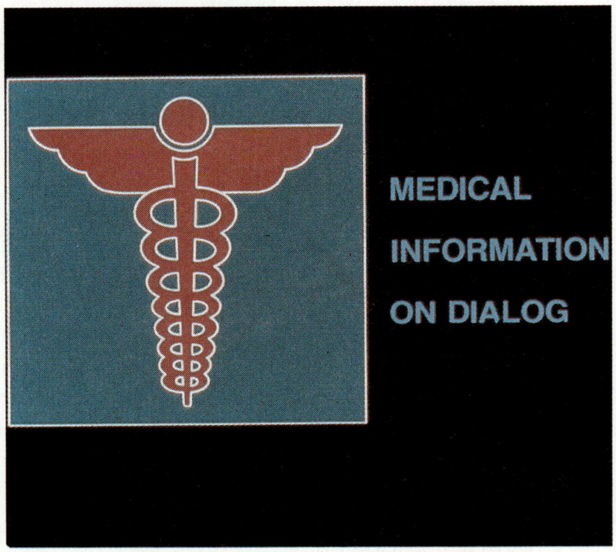

Using Medline on the DIALOG information service, a physician or researcher can access abstracts of journal articles on almost any medical subject.

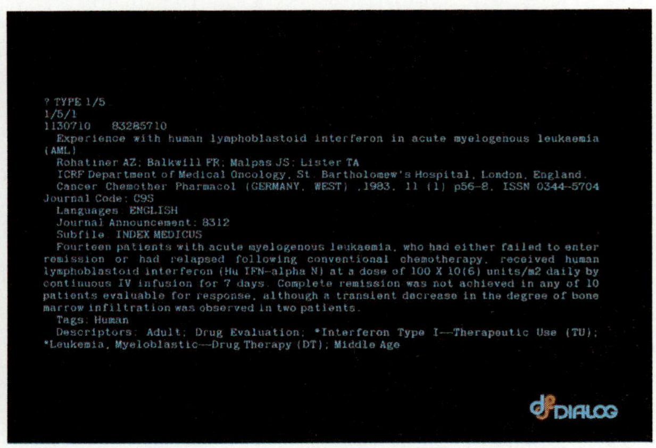

ZAP Mail is a form of electronic mail that allows a user to send a document across the United States in the same day.

works can handle conferences or other multiple-user sessions. Users interact for informal "gab" sessions usually through CompuServe or The Source. On CompuServe, a citizens' band simulator program has 40 channels for conversation among users. CompuServe estimates that nearly one-half of their subscribers regularly use the CB simulator. On The Source, informal teleconferencing is available on the CHAT option.

For formal teleconferencing, real time or delayed conferences may be arranged. In a **real time conference**, all participants are actually logged onto the system at the same time. In a **delayed conference**, participants' comments are stored sequentially as they are entered. A delayed conference can last for months while participants formulate replies to comments already made by others. Normally, a real time conference would be used for a pressing topic that requires a quick resolution, and the delayed conference might be used for philosophical or policy questions that do not require immediate decisions.

Electronic Mail

An exciting area of telecommunications is **electronic mail**—that is, sending letters, documents, and messages to other users via a personal computer. Electronic mail offers many advantages over written mail and telephone calls. It is much faster than written mail because it moves electronically. Electronic mail can be much cheaper if the costs of dictating, typing, proofreading, and mailing a letter are considered. Using electronic mail, a user can type a letter from a keyboard and another user can read it the same day.

I can't think of anything that would possibly prevent e-mail [electronic mail] from becoming a multi-billion-dollar industry by the early 1990s.

Michael Cavanaugh, Director of the Electronic Mail Association

(As quoted in "Electronic Mail Firms in Survival Fight," *USA Today,* March 11, 1985, pp. 1B–2B.)

Electronic mail can help solve the problem known as *telephone tag.* In telephone tag, one person calls a second, does not find his or her party, and leaves a message. When the second person returns the call, the original caller is out, and another message is left. This process can continue for several days. With electronic mail, a more substantive message can be left, possibly eliminating the necessity of a return call.

Essentially, three types of electronic mail are available today. First, the commercial variety—such as ZAP Mail offered by Federal Express—sends a facsimile of a letter or document cross-country in one day. Neither party needs access to a personal computer or terminal. Second, electronic mail that is internal to an organization requires some form of personal computer network so that organization members can quickly and easily communicate with one another. This type of electronic mail is extremely important to the management of the organization and the realization of its goals.

Finally, the third type of electronic mail is available to subscribers of CompuServe and The Source. Users can communicate with any other subscriber through these electronic mail services. The CompuServe electronic mail service is called EasyPlex, and the corresponding service on The Source is called SMAIL. With either service, a subscriber can send a "letter" to another subscriber by use of the recipient's account number. Subscribers of either service who write articles that are published in newspapers or magazines often include their account numbers at the end of the article to invite electronic mail comments from other subscribers.

Business Services

Businesses are quick to take advantage of any new avenue of communication for advertising and sales purposes. This is especially true of telecommunications. With telecommunications, users can view and purchase various services and products. **Videotex**—or viewdata or viewtron—is currently a small industry with the potential for enormous growth over the coming years. In February 1984, CBS, Sears, and IBM formed a cooperative group to move into videotex. The three companies felt that no one industry could do the job right and that a successful approach to the market required all three companies to bring their individual expertise to the group. The impact of this group in the videotex marketplace will soon be felt.

Currently, videotex appears in the following three areas:

1. Shopping at home for goods and services.
2. Banking at home.
3. Managing stocks and bonds at home.

CompuServe and The Source offer shop-at-home services for subscribers. CompuStore and the Electronic Mall both offer a wide range of products on CompuServe. The Source offers the same services with CompuStore and CHESS (Computer Home Economic Supply Service). Available on both major telecommunications operations, CompuStore offers over 60,000 different products with over 2,000 brand names.

Over 60 banks across the country offer home banking, or **electronic funds transfer**, services to their customers. A customer can establish automatic bill-paying with the bank, pay bills by computer as they are due, or

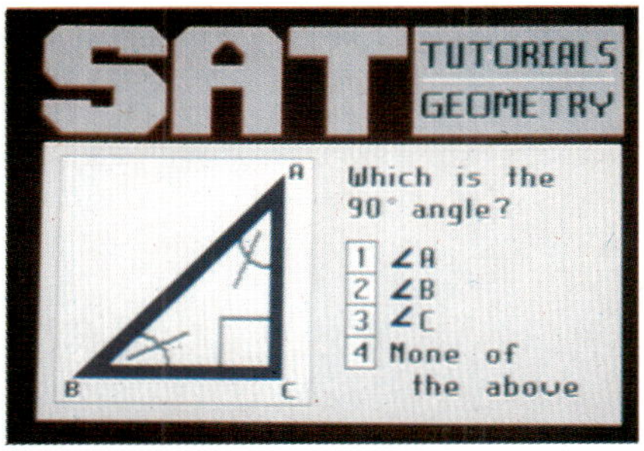

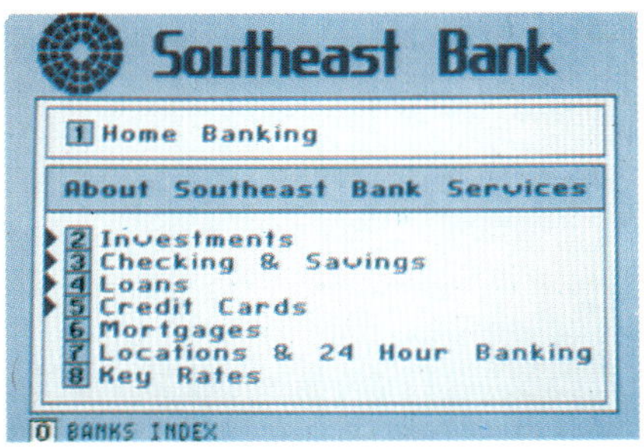

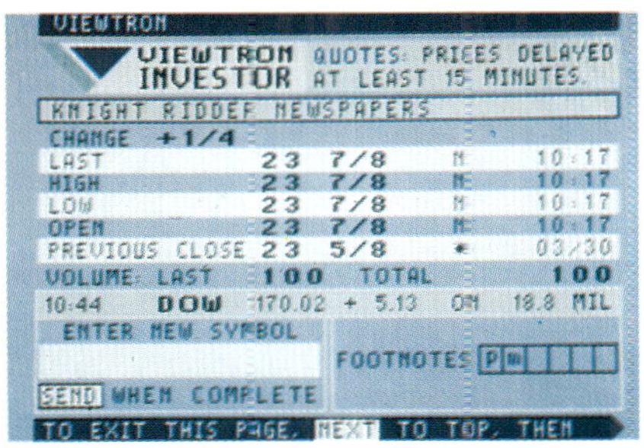

Videotex can be used for many purposes, including banking, purchasing tickets to sporting and entertainment events, and obtaining up-to-date stock market quotes.

transfer funds among various types of accounts—for example, checking, savings, money market, IRA (individual retirement account), and so on. The current status of a customer's bank account can be transmitted to his or her personal computer. People have many excuses for not taking advantage of this service, including fears that computer criminals may break into an account or the initial startup cost may be prohibitive for those who do not own a personal computer. However, many banking executives see it as the wave of the future. CompuServe offers three banks and a money market fund for subscribers. Bank of America and Chemical Bank both offer home banking services to their customers.

Another form of electronic funds transfer is electronic portfolio manage-

Videotex is a classic consumer-marketing business. Our concept is to tie this to the home computer market.

Charles F. Moran, Vice-president of corporate planning at Sears, Roebuck and Company

(As quoted in "Three Big Backers Give Videotex a Shot at Success," *Business Week,* February 27, 1984, pp. 36–37.)

Research into videotex may soon allow anyone with a telephone and television set to take advantage of the many opportunities offered by this service.

ment. More people are handling their stock portfolios via computer than ever before. The simplest form of help consists of computer network information that gives up-to-the-minute stock quotes. More sophisticated systems give stock forecasts and analyses. Finally, stock transactions can be accomplished using a personal computer, thereby giving users ultimate control over their investment portfolios.

Telecommuting

Early telecommunications involved the use of a terminal to access a mainframe. The introduction of the personal computer only made telecommunications easier because access to a mainframe was not required. Now, a user can work on a personal computer at home, store the results on disk, and then download them to the mainframe at work.

Basically, three types of **telecommuting** workers exist—individuals who access a mainframe using their personal computers to avoid a trip to the office; individuals who use their home computers to continue or finish work begun at the office; and people who work at home computers most of the time and go into the office only occasionally to review their work with a supervisor. For the first two types of telecommuter, a home computer is a convenience that allows them to complete their work quickly and easily. Working at home is a way of life for the third type of telecommuter. He or she can raise a family, save money on commuting costs, or live in a rural setting and still work in a computer-related field.

Telecommuting has its problems. For example, accessing a free line into the mainframe may be difficult. Mainframes usually have a limited number of incoming lines, which can often be overloaded. On the personal side, the user's family may not appreciate the fact that the telephone is tied up by the computer for long periods of time (at least this was true in the case of the author!).

The individual who uses a home computer to complete work begun at the office faces problems with accessing the data bases on the office mainframe. These mainframes may not be set up for access from the outside, and the data bases may not be in a form that is easily used on a personal computer. Solving these problems requires a change of policy by the data processing department toward outside access.

For the telecommuter who works at home most of the time, a presumably perfect work situation has its own set of problems. Inadequate time management and lack of interaction with co-workers and superiors in the office may cause workers to return to the office on a full-time basis.

MAKING THE CONNECTION

To take advantage of the many opportunities for telecommunicating, a user must first have the proper hardware and software. For an individual user, the hardware includes a personal computer or terminal, a telephone, and a modem. For large computers, the modem is still needed, but the telephone line may be replaced by other types of communications links. In this section, we cover some technical aspects and terminology of telecommunications. Although the discussion emphasizes the use of a personal computer or terminal to telecommunicate, much of the discussion also holds true for communications between larger computers.

Personal Computer or Terminal

A **computer terminal** is a "dumb" version of a personal computer. Even though it has a keyboard and video screen, the terminal does not have any form of secondary storage or a CPU. The original form of a terminal was the **teletype (TTY)**, which delivered news to radio stations and newspapers. A TTY had a keyboard and printhead, and its output was usually printed on rolls of inexpensive yellow paper.

A terminal can be used only for simple telecommunications, because it can only respond to another computer's signal. Terminals cannot run programs separately or store information received from another computer. The simplest form of communications software merely converts a personal computer into a dumb terminal—that is, a terminal with no secondary storage or a CPU. More advanced software greatly expands the potential uses of the personal computer.

Communications Links

For over 100 years, the telephone has been a useful form of voice communication that converts audible tones into electrical signals. It would be nice if the electrical signals generated by the computer could be sent directly over a telephone line. However, this is impossible, because the two types of signals are very different. Computer signals sent over telephone lines must be converted into the appropriate telephone signals. This conversion is handled by the modem.

Until recently, the telephone lines that transmitted the converted signal were made of copper, which resulted in bulky combinations of wire. Now, **fiber optics** that use flexible glass rods to carry the information are used. Fiber optics are much more efficient than copper wire and reduce the bulk tremendously.

Other forms of communications that are used to transfer data include satellite links, coaxial cable, and microwaves. With **satellite links**, voices and data are sent over great distances. A **coaxial cable** is a large number of copper wires surrounded by a metallic shield. Coaxial cable can send data at high speeds, and the shield protects it from outside influences. Finally, with **microwave relays**, voices and data can be sent over line-of-sight distances—that is, straight lines between microwave towers.

Data Conversion

Whether computer data are sent from a personal computer over a telephone line or from a mainframe via coaxial cable, a modem is necessary to convert the computer signals into telephone signals. Recall that the information in a computer is stored and manipulated in the form of bits. (A bit is an electronic pulse—one—or the absence of a pulse—zero.) Before the bits can be transmitted over a telephone line, the **modem** must translate them into a form the telephone can accommodate. This translation process has the following two steps:

1. Conversion of data from parallel form to serial form.
2. Conversion of data from digital form to analog form.

Parallel to Serial Conversion Recall that data in a **parallel form** are processed 8 or 16 bits at a time, and data in a **serial form** are processed one bit at a time. Computers process data in a parallel form, but a telephone line can only accept data in a serial form. The conversion from parallel to serial form is performed by an **RS-232C card** in the computer. The name *RS-232C* refers to a standard pin configuration in a plug, and the card is either part of the computer or it can be inserted separately. The **serial port** connects the cable from the modem with the RS-232C card, and the parallel form data in the computer are converted to a serial stream of bits that is sent to the modem. The conversion of data from a parallel form to a serial form is demonstrated in Figure 13-2.

Digital to Analog Conversion Recall that **analog** refers to a physical relationship that represents data. In this case, the data are represented as an audio signal that the telephone line can carry. The translation of data from digital form to analog form is carried out by the modem. (Remember, the *modem* is so named because it **mo**dulates and **dem**odulates computer data.) When a bit is modulated, it is converted into a particular sound frequency—one frequency to represent the digit zero, and another frequency to represent the digit one. When these frequencies are demodulated, they are con-

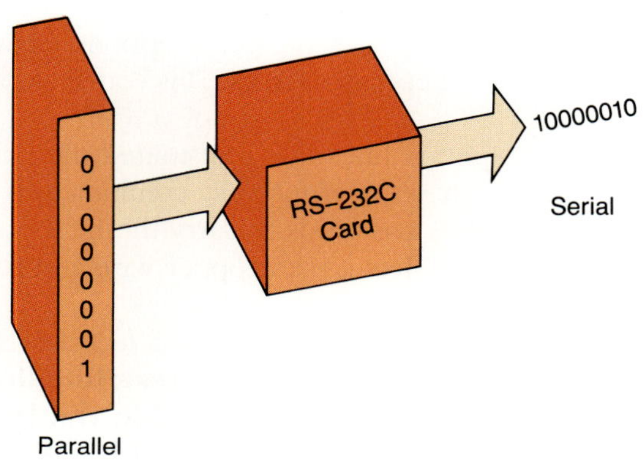

FIGURE 13-2
Conversion of Data from Parallel to Serial Form

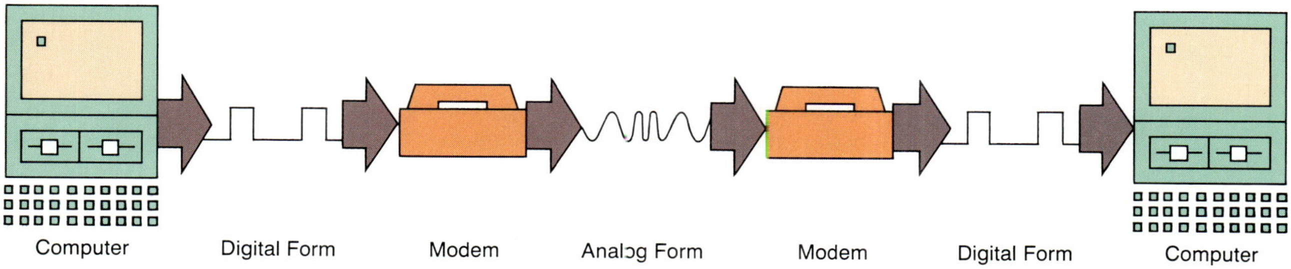

FIGURE 13-3 Communication between Computers

verted back into zeros or ones. Figure 13-3 demonstrates the process of sending information from one computer to another over telephone lines.

When a character that is stored in one computer in binary form is transmitted to another computer over a telephone line, 10 bits must be modulated and demodulated. The ASCII representation of the character takes 8 bits. A **start bit** before the character notifies the receiving computer that a new character is coming. A **stop bit** after the character notifies the computer when the character is complete. Figure 13-4 shows three different representations of the letter A (01000001 in ASCII). A start bit of zero appears at the beginning of each representation, and a stop bit of one appears at the end of each representation. The first representation is in binary form. The bits are also shown in digital form as they exist before modulation and then as sound waves after modulation. In all three representations, the bits that represent the character are shown in a box to distinguish them from the start and stop bits. The demodulation process is simply the reverse of modulation—the sound waves are converted into pulses, which are equivalent to the character representation.

Asynchronous, or nonsynchronized, **communication** uses start and stop bits to define characters in the communication process. This form is most often used in communications between a personal computer and a mainframe or between two personal computers, because it does not require that the two computers be synchronized in the rate at which they process information. Mainframe-to-mainframe communication is often synchronous—that is, the timing of the computers is matched. **Synchronous communication** means large amounts of data can be transmitted without start and stop bits.

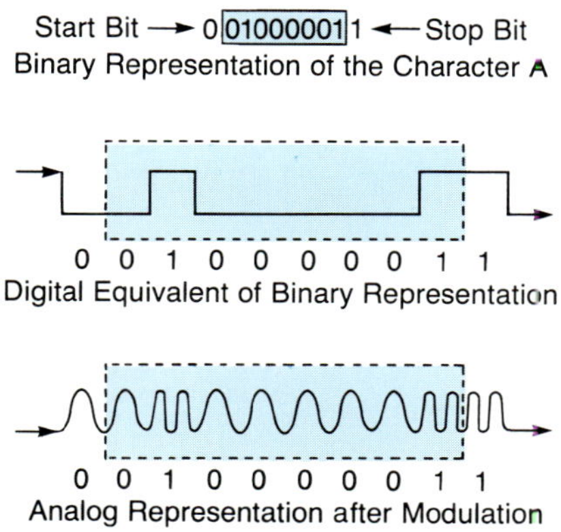

FIGURE 13-4 Demonstration of Modulation Process

Using a Modem

Communication with a modem can be made in one of three modes—simplex, half-duplex, or full-duplex. Communication in *only* one direction is in the **simplex mode**. Communication between computers is in the **half-duplex mode** if only one computer can send information at any one time. If both computers can send information at the same time, communication is in the **full-duplex mode**. We can imagine the half-duplex mode as a one-way bridge that allows only one car to pass at a time, and the full-duplex mode as a two-way bridge that allows cars to pass in both directions at the same time. When half-duplex is used, the sending computer usually shows the signal that is transmitted on the screen. However, with full-duplex, the receiving computer sends the signal back to the sending computer's screen. The accuracy of the signal received can be checked in full-duplex, because it is sent back to the originating computer.

Modems can usually be switched to accommodate either half- or full-duplex communications. Simplex mode is seldom used. Most communications involving personal computers use the full-duplex mode. Figure 13-5 shows both half-duplex and full-duplex communications between computers.

It is very easy to tell if a modem is set to the wrong mode by observing the output on the screen. If the modem is set at half-duplex when it should be at full-duplex, *two* of everything appears on the screen. The half-duplex modem puts one set there, and the receiving computer sends one set back. On the other hand, if the modem is set at full-duplex when it should be at half-duplex, nothing appears on the screen. The full-duplex modem does *not* show input on the screen, and the receiving computer does not send it back.

A modem can also be switched between the originate and answer modes. These modes control the channel that each computer uses to transmit data. Two computers that communicate in the full-duplex mode cannot both send information using the same audio frequencies. Therefore, one computer must be in the **originate mode** and use one pair of audio frequencies to represent zeros and ones. The other computer must be in the **answer mode** and use another pair of audio frequencies to represent zeros and ones. As a result, the modem can send and receive information at the same time without any confusion about which signal is which. In most communications involving personal computers, the user calls into a host computer, so the user's modem should be set to the originate mode. The host computer's modem would be switched to the answer mode.

The **protocol** for any communication between computers is the set of rules that the two computers follow in sending and receiving information. The continuing standardization of modems has made protocol less important than it once was.

FIGURE 13-5
Types of Computer Communications

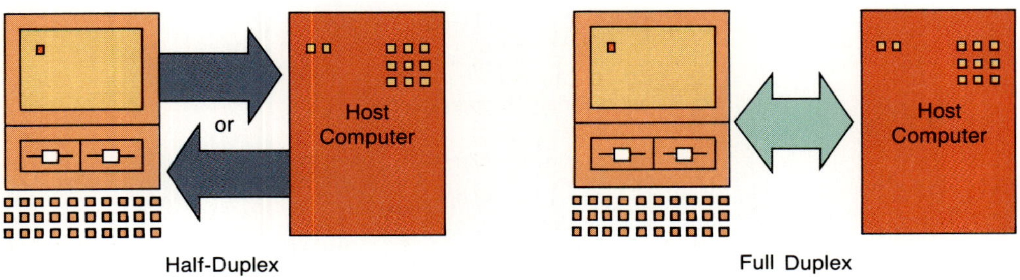

Types of Modems

Modems can be classified in the following three ways:

1. By the type of connection they make with the phone set.
2. By the speed at which they send and receive information.
3. By whether or not they are "intelligent" modems.

Let us consider each classification in order.

An **acoustical coupler** modem is built so that a desk phone's handset can be "plugged" in to a pair of rubber cups. The handset sends and receives signals from the modem when it is inserted into the rubber cups of the acoustical coupler. Acoustical couplers are the least expensive form of modem, but they have problems associated with outside noises that leak into the transmission of information.

Another type of modem connection is the **direct-connect modem**, which is connected directly to the telephone line. This type of modem, which is the fastest and most versatile modem, is usually used with personal computers.

The speed at which modems can send and receive information is measured by the baud rate. The **baud rate** is the number of bits per second that can be transmitted. Baud rates of 300–1,200 bits per second are standard for personal computer modems. (Modems with a baud rate of 2,400 bits per second are now available. Modems with baud rates of 9,600 bits per second may be available in the near future.) Because each character in asynchronous communication is 10 bits, a baud rate of 300 bits per second equals 30 characters per second. Similarly, a baud rate of 1,200 bits per second equals 120 characters per second. Acoustical couplers operate at low baud rates, whereas direct-connect modems can operate at the 1,200–2,400 bits per second rates. For many personal computer communications, a baud rate of 300 bits per second is acceptable, but higher baud rates are essential if large amounts of information are transmitted.

With any standard telephone handset plugged into an acoustical modem, a computer user can communicate with another computer.

With this prototype communications unit, a U.S. Army infantryman can communicate directly from the field with his superiors at headquarters.

An intelligent modem can handle more operations than just translating between digital and binary forms of information. With **auto-dial** and **auto-answer** capabilities, an intelligent modem can be programmed to dial another phone or answer your phone, to hang up the phone if a busy signal is reached, or even to dial a second number if the first number is busy. Because only direct-connect modems are intelligent, the reasons for their popularity are fairly clear.

Communications Software

A personal computer cannot send or receive information without special instructions known as **communications software**. The software can convert the personal computer into either a "dumb" or a "smart" terminal depending on how the software uses the personal computer's secondary storage and CPU. If the software merely instructs the computer to perform the same actions as a TTY terminal, then the personal computer is converted into a "dumb" terminal. In other words, the personal computer receives information from the host computer, displays it on the screen, and sends data or instructions from the keyboard back to the host computer.

On the other hand, if the communications software uses the personal computer's secondary storage and CPU to yield a terminal that is superior to a TTY terminal, then the personal computer is a "smart" terminal. The software may allow the user to save on disk any host computer information that appears on the personal computer's screen. This process is used for *downloading* software and other information. The software can also allow the user to *upload* information from a personal computer disk to the host computer. Many communications software packages can also print the information that appears on the screen for future reference.

Telecomputing allows me to use information when I need to, without having to wait for some outside company or service to be available to work with me.

Dennis Hayes, Chairman of Hayes Microcomputer Products, Inc.

(As quoted in "Dennis Hayes on Data Banks, AT&T, and the Future of Telecomputing," *Personal Computing,* February 1983, p. 39.)

Figure 13-6 shows the menu for HBJ: TALK, which simulates the conversion of a personal computer into a "smart" terminal. In the menu, settings for the communication are given. In Figure 13-6, the baud rate is 300, and 7 data

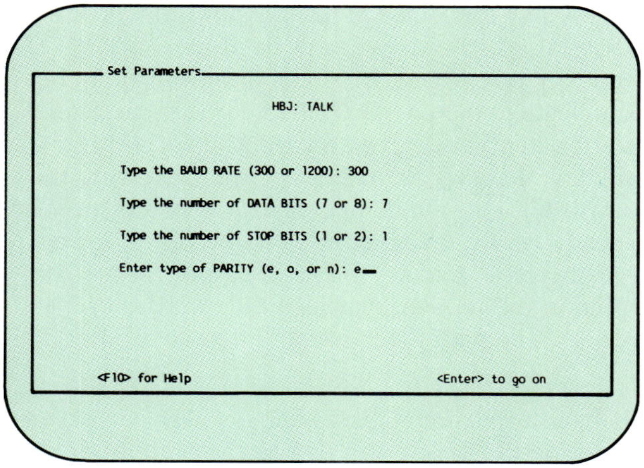

FIGURE 13-6
Menu for HBJ: TALK Communications Package

bits are used, along with one stop bit and even parity. (Recall from Chapter 8 that a parity bit is used to check data transmissions by ensuring that the number of bits in each byte is either even or odd.) These settings can be changed by the user if required by the host. Standard, or default, settings in most communications packages are set to work for most applications, so the user need not worry about them.

SELECTING A MODEM AND COMMUNICATIONS SOFTWARE

As with any software, the communications package must be compatible with a personal computer, but it must also be compatible with an intelligent modem. With a compatible combination of communications software and intelligent modem, the computer can be instructed to dial numbers that are stored in the modem's memory, to hang up or to dial another number if the first is busy, to send data if another modem is reached, to answer a call and receive data from another modem, and to perform similar functions depending on the individual modem and communications package.

A popular line of direct-connect modems is marketed by Hayes Microcomputer Products under the names Smartmodem and Micromodem. Because of their popularity, many communications packages have been written to work with them. Numerous other modems and compatible software work with various types of personal computers. When buying a modem and a communications package, a prospective user should do the following:

1. Determine the purposes for the communications software. For example, a user might want to go on-line with CompuServe or The Source or to transfer large amounts of work-related data.
2. Find software that serves the purposes determined in step 1 and that is compatible with the user's personal computer. Test the software at the computer store to ensure that it is easy to use and actually fits the user's needs.
3. Find a modem that is compatible with the software found in step 2 and that is sufficiently "intelligent" to meet the user's needs.

The user should not pay extra money to have auto-answer if this function will not be used. The question of baud rate also depends on the user's needs. If large amounts of information are downloaded or uploaded, then a 1,200 or 2,400 baud modem is a must. A 300 baud modem is adequate for most users and usually costs significantly less than a 1,200 baud modem. Make sure that an RS-232C card is built into the computer. If it is not, it must be purchased separately before the computer can be used for telecommunications. The cable that fits the RS-232C port in the computer and the plug in the modem may also be purchased separately if it does not come with the modem.

Once the modem and the software are in place, then the user can telecommunicate simply by connecting the phone and dialing the number of a national data bank, a bulletin board, the mainframe at work, or another personal computer user.

REVIEW OF KEY POINTS

- A computer that is combined with a telecommunications link, a modem, and communications software can communicate with other computers.
- The use of a computer for communications is known as telecommunications.
- Two or more computers linked together via a communications medium form a computer network.
- Popular types of computer networks are ring and star networks.
- Distributed data processing uses small computers to handle local processing and to relieve a central mainframe or minicomputer of some processing chores.
- Important uses of telecommunications for personal computers include finding information, interacting with other users, sending electronic mail, shopping and banking, and working from home.
- CompuServe and The Source are general purpose information services through which a user can carry out most telecommunications functions.
- National data bases, news services, and specialized networks are sources of information.
- A user can interact with other users through electronic bulletin boards and teleconferences.
- With electronic mail, a computer user can send messages and documents long distances instantaneously or communicate more efficiently with other users in the same office or local network.
- A computer user can buy goods and services, bank, and manage a stock portfolio with a computer.
- The number of individuals working at home has increased with the use of personal computers and communications packages.
- A modem translates the electronic form of information in a computer to the audio form transmitted on a telephone line, and vice versa.
- Communications software can turn a personal computer into a "smart" terminal.
- The baud rate is the number of bits per second that can be transmitted on a telephone line.
- Personal computers use asynchronous communications with start and stop bits.
- A modem and software must match the user's personal computer and fit the user's needs.

KEY TERMS

acoustical coupler
analog
answer mode
asynchronous communication
auto-answer
auto-dial
baud rate
carrier tone
coaxial cable
communications software
computer terminal
delayed conference
direct-connect modem
distributed data bases
distributed data processing (DDP)
downloaded
electronic bulletin board
electronic funds transfer
electronic mail
fiber optics
full-duplex mode
half-duplex mode
host computer
leased lines
microwave relays
modem
network
on-line
originate mode
parallel form
password
protocol
real time conference
ring network
RS-232C card
satellite links
serial form
serial port
simplex mode
star network
start bit
stop bit
synchronous communication
system operator (sysop)
telecommunications
telecommuting
teletype (TTY)
uploaded
user number
videotex

REVIEW QUESTIONS

1. Name the four elements of a telecommunications system. Why is each element necessary?
2. Why are computer networks useful? Is your computer center part of a network? If so, determine what type of network and what other computers are part of the network.
3. Why are distributed data processing and distributed data bases closely linked? List the advantages and disadvantages of DDP.
4. List the five major categories of telecommunications use. Which do you think you would most likely use?
5. Why do we say that CompuServe and The Source have elements of all five categories of telecommunications use?
6. What type of data base would you most likely want to access? What type would you probably not want to access?
7. Visit a computer store and ask if a local bulletin board exists. If one does exist, find out who sponsors it.
8. Why is a modem necessary in the telecommunications process? What function does communications software perform?
9. How do half-duplex communications differ from full-duplex communications? What are the functions of the answer mode and originate mode?
10. How is a "dumb" terminal different from a "smart" terminal? Why is software necessary for a "smart" terminal?

Hands On

HBJ: TALK

Most communications software packages make the connection between the personal computer or terminal and another computer. HBJ: TALK is a simulator communications software package that simulates both the electronic connection over a telephone line *and* the response from a host computer. HBJ: TALK was written as a simulator for two reasons. First, not every personal computer has a modem. Without a modem, a standard communications package is useless. Second, even if a modem is available with your personal computer, accessing mainframes or national information networks requires a user account that is charged for the time used. Not everyone has such an account available.

Through the HBJ: TALK simulator, you can become familiar with making the connection with a national information network and using a local bulletin board or an electronic mail service. The wide range of possibilities that are open to you through communications is demonstrated *without* a modem and account number.

Using HBJ: TALK

The use of HBJ: TALK (or any communications software) is divided into the following two phases:

1. Making the connection with a host computer and accessing information.
2. Reading and leaving messages and sending electronic mail.

To begin this process on HBJ: TALK, boot the HBJ systems disk and choose option 5 from the HBJ main menu.

You can make a simulated connection by entering your name and password when requested by completion aids. The password, which must be 8–24 characters long, should be written down, because it is requested at a later point in the connection process. Press ⟨Enter⟩ after each entry. At this point, the package assigns you a six-digit ID number, which you should also write down for later reference. Before dialing the simulated information service, assign the telecommunications settings including the baud rate, the number of data and stop bits, and the parity. The following values are acceptable settings:

Baud rate: 300 or 1,200

Data bits: 7 or 8

Stop bits: 1

Parity: e, o, or n (even, odd, or none)

Entering any other values generates another request for these settings.

Accessing the Simulated Information Service

After you have entered your name and password, been assigned a user ID number, and entered acceptable telecommunications settings, you can access the simulated information service. Enter one of two phone numbers—555-2938 or 555-6751—to be dialed by the communications package. The dialing process is activated when you press ⟨Alt⟩⟨D⟩ (or ⟨Ctrl⟩⟨d⟩).

When the correct phone number is entered and dialed, a *carrier tone* is heard for approximately 5 seconds, and then the information service is accessed. Once this occurs, you need only select from the various menus to obtain information, read or leave messages on the bulletin board, or use electronic mail.

Using the Menus

The first menu that appears on the information service is the main menu, which has the following four choices:

1. News/Financial
2. Sports/Entertainment
3. Bulletin Boards
4. Electronic Mail

You may access any service by entering the appropriate number when a selection is requested. You can either return to a previous menu by entering the letter P, or you can return to the main menu by entering the letter M. On-screen help is available by entering the letter H from the information service main menu. Finally, the information service is exited by entering OFF or BYE at a selection point. These letter commands are referred to as *navigation commands*.

A series of control commands allows the user to control scrolling. *Scrolling* is up and down movement of information on the screen. These control commands include stopping the scroll to review the information on the screen by pressing ⟨Ctrl⟩⟨s⟩, restarting the scroll with ⟨Ctrl⟩⟨r⟩, and reversing the direction of the scroll with ⟨Ctrl⟩⟨b⟩.

The Sub-Menus

If option 1 is selected from the main menu, the following sub-menu of news and financial information appears:

1. National
2. World
3. Financial
4. Dow Jones Averages

The first and second options present sample headlines on the national and world scene, respectively, and the third option presents U.S. financial news. The fourth option presents opening and closing Dow Jones averages for a selected group of stocks.

If option 2 is selected from the main menu, the screen presents the following sub-menu of choices related to sports or entertainment:

1. Team Standings
2. Movie Mania
3. Music Happenings

Sub-menus for the first option allow you to check team standings for various sports, and the second option offers reviews of both modern and classic movies. The third option offers information on various musical topics.

If you choose the third option from the main menu, a sub-menu relating to the information service bulletin board appears:

1. Jobs
2. Shopping
3. Personal/Miscellaneous

If you select one of these options, you can either read existing messages or post messages of your own.

Finally, if you select the electronic mail option, you see the following sub-menu related to the type of message you want to send or receive:

1. Private Message
2. Public Forum

If you choose the first option, you can either read or post private messages. On the other hand, if the second option is chosen, the messages can be accessed by the public.

Exiting the Package

As mentioned earlier, the information service can be exited at any menu if you simply enter OFF or BYE. To exit HBJ: TALK, press ⟨Esc⟩.

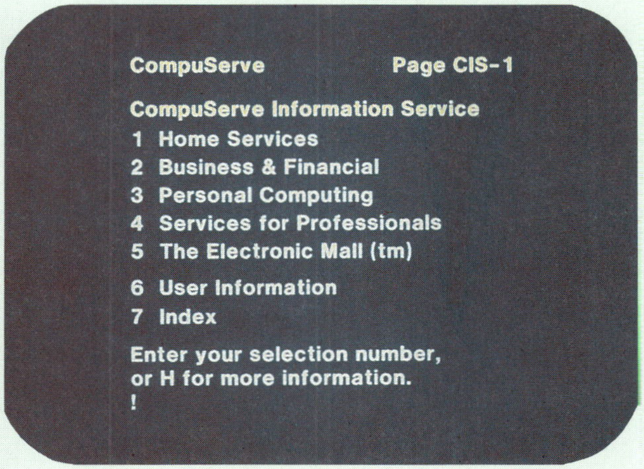

Using a personal computer, a modem, and a communications software package, individuals can access such national networks as CompuServe.

Block 4

PROGRAMMING

Chapter 3 contained a brief introduction to the programming of computers to solve problems. Block 4 discusses this topic in more detail. Although software packages may be used to accomplish tasks on the computer, some situations may require an individual to write programs. These situations usually involve specialized problems or tasks for which no software has been written. As an introduction to the art and science of programming, the next four chapters cover three facets of programming—problem solving with programs, types of computer languages, and a short course in the BASIC language. These chapters will not turn you into an accomplished programmer, but after reading them you will be aware of the pleasures and challenges of computer programming.

We have emphasized the use of software packages on personal computers, but sometimes individual programming may be necessary. For example, a user may have a problem too specific to be addressed by a commercial software company, or the user may find that existing software does not suit his or her needs. In this chapter, we cover the process of writing a program for a computer without discussing the actual language needed, because a logical plan is needed first to write a program in any language. This plan involves identifying the problem, developing a procedure for solving the problem, converting the procedure into a program, and running the program on a computer. Flowcharts and pseudocode help in the planning of a computer program, and various examples demonstrate the use of flowcharts and pseudocode.

14

Solving Problems with Computers

STUDY OBJECTIVES

After reading this chapter, you should be able to

- Understand the step-by-step nature of a computer program.
- Understand the concept of an algorithm and how important it is to the process of computer programming.
- Understand the steps to follow in writing a computer program.
- Use flowcharts and pseudocode to convert an algorithm into a form that can then be programmed.
- Recognize the various flowchart symbols that are used in program planning.
- Distinguish between translation of a high-level language into machine language and the actual execution of the program.
- Develop an algorithm for a problem and then convert that algorithm into a flowchart and pseudocode.

A STEP-BY-STEP APPROACH TO PROGRAMMING

The manipulation of symbols by a computer is based on instructions that are given to the computer by a human. Without these instructions, called a **program**, the computer is merely a collection of copper wires and silicon chips that can do absolutely nothing. Every computer package discussed so far—word processing, graphics, spreadsheets, accounting, data base management, and telecommunications—is composed of one or more programs.

The process of developing a program is called **programming**. A programmer must first develop a logical sequence of steps to accomplish a desired task. Then, with a knowledge of the rules and vocabulary of a computer language, the programmer turns the logical sequence of steps into a program.

Why Learn to Program?

With thousands of computer software packages on the market, a user may never need programming knowledge to solve problems on a computer. However, by learning to write programs, a user can take advantage of the full potential of the computer. It is another road to computer literacy.

A user with programming knowledge can expand the capabilities of commercial software packages. A user can also solve problems that software companies did not consider essential enough to include in a package. User-written programs can solve problems for which no package currently exists. Finally, programming knowledge gives the user the freedom of individual expression and creativity on the computer.

Programming on personal computers is now taught in many elementary and middle schools.

HOMEMADE PROGRAMS

No matter how many personal budgeting and financial management packages are available on the market today, the software still may not solve everyone's problems. When retired IBM engineer Elmer "Skip" Pape could not find a suitable package, he wrote his own program. Designed over a six-month period, his program handles all of his financial affairs—even tracking investments and managing assets and liabilities. On Pape's program, a change in the value of one security is reflected in his net worth. Pape says, "I think the stock part is the most valuable. It's an area I like to keep a close eye on."

SOURCE: Mark Lewyn, "How Computers Can Manage Money," *USA Today,* July 27, 1984, p. B-3.

The greatest number of user-written programs is found in the area of accounting. Many companies and individuals have discovered that standard accounting packages do not fit the way they manage money. Often, these companies or individuals purchase a commercial package and then change the program to fit their specific needs. In this way, they can take advantage of the package's many powerful options and still solve their special problems.

Some packages are structured so that a user can use the package commands to turn a step-by-step solution procedure into a separate program. In other words, a user can write a program using the package commands. A popular relational data base package, dBase II, is an example of this type of software. Not only is dBase II an excellent data base management package, but its programming language allows a user to develop the logic necessary to manage data satisfactorily and generate needed reports.

The Programming Process

The process of writing a computer program can be viewed as solving a problem. The problem is the task the user wants the computer to perform. The solution is the development of a sequence of steps using the rules and vocabulary of the computer language. The key to developing this sequence of steps is to break the problem up into small pieces, rather than approaching it as a whole. Each small piece may then be viewed as a single step in the sequence that will solve the problem. This step-by-step solution plan in computer programming is called the **logic** of the program. Often, the failure of a program can be traced to the programmer's having written the program before developing an appropriate plan for solving the problem.

Program development can be divided into the following sequence of steps:

Step 1: Identifying the problem
Step 2: Developing the algorithm
Step 3: Converting the algorithm to flowchart or pseudocode
Step 4: Writing the program
Step 5: Entering the program into the computer
Step 6: Translating the program into machine language
Step 7: Executing the program with test data
Step 8: Debugging the program using test data
Step 9: Using the program with actual data

If you don't know what your program is supposed to do, you better not start writing it.

Edsger W. Dijkstra

(As quoted in *The Official Rules* by Paul Dickson, Dell Publishing Company, New York, 1978, p. 37.)

Each step is discussed in detail later in this chapter. Not all of the terms used in these steps are familiar now, but they will be explained as you progress through the chapter.

Programming as Part of Systems Analysis

Chapter 4 included a discussion of the systems analysis process. Recall that systems analysis was also portrayed as a step-by-step process, as follows:

1. Problem definition
2. Feasibility study
3. Analysis
4. System design
5. Detailed design
6. Implementation
7. Maintenance

The steps for program development overlap the systems analysis procedure. In fact, writing any program of a practical size—such as a word processor or spreadsheet program—requires the completion of the first four steps of the systems analysis process *before* the program may actually be written. Table 14-1 compares the systems analysis and programming procedures, showing the overlap between the two.

From Table 14-1, we can see that the actual process of writing a program (program development steps 3–8) takes place only after a great deal of systems analysis has been completed. This is an important concept: Regardless of how well a program is written, its objective will not be achieved if it is written

Table 14-1 COMPARISON OF SYSTEMS ANALYSIS AND PROGRAMMING PROCEDURES

Systems Analysis	*Program Development*
1. Problem definition 2. Feasibility study 3. Analysis	1. Identifying the problem
4. System design	2. Developing the algorithm
5. Detailed design	3. Converting the algorithm to flowchart or pseudocode 4. Writing the program 5. Entering the program into the computer 6. Translating the program into machine language 7. Executing the program with test data 8. Debugging the program using test data
6. Implementation	9. Using the program with actual data
7. Maintenance	

CHRIS CRAWFORD ON PROGRAMMING

As one of the chief programmers responsible for the exciting games developed by Atari, Chris Crawford has written many programs. According to Crawford, if you can write a comprehensible paragraph, you can learn to program a computer. He lists these reasons to learn programming:

1. **To enjoy as a hobby**
2. **To learn logical thinking**
3. **To sharpen your thinking**
4. **To learn the importance of precise communications**

As a hobby, programming can be as enjoyable and creative as woodworking, knitting, or painting. Logical thinking is important for people to be better problem solvers. Crawford compares computer languages with Latin—both are closed, formal, logical forms of communication with limited but precise syntax. Computer language also enables the programmer to express ideas—such as mathematical formulas—that are too clumsy to express in English. Finally, communication with a computer requires clarity and precision. A computer will not perform a desired task unless you express yourself clearly and in the proper syntax.

SOURCE: Chris Crawford, "Why You Should Learn to Program," ***Popular Computing,*** **September 1983, pp. 153–56.**

for the *wrong* process. (In Chapter 18, we discuss how systems analysis was involved in the programming of the software packages available with this text.)

PROGRAM DEVELOPMENT

We should now look closely at the program development steps to determine what is involved in each step. To demonstrate how each step fits into the programming process, we use an example involving the computation of the average score of a student who has taken five quizzes during a school term and the determination of whether that score is less than the passing value of 60. If a student's score is less than 60, then a message from the computer indicates that the student has failed the course. Regardless of the score, both the score and the student's name are printed.

Step 1: Identifying the Problem

The first step of program development is the most important: It is virtually impossible to write a computer program without *identifying and clearly understanding* the problem to be solved. Fuzzy thinking at this stage can cause many problems for the programmer. For example, the programmer may write a program that does not correctly solve the problem at hand, or that correctly solves the wrong problem, or a combination of both! Identifying the problem may often require only a verbal statement of what the *objective* is. At other times, the objective and other important factors of the problem should be in writing. Complex problems may require a formal written description of the problem and a detailed list of other items that must be considered when writing the program. In this last situation, systems analysis and design are extremely important to ensure that the programming process results in the appropriate program.

The first step in the program development process should also include an identification of the data to be *input* to the program and the desired results to be *output* from the program. Often, these two items are specified by an external person or agency. Much grief can be avoided by incorporating these input/output requirements into this early stage of program development.

When the program is complete (step 9), the programmer should always return to step 1 to ensure that the problem solved is also the problem identified in step 1. This step may seem obvious, but it is not carried out by all programmers. To avoid frustration and problems, programmers should check program results against the original program objectives.

For the grade computation example, the objective of the program is to find the average of the five quiz scores and to determine if the average is less than 60. In this case, the problem identification part of writing our program is straightforward—an unusual situation.

Step 2: Developing the Algorithm

Step 2 in program development is to work out a step-by-step solution for the problem at hand. This step-by-step solution, called an **algorithm**, expresses the logic of the program in written form. Unless the programmer has a complete understanding of how to solve the problem, he or she will be unable to write the desired program.

We use algorithms quite often in our daily activities. Perhaps the most commonly used algorithm is a recipe for cooking. You probably would not consider a recipe an algorithm, but it is just that—a step-by-step description of the actions necessary to perform a task (for example, cooking a main dish, a vegetable, or a dessert). An example of a cake mix recipe as an algorithm is shown below:

Step 1: Preheat oven to 350 degrees.

Step 2: Generously grease and flour pan.

Step 3: Empty mix into large bowl; add 1 cup of water and 2 eggs and blend until moist.

Step 4: Beat vigorously for 300 strokes and pour into pan.

Step 5: Bake at 350 degrees until done. Cake is done if toothpick inserted in center comes out clean.

You can probably think of numerous other situations in which you have received a step-by-step list of instructions to perform some task.

The key difference between algorithms written by humans for other humans and those written by humans for computers lies in the level of understanding that the recipient of the algorithm presumably has. When an algorithm is written for use by humans, a certain degree of reasoning is usually assumed that will keep the user from taking an instruction literally or to an extreme. For example, in the cake mix recipe, the instruction to blend until moist assumes that we can decide when to stop blending. The cake mix instructions also assume that the user knows the meaning of certain terms or can find out the meaning. For example, we know the meaning of "preheat."

Computers cannot reason or recognize the meanings of words that are not in their limited vocabularies. For computers, algorithms must be written very precisely. Strange things can happen when the computer does what the pro-

Many retail computer stores offer lessons in programming to the general public.

grammer *tells* it to do *rather* than what the programmer *wants* it to do! For example, if a computer is told to repeat some operation, but is not told when to cease the repetition, the computer will repeat the action until the program is aborted. The need for a logical plan for the program should be obvious.

In this step, a novice programmer must learn to think in a logical fashion, breaking a procedure down into a sequence of small steps that a computer can understand. Many persons can state a general procedure for solving a problem on the computer, but they sometimes find that breaking this general procedure into smaller steps is difficult. Unfortunately, no quick, easy way to learn this skill exists. The best way to learn the skill is to start with simple examples—such as those discussed here—and then move on to more complex examples. Learning this skill is much like learning to snow ski, surf, or play racquetball—by *doing* rather than by watching. Reading this or any other text or observing your professor develop algorithms is not enough; you must "get your hands dirty" and develop algorithms yourself.

We now look at an algorithm for computing the average score on five quizzes. We already have our objective—to find the average of the five quiz scores and to determine if the average is less than 60. First, we state a general procedure to solve the problem, and then we break this general procedure down into a series of steps.

The general procedure to find the average value of a group of values is as follows: First, input a student's name and quiz scores. Second, find the sum of the quiz scores and divide the sum by five to find the average. Third, determine if the average is less than 60; if so, output a message. In all cases, output the student's name and average.

This statement of the general procedure may be understandable to you, but it is not yet in a form that can be used to write a computer program. The general procedure must be converted into specific steps that compose the desired algorithm, as follows:

Step 1: Input student's name and five quiz scores.

Step 2: Sum the five scores and divide the sum by 5 to find the average.

Step 3: Check to see if the average is less than 60; if so, output a message that student is failing.

Step 4: Output student's name and average.

Note that if the number of quizzes given during the term is changed, then the algorithm also must be changed to account for the different number of scores.

We can state this algorithm with specific information. Assume student George Burdell has exam scores of 57, 60, 55, 63, and 60. The above algorithm is stated as follows:

Step 1: Input "George Burdell" and 57, 60, 55, 63, and 60.

Step 2: Sum 57, 60, 55, 63, and 60 to obtain 295; divide this by 5 to find an average of 59.

Step 3: Is 59 less than 60? Yes, so output a message that this student is failing.

Step 4: Output "George Burdell" and 59.

Step 3: Converting the Algorithm to Flowchart or Pseudocode

Once we have an algorithm, we are well on the way to writing a program to perform the desired task. However, we must go one step further to ensure that the program actually represents the algorithm developed in step 2. We must convert the algorithm to an intermediate form, from which we can prepare the actual program.

The algorithm can be converted into either a written form or a pictorial form, or both. The written form is called a **pseudocode**, and the pictorial form is a **flowchart**.

The conversion of an algorithm to pseudocode involves actually writing a program in English rather than in a computer language. With this conversion, the program can ensure that the logic is correct. In step 4, the pseudocode is translated into the desired computer language. (Computer programmers often find that the development of an algorithm and its conversion to pseudocode occur in one step because they write the algorithm as pseudocode to begin with.) A pseudocode program is useful for two reasons. First, it may be used to *simplify* the logic of the algorithm. Second, it provides a relatively direct link between the algorithm and the computer program because English language instructions are converted into computer language program instructions.

No set rules exist for writing pseudocode. The method for converting the algorithm to the computer program should be an individual one. However, the pseudocode should be a set of clearly defined steps from which the reader can easily see the next step to be taken under any possible circumstances. The language and syntax should be consistent, so that you can always understand your own pseudocode. As an example of pseudocode, assume a programmer wants the computer to solve the quiz score averaging problem. A possible pseudocode for this situation is as follows

```
Begin program;
Input name and five scores;
Let total = score 1 + score 2 + score 3 + score 4 + score 5;
Let average = total/5;
If average < 60, then output message that student is failing;
Output name and average;
End program.
```

In this pseudocode, the name and quiz scores are input. The scores are then summed and the sum is divided by 5. If the resulting average score is less than 60, then a failing message is output. In any case, the student's name and average are output. (We use semicolons here to denote the end of a pseudocode statement, but you may wish to use other punctuation.)

The pseudocode for this problem is a simple example because the steps of the pseudocode follow one another in a constant downward flow. Later examples demonstrate situations in which the flow of control is more complicated. Remember, the pseudocode expresses an algorithm to the programmer the way a computer language used by the programmer expresses the algorithm to the computer.

A flowchart is a pictorial representation of an algorithm that clearly demonstrates the flow of control in the final program. Often, this flow of control is difficult to follow by reading the computer program. For this reason, a flowchart may be helpful to the programmer and to anyone else who looks at the program.

A standard set of flowchart symbols is used with computers. The actual flow of control is designated by arrows, which connect the symbols. We will use the set of symbols shown in Figure 14-1.

FIGURE 14-1
Flowchart Symbols

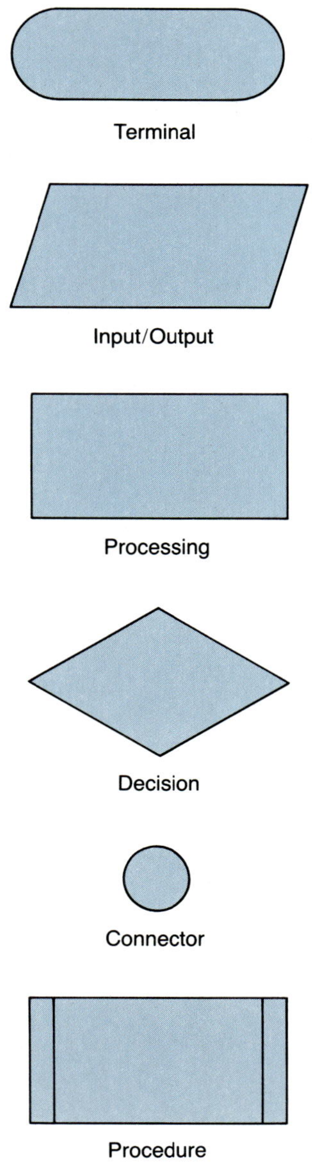

The **terminal symbol** is used to show the starting or stopping point of a flowchart. It shows a reader where the flow of control begins and ends. The following terminal symbol indicates the beginning of a flowchart:

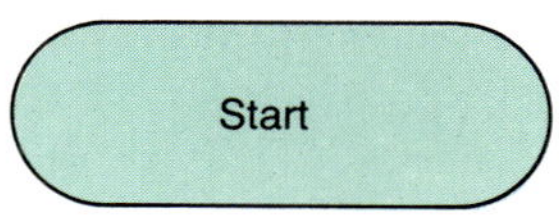

Terminal Symbol

To communicate with the program, input and output are necessary. The **input/output symbol** can be used for either operation regardless of the input or output method. The following symbol shows that the values of X and Y are input.

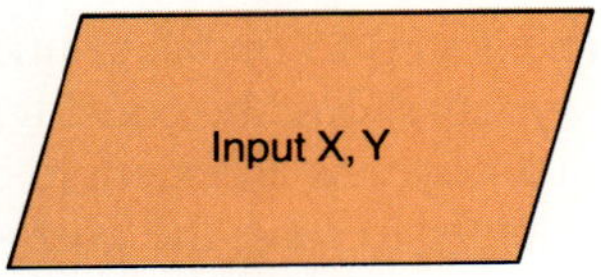

Input/Output Symbol

The **processing symbol** is a very important symbol in any flowchart. This symbol shows all calculations and often represents the operations that must be accomplished. In the following processing symbol, the quantity Z is set equal to the sum of X and Y.

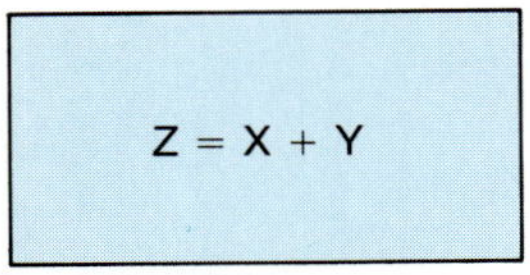

Processing Symbol

The **decision symbol** is used to denote a decision. Without decisions, the program's flow of control moves directly from statement to statement in the order in which the statements are entered. A decision in a computer program changes the program's flow of control. Using a decision, direction can be changed to skip around one segment or to repeat one segment. With decisions, a program segment may be selected for execution from among two or more program segments depending on the logic of the program and the data that are input. For example, suppose that if X is greater than Y, then X is output; but if X is not greater than Y, then Y is output. The decision symbol would represent this logic as follows:

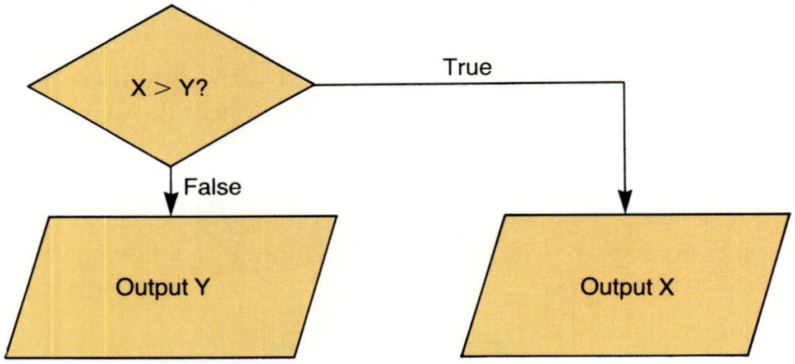

Decision Symbol

If the flow of control requires that distant portions of the flowchart be connected, then the **connector symbol** is used. In the flowchart, an arrow points to a connector, which contains a number. Control is then transferred to the connector with the same number elsewhere in the program. This symbol is useful for complicated programs that have many connections. In the example below, one alternative of a decision symbol is a connector. This connector is also shown elsewhere in the program, as follows:

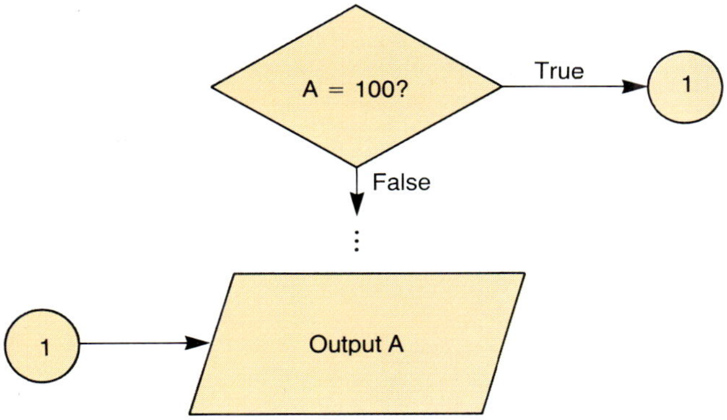

Use of Connector Symbol

> **Anybody who can write a comprehensible paragraph can write a workable program.**
>
> ***Chris Crawford, manager of games research at Atari Corporate Research***
> ("Why You Should Learn to Program," *Popular Computing,* September 1983, pp. 153–56.)

In some situations, a particular procedure is included in the flow of control, but the logic of this procedure is actually flowcharted separately. When this happens, a **procedure symbol** is used to designate a separate flowchart.

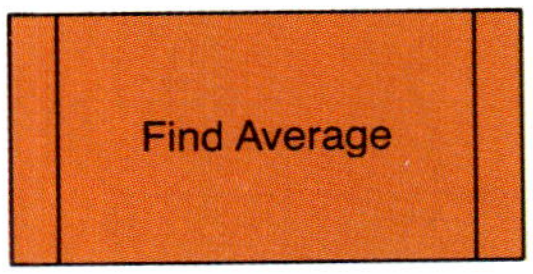

Procedure Symbol

Before we look at a flowchart for the quiz score averaging problem, consider the flowchart in Figure 14-2 (page 368), which depicts the college registration process. Note that the process goes back to the advisor if a desired course is not available. If this process of selecting courses, determining if they are available, and returning to the advisor if one or more is not available is repeated more than once, then it is called a loop. A **loop** is the repetition of one or more actions. The loop in Figure 14-2 could be endless, because the student may never register for all the courses desired. The programmer should be alert for an endless loop. Checks should be inserted to ensure that the loop will eventually stop.

To demonstrate the use of psuedocode and flowcharts, we use the quiz score averaging problem as an example. The flowchart for the algorithm developed earlier appears in Figure 14-3.

Step 4: Writing the Program

In this step, we discuss the use of a language in the preparation of a program. Steps 1–3 were language independent—they could be followed by any programmer regardless of the language to be used. However, at this point, the programmer must use a specific language that a computer can understand. The success of this step depends a great deal on the quality of the previous steps.

Every language has its own **syntactical (grammatical) form** and vocabulary. For example, one syntactical rule in the English language is that subject–verb agreement must exist in a sentence. Computer languages also have syntactical rules and vocabularies that the programmer must follow in the

FIGURE 14-2
Registration Process

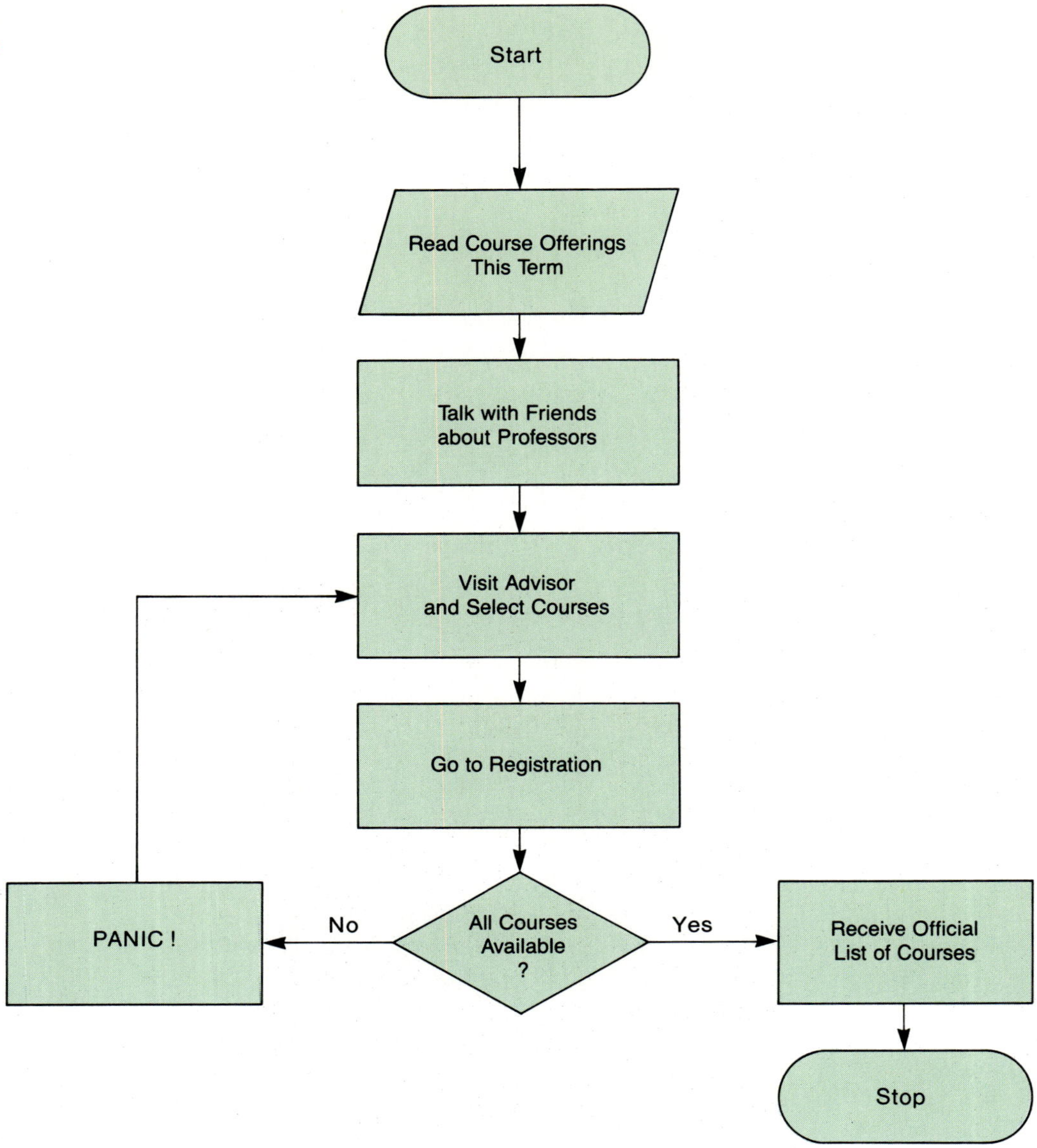

preparation of the program. A program's logic will usually be the same regardless of the language used, but the programmer must ensure that both the logic and the syntax of a program are correct before the program is used.

Further discussion of this step in the program development process is included in Chapters 16 and 17, which cover the BASIC computer language. When we learn the vocabulary and syntax of BASIC, we can convert the logic embodied in the flowchart and pseudocode into a written BASIC program.

Step 5: Entering the Program into the Computer

After the program is written in a computer language, it must be entered into the computer. Any of the various input methods discussed in Chapter 7 can be used, but most programming is performed either on a personal computer or on a terminal that is linked to a mainframe.

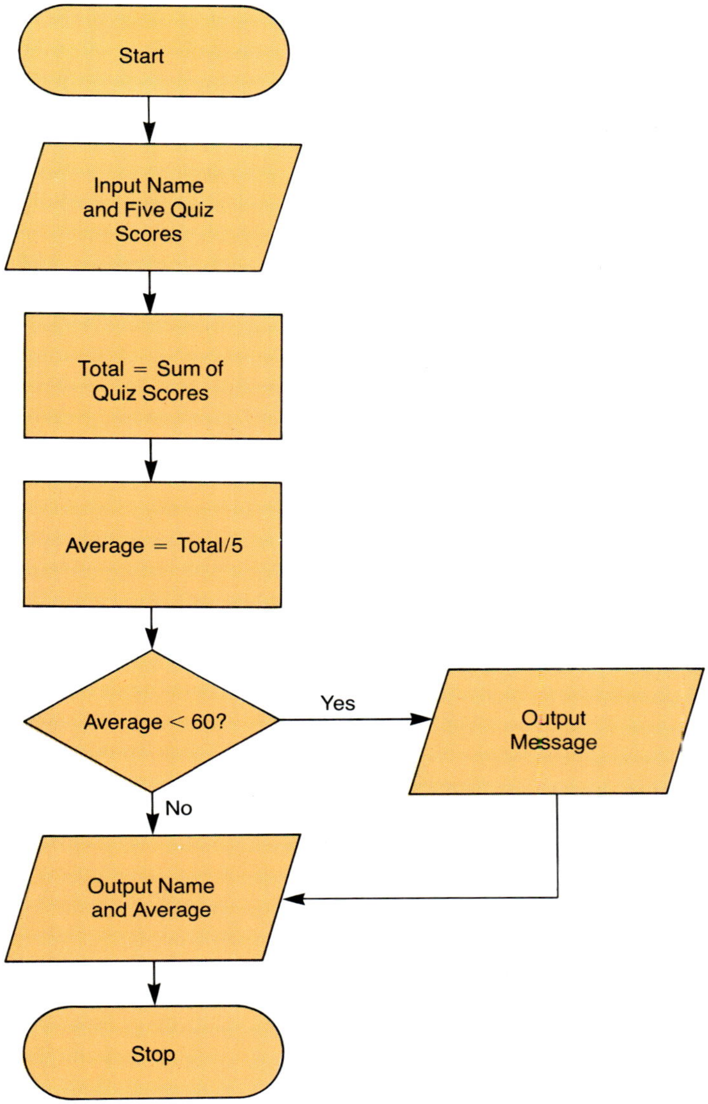

FIGURE 14-3
Flowchart for Quiz Score Averaging Problem

During this stage, typing errors can occur when a written program is entered into the computer. With most languages, typing errors are usually not discovered until step 6 of the program development process.

Step 6: Translating the Program into Machine Language

English-like computer languages (such as BASIC) are **high-level languages** because they are on the programmer's level. High-level languages must be translated into **machine language**, which the computer understands. (Recall that the computer works with data and instructions in the form of zeros and ones.) The translation process is diagramed in Figure 14-4, which shows the translator as a software program that can change a high-level language program into a machine language program.

Depending on the type of language and application, two methods are used for the translation process—interpretation and compilation. With **interpretation**, each statement is individually converted into an equivalent ma-

FIGURE 14-4
Computer Language Translation Process

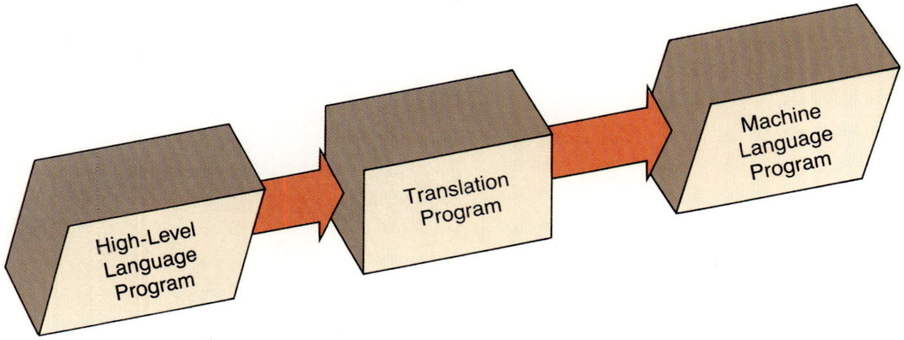

chine language statement during execution. BASIC is the best example of an interpreted language. Because the computer attempts to translate each statement individually, the user can check a statement or set of statements to determine if a syntax or vocabulary error has occurred. If a statement cannot be translated because of an error, the user is notified to correct and reenter the statement. Figure 14-5 shows the statement interpretation process in flowchart form.

In **compilation**, the entire program is considered as a whole in the translation process. After the entire high-level language program is entered, it is called the **source program**. When the source program is compiled into a machine language program, it is the **object code**. Compilation has an advantage over interpretation in that a compiled program runs faster than an interpreted program once all errors are corrected. However, syntax and vocabu-

FIGURE 14-5
Statement Interpretation Process

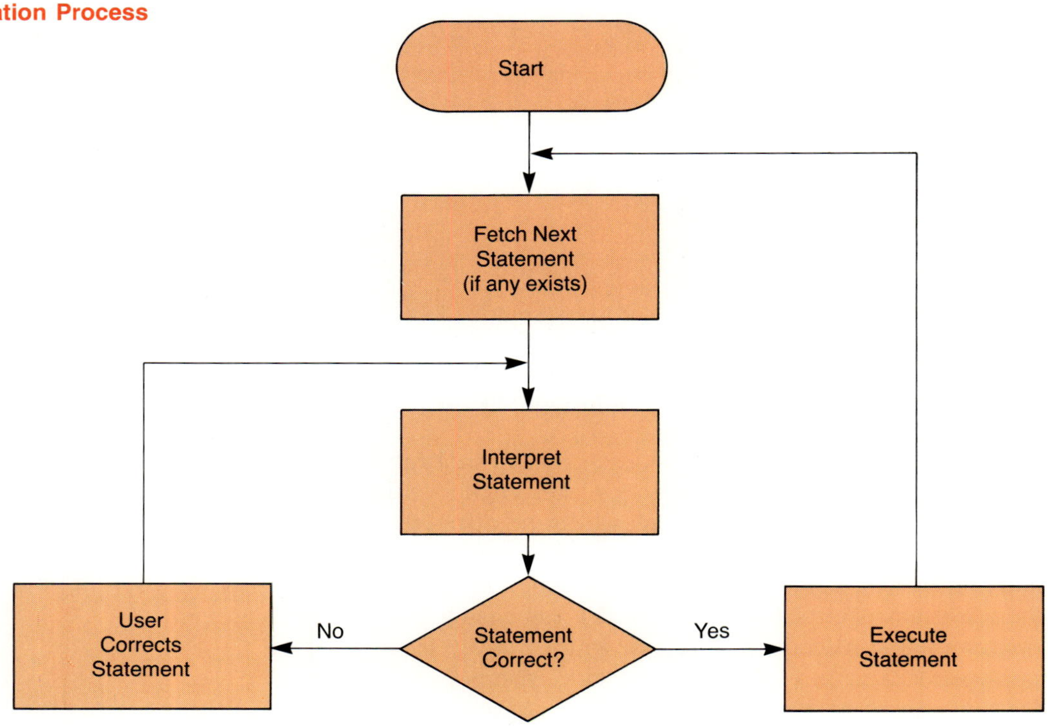

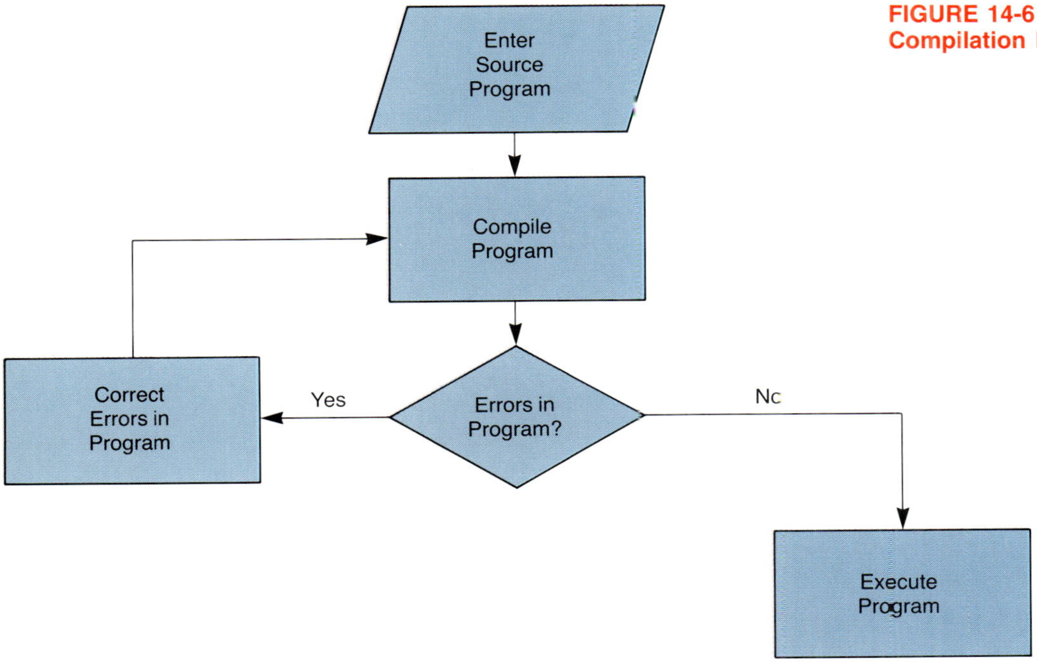

FIGURE 14-6
Compilation Process

lary errors cannot be found unless the entire program is considered and the computer attempts to compile it into object code. Figure 14-6 shows the compilation process in flowchart form.

Most high-level languages are compiled rather than interpreted. BASIC is the major exception to this trend, but even some versions of BASIC available for personal computers can be compiled. A compiled program is a faster-running version of the program that can generate an object code. For commercial purposes, it is sometimes advantageous to send a program's object code to another user, because it cannot be changed or copied.

Step 7: Executing the Program with Test Data

After the source program is translated into machine language without vocabulary or syntax errors, the resulting machine language program is ready for execution. When the user gives the command for execution, the machine language program instructions are actually carried out by the computer. Although the program may not contain syntax or vocabulary errors, it still may be incorrect either in the manner in which the program carries out the logic or in the logic itself. To find and correct the errors that occur during program execution, the programmer must test the program using test data.

Test data are used in hand calculations to determine in advance the results expected from the program. If the program results differ from the results of the hand calculations, then an error exists in the program logic or in the hand calculations. If the hand calculations are verified, then the program logic must be checked. We discuss this procedure in more detail in the section on debugging programs. For test data, we use George Burdell and quiz scores of 57, 60, 55, 63, and 60 from the quiz score averaging problem. An average of 59 is easily calculated by hand. Any program written should compute the same value.

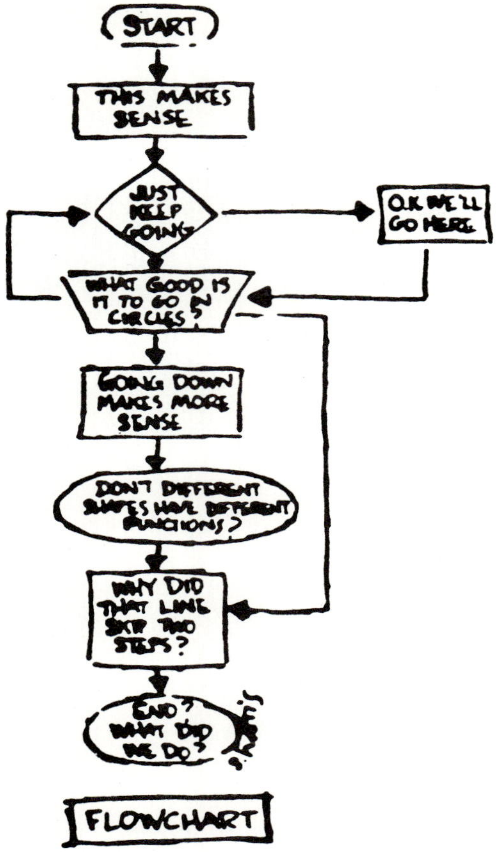

In addition to problems with program logic, other errors can occur during execution, including the incorrect use of data or an inadvertent user request that the computer perform a meaningless operation. A common example of a meaningless operation is division by zero. Such errors cause the computer to generate an error message. The program executes up to the error point, and a message appears on the screen as to the cause of the abnormal termination of program execution. Test data should be chosen so that all portions of a program are tested. Otherwise, errors in a section of the program that is not tested will not be discovered.

An error that occurs during execution is often not easy to find and correct. The user must go through the debugging process described in detail in the next section. If the program executes properly with test data, the programmer can skip the next step and proceed to step 9.

Step 8: Debugging the Program Using Test Data

A programmer must find and correct any error encountered during program execution. The process of tracking down execution errors and correcting them is referred to as the **debugging process**. When a program finally runs error-free, it is said to be *debugged.* Syntax or vocabulary errors found at the translation stage are easy to fix, and are therefore *not* program "bugs."

The debugging process should always follow the same steps, regardless of the type of error encountered. Checking a program for execution errors requires a return to the algorithm development step (step 2) to check the logic of the algorithm using the test data. If the algorithm logic is in error, it is corrected and the following steps are taken:

Correct the flowchart and pseudocode.

Correct the high-level language version of the program.

Reenter the program or correct the version of the program that is stored in the computer.

Translate the new version of the program into machine language.

After these steps are completed, the programmer can attempt to execute the program again with the test data.

If the algorithm logic appears to be correct, then the pseudocode and flowchart must be checked with the test data to determine the error. If the error is found and corrected in the pseudocode and flowchart, the high-level language program must be corrected before translation and execution are attempted again. Finally, if the error is not found in the pseudocode and flowchart, the high-level language program is checked with test data to find and correct the error before compiling and executing the program again. Throughout the debugging process, the user must perform each step of the program the way the computer would—*exactly* as stated in the algorithm, pseudocode, flowchart, and high-level language program. This process is also called a **desk check** of each form of the program.

Step 9: Using the Program with Actual Data

After the high-level language program is translated into machine language and executed correctly with test data, the program can be executed with actual data. Computing the average quiz scores involves executing the program for each student in the class.

At this stage, the programmer must determine whether the results meet the objectives outlined in step 1. If the program does not meet the user's needs, then the programmer must analyze the results and the objectives to find out where they diverge. Following the analysis, the programmer should retrace the program development procedure, making any necessary changes in the algorithm, flowchart, pseudocode, and the high-level language program, so the results satisfy the final user.

The entire program development procedure is illustrated in flowchart form in Figure 14-7. This flowchart summarizes all of the steps and decisions that must be made before a program is finished.

PROBLEM-SOLVING EXAMPLES

Now that we have discussed a step-by-step approach to problem solving using the computer, we can apply the procedure to two additional examples. This discussion centers on the first three steps in the program development procedure.

Step 1: Identifying the problem

Step 2: Developing the algorithm

Step 3: Converting the algorithm to flowchart or pseudocode

FIGURE 14-7
Flowchart of Program Development Procedure

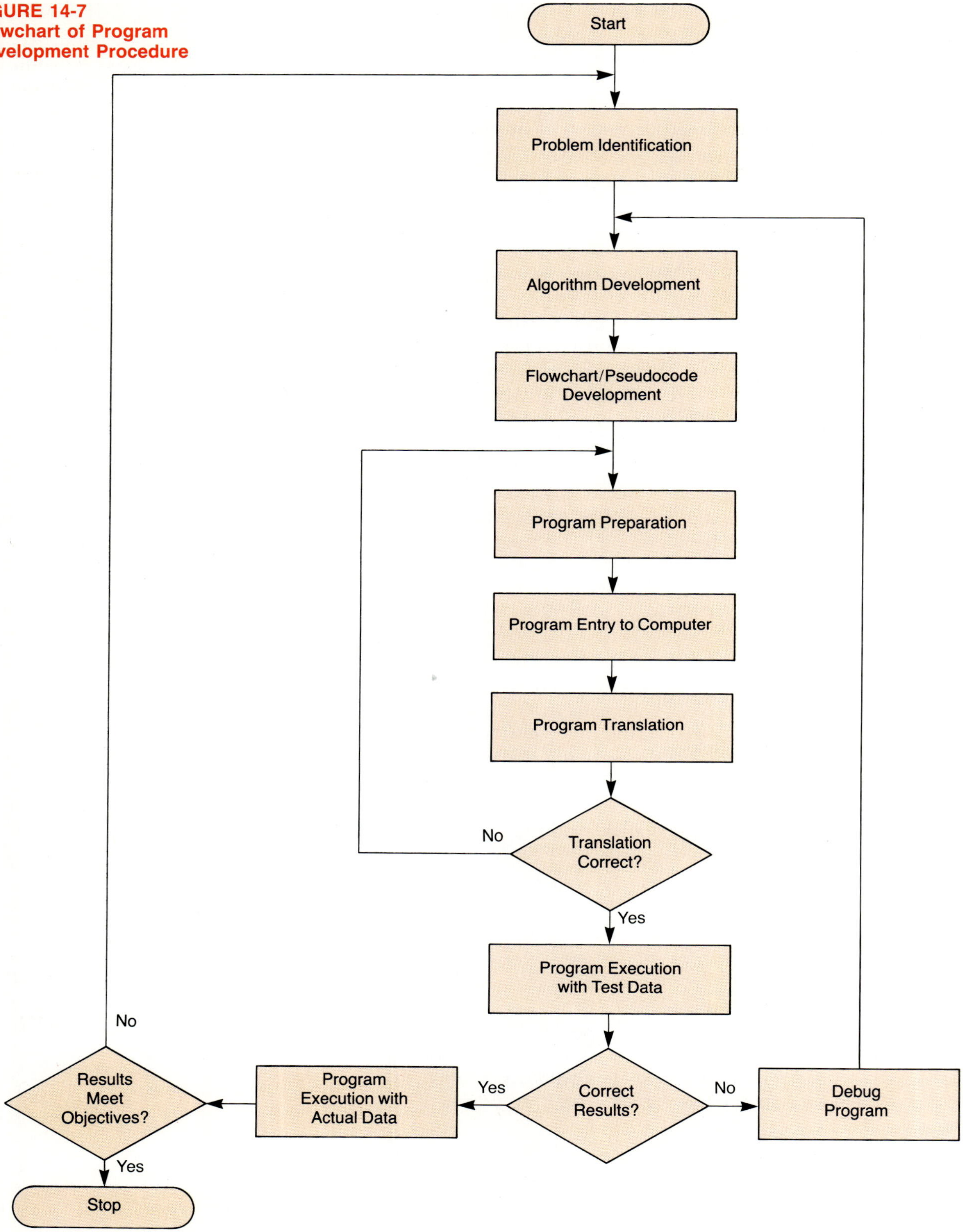

We carry both examples into Chapters 16 and 17, in which we actually write programs to go with the algorithms, flowcharts, and pseudocodes discussed in this section.

We consider the following two examples:

1. An extension of our quiz score averaging example that will average scores for many students rather than for just one student.
2. A computation of take-home pay for employees who are paid on an hourly basis.

The latter example will account for the effects of overtime on employees' gross pay and of deductions on their take-home pay. Both examples use the concept of a loop, which allows a process to be repeated many times. A loop may be defined as *the process of repeatedly executing one or more steps of an algorithm or program.* A loop is an important programming concept because most programs perform some repeated task. Before going into these two examples, we should look at loops.

To repeat some action successfully, a loop must have the following three parts:

1. A loop termination decision
2. A body (the steps to be repeated)
3. A transfer back to the beginning of the loop

The **loop termination decision** determines when the loop ends. Without a loop termination decision, a computer will repeat a loop endlessly. The **body** of the loop is the step or steps of the algorithm that are repeated. The body of the loop may be a simple counting mechanism, or it may be a fairly complicated situation, as in our second example in which gross and take-home pay are repeatedly calculated for several employees. Finally, the **transfer** returns control to the beginning of the loop so a new repetition can begin. Figure 14-8 shows a flowchart of a loop with these three parts.

Figure 14-8 shows the loop termination decision in a decision symbol, which indicates a test of some condition and a decision on whether or not to

I wanted some objective data to back up my personal feelings. So I wrote my own computer program.

Richard Flutie

(As quoted in "The Computer Fortunes of Doug Flutie," *Personal Computing,* April 1985, p. 35.)

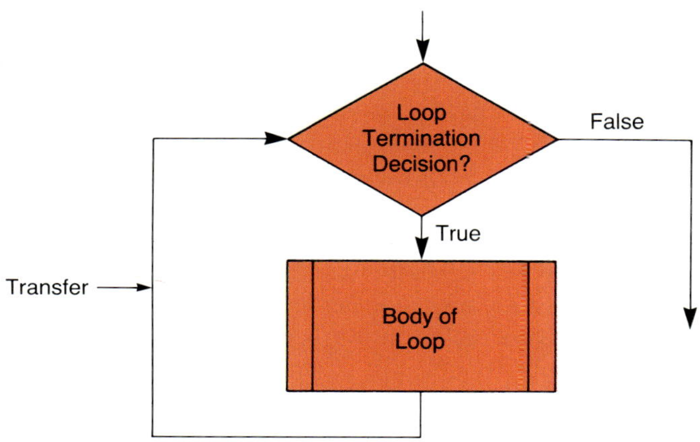

FIGURE 14-8
General Flowchart of Loop

continue. If the condition is true, the body of the loop is executed, and control is transferred back to the loop termination decision. If the condition is false, control is transferred out of the loop and the loop ends.

Two basic types of loops are differentiated by the position of the loop termination decision in relation to the body of the loop. The loop shown in Figure 14-8 is a **pre-test loop**, because the loop termination decision occurs *before* the body of the loop. A loop termination decision that occurs *after* the body of the loop indicates a **post-test loop**. Figure 14-9 shows a flowchart for a post-test loop. Although both loops can be used in many situations, the pre-test loop is used predominately. We use only the pre-test loop in our programming examples. The two examples that follow demonstrate the use of the pre-test loop for counting and for determining when all data have been input.

Averaging Scores for Many Students

In this example, we expand our quiz score example from one student to more than one student. The total number of students is input first, followed by the name and five quiz scores for each student. Missed quizzes rate a zero score. The output includes a message if the student fails the course (that is, averages less than 60), the student's name and quiz average, and the class average of all quiz scores. For example, if 24 students are in the class, the professor first inputs the number of students. Then, the professor inputs each student's name and five quiz scores. The program must compute the average score for each of the 24 students and keep a running sum of these averages to compute an overall average at the end of the program. After all 24 students' quiz scores are averaged, the sum of the averages is divided by 24 to find the class average.

The first step is to identify the problem, which in this case, is easy to do. The problem is as follows: For some number of students, find each student's average quiz score, output a message if this average is less than 60, output the student's name and quiz average, and, after all students have been processed, output the average quiz score for all students.

The following algorithm for this example simply extends the algorithm shown on page 364 to account for more than one student and for computing a class average of all quizzes:

Step 1: Input number of students.
Step 2: Set student counter to one and sum of averages to zero.
Step 3: Check to see if counter is less than or equal to the number of students. If it is, then add one to student counter and go to step 4; otherwise, go to step 9.
Step 4: Input a student's name and five quiz scores.
Step 5: Sum the five scores and divide the sum by 5 to find the average.
Step 6: Check to see if the average is less than 60; if so, output a message that student is failing.
Step 7: Output student's name and average.
Step 8: Add average quiz score to sum of averages and return to step 3.
Step 9: Divide sum of averages by number of students and output the result as average quiz score for class.

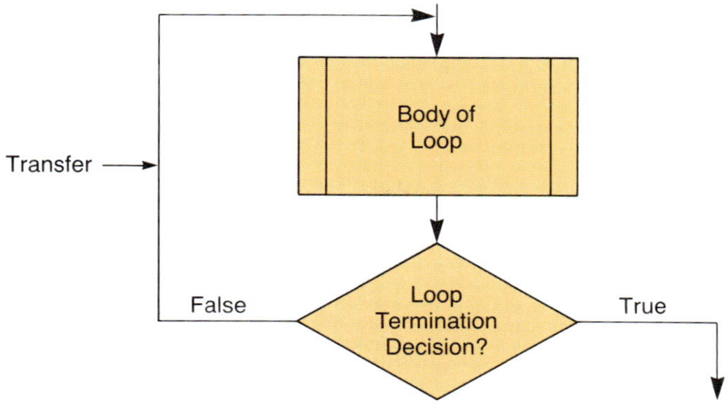

FIGURE 14-9
Post-Test Loop

Note that steps 4–7 are the same as before, but that steps 1–3 and 8–9 handle the loop and the new input and output.

Let us discuss how the new steps in this algorithm fit the concept of a loop. Step 1 simply inputs the number of students in the class, and step 2 **initializes** the student counter to one and the sum of averages to zero. A student counter counts the students as their scores are processed so we know when all students have been processed. The sum of averages is needed to sum the individual student averages to compute an overall class average. The user must initialize the student counter and sum of averages so that they start at the correct values. The initialization is part of the program because the computer cannot by itself start counters and sums at any specific value.

In step 3, the beginning of the loop, the student counter is compared to

Programming knowledge can enhance a person's problem-solving and communications capabilities.

the number of students input. If the student counter is less than or equal to the number of students in the class, the counter is incremented and the loop is continued; if it is not, the loop is terminated. Steps 4–7 are the same as before. Step 8 adds the student's average to the sum of averages and returns control to step 3. Steps 3–8 constitute the body of the loop.

Step 9 occurs after the loop and handles the computation of the class quiz average by dividing the sum of averages value by the number of students input in step 1. We assume that the professor would *never* enter a zero number of students, because an error would occur in step 9 when the class quiz average is computed.

We now look at this same algorithm in flowchart form in Figure 14–10 and in pseudocode form. Note in the flowchart that the loop termination decision is *before* the body of the loop, making it a pre-test loop. In this case, the loop termination decision is based on a counter becoming greater than some value. The loop in Figure 14-10 is a very common type of loop.

In Figure 14-10, a decision symbol designates the loop termination decision that either returns control to the input statement or transfers control out of the loop to the calculation of class average. Because the calculation for each student is the same here as it was in Figure 14-3, a procedure block is used in the flowchart to denote this process.

The pseudocode for our example is as follows:

```
Begin program;
Input number of students;
Let student counter = 1 and sum of averages = 0;
While student counter ≤ number of students, repeat the following:
    Add one to the student counter;
    Input name and five scores;
    Let total = score 1 + score 2 + score 3 + score 4 + score 5;
    Let average = total/5;
    If average < 60, then output message that student is failing;
    Output name and average;
    Add average to sum of averages;
End repeat.
Let class average = sum of averages/number of students;
Output class average;
End program.
```

In this pseudocode, the statement "While student counter . . . repeat the following:" handles both the loop termination and the repetition. The use of the word *while* in pseudocode characterizes this loop as a *pre-test* loop, because the loop continues *while* a condition is true. The body of the loop is indented to show what is repeated, and an "end repeat" statement indicates the end of the body of the loop. If the student counter is greater than the number of students, then the loop terminates and control goes to the statement after the "end repeat" statement.

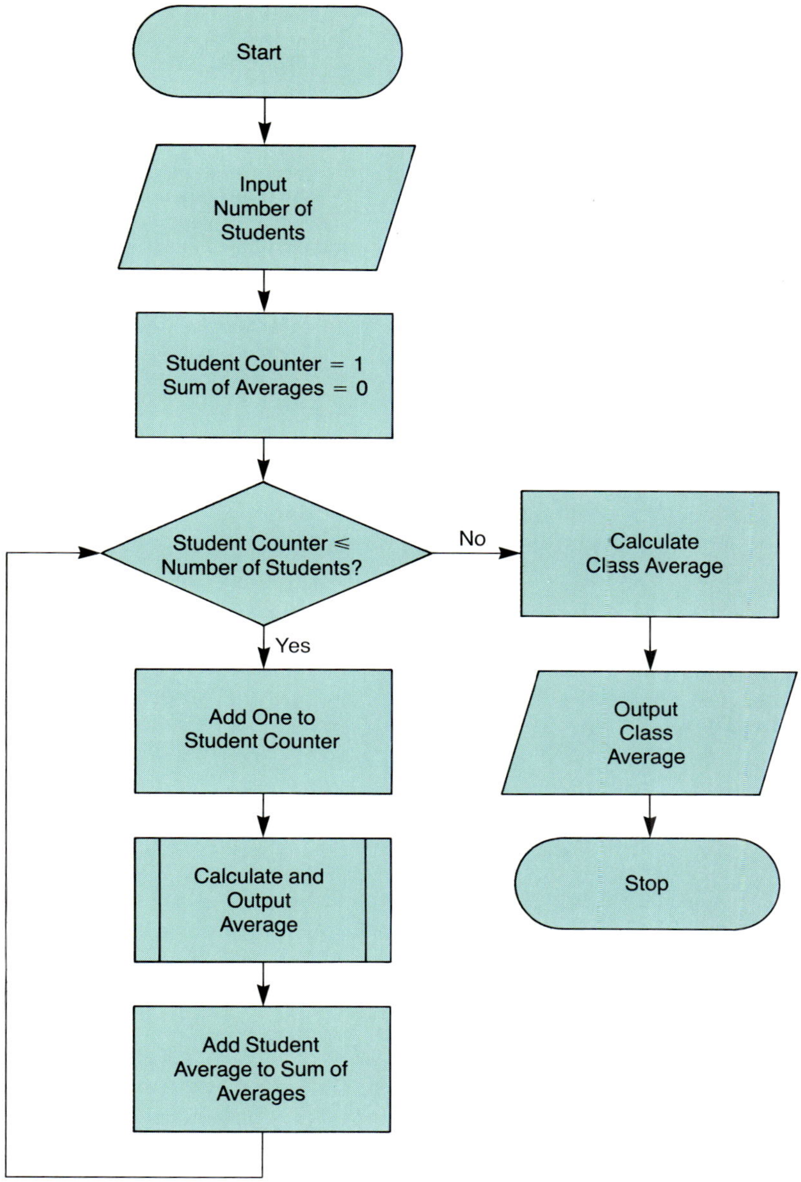

FIGURE 14-10
Flowchart for Average Quiz Scores for Many Students

Let us examine step-by-step how this pseudocode works. Consider a class with three students. The class total of three is input first, the number of students counter is set to 1, and the sum of averages is set to 0. The student counter is less than or equal to 3, so the body of the loop is executed. The student counter increases to 2, and the first student's name and quiz scores are input. The quiz scores are averaged to 59. Because this value is less than 60, a message is output that the student is failing. The student's name and average are output, and 59 is added to the sum of averages. The student counter is still less than or equal to 3, so a repetition of the loop occurs. The student counter increases to 3, and the second student's name and scores are

Table 14-2 CALCULATIONS IN PSEUDOCODE

Step	*Calculation*
Before loop	student counter = 1 sum of averages = 0
First execution	student counter = 1 + 1 = 2 sum of averages = 0 + 59 = 59
Second execution	student counter = 2 + 1 = 3 sum of averages = 59 + 71 = 130
Third execution	student counter = 3 + 1 = 4 sum of averages = 130 + 80 = 210
After loop	class average = 210/3 = 70

input. Assume that the second student's average is 71. The student's name and average are output, and the sum of averages becomes 130 (59 + 71). Because the student counter is still less than or equal to 3, we repeat the process.

The student counter increases to 4, and the third student's name and scores are input. Assume this student's average is 80. The student's name and average are output, and the sum of averages equals 210. The student counter is now greater than 3, so the loop is not repeated. Instead, the class average is computed as 70 (210/3). This value is output and the program ends. Table 14-2 shows the calculations that are made at each step of the pseudocode.

Take-Home Pay Calculation

Take-home pay for most hourly employees depends on gross pay (pay before deductions) and the amount of deductions for withholding taxes, Social Security, health insurance, and so on. Gross pay itself depends on regular pay for up to 40 hours of work each week and overtime pay for hours each week in excess of 40. In this example, we assume that employees are paid time-and-a-half for overtime—that is, 1.5 times the regular wage rate. We also assume that withholding is 10% of gross pay, Social Security is 7% of gross pay, and health insurance is $10 per week. The objective of this program is two-fold: First, compute each employee's gross pay based on the number of hours worked and the employee's wage rate. Second, compute and output take-home pay by computing deductions and subtracting them from gross pay. This procedure is performed for an *unknown* number of employees. This statement of the program's objective satisfies step 1 of our program development procedure.

Step two involves developing an algorithm, which in this case, has the following three major parts:

1. Enter each employee's name, wage rate, and number of hours worked in the week, and compute gross pay by multiplying the wage rate by the number of hours worked if the number is 40 or less. If the number of hours worked is greater than 40, multiply the wage rate by 40 and add this amount to overtime pay. Overtime pay equals the number of hours worked *over* 40 multiplied by 1.5.

2. Compute deductions as 17% of gross pay plus $10, and subtract this value from gross pay.
3. Repeat this process for all employees.

". . . and in 1/10,000th of a second, it can compound the programmer's error 87,500 times!"

Part 3 is carried out by repeating a loop of data input and calculations only when valid employee names are input. When an invalid name—for example, "out of data"—is entered, this generally means that no more employees will be processed and the loop ends. A loop that depends on an invalid data item for its termination is a common technique in programming. The actual algorithm for the take-home pay calculation is as follows:

Step 1: Input employee name, wage rate, and hours worked.

Step 2: If employee name is valid, then go to step 3; otherwise stop.

Step 3: If employee hours are not greater than 40, then gross pay = employee hours × wage rate; otherwise, gross pay = 40 × wage rate + [(employee hours − 40) × 1.5 × wage rate].

Step 4: Compute deductions as 0.17 × gross pay + 10.

Step 5: Compute take-home pay as gross pay − deductions.

Step 6: Output employee name, gross pay, and take-home pay and go to step 1.

The flowchart for this algorithm is shown in Figure 14-11.

In Figure 14-11, the loop for the take-home pay calculation is a pre-test loop. When an invalid data item is input, the repetition stops *before* going through the loop. A pre-test loop is required when the number of times a loop will be repeated is unknown.

The pseudocode for the take-home pay calculation follows:

```
Begin program;
While name is valid, repeat the following:
        Input employee name, wage rate, and hours worked;
        If hours worked ≤ 40, then gross pay = hours worked ×
        wage rate;
        Otherwise, gross pay = 40 × wage rate − [(hours worked −
        40) × wage rate × 1.5];
        Deductions = 0.17 × gross pay + 10;
        Take-home pay = gross pay − deductions;
        Output employee name, gross pay, and take-home pay;
End repeat.
End program.
```

Both the pseudocode and the flowchart are straightforward translations of the algorithm. As long as a valid employee name is input by the user, the loop repeats. If an invalid name is input, the loop terminates.

A Look Ahead

Having developed flowcharts and pseudocode for the examples in this chapter, we now look ahead to the next three chapters. Chapter 15 presents a

FIGURE 14-11
Flowchart for Take-Home Pay Calculation

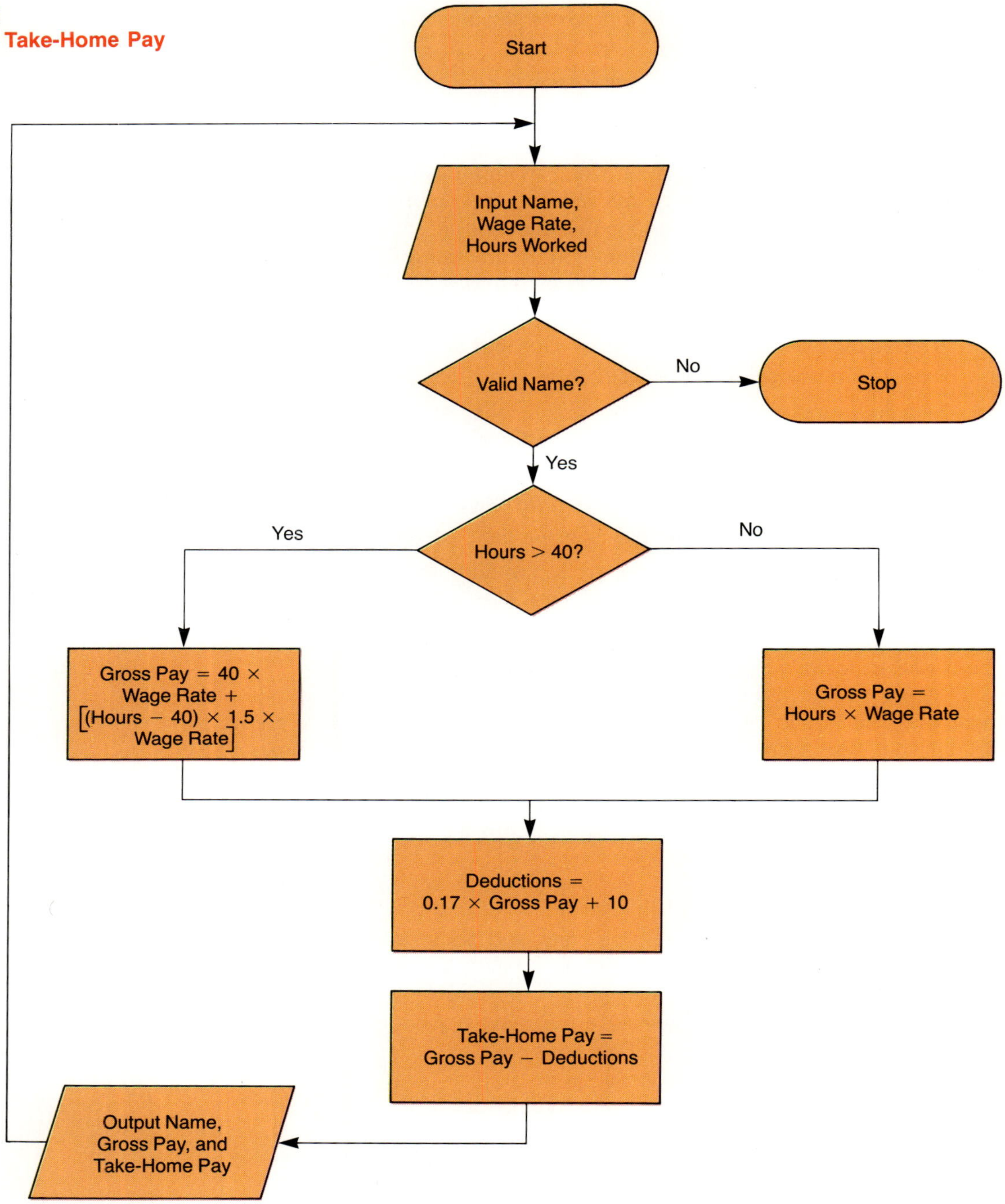

survey of computer languages, in which we use the quiz score averaging problem for multiple students as an example. This problem is programmed in several languages, to demonstrate the differences in vocabulary and syntax for the same logic. In Chapters 16 and 17, we present a short course in programming in BASIC, concentrating on the three examples presented in this chapter.

REVIEW OF KEY POINTS

- Programming a computer can be a useful and enjoyable way of accomplishing the tasks that commercial software is not designed to do.
- A program consists of instructions to the computer.
- The programming process can be viewed as a nine-step procedure that overlaps systems analysis and design.
- Problem identification and algorithm development are crucial steps in developing program logic.
- Developing flowcharts and pseudocode are two ways of converting an algorithm into a form that is easily programmed.
- After the program is written in a high-level language, it must be entered into the computer, translated into machine language, debugged, and then executed with actual data.
- The loop is an important concept in programming.
- Two important types of loops are the pre-test loop and the post-test loop.
- A pre-test loop is required when the loop will be repeated an unknown number of times, but the post-test loop can be used when the number of repetitions is known.
- All counters and sums must be initialized in the program because the computer cannot set them to a desired value by itself.

KEY TERMS

algorithm
body (of the loop)
compilation
connector symbol
debugging process
decision symbol
desk check
flowchart
high-level languages
initializes
input/output symbol
interpretation
logic
loop
loop termination decision
machine language
object code
post-test loop
pre-test loop
procedure symbol
processing symbol
program
programming
pseudocode
source program
syntactical (grammatical) form
terminal symbol
test data
transfer

REVIEW QUESTIONS

1. Give three reasons for learning to write computer programs.
2. What is an algorithm? Discuss how an algorithm in your everyday life fits our definition of algorithm.
3. How is the programming procedure presented in this chapter related to the systems analysis process?
4. Why do we use a pseudocode or flowchart as an intermediate step between an algorithm and a computer program?
5. Flowchart your algorithm from question 2 and rewrite it in pseudocode.
6. Why must a computer program be translated into machine language? Explain the difference between interpretation and compilation.
7. Why do we use test data in the debugging process?
8. How is a loop an important concept in programming? Describe a process in your life that requires looping.
9. Walk through the take-home pay flowchart and pseudocode with employee Gwen Hollander, who works 44 hours this week at a wage rate of $9.50 per hour.
10. Develop the algorithm, write a pseudocode, and draw the flowchart to average the scores of many students who take an *unknown* number of quizzes (all students take at least one quiz).

HERO 1

Currently, the most common way to give a computer instructions is through a computer language. Therefore, in this chapter, we discuss why computer languages are needed. Six languages—FORTRAN, COBOL, PL/I, BASIC, Pascal, and C—are discussed in detail, and examples of each are shown. We also discuss several other languages in less detail. The chapter emphasizes how each language fits into the following five language classifications: high-level versus low-level; interpreted versus compiled; interactive versus batch; procedural versus nonprocedural; and structured versus unstructured. Finally, we discuss how artificial intelligence applies to our use of the computer.

15

A Survey of Computer Languages

STUDY OBJECTIVES

After reading this chapter, you should be able to

- Understand the need for computer languages for communications with computers.
- Recognize the various classifications of computer languages.
- Understand the difference between a high-level and a low-level language.
- Differentiate between a compiled language and an interpreted language.
- Distinguish a batch language from an interactive language.
- Understand the three levels of structured programs.
- Define artificial intelligence.
- Discuss natural language and expert systems.

THE NEED FOR COMPUTER LANGUAGES

One of the first complaints that is often heard from new users of computers concerns learning a computer language. In most cases, a novice user is uncomfortable with learning a new grammar and syntax just to give the computer the simplest instructions. Users can solve problems on the computer with software packages without knowing a computer language. However, if the user must write a computer program—perhaps for the reasons discussed in Chapter 14—then he or she must master a computer language.

Why not just give the computer commands in English like in science fiction movies? Research is ongoing in the use of English or other natural languages with computers. However, for now, we must use one of the variety of computer languages to communicate with the computer. English cannot be used because it is too ambiguous for the computer to handle. Many words in English have multiple meanings that depend on the context in which they are used. For example, the computer would have trouble with the following two commands: "Choose the item on the right side of the table" and "Mail this package right away." In the first case, the word *right* refers to a physical location, and in the second case, the same word means "immediately."

The human brain is an amazing computer that can decipher the appropriate meaning of a word based on the context in which it is used. Electronic computers are not nearly that sophisticated. For that reason, we must use a computer language with a restricted vocabulary and a specific grammar that allows little room for misinterpretation by the computer. The limited vocabulary and rigid grammatical form also make computer languages much easier to learn than a foreign language.

Why So Many Computer Languages?

New computer users often ask why so many languages exist. At first glance, these new users seem to have a point—over 200 computer languages are available for use on mainframes, minicomputers, and personal computers. Some languages even have specific dialects that depend on the type of computer in use. Some are special purpose languages and others are general purpose. A **special purpose language** handles a specific task. For example, SLAM (Simulation Language for Alternative Modeling) was developed so that practitioners and researchers could use the computer to simulate economic or physical conditions. On the other hand, a **general purpose language** can do many different tasks, from computing payrolls to computing satellite orbits.

Many languages exist for the same reason that a carpenter has more tools than just a hammer and saw. A house can be built with just these two tools, but a full range of tools makes the job easier and more efficient. Similarly, every program could probably be written with a single language, but multiple languages allow us to use the most efficient language for each programming problem. Some languages are better for scientific problems, some for business applications, some for lists, some for textual material, and still others for educational purposes. Because each language is slanted toward a specific area, it works better to solve a problem in that area. We cannot say that one computer language is better than all others any more than we can say that English is better than all other languages. However, *once you have learned a computer language, it is much easier to learn any other computer language.*

It does not matter which language you learn first; other languages are easy to pick up.

Classifying Languages

Computer languages are easier to understand if we classify them by type and use. Referring to a computer language as special purpose or general purpose is one way of classifying it. However, several other methods of classification are used as well.

In addition to classifying a language as special purpose or general purpose, the following five classifications help to differentiate among computer languages:

1. High-level languages versus low-level languages
2. Compiled languages versus interpreted languages
3. Interactive languages versus batch languages
4. Procedural languages versus nonprocedural languages
5. Structured languages versus unstructured languages

High-Level Languages Versus Low-Level Languages Recall that a computer actually works with instructions in a binary form called **machine language**. Writing a computer program in machine language is an extremely tedious task. The closest language to machine language that does not work strictly with numbers is assembly language. **Assembly language** is a series of **mnemonics**—that is, words which imply their action—that are combined with addresses of computer locations to carry out instructions. Examples of mnemonics are LD for load, ADD for add, and DEC for decrease by one. Machine and assembly languages are called **low-level languages** because they are written at the machine's level. On the other hand, languages—such as BASIC—that use English-like instructions to the computer to carry out a series of machine-level commands are called **high-level languages**. High-level languages are at the programmer's level rather than at the machine's level.

What seems to be the key distinction [between computers and humans] is that computers operate on algorithms and people operate on heuristics.

Dr. Natalie Dehn, researcher in artificial intelligence
(As quoted in "Natalie Dehn Reflects on Artificial Intelligence," *Personal Computing,* June 1983, p. 51.)

Compiled Languages Versus Interpreted Languages Recall from Chapter 14 that a high-level language must be translated into machine language before it can be used by the computer. This translation occurs in one of two ways. If each instruction is translated individually as it is executed, then we are using an **interpreted language**. On the other hand, if the program is translated as a unit into a complete machine language program that can then be executed, a **compiled language** is used. An interpreted language can give the user instant feedback about the validity of any statement as it is executed. It also allows the user to test a single statement or group of statements before those statements are incorporated into the program. The disadvantage of an interpreted language is that it executes much more slowly than a compiled language, because each statement must be interpreted every time it is encountered during program execution. The advantages and disadvantages of a compiled language tend to be the opposite of those for an interpreted language. Compiled languages execute quickly but give the user no feedback on statement errors until the entire program is entered and com-

The cleaner and more comprehensible a program is, the less likely that it will be bugged and the easier it will be to change and improve [as well as debug].

Peter Norton, developer of the Norton Utilities software package

(As quoted in "PC Languages: The Living and the Dead," *PC Magazine,* September 1983, pp. 99–101.)

piled. Interpreted languages are excellent for teaching purposes, but compiled languages are usually needed for commercial purposes. BASIC is the best example of an interpreted language; most other languages are compiled.

Interactive Languages Versus Batch Languages If a user can communicate directly with the computer while a program is entered or executed, then the program is written in an **interactive language**. On the other hand, a program that is entered, translated, and executed without intervention from the user is written in a **batch language**. Interactive languages allow a user to edit, or make changes, in the program while it is entered or executed. They also allow the user to detect errors as they occur. On the other hand, batch languages force the user to work back and forth between the translation/execution steps and the edit/error correction steps. In other words, an interactive program tells you when an error occurs and gives you a facility to correct that error easily. A batch program points out all the errors at one time and forces the user to enter a special editing program to correct the errors. A batch program can only be tried again as a whole after the errors are corrected. Interactive languages include BASIC, APL, LOGO, Pilot, Smalltalk, and some forms of Pascal. Most other languages are batch languages.

Procedural Languages Versus Nonprocedural Languages A language that requires the program to give instructions on what should be done and how it should be done is a **procedural language**. On the other hand, a **nonprocedural language** only requires the user to define the desired task, without a step-by-step procedure. Currently, only a few special packages qualify as nonprocedural languages; most other commonly used languages are procedural. Some data base packages offer nonprocedural languages as a means of finding information.

Structured Languages Versus Unstructured Languages To understand the difference between structured and unstructured languages, we must discuss the concept of **structured programming**. A structured program is written in modules or blocks that have few, if any, transfers of control between them. The program logic for a structured program is easy to follow and understand. The correction of such programs is also much easier.

Structured programming was first suggested by Dutch Professor Edsger W. Dijkstra. Dijkstra suggested that all programs use one of the following three basic building blocks:

1. A processing block
2. A repetition or loop block
3. A decision block

The three types of programming blocks are shown in flowchart form in Figure 15-1.

If we work only with these three types of programming blocks, how do we write highly sophisticated programs? The answer lies in combining these three types of programming blocks to perform whatever task we desire. For example, a decision block could have a processing block as one alternative and a loop block as the other alternative. With this combination, the structured programming form is retained, but a variety of logic is incorporated into a program.

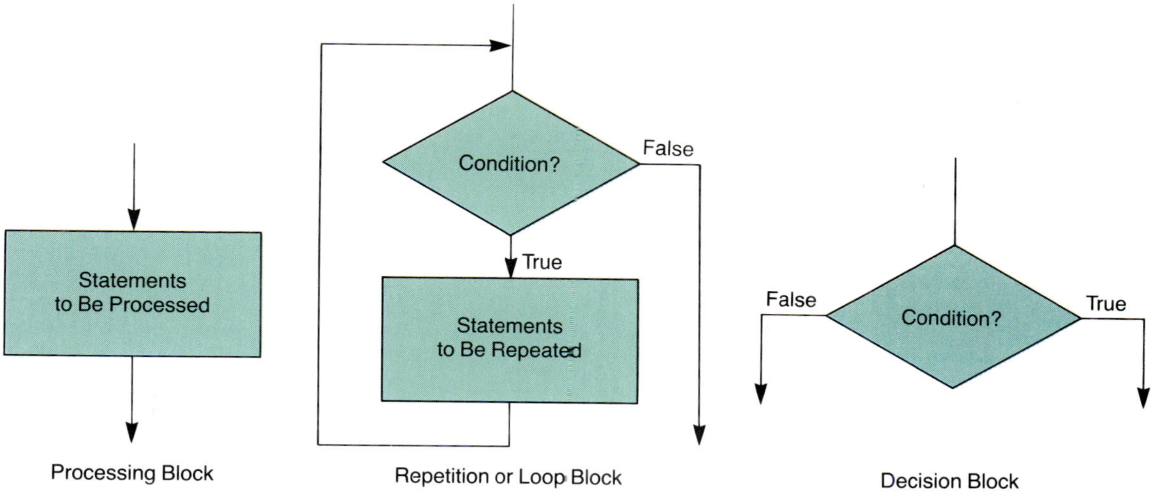

FIGURE 15-1
Types of Programming Blocks

A crucial type of statement that is not found in structured programming is the transfer statement. (The usual form of a transfer is the **GO TO statement**, which sends control to another part of the program.) The concept of structured programming can be described as "GO TO-less programming." Another aspect of structured programming is that the blocks have only one entry and one exit. The program cannot jump into or out of the middle of a block. Instead, entry to a block is at a single point, and exit is at another single point. The lack of transfer statements reduces the complexity of programs enormously.

Unstructured programs are often more difficult to debug, more difficult for a reader to follow, and less efficient in their execution than structured programs. The use of the GO TO statement can cause a program to have what is called *spaghetti code*. The name comes from the fact that if all GO TO statements were connected with lines to the object of the GO TO, the result would resemble a pile of spaghetti! The overuse of GO TO statements in unstructured programs results from the programmer's lack of planning and a failure to use the systems analysis approach to program design.

Structured programming is usually combined with **top-down design** another approach to writing programs. Top-down design in computer programs involves breaking large, complex problems into small pieces. In a computer program, this means writing the program in small segments, or **modules**, each of which performs a specific task. Each module can then be checked and debugged separately to ensure that it performs the desired task. When the individual modules are put together, they solve the large problem for which the program is developed.

The differences between structured and unstructured languages exist at three levels. First, structured programs are difficult to write in some languages because these languages do not have the statements necessary to avoid use of the GO TO statements. In some cases, separate modules for individual tasks cannot be developed. Such languages—like older versions of BASIC and FORTRAN—are unstructured. At a second level, some languages allow a user to write either structured or unstructured programs. This second

DISASTER
The Unstructured Program

In 1968, long before I wrote this text, I began my programming using FORTRAN 66 on cards and teletype terminals. Because FORTRAN 66 was an unstructured language, I learned several bad programming habits, including the overuse of the GO TO statement. Until structured languages were available, I wrote in various versions of FORTRAN 66.

One of my FORTRAN 66 projects was a long program to solve a complex mathematical problem involving the repetition of an algorithm with numerous decisions. Several years after completing this project, I wanted to convert the program into a structured program. In so doing, I discovered what may be the height of unstructured programming: In one program segment consisting of eight statements, five involved a GO TO statement. Trying to trace the underlying logic of these five GO TO statements was almost as bad as removing a backlash from a fishing reel! Needless to say, I now write only structured programs.

PROGRAMMING LANGUAGES
A Short History

In the late 1940s and early 1950s, programming on computers was performed by connecting wires and throwing switches so that the computer could solve a specific problem. When the computer had solved one problem, the programmer changed the connections and threw a new set of switches to solve a different problem. This extremely slow and inefficient process improved with the use of binary numbers to direct the same operations. When working with binary numbers quickly became unwieldy, programmers used octal (base 8) and hexadecimal (base 16) notation to represent the patterns of zeros and ones.

Programming improved even more with the use of abbreviations for the operations previously denoted by binary, octal, or hexadecimal numbers. For example, instead of entering a hexadecimal number to designate multiplication, programmers could use a mnemonic abbreviation like MUL to represent the operation. However, even with mnemonic instructions, the programmer needed a detailed understanding of the computer's operations. This situation limited the access to a computer.

With the introduction of high-level languages, more people could actually be involved with the computer. Using high-level languages required a translation program that would perform the following series of operations:

Analyze the vocabulary of the high-level language.

Check the syntax.

Relate the names used by the programmer for various quantities to storage locations.

Find the operations that are called for in a library of such operations.

Generate the appropriate machine code.

Programs that could translate high-level languages into machine code were called **compilers** or **interpreters**, depending on the method of the translation.

The time line below shows when the various high-level languages were introduced, beginning with the first high-level language, FORTRAN.

SOURCE: Bill Machrone, "Micro-Linguistics: Languages for the PC," *PC Magazine*, September 1983, pp. 115–27; Bernard Cole, "The Family Tree of Computer Languages," *Popular Computing*, September 1983, pp. 82–88.

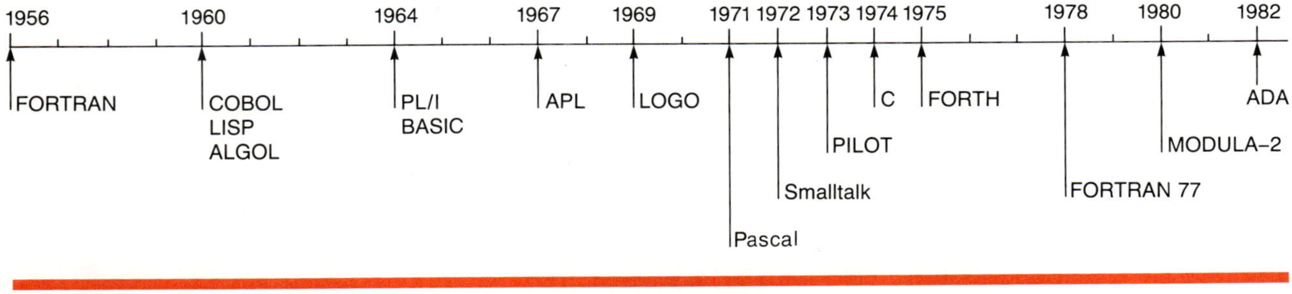

Table 15-1 LANGUAGE CLASSIFICATIONS

Classification	*Options*
Level	High or low
Translation	Compiled or interpreted
Interaction	Interactive or batch
Structure	Unstructured, structure possible, or structure required
Procedure	Procedural or nonprocedural

group of languages contains most or all of the statements necessary to write structured programs. However, the programmer can still use an unstructured approach to programming. The majority of modern computer languages fall into this category—that is, between the languages in which a structured program cannot be written and the next category, languages that *require* a structured form. In this last group of languages, the programmer cannot use any unstructured approach to programming, including the GO TO statement. The best example of this type of language is Pascal, which has become very popular over the last five years.

Table 15-1 summarizes the computer language classifications we have just discussed. As we consider each language in this chapter, we comment on whether it is a compiled or an interpreted language; whether it is an interactive or a batch language; and whether it is an unstructured language, one that allows but does not require structure, or one that requires structure. All languages discussed in this chapter—except machine language and assembly language—are high-level languages; all are procedural languages.

LOW-LEVEL COMPUTER LANGUAGES

Two types of low-level computer languages exist—machine language and assembly language. Machine language can be expressed in binary, octal, or hexadecimal numbers, and assembly language is made up of abbreviations of commands. When machine language is used, the programmer specifies everything that the computer must know using the binary number system or an octal or hexadecimal equivalent. With assembly language, the programmer does not use numbers for instructions. He or she still works close to the computer's level of communication, but a translation program called an **assembler** handles many tedious chores associated with using machine language.

Assembly language programming is an extravagant waste of human talent and should be avoided whenever possible.

Peter Norton

(As quoted in "PC Languages: The Living and the Dead," *PC Magazine,* September 1983, pp. 99–101.)

Because low-level languages are so close to the machine, the specific language used depends on the type of computer or chip. For example, the machine or assembly language for an IBM mainframe is quite different from that for a UNIVAC computer. Similarly, the assembly language for the Z80 chip used in Radio Shack and CP/M machines is different from the language used for the Intel 8088 chip used in the IBM PC and compatible machines.

An advantage of using an assembly language (almost no one bothers with machine languages today) is that the user has complete control over the computer's inner workings. Assembly language also executes faster than any high-level language. In fact, many commercial packages—such as word processing, spreadsheet, and data base manager packages—are written in assem-

Table 15-2 MACHINE LANGUAGE PROGRAM

Step	*Machine Language Statement*	*Instruction*
1	00100001 00000000 00000000	Load total register with 0.
2	00000001 00000000 01100100	Load current number register with 100.
3	00001001	Add current number register to total register.
4	00010101	Subtract 1 from current number register.
5	00100000 11111100	If current number register is not 0, then go back to 3.

(SOURCE: William Barden, Jr., "What Language Is Best for You?" *Popular Computing*, February 1982, pp. 68–69. Reprinted by permission of the author.)

Table 15-3 ASSEMBLY LANGUAGE PROGRAM

Symbolic Instructions		*Remarks*
	LD HL,Ø	;LOAD TOTAL WITH Ø
	LD BC,1ØØ	;LOAD CURRENT WITH 1ØØ
LOOP	ADD HL,BC	;ADD CURRENT TO TOTAL
	DEC C	;CURRENT-1 TO CURRENT
	JR NZ,LOOP	;GO IF CURRENT NOT Ø

(SOURCE: William Barden, Jr., "What Language Is Best for You?" *Popular Computing*, February 1982, pp. 68–69. Reprinted by permission of the author.)

bly language. This speed and control are two reasons why many companies using the IBM Series 370 computers and their successors require that programmers be knowledgeable in 370 Assembly Language. (Check any metropolitan newspaper. Along with COBOL, 370 Assembly Language is often mentioned in job openings for programmers.)

On the negative side, because each assembly language is different, a program cannot be moved from one type of computer to another. An entirely new program must be written in the new computer's assembly language. Writing programs in assembly language usually takes much longer than writing in a high-level language, because the programmer must provide specifically for many operations in assembly language that a high-level language automatically covers.

Tables 15-2 and 15-3 show machine language and assembly language programs, respectively, for the summation of the numbers from 1 to 100. The languages used here are for the Z80 chip used in many 8-bit computers.

HIGH-LEVEL COMPUTER LANGUAGES

With the advent of high-level languages and compilers, many people who did not understand the details of the computer could write programs. The first high-level language, FORTRAN, was introduced in 1956. Since then, numerous high-level languages have been introduced either as general purpose or special purpose languages. In this section, we discuss in detail some popular high-level languages—FORTRAN, COBOL, PL/I, BASIC, Pascal, and C—in order of introduction. We also discuss other special purpose languages and languages that are not as popular.

FORTRAN

The oldest high-level language, FORTRAN, was originally developed by an IBM-sponsored committee headed by John Backus. FORTRAN is designed to meet the needs of users in the scientific, mathematical, and engineering community who want to write programs without learning an assembly language. In fact, the name FORTRAN comes from the name FORmula TRANslator. FORTRAN can easily convert a user's equation or formula into a statement that can be executed by the computer. First released in 1956 as FORTRAN I, FORTRAN has been standardized twice by the American National Standards Institute (ANSI). ANSI is the scientific body that decides which version of a language is the standard. In 1966, the first standard version was FORTRAN IV, or FORTRAN 66; the 1978 version is FORTRAN 77. The remainder of this discussion concerns the latest version of FORTRAN, because it is available on all mainframes and is much more versatile than earlier versions. Unfortunately, personal computer software vendors have not been as quick to release complete versions of FORTRAN 77.

FORTRAN is a compiled language. In other words, the entire program is entered before any syntax or vocabulary mistakes may be detected. On the other hand, once compiled and debugged, FORTRAN is one of the fastest (if not *the* fastest) high-level languages in executing program instructions. FORTRAN is also a batch language, so user interaction is impossible during program entry or execution.

FORTRAN was developed especially for users who want to solve mathematical, scientific, and engineering problems on the computer.

FORTRAN was often criticized as an unstructured language that could not handle textual material and that was difficult to use when data were input from a terminal. These criticisms were true of FORTRAN's early versions. However, with FORTRAN 77, the programmer can write structured programs that manipulate textual material as well as carry out scientific and mathematical calculations. The latest version of the language also simplified data entry from a terminal. Top-down design using modules, or **subroutines**, is easy to implement in FORTRAN. Subroutines can be written and tested separately from the **main program**, which manages the subroutines that perform the actual work.

As an example of how FORTRAN converts a formula into a program statement, consider the computation of the value of y, where $y = 5.x^2 + x/8. - 10.$ In FORTRAN, this equation is

```
Y = 5.*X**2 + X/8. - 10.
```

where * means multiplication, ** means raised to the power of, + indicates addition, / indicates division, and − means subtraction. Figure 15-2 shows a FORTRAN program for computing quiz score averages for several students.

The program in Figure 15-2 follows the pseudocode closely, but several statements are noteworthy. First, statements beginning with an asterisk (*) are **comment statements** that explain the computer statements. This **documentation** is useful for explaining the program logic. The three statements that begin with INTEGER, CHARACTER, and REAL declare that the memory location names—usually referred to as **variables**—are whole numbers, characters, and decimal numbers, respectively. The DO 100 statement is equivalent to the WHILE . . . repeat pseudocode statement, which repeats the loop and counts the number of repetitions. The 100 CONTINUE statement has a numeric **label** and indicates the end of the body of the loop.

FIGURE 15-2
FORTRAN Program to Compute Quiz Score Averages

```
* PROGRAM TO COMPUTE QUIZ AVERAGE FOR MULTIPLE STUDENTS
      INTEGER NUMSTU
      CHARACTER*30 NAME
      REAL SCORE1,SCORE2,SCORE3,SCORE4,SCORE5,QAVE,CAVE,TOTAL,CTOTAL
      CTOTAL = 0
      READ *,NUMSTU
      DO 100 I = 1,NUMSTU
        READ *,NAME,SCORE1,SCORE2,SCORE3,SCORE4,SCORE5
        TOTAL = SCORE1 + SCORE2 + SCORE3 + SCORE4 + SCORE5
        QAVE = TOTAL/5.
* READ NAME AND QUIZ SCORES, TOTAL SCORES AND FIND AVERAGE
        IF(QAVE.LT.60.)THEN
          PRINT *,'STUDENT HAS FAILED'
        ENDIF
* CHECK TO SEE IF STUDENT IS FAILING
        PRINT *,'QUIZ AVERAGE FOR: ',NAME,' IS ',QAVE
        CTOTAL = CTOTAL + QAVE
100   CONTINUE
      CAVE = CTOTAL/NUMSTU
      PRINT *,'CLASS AVERAGE IS ',CAVE
* COMPUTE AND OUTPUT CLASS AVERAGE
      END
```

COBOL

FORTRAN I was clearly not adequate for the data processing needs of business and government. To remedy this situation, a group of computer users from business, government, and academia met with representatives of the computer industry in 1959 to discuss their computing needs. This group, CODASYL (Conference on Data Systems Languages), developed COBOL (COmmon Business Oriented Language). The "common" in COBOL refers to the ability to run the language on many different computers. Since COBOL's introduction in 1960, more software has been written in that language than in any other.

COBOL is often used for business applications on mainframes because the language can organize and manipulate large amounts of data. Approximately one-half of the language is dedicated to file-handling that is similar to the data base management packages. In addition to superior file-handling capabilities, COBOL has a sort module, which reorganizes data files. COBOL also provides arithmetic commands for addition, subtraction, multiplication, and so on.

COBOL programs are strikingly similar to English prose. This similarity is not accidental; it was built into the language on purpose. A nonprogrammer business person can pick up a COBOL program and at least understand its purpose, if not all of the logic. For example, the following program segment clearly computes the gross pay for an hourly employee using either a regular time or an overtime computation.

COBOL is the computer language of business.

```
IF EMPLOYEE-HOURS ARE GREATER THAN 40
  PERFORM REGULAR-TIME-GROSS-PAY-ROUTINE,
ELSE
  PERFORM OVERTIME-GROSS-PAY-ROUTINE.
```

The use of English-like vocabulary and syntax make a program easier to maintain. Software maintenance is an important part of a programmer's job. **Maintenance** includes fixing bugs that are discovered during program execution, adding features to the program, altering parts of the program, and performing any other activities to keep the program responsive to current needs. Maintenance of previously written programs uses an estimated 70% of a programmer's time. Because COBOL is easy to understand, it is also easy to maintain. COBOL is essentially a **self-documenting language**, because the user does not need comments to explain what the program is doing.

COBOL has been criticized for its wordy and repetitive nature and for the fact that short programs are difficult to write in COBOL. These criticisms relate to the same features that are stated as advantages. COBOL was designed as a *business language* not a programming language, and as such, it is not meant for general programming.

COBOL compilers for personal computers cannot currently offer the same range of features offered on a mainframe because the compilers take up much computer memory. COBOL users must shop carefully to ensure that a compiler program contains all desired features.

COBOL is a compiled batch language that may or may not be structured, depending on the programmer. Figure 15-3 shows a portion of a COBOL program for the same example shown in the FORTRAN program on page 394. Only a portion of the program is shown, because the entire program would take several pages.

PL/I

Following the introduction of FORTRAN and COBOL, IBM developed a language which it hoped would combine the best features of those languages. PL/I (Programming Language/I), introduced in 1964, was the first high-level language that allowed structured programming but was still a very flexible language. PL/I combines the scientific computation aspects of FORTRAN, the file-handling capability of COBOL, and superior text-handling capabilities.

Because it has all these capabilities, PL/I supports a large number of statements. Users joke that any PL/I task can be accomplished in at least three ways. This situation makes PL/I difficult for beginners to learn. Although IBM marketed the language as a replacement for both FORTRAN and COBOL, PL/I is not as widely accepted as its developers hoped.

A recent standardization committee produced a subset of PL/I that reduced the size of the language so that it could run on personal computers. Other subsets of the language that retain the basic form can be taught to beginning programmers without overwhelming them. A subset called PL/M was written by Gary Kildall for Intel's 8080 chip. Kildall also wrote in PL/M the original version of the CP/M personal computer operating system. Kildall's company, Digital Research, currently provides a version of PL/I for personal computers that use CP/M.

PL/I is a compiled language that contains all the statements necessary to write structured programs. It is also a batch language—that is, user interaction with the language is impossible during program entry or execution.

```
PROCEDURE DIVISION.
MAIN-PROC.
    PERFORM OPEN-EM.
    WRITE PRINT-LINE FROM HEADING-LINE AFTER ADVANCING PAGE.
    READ GRADE-TRANSACTIONS
        AT END MOVE ZERO TO CLASS-AVERAGE.
    PERFORM PROCESS-RECORDS UNTIL FILE-STATUS IS EQUAL TO "10".
    WRITE PRINT-LINE FROM TOTAL-LINE AFTER ADVANCING 2.
    PERFORM CLOSE-EM.
    STOP RUN.
OPEN-EM.
    OPEN INPUT GRADE-TRANSACTIONS
         OUTPUT PRINT-FILE.
PROCESS-RECORDS.
    MOVE STUDENT-NAME OF INPUT-LINE TO
         STUDENT-NAME OF DETAIL-LINE.
    ADD SCORE OF INPUT-LINE (1), SCORE OF INPUT-LINE (2),
        SCORE OF INPUT-LINE (3), SCORE OF INPUT-LINE (4),
        SCORE OF INPUT-LINE (5) GIVING TOTAL-SCORE.
    MULTIPLY TOTAL-SCORE BY 0.20 GIVING AVERAGE.
    IF AVERAGE IS LESS THAN 60,
        MOVE "FAILED" TO COMMENT,
      ELSE MOVE SPACES TO COMMENT.
    MOVE AVERAGE TO STUDENT-AVERAGE.
    WRITE PRINT-LINE FROM DETAIL-LINE.
    ADD 5 TO CLASS-COUNT.
    ADD TOTAL-SCORE TO CLASS-TOTAL.
    READ GRADE-TRANSACTIONS;
        AT END DIVIDE CLASS-TOTAL BY CLASS-COUNT
               GIVING CLASS-AVERAGE.
CLOSE-EM.
    CLOSE GRADE-TRANSACTIONS
          PRINT-FILE.
END PROGRAM.
```

FIGURE 15-3
Portion of COBOL Program to Compute Quiz Score Averages

Figure 15-4 shows a PL/I program to compute quiz score averages for multiple students. Note that the PL/I program allows meaningful variable names and that an underline takes the place of a blank space in a variable name.

BASIC

When IBM introduced PL/I as a language that attempted to combine the best features of COBOL and FORTRAN, two professors at Dartmouth College introduced a language that went in another direction. John Kemeny and Thomas Kurtz wanted a computer language for their students that would be easy to learn and still retain the formula translation characteristics of FORTRAN. Kemeny and Kurtz called their new language BASIC (Beginner's All-purpose Symbolic Instruction Code), a scaled-down version of FORTRAN.

BASIC is a simple language, in which programs can be written with as few as seven statement types. An interpreted language, BASIC is easy for students to use because errors are signaled to the user during execution. For ease of use and simplicity, BASIC was chosen by early personal computer manufac-

```
GRADES:PROCEDURE OPTIONS (MAIN);
      DCL STUDENT_NAME CHAR(30)
         (STUDENT_COUNTER,
         QUIZ1,QUIZ2,QUIZ3,QUIZ4,QUIZ5,
         STUDENT_AVERAGE,CLASS_AVERAGE,QUIZ_TOTAL,
         NUMBER_STUDENTS,CLASS_TOTAL,
         I , NUMBER_STUDENTS) REAL (6),
         MESSAGE CHAR (7);
CLASS_TOTAL = 0.;
GET LIST(NUMBER_STUDENTS);
DO I = 1 TO NUMBER_STUDENTS;
      GET LIST(STUDENT_NAME, QUIZ1, QUIZ2, QUIZ3, QUIZ4, QUIZ5);
      QUIZ_TOTAL = QUIZ1 + QUIZ2 + QUIZ3 + QUIZ4 + QUIZ5;
      QUIZ_AVERAGE = QUIZ_TOTAL/5.0;
      IF QUIZ_AVERAGE < 60. THEN MESSAGE = 'FAILING';
         ELSE MESSAGE = '';
      PUT SKIP LIST(MESSAGE, STUDENT_NAME, QUIZ_AVERAGE);
      CLASS_TOTAL = CLASS_TOTAL + QUIZ_AVERAGE;
END;
CLASS_AVERAGE = CLASS_TOTAL/NUMBER_STUDENTS;
PUT SKIP LIST('CLASS AVERAGE = ', CLASS_AVERAGE);
END GRADES;
```

FIGURE 15-4
PL/I Program to Compute Quiz Score Averages

turers. The earliest Apple and Radio Shack computers always included BASIC on cassette or disk.

The current versions of BASIC found on personal computers are far different from the simple language that Kemeny and Kurtz originally developed. Many new commands have transformed the language from a beginner's instructional language into one that can be used to write commercial software. Such advanced commands as PEEK and POKE are used either to check the contents of a single memory location or to change those contents.

Even with the new commands, BASIC is an interpreted language that is highly interactive. Programs in BASIC are easy to write and debug. A user can write one or more statements of a BASIC program and try them out before incorporating them into the program. BASIC is often chosen as a first computer language. However, because BASIC is interpreted, it runs much slower than compiled languages. (Compiled versions of the language are now available if speed is important—such as in commercial software.)

The greatest criticism of BASIC (other than its slow execution speed) is that many of its older versions were unstructured. This absence of structure was due to the lack of appropriate statement forms necessary to write structured programs. In other words, the programmer had to use the GO TO statement. BASIC's interactive nature made it easy to write unstructured programs when the programmer's preliminary planning was not sufficient. The most popular current version of BASIC for personal computers, Microsoft BASIC, falls into the middle group of languages—that is, the user can write, but is not required to write, a structured program with it. Kemeny and Kurtz have developed a new form of BASIC—True BASIC—which is a completely structured language similar to Pascal.

A criticism of BASIC for personal computers is the lack of standardization, which is answered to some extent by the almost universal availability of

BASIC was developed at the Dartmouth College computer center in 1964 by John Kemeny and Tom Kurtz (shown here with student).

COMPUTING A DEAL
Flutie Signs with the Pros

In 1984, when Doug Flutie completed the nationally televised, last-second 64-yard touchdown pass that defeated the University of Miami, he was an overnight sensation. The Boston College quarterback won the Heisman Trophy that year and signed a professional football contract worth over $1.3 million per year for four years. Although Doug surely was responsible for the fame he received, his fortune can be attributed to his father, Richard Flutie, and the computer programs he wrote to help Doug choose an agent and structure a contract.

Richard first developed a program that ranked each possible agent on the basis of various categories, which included experience in direct negotiations with professional football teams, tax expertise, entertainment connections, integrity, and so on. On the basis of his ranking, Boston attorney Bob Woolf was chosen to handle Doug's negotiations with both the National Football League (NFL) and the United States Football League (USFL).

Next, Richard analyzed the contracts of all the players drafted by the 28 NFL teams in 1982 and 1983. Using this analysis, Richard could plot a curve that demonstrated Doug's potential value to the NFL. Richard also used this information to determine how his son's contract should be structured to achieve maximum take-home pay.

As a result of Doug's athletic ability and his father's computing talents, Doug signed with the USFL New Jersey Generals as the highest paid rookie in professional football history.

SOURCE: Sue Mott, "The Computer Fortunes of Doug Flutie," *Personal Computing*, April 1985, p. 35. Reprinted with permission from *Personal Computing*, April 1985, p. 35. Copyright 1985, Hayden Publishing Company.

```
50 REM THIS PROGRAM INPUTS QUIZ SCORES AND FINDS THE AVERAGE SCORE FOR
ALL STUDENTS IN THE CLASS. IT ALSO COMPUTES THE CLASS AVERAGE.
70 INPUT "ENTER NUMBER OF STUDENTS IN CLASS: ";NUMBER
80 CLASSTOTAL = 0 'INITIALIZE CLASS TOTAL TO ZERO
90 FOR I = 1 TO NUMBER 'REPEAT THE FOLLOWING FOR EACH STUDENT
100   INPUT "NAME AND SCORES: ";STUDENT$,SCORE1,SCORE2,SCORE3,SCORE4,
SCORE5
200   AVERAGE = (SCORE1+SCORE2+SCORE3+SCORE4+SCORE5)/5 'FIND AVERAGE
SCORE
300   IF AVERAGE < 60 THEN PRINT "STUDENT IS FAILING" 'CHECK AVERAGE
400   PRINT "STUDENT'S NAME: ";STUDENT$
500   PRINT "STUDENT'S AVERAGE: ";AVERAGE
600   CLASSTOTAL = CLASSTOTAL + AVERAGE 'ADD STUDENT AVERAGE TO CLASS
      TOTAL
700 NEXT I
800 CLASSAVERAGE = CLASSTOTAL/NUMBER 'COMPUTE CLASS AVERAGE
900 PRINT "CLASS AVERAGE = ";CLASSAVERAGE
```

FIGURE 15-5
BASIC Program to Compute Quiz Score Averages

Microsoft BASIC for personal computers. This language is built-in on the IBM PC and is available for IBM compatibles and the Apple Macintosh computers. Apple uses a different version of BASIC for its Apple II series, which is a problem if the user wants to convert a BASIC program from an Apple IIe or IIc to another machine.

Figure 15-5 contains a Microsoft BASIC version of the quiz score averaging program. Note that this BASIC program has **line numbers**, which are used for identification. Line numbers can also be quite useful during the interpretation and debugging processes. In BASIC, information can be given about any program statement using the REM statement. The apostrophe (') is also used to begin a comment on the same line as the statement it references.

Pascal

In 1971, a Swiss computer scientist named Niklaus Wirth introduced a teaching language that he called Pascal, after the French mathematician. Pascal is now a popular language for teaching introductory computer science. This popularity is due to the fact that Pascal *must* be written in a structured manner, so students never learn to write poorly designed programs.

Pascal has a clean, block-structure approach to programming, which makes the language easy to use and learn. Pascal is also a **strongly typed language**, which means that all variable names must be declared at the beginning of the program. The computer must be told what each variable name represents—the type of quantity, whole numbers, decimal numbers, text, and so on. Because of this approach, the user must think through the program before it is written. In comparison, BASIC and FORTRAN are **weakly typed languages** that do not require a declaration of variable types. All Pascal programs follow the order shown below:

```
PROGRAM program name;
VAR
        variable declarations
BEGIN
        program logic
END.
```

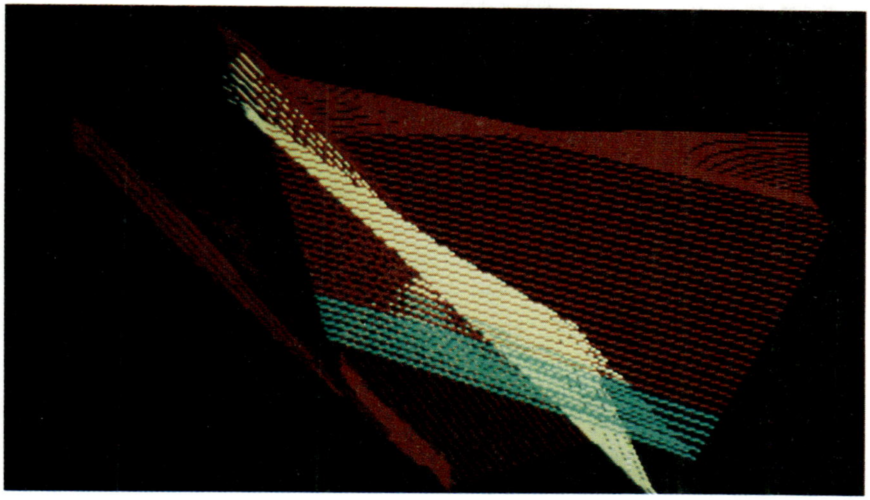

These graphics were produced from a program written in Pascal.

Pascal programs must have a PROGRAM statement that names the program, a VAR statement that comes before the variable declarations, and a BEGIN statement that defines the beginning of the actual program logic. The program always ends with an END statement. Other BEGIN and END statements can define blocks of material within the main program. Pascal also lends itself well to top-down design through the definition of a **procedure**, which can perform some specific task.

Because of these advantages, Pascal is used for many purposes other than instruction. Commercial software is now available in Pascal, as is the UCSD

FIGURE 15-6
Pascal Program to Compute Quiz Score Averages

```
PROGRAM Average(Input,Output)
VAR
      Numberstudent,I,K: INTEGER;
      Studentaverage,Classaverage,Classtotal,Score1,Score2,Score3,Score4,
      Score5: REAL;
      Studentname: Packed array(1..20) of CHAR;
BEGIN
      READLN(Numberstudent);
      Classtotal :=0
      FOR I := 1 TO Numberstudent DO
            BEGIN
            FOR K := 1 to 20 DO
                READ(Studentname(K));
            READLN(Score1,Score2,Score3,Score4,Score5);
            Studentaverage := (Score1+Score2+Score3+Score4+Score5)/5.;
            IF Studentaverage < 60 THEN WRITELN('Student has failed');
            WRITELN('Average for student named ',Studentname,' is '
            ,Studentaverage);
            Classtotal := Classtotal + Studentaverage;
            END
      Classaverage := Classtotal/Numberstudent;
      WRITELN('Class average is ',Classaverage);
END.
```

p-system operating system. With these additional uses of Pascal, the original language has expanded, and nonstandard forms of Pascal now exist. To remedy the need for extensions to Pascal, Wirth introduced a new language that meets the needs of software developers. This new language, called Modula-2, is discussed in the next section.

We said earlier that Pascal is a structured language with which a user cannot write an unstructured program. Most versions of Pascal are compiled, but an interpreted, interactive version was released for the Apple Macintosh. The Macintosh version is much like BASIC in that parts of a program can be tested before they are incorporated into the main program. Figure 15-6 shows a Pascal version of the quiz score averaging program.

Note that the Pascal program allows both upper- and lower-case letters where previous examples use only upper-case letters. The words in all upper-case letters are **keywords**, which are part of the syntax of Pascal. The program statements after the keyword VAR are the variable declaration statements required in Pascal, and the FOR statement handles the counting loop.

Pascal also allows the names of the various quantities—such as student average and class average (variables)—to be written out like COBOL, compared with FORTRAN and some versions of BASIC, which restrict the number of letters in a name. Both characteristics make Pascal a self-documenting language. Self-documenting languages like COBOL and Pascal are easy to maintain.

C

For writing operating systems, a favorite language of programmers is the C language. C was developed at Bell Labs in 1974 by Brian Kernighan and Dennis Ritchie. These two authors supposedly looked at all programming languages and chose the most desirable features of each. As with Pascal, C has a block structure that requires structured programming. However, C differs from other high-level languages in the degree to which the computer can be controlled with the language. In a sense, C is a cross between a high-level

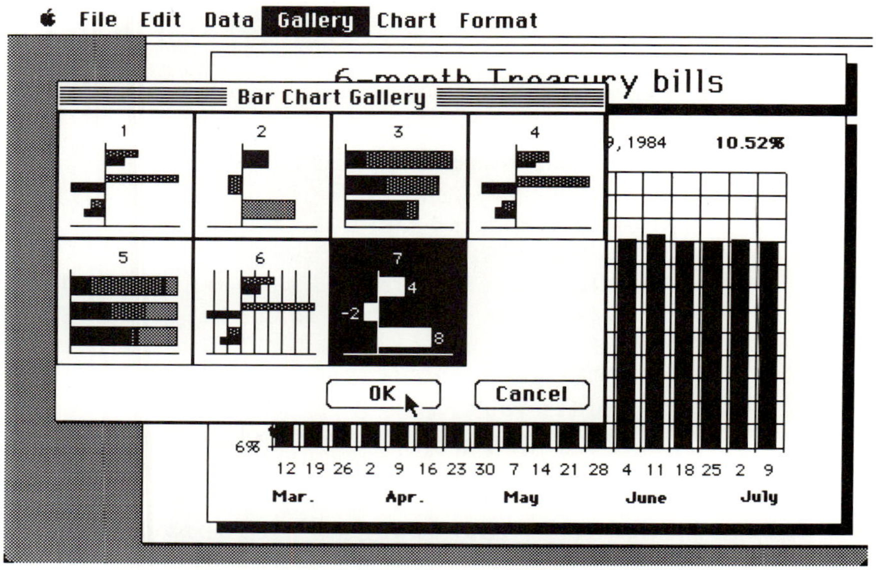

The popular Multiplan spreadsheet is written in the C computer language. Multiplan is shown here in its implementation for the Apple Macintosh.

```
main ()
{
char  name[20];
int   students=0, grades[5];
float average, class_total=0;
printf("------- NAME ------- AVERAGE\n");
while (scanf("%20s%d%d%d%d%d",
          name,grades,grades+1,grades+2,grades+3,grades+4) != EOF)
    {
    average = (grades[0]+grades[1]+grades[2]+grades[3]+
       grades[4]) * 0.20;
    printf("%-20s    %5.2f %s\n",
           name,average,(average<60.0?"Failed":" "));
    students++;
    class_total += average;
    }
printf("\nClass average is %5.2f\n",class_total/students);
return(0);
}
```

FIGURE 15-7
C Program to Compute Quiz Score Averages

language and an assembly language; some people refer to it as a *middle-level language*. A distinguishing feature of C is that it uses functions to perform most of its operations. **Functions** are short programs that are stored in a computer memory library, which may be accessed by the language as needed to perform specific tasks. Today, versions of C are available for all types of computers—from personal computers to CRAY-1 supercomputers.

The C language produces extremely fast machine language code, has greater control of the machine than any other language, and is easily portable. More software is written every day in C, including Microsoft's Xenix operating system for such machines as the IBM PC and the Radio Shack Model 16. Microsoft's popular Multiplan spreadsheet package is written in C. The IBM software that accompanies this text is written in C for fast execution and portability.

The C language is criticized because understanding a C program written by someone else can be difficult. In fact, some people have suggested that the language name stands for "Cryptic"! Critics also suggest that programs written in C should have one comment for each program statement to facilitate program maintenance. C was designed for systems programming, not for learning programming. However, with its power and speed, C is a popular language for advanced programming projects.

C is a structured language in the Pascal mold because it is difficult to write unstructured programs using C. It is also a batch language that must be compiled before it is executed. Figure 15-7 shows the C version of the quiz score averaging program.

OTHER HIGH-LEVEL LANGUAGES

In addition to the six languages we have just discussed, numerous other languages are available on mainframes, minicomputers, and personal computers. In this section, we briefly cover several other high-level languages. Some are general purpose languages, but most are special purpose languages that make communications with the computer easier when a specific task must be accomplished. Again, we discuss the languages in the order of their introduction.

LISP

LISP (LISt Processor) was developed in 1960 specifically for processing lists. The language approaches everything from sentences to mathematical formulas as lists. LISP is quite useful in the area of artificial intelligence, which we discuss later in this chapter. LISP is also the parent to LOGO, a popular educational language that is also discussed later in this section.

ALGOL

The parent of Pascal and other block languages is ALGOL (ALGOrithmic Language). This language, which was very popular in Europe in the 1960s, is similar to FORTRAN except for its structured style. It is a general purpose language like FORTRAN or PL/I.

APL

APL (A Programming Language) is a special purpose language used for mathematical and scientific formulas. With special symbols—like Greek letters and overstrike characters—APL can accomplish in one line what other languages might take 10 lines to do. APL is also an interpreted language that is easy to use. However, it can be difficult to decipher because of its special symbols and compact form. In fact, compared with APL, the C language is very easy to read!

LOGO

For ease of use, LOGO probably ranks first among all languages. Preschool children learn how to move the special LOGO graphics cursor around on the screen to trace patterns. The cursor, called a **turtle**, is moved via simple geometric commands. For example, the following commands

```
FORWARD 60
RIGHT 120
```

The LOGO computer language can be learned quickly even by pre-school children, who move the "turtle" cursor with simple commands.

instruct the turtle to move 60 steps forward and then turn right at an angle of 120 degrees. If we repeat this command three times as shown,

```
REPEAT 3 (FORWARD 60
  RIGHT 120)
```

the turtle draws an equilateral triangle.

Using other commands—such as GROW and EDIT—a user can draw sophisticated figures on the screen, and at the same time, learn the concept of programming logic. With more advanced commands, LOGO can be used for nongraphic programming tasks similar to those performed by other high-level languages. LOGO users can also generate new commands by combining available commands, so the language can expand to meet users' needs. Because LOGO was developed by the MIT Artificial Intelligence Laboratory as a dialect of LISP, these commands are based on the same list processing concepts used in LISP.

Smalltalk

This language is the predecessor of Apple's desk metaphor, which uses menus with icons to help the user choose an option. Smalltalk was developed at the Xerox Palo Alto Research Center in 1972 based on the ideas of a University of Utah graduate student named Alan Kay. Kay wanted to implement the notion that the computer works by sending messages when he considered the idea of an **object-oriented language**, the basis for Smalltalk.

PILOT

BASIC was originally designed for student use, but it is now a very sophisticated language. Currently, an easier language to learn is PILOT (Programmed Inquiry Learning or Teaching). This language was developed for instructional situations and is not as complex as the modern versions of BASIC.

Forth

Forth was originally developed by an astronomer to control his telescopes. It is a very fast, high-level language that has a small, but devoted following of

THE LOGO CHALLENGE
Will BASIC Survive?

BASIC has been the language of the personal computer for as long as these machines have been in use. However, successful implementations of LOGO for various types of personal computers are challenging BASIC's domination.

The reason for the increasing use of LOGO can be traced to the backgrounds of both languages. BASIC was first developed to squeeze as much power as possible into the limited memory capacities of the early personal computers. In other words, BASIC was developed with the machine in mind rather than the user. As more computing power was available on personal computers, BASIC was expanded by the addition of functions and features. (True BASIC is an exception to this approach.) The language has retained many of its original machine-oriented characteristics.

The designers of LOGO were optimistic about the future of computing power. They believed that increased power could be tapped to make programming languages easier to use and understand. LOGO designers first considered how humans perform tasks, and then they created the easiest possible computer language. LOGO was designed with the user, not the computer, in mind. This ease of use has resulted in an image problem for LOGO, because many people find it hard to believe that such an easy language can also be a powerful problem-solving tool. Will personal computer versions of LOGO be found in the business and scientific world as well as the classroom? Only time will tell.

SOURCE: Winn L. Rosch, "BASIC Survival and the LOGO Challenge," *PC Magazine*, May 15, 1984, p. 189.

users. Forth is different from other languages because it uses **reverse Polish notation (RPN)** like that used on Hewlett-Packard calculators. In RPN, 3 4 + 5 × means to add 3 and 4 to get 7, and then to multiply this value by 5 to obtain 35. Although programmers have reported significant increases in productivity with Forth, most programmers will probably not switch to this somewhat different language.

Modula-2

Niklaus Wirth invented Pascal to teach correct programming methods. However, Pascal is also used commercially, which requires an expanded version of the language. To meet the need for an extended Pascal, Wirth developed Modula-2. This language looks very much like Pascal, but it is used for systems development.

Ada

Named for Lady Ada Lovelace—the first programmer and co-worker of Charles Babbage—Ada was developed for use by the U.S. Department of Defense. The Department of Defense felt that all military software should be written in one language, so Ada was developed over a period of several years. Much like Pascal, Ada is a structured language. However, it has many more features than Pascal, because it is designed to meet the needs of military

All Department of Defense software development is now carried out in Ada.

programmers. Because of the tremendous amount of software developed for military computers, Ada should soon be an important language in programming.

ARTIFICIAL INTELLIGENCE

Why can't human languages be used to give the computer instructions? We have pointed out some reasons why—the large vocabulary in most human languages, the often inconsistent syntax, the many idioms, and the general ambiguity involved with such languages. However, these problems have not stopped researchers from attempting to use **natural languages** to give instructions to a computer. The research on the use of natural languages is an important part of a larger field of research known as artificial intelligence. In general, **artificial intelligence (AI)** is trying to build computer hardware and software systems that exhibit the same type of intelligence-related capabilities as humans—for example, listening, reading, speaking, solving problems, and making inferences.

More and more, we will want the machine to adapt to our needs without being instructed to do so.

Michael Crichton, author and film maker

(As quoted in "Make Software Softer or the Programmable Program," Business Software '84 Advertising Supplement, *Business Week,* September 17, 1984, pp. C–F.)

Artificial intelligence may be the most important area of computer research today. In the field of **robotics** (discussed in Chapter 6), AI has already been of practical use. Artificial intelligence is one of the fastest growing high-tech areas. The September 7, 1984 issue of *USA Today,* showed that AI was growing at an annual rate of 300%, $1\frac{1}{2}$ times faster than the second fastest growth industry. Many companies spend large amounts of money either to develop AI systems or to purchase systems developed by other companies. In addition to robotics, natural language systems and expert systems have received much attention.

DR. COMPUTER

Diagnosing diseases and suggesting treatments to doctors were among the first applications that occurred to artificial intelligence (AI) researchers. With steady funding coming from the National Institutes of Health (NIH), AI expert systems have been developed that can aid doctors in treating a wide variety of diseases. Persuading computer-shy doctors to accept these systems, however, is another matter.

William R. Baker, who approved the spending of \$60 million to develop medical expert systems during his 12 years at NIH, has left government service, determined to move that technology into the doctor's office. With the help of a lawyer and a young venture broker, he is raising \$4 million to launch Knowledge Research Associates. "I never expected to get into the computer business," says the 62-year-old biomedical engineer.

Baker believes his new Potomac, Maryland, company will succeed. Once expert systems are licensed from their academic developers, he expects to coax the medical community into using the systems by first selling them to respected medical centers and teaching hospitals. Eventually, Baker says, the market will be "individual physicians."

Baker has plans for two initial products—AI/RHEUM, a tool for diagnosing arthritis and rheumatism, developed at the University of Missouri and Rutgers University, and CLINFO, a data management system for clinical investigators, developed by Baker himself. He also wants to market CADUCEUS II, an internal-medicine diagnostic system from the University of Pittsburgh.

Doctors will accept these systems only if they work, Baker says, "in a collegial manner, as a doctor would converse with a colleague." And if they do, the market will explode, Baker predicts. "By the turn of the century, every physician will be dealing with some kind of computer expert."

SOURCE: "Getting Doctors to Consult Electronic Advisers," *Business Week,* July 9, 1984, p. 57. Reprinted from the July 9, 1984 issue of *Business Week* by special permission, © 1984 by McGraw-Hill, Inc.

Robotics and Artificial Intelligence

1 The SCARAB (Submersible Craft Assisting Repair and Burial) is a remotely operated vehicle that provides information to its operator via television cameras, sonar, and other sensors. SCARAB helped searchers recover the "black Box" from the Air India jet that crashed into the Atlantic Ocean.

2 HERO, Jr., a fully preprogrammed personal robot with an on-board computer control system, is available in kit form.

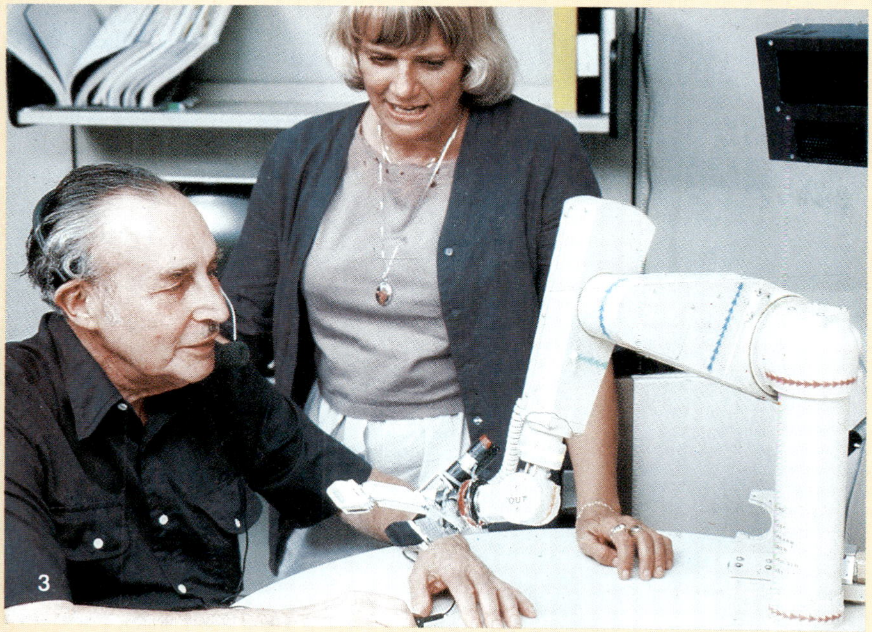

3 **Handicapped persons may soon benefit from research in combining voice communications with a robot arm.**

4 **Dr. Yik San Kwoh, Memorial Medical Center of Long Beach, California, demonstrates the world's first surgical application of robotic technology. This robotic arm will be programmed to reach the exact spot where a needle is inserted to diagnose or treat a brain tumor.**

These three images are different computer versions of the same scene. 5a A digitized image of a suburban house is shown. 5b The same scene is shown after the straight lines are sorted according to length and contrast. 5c Finally, a segmentation of the same scene by color and texture is shown. When these images are combined with general information on the house and its surroundings, the computer can "see" the scene.

6 **This multi-fingered robot hand can handle many kinds of objects skillfully and gently.**

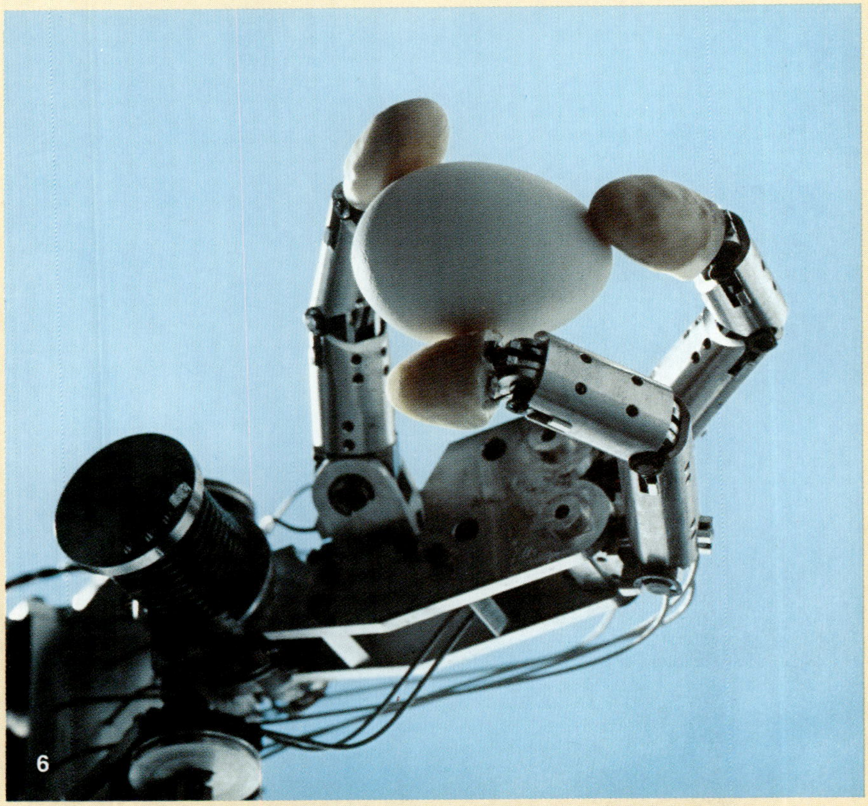

7 **In aerospace manufacturing operations, a precisely programmed robot arm can inspect welding to ensure that it meets required standards.**

8 **Robots that install various chips and components are very important in the manufacture of computer circuit boards.**

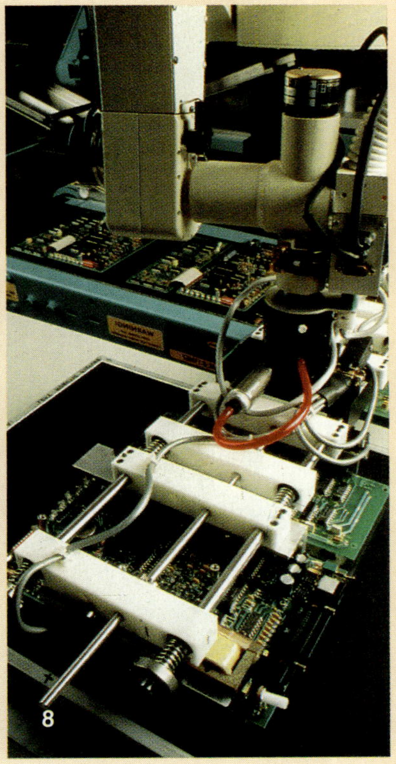

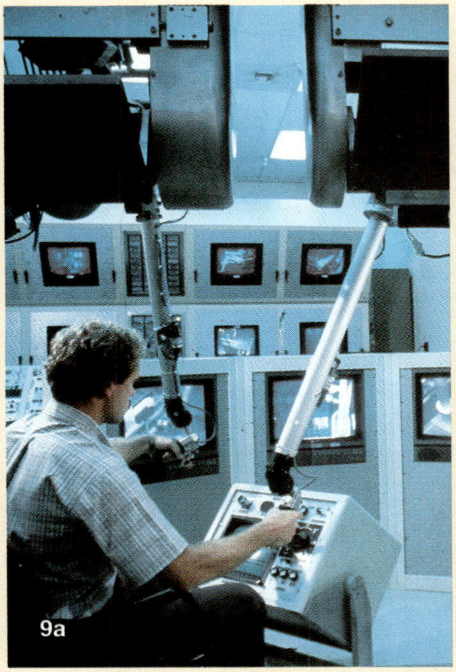

9a

9b

Using a robotic "master" unit in a control room (9a), a human operator controls the robot "slave" unit in an adjoining room (9b) and avoids contact with hazardous materials.

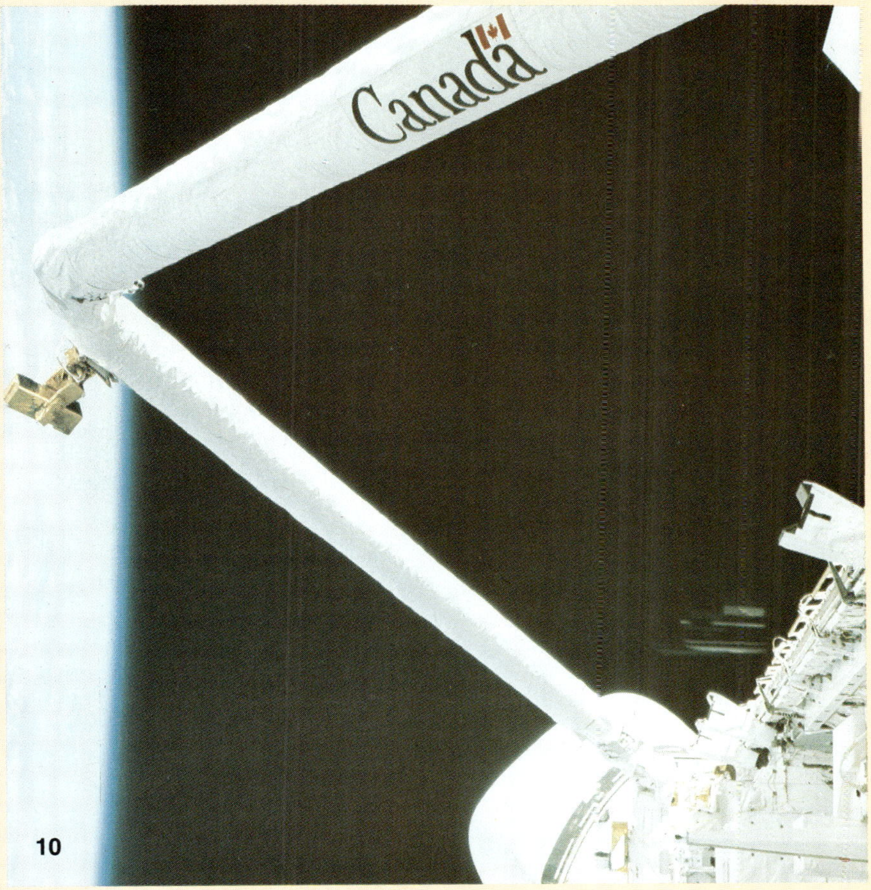

10 The remote manipulator system (RMS) arm on the space shuttle Columbia handles various cargoes. A remotely operated television camera is near the "elbow."

Natural Language Systems

With a natural language AI system, a user need not learn a special computer language to give the computer instructions. For example, a manager could access a data base simply by typing in his or her questions in "plain" English. For example, the question, "How many female employees have been hired since January first?" would be answered by the computer with the appropriate number. If the computer were then asked, "How many are paid more than $30,000 per year?" it would know immediately that the question referred to the women hired since January 1.

Two approaches are helping to solve the natural language system problem. In one approach, the computer analyzes each letter and word to determine the meaning of the sentence. This analytical approach already exists as a mainframe software package called Cognitive Systems, which is used by several large corporations. In the second approach, the computer compares a sentence that is input to other sentences that are stored in the computer to determine the meaning of the sentence. If an exact match is not found, then the closest match is used. One shortcoming of this natural language system is that the question about number of females "hired" can be confused with a question about the number "fired," because the two words are very similar.

Expert Systems

Creating an expert system involves storing in the computer all of the knowledge and rules from several experts on a given subject. The computer is then an "expert" on that subject, combining the knowledge and rules to aid humans in decision making. Expert systems are successfully used in searching for oil, diagnosing medical problems, finding problems with large machinery, and giving advice on business decisions. An expert system called MYCIN was developed at Stanford Medical School to help doctors diagnose patient

JAPAN AND THE FIFTH GENERATION

For several years, Japan has been a leader in the automobile and electronics industries, but not in computers. Japanese manufacturers make many of the chips used in American-made machines, but their own machines have made few inroads into the computer market. Now, the Japanese plan to "leapfrog" U.S. companies by starting work on fifth generation computers. In a recent announcement, the Japanese government and computer industry stated that they have teamed up to develop the fifth generation of computers before the end of this century. The Japanese Ministry of International Trade and Industry has pooled its resources with eight of the country's largest electronics companies to form the Institute for New Generation Computer Technology. This institute is committed to the development of the necessary hardware and software for the fifth generation machine.

These computers will be much faster and smarter than anything available today, incorporating many artificial intelligence concepts. A fifth generation computer should be able to

Listen when the user talks and then do what it is told.

Help program itself.

Make logical inferences.

Translate between languages.

Treat graphics like words.

Learn from its own experience.

To do this, the fifth generation computer will use parallel processing rather than today's standard serial processing. Parallel processing can work on multiple instructions simultaneously, but serial processing can only work with one instruction at a time. This new computer will be 70 times faster than the current supercomputers and store up to 3,000 times as much information.

SOURCE: Jim Schefter, "Fifth-Generation Computers," ***Popular Science,*** **April 1983, pp. 79–81.**

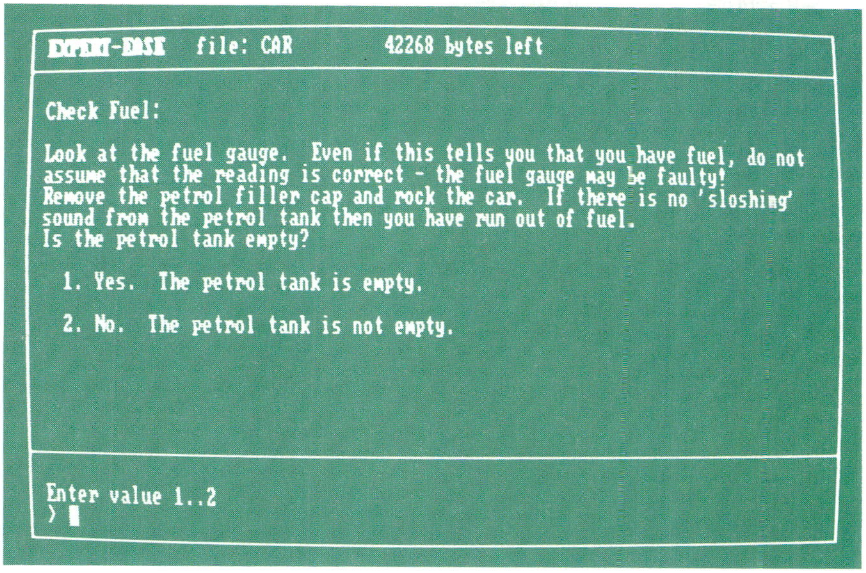

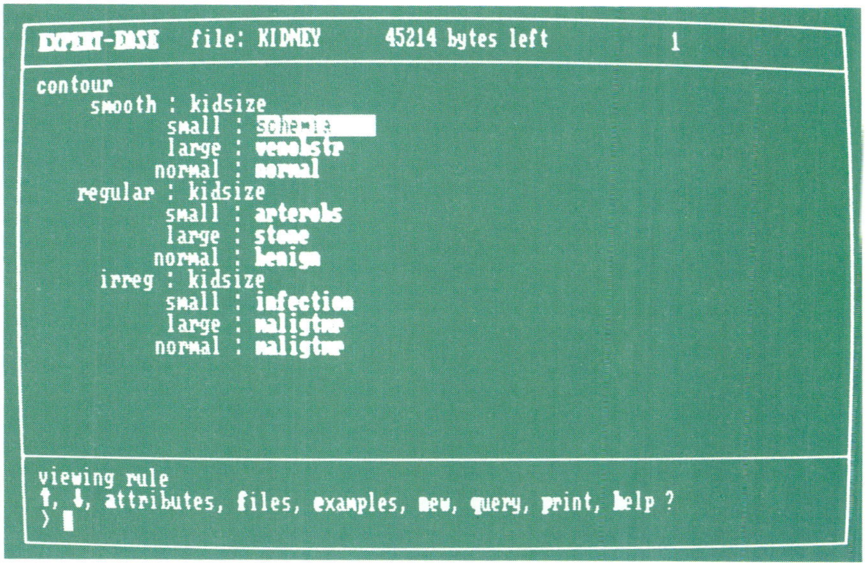

Expert-Ease is an expert system that has widely diverse applications, for example, diagnosing problems in automobiles or kidneys.

ills. MYCIN reviews the patient's symptoms with the physician and makes suggestions for testing, diagnosis, and treatment. Another medical-related expert system, PUFF, is aimed at pulmonary disease.

All expert systems have two parts—a knowledge base and an inference mechanism. The knowledge base includes the facts, judgments, rules, intuition, and experience provided by the group of experts. In the medical expert systems discussed above, the knowledge base would include all information from a group of physicians about various diseases. This information is then interpreted by the inference mechanism, which performs deductive reasoning to develop advice or more questions, or both. The knowledge base can be considered a map and the inference mechanism the rules that are used to follow the map. Because the combined knowledge base and inference mech-

[The] computer as servant will mature to computer "agent" or guide. A little guide in the computer will anticipate what you might want, suggest things you might do, or watch your patterns and say, "You normally do it this way so I'll just assume you want to do it that way unless you ask me otherwise."

Steven Jobs, co-founder of Apple Computer, Inc.

(As quoted in "Computer Will Grow from Servant to Guide," *USA Today,* August 2, 1984, p. 13A.)

anism can be very large, most expert systems run on mainframe or large minicomputers. However, at least one expert system is designed to run on personal computers.

Most artificial intelligence systems use the LISP (LISt Processor) language for software development. LISP works with a sentence or question as a list of letters. AI systems use LISP because it handles data strings of unpredictable size more easily and efficiently than any other language. LISP was developed in the late 1950s by one of the first artificial intelligence researchers, John McCarthy. In addition to developing LISP, McCarthy is also credited with coining the term *artificial intelligence.*

Many people feel that artificial intelligence is the future of computing. Certainly, it has the potential to make computer use much easier. Whether the research ever produces robots like C-3PO and R2-D2 of *Star Wars* remains to be seen.

REVIEW OF KEY POINTS

- Computer languages are needed to communicate with computers because computers cannot understand human languages.
- Computer languages may be classified according to level, manner of translation into machine language, level of user interaction, whether or not the user must provide the logic, and degree of structured support.
- Structured languages are favored for programming because high-quality programs result more often.
- Machine and assembly languages are low-level computer languages; all other languages are high-level computer languages.
- FORTRAN is primarily a scientific language, COBOL is primarily business oriented, and PL/I is a combination of these two.
- BASIC is an interpreted, interactive language that is very easy to learn, use, and debug. However, unstructured programs can easily be written in BASIC.
- Pascal is a highly structured language that is favored for instructional purposes.
- The C language is a middle-level language popular for systems programming.
- Numerous special purpose languages are available to fit a particular programming need.
- Artificial intelligence is the process of having the computer perform actions that require intelligence.
- Artificial intelligence is used in the areas of robotics, natural language systems, and expert systems.
- LISP (for LISt Processor) is the favored language for artificial intelligence applications.

KEY TERMS

artificial intelligence (AI)
assembler
assembly language
batch language
comment statements
compiled language
compilers
documentation
functions
general purpose language
GO TO statement
high-level languages
interactive language
interpreted language
interpreters
keywords
label
line numbers
low-level languages
machine language
main program
maintenance
mnemonics
modules
natural languages
nonprocedural language
object-oriented language
procedural language
procedure
reverse Polish notation (RPN)
robotics
self-documenting language
special purpose language
strongly typed language
structured programming
subroutines
top-down design
turtle
variables
weakly typed language

REVIEW QUESTIONS

1. Explain why we cannot currently use a human language to communicate with a computer except in special circumstances.
2. Name the five ways to classify computer languages.
3. Why are machine and assembly languages called low-level languages? When is an assembly language a useful computer language?
4. How is a compiled language different from an interpreted language? Why does the interpreted language execute more slowly than a compiled language?
5. List the three levels of structure in languages. Why is BASIC often referred to as an unstructured language?
6. Why is FORTRAN often considered a scientific language? Why is COBOL considered a self-documenting language?
7. Explain how BASIC became the language of personal computers. What is the unofficial standard form of BASIC for personal computers?
8. Why is Pascal often the language chosen for teaching programming? What languages are similar to Pascal but are used for commercial or defense purposes?
9. Define *artificial intelligence* and list four areas in which it is applied. What does LISP have to do with AI?
10. What is a natural language system? What is an expert system? Give an application of each.

PICTURE DO YOU WANT TO SHOW?

16

Introduction to BASIC

After discussing programming logic and programming languages, we can now take up the actual programming process in a high-level computer language. This chapter introduces the BASIC computer language and the many tasks it can perform. The chapter has a structured approach to BASIC that demonstrates how to avoid the GO TO statement. This structured approach emphasizes the three building blocks of programs—the processing block, the decision block, and the repetition block. The Microsoft version of BASIC is used, because it is closest to an industry standard.

STUDY OBJECTIVES

After reading this chapter, you should be able to

- Understand the form of a BASIC program.
- Use such system commands as RUN, LIST, AUTO, SAVE, and LOAD.
- Use the INPUT, REM, assignment, and PRINT statements to write the processing block of a program.
- Understand the correct use of the IF–THEN statement to carry out a decision within the BASIC program.
- Understand the correct use of the FOR loop to repeat a set of instructions a definite number of times.

INTRODUCTION

Recall from Chapter 15 that BASIC (Beginner's All-purpose Symbolic Instruction Code) was developed by two Dartmouth professors in 1964 to help their students learn programming. Today, BASIC is the primary language for personal computers, and it is used much more than just in the classroom. Given its popularity and the ease with which this language can be learned, BASIC is the subject of our short course in a programming language. We present only an introduction to programming in BASIC. Books specifically about programming in BASIC contain detailed information not covered here.

Critics contend that BASIC has too many versions to be a standard language. This criticism was certainly true in the early years of programming in BASIC on personal computers. Currently, Microsoft produces a version of BASIC called Microsoft BASIC, which is standard on the IBM PC and compatible machines, the Apple Macintosh, and the Radio Shack (Tandy) computers. The Apple II series of computers uses AppleSoft BASIC, which differs from Microsoft BASIC in some advanced instructions. In this chapter, we discuss Microsoft BASIC in its simplest form, which is not much different from AppleSoft BASIC. Chapter 17 discusses more advanced topics in Microsoft BASIC.

A Structured Approach to BASIC

BASIC is also criticized because it is an unstructured language—that is, a language that involves the use of the GO TO instruction. Microsoft BASIC is not as highly structured as Pascal. However, it does fall into that middle category of languages, in which structured programs *can* be written if the programmer so desires. Therefore, our discussion emphasizes a structured approach to BASIC, avoiding the use of the GO TO statement.

Recall from Chapter 15 that a structured approach to programming uses three types of building blocks to write computer programs—the processing block, the decision block, and the repetition block. In this chapter, we demonstrate how each block contributes to a structured program in BASIC. We discuss the types of statements that fit into each block and write progressively more complex programs throughout the chapter.

A FIRST PROGRAM

Because BASIC is such an easy language to understand and to learn, we can begin by writing a very simple program and then explaining it. This first program is designed to read a student's name and five quiz scores and then to output this same information with appropriate labels. This program is shown in Figure 16-1.

The program in Figure 16-1 has three program statements—one INPUT statement and two PRINT statements. The INPUT statement reads a student's name into a variable called STUDENT$ and his or her scores into the variables SCORE1, SCORE2, and so on. The PRINT statements output the name and scores with labels enclosed in quotation marks. The line numbers before each statement are required for a BASIC program to order the statements in the proper sequence. This program was entered from the keyboard. After each line is entered, the RETURN, ENTER, or ↵ key is pressed to send the

FIGURE 16-1
Program to Input and Output Students' Names and Quiz Scores

```
100 INPUT STUDENT$,SCORE1,SCORE2,SCORE3,SCORE4,SCORE5
200 PRINT "STUDENT'S NAME: ";STUDENT$
300 PRINT "STUDENT'S SCORES: ";SCORE1,SCORE2,SCORE3,SCORE4,SCORE5
```

BASIC AND THE FIRST PERSONAL COMPUTER

Why is BASIC synonymous with personal computers today? It started in the early 1970s, when two Seattle teenagers named Bill Gates and Paul Allen worked for a computer firm. Gates and Allen were among the first hackers who spent almost every waking hour figuring out how mainframe and minicomputer operating systems worked. They had convinced a Seattle computer firm to let them work on the company's PDP-10 minicomputer to solve the company's systems problems. Their success in this project made a name for them.

Two years later, after both men had tried college, they read about the first personal computer—the Altair. The Altair, which used an Intel 8080 chip, was built by a firm called MITS. Gates and Allen called MITS and proposed that they develop a version of BASIC that would run on the Altair personal computer. Because they did not have an Altair computer, Allen used that computer's specifications to develop a simulated Altair on the PDP minicomputer. Using this simulated Altair, the two developed a form of BASIC which they thought would work on the real computer. Less than two months after the original contact with MITS, the software was finished, and Gates and Allen were on a plane to Albuquerque to demonstrate their Altair BASIC for MITS. In true storybook fashion, the BASIC worked the first time it was loaded on the Altair, even though Gates and Allen had never seen one before.

After this success, Gates and Allen formed a company called Microsoft to market their version of BASIC—the rest is history. Today, Microsoft BASIC is an industry standard, and the MS-DOS operating system that Microsoft developed for the IBM PC is also an industry standard for 16-bit computers. Who would believe that the company's founders, Bill Gates and Paul Allen, are barely into their 30s!

SOURCE: Paul Somerson, "In Defense of BASIC," *PC Magazine*, September 1983, p. 331.

Bill Gates and Paul Allen, the founders of Microsoft, are the developers of the first BASIC for personal computers.

statement to the computer—in this book, we refer to that key as the ENTER key.

To execute this program after it is typed into the computer, the user types in the RUN command and presses ENTER. The program then requests a name and quiz scores by displaying a question mark on the screen. If the name and scores are entered as follows

```
? ASHLEY HYATT,75,83,92,88,95
```

then the following output appears on the screen when the ENTER key is pressed after the last score is typed:

```
STUDENT'S NAME: ASHLEY HYATT
STUDENT'S SCORES: 75 83 92 88 95
```

(You can see how this program and the RUN command work by entering the

I swore off computers for about a year and a half—the end of the ninth grade and all of the tenth. I tried to be normal, the best I could.

William Gates, President of Microsoft

(As quoted in *Popular Computing*, October 1984, p. 110.)

program into either a mainframe computer from a terminal or into a personal computer. After the program is entered, use the LIST command to have it listed on the screen. Check with your instructor as to whether the variable names used here will work on your system. If not, substitute two letters or a letter and a digit for each.)

BASIC Program Statements

BASIC is easy to learn because its syntax, or grammar, is so simple. In its simplest form, BASIC does not restrict the placement of its program statements as FORTRAN does nor does it require special punctuation like Pascal. The general form of a BASIC statement is

Line number *instruction*

The line number must be a positive number between 1 and 99999 with no decimal.

A statement or command—such as RUN—is not entered to the computer's CPU until the ENTER key is pressed. Until the ENTER key is pressed, the statement may be changed using the left arrow or BACKSPACE key to delete as much of the statement as needed and typing in the correct statement. After the ENTER key is pressed, the statement may be corrected by entering a new statement with the *same* line number as the incorrect statement. A statement can also be deleted by simply entering DELETE and the line number. For example, the following statement deletes the first statement in the Figure 16-1 program:

```
DELETE 100
```

Line numbers in increasing order determine the position of each statement in the program. In other words, a statement with line number 20 is executed before a statement with line number 300 regardless of when they are entered. Often, program statement line numbers initially increase by 100, so that additional statements are easily entered later if necessary. For example, we can add a heading to the program in Figure 16-1 by entering the following statement:

```
60 PRINT "LISTING OF STUDENT NAMES AND QUIZ SCORES"
```

If we entered the LIST command, the result on the screen would be as follows:

```
60 PRINT "LISTING OF STUDENT NAMES AND QUIZ SCORES"
100 INPUT STUDENT$,SCORE1,SCORE2,SCORE3,SCORE4,SCORE5
200 PRINT "STUDENT'S NAME: ";STUDENT$
300 PRINT "STUDENT'S SCORES: ";SCORE1;SCORE2;SCORE3;SCORE4;SCORE5
```

BASIC orders the statements by line number. BASIC usually has an AUTO command, which automatically numbers the statements as they are entered if the user implements this command before entering the program instructions.

The BASIC Program

A BASIC program of numbered statements is not executed until the RUN command is entered. Each statement is then interpreted and checked for errors. If no errors exist in the statement, then the actual execution occurs. For example, assume that the first statement of the program in Figure 16-1 was entered as follows:

```
100 INPUR STUDENT$,SCORE1,SCORE2,SCORE3,SCORE4,SCORE5
```

The misspelling error would be noted when the RUN command is entered, as shown:

```
RUN
LISTING OF STUDENT NAMES AND QUIZ SCORES
SYNTAX ERROR IN 100
```

Using the LIST command, program statement 100 would be shown and the error corrected.

In BASIC, the entire program does *not* have to be entered before it is executed. The user may enter a section of the program, enter RUN to try it out, and if it executes as expected, enter more of the program. The program in Figure 16-1 is an example of this feature because it contains only the first three statements of a larger program.

System Commands

The RUN, LIST, DELETE, and AUTO commands are examples of system commands. A **system command** results in some action by the BASIC program. Four other important system commands in BASIC are NEW, SAVE, LOAD, and SYSTEM.

The NEW command clears the previous program from memory so a new program can be entered. On the other hand, the SAVE command saves the previous program. The SAVE command combined with a name in quotation marks stores the current BASIC program on disk. For example, the following statement

```
SAVE "FIRSTPGM"
```

stores the current BASIC program on disk under the name FIRSTPGM.

If the user wished to add more to this program at a later time, the LOAD command transfers the program from disk to the CPU. For FIRSTPGM, this command is as follows:

```
LOAD "FIRSTPGM"
```

Finally, if the user wishes to exit from BASIC and return to the operating system, Microsoft BASIC uses the SYSTEM command.

MEMORY CELLS, CONSTANTS, AND VARIABLES

Recall that a *conceptual computer* has an input unit, a processing unit, an output unit, and a secondary storage unit. Within the processing unit, the internal memory unit and the data it contains are extremely important because they are used by the other three units. A programmer can view computer memory as a large number of boxes arranged in a manner similar to post office boxes, or cubbyholes. These storage locations in a computer are called **memory cells**. This concept is shown in Figure 16-2.

Memory Cells

Only one data item can be stored in each memory cell at one time. This concept is similar to writing a number on a card and then placing that card in a cubbyhole that only has room for one card. This card remains in the cubbyhole until replaced by another card.

Nondestructive fetch and **destructive replacement** are important memory cell concepts. The contents of a memory cell can be read and used without being destroyed. However, if the contents are replaced by a new value, then the old value is destroyed. The new value is effectively written

FIGURE 16-2
Computer Memory Cells

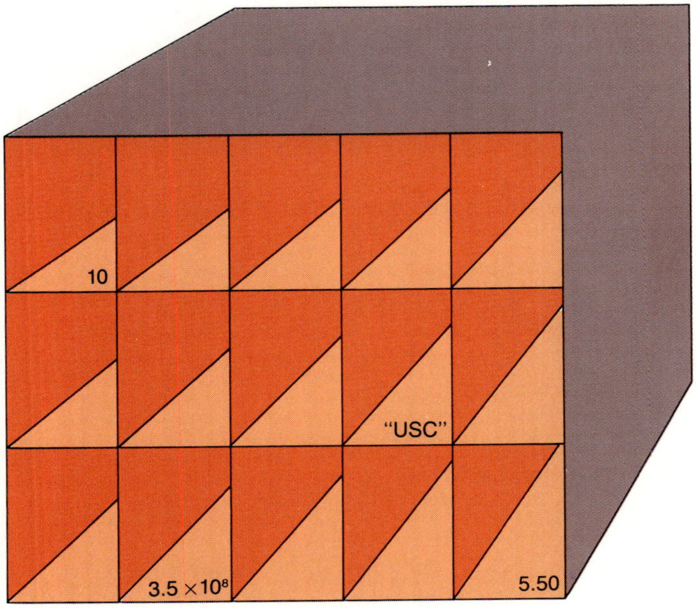

over the old. In other words, the cubbyhole card can be fetched and read and not destroyed. However, the first card must be destroyed before a new card is placed in the cubbyhole. The difference between nondestructive fetch and destructive replacement is illustrated as follows:

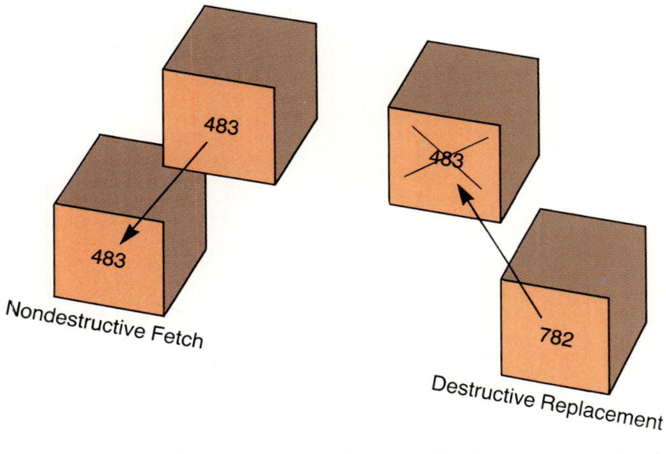

Constants

The data that are placed in memory cells are called **constants**. In the diagram illustrating nondestructive fetch, the constant 483 remains in the first memory cell after being fetched and read. In the example of destructive replacement, the constant 782 is written into the cell, destroying the old constant.

Because a computer is a data manipulator—not just a high-powered adding machine—different types of constants exist for different purposes. The BASIC language has numerical constants and string constants. A **numerical constant** is a positive or negative number such as 1001.045 or −18.5. Three types of numerical constants exist—single precision, double precision, and integer. A single-precision (also called *real*) constant is a decimal number that has up to eight digits. A double-precision constant may contain up to 16 digits and a decimal. An integer constant is any whole number without a decimal in the range −32768 to +32767. As we explain the BASIC language, we will only work with single-precision constants.

A **string constant** is a string of ASCII symbols or characters that are enclosed in quotation marks. For example, a string constant can be "120 HILLTOP RD." A string constant may contain any combination of the letters A–Z, the digits 0–9, and numerous special characters—such as $, #, and &. The example in the preceding sentence contains all three—digits, letters, and a special character (the period).

You should remember that a number stored as a numerical constant is different from the same number stored in string form. Numerical constants can be used in arithmetic operations—addition, subtraction, multiplication, and so on—whereas string constants *cannot* be used in such operations. For example, two numbers stored as string constants cannot be multiplied. String constants primarily provide for the input, output, and manipulation of sets, or *strings,* of characters.

Variables

Because data are stored in memory cells, the computer and the programmer must refer to a particular memory cell to perform a desired operation. The programmer gives memory cells names for identification.

A memory cell in a computer program is a **variable**. The term is derived from the *variability* of the values in the memory cell. A memory cell's location remains the same, but it may contain different values at different times during the execution of the program. For example, assume a memory cell called NUMBER has a value of 10 stored in it, shown as follows:

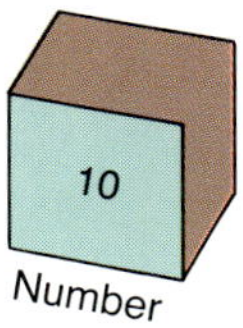

The programmer can change the value stored in NUMBER by using the appropriate BASIC statements and referring to NUMBER by name. Note that the name of the memory cell and its contents are *not* the same. A memory cell called B does *not* contain the symbol "B." Assume the memory cell (variable) called NUMBER begins a program with a value of 10, and that during the program, this value changes to 0, and then to −20. We show these changes schematically as follows:

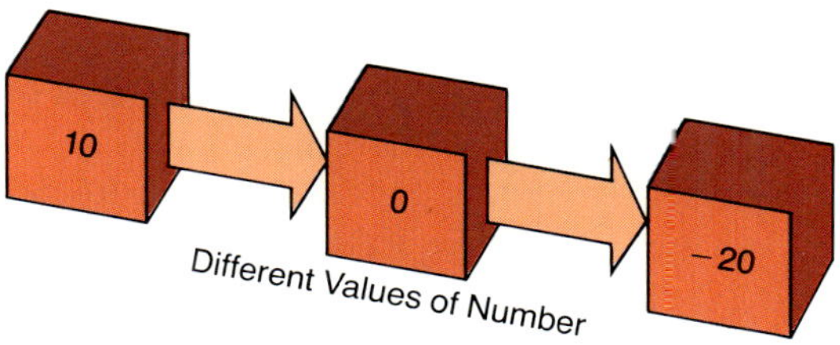

These changes are accomplished through the destructive replacement characteristic of memory cells.

COMPARISONS
BASIC and True BASIC

In 1964, John Kemeny and Thomas Kurtz invented BASIC at Dartmouth College. Today, BASIC is the most widely used computer language in the world, due largely to the inclusion of BASIC with the first personal computer in 1975 and the subsequent explosion of personal computer use. Currently, BASIC is available on all varieties of personal computers, usually included with the computer's operating system at no additional cost.

Although BASIC is popular, most current versions retain many unstructured features and the use of line numbers characteristic of the original BASIC, which was developed for time-sharing applications on mainframe computers. No official version of BASIC has been developed, but several forms of BASIC were patterned after a previous form. This lack of a single, structured version of the language has made the transfer of programs between computers and in educational uses quite difficult. For example, the College Board chose Pascal over BASIC for its advanced college placement exam because a structured form of BASIC did not exist.

In response to the need for a new BASIC, the pair that came up with the original version—Kemeny and Kurtz—have developed a new, highly structured form of BASIC, which they have named True BASIC. This language is very similar to Dartmouth's Structured BASIC and to the ANSI standard version of BASIC. True BASIC is highly structured like Pascal, but it does not require that all variables be declared. It allows, but does not require, line numbers and uses subroutines called out by name rather than by line number. Structured features of True BASIC include the CASE structure, which selects from among numerous alternatives, and the EXIT FOR instruction, which lets the program exit from the middle of the loop without using a GO TO statement. As an example of this last feature, consider the following True BASIC program, which allows a user to guess a random number.

```
! Play Guess My Number
!
LET secret = int(rnd*20 + 1)
PRINT "I have a secret number"
!
FOR try = 1 to 10
      PRINT
      PRINT "Guess my number (1-20)";
      INPUT guess
      IF guess = secret THEN EXIT FOR
      PRINT "That's not it."
      PRINT 10-try;"tries left"
NEXT try
!
IF guess = secret THEN PRINT "That's it!"
END
```

A *variable,* or a *variable name,* in a program refers to a memory cell in the computer. The *value of a variable* in a program is the *current value* in the memory cell. For this reason, we often use the terms *memory cell* and *variable* interchangeably.

Memory cells are *never* empty. The quantity can be zero, a value the programmer or user has placed there, or a value from a previous use of the memory cell. In any program, unless the value in a memory cell is changed from its last use, it retains its previous value. When a series of numbers are summed, the memory cell that is holding the sum must be **initialized** to zero. Otherwise, the sum may begin at some nonzero value.

Variable Types

A direct relationship exists between the type of constant stored in a memory cell and the variable name in a program for that memory cell. Therefore, in

Tom Kurtz and John Kemeny developed the first version of BASIC in 1964 and the most recent version—True BASIC—in 1985.

In this True BASIC program, an exclamation point is used to begin comment statements, and reserved words (see p. 426) are shown in all capital letters. (True BASIC has 20 reserved words, compared with almost 160 in Microsoft BASIC.) A secret number is randomly selected at the beginning of the program, and a FOR loop gives the user 10 tries to guess the answer. If the answer is found, the EXIT FOR instruction transfers control to the line after the FOR loop, where an IF statement checks to determine if the user has guessed the correct answer.

In addition to its structured capabilities, True BASIC has highly developed graphics capabilities that are transferable between machines. It also allows a subroutine to call itself to perform an operation numerous times.

With these advantages, how True BASIC will fare in competition with currently available versions of BASIC is unknown. Current versions are usually included with a personal computer, but True BASIC must be purchased separately from the computer and the operating system. On the other hand, some education systems are beginning to adopt True BASIC. Students exposed to it as a beginning language may be willing to pay the extra amount to have this language on their personal computers. It is definitely a language to keep your eye on in the future!

SOURCE: Andrew Fluegelman, "In Quest of True BASIC," *PC Magazine*, November 1984, pp. 120–28; George Stewart, "True BASIC," *Popular Computing*, November 1984, pp. 95–107. Program reprinted with permission from the November 1984 issue of *Popular Computing* magazine. Copyright © by McGraw-Hill, Inc., New York 10020. All rights reserved.

our discussion of numerical or string variable types, remember that numerical or string constants are stored in the memory cell.

Variable names in BASIC are combinations of the letters A–Z and the digits 0–9. No special characters other than a period (.) are allowed in variable names, which must *always* start with a letter. In some forms of BASIC, only two characters are recognized as variable names, whereas other versions use up to 40 characters in a name. A user may designate longer variable names than the maximum, *but* the computer recognizes only the maximum number of letters and digits. For example, in versions of BASIC that only use two letters and symbols, the name LONG is recognized as LO. LONG and LOPE would be the same variable in this situation. In this discussion, we use the 40-character variable names accepted by Microsoft BASIC, which runs on many personal computers. You may have to modify the variable names we use in this chapter to fit your system.

Names of numerical variables must be differentiated from string variables to ensure that the correct type of constant is stored. Therefore, a dollar sign ($) must be added to the end of each string variable name. For example, STUDENT$ is a string variable, but NUMBER is a numerical variable. If necessary, numerical variables can be further differentiated by adding the percent sign (%) to a variable that represents an integer constant, an exclamation point (!) to variables that represent single-precision constants, and a pound sign (#) to variables that represent double-precision constants. A variable name with no symbol at the end is considered single precision. We consider only this type of numerical variable here.

Often, variable names indicate the quantity that is represented. This practice is easy if the version of BASIC in use allows variable names with up to 40 characters. On the other hand, with a version of BASIC that allows only two characters in a name, a little more thought to variable names is necessary. For example, GROSSPAY would be a descriptive variable name to represent gross pay in Microsoft BASIC, but GP would be a good choice of a two-letter variable name. Unfortunately, when only two characters are allowed per variable name, most meaningful names are used very quickly. Even in a short program, the user may need to use any two available characters.

A variable name may not be one of almost 160 BASIC **reserved words**, which are used to give commands to the computer. We have already seen some examples of reserved words—RUN, LIST, PRINT, and INPUT. We could not use NAME$ as a variable for the student's name in Figure 16-1 because NAME is a reserved word. A syntax error in a statement that is apparently correct may be the use of a reserved word. A variable name that begins with a reserved word or that contains a reserved word is valid. For example, STUDENTNAME$ would be a valid variable name.

Now that we know what a simple BASIC program looks like and how variable names are chosen, we can examine how more complex programs are written.

THE PROCESSING BLOCK

Programs can be written as a combination of processing blocks, decision blocks, and repetition blocks. Therefore, to write a BASIC program, we must see how BASIC instructions can build each block. The first block we consider is the **processing block**, which can represent the input statements that allow data entry, assignment statements that allow calculations with the data, and output statements that display the results on the screen or print them.

The INPUT Statement

The INPUT statement in BASIC allows the user to enter data from the keyboard. If values or strings are entered, then one program can execute multiple runs using different data each time without a change in program logic. Such a flexible program is more useful than one with program instructions that must change when the data change. (A method of placing data in the program itself is discussed in Chapter 17.)

The form of the INPUT statement is

Line number INPUT *variable list*

where *variable list* is a list of variable names separated by commas. For example, the INPUT statement in Figure 16-1,

```
100 INPUT STUDENT$,SCORE1,SCORE2,SCORE3,SCORE4,SCORE5
```

shows that one string constant and five numerical constants will be entered from the keyboard in that order.

When BASIC is ready for input from the keyboard, a question mark appears on the screen, with the cursor to the right of it. Data are typed in at this point. Several data items placed on one line must be separated by commas. If the user does not place all data on one line, BASIC displays two question marks to inform the user that more data are expected. Finally, if unnecessary data are entered, BASIC displays a message that the additional data have been ignored.

For the example INPUT statement, the data entry appears as follows

```
? ASHLEY HYATT,75,83,92,88,95
```

where STUDENT$ equals ASHLEY HYATT, SCORE1 equals 75, SCORE2 equals 83, and so on. The string constant ASHLEY HYATT can also be entered as data enclosed in quotation marks. For this reason, the following entry would also be correct:

```
? "ASHLEY HYATT",75,83,92,88,95
```

If the *wrong* type of data is entered, BASIC asks that the data be reentered.

The INPUT statement can be made more "user-friendly" by the addition of the user prompt and the semicolon (;). The **user prompt** is a string constant that is included in the INPUT statement to prompt the user to enter the needed data. For example, the following statement prompts the user to enter a student's name and five quiz scores:

```
100 INPUT "ENTER NAME AND SCORES: ";STUDENT$,SCORE1,SCORE2,SCORE3
SCORE4,SCORE5
```

Note that the new statement 100 extends beyond one line. Because BASIC allows up to 225 characters per statement, it is *not* necessary for the user to select the breakpoint of the line. BASIC automatically wraps the statement around to the next line. The input to this statement would be as follows:

```
ENTER NAME AND SCORES: ? ASHLEY HYATT,75,83,92,88,95
```

Assignment Statements

Two basic methods exist for giving a memory cell a value. We have just considered the first method, in which the value may be *input* into the cell. Second, the value may be *assigned* in the program via an assignment statement. The **assignment statement** is used when the programmer wishes to give a variable one initial value that will be used throughout the program, or when a variable is assigned a new value as the result of a computation or operation. For example, the following statement assigns the name "CHRIS PATRICK" to the variable STUDENT$:

```
110 STUDENT$ = "CHRIS PATRICK"
```

The assignment statement has the following three parts:

1. The variable that is assigned the value.
2. An equals sign (=).
3. The variable or expression whose value is assigned to the variable in 1.

The general form of the assignment statement is as follows:

Line number   LET *variable* = *Variable or expression*

The variable that is assigned a value is to the left of the equals sign, and the variable or expression appears on the right. This important rule must be followed in the assignment statement. (The word LET is optional in BASIC assignment statements and is *not* used in this discussion.)

The term *expression,* common in algebra, is defined as a combination of two or more variables and/or one or more constants and operators. We have already encountered variables and constants, but operators are new. An **operator** combines two variables or constants. In our discussion, we consider only arithmetic operators, which appear in Table 16-1.

We construct arithmetic expressions by combining variables, constants, and arithmetic operators. The following expressions are valid:

X + 2. − Z

3*M − L^2

113.

Note that the last expression contains only one constant. This expression is valid according to our definition and is very useful in assignment statements.

Table 16-1 ARITHMETIC OPERATORS

Operator	*Function*	*Example*	*Result*
^	Raise to a power	L^2	L raised to the second power
*	Multiplication	M*3	M multiplied by 3
/	Division	R/5.	R divided by 5.
+	Addition	X + Y	X added to Y
−	Subtraction	A − 10	10 subtracted from A

In what order are operators used in BASIC? For example, consider the following expression:

$$F + V*D + S*D\^{}2$$

In this or any expression in BASIC, the **hierarchy of operations** controls the order in which operations are performed. The hierarchy of operations in BASIC is

1. Expressions in parentheses
2. Raising a number to a power
3. Multiplication or division
4. Addition or subtraction

No parentheses appear in our example, so the first operation performed is raising D to the second power. Then, V is multiplied by D, S is multiplied by D^2, and F is added to the two products. Parentheses can have a dramatic effect on an expression. For example, consider the same expression with parentheses around F + V:

$$(F + V)*D + S*D\^{}2$$

Now, F and V are summed *before* being multiplied by D, which yields a different result from the first expression.

The only operation for string variables and constants is combining two strings into one, which is performed using the plus sign (+). This operation adds the second string variable or constant to the end of the first. For example, the result of the expression "GO" + "DOGS" is "GO DOGS". No other operators—multiplication, division, subtraction, or raising to a power—has any meaning in operations with strings.

Table 16-2 contains examples of valid assignment instructions and their results. In the last example, the value in a memory cell (K) is increased by one, and this new value replaces the previous value in the memory cell. Remember this key concept: The value of a memory cell on the right-hand

Table 16-2 EXAMPLES OF VALID ASSIGNMENT INSTRUCTIONS

Assignment Instruction	*Result*
`X = Y`	Current value of Y is placed in X.
`I = J + K`	Current values of J and K are summed and placed in I.
`Q = R^2`	Current value of R is squared and placed in Q.
`KT = Ø`	KT is set equal to 0.
`N$ = "NEW YORK"`	The string variable N$ is set equal to "NEW YORK".
`T$ = N$ + " CITY"`	Stores "NEW YORK CITY" in the string variable T$.
`K = K + 1`	Old value of K is increased by one to form a new value of K.

side of the equals sign is the current value of that memory cell, and the value on the left-hand side of the equals sign is the new value of the memory cell. The computer makes any needed calculations on the right-hand side of the equals sign using current values. That resulting value is placed in the memory cell on the left-hand side of the equals sign. This procedure does not confuse the old and new values of the same memory cell.

One major syntax error often occurs in the use of assignment statements: *an expression may never appear on the left-hand side of the equals sign.*

The following assignment statement is *invalid:*

$$X + Y = Z + Q$$

The expression of two variables and an operator on the left-hand side of the equals sign violates the rule.

In our quiz score averaging program, we could find the average of those five scores simply by adding an assignment statement to the program. This statement would be as follows:

```
400 AVERAGE = (SCORE1+SCORE2+SCORE3+SCORE4+SCORE5)/5
```

The parentheses force the program to sum the quiz scores *first* and then divide the sum by five. If the parentheses are deleted, then only the *last* quiz score—SCORE5—is divided by five, because division is performed before addition.

REMark Statements

A program's objective and logic are usually clear to the programmer, but they may not be clear to other users. To explain a program and its logic to other users, programmers use the **remark**. A remark can appear in a program in one of two ways. First, a separate remark statement that begins with REM is a remark for documentation purposes only and is not part of the program. This type of remark can be used at the beginning of a program to explain the program's purpose, or within the program to separate the program's parts. Second, a remark can be added at the end of a statement, set off by an *apostrophe* ('). The after-statement remark is used to explain that statement's logic. Examples of both types of remarks in the quiz score averaging program are shown below:

```
50 REM THIS PROGRAM INPUTS QUIZ SCORES AND FINDS THE AVERAGE SCORE
 .
 .
 .
400 AVERAGE = (SCORE1+SCORE2+SCORE3+SCORE4+SCORE5)/5 'FIND THE
AVERAGE SCORE
```

The PRINT Statement

Once the user obtains the desired results from the program, he or she needs those results as output. This output is generated by the PRINT statement.

Like the INPUT statement, the PRINT statement has two parts—the key-

```
50 REM THIS PROGRAM INPUTS QUIZ SCORES AND FINDS THE AVERAGE SCORE
60 PRINT "LISTING OF STUDENT NAMES AND QUIZ SCORES"
100 INPUT "ENTER NAME AND SCORES: ";STUDENT$,SCORE1,SCORE2,SCORE3,
SCORE4,SCORE5
200 PRINT "STUDENT'S NAME: ";STUDENT$
300 PRINT "STUDENT'S SCORES: ";SCORE1;SCORE2;SCORE3;SCORE4;SCORE5
400 AVERAGE = (SCORE1+SCORE2+SCORE3+SCORE4+SCORE5)/5 'FIND THE
AVERAGE SCORE
500 PRINT "STUDENT'S AVERAGE SCORE IS: ";AVERAGE
```

FIGURE 16-3
Quiz Score Averaging Program

word PRINT and a list of variables and/or constants separated by commas or semicolons. The general form of the PRINT statement is as follows:

Line number PRINT *variable and/or constant list*

The following PRINT statement example also appears in the program in Figure 16-1

```
200 PRINT "STUDENT'S NAME: ";STUDENT$
```

where the variable STUDENT$ is output with the string constant "STUDENT'S NAME: " as a label.

In the PRINT statement, a **label** is any string constant enclosed in a pair of quotation marks. The label, which is like the user prompt in the INPUT statement, is printed exactly as shown in the program. In the quiz score averaging program, a label in the PRINT statement describes the student's name and quiz scores. If output also includes the student's average with a label, the complete program would look like the one in Figure 16-3. If this program is executed with the following data as

```
ENTER NAME AND SCORES:? ASHLEY HYATT,75,83,92,88,95
```

the program output is as follows:

```
LISTING OF STUDENT NAMES AND QUIZ SCORES
STUDENT'S NAME: ASHLEY HYATT
STUDENT'S SCORES: 75 83 92 88 95
STUDENT'S AVERAGE SCORE IS: 86.6
```

The exact spacing between labels or variables is controlled by BASIC **PRINT zones**, each of which is 14 spaces wide. When variables or string constants are separated by *commas,* then each new variable or string constant is placed at the beginning of a new zone. (Zones begin in columns 1, 15, 29, 43, and 57.) On the other hand, when variables or constants are separated by *semicolons,* then printing continues with only one or two intervening spaces. If a PRINT statement ends with a semicolon, then new output begins on the same line. As an example of this difference in printing consider the following PRINT statement from Figure 16-3 that uses commas to separate data items instead of semicolons:

```
300 PRINT "STUDENT'S SCORES: ",SCORE1,SCORE2,SCORE3,SCORE4,SCORE5
```

If the program in Figure 16-3 is executed with the same data and with the new line 300, the output would appear as follows:

```
LISTING OF STUDENT NAMES AND QUIZ SCORES
STUDENT'S NAME: ASHLEY HYATT
STUDENT'S SCORES:            75              83              92
 88           95
STUDENT'S AVERAGE SCORE IS: 86.6
```

STOP and END Statements

STOP and END statements are used to terminate a program at a point other than after all instructions have been executed. If either statement is encountered, program execution terminates. The difference between the two statements lies in the message displayed by BASIC when they are executed. Because the END statement is considered the "normal" end of execution by BASIC, an OK is displayed when this statement is encountered. On the other hand, a STOP statement results in a "BREAK IN LINE nnnnn" message which indicates that the program has terminated abnormally. The STOP statement usually indicates that a logic error occurred and that the programmer wanted execution to terminate at this point.

THE DECISION BLOCK

The second block with which we can construct a structured program in BASIC is the decision block. A **decision block** chooses between alternative program sections based on whether a condition is true or false. Without the decision block, the program could never perform different instructions under different conditions. In our quiz score averaging program, if we want to determine whether a computed quiz average is less than 60, we use a decision block. If the average score is less than 60, a message that the student is failing can be displayed. The flowchart for this decision is shown in Figure 16-4.

The quiz score decision is a **one-alternative decision**. If the condition is true, then a message is displayed, but if the condition is false, then no special action is taken. On the other hand, if one alternative is taken for a true condition and another for a false condition, then a **two-alternative decision** results. (We discuss two-alternative decisions in Chapter 17.)

The one-alternative decision block is implemented in BASIC by the IF–THEN statement. The form of the IF–THEN statement is as follows:

Line number IF *condition* THEN *instruction for true condition*

The following example of this type of statement checks if a student's average is less than 60.

```
450 IF AVERAGE < 60 THEN PRINT "STUDENT IS FAILING"
```

The condition part of the IF–THEN statement compares two numeric variables, expressions, or constants, or two string variables, expressions, or constants. The part of the statement *after* the THEN is the instruction for the true condition, which is executed. The instruction may be only a line number, to which control is transferred. If the condition is false, control is transferred immediately to the next statement in the program with no action being taken.

The comparison of the variables or constants is performed through a **relational operator**. The six relational operators and their meanings for nu-

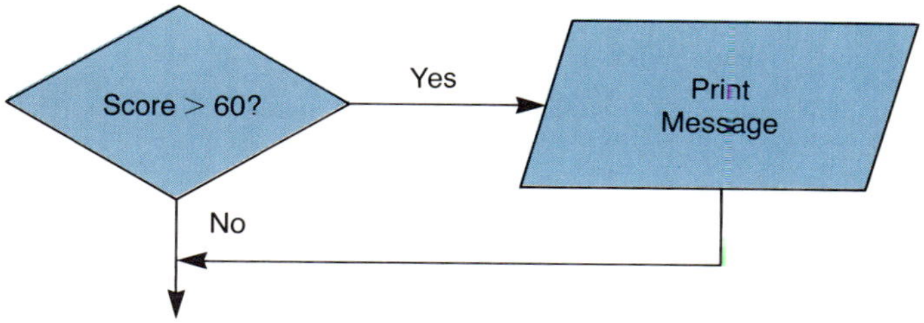

FIGURE 16-4
Quiz Score Decision

meric and string variables are shown in Table 16-3. Examples of relational operators that could form the conditional part of an IF–THEN statement are shown in Table 16-4.

The comparison of numeric variables or constants is easy to understand, but the comparison of string variables or constants depends on the ASCII ordering of symbols. If the string variables or constants are single symbols like B or &, then the comparison simply determines which symbol comes first in the ASCII ordering. (See the Appendix at the end of this book for the ASCII ordering.) If the string variables or constants have two or more symbols, then a symbol-by-symbol comparison occurs, similar to alphabetizing words. For example, APPLE would precede APTITUDE because P comes before T in the ASCII ordering. If all symbols are the same, then the two string variables or constants are the same.

Assume the following statement is added to the BASIC program shown in Figure 16-3:

```
450 IF AVERAGE < 60 THEN PRINT "STUDENT IS FAILING"
```

Table 16-3 RELATIONAL OPERATORS AND MEANINGS

Relational Operator	*Numeric Meaning*	*String Meaning*
<	Less than	Precedes
>	Greater than	Follows
=	Equals	Is the same as
< > or ><	Not equal	Different
= < or <=	Less than or equal to	Precedes or is the same as
= > or >=	Greater than or equal to	Follows or is the same as

Table 16-4 EXAMPLES OF USING RELATIONAL OPERATORS

Condition	*Meaning*
`A < B`	Is variable A less than variable B?
`K >= 100`	Is variable K greater than or equal to 100?
`XX = 2.5`	Is variable XX equal to 2.5?
`Q$ > "D"`	Does string variable Q$ follow the letter D?
`"AA" <= R$`	Is the string constant AA before or the same as the string variable RS?

```
50 REM THIS PROGRAM INPUTS QUIZ SCORES AND FINDS THE AVERAGE SCORE
60 PRINT "LISTING OF STUDENT NAMES AND QUIZ SCORES"
100 INPUT "ENTER NAME AND SCORES: ";STUDENT$,SCORE1,SCORE2,SCORE3,
SCORE4,SCORE5
200 PRINT "STUDENT'S NAME: ";STUDENT$
300 PRINT "STUDENT'S SCORES: ";SCORE1;SCORE2;SCORE3;SCORE4;SCORE5
400 AVERAGE = (SCORE1+SCORE2+SCORE3+SCORE4+SCORE5)/5 'FIND THE
AVERAGE SCORE
450 IF AVERAGE < 60 THEN PRINT "STUDENT IS FAILING"
500 PRINT "STUDENT'S AVERAGE SCORE IS: ";AVERAGE
```

FIGURE 16-5
Quiz Score Averaging Program with Decision Block

where AVERAGE is the variable that stores the average quiz score. The program in Figure 16-5 results. We now enter data on student George Burdell, whose quiz scores are 57, 60, 55, 63, and 60. The program yields the following output:

```
LISTING OF STUDENT NAMES AND QUIZ SCORES
STUDENT'S NAME: GEORGE BURDELL
STUDENT'S SCORES: 57  60  55  63  60
STUDENT IS FAILING
STUDENT'S AVERAGE SCORE IS: 59
```

In BASIC, multiple instructions can be combined in one statement. The additional instructions, separated by the colon (:), are executed in the order in which they occur. For example, the following IF–THEN statement checks whether the variable XX is less than 25. If XX is less than 25, then XX is increased by 20 *and* output by a PRINT instruction after the assignment instruction. Control is then transferred to the next statement. If XX is *not* less than 25, control immediately goes to the next statement.

```
100 IF XX < 25 THEN XX = XX + 20: PRINT "XX = "; XX
```

Only instructions in the *same* program statement are affected by the IF–THEN statement. Therefore, placing multiple instructions on the same line using the colon is a very useful facility in BASIC.

THE REPETITION BLOCK

The third block that can be used to make up a structured program is the **repetition block**, which is equivalent to the loop in a flowchart. It also corresponds to the "While . . . repeat" or "Repeat the following until . . . " statements in pseudocode. In any case, the repetition block causes an action to be repeated some number of times. Recall from our discussion of loops in Chapter 14 that all loops have the following three parts:

1. A loop termination decision
2. A body
3. A transfer back to the beginning of the loop

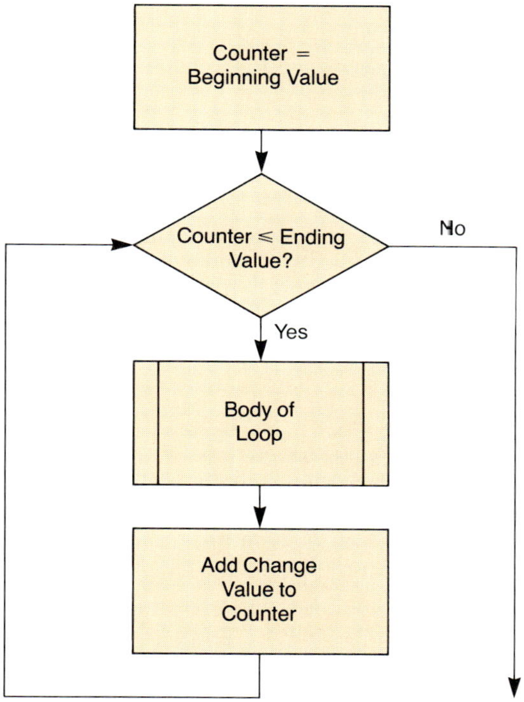

FIGURE 16-6
FOR Loop Flowchart

Two types of loops occur in BASIC—the FOR loop and the WHILE loop We consider the FOR loop here and the WHILE loop in Chapter 17.

The FOR Loop

A common programming situation involves a loop that is repeated a specified number of times. The **FOR loop** has a **counter** that controls the termination of the loop. In a flowchart, this type of loop uses a *counter variable* to count the number of times the loop repeats. The counter is increased or decreased by adding or subtracting a value each time through the loop, as shown in Figure 16-6.

Because the loop termination decision in Figure 16-6 comes before the body of the loop, it is a pre-test loop. An example of the FOR loop in BASIC that sums the whole numbers from one to ten is shown in Figure 16-7. Note that the body of the FOR loop is indented; this helps a reader understand what is being repeated. The output for this program is as follows:

```
SUM IS: 55
```

The general form of the FOR loop appears on page 436.

```
100 SUM = 0
200 FOR I = 1 TO 10 STEP 1
300  SUM = SUM + I
400 NEXT I
500 PRINT "SUM IS: "; SUM
```

FIGURE 16-7
Example of FOR Loop

BASIC is really the only language that lends itself to change by program users who aren't also program developers.

Peter Norton, developer of the Norton Utilities software package

(As quoted in "PC Languages: The Living and the Dead," *PC Magazine,* September 1983, pp. 99–101.)

Line number FOR *variable* = *begin* TO *end* STEP *change*
body of loop
Line number NEXT *variable*

where variable = the loop's counter variable
begin = the variable's beginning value
end = the variable's ending value
change = the amount the counter variable changes each time through the loop. (If the STEP part of the statement is deleted, the change value is assumed to be one.)
NEXT = the end of the FOR loop

Figure 16-8 points out the parts of the FOR loop. In a FOR loop, the FOR statement adds the change value to the current value of the variable. This new value is compared with the ending value to determine if the loop should be terminated. The NEXT statement transfers control back to the FOR statement after the body of the loop is executed. If the loop is terminated, control is transferred to the statement in the program that follows the NEXT statement.

Note that the STEP part of our FOR loop example equals one. If the change value is one, it need not be stated. We showed it here for purposes of demonstration. The program to count backwards from 10 to 1 and output the values would be

```
100 FOR I = 10 TO 1 STEP -1
200   PRINT I;
300 NEXT I
```

and the program's output would be as follows:

```
10 9 8 7 6 5 4 3 2 1
```

(Note that the numbers are all on one line with only one space between each value. This spacing occurs because a semicolon appears after the PRINT statement.) The STEP part of the statement is necessary in this case to have the loop count backwards. Without the STEP part, the loop would not execute. For example, if we changed line number 100 in the above FOR loop to

```
100 FOR I = 10 TO 5
```

the program would generate no output. The loop terminates immediately because the beginning value, 10, is greater than the ending value, 5. The loop does not repeat at all in this case.

We can now add a FOR loop to our original quiz score averaging program to input and display data on multiple students and to compute an average for

FIGURE 16-8
Parts of the FOR Loop

```
100 SUM = 0
200 FOR I = 1 TO 10 STEP 1      (I = variable, 1 = begin, 10 = end, and STEP 1 = change)
300   SUM = SUM + I        (body of loop)
400 NEXT I      (NEXT statement)
500 PRINT "SUM IS: "; SUM
```

A GUIDE TO DEBUGGING

In the process of writing computer programs to solve problems, the debugging stage is often the most frustrating step. This stage occurs after the program is entered into the computer and checked with test data. Even when a program is carefully planned using pseudocode and flowcharts and then carefully coded in a computer language, bugs can slip into the program. Many professional programmers have developed procedures that help make the debugging stage less time-consuming and frustrating. Some of these procedures are as follows:

Keep a journal. By recording events that occur during the program testing process in a journal, the programmer can link together seemingly unrelated events or record solutions to problems. Even if the journal entries do not immediately help the programmer, they may help at some later date.

Keep a run log. By tracking all problems that occur in program development, a programmer can look back to see if one problem occurred more than once. If the problem is a recurring one, then the run log can help the programmer correlate the problem.

Record dates and times. By entering the date and time of an event or output, a programmer can confirm a sequence of events.

Keep time. Often, a programmer is so involved in the debugging process that he or she loses track of time. If too much time is used to debug a program, the programmer may need to rethink the approach to the problem.

File results. By filing output and listings, a programmer can prepare in advance to solve problems.

Learn from other people. By watching and listening to other programmers, a programmer can learn better programming habits and techniques.

SOURCE: Gerald M. Weinberg, "Debugging Bad Habits," *PC Magazine*, June 12, 1984, pp. 431–33.

each student. We start with the statements in Figure 16-5 and simply add the necessary statements to input the number of students, execute the FOR loop, and compute a class average. The resulting program is shown in Figure 16-9. Because the instructor uses the output from this program to assign final grades, a printed copy of the output is needed. Therefore, we replace the PRINT statement with the LPRINT statement, which causes output to go to the printer rather than to the screen. Similarly, the LLIST statement causes a program to be listed by the printer rather than on the screen.

FIGURE 16-9
Multiple Student Quiz Score Averaging Program

```
50 REM THIS PROGRAM INPUTS QUIZ SCORES AND FINDS THE AVERAGE SCORE
60 LPRINT "LISTING OF STUDENT NAMES AND QUIZ SCORES"
70 INPUT "ENTER THE NUMBER OF STUDENTS IN CLASS: ";NUMBER
80 CLASSTOTAL = 0 'INITIALIZE CLASS TOTAL TO ZERO
90 FOR I = 1 TO NUMBER 'REPEAT THE FOLLOWING FOR EACH STUDENT
100    INPUT "ENTER NAME AND SCORES: ";STUDENT$,SCORE1,SCORE2,SCORE3,
SCORE4,SCORE5
200    LPRINT "STUDENT'S NAME: ";STUDENT$
300    LPRINT "STUDENT'S SCORES: ";SCORE1,SCORE2,SCORE3,SCORE4,SCORE5
400    AVERAGE = (SCORE1+SCORE2+SCORE3+SCORE4+SCORE5)/5 'FIND THE
AVERAGE SCORE
450    IF AVERAGE < 60 THEN LPRINT "STUDENT IS FAILING"
500    LPRINT "STUDENT'S AVERAGE SCORE IS: ";AVERAGE
700    CLASSTOTAL = CLASSTOTAL + AVERAGE 'ADD STUDENT AVERAGE
TO CLASS TOTAL
800 NEXT I
900 CLASSAVERAGE = CLASSTOTAL/NUMBER 'COMPUTE CLASS AVERAGE
1000 LPRINT "CLASS AVERAGE IS: ";CLASSAVERAGE
```

BASIC programs can be used to generate computer art.

Assume we execute this program using three students' quiz scores. The input would be as follows:

```
ENTER THE NUMBER OF STUDENTS IN CLASS:? 3
ENTER NAME AND SCORES:? SAM JONES,42,62,65,60,55
ENTER NAME AND SCORES:? CATHY SMITH,70,80,63,67,75
ENTER NAME AND SCORES:? BEN SIBLEY,65,83,87,82,83
```

The printed output from this program is shown in Figure 16-10.

A Look Ahead

This chapter has presented the fundamental building blocks needed to write computer programs in the BASIC language. In Chapter 17, this discussion is continued, as we take up the more advanced topics in BASIC that are needed to write complex programs.

```
LISTING OF STUDENT NAMES AND QUIZ SCORES
STUDENT'S NAME: SAM JONES
STUDENT'S SCORES: 42  62  65  60  55
STUDENT IS FAILING
STUDENT'S AVERAGE SCORE IS:  56.8
STUDENT'S NAME: CATHY SMITH
STUDENT'S SCORES: 70  80  63  67  75
STUDENT'S AVERAGE SCORE IS:  71
STUDENT'S NAME: BEN SIBLEY
STUDENT'S SCORES: 65  83  87  82  83
STUDENT'S AVERAGE SCORE IS:  80
CLASS AVERAGE IS:  69.26667
```

FIGURE 16-10
Output from Multiple Student Quiz Score Averaging Program

REVIEW OF KEY POINTS

- Because of its simple syntax and interactive nature, BASIC is an easy computer language to learn.
- Structured programs may be written in BASIC.
- Data and information are stored in memory cells, or variables, which are named by the user.
- Two types of variables exist in BASIC—numerical and string.
- A program in BASIC has numbered statements that contain instructions.
- The processing block in BASIC has input, output, and assignment statements.
- Expressions in BASIC contain variables, constants, and operators.
- The arithmetic operators in BASIC are addition (+), subtraction (−), division (/), multiplication (∗), and raising to a power (^).
- The hierarchy of operations defines the order in which the arithmetic operators are evaluated.
- String variables and constants can be combined using the plus sign (+).
- The decision block for the one-alternative decision uses an IF–THEN statement.
- The repetition block for counting uses a FOR loop.

KEY TERMS

assignment statement
constants
counter
decision block
destructive replacement
FOR loop
hierarchy of operations
initialized
label
memory cells
nondestructive fetch
numerical constant
one-alternative decision
operator
PRINT zones
processing block
relational operator
remark
repetition block
reserved words
string constant
system command
two-alternative decision
user prompt
variable

REVIEW QUESTIONS

1. Why do we say that BASIC has a simple syntax? What version of BASIC is used in this book?
2. How is a constant different from a variable? What are the four types of constants in BASIC?
3. What are the arithmetic operators in BASIC? Give the hierarchy of operations.
4. How are relational operators related to the IF–THEN statement?
5. Write a program to input the dimensions of a room and to compute and output the square yards of carpet needed to cover the floor.
6. Write a program to input the dimensions of a room and the number and size of the windows and doors in the room, and to compute and output the square feet of wallpaper needed to cover the walls (assume 8-foot ceilings).
7. Write a program to input a taxpayer's name, number of dependents, and age. If the taxpayer is older than 65, increase the number of dependents by one. Output the name, age, and revised number of dependents.
8. Write a program to compute and output the sum of the odd numbers from 1 to 100.
9. Write a program to input and sum students' scores on 10 quizzes. Use this sum to find and output the average score.

Chapter 16 was an introductory discussion of the BASIC language, covering such topics as types of constants and variables, the processing block, the decision block, and the repetition block. This chapter continues that discussion with advanced topics, including the IF–THEN–ELSE statement, the WHILE loop, nested FOR loops, arrays, subroutines and functions, and files.

17

More BASIC

STUDY OBJECTIVES

After reading this chapter, you should be able to

- Use the IF–THEN–ELSE statement to execute one of two alternatives for a decision.
- Work with WHILE loops to repeat a series of statements.
- Use the INPUT loop to input an unknown number of data items.
- Use nested FOR loops to execute a loop within a loop.
- Use arrays to work with lists of numbers or strings.
- Use subroutines and functions to break a complex program into smaller parts.
- Manipulate strings of data using functions.
- Work with files to store data.
- Write sophisticated BASIC programs and understand BASIC programs written by other users.

LOOPS AND DECISIONS

In Chapter 16, we discussed how the IF–THEN statement is used in the decision block and how the FOR loop is used to repeat one or more BASIC statements. This section continues that discussion of decisions and loops with coverage of the IF–THEN–ELSE statement, the WHILE loop, and nested FOR loops. The IF–THEN–ELSE statement is used to make two-alternative decisions, and the WHILE loop implements loops using a termination decision other than the condition of a counter. Nested FOR loops are used to program loops within loops.

Our discussion of the IF–THEN–ELSE statement and WHILE loop uses the second programming example from Chapter 14—computing gross and net pay based on an employee's wage rate, hours worked, and deductions. We first use the IF–THEN–ELSE statement to make this computation for one employee and then use a special form of the WHILE loop—the INPUT loop—to repeat the computation for many employees.

IF–THEN–ELSE Statement

The calculation of an employee's gross pay is a two-alternative decision—that is, calculations must be made for both a true and a false alternative. In the calculation of gross pay, if the hours worked are less than or equal to 40 hours, the employee's gross pay equals the number of hours worked multiplied by his or her wage rate. On the other hand, if the hours worked are greater than 40 hours, the employee is paid his or her regular wage rate for the first 40 hours and $1\frac{1}{2}$ times the regular wage rate multiplied by the number of hours over 40. The flowchart for this type of decision is shown in Figure 17-1.

In BASIC, the two-alternative decision is handled through the **IF–THEN–ELSE statement**, which has the following form:

Line number IF *condition* THEN *true instruction* ELSE *false instruction*

where the *condition* has the same form as the IF–THEN statement condition. If this condition is true, then the instruction after the THEN is executed and control passes to the next statement. However, if the condition is false, then the instruction after the ELSE is executed and control passes to the next statement. For the gross pay calculation example, the appropriate INPUT, IF–THEN–ELSE, REM, and PRINT statements are shown in Figure 17-2.

FIGURE 17-1
Two-Alternative Flowchart

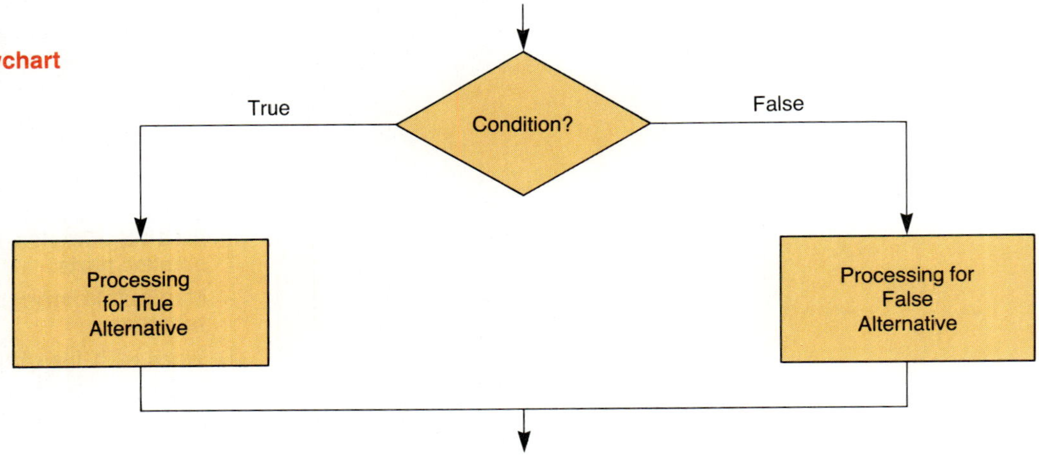

```
200 INPUT "ENTER NAME, WAGE RATE, AND HOURS WORKED: ";EMPLOYEE$,WAGE,
HOURS
400 IF HOURS <= 40 THEN GROSSPAY = HOURS*WAGE ELSE GROSSPAY =
40*WAGE + (HOURS - 40)*1.5*WAGE
500 REM IF HOURS <= 40 USE REGULAR TIME; OTHERWISE USE OVERTIME
700 PRINT "EMPLOYEE NAME IS: ";EMPLOYEE$:PRINT "GROSS PAY IS:$
";GROSSPAY
```

FIGURE 17-2
Gross Pay Calculation Program Using the IF–THEN–ELSE Statement

Note that line 400, which implements the IF–THEN–ELSE statement to determine gross pay, carries over to a second line. Because both the IF–THEN and IF–THEN–ELSE instructions *only* affect the statements in which they appear, multiple lines may be needed to implement both the true and false alternatives. This causes no problem because a program statement can have up to 255 characters. Statement 700 combines multiple instructions using the colon. By using up to 255 characters in a statement and combining instructions with the colon, a user can combine long sets of instructions into one statement. No colon is needed between the THEN instruction and the ELSE because both are part of the same IF–THEN–ELSE statement.

Adding to Figure 17-2 the statements necessary to compute net pay by subtracting deductions from gross pay gives us the program shown in Figure 17-3. If the program in Figure 17-3 is executed, the input is as follows:

```
ENTER NAME, WAGE RATE, AND HOURS WORKED:? JOSEPH JONES,10.0,43
```

The output from this program is:

```
EMPLOYEE NAME IS: JOSEPH JONES
GROSS PAY IS:$ 445
NET PAY IS:$ 359.35
```

Because Jones worked more than 40 hours in one week, the overtime (ELSE) alternative is selected. If the program is executed for an employee who did *not* work overtime, the following input

```
ENTER NAME, WAGE RATE, AND HOURS WORKED:? NED JACKSON,8.0,30
```

generates the output at the top of the next page.

FIGURE 17-3
Program to Calculate Gross and Net Pay

```
200 INPUT "ENTER NAME, WAGE RATE, AND HOURS WORKED: ";EMPLOYEE$,WAGE,
HOURS
400 IF HOURS <= 40 THEN GROSSPAY = HOURS*WAGE ELSE GROSSPAY =
40*WAGE + (HOURS - 40)*1.5*WAGE
500 REM IF HOURS <= 40 USE REGULAR TIME; OTHERWISE USE OVERTIME
600 NETPAY = GROSSPAY - .1*GROSSPAY - .07*GROSSPAY - 10
650 REM NET PAY = GROSS PAY - TAXES - SOCIAL SECURITY - HEALTH
INSURANCE
700 PRINT "EMPLOYEE NAME IS: ";EMPLOYEE$:PRINT "GROSS PAY IS:$
";GROSSPAY
800 PRINT "NET PAY IS:$ ";NETPAY
```

```
EMPLOYEE NAME IS: NED JACKSON
GROSS PAY IS:$ 240
NET PAY IS:$ 189.20
```

These data implement the regular time (THEN) alternative.

The WHILE Loop

The program shown in Figure 17-3 easily calculates the gross and net pay for one employee at a time. However, most businesses need programs that make these calculations for many employees. If the number of employees is known, then a FOR loop is appropriate. If the number of employees is unknown before the data are entered, then the **WHILE loop** is necessary. This loop continues *while* some condition is true. When this condition becomes false, the loop terminates. The flowchart of the WHILE loop is shown in Figure 17-4.

The WHILE loop in Figure 17-4 is a pre-test loop, because the loop termination decision comes before the body of the loop. (Recall that the FOR loop was also a pre-test loop that used a counter for loop termination.) The WHILE loop can use a counter or some *other* condition—such as the value of a variable or sum—to terminate the loop.

To execute the WHILE loop in BASIC, we use the WHILE–WEND block. The general form of the WHILE–WEND block is shown below:

line number	WHILE *condition*
	body of loop
line number	WEND

Beginning programmers can write games in BASIC to produce both graphics and sound.

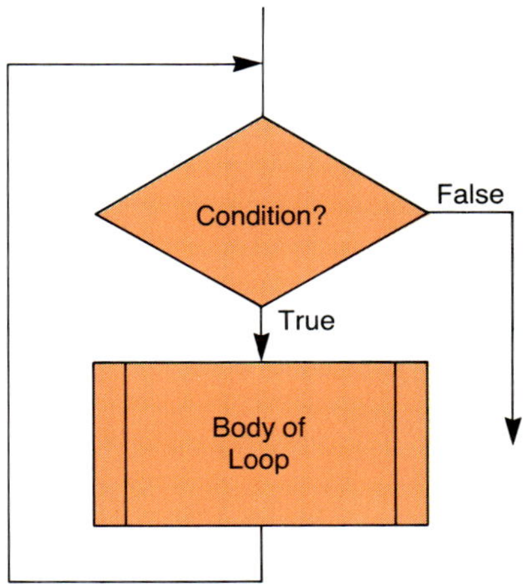

FIGURE 17-4
WHILE Loop Flowchart

The type of condition in the WHILE statement is the same as that used in the IF–THEN statement. Note that if the condition that is tested is true, then control is transferred to the body of the loop for a repetition of the loop. On the other hand, if the condition is false, then control is transferred out of the loop to the next statement after the WEND statement.

THE PRINT USING STATEMENT

In many situations, the form used by BASIC to output numbers is not acceptable. The output may not fit the user's needs, or it may not appropriately represent the values that are output. For example, a calculation may result in output of 1.6578 when the degree of accuracy of the data calls for only two places to the right of the decimal. Output that represents dollars and cents needs a dollar sign. Finally, the number may be so large that including commas would help the user understand the value. BASIC has a *formatting* command that allows the user to control the form of the output. This PRINT USING statement has the following form

PRINT USING *format string;list of variables*

where the format string designates the form of output for the list of variables.

Several types of format strings are available, but we only consider the control of numeric output using the pound sign (#). The pound sign represents each digit position. For example, assume that VALUE = 365.5478 and SIZE = 23456.23. Consider the program segment and associated output at the end of this box. In the first case, the digits to the right of the decimal were rounded to two digits. The same thing occurred in the second case, but the dollar sign was added. In the last example, a comma was added to the number.

These are only three of the many formatting combinations that can be used to control output in BASIC. Check your BASIC manual to find others.

```
50  VALUE = 365.5478:SIZE=23456.23
100  PRINT USING "###.##";VALUE
200  PRINT USING "$$###.##";VALUE
300  PRINT USING "#####,.##";SIZE


365.55
 $365.55
23,456.23
```

To illustrate the WHILE–WEND block, we show a program that initializes variable X to 10. The value 2 is repeatedly subtracted from X *while* X is greater than zero. When X is no longer greater than zero, the loop ceases to operate. The statements to do this are as follows:

```
100 X = 10
200 WHILE X > 0
300   PRINT X;
400   X = X - 2
500 WEND
```

The output for this program is shown below:

```
10 8 6 4 2
```

The values that are output stop when X equals zero, the point at which the loop is terminated by the WHILE statement. Note that the body of the loop is indented; this helps a reader see what is repeated.

Another example of the WHILE loop is a program to compute and output the sum of the squares of the integers—1, 2, 3, and so on—*while* this sum is less than or equal to 300. The program for this example is shown in Figure 17-5. Note that because we are explicitly working with integers in this example, we have added the % suffix to the variables to restrict them to integers. If this program is executed, the following output occurs:

```
1 1
2 5
3 14
4 30
5 55
6 91
7 140
8 204
9 285
```

The INPUT Loop

To implement a loop to compute gross pay and net pay for an unknown number of employees, we use a special form of the WHILE loop known as the **INPUT loop**. This loop is used to input an *unknown number* of data items. To signal the end of data, a special data item called a **trailer record** is used. The trailer record matches the condition that terminates the loop. For example, if a student is allowed to take between one and five quizzes during an academic term, then the exact number of quizzes each student will take is

FIGURE 17-5
Program to Compute Sum of Squares

```
50 REM PROGRAM TO COMPUTE SUM OF SQUARES
100 SUMSQS% = 1 'INITIALIZE SUM OF SQUARES
200 COUNTER% = 1 'INITIALIZE COUNTER
300 WHILE SUMSQS% <= 300 'REPEAT WHILE SUM OF SQUARES <= 300
400   PRINT COUNTER%; SUMSQS% 'OUTPUT VALUE OF COUNTER AND SUM OF
SQUARES
500   COUNTER% = COUNTER% + 1 'INCREMENT COUNTER
600   SUMSQS% = SUMSQS% + COUNTER%^2 'SQUARE COUNTER AND ADD TO SUM
700 WEND 'END OF LOOP
```

unknown. In this case, to signal the end of quiz scores for a particular student, the trailer record might have a negative quiz score, because quiz scores are normally positive (or zero, at worst!). When this negative value is encountered by the WHILE statement, it signals the computer that no more data are coming and that the INPUT loop is terminated. A FOR loop could not be used in this situation because the number of times the loop is repeated is unknown in advance. The general form of the INPUT loop is as follows:

Line number INPUT *data item*
Line number WHILE *data item* <> *trailer record*
    body of loop
Line number   INPUT *data item*
Line number WEND

Note that the general form of the INPUT loop has one INPUT statement before the loop and one in the loop itself. The first INPUT statement initiates the INPUT loop by giving it a value to test in the WHILE statement. The INPUT statement that is in the loop is repeated. When the trailer record is encountered, the loop terminates and transfers control to the statement after the WEND statement.

Because we enter employee names, wage rates, and hours worked to calculate gross pay and net pay, we can use any of these variables as the signal data in the trailer record. Let us assume that the trailer record has the string constant OUT OF DATA in place of employee name. We can determine when this string constant is encountered by using a WHILE statement of the following form

```
WHILE EMPLOYEE$ <> "OUT OF DATA"
```

where EMPLOYEE$ is the employee name variable. This program incorporates the program shown in Figure 17-3 into an INPUT loop in Figure 17-6.

FIGURE 17-6
Program for Unknown Number of Employees

```
100 REM THIS PROGRAM COMPUTES GROSS AND NET PAY FOR AN UNKNOWN NUMBER OF
110 REM EMPLOYEES. THE LAST DATA RECORD HAS "OUT OF DATA" FOR AN
120 REM EMPLOYEE NAME
200 INPUT "ENTER NAME, WAGE RATE, AND HOURS WORKED: ";EMPLOYEE$,WAGE,
HOURS
300 WHILE EMPLOYEE$ <> "OUT OF DATA"
400    IF HOURS <= 40 THEN GROSSPAY = HOURS*WAGE ELSE GROSSPAY =
40*WAGE + (HOURS - 40)*1.5*WAGE
500    REM IF HOURS <= 40 USE REGULAR TIME; OTHERWISE USE OVERTIME
600    NETPAY = GROSSPAY - .1*GROSSPAY - .07*GROSSPAY - 10
650    REM NET PAY = GROSS PAY - TAXES - SOCIAL SECURITY - HEALTH
INSURANCE
700    PRINT "EMPLOYEE NAME IS: ";EMPLOYEE$:PRINT "GROSS PAY IS:$
";GROSSPAY
800    PRINT "NET PAY IS:$ ";NETPAY
900    INPUT "ENTER NAME, WAGE RATE, AND HOURS WORKED: ";EMPLOYEE$,WAGE,
HOURS
1000 WEND
```

Blackjack is one of many games that can be written in BASIC.

In the program in Figure 17-6, the instruction in line 200 is the first INPUT statement, and the WHILE decision appears in line 300. Lines 400–800 are made up of an IF–THEN–ELSE statement that computes the gross pay, a statement that computes net pay, and three PRINT statements that output the results for each employee. Line 900 is the INPUT statement within the loop, and line 1000 is the WEND instruction that transfers control back to the beginning of the loop.

Assume the program in Figure 17-6 is executed for two employees. The input would be as shown below

```
ENTER NAME, WAGE RATE, AND HOURS WORKED:? JOSEPH JONES,10.0,43
ENTER NAME, WAGE RATE, AND HOURS WORKED:? NED JACKSON,8.0,30
ENTER NAME, WAGE RATE, AND HOURS WORKED:? OUT OF DATA,0,0
```

and the output would appear as follows:

```
EMPLOYEE NAME IS: JOSEPH JONES
GROSS PAY IS:$ 445
NET PAY IS:$ 359.35
EMPLOYEE NAME IS: NED JACKSON
GROSS PAY IS:$ 240
NET PAY IS:$ 189.20
```

In the data for the trailer record, we use OUT OF DATA for the employee name and dummy values (two zeros) for the other data items. **Dummy values** merely satisfy the INPUT statement. In BASIC, every variable in the input list must have a data item. Otherwise, BASIC displays two question marks (??) on the screen to remind the user to enter the missing data.

Nested FOR Loops

Sometimes, a program may need a loop within a loop. The loops can be two FOR loops, two WHILE loops, or a combination of the two types. This section

```
50 REM THIS PROGRAM COMPUTES SUM OF INNER AND OUTER COUNTER VARIABLES
100 OSUM = 0 'INITIALIZE SUM OF OUTER COUNTER VARIABLE TO ZERO
200 ISUM = 0 'INITIALIZE SUM OF INNER COUNTER VARIABLE TO ZERO
300 FOR I = 1 TO 5 'RUN OUTER COUNTER FROM 1 TO 5
400    FOR K = 10 TO 100 STEP 10 'RUN INNER COUNTER FROM 10 TO 100
BY TENS
500       ISUM = ISUM + K 'ADD INNER COUNTER TO INNER SUM
600    NEXT K 'END OF INNER LOOP
700    OSUM = OSUM + I 'ADD OUTER COUNTER TO OUTER SUM
800 NEXT I 'END OUTER FOR LOOP
900 PRINT "INNER SUM = ";ISUM; "OUTER SUM = ";OSUM 'OUTPUT INNER AND
OUTER SUMS
```

FIGURE 17-7
Using Nested FOR Loops

covers the first case—two FOR loops—because that situation is quite common.

A FOR loop within a FOR loop is commonly referred to as **nested FOR loops**. When this combination is used, the inner FOR loop calculates all its values for each value of the outer FOR loop. Different counter variables must be used for the outer and inner loops, and the inner FOR loop must always be finished before the outer FOR loop. The example in Figure 17-7 demonstrates the proper use of nested FOR loops to sum the values of both the inner and outer counter variables.

If the program in Figure 17-7 is executed, the result is as follows:

```
INNER SUM = 2750 OUTER SUM = 15
```

The sum of the values 10, 20, . . . , 100 is only 550, but this sum is repeated five times by the outer loop to arrive at a total value of 2,750.

The GO TO Statement

In our discussion of decision blocks and repetition blocks, we have avoided the use of the GO TO statement, because our objective is a *structured* program. However, for completeness, we now briefly demonstrate the use of this unstructured instruction. The GO TO statement causes control to transfer unconditionally to the line number that is included in the instruction. For example, the following program statement

```
1000 GO TO 200
```

causes control of the program to transfer to line 200. Use of the GO TO statement is discouraged because it can lead to loosely structured—and often bad—programs.

FUNCTIONS

We can perform some specific operations with both numeric and string variables by using the functions that are built into BASIC. These **functions** include such numeric operations as finding the square root of a value, finding the absolute value of a value, and finding the trigonometric sine of an angle. String functions include such operations as finding the leftmost or rightmost set of char-

Table 17-1 EXAMPLES OF USING FUNCTIONS

Use of Functions	*Result*
`X = ABS(Y)`	Sets X equal to the absolute value of Y
`K = INT(5.4)`	Makes K equal to the integer part of 5.4, which is 5
`QQ = LOG(RR)`	Sets QQ equal to the natural logarithm of RR
`PRINT SQR(441)`	Outputs the square root of 441
`PRINT SIN(X)`	Outputs the sine of angle X
`T$ = RIGHT$(A$,3)`	Sets T$ equal to the last 3 characters in A$
`R$ = LEFT$(A$,4)`	Sets R$ equal to the first 4 characters in A$
`S$ = MID$(A$,3,10)`	Sets S$ equal to 10 characters of A$ beginning with the third character
`PRINT STRING$(5,"* ")`	Outputs five asterisks (*****)
`K = LEN(G$)`	Makes K equal to the number of characters in G$
`PRINT CHR$(65)`	Outputs the sixty-fifth ASCII character, which is A

acters in a string, creating a string of identical characters, or generating a specific ASCII character.

In most numeric and string functions, an **argument** gives the function the information it needs. For example, in finding the square root of 49, the argument of the SQR function is 49. The 49 is placed in parentheses after SQR—that is, SQR(49)—and the function becomes the square root of 49, or 7. The function is said to *return* this value. An example of a string function is LEFT$("BULLDOGS",4), which returns the first four characters of the string variable or constant, in this case, BULL. The function name and argument may be used the way a variable is used, except that it cannot be placed on the left-hand side of an assignment statement. A function can be output using the PRINT statement, or it can be placed on the right-hand side of an assignment statement by itself or as part of an expression. It can also be used in an IF–THEN or an IF–THEN–ELSE statement or in a WHILE or a FOR loop. Some popular function uses are shown in Table 17-1. Numerous other functions available in BASIC can be found in any user's guide that comes with a personal computer. These functions can help accomplish many tasks in programming.

As an example of using functions, consider the small program shown in Figure 17-8, which generates a table of the square roots of the numbers 1–10 using the SQR function and a FOR loop. If the program in Figure 17-8 is executed, the output at the top of the next page results.

FIGURE 17-8
Program to Output Square Roots

```
100 REM THIS PROGRAM OUTPUTS THE SQUARE ROOTS OF THE NUMBERS 1 THROUGH 10
200 FOR X = 1 TO 10 'LOOP FROM 1 TO 10
300    PRINT X;SQR(X) 'OUTPUT VALUE AND ITS SQUARE ROOT
400 NEXT X 'END OF LOOP
```

```
1   1
2   1.414214
3   1.732051
4   2
5   2.236068
6   2.44949
7   2.645751
8   2.828427
9   3
10  3.162278
```

The RIGHT$, LEFT$, and MID$ functions allow the user to extract part of a string variable or constant. For example, if TEAM$ = "DODGERS," then RIGHT$(TEAM$,4) equals "GERS," LEFT$(TEAM$,3) equals "DOD," and MID$ (TEAM$,2,4) equals "ODGE." Combining these functions with the addition operation to combine strings or parts of strings, the user can generate new strings of any form or length. For example, if GA$ = LEFT$(TEAM$,2) + MID$(TEAM$,4,1) + RIGHT$(TEAM$,1), then GA$ = "DOGS." The LEN function allows a user to determine the length of a string variable or constant. For TEAM$, LEN(TEAM$) returns a value of 7, because TEAM$ has 7 characters. Finally, the CHR$ function is useful for generating various ASCII characters. This function is especially important in generating graphics by combining

BASIC ART AND SOUND

Programming in BASIC on a personal computer that has graphics and sound capabilities means that both art and music can be generated. Art is the result of BASIC commands that cause colors and shapes to appear on the screen and instructions that allow the generation of user-developed characters. Sound capabilities result in music or sound effects for games or other programs.

In BASIC, graphics may be block graphics characters, which correspond to ASCII positions 176–223, or they may be generated by direct control of the picture elements, or pixels, on the screen. Computers with graphics capabilities can control the individual pixels on the screen through various commands, but computers without the necessary hardware are restricted to block graphics. For computers that can control the screen's pixels, a series of BASIC instructions allow the creation of sophisticated art. These commands include COLOR, LINE, DRAW, CIRCLE, PAINT, PSET, and PRESET. These commands, with the exception of the last two, are self-explanatory. The last two commands enable the programmer either to set a pixel "on" (PSET) or to turn it off (PRESET). By working with PSET and PRESET and using a coordinate system that identifies each individual pixel, a wide variety of figures can be created on the screen. Some computers support a *graphics definition language (GDL),* which allows the programmer to use the DRAW command with the GDL to facilitate drawing and animation.

Sound in BASIC is generated using one of two commands—SOUND and PLAY. The SOUND command generates a sound of a specified frequency for a selected length of time. This command can be used to produce beeps, buzzes, or almost any type of sound depending on the frequency and length. On the other hand, music is best produced in BASIC using the PLAY command. When combined with a character string showing the notes and tempo, the PLAY command can be used to produce melodies. For example, the following statements produce the first part of "Jingle Bells" when executed:

```
10  JBELL$ = "MNT180L403DBAG MLD2D4MN
D8D8DBAG"
20  PLAY JBELL$
```

SOURCE: *ITT Advanced BASIC,* ITT Information Systems, 1984, pp. 7-1–7-43, 8-1–8-34.

two or more of the extended ASCII character set elements—that is, positions 176–223. For example, CHR$(219) corresponds to a solid black box (■). Similarly, CHR$(179) corresponds to a vertical line (|). Various pictures can be created by combining these extended ASCII characters using the CHR$ function and the addition operator.

ARRAYS

Many programming applications involve the use of a list or a table. Mailing lists, membership lists, and tax tables are all examples of programming situations that might require a list or table. The difference between a list and a table is the number of columns. A **list** is a single column of elements, and a **table** has more than one column of elements. For example, a membership list has a column of names, with each name making up a row of the list. A tax table has multiple columns and rows. Each column corresponds to an income range, and each row corresponds to a taxpayer's filing status—single, head of household, and so on. To find the tax for a particular income range and filing status, a taxpayer merely finds the appropriate row and column.

In programming, lists and tables are called **arrays**. A list is a **one-dimensional array**, and a table is a **two-dimensional array**. Figure 17-9 shows a one-dimensional string array and a two-dimensional numeric array. For this introduction to BASIC, we restrict ourselves to one-dimensional arrays, but the approach is the same for two-dimensional arrays.

In BASIC, each element of a one-dimensional array is identified by an **index**, which is the position of the element in the list. The index is placed in parentheses after the array name, which is the name of the entire list. As a result, each element is identified by the array name and the appropriate index. In the one-dimensional array in Figure 17-9 called HH$, the third element is HH$(3), and the fifth element is HH$(5). The value in the parentheses is also called the **subscript**, which must be an integer variable or constant. Three important operations in using arrays are declaration of arrays, input/output for arrays, and manipulation of data using arrays.

Declaring an Array

In BASIC, an array should first be *declared* through the use of the DIM statement. The DIM statement reserves storage space for the array and notifies the

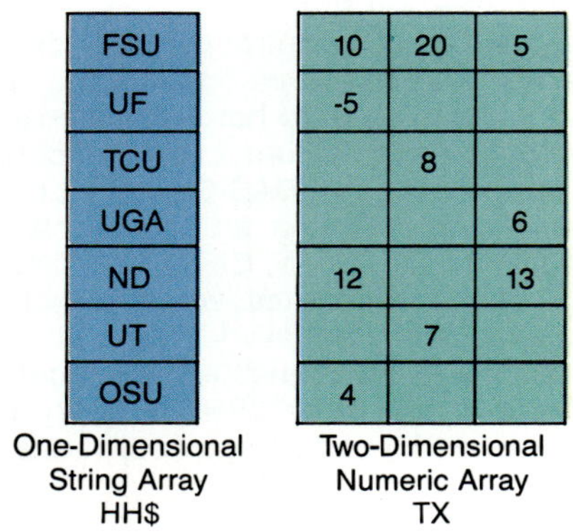

FIGURE 17-9
Examples of Arrays

CPU that this variable name refers to multiple elements. The general form of the DIM statement is as follows:

DIM *var1(number of elements),var2(number of elements)*, . . .

For example, to declare a string array SCHOOL$ that holds 100 elements and a numeric variable VALUE that holds 50 elements, the DIM statement would be as follows:

```
100 DIM SCHOOL$(100),VALUE(50)
```

The DIM statement is used at the beginning of the program so that arrays are declared before they are used.

Input/Output for Arrays

The easiest way to input and output arrays is through a FOR loop in which the counter variable matches the index values of the array. The BASIC program in Figure 17-10 is an example of declaring an array and then using FOR loops for input and output. In this example, a 10-element array is entered, but the output contains only the even numbered elements.

Note that the program in Figure 17-10 uses a new form of input, the READ statement. The READ statement works like the INPUT statement with one key difference: The data for a READ statement are included *in the program* in a numbered DATA statement. With the READ statement, a program can be run without the user's entering data from a keyboard.

If the program in Figure 17-10 is executed, the output would be

```
3.03 1.45 6.66 1.87 9.01
```

where the second, fourth, sixth, and eighth elements of the list in the DATA statement are output.

Manipulating Data with Arrays

Numerous operations can be performed on data using arrays, including finding a particular element in an array, matching elements from two arrays, and sorting an array. **Sorting an array** means arranging the array from smallest to largest.

As an example of data manipulation using an array, consider the problem of finding the largest value in an array. The program should use a FOR loop to search the array and a **temporary variable** to store the largest value found at each step of the search. The temporary variable is initially set equal to the first element in the array, and the search starts with the second element. If the search yields a value that is larger than the temporary variable, then the

FIGURE 17-10
Array Input and Output Program

```
100 REM THIS PROGRAM DECLARES, INPUTS, AND THEN OUTPUTS AN ARRAY
200 DIM A(10)   'DIMENSION THE ARRAY FOR 10 ELEMENTS
300 FOR I = 1 TO 10   'BEGIN FOR LOOP TO READ DATA
400   READ A(I)   'READ EACH ELEMENT FROM DATA STATEMENT
500 NEXT I 'END READ LOOP
600 FOR K = 2 TO 10 STEP 2   'OUTPUT EVERY OTHER ELEMENT
700   PRINT A(K); 'PRINT ELEMENTS ON SAME LINE
800 NEXT K   'END OUTPUT LOOP
900 DATA 4.5,3.03,7.1,1.45,8.95,6.66,7.32,1.87,3.00,9.01
```

```
100 REM THIS PROGRAM FINDS THE LARGEST VALUE IN A LIST
200 DIM V(100) 'DECLARE LIST TO HOLD 100 VALUES
300 INPUT "ENTER THE NUMBER OF ELEMENTS IN THE LIST ";M  'M = ELEMENTS
IN LIST
400 PRINT "ENTER THE ELEMENTS IN THE LIST"
500 FOR I = 1 TO M 'ENTER EACH ELEMENT USING FOR LOOP
600   INPUT V(I)  'ENTER ITH ELEMENT
700 NEXT I  'END OF INPUT LOOP
800 REM START SEARCH WITH TEMPORARY VARIABLE EQUAL TO FIRST ELEMENT
IN LIST
900 TT = V(1)
1000 FOR K = 2 TO M 'NOW SEARCH BEGINNING WITH SECOND ELEMENT
1100   IF V(K) > TT THEN TT = V(K)  'IF ELEMENT LARGER, THEN CHANGE
TEMPORARY VARIABLE
1200 NEXT K 'END OF SEARCH LOOP
1300 PRINT "THE LARGEST VALUE IN THE LIST IS: ";TT
```

FIGURE 17-11
Program to Find the Largest Value in a List

temporary variable is set equal to that larger value. When the FOR loop is completed, the temporary variable is the largest value in the array. Figure 17-11 shows the BASIC program that implements this logic.

If the program in Figure 17-11 is executed with an array of six elements, the results would be as follows:

```
ENTER THE NUMBER OF ELEMENTS IN THE LIST? 6
ENTER THE ELEMENTS IN THE LIST
? 15
? 18
? 10
? 13
? 20
? 17
THE LARGEST VALUE IN THE LIST IS: 20
```

In this program, the temporary variable, TT, is initially equal to 15, then changed to 18, and finally changed to 20, which is the largest value.

SUBPROGRAMS

The discussion of top-down design in Chapter 15 included the concept of modules, which break a large program into manageable pieces. In BASIC, top-down design is implemented with subroutines and user-defined functions. A **subroutine** is a section of a program that carries out a specific piece of logic. A **user-defined function** is like a function that is provided by BASIC but is defined by the user.

Subroutines

For a program to use a subroutine, the program must first "call" the subroutine using the GOSUB statement. When a GOSUB is encountered, control of the program is transferred to the line number in the GOSUB statement. The general form of the GOSUB instruction is as follows:

Line number GOSUB *Line number of first line of subroutine*

An example of a GOSUB instruction is

```
1000 GOSUB 1800
```

where 1800 is the line number of the first line of the subroutine.

The subroutine begins at the line number referenced by the GOSUB instruction. After the subroutine is executed, the RETURN instruction returns control to the statement immediately following the GOSUB instruction. The last instruction in any subroutine must *always* be the RETURN instruction. Without the RETURN instruction, program statements that follow the subroutine are executed as part of the subroutine.

As an example of a subroutine, consider the program in Figure 17-12, which combines the program in Figure 17-10 with an output subroutine. This program inputs an array of values, finds and prints the largest value in the array, and then prints the entire array. Subroutines are used for the input, the largest value search, and the output of the array. The main program contains only the GOSUB instructions, and the subroutines handle the specific logic.

FIGURE 17-12
BASIC Program Using Subroutines

```
100 REM PROGRAM TO INPUT AND OUTPUT A LIST; ALSO FIND AND OUTPUT LARGEST
110 REM VALUE
200 DIM V(100)  'DECLARE LIST FOR 100 ELEMENTS
300 INPUT "ENTER THE NUMBER OF ELEMENTS IN THE LIST ";M
400 GOSUB 800  'USE SUBROUTINE TO INPUT DATA TO LIST
500 GOSUB 1300  'USE SUBROUTINE TO FIND AND OUTPUT LARGEST VALUE IN LIST
600 GOSUB 2000  'USE SUBROUTINE TO OUTPUT ELEMENTS IN THE LIST
700 END  'END MAIN PROGRAM--SUBROUTINES FOLLOW
800 PRINT "ENTER THE ELEMENTS IN THE LIST"  'BEGINNING OF INPUT
SUBROUTINE
900 FOR I = 1 TO M  'USE FOR LOOP TO INPUT ELEMENTS OF LIST
1000   INPUT V(I)  'INPUT EACH ELEMENT OF LIST
1100 NEXT I  'END OF INPUT LOOP
1200 RETURN  'END OF INPUT SUBROUTINE
1300 REM BEGINNING OF SUBROUTINE TO FIND AND OUTPUT THE LARGEST ELEMENT
IN LIST
1400 TT = V(1)  'INITIALLY SET TEMPORARY VARIABLE EQUAL TO FIRST
ELEMENT
1500 FOR K = 2 TO M  'START SEARCH WITH SECOND ELEMENT IN LIST
1600   IF V(K) > TT THEN TT = V(K)  'IF ELEMENT IS LARGER, THEN CHANGE
TEMPORARY VARIABLE
1700 NEXT K  'END SEARCH LOOP
1800 PRINT "THE LARGEST VALUE IN THE LIST IS: ";TT
1900 RETURN  'END OF SUBROUTINE TO FIND LARGEST VALUE IN LIST
2000 REM BEGINNING OF OUTPUT SUBROUTINE
2100 PRINT "THESE ARE THE ELEMENTS IN THE LIST"  'LABEL THE OUTPUT
2200 FOR I = 1 TO M  'USE FOR LOOP TO OUTPUT ELEMENTS OF LIST
2300   PRINT V(I);  'OUTPUT EACH ELEMENT ON SAME LINE
2400 NEXT I  'END OF OUTPUT LOOP
2500 RETURN  'END OF LIST OUTPUT SUBROUTINE
```

THE WIZARD OF ID By Parker and Hart

Using this logic, the programmer breaks the large problem into small pieces and writes a subroutine for each piece. After each piece is programmed and tested individually, it is added to the main program with confidence that the logic is correct.

Note that the END statement is used to terminate the main program. Without the END statement, program control would continue through the subroutines a second time. If the program in Figure 17-12 is executed with the data for Figure 17-11, the results would be as follows:

```
ENTER THE NUMBER OF ELEMENTS IN THE LIST? 6
ENTER THE ELEMENTS IN THE LIST
? 15
? 18
? 10
? 13
? 20
? 17
THE LARGEST VALUE IN THE LIST IS: 20
THESE ARE THE ELEMENTS IN THE LIST
 15  18  10  13  20  17
```

User-Defined Functions

A user-defined function is any valid operation that the user defines as a function. For example, the user may wish to find the average of five values that appear in several places in a BASIC program without repeating the statements to do this in every place. To avoid the repetition of the averaging statement, the user defines a function called FNAVERAGE(V1,V2,V3,V4,V5), where V1, V2, . . . , V5 are the arguments used by the function. All user-defined functions must begin with FN and end with a valid variable name. The general form of the function definition statement is as follows:

Line number   DEF FN*name*(*argument list*) = *expression*

The definition statement for FNAVERAGE is as follows:

```
500 DEF FNAVERAGE(V1,V2,V3,V4,V5) = (V1 + V2 + V3 + V4 + V5)/5
```

PEEKS AND POKES

Two common terms in BASIC—PEEK and POKE—sound like they have nothing to do with programming. Contrary to what you might think on first hearing about PEEKs and POKEs, they are useful in BASIC. The PEEK function allows the programmer to determine the contents of a particular memory cell by giving the address of that memory cell as the argument of the PEEK function. For example, if the programmer wanted to know the contents of memory cell 60,000 (memory addresses in BASIC are numbered from 0–65,536), he or she could use the following statements:

```
100  A = PEEK(60000)
200  PRINT "CONTENTS OF CELL ARE ";A
```

When a PEEK is used, the output is a number between 0 and 255, which corresponds to the number of the ASCII character stored in that cell.

The complementary statement to the PEEK function is the POKE statement. The POKE statement places a character in a particular memory location. The POKE statement must be used carefully, because the programmer may overwrite information that the computer needs. One fairly safe use of POKE is to display characters on the screen without using the keyboard. The following program places the letter "A" in the upper left-hand corner of an IBM or IBM compatible personal computer:

```
10 DEF SEG = &HB800
20 POKE 0,65
```

This two-line program lines up the memory addresses using the DEF SEG statement. It then POKEs the decimal number (65) corresponding to "A" into memory location zero, which is the upper left-hand corner of the screen. Any desired character can be POKEd onto the screen by replacing 65 with the appropriate value. The memory locations on the screen into which the characters can be placed are numbered from 0–3,998 using the even numbers. After you run this program, try a PEEK into the same memory location. The result should be the same value you POKEd earlier.

A user-defined function can be used at any point in the program *after* it is defined. For example, a use of FNAVERAGE would be

```
1000 QUIZAVERAGE = FNAVERAGE(SCORE1,SCORE2,SCORE3,SCORE4,SCORE5)
```

where SCORE1, SCORE2, . . . , SCORE5 have been entered or assigned a value.

FILES

A computer has a limited amount of internal memory, which is further restricted by the 64K limit that BASIC places on the total memory that it can use. For this reason, input and output in BASIC are often stored in files. Recall that a **file** is a collection of information stored as records, usually on a secondary storage device such as a disk. A record is a group of constants that are placed on the file by a single output statement.

Files in BASIC must first be opened—that is, contact must be made with the operating system to input information from the file or to output information to the file. An OPEN statement precedes the first reference to the file in a program. The general form of the OPEN statement is

Line number OPEN *"filename"* FOR *INPUT or OUTPUT* AS *#n*

where *filename* is eight letters or less and $n = 1$, 2, and 3.

An example of an OPEN statement is as follows:

The Please data base management software is one of many packages written in BASIC.

```
100 OPEN "DATAFILE" FOR OUTPUT AS #1
```

This OPEN statement opens a file named DATAFILE, which will be used for output. The computer refers to this as file number 1, and any further statements to input or output from or to this file must use this file number. A file must already exist to be used for input, and a file must be created to use for output. For example, the OPEN statement shown above prepares the file named DATAFILE to receive information from a program. Later, this file can be used for another program's input.

After a file is opened for output, information is placed there using a WRITE statement. The WRITE statement is like the PRINT statement, *except* that it places a comma after each item that is output. Because commas must separate data items that are input, information placed on a file by the WRITE statement can also be used as input to another file. The general form of the WRITE statement is

Line number WRITE #*n*, *variable list*

where $n = 1, 2,$ or 3.

Assume we want to place the following record on DATAFILE:

```
"ASHLEY HYATT",15,"F"
```

"WELL... I GUESS THAT PROGRAM WASN'T COMPATIBLE WITH MY COMPUTER!"

The following program statements accomplish this after DATAFILE is opened as file number 1:

```
200 STUDENT$ = "ASHLEY HYATT"
210 AGE = 15
220 SEX$ = "F"
230 WRITE #1, STUDENT$,AGE,SEX$
240 CLOSE #1
```

The WRITE #1 statement outputs the information to the file called DATAFILE, which was designated file number 1 by the OPEN statement.

After all information is output to the file, it must be closed by the CLOSE statement. A complete program to create DATAFILE using input from the keyboard is shown in Figure 17-13. A FOR loop for a given number of records is used to input the data and then to output them to the file. If the program in Figure 17-13 is executed and five records are entered, the input would appear as follows:

```
ENTER THE NUMBER OF RECORDS TO BE ON FILE? 5
ENTER NAME, AGE AND SEX FOR EACH STUDENT ? JOSEFH SMITH,22,M
ENTER NAME, AGE AND SEX FOR EACH STUDENT ? ALICE JONES,21,F
ENTER NAME, AGE AND SEX FOR EACH STUDENT ? CHRIS PATRICK,20,M
ENTER NAME, AGE AND SEX FOR EACH STUDENT ? BETH ELSEY,23,F
ENTER NAME, AGE AND SEX FOR EACH STUDENT ? CAROLYN MYERS,23,F
```

```
50 REM PROGRAM TO SET UP FILE CALLED DATAFILE
100 OPEN "DATAFILE" FOR OUTPUT AS #1   'OPEN THE FILE
200 INPUT "ENTER THE NUMBER OF RECORDS TO BE ON FILE ";NUMRECORDS
300 WRITE #1, NUMRECORDS   'FIRST RECORD ON FILE IS THE NUMBER OF
STUDENT RECORDS
400 FOR I = 1 TO NUMRECORDS   'USE FOR LOOP TO INPUT RECORDS AND PUT ON
FILE
500   INPUT "ENTER NAME, AGE AND SEX FOR EACH STUDENT ";STUDENT$,AGE,
SEX$
600   WRITE #1,STUDENT$,AGE,SEX$   'PUT RECORD ON THE FILE
700 NEXT I   'END OF FOR LOOP
800 CLOSE #1   'CLOSE THE FILE
```

FIGURE 17-13
Program to Create a File

If we now wanted to input data from DATAFILE to the screen, we would open the file for input and use the INPUT *#n* and PRINT statements to display the file data. The INPUT *#n* statement has the same form as the WRITE *#n* statement. The program to do this is shown in Figure 17-14. The number of records on DATAFILE is first input from the file, and then a FOR loop is used to input the records from the file.

Note that we use different variable names for the input program from the names used in the program that created the file. The computer is not confused, because these are two different programs. Similarly, opening DATAFILE for input as file number 2 causes no problems as long as we are consistent about the file number used throughout a particular program. If the input program in Figure 17-14 is executed, the output would be as follows:

```
NAME: JOSEPH SMITH AGE: 22 SEX: M
NAME: ALICE JONES AGE: 21 SEX: F
NAME: CHRIS PATRICK AGE: 20 SEX: M
NAME: BETH ELSEY AGE: 23 SEX: F
NAME: CAROLYN MYERS AGE: 23 SEX: F
```

FIGURE 17-14
BASIC Program to Input Data from a File

```
100 OPEN "DATAFILE" FOR INPUT AS #2   'OPEN FILE FOR INPUT
200 INPUT #2, NUMBER   'READ NUMBER OF STUDENT RECORDS ON THE FILE
300 FOR I = 1 TO NUMBER   'USE FOR LOOP TO INPUT STUDENT RECORDS FROM
FILE
400   INPUT #2, STUDENTNAME$,YEARS,BOYGIRL$   'INPUT RECORD FROM FILE
500   PRINT "NAME: ";STUDENTNAME$;" AGE: ";YEARS;" SEX: ";BOYGIRL$
'OUTPUT DATA
600 NEXT I   'END OF FOR LOOP
700 CLOSE #2   'CLOSE THE FILE
```

REVIEW OF KEY POINTS

- The IF–THEN–ELSE statement can be used to execute one of two alternatives in a decision block.
- The WHILE loop can be used when some condition other than a counter is used to control a loop.
- The INPUT loop can be used to input an unknown number of data items using a trailer record for termination.
- Nested FOR loops can be used to execute one loop within another.
- The GO TO statement can be used for an unconditional transfer of program control, but its use often leads to poorly designed programs.
- A function can be used to perform a special operation—such as finding the square root of a number or finding the leftmost characters in a string.
- An array is a list of numbers or strings, the length of which must be declared at the beginning of a program.
- The READ statement can be used to read data from a DATA statement in the program.
- A subroutine is a program that is called by the main program to perform one or more processing operations.
- A user-defined function is a function that is provided by BASIC but defined by the user to perform a special operation.
- A file is a collection of data arranged as records. Information can be output to a file and then input from a file as data.

KEY TERMS

argument
arrays
dummy values
file
functions
IF–THEN–ELSE statement
index
INPUT loop
list
nested FOR loops
one-dimensional array
sorting an array
subroutine
subscript
table
temporary variable
trailer record
two-dimensional array
user-defined function
WHILE loop

REVIEW QUESTIONS

1. Why is a WHILE loop used to input an unknown number of data items?
2. Why must an array be declared in terms of the number of elements it holds?
3. What is the difference between a function and a subroutine? Explain the best way to enter data into an array.
4. Why would a user wish to define a function?
5. Why would a user want to output information to a file?
6. Write a program to input a student's name and an unknown number of quiz scores. The program should then compute and output the average quiz score.
7. Write a program to input a string constant. The program should then determine whether the first three characters of the string are the same as the last three characters.
8. Write a program to input a list of student names. After the list is entered, a single name is input, and the program should determine if this name is on the list.
9. Rewrite the program in Question 8 using subroutines or user-defined functions, or both.
10. Write a program that uses a WHILE loop to input an unknown number of student names and ages. These data should then be output to a file called STUDENTNAMES, and the number of records should be counted. Write a second program to input and display these file data on the screen.

A GUIDE TO BUYING A PERSONAL COMPUTER

If you don't have a personal computer at your disposal, you may be thinking about purchasing one. Today, increasing numbers of people are deciding that they want a computer for home or business use. Eventually, an estimated 20% of all U.S. households will have some variety of personal computer. This percentage will be much higher in business as companies find that the computer can save money and increase profits.

Because consumers have so many makes and models of computers to choose from, a computer purchase may require more research from the prospective owner than a purchase of, say, an automobile or a television. All personal computers do not handle the same tasks with equal effectiveness. For example, a machine that is great for games and graphics may not be suitable for word processing. The computer you purchase should suit your computing needs the way the type of vehicle (car, van, truck, sports car, and so on) you buy fits your transportation needs.

This special section on buying a personal computer is included to show you what is involved in such a purchase. We have devised a six-step process that may be helpful in your selection of a personal computer. The actual brand of computer that you choose depends on the results of this procedure and the price that you can pay. This step-by-step approach is similar to the systems approach to problem solving discussed in Chapter 4, because the overall computer system is considered in the decision rather than separate computer components. Our six steps for buying a computer system are as follows:

1. Learn about the capabilities and limitations of computers.
2. Define the tasks for which your personal computer will be used.
3. Determine which software packages will accomplish these tasks.
4. Determine which hardware systems will support the software you selected in step 3.
5. Find suppliers that can provide the desired hardware and software.
6. Purchase this software and hardware system.

In this procedure, you first learn enough about computers to know what they can and cannot do and then define your needs. Your needs may include becoming computer literate, keeping a personal budget, learning to program, or handling a business. After determining your needs, you can then find the appropriate software packages to meet those needs. Because of the variety of software available today, this step requires the most time and research. Often, this step results in a list of software from which a subjective choice must be made. Once you have selected the software that meets your needs, you have also narrowed your choice of computers, because not all computers run all software. Finally, you find the suppliers that carry the desired software and hardware and purchase the equipment. We discuss each step in detail in this special section.

You should remember that the original purchase of hardware and software is just the beginning. Additional software packages may be purchased as you find more uses for the computer, or additional hardware devices may expand the uses of the computer system. For example, a buyer who uses the computer for home record keeping may add a spreadsheet package or a letter quality printer to enhance the use of the computer. Possible additions should be considered in the original plan and an expandable computer system should be purchased. By planning ahead, you will not be locked out of the future.

THE PERSONAL COMPUTER

A Short History

The term *personal computer* was coined by computer scientist Alan Kay in a 1972 paper titled "A Personal Computer for Children of All Ages." As a result of Kay's work, Xerox built a personal computer called the Alto, which it never released. Other established computer companies also considered the concept of a personal computer, but they decided that no market existed for such a machine. Finally, in 1975, an Albuquerque, New Mexico, company called MITS released the first personal computer in kit form. This machine, named the Altair after a planet in the *Star Trek* TV series, had only 1K of memory and was very slow by today's standards. MITS received 5,000 orders for the Altair after it was pictured on the cover of *Popular Electronics.* A pioneer in the field and current computer science publisher Rodney Zaks remarked, "Never before had such a powerful tool been invented and so few people realized what it could do."*

Although MITS was the first to come out with a personal computer, companies like Apple, Radio Shack, and Commodore popularized its use. These companies were among the nearly 100 companies that rushed personal computers onto the market in the years immediately after MITS offered the first one.

Apple's success story is particularly amazing. Apple was formed by two young Californians, Steve Jobs and Steve Wozniak, who built the first Apple computer in their garage. In 1978, Apple offered a disk drive to accompany the original Apple II. This key breakthrough, along with the VisiCalc software package that was offered only on the Apple, allowed the company to leapfrog over Radio Shack and Commodore into first place in sales among the pioneer companies.

The next breakthrough was the release of the IBM PC in 1981. Although not an innovation technologically, the IBM PC was almost immediately an industry standard that legitimized the personal computer concept. Today, the industry is divided into three groups of computers—IBM PC and compatible machines; Apples (IIe, IIc, and Macintosh); and others [Commodore, Atari, Radio Shack (Tandy), Kaypro, and so on]. Experts believe the industry will narrow down, like the automobile industry, with only a few companies surviving the "shakeout."

*John Hillkirk, "Computer Legends after a Decade," *USA Today*, June 18, 1984, p. B3.

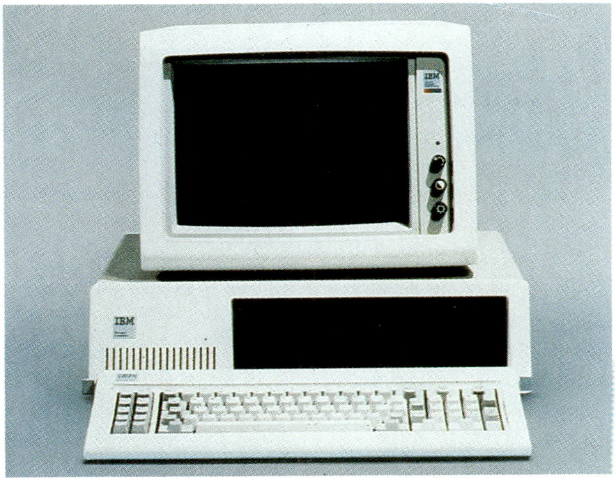

The IBM Personal Computer (PC), now an industry standard, has made IBM the leading personal computer manufacturer.

STEP 1: LEARN ABOUT COMPUTER CAPABILITIES

Before purchasing a computer, a prospective user should spend some time learning about computers. In other words, he or she should become *computer literate.* This education can be accomplished by taking a course at a local college or technical school, by reading a book such as this one, by reading various computer magazines, or by attending local computer users' group meetings. The buyer will then know what tasks they can expect a computer to perform and will learn the necessary hardware and software terminology. A prospective buyer can determine computer needs only after he or she is computer literate.

STEP 2: DEFINE NEEDS

Often, a buyer purchases a computer without defining a clear need. The purchaser may buy a computer simply because everyone else is doing so. Because the personal computer is a tool, the prospective purchaser must define what its uses will be before moving any further. A person does not normally buy an expensive woodworking tool—such as a lathe or table saw—unless a need exists. The same should also be true of a computer. It is a versatile machine—for example, it can be used for games, education, word processing, programming, and financial analysis. Most people will have multiple needs for the computer. In the decision process, these needs should be ranked according to use so the buyer can determine the most appropriate computer without over- or underbuying.

Types of Computer Needs

Most people find that their computer needs fall into one of the following three categories:

1. Recreation/Computer Literacy
2. Personal Record Keeping/Education
3. Business Computing

The Commodore 64 personal computer system is very popular for computer literacy or recreational purposes.

Examples of computers that are used in many educational environments, as well as for home and business computing, are the IBM AT (left) and the Apple IIe (right).

Recreation/computer literacy includes game-playing, learning to use a keyboard, or learning to program. Personal record keeping/education is the use of the computer for home budgeting, correspondence, telecommunications, and volunteer activities. This category also includes the use of the personal computer for education and personal advancement using such software packages as math drill, computer-aided instruction, and SAT review. Finally, business computing includes the use of the computer in small and large businesses to manage costs and increase profits.

Other classifications of computer use exist, but these three match up very well with software and hardware selection. We relate these three categories to our selection of software and hardware to help in the following two steps of the purchasing process.

STEP 3: SELECT SOFTWARE PACKAGES

Once a prospective buyer has determined his or her computer needs, the software package search begins. Remember that without software, the computer can do nothing. Because the software actually makes the computer perform the desired tasks, it should be selected first. A prospective buyer should try to match needs and his or her level of expertise with the software rather than just buying the most popular package on the market. For example, several popular word processing packages each cost $300 or more, but many less expensive and less sophisticated word processing packages can handle many users' writing needs. These inexpensive packages are adequate for home correspondence or for writing short papers. However, if the user is writing the Great American Novel (or textbook), then he or she may indeed need a sophisticated word processing package to handle the volume and complexity of the work.

Methods of Selecting Software

A user may select software packages in several ways, including reading computer magazines that review various software packages, discussing software with members of a users' group, attending a computer literacy course at a local college or technical school, or explaining your needs to a computer store salesperson. Computer software research may require more than one of these avenues.

[In choosing a particular personal computer] once you have specified an intended use for the computer, there are fewer choices.

Rodney Zaks, President and founder of Sybex Books
(As quoted in "Some Clarification on Consumer Confusion," *Personal Computing,* November 1983, pp. 56–63, 217–18.)

Computer Magazines Some well-known computer magazines, which are listed in Table 10-1 (page 233), often review individual packages, listing specific capabilities and/or drawbacks. Occasionally, a computer magazine reviews an entire class of software, comparing the available packages on a feature-by-feature basis. Some magazines offer yearly directories of software, and software directories list all available software. For example, the *PC Telemart Software Directory* has over 1,200 pages of software listings categorized according to use and computer. These reviews and directories can be invaluable in the search for software that fit certain needs.

Users' Groups After this research, a prospective buyer may obtain additional information on various packages by visiting a computer users' group meeting and asking questions. The members of such a group are usually more than happy to discuss and even demonstrate the software that they own. A prospective buyer can talk to experienced users about problems they have faced, look at the types of software that they use, and, possibly, try out some software and hardware in a friendly environment. Meeting times of users' groups can be found by contacting a computer store or watching for notices in the newspaper.

Taking a Computer Literacy Course Many colleges, universities, and technical schools now offer either noncredit short courses or night classes in computer literacy. By taking a computer literacy course, an individual can learn a great deal about computer hardware, software, and applications. This knowledge can then be applied to the software selection process.

You should buy a computer because of what it will do—which, in fact, means what software is available for it.

Clive Sinclair, developer of the Timex/Sinclair computers
(As quoted in "Some Clarification on Consumer Confusion," *Personal Computing,* November 1983, pp. 56–63, 217–18.)

Visiting a Computer Store Visiting a computer store can be very helpful if someone there is knowledgeable about your specific computer need. It is often wise to make an appointment. The salesperson should walk a prospective buyer through the packages that appear to fit his or her needs. The buyer should run some test data through the software. Ease of use and applicability to the specific problem are two important criteria for deciding whether a software package is appropriate. This demonstration should also include a review of the user's manual and any other documentation that accompanies the software. If the user's manual and other documentation are difficult to follow, then the package may not fit your needs.

Even after all the research and testing, an objective choice between two or more packages may not be possible. The choice may depend on price or the ease of use.

STEP 4: SELECT HARDWARE

After software needs are determined, the buyer should select the hardware that will run the software. Because not all computers run all software, this matching process is important. Computers differ in the number of bits they can manipulate (8 or 16), the amount of memory they have (64K, 128K, 256K, or more), and the operating system that directs the computer operations (CP/M, MS-DOS, or proprietary). For example, it is impossible to run 16-bit, MS-DOS software that requires 128K memory on an 8-bit, CP/M computer with only 64K memory, and vice

The Kaypro 2 is a CP/M-based computer.

versa. Some examples of each type of computer are shown in Table 1.

To select personal computer hardware, a buyer must be aware of its component parts. Personal computer hardware components include the central processing unit (CPU), keyboard, monitor, modem, secondary storage units, a printer, and alternate input devices like the joystick, as shown in the figure on the next page. Because the keyboard and CPU come with the computer, the decisions facing the computer buyer involve the amount of internal and secondary storage, the type of monitor, the type of modem, the type of printer, and whether the system can expand.

Amount of Internal and Secondary Storage

The amount of internal and secondary storage needed has increased as a result of more sophisticated software and more reasons for users to store data on a computer. At one time, 48K of RAM and a cassette recorder or one 140K disk drive was more than enough for most needs. However, current users often need 256K or more of RAM and two 360K floppy disk drives or one floppy drive and a 10 Mbyte hard disk drive. The amount of internal and secondary storage that is needed depends on the software and the projected uses of the computer. Some popular software packages require 320K of RAM, so this amount should be considered in the purchase. Similarly, if the user needs large amounts of secondary storage, then a hard disk drive should be seriously considered. Cassette storage is still available on inexpensive computers, but the cost of a disk drive has dropped enough to make it competitive with cassette storage.

Table 1

Number of Bits	*Operating System*	*Memory*	*Computer*
8	CP/M	128K	Kaypro 2
8	Proprietary	64K	Commodore 64
16	MS-DOS	256K or more	IBM PC
16	Proprietary	128K or more	Apple Macintosh

FIGURE PC-1
Personal Computer Components

A buyer should also consider the possibility of expanding the system. For example, how easy is it to add extra RAM to the system? Can a hard disk drive be easily substituted for an existing floppy disk drive?

Choosing a Monitor and a Printer

The choice of a monitor and a printer is discussed in detail in Chapter 7, but we review the options here. For the video screen, the user can choose a monochrome (one color) monitor, a full color monitor, or a television monitor. If the buyer chooses a portable computer with a built-in video screen, then the monitor decision is already made. Some monitors are specially built to be attached to the computer and therefore can display up to 80 characters across the screen with high-quality resolution. On the other hand, a television monitor cannot display more than 40 characters clearly. Many computers used for game-playing or for learning to program are built to work only with 40 columns (or less). These computers are adequate for programming or games, but the 80-column screen is necessary for word processing or financial analysis packages. Buyers should be aware that the use of a color monitor may require a special addition to the CPU on some computers.

Two types of printers are available—dot matrix printers and daisy wheel printers. A dot matrix printer uses tiny dots to form characters on paper, and a daisy wheel printer uses fully formed characters on a spinning wheel. The dot matrix printer, which is the less expensive of the two, is usually satisfactory for most situations. On the other hand, if letter quality print is required for formal correspondence, then the daisy wheel printer is needed.

A printer that is selected to accompany a word processing package should be chosen carefully. A word processing package that supports boldface type, underlining, subscripts, superscripts, and multiple fonts is a waste if the printer does not also support these features.

Modem

Although the selection of a modem was discussed in detail in Chapter 13, we review it here. Modems are usually classified as either 300 baud (30 characters per second), 1,200 baud (120 cps), or 2,400 baud (240 cps) and as either external or internal. A 300-baud, external modem is generally adequate (high-volume business uses will require more). In fact, users with a 1,200-

The Apple Macintosh—with its mouse input, high-quality graphics, and innovative use of icons—has many loyal users.

baud modem are charged extra for such services as CompuServe and The Source. In any case, remember that communications software is needed to implement the modem.

A Package Approach

With the exception of the modem, all the components discussed here are necessary for full use of a computer, and they should be included in the computer purchase. The systems approach should be used to make the hardware purchase. Sometimes, suppliers may promise to back-order some component of hardware, which means that it must be ordered from the factory. This chancy process can leave a user unable to perform the operations for which the computer system is purchased in the first place. For example, if a special printer is required for a new type of computer system, that system may be useless until the printer arrives. If a computer system is purchased as a whole, the buyer can avoid missing necessary components.

Price Factors

Personal computers can be classified according to price and the user needs for which they are appropriate. Because of additional requirements for memory and storage, prices increase from game-playing computers to business record-keeping computers. Table 2 gives price ranges and examples of computers that fit our three categories of computer use.

Table 2

Needs	*Price Range*	*Examples*
Recreation/computer literacy	Up to $1,000	Commodore, Atari, and Radio Shack Color Computer
Personal record keeping/education	$1,000–$2,000	Apple IIe, Radio Shack Model 4, Apple IIc, Tandy 1000, and Kaypro 2
Business computing	Over $2,000	IBM PC, Apple Macintosh, ITT Xtra, TI Professional, Compaq, AT&T, and Tandy 2000

Take the main thing you want to get done—word processing, say. Get the store to configure the machine and let you use it that way before you buy it.

William Gates, Chairman of Microsoft Corporation

(As quoted in "Some Clarification on Consumer Confusion," *Personal Computing,* November 1983, pp. 56–63, 217–18.)

The prices in the table include the CPU, keyboard, monitor, some form of secondary storage, and a printer. For recreation and computer literacy, secondary storage is usually in cartridges (for games) or cassette tapes, but in the personal record keeping/education category, at least one disk drive is necessary to run the available software. Finally, business computing requires two disk drives or one disk drive and a hard disk to store the necessary information. Although the inexpensive machines can often be upgraded by adding memory and disk drives, the final cost may be the same as a comparable system with a high initial cost.

Overlap

Some overlap does exist between computers and the types of work they perform. For example, in the table, the Apple IIe and Radio Shack Model 4 are classified as personal record keeping/education computers, but they are also used in numerous small business situations. Similarly, the IBM PC and Apple Macintosh are listed as business computing machines, but they are used in many educational situations and for personal finances and record keeping. These general classifications are meant to help you understand the *predominant* use of the computers.

The Tandy 1000 is an economical IBM compatible computer that can be used for home or business record keeping.

"IBM COMPATIBLE" What Does It Mean?

A purchase of hardware often centers around its compatibility. An IBM compatible personal computer uses the same operating system (MS-DOS) and the same Intel 8086 family of chips as the IBM PC. These computers may offer different features than the IBM PC—such as a different keyboard or graphics capabilities—or they may have a lower price than the IBM PC. The degree of compatibility varies from machine to machine, but generally, three levels of compatibility exist—operationally compatible, data-compatible, and MS-DOS compatible.

An operationally compatible computer is built as much like the IBM PC as possible without violating the copyright laws. These machines, which are virtually interchangeable with the IBM PC in terms of software and add-on hardware, run almost any program that the IBM PC runs. We say "almost" because some software packages use the copyrighted features of the PC and therefore cannot run on other computers. Examples of operationally compatible computers are Compaq, the Tandy 1000, the Corona, and the ITT Xtra.

A data-compatible computer also uses the same type of chip and operating system as the IBM PC, and it reads and/or writes the same disks as an IBM PC. However, these machines cannot run all IBM software nor can they accept IBM add-on hardware. They also have different interfaces for keyboard, sound, and display. A buyer should determine whether a piece of needed IBM software can run on the data-compatible machine. Some manufacturers have added a feature to their computers' operating systems that allow the machines to run more IBM software. Examples of data-compatible computers are the TI Professional, the Tandy 2000, and the DEC Rainbow 100.

The MS-DOS compatible machines use the same CPU chip and operating system as the IBM PC. However, these machines will not accept IBM add-on hardware or IBM data disks, and they run MS-DOS software that is modified to their special data format. Examples of MS-DOS compatible machines are NEC Advanced Personal Computer, the Grid Compass, and the Hewlett-Packard 150.

These three very different levels of compatibility require that a buyer test needed software on the machines under consideration. Buying a $2,000 "IBM compatible" machine that does not run the needed software can be an expensive mistake.

SOURCE: Michael J. Miller, "Special Report: IBM Compatibility," *Popular Computing,* April 1984, pp. 106–111.

The Texas Instruments Professional Computer (left) is an IBM data-compatible personal computer that can read IBM data disks.

The ITT Xtra (right) is operationally compatible with the IBM PC because it can run software written for the IBM.

Hardware Trends

The two lower priced categories in Table 2 (page 469) contain a wide variety of computers. However, in the business computing category, manufacturers lean toward IBM PC compatibility. The majority of business computers sold today are IBM compatibles, and over 5,000 pieces of software can be run on these machines. The exceptions to this trend are the extremely successful Apple Macintosh, and the Kaypro 8-bit, CP/M computers.

PORTABLE COMPUTERS

All personal computers are, to some extent, "portable." Today, an entire class of truly portable computers exists—transportables, briefcase portables, and notebook portables. Transportable computers are complete, but smaller, versions of the desk-top computer. These computers use a small-screen VDT (9 inches or less) for display, along with full-size keyboard and disk drives. One drawback to this type of system is that the screen may be hard to read when the full 80 characters are used for word processing or spreadsheet analysis. Although these computers can be transported, they usually weigh over 20 pounds (some weigh over 40 pounds!). Such computers probably could not be carried around all day. Examples of this type of computer are the Compaq, the IBM Portable, the TI Professional Portable, the Kaypro series, and the Apple IIc.

The notebook (or handheld) portables use a one-line display with varying column widths and a miniature keyboard. Because these computers are battery powered, their memory is nonvolatile—that is, it does not disappear when the computer is turned off. Although these computers are not suitable for running full-scale software, they often have software built into ROM that can be used for entering and running BASIC programs. Weighing in at less than 1 pound, they can be useful for making quick calculations in a previously developed program.

As the name implies, a briefcase portable computer fits into the average briefcase. These computers usually have a pop-up flat screen that utilizes a liquid crystal diode (LCD) display that is 80 columns wide and 8–25 lines long. Many of these machines have popular programs stored in ROM, but the amount of RAM available to the user is restricted in some cases. Some, but not all, have built-in disk drives or bubble memory for data storage. Briefcase portables may be easily carried around because they usually weigh less than 10 pounds. Because many of these machines combine small size with a high level of computing performance, this category of machine will likely become the true "portable." Examples of briefcase portables include the Tandy 200, the TI Pro-Lite, the HP Portable, the Epson Geneva, and the Data General One.

SOURCE: Edward Foster, "When IS a Computer Portable?", *Personal Computing,* March 1985, p. 85.

The Compaq (left) is a popular IBM compatible transportable personal computer.

The Tandy 100 briefcase portable computer (right) has several built-in applications software programs.

When considering a software–hardware combination, a buyer may find a computer that comes with *bundled software*—that is, one or more software packages that are included with the computer at no extra cost. If the software that you have selected is bundled with a computer, the combination may be worth considering. On the other hand, if the computer does not include desired software or if part of the software bundle does not fit the buyer's needs, then the combination may have hidden costs that could be avoided with another hardware selection.

In the next two years, sales of these little lap-size computers are going to outdo the desk tops.

Wayne Green, founder of* Byte *magazine and numerous other computer magazines
(As quoted in *USA Today*.)

STEP 5: SELECT A SUPPLIER

Once software and hardware are selected, the buyer must choose a supplier (or suppliers) from which to make the purchases. People usually buy computer hardware and software from a computer store, from a department or discount store, or by mail order. A computer store usually stocks a range of computer hardware and software, and its staff is usually (but not always) knowledgeable about the equipment they sell. For a novice in computers, a computer store might be a good place to learn about the various types of hardware and software. A department or discount store may have a special computer department or it may just include computers with electronic equipment. The selection is probably less than in a computer store, and the staff may not be as knowledgeable. The buyer must know more about what he or she desires to make up for the sales staff's lack of knowledge. However, the prices may be lower in a department or discount store than in a computer store.

The least expensive way to buy computer software and hardware is by mail. Various computer magazines carry numerous advertisements for software and hardware at prices that are quite a bit less than the list price. Although a buyer may save a great deal of money by using a mail order company, he or she must be well informed and experienced to select hardware and software by mail. Software purchased from a mail-order house cannot be tested before it is purchased, and once opened, it cannot be returned to the company.

BUYING BY MAIL

Buyers should consider the following advice for buying computer hardware and software by mail:

Make sure incidental costs—such as shipping and handling—do not increase the mail order price above a local supplier's price.

If the mail order price is a great deal lower than a local supplier's price, check the description carefully to ensure that you are actually getting what you want.

Consider buying elsewhere if the company does not offer refunds or exchanges.

Make sure that the company has a toll-free (800) phone number and that it is willing to answer questions about its product.

Keep all transaction records in case a problem should arise.

Remember that you are entitled to a full refund if the merchandise is not delivered within 30 days of payment.

SOURCE: Mark Lewyn, "Mail-Order Computer Deals: Savings vs. Risks," *USA Today*, August 2, 1984, p. 3B.

Service Factors

A key point to consider in selecting a hardware supplier is service. A computer is generally a trouble-free machine with few moving parts, but service *will* be needed sooner or later. Computer stores have repair services to handle most problems, but a discount or department store probably does not. Most equipment has a 90-day warranty, which will be honored by the computer store on equipment that it sells. However, equipment purchased from another source may need to be returned to the factory at the buyer's expense.

STEP 6: PURCHASE THE SYSTEM

The actual purchase of hardware and software is the final step in our guide to buying a personal computer. Before this purchase is made, the buyer should consider the following checklist to ensure that he or she is buying a ready-to-use system that will not have to be returned for extra items (this checklist includes questions for the supplier as well as items that must be included in the purchase):

1. Is the software copy protected? If so, is a backup copy included in the package or must it be ordered from the manufacturer? Is the manufacturer's backup an added cost?
2. Is supplemental software needed to receive full benefit from a software package or is it an all-in-one package (for example, is a spelling-checker included in a word processing package?)?
3. If graphics are an important consideration, can they be shown on the monitor without additional devices? If not, what additional hardware is needed? What is the additional cost, and is installation included?
4. Are all printer and monitor cables included in the system or are they purchased separately?
5. Are additional interface cards or boards needed to run the printer or monitor? Are the connections sufficient to hook up a modem and a printer at the same time? If not, what do these interfaces cost?
6. Is communications software included with the modem? If not, what is the cost of communications software that is compatible with the computer?
7. Can the system be expanded in the future by adding memory or disk drives, especially a hard disk?
8. Is the cost of an initial blank floppy disk or cassette tape included in the purchase price? Similarly, is printer paper included in the cost estimate?

Once the questions in this checklist are answered satisfactorily, the purchase can be made and the system should run immediately after installation in the home or office. If any answers imply that additional equipment or purchases are needed for the desired system, then more research might be necessary before the final purchase is made.

BUYING A USED COMPUTER

Because increasing numbers of computer users are moving up to more expensive computers, used or "pre-owned" computers are often available at reduced prices. Although these machines are usually not state-of-the-art computers, they *will* serve the purposes for which they were built. A used computer is like an old pickup truck. It may not be slick and new, but it still does its job. For example, this textbook was written on an old 48K, 8-bit machine that would probably sell for less than $1,000 on the used computer market. A new 16-bit, IBM compatible computer with a full-color monitor sits on a desk nearby, but the older machine is adequate for writing the book.

A buyer should consider a few rules in selecting a pre-owned computer. First, determine the cost of a comparable new machine. With the constant decrease in computer prices, a new machine may not cost that much more than the older machine. If the price of the used machine is significantly lower, then follow these steps:

Unless you are a computer expert, find a friend or hire a consultant to help you check the machine out.

Look at the case of the computer. Is it marked up or does it appear from the mounting screws that the case has been frequently removed? Either situation may suggest problems.

Turn the unit on and attempt to boot the operating system. If the system has problems with this simple operation, then the computer should not be considered.

Check the keyboard. Dust between the keys may cause problems at a later date. Do the keys work easily, without resulting in extra or extraneous letters? If not, problems with the keyboard may make its use difficult.

If a printer is included with the machine, test it. Check the quality of symbols and whether any problems with the paper advance exist.

Test the disk drive. Can it copy a disk from one drive to another without several retries? Does it run quietly? If the answer is no to either question, then the disk drive may be a problem later.

If this test shows no apparent problems with the hardware, then the pre-owned computer may be the right buy.

SOURCE: Edward Joyce, "Negotiating the Course to Used Computerdom," *PC Magazine*, July 10, 1984, pp. 271–89.

After the personal computer is purchased, the buyer should immediately "burn in" the machine by running it for several hours. Because computer chips either fail during the first 50–100 hours of operation or not at all, running a repetitive program on the computer overnight is a good idea. The user improves the chance of catching a problem while the computer is still within the 90-day warranty. After this process, the software should also be tested to detect problems not found during the test use phase. Once the "burn-in" phase is over and the software is tested, this wonderful mind tool is ready for use.

Deal with people who understand computers and can be helpful when you need help.

John Roach, Chairman of Tandy Corporation

(As quoted in "Some Clarification on Consumer Confusion," *Personal Computing*, November 1983, pp. 56–63, 217–18.)

MEMOREX 3683
MEMOREX 3680

Block 5

INFORMATION SYSTEMS

Chapter 4 contained a survey of systems in general and information systems in particular. That discussion defined management information systems (MIS) as a broad category of information systems that aid in the management of an organization. We discussed five subsystems of MIS—management support systems (MSS), decision support systems (DSS), accounting information systems (AIS), office information systems (OIS), and data manipulation and reporting systems. We also discussed the systems analysis and design process, which is used to develop information systems. Block 5 includes a chapter on both major topics. Chapter 18 discusses the systems analysis and design process in detail using a case involving a software–hardware selection and an example of software development.

Chapter 19 examines management information systems, which are extremely important to managers today. We cover in detail three of the subsets of MIS—MSS, DSS, and OIS—and show how these systems improve decision making and the flow of work in organizations. Included is a discussion of local area networks, office automation, and data bases as part of the modern office environment.

The introduction to systems in Chapter 4 defined the concept of a system, discussed the systems approach to problem solving, presented the various information systems in organizations, and outlined the systems analysis and design method of building information systems. This chapter fills in the details of the systems analysis and design outline through a case study involving a software–hardware selection and an example of software development. The various tools used by the systems analyst are explained in these two examples. This chapter will not make you a systems analyst, but it will make you aware of the work that goes into the development of any information system.

18 Systems Analysis and Design

STUDY OBJECTIVES

After reading this chapter, you should be able to

- Understand the role of the systems analyst in the systems analysis and design process.
- Relate the steps in the systems analysis and design process.
- Understand the problem identification step and how it differs from a solution to the problem.
- Explain the feasibility study and what constitutes a successful outcome.
- Point out the system that is considered in the analysis step.
- Understand what is required in the analysis stage of the systems analysis and design process.
- Understand how the systems design step differs from the detailed design step.
- Understand how the implementation step utilizes the output from the previous steps.
- Explain the use of special systems analysis and design tools.

REVIEW OF SYSTEMS ANALYSIS AND DESIGN

In Chapter 4, we defined a **system** as *a group of elements organized for the purpose of achieving a particular goal.* An **information system** is a special type of system that involves the processing of data into information useful to managers of the organization or to interested third parties. Because data processing is mostly automated through the use of computers, we discuss *computerized* information systems in this chapter.

The **systems analysis and design process** is used to develop new information systems or to solve a problem in an existing system. The individuals who perform this task are **systems analysts**. The analyst must work with the users of the system, the programmers or the software and hardware suppliers, and the managers of the organization. Because each group views the problem differently, the analyst must act as an intermediary among the three groups. The analyst must understand the problem from the user's viewpoint. He or she must also understand how the programmers or the software and hardware suppliers can solve the user's problem. Finally, the analyst must make decisions within management's budgetary constraints. This relationship, originally shown as Figure 4-8, is repeated here in Figure 18-1.

The systems analysis and design process can be portrayed as a seven-step process. The seven steps are listed in Table 18-1, along with the objective of each step.

These seven steps were discussed in Chapter 4—you should read that material again if the details of each step are not clear to you. However, we will discuss the analysis step in more detail here, because it is the most difficult to understand.

I am persuaded that top-down design is the most important new programming formalization of the decade [1970s].

Frederick P. Brooks, Jr.

(*The Mythical Man-Month* as excerpted in *PC Magazine,* September 1983, pp. 212–40.)

Many people cannot decide exactly which system is being analyzed—the current system, a replacement system, or an entirely new system. Often, individuals do not understand the actual analysis process. In the first case, if the current manual system is being converted to an automated system, then the analyst must first understand the manual system completely. The manual sys-

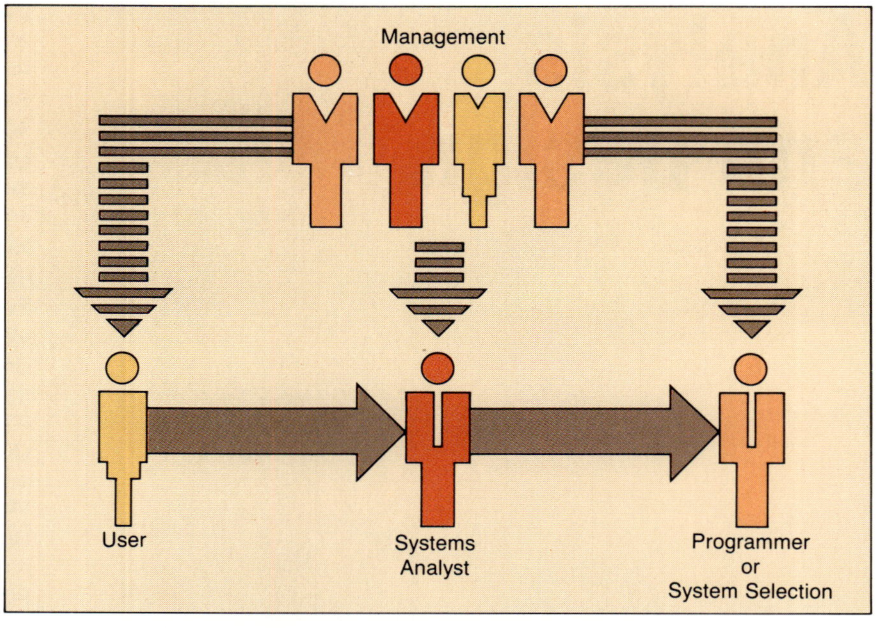

FIGURE 18-1
The Role of the Systems Analyst
[Adapted from William S. Davis, *Systems Analysis and Design* (Reading, MA: Addison-Wesley, 1983), p. 6.]

Table 18-1 SEVEN-STEP SYSTEMS ANALYSIS AND DESIGN

Step	*Objective*
1. Problem definition	To define the problem to be solved or the new system to be designed
2. Feasibility study	To determine whether the problem can be solved within budgetary constraints and to make an initial recommendation
3. Analysis	To develop a logical description of the system being designed
4. System design	To develop a high-level physical design for the recommended system
5. Detailed design	To refine the physical design so that all details can be implemented
6. Implementation	To write software or acquire the software and hardware described in the previous steps
7. Maintenance	To ensure that the system works properly and is updated as needed

tem is analyzed so that the functions currently performed are also performed in the new automated system.

If a manual or automated system is being replaced by a new system, then both the current and new systems must be analyzed. The important part of this analysis is determining the current system's input and output, because any new system must use the same input to produce identical output. The new system must be analyzed to determine how the input data flow logically through the system to generate the needed output.

THE STRUCTURED WALK-THROUGH

The systems analysis and design procedure emphasizes planning for all possible situations. However, oversights may occur because the systems analyst or programmer is too close to the project. To avoid these errors, project members can use the structured walk-through—a review of an analyst's or programmer's work by his or her peers. Such a review does not include management, so the developer is not evaluated by supervisors until the project is in final form. The structured walk-through is designed to find errors in the system design or program in an atmosphere that avoids faultfinding on the part of the reviewers and defensiveness on the part of the developer. The emphasis is on helping the developer find possible problems at an early stage of development, not in the final product.

In a structured walk-through, the developer's fellow project members help him or her analyze the project design or program. Because reviewers are provided with information on the project, they are expected to come to the walk-through with questions in mind. In the walk-through, the developer explains the project, giving a brief tutorial on how it will work. He or she then "walks" the reviewers through the design or program, step-by-step, to simulate all of its functions. During this manual execution of the project, the reviewers may develop more questions for the designer.

After the manual simulation, the reviewers summarize their joint concerns with an eye toward generating problems to be solved, rather than finding solutions. The developer must ensure that the reviewers' concerns are successfully resolved and that the reviewers are notified of the corrective action. More than one such walk-through may be necessary to resolve major questions that may arise or to review the same project at a later stage of development.

SOURCE: *Improved Programming Technologies: Management Overview,* IBM IPTO Support Group, Zostermeer, Netherlands, 1975, pp. 29–32.

"Sure you can become a systems analyst if you want to—but tell Daddy, what *is* a systems analyst?"

If an entirely new system is being designed, then the analyst must first develop a logical model of the new system, complete with the input data, the data flows through the model, and the required output.

Regardless of the system considered—current or new—the analysis step must produce a logical definition of that system. The systems analyst must be careful not to jump past this step to consider the physical definitions in the system design step. Problems can easily occur if the data and data flows within the system are not clearly defined.

The systems analyst uses several tools in the analysis process, including data dictionaries, data flow diagrams, systems flowcharts, the HIPO technique, and structure charts. The uses of these tools are explained in two examples of systems analysis and design. The first case involves the conversion of a manual system to an automated system that produces the same results. In the second example, we examine the development of a completely new system—the word processing software that accompanies this textbook. Our examples are simple cases. Often, such projects require a team of people with different backgrounds and take many months to complete. Figure 18-2 is a diagram of the systems analysis and design process, including the output required from each step as well as the tools used there.

THE MYERS FURNITURE COMPANY CASE

In the early 1950s, Len Myers established the Myers Furniture Company in Dothan, Alabama, to build and distribute pine furniture products. The company enjoyed almost immediate success because pine furniture was quite popular at that time, and because that Sun Belt area's population grew quickly. After nearly 30 years of operating in Dothan, Myers opened the Anniston division in the northern part of Alabama to take advantage of individual furniture makers in that area. Both the Dothan and Anniston divisions

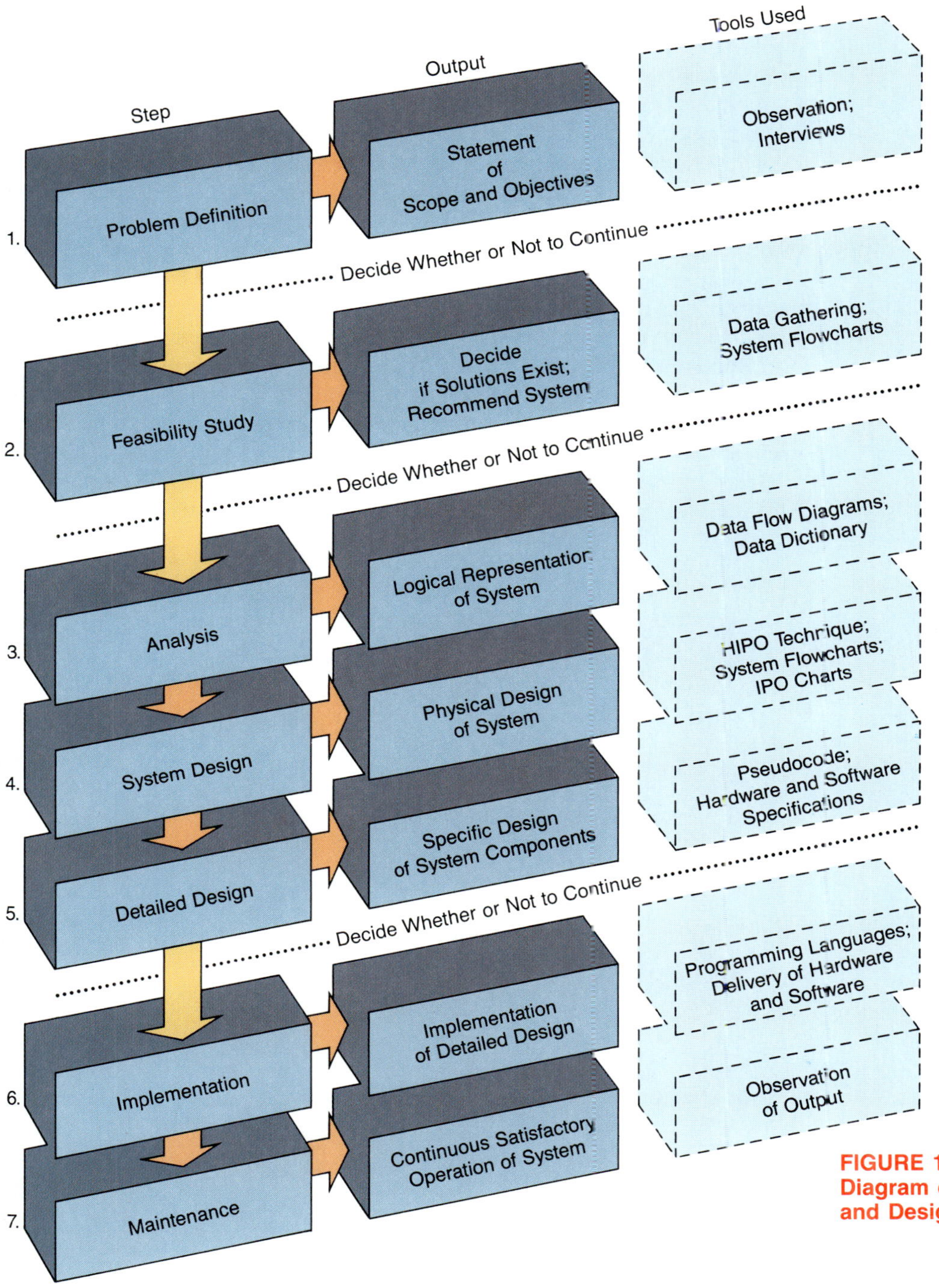

FIGURE 18-2
Diagram of Systems Analysis and Design Process

are wholesale operations that sell only to furniture stores. In addition to manufacturing furniture, the Anniston division purchases furniture from individual makers.

The Anniston division of Myers Furniture Company has annual sales of $750,000 and employs three managers, a secretary, and varying numbers of crew chiefs and furniture makers. The last group varies in size according to the level of sales and availability of furniture from outside sources. Figure 18-3 shows the chain of command of the Anniston division of the Myers Furniture Company.

Myers Furniture Company was purchased by an international conglomerate, which may close the Anniston division because it is only marginally profitable at best. A recent fire at Anniston caused over $250,000 in damage. On a visit to Anniston, auditors for the new owner found that the managers knew the furniture business quite well, and they produced a quality product. However, definite administrative and record-keeping problems existed. The three managers and the secretary manually gathered the division's accounting and administrative data and mailed it to Dothan once a week. The data were processed on the company's mainframe computer and then sent back to the Anniston division. This procedure resulted in a two-week lag between the submission of data and the return of processed information to Anniston's managers.

Given the quality of the product and the Anniston managers' enthusiasm, corporate management decided to investigate a system design for the division

FIGURE 18-3 Anniston Division Chain of Command

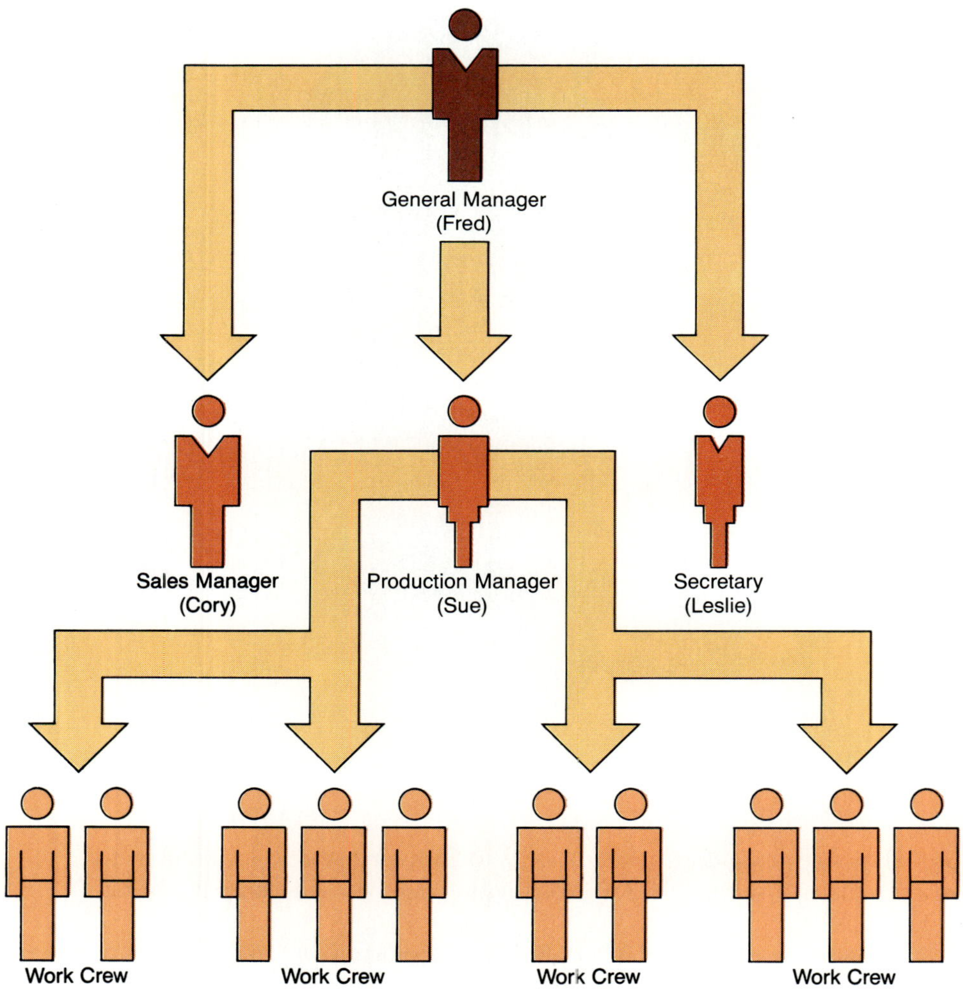

that would reduce its overhead costs and thereby enable the division to show a profit. The corporation assigned a systems analyst from its home office to the project.

Step 1: Problem Definition

The analyst correctly began her systems analysis and design project with **problem definition**. Corporate management informed her that the Anniston division of the Myers Furniture Company was unprofitable, apparently due to a lack of record keeping and good business practices. The analyst noted these opinions but did not make any decisions. The analyst then went to Dothan's mainframe operation to consult the individual in charge of processing Anniston's weekly data. These data include the number of each style of furniture in inventory. The mainframe processed the data and prepared summary reports based on shipments to the factory, sales, and production. The reports were correct, but by the time Anniston received them, the reports were out of date. After these interviews and a discussion with Len Myers, the analyst understood the Dothan end of the operation.

The analyst's next stop was Anniston. She received a tour of the operation from Fred, the general manager, who explained that over 1,000 pieces of

In the systems analysis and design process, the problem definition step is extremely important to ensure that the systems analyst understands the problem being solved.

furniture in 50 different styles were in stock. A sales force that covered the eastern half of the United States constantly needed current availabilities of various styles of furniture. Unfortunately, this information was contained only in the two-week-old reports generated by the mainframe at the home operation. In fact, the Anniston division lost a big sale to a major department store because of uncertainty over inventory. The division simply could not keep up with the constant changes in inventory due to production, purchases from outside sources, and sales.

After the tour and discussion, the analyst examined the type of computer output received each week from the Dothan office. The output certainly contained the information submitted from Anniston each week, but it was not current. The output's format also made certain information on particular furniture styles difficult to find.

Over lunch, Fred gave the analyst more thoughts on the problem definition. First, any new system of inventory control must be easy to use and relatively inexpensive. Obviously, the parent company will not invest a great deal of money in a new inventory system for an operation that might close. Fred had previously suggested that the company install a terminal connected to the home office mainframe by telephone lines, but the request was denied. Second, any new system should eventually handle payroll. Payroll is often difficult to process, because factory workers' wages are based on the number of pieces of furniture produced.

Based on all these conversations, the analyst concluded that the problem was timing—that is, the reports were out-of-date when received and therefore useless to the Anniston division. A new system should give the managers up-to-date information on their inventory *and* reduce administrative costs.

When the analyst met with Fred again, she outlined the problem, along with the restrictions on any new system that would solve the problem. She stated that the new system

1. Must provide managers with up-to-date inventory information.
2. Must be easy to use.
3. Must be relatively inexpensive.
4. Should be expandable to handle payroll.

After Fred read the analyst's statement of the problem, he reiterated the ease of use criterion. No one at the Anniston plant had any experience with computers, so any new system must be *extremely* easy to use and virtually impossible to ruin. He made several other suggestions, which the analyst incorporated in a revised statement of the problem.

The analyst submitted a statement of scope and objectives (shown in Figure 18-4) to the corporation to obtain approval for a feasibility study. She estimated that the study would take a week and cost $500. The corporation approved the feasibility study but stated that the entire project cannot cost more than $10,000, including the $500 for the feasibility study and the $500 for the time already expended.

Note that the analyst listened to key parties in this case and gathered enough preliminary information to determine the *real* problem with the Anniston division. Analysts must ask the right questions and listen carefully to

Statement of Scope and Objectives
March 11, 1986

The Project: Record keeping at Myers Furniture Company—Anniston division.

The Problem: Inventory updating is not current leading to lost sales and excessive record-keeping expenses.

Project Objectives: To develop an improved method of updating inventory.

Project Scope: The development cost of this project cannot exceed $10,000.

Preliminary Ideas: Use a terminal to transmit data to mainframe at home office; use a personal computer to process data locally.

Feasibility Study: To investigate possible improvements to the inventory record-keeping system, a feasibility study should be carried out at a cost not to exceed $500.

FIGURE 18-4
Statement of Scope and Objectives

the answers. Often, an interested person's statement of the problem also includes his or her solution to the problem. For example, Fred suggested using a terminal to transmit information to the home office. The analyst must listen to these suggestions, but she must also concentrate on defining the problem, leaving the solutions for a later step. In this situation, the problem was not poor record keeping, but a lack of an interactive, real time inventory system. In such a system, data are entered from a keyboard as they are available, and results are output at a video display terminal or printer almost instantaneously.

Step 2: Feasibility Study

In the **feasibility study**, the analyst determines whether an acceptable solution to the problem exists. He or she must perform a "quickie" version of the entire systems analysis and design process. The feasibility study includes technical, operational, and economic aspects of the problem. Technical feasibility means that the technology to solve the problem exists, and operations feasibility means that the problem can be solved within the operational restrictions of the current environment. Finally, economic feasibility means that solving the problem is an economically wise decision. The systems analyst in our example used the following seven-step process in her feasibility study:

1. Clarify the scope and objectives stated in the problem definition.
2. Study the existing system.
3. Develop a high-level model of the existing system.
4. Redefine the scope and objectives.
5. Develop alternate solutions.
6. Recommend a course of action and possibly a new system.
7. Write and present the feasibility study.

To clarify the scope and objectives, the analyst interviewed Fred again and then discussed the problem with Anniston's sales manager and production manager. Each interview involved the analyst's statement of scope and objectives, but she still gathered facts on the current operation. From these interviews, the analyst learned that each manager spent a great deal of time on record-keeping and inventory-updating duties. Much of this time was charged to the company as overtime, which was a significant part of the high administrative costs experienced by this division. The managers were frustrated with this record keeping, because they consider themselves builders of fine furniture, not bookkeepers.

The study of the current system also included interviews with the secretary, crew chiefs, and factory workers. The systems analyst also observed the current system, read operations manuals, and examined the records and record-keeping procedures. With this information, she could build a model of the existing system. A **model** is *a simplified version of the system* that allows the analyst to understand the system's important parts.

A **systems flowchart** can demonstrate the flows of information and control in the existing system. A systems flowchart uses arrows and the standard set of symbols shown in Figure 18-5. Using the information she has gathered

FIGURE 18-5
Systems Flowchart Symbols

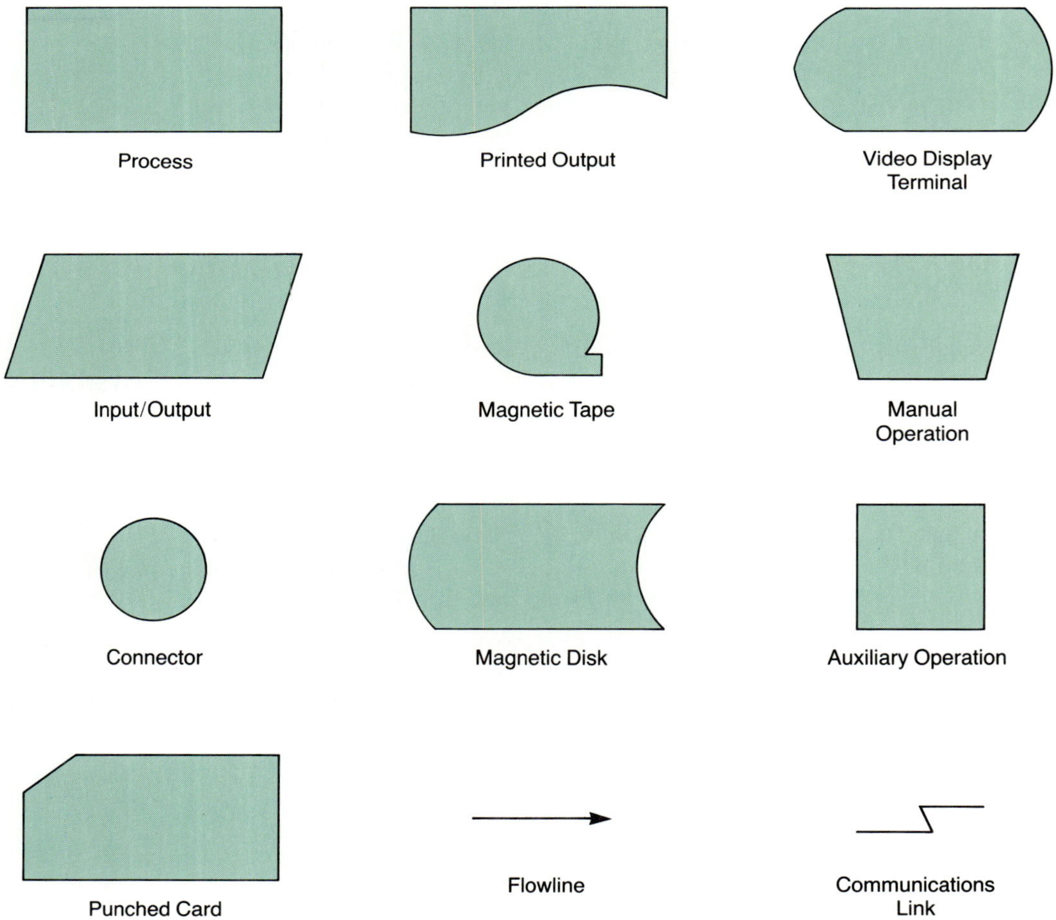

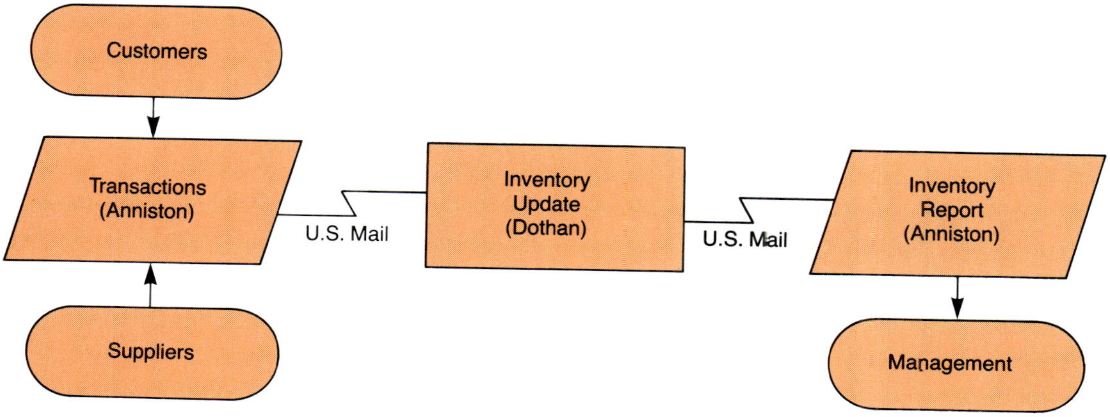

FIGURE 18-6
Overview Systems Flowchart

during her interviews and observations, the analyst can develop a systems flowchart that describes the physical operation of the current system. In Figure 18-6, only a general overview of the system is depicted, and the actual detail in each box is ignored. This kind of flowchart is useful to gain an understanding of the overall system. In Figure 18-7, the detail in each box in the overview flowchart is shown. These two flowcharts demonstrate the **top-down approach** to systems analysis and design—that is, the overall system is studied first, and detail is added as the project continues.

In the systems flowchart in Figure 18-7, three copies of sales reports, suppliers' invoices for furniture received, and production counts were processed manually in Anniston, but only one copy of each form remained there. The other two copies of each form were mailed to Dothan for processing on the home office mainframe. One copy of the sales report was used to update

ANOTHER VIEW
Floyd Read

To help you understand the job of the systems analyst, we have interviewed a working systems analyst. Floyd Read has a bachelor's degree in Business Administration and nearly 20 years of computer experience. Read is a Senior Analyst/Programmer for a medium-sized (1,000 employees) production facility.

What responsibilities does your job include?
READ: My job can be thought of as falling into three main categories—new system design; feasibility studies on new projects proposed by top management; and maintenance of current systems. However, the three tend to blend together.

What do you mean by that?
READ: Well, I may be working on a major design project like the one I just finished and a feasibility study of a "hot" idea will be requested. In that case, I have to stop the design work and perform the feasibility study. Also, a problem with an existing system can occur at any time and fixing that takes precedence over everything else.

Your title is Analyst/Programmer. Does that mean you do both?
READ: Yes. I can take a project all the way from feasibility study through to final programming and testing. The jobs are often combined in small- to medium-sized operations such as ours, but in bigger organizations, the positions are often separated. Sometimes I work as the lead analyst on a team of three or four analysts, and other times, I work alone on small projects.

What would you like to tell our readers about being a systems analyst?
READ: If you can keep your cool during periods of stress, it's an exciting and rewarding career.

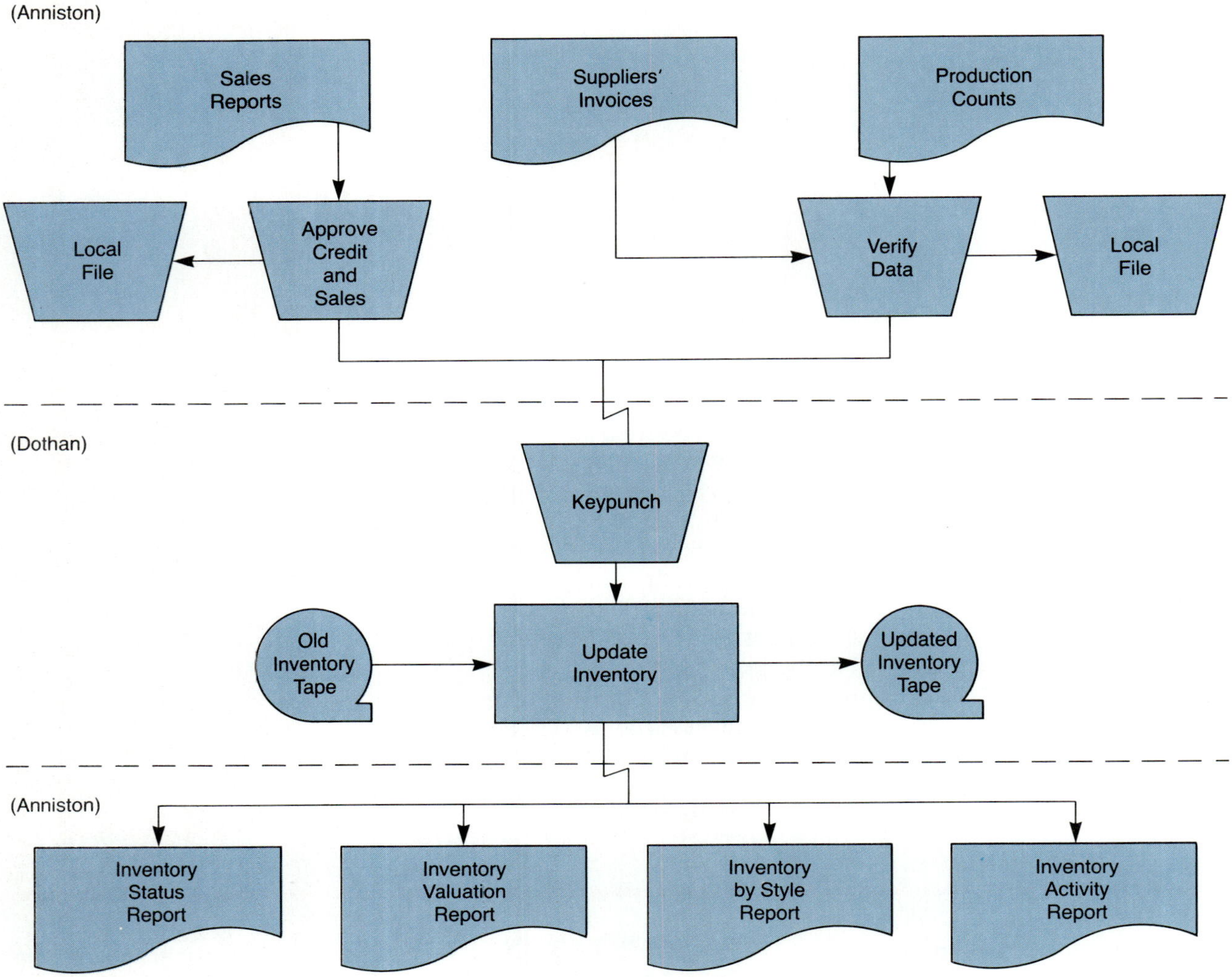

FIGURE 18-7
Detailed Systems Flowchart of Existing System

accounts receivable (money owed to Myers Furniture Company by customers), and one copy of the suppliers' invoice was used to update accounts payable (money owed by Myers Furniture Company to suppliers). One copy of the production count was stored on magnetic disk as part of the production record. The data on the other copy of each item were keypunched onto computer cards. The computer cards that contained the data on furniture received, sales, and production were then processed to update the old inventory status stored on magnetic tape. After the magnetic tape was updated, four reports were sent to Anniston.

Although the systems flowchart depicts the physical movement of data to and from the Anniston division, developing a high-level system model requires an understanding of the data flow in a **data flow diagram**. This diagram has its own set of symbols—shown in Figure 18-8—which depict the sources and destinations, the processes, the data stores, and data flows within

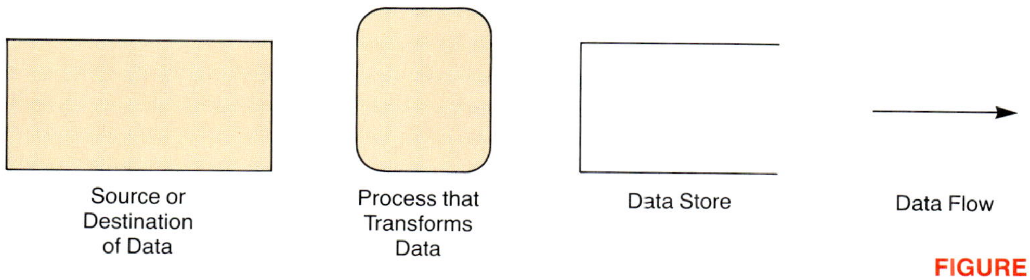

FIGURE 18-8
Data Flow Diagram Symbols

the system. Table 18-2 shows the corresponding data flow elements in the Myers Furniture Company system. Using the data flow diagram symbols shown in Figure 18-8 and the data flow elements shown in Table 18-2, the analyst can construct a data flow diagram of the current system at the Anniston division, shown in Figure 18-9.

The data flow diagram shown in Figure 18-9 is a logical model of the current system that, when combined with the systems flowchart in Figure 18-7, gives the analyst a clear picture of the Anniston division's operations. After the two diagrams were explained to Fred, he agreed that they portrayed the current system. He emphasized that the most important aspect of a new system was ease of use while reducing record keeping and updating inventory on a real time basis.

In each conference, the analyst and a manager learned something from each other. Initially, both were ignorant of the other's role. However, during discussions, each learned a great deal about the other's job and what a new system could and could not do. As a result of this process of problem definition and study of the current system, the analyst was an expert on Anniston's inventory system. A systems analyst must learn as much as possible to do a good job in the later stages of the systems analysis and design process. In fact, without a thorough understanding of the underlying concepts of Anniston's inventory system, the analyst could not proceed to the next step in the feasibility study—development of alternative solutions.

The analyst can now determine whether any solutions exist for the inventory control problem defined earlier. If no solutions to the problem exist, the study is terminated, and only a small investment was made in the problem definition and feasibility study. If only one solution exists, then the remainder of the study is dedicated to designing this one solution. Usually, multiple

Table 18-2 DATA FLOW ELEMENTS FOR MYERS FURNITURE COMPANY

Sources and Destinations	*Processes*	*Data Stores*	*Data Flows*
Customers	Process transactions and production counts	Local inventory	Transactions (receipts and sales)
Independent furniture makers	Transmit data	Master inventory	Production count
Factory workers	Update files		Processed transactions and production counts
Management	Generate reports		Reports
	Transmit reports		

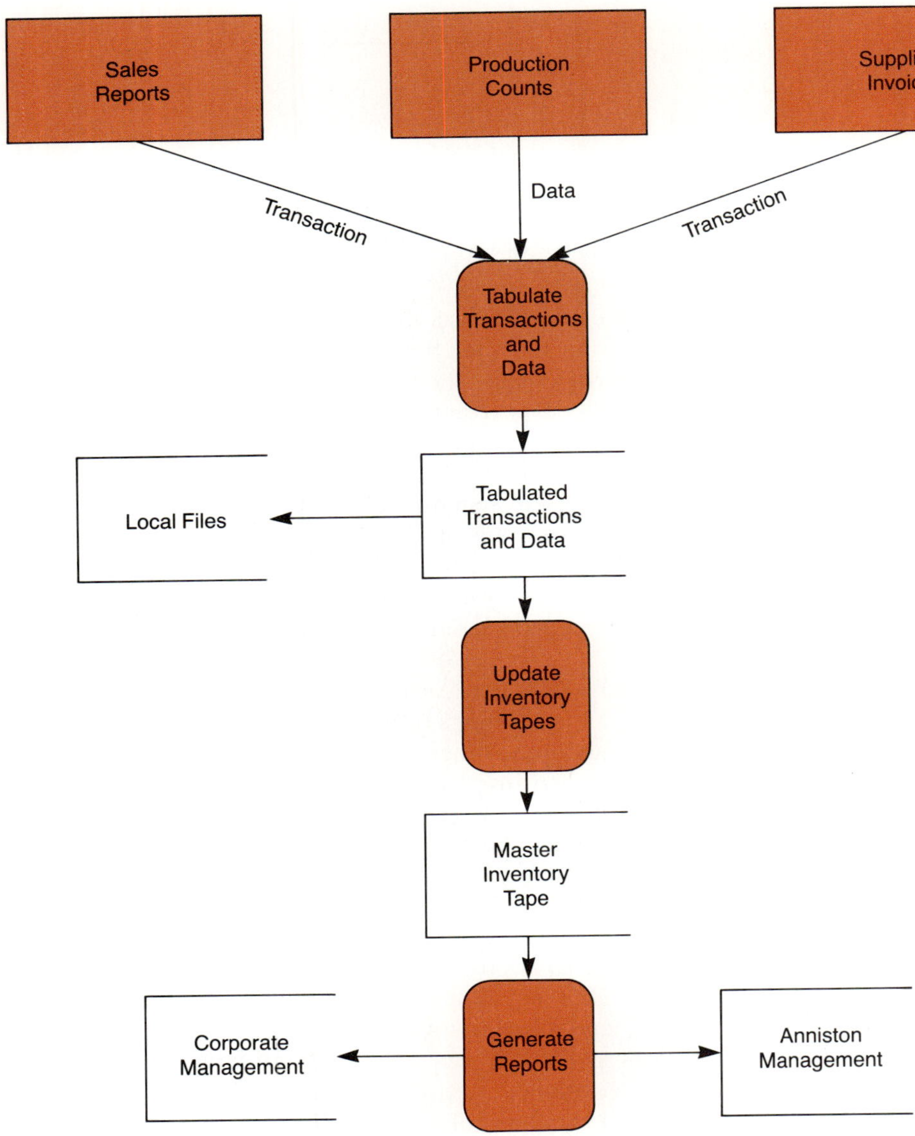

FIGURE 18-9
Data Flow Diagram of Anniston Division's System

solutions can be found for a problem. Recall from Chapter 4 that three types of solutions are usually considered—a low-cost "bare-bones" solution; an intermediate solution that meets all stated requirements; and an expensive solution that extends beyond the current needs. For the Anniston division of the Myers Furniture Company, the analyst developed the following three possible solutions:

1. Upgrade the current manual system so that inventory updating is done manually in Anniston and not sent to Dothan.
2. Install a personal computer at the Anniston division that can update the local inventory and communicate with the mainframe in Dothan on a weekly basis to update the master inventory records.

3. Install a terminal in Anniston that would transmit data and receive reports over business quality telephone lines. This terminal would be tied into the Dothan mainframe, which would update inventory daily. Inventory reports would then be returned to Anniston by telephone lines and printed there.

The analyst first discussed each alternative with Fred and the other managers. The first alternative was unanimously rejected. All three managers felt that a totally manual system would require more time than the current system, and would therefore result in higher overtime charges. The first alternative would only delay a permanent solution to the problem.

The choice between the second and third options was not as clear-cut. Fred liked the idea of having a terminal connected to Dothan's mainframe. When he expressed concern about programming a personal computer, the analyst explained that software packages would be used and that no programming would be necessary. Sales manager Cory favored the personal computer because he must respond quickly to telephone calls from salespeople. He did not want to put a salesperson on "hold" and sort through a pile of output to answer a question. Production manager Sue noted that someone would still have to compile sales and production data each day and transmit it to the home office. Finally, all three managers were concerned that the mainframe might be "down" during the business day, requiring someone to work overtime to enter the data. Dothan often used this excuse when inventory reports took longer than usual to be returned. Finally, the mainframe terminal could not handle the payroll.

After listening to the managers' comments, the analyst prepared a rough cost–benefit analysis comparing the latter two alternatives with the current system. The cost values in this analysis were based on the analyst's knowledge of the computer hardware and software market and estimates of current costs supplied by Anniston's managers. This cost–benefit analysis is shown in Table 18-3.

Table 18-3 COST–BENEFIT ANALYSIS

	Current System	*Alternatives* Terminal	Personal Computer
Initial Development Costs			
Hardware	$ 0	$1 500	$7,000
Software	0	0	500
Total	$ 0	$1 500	$7,500
Yearly Operating Costs			
Phone lines	$ 0	$3,500	$ 500
Supplies	250	1,000	500
Labor (overtime)	2,000	0	0
Maintenance	0	50	250
Lost sales	4,000	0	0
Total	$6,250	$4,550	$1,250
Annual Cost Savings	$ 0	$1,700	$5,000

FIGURE 18-10
Cost Comparison of Alternatives

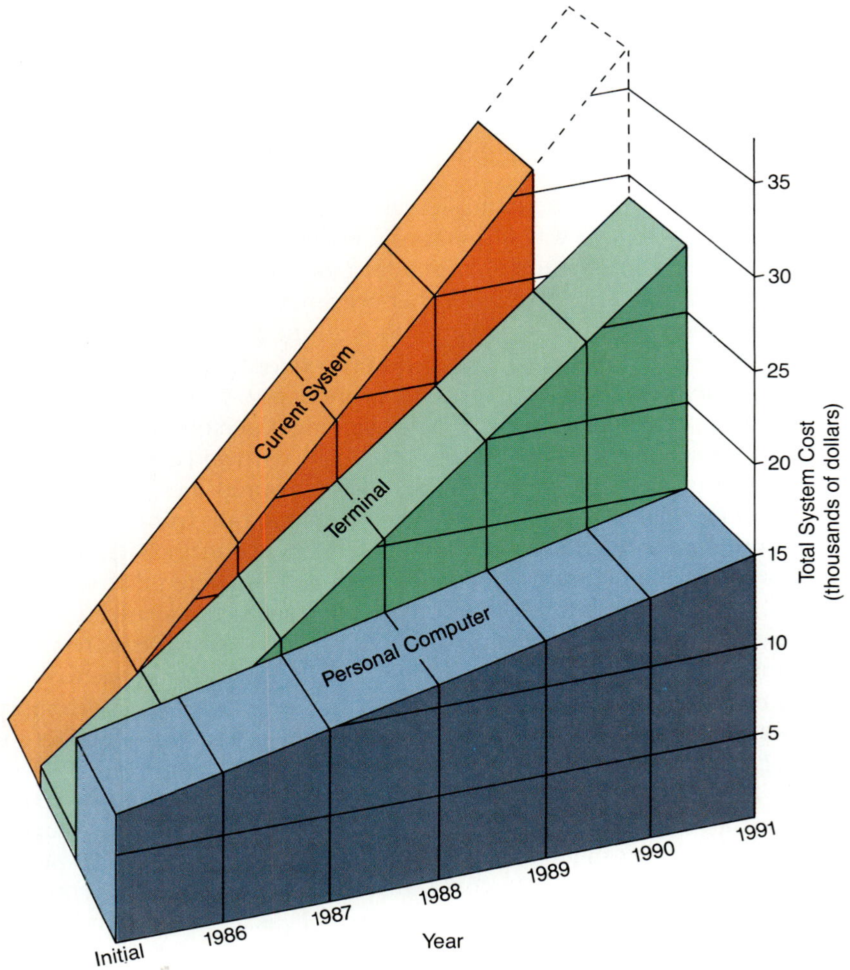

A graph of the values shown in Table 18-3 appears in Figure 18-10. The graph clearly shows that the terminal is initially cheaper, but that the cost savings of the personal computer overtake both the current system and the proposed terminal system by the end of the second year, with savings increasing every year thereafter. At this point, the analyst recommended that the personal computer system be selected. Remember, this recommendation is by no means final; it is based only on the feasibility analysis.

In her feasibility report, the analyst concluded that the problem defined earlier could be solved with a computer system. She also made a *preliminary* recommendation that a personal computer be used to give Anniston division's management an up-to-date inventory report. A rough implementation schedule, shown in Table 18-4, was included in the feasibility report. This schedule should help the analyst estimate the project's cost and show local and corporate management approximately how much time the project will take. In this case, less than six weeks would be required to analyze, design, and implement the recommended system.

Based on this implementation schedule and the estimated initial cost of the personal computer system, the analyst estimated the total cost of the new system at $10,450 ($7,500 for the computer system, 5.4 weeks at

Table 18-4 ROUGH IMPLEMENTATION SCHEDULE

Activity	*Time Required (weeks)*	*Elapsed Time*
Feasibility study	1.0	1.0
Analysis	2.0	3.0
System design	1.0	4.0
Detailed design	1.0	5.0
Implementation	0.4	5.4

$500/week = $2,700 for the systems analysis and design, and $250 already incurred for problem definition). Although the estimate is $450 more than the parent company's limit, the analyst felt comfortable with this recommendation because of the large cost savings in future years.

After examining the analyst's feasibility report, corporate management decided to proceed with the systems analysis and design. The project could still be terminated at any time up to the implementation stage, if necessary. The cost of termination would be limited to the time spent by the analyst.

Step 3: Analysis

The feasibility study provides an outline of a system, and the **analysis** step fills in the details. Every step of the recommended system must be accounted for and included in the overall analysis. For example, the primary objectives of Anniston's new system, as defined in the feasibility study, are as follows:

1. To provide current inventory information.
2. To save time and effort in record-keeping activities.

After the problem is defined, the next steps in systems analysis and design are the feasibility study and analysis.

The system should also be easy to use and expandable to other activities.

These objectives can be accomplished through reports to management sent in printed form or displayed on a home office terminal. Additional inventory information can be printed out for study at a later date. The analyst must determine the exact contents of each report and develop a more detailed list of data elements and data flows. For example, the analysis must answer the following questions: What is counted in inventory for a particular style of furniture? Does this quantity have any other names or "aliases"? How is this quantity used in generating reports?

In Anniston, the analyst first considered the needed output—that is, the reports that the system must generate. Table 18-5 lists examples of the reports that the analyst found in her research, along with a short explanation of each.

Next, she analyzed the data elements used to generate these reports by writing a data dictionary. A **data dictionary** contains information about data and explains the uses of each type of data. The data dictionary and a list of data elements constitute the **formal documentation** of the analysis. Table 18-6 lists some data elements that the analyst found. Each data element has one page of the data dictionary, which shows the data stores, data flows, and the reports in which this data element can be found. Any aliases of the data element are given, as well as the form of the data. A sample data dictionary page appears in Figure 18-11.

After data elements were analyzed, data flows were diagramed in detail. Each element of the data flow diagram in the feasibility report was broken down into its component parts. For example, the analyst magnified the section of the data flow diagram associated with production, showing its component parts. As a result, a new data flow diagram was created with data stores

Table 18-5 EXAMPLES OF NEEDED REPORTS FOR ANNISTON DIVISION

Report	*Explanation of Contents*
Picking tickets	An order for a factory worker to pick certain numbers of various styles of furniture to fill an order
Customer invoices	A statement of the number and price of furniture that is shipped
Sales reports	A summary report for sales of each style of furniture
Inventory status report	A list of the amount of each style of furniture currently in stock

Table 18-6 PARTIAL LIST OF DATA ELEMENTS

Discount price	Quantity on hand
Open orders	Transfers in
Product description	Transfers out
Product number	Total month-to-date (MTD) sales
Product price	Total quantity
Quantity available	Total value
Quantity back-ordered	Total year-to-date (YTD) sales

Name:	Quantity on hand
Aliases:	Total furniture, furniture on hand, inventory total
Description:	Amount of each style of furniture currently in stock
Form:	Numeric; maximum value = 10,000
Location:	Inventory status report, inventory valuation report, price list, inventory activity report

FIGURE 18-11
Data Dictionary Page

and flows that were concerned only with production. The analyst's production data flow diagram is shown in Figure 18-12.

After the formal documentation was completed, Anniston's managers reviewed the data dictionary and the various data flow diagrams. This learning experience for both parties resulted in several changes in data dictionary items and the data flow diagrams. With Fred's approval of these changes, the analyst could assume that the logic underlying the data dictionary and data flow diagrams was correct. As a result, the analyst's picture of Anniston's operations was clear enough for her to design the new system.

Step 4: System Design

The objective of the analysis step was to develop a logical view of a new system using a data dictionary and data flow diagrams, first for the system as a whole and then for the parts of the system. The **system design** step produces a high-level physical design of the new system that includes its actual parts. This type of design, often referred to as a *black box design,* shows a system that performs the needed functions but does not consider exactly how those functions actually work. Such a design should include a systems flowchart of the recommended system.

Using the detailed study of the recommended system from the analysis stage, the analyst can design the recommended system. Usually, three versions of the recommended system are designed—a fully automated system, a combination manual and automated system, and a manual system. A fully automated system would perform all needed operations without human intervention, and a combination manual and automated system would require human intervention at some stages.

Recall that the systems analyst recommended the use of a personal computer to handle the inventory reports for the Anniston office that are now prepared in the home office. As an aid to the design of this system, the analyst developed the systems flowchart in Figure 18-13, which shows the various components of the recommended system. In the systems flowchart, note that a telecommunications link is used to transmit information to the home office every week. Using this method, the home office receives the same information as before, but it is sent by telephone instead of by mail. The Anniston division has its own processing, which is backed up by the tape storage in the home office. The components of the recommended system are designated only in general terms. The actual selection of make and model of hardware occurs in the detailed design step.

The systems flowchart in Figure 18-13 represents a combined manual and automated system. Theoretically, the analyst should also develop system flowcharts for the fully automated option and the manual option, but in this case, she chose not to do so. The manual option was discarded in the feasibility study, and the fully automated option was apparently unworkable from a price and manpower viewpoint. At this stage, the analyst did not change any of her cost estimates, because the costs of the recommended system and the analysis seemed to be within the budget.

FIGURE 18-12
Data Flow Diagram for Production Count

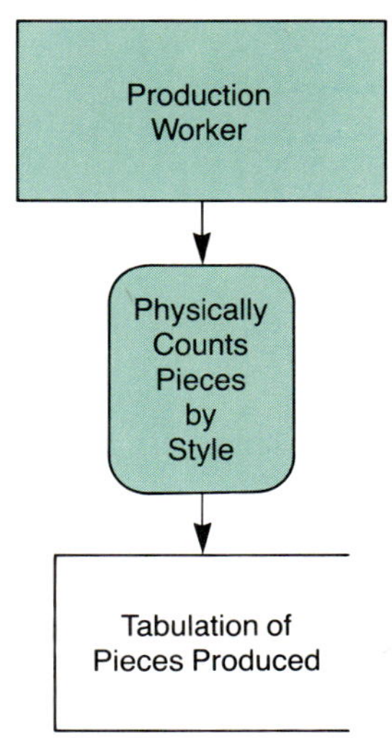

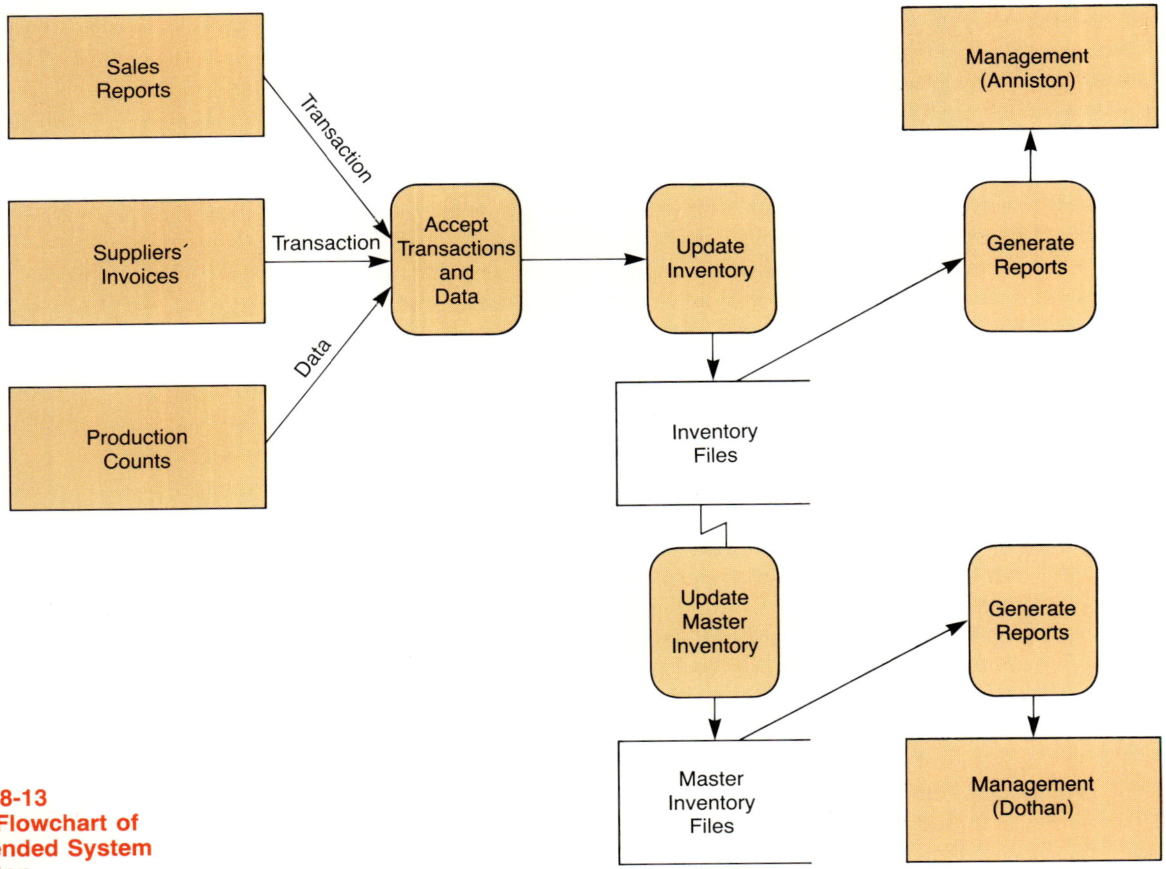

FIGURE 18-13
Systems Flowchart of Recommended System for Anniston

Developing a system design requires close contact between the systems analyst and the user of the system.

The analyst then defined the system physically by determining software and hardware needs. The logical design developed in the analysis step guided the selection of software. The analyst found software that provided the reports listed in Table 18-5 (page 496) and the data stores and flows noted in the data flow diagrams. Once the software was selected, the analyst looked for hardware that would accomplish the following tasks:

1. Run the software.
2. Meet the secondary storage needs of the Anniston division.
3. Print the output and transmit information to and from the home office.

The systems analyst concluded that the Anniston division's hardware system should include the following components:

1. A central processing unit (CPU) with at least 256 Kbytes of internal memory to run the projected software.
2. A high-resolution monitor.
3. A secondary storage capacity in excess of 1000 Kbytes to handle the division's information storage needs.
4. A high-speed printer to handle 132-column (computer) paper.
5. A high-speed (at least 120 cps) modem for telecommunications with the home office.
6. A business-quality phone line to handle telecommunications of data via telephone.

Anniston's managers want the system purchased from a local firm that can train the division's employees and maintain the equipment after installation.

Step 5: Detailed Design

After Anniston managers approved the high-level design, the analyst researched software and hardware that would fit the design's requirements. Her research started with an inventory control software package that would provide all data requirements for Anniston and be easy to use. The system she selected ran on computers that used an MS-DOS operating system and required 256 Kbytes of internal memory and a 10 Mbyte hard disk. This software package also met the management requirements in the following ways:

1. Because the user could select from a menu of commands by entering a single digit, the package was easy to use.
2. The software package could expand to include other financial and accounting applications.
3. The software package did not require a knowledge of accounting principles.
4. The software manufacturer had an 800 (toll-free) phone number for user support and offered free corrections and revisions to the package if necessary.

PC INTERACTIVE SYSTEMS

The keynote of modern systems development is the highly structured approach that is used to develop large-scale systems. The structured approach pervades every aspect of the development process, from the hierarchy of the project team to the system flowcharts to the program code itself. The complexity of a large software design and the development project requires a structured approach to ensure that nothing is left to chance. Because such large-scale projects are usually designed for multiple users on an expensive mainframe computer, the end result is often a compromise between the exact needs of the users and the economic and technical realities of the data processing environment.

The structured approach may be necessary in large-scale systems development, but simpler projects may need to be developed using a personal computer. In this environment, the PC user is the end user, systems analyst, programmer, computer operator, and data input clerk—all in one. This user is interested in the application and not in the technical aspects of systems design. As a result, he or she may use a trial and error method with such ready-made application tools as spreadsheets, word processing packages, or data base management packages. Flexibility is the key word in the trial and error process as the user interacts with the personal computer and tries out a series of formulas to see if they provide needed answers. In this process, the user quite often arrives at a better understanding of the problem. Because the personal computer user is often the sole user of the system, he or she need not compromise on the results of the system.

The accompanying table compares the structured approach used in large-scale systems development to the interactive approach of systems development used with personal computers.

Structured Development	*Interactive Development*
Planned	Spontaneous
Efficient	Inefficient
Compromising	Uncompromising
Certain	Quick
Dominated by technical experts	Dominated by applications experts

SOURCE: David Dee, "Developing PC Applications," ***Datamation,*** **February 15, 1985, pp. 112–16. Table reprinted with permission of** ***Datamation®*** **magazine, © copyright by Technical Publishing Company, a Dun & Bradstreet company, 1985. All rights reserved.**

The analyst then researched various computers that would run the selected software package. She excluded machines that did not use an MS-DOS operating system and that did not have the required internal memory or hard disk options. Finally, the analyst considered the availability of staff training and after-sale maintenance.

The analyst's research led her to MS-DOS machines that used a 16-bit Intel chip—such as the 8086, 8088, or the 80186. Such machines are often referred to as *IBM compatible*. She seriously considered the Apple Macintosh because of its ease of use. However, because the desired software was not available for the Macintosh, or any other mouse-driven or touch screen machine, she discarded the idea of using such a system. The analyst finally suggested that an IBM or any one of several IBM compatible machines would fit Anniston's needs. The computers she suggested were available from a local supplier who offered 10 hours of on-site training for users and a factory-trained repair staff for any maintenance problems. This supplier also had a reputation for answering customers' questions long after the sale was made.

All three Anniston managers accompanied the analyst to the supplier for a demonstration of the selected software with several computers. Each manager brought sample data, questions, and reports to test the software and hardware. The salesperson had the entire day to demonstrate the system, and the home office mainframe was available to test communications with the

After selecting appropriate software, a systems analyst researches hardware components and finds a supplier to provide the entire system.

new system. After trying several IBM compatible computers, the managers settled on the system that was the easiest to use and offered the most features for the money. Because this machine was produced by a large, stable company, support in later years was not a worry.

The managers spent the rest of the day testing the inventory system with their sample data. The menu-driven software worked quite well and appeared to satisfy their needs. Questions on the inventory system application were resolved by a call to the manufacturer's toll-free number. Cost figures on the computer, a 132-column printer, and a 120 cps modem selected by the analyst are shown in Table 18-7.

Table 18-7 HARDWARE COST FIGURES

Hardware Component	*Cost*
System unit (IBM compatible)	$3,895
Full color monitor	580
Color/graphics card	235
Printer adapter	75
132-column printer	800
Printer cable	45
120 cps internal modem	600
Total Cost	$6,230

A full color monitor was included in the system so that color graphics packages could be used in future applications. For example, the Anniston managers could make budget projections and view the results of various changes on a multicolor graph. No additional communications software was necessary, because the internal modem included this software. The total cost of the software–hardware package recommended by the analyst is shown below:

Inventory control software package	$ 800
Total hardware cost	6,230
Total system cost	$7,030

The parent company reviewed the final recommendations, noted that the cost was below the estimate in the feasibility study, and approved the purchase of the system.

Step 6: Implementation

Before the system was installed, the analyst consulted with the Anniston managers to determine the system's location. The analyst noted that the system should be located so that its users would not disturb other workers. Because the supply room was centrally located and had the necessary electrical outlets and telephone jacks, it was cleaned out to make room for the installation of the computer.

The analyst arranged for a telephone company to install another business quality phone line for telecommunications with the home office. She also made an appointment with the supplier to install the computer, printer, modem, and software package. The analyst then returned to the corporation's home office, with the understanding that she would return to Anniston on the day of installation.

Implementation of a new hardware and software system (left) involves a training process for users. Maintenance (right) can involve both repair of hardware components and correction of problems in software.

The analyst followed up the selection of hardware and software by making the actual purchase and preparing for the installation. By preparing the way for the computer, she ensured that the initial use of the computer would be a good experience. She was also present at the installation to ease the computer's introduction. A new user is easily discouraged if problems with the computer occur when it is installed. If the analyst could not solve the problems, she knew who to call—the supplier, the hardware manufacturer, or the software company. The supplier's training sessions enabled the managers to overcome their initial fears of the computer.

Step 7: Maintenance

The analyst's operating costs for the personal computer system included maintenance costs. The hardware had a 90-day warranty that covered any initial problems. After this period, the company could buy a maintenance agreement to cover any problems or simply take the computer in for repair when necessary. Because personal computers generally require very little maintenance after the warranty period, the analyst suggested that Anniston not buy an extended service agreement. The amount included in the operating cost for maintenance was placed in a fund to pay for any large future repairs—such as major disk drive repairs.

Postscript

The system that the analyst designed for the Anniston division of the Myers Furniture Company enabled the company to save money on administrative costs and have up-to-date inventory information on hand. Six months after installation, the analyst spent another week in Anniston to help the managers select and install a payroll system that would handle the payment of furniture workers on a piece-rate system.

SOFTWARE CONSTRUCTION

The Effects of Manpower and Time

When the development of a software project falls behind schedule due to poor design or unforeseen problems in writing the software, management often adds more manpower to the project to speed up the process. However, this may actually have a negative effect on the project. In his book on systems analysis and design, Frederick P. Brooks states Brooks' Law:

Adding manpower to a late software project makes it later.

Brooks, the so-called "father" of the OS/360 operating system used on the IBM System 360 mainframe and its successors, reasons that men and months are interchangeable commodities only when a task can be divided between them with no communications necessary to carry out the task. This may be true of reaping wheat or picking cotton, but it is not even approximately true of software development using the systems approach.

Software development is inherently a systems effort with much communication. As such, the decrease in individual task time brought about by adding manpower is quickly dominated by the increase in communications efforts required by the complex interrelationships that exist in any large-scale project. The number of months depends on the project's sequential constraints, and the maximum number of workers depends on the number of independent subtasks. From these two quantities, schedules that require less manpower and more time can be established, but the reverse is seldom possible!

SOURCE: Frederick P. Brooks, Jr., *The Mythical Man-Month* as excerpted in *PC Magazine*, September 1983, pp. 212–40.

DEVELOPING A SOFTWARE SYSTEM

The Myers Furniture Company case involved the analysis and design of a small computer system for a business. Another type of systems analysis and design involves the development of a software system by writing computer programs. In this section, we discuss this second use of systems analysis and design.

Most cases of software development involve a new system—either the automation of a manual system or the creation of an entirely new system. Occasionally, an old system is redone, but this situation is less common. The approach to software development is similar to that discussed in the Myers Furniture Company's systems analysis and design. The difference between the design of a software–hardware system and the development of software lies predominantly in the system design, detailed design, and implementation steps of the process. Therefore, we concentrate on these three steps in our discussion of software development.

Additional Tools

In software development, the analyst must use additional tools to design the system. In addition to the systems flowchart, data flow diagrams, and a data dictionary, software development requires the use of the Hierarchical Input/Process/Output (HIPO) Technique, hierarchy charts, Input/Process/Output (IPO) Charts, structure charts, and pseudocode. We illustrate the use of each tool in the development of the word processing package available with this book. Although this section is not a complete case study like the Myers Furniture Company case, the development of the word processing package can explain the use of these additional tools.

The **Hierarchical Input/Process/Output (HIPO) technique** is used in the systems design stage to develop the high-level design of the recommended system. The analyst uses two types of charts—hierarchy charts and IPO charts—to develop specifications for the programs in the software package. A **hierarchy chart** breaks the software package into smaller pieces until

FIGURE 18-14
Hierarchy Chart for Word Processing Software

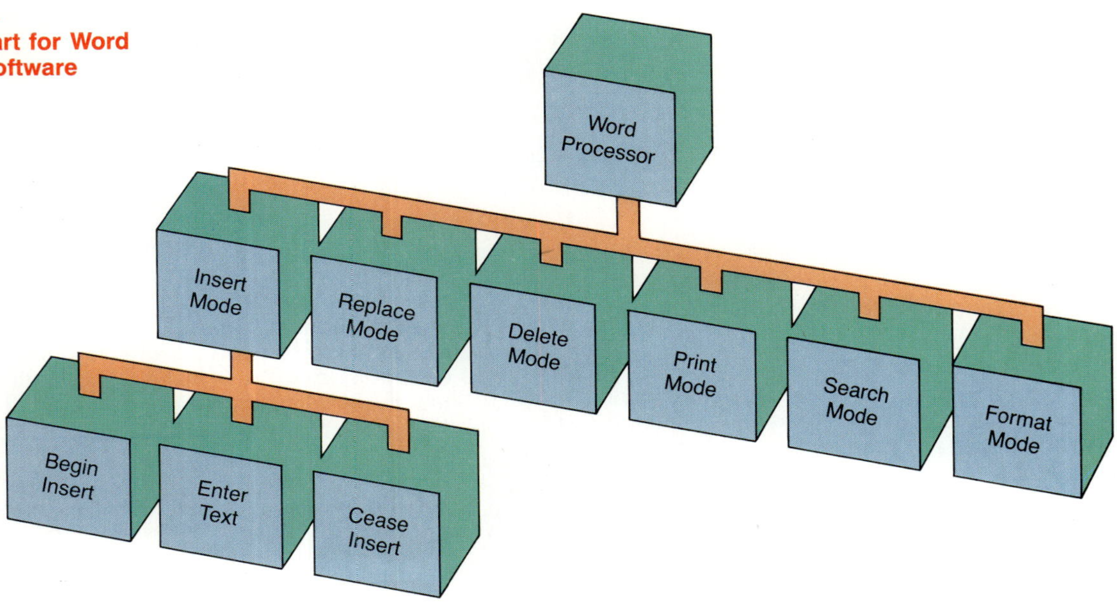

a program can be written to implement each piece of the package. For example, Figure 18-14 shows the first-level hierarchy chart for the word processing package. The main package is broken down into blocks, or **modules**—one for each function of the package. Additional hierarchy charts are then developed for each module. This division process continues until the modules cannot be subdivided any further. In Figure 18-14, the Insert Mode module is divided into another level of modules.

For each module in the hierarchy chart, the analyst develops an **Input/Process/Output (IPO) chart**. The IPO chart shows the input to the module, the processing that takes place in the module, and the output from the module. The data dictionary developed in the analysis step provides the input to the module, and the algorithms devised in the program development process are the source of the processes in each IPO chart. Figure 18-15 demonstrates the IPO chart for the Insert Mode module.

Structure charts combine some features of the hierarchy chart and the IPO chart. The structure chart demonstrates the top-down design of the program and shows the input to each module on the lines leading to the module. Looking at a structure chart, the analyst can quickly see the connections between modules and the input to each lower level module. Figure 18-16 demonstrates a structure chart for the first-level modules of the word processing package.

The results of the HIPO technique and the structure charts are used in the detailed design stage of software development. The next step is usually converting the modules into **pseudocode**, or programs written in a form of English. In pseudocode, the analyst can concentrate on the input, processing, and output of the design without worrying about the vocabulary and syntax of a high-level language. For the word processing Insert Mode module, a section of pseudocode might read as follows:

```
While insert mode is "on" repeat the following:
      Add characters after the beginning of insert;
End repeat.
```

To develop an individualized personal computer application, a personal computer user must be a combination systems analyst, programmer, computer operator, and data entry clerk.

IPO Chart

System: Word Processing

Module: Insert

Called by: Main program

Calls: Begin Insert
Enter Text
Cease Insert

Input: Begin Insert

Process: Text is inserted into middle of existing text.

Output: Text added to document

FIGURE 18-15
IPO Chart for Insert Mode

FIGURE 18-16
Structure Chart

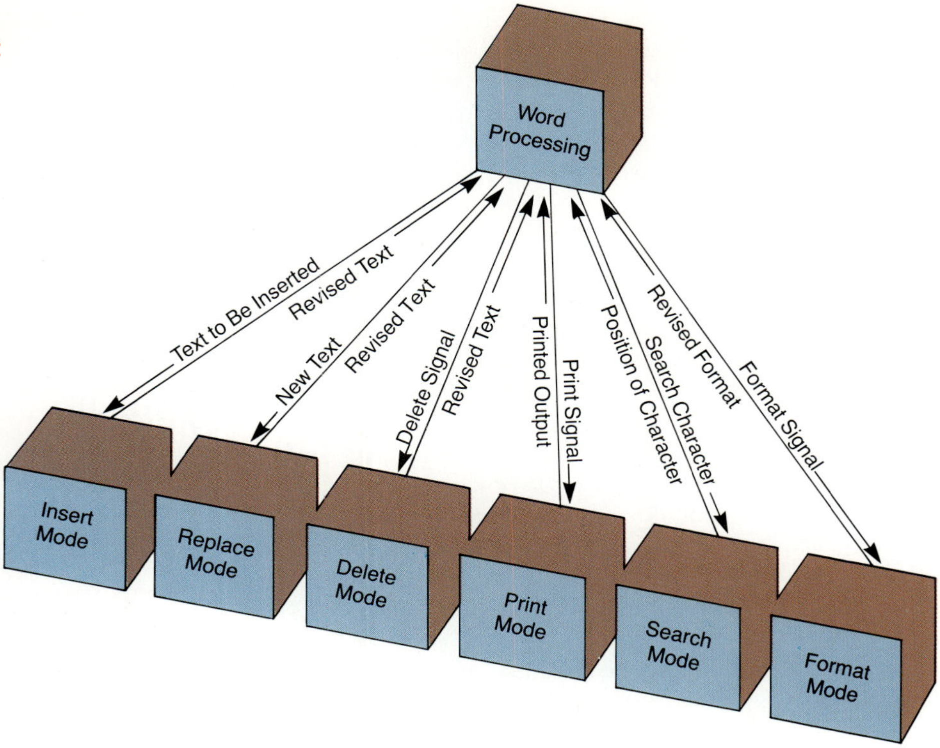

Using the pseudocode version of the program, the programmer can easily write the final high-level language version of the program in the implementation stage. The word processing package that accompanies this text uses the C language, so the pseudocode was coded into the C language before the package was tested and eventually used.

REVIEW OF KEY POINTS

- The systems analyst is responsible for analyzing and designing information systems.
- Structured systems analysis and design is a seven-step process.
- Problem identification involves learning about the current system and determining its scope and objectives.
- In the feasibility study, the analyst determines if the problem can be solved and makes an initial recommendation.
- Systems flowcharts and data flow diagrams are used in the feasibility study to develop a model of the current system.
- A cost–benefit analysis and rough implementation schedule are included with the feasibility study.
- In the analysis step, the systems analyst develops a logical model of the system being studied.
- A data dictionary is useful in the analysis of the system.
- The system design step develops a high-level physical design of the system.
- The detailed design step uses the high-level design to develop specific details of the system.
- The implementation and maintenance steps put the detailed design into action and ensure that it continues to operate correctly.
- Software design is an important type of systems analysis and design.
- Additional tools used in systems analysis and design are the HIPO technique, hierarchy charts, IPO charts, structure charts, and pseudocode.

KEY TERMS

analysis
data dictionary
data flow diagram
feasibility study
formal documentation
Hierarchical Input/Process/Output (HIPO) technique
hierarchy chart
information system
Input/Process/Output (IPO) chart
model
modules
problem definition
pseudocode
structure charts
structured walk-through
system
system design
systems analysis and design process
systems analysts
systems flowchart
top-down approach

REVIEW QUESTIONS

1. Why is systems analysis and design used to select hardware and software for a small business?
2. Why is interviewing an important tool during the problem definition step of systems analysis?
3. How does model-building fit into the systems analysis and design process? How is a logical model different from a physical model?
4. Why is the feasibility study described as a scaled-down version of the entire systems analysis process?
5. How does the analyst decide which system should be studied during the analysis step? What does the data dictionary have to do with the analysis step?
6. What is the objective of the system design step? What tools are used by the analyst in this step?
7. What design tools are used in software design that might not be used in software–hardware selection?
8. How does the detailed design step relate to the system design step? How does this relationship differ in software–hardware selection and software development?
9. What is the difference between the implementation and maintenance steps?
10. What is the difference between a HIPO chart and a structure chart? In what step is pseudocode used?

A management information system is important in any organization because it ensures the adequate flow of information to managers who make decisions. This chapter on management information systems covers in detail three subsystems of the overall information system—management support systems, decision support systems, and office information systems. We discuss the overall management information system in an organization as well as the similarities and differences between management support systems and decision support systems. The functions of an office information system and how that system supports an organization's management information system are explained. Because a computer information system of any type is impossible without data bases and computer networks, these topics are also included in this chapter.

19

Management Information Systems in Organizations

STUDY OBJECTIVES

After reading this chapter, you should be able to

- Understand the importance of management information systems in organizations.
- Understand what a management information system is and how it provides managers with information.
- Discuss the reports produced by a management support system and the purpose of each report.
- Explain how each part of a decision support system helps in managerial decision making.
- Explain the differences between a management support system and a decision support system.
- Understand the functions of the office information system and how it supports the management information system.
- Explain how data bases and computer networks support the management information system.

MANAGEMENT INFORMATION SYSTEMS

Chapter 4 introduced the concept of systems, with particular emphasis on information systems. An **information system** has as its goal the conversion of data into information that is useful to an organization's managers or to external interested third parties.

An organization must be managed efficiently to survive. A key ingredient in the management of any organization is its arrangement of information systems. Before computers, manual information systems included typewritten reports, verbal reports, and any informal information that the manager could glean from the organization's "grapevine." These information sources are still important, but current management also needs automated or computerized information systems. Automated information systems handle the large quantities of data and information that today's manager needs to allow him or her to make timely decisions.

The **management information system (MIS)** is "an integrated, user–machine system for providing information to support operations, management, and decision-making functions in an organization."[1] In Chapter 4, we noted that a management information system has at least five subsystems, each of which serves a special need within the organization. Figure 19-1 shows the relationship between the MIS and these five subsystems—the management support system, the decision support system, the accounting information system, the office information system, and the data manipulation and reporting system. Because the accounting information system is specialized, it is not discussed here. The data manipulation and reporting system was discussed in Chapter 4. Therefore, this subsystem is also not discussed further here. We concentrate on the management support systems and decision sup-

[1] Gordon B. Davis and Margaret H. Olson, *Management Information Systems,* 2nd ed. (New York: McGraw-Hill, 1985), p. 6.

FIGURE 19-1
Relationship of Information Subsystems in an Organization

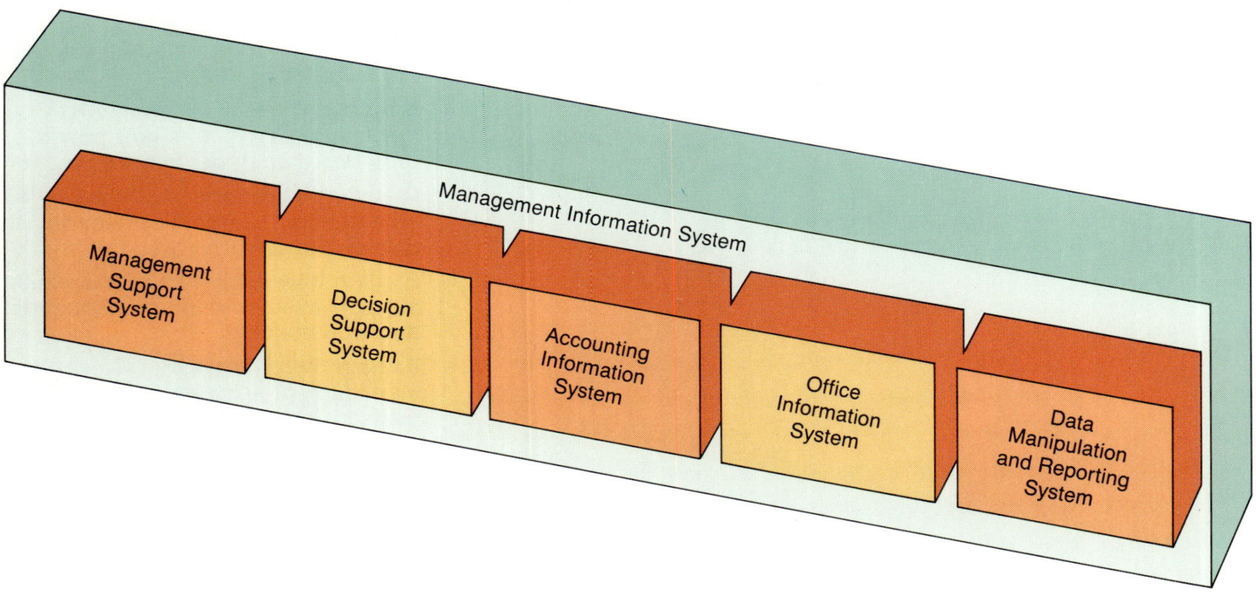

port systems and how these two systems are supported by the office information system.

Overview of the Management Information System

To understand the current role of the management information system, we must look at its evolution. The computer was first used by management in the area of electronic data processing (EDP). **Electronic data processing (EDP)** processed raw data into useful information. Examples of EDP tasks include computing payrolls, writing checks, updating inventory records based on sales and receipts, and updating student records at the end of each academic term. Although EDP was certainly a positive step toward providing information to managers, it did not always provide the information in a usable form. Managers often suffered from a malady known as *information overload* due to the tremendous amount of information generated by EDP. Management information systems were developed in organizations to make EDP results more useful. Instead of searching through pages of computer output for the needed information, a manager can use MIS results, which provide this information in a readily usable form.

Today, most large organizations have MIS Departments that handle their data processing and information needs. An MIS Department is a service center that accepts projects from other departments much as a consulting firm would take on projects from an outside client. The department's personnel usually includes systems analysts, applications programmers, data base specialists, and other computer specialists. The MIS staff uses the systems analysis and design procedure to automate manual procedures, revise existing information systems, or develop entirely new systems for organizational clients.

MIS Subsystems

As the demand for management information systems grew, the number of its subsystems also increased. The **management support system (MSS)** primarily provides information to managers on a timely basis or as needed in report form. The management support system is the oldest MIS subsystem and also the most highly developed. Because the management support system was the management information system's first subsystem, MSS is often confused with MIS.

When a manager needs more information than that found in reports, he or she may use a decision support system. A **decision support system (DSS)** manipulates data through mathematical or graphic models so that the manager can answer questions that may be raised by information provided in a report.

An **office information system (OIS)**—often referred to as **office automation**—provides a free flow of information throughout the organization. Office information systems began with the introduction of the electric typewriter and dictaphone. OIS now includes many computerized office machines, which are often connected as a network. OIS has the following four functions, which facilitate the flow of information.

1. Text and transaction processing
2. Document distribution through electronic mail
3. Electronic filing
4. Access to internal and external data bases

Increasingly, companies are recognizing that information systems used strategically are a key to corporate survival and a new factor in corporate strategic planning.

F. Warren McFarlan, Professor of business administration at Harvard University Business School

(As quoted in "Business Is Turning Data into a Potent Strategic Weapon," *Business Week,* August 22, 1983, pp. 92–95.)

The relationship among the three subsystems—that is, MSS, DSS, and OIS—and the data base is shown in Figure 19-2. The OIS function numbers correspond to the previous list of OIS functions. Figure 19-2 shows how MSS, DSS, OIS, and a data base form a management information system that supports managerial decision making. The actual flow of information, denoted by the arrows, is handled by a network. In this diagram, the decision-making process starts with data from internal and external sources.

Some data must be prepared through transaction processing (OIS) before it is ready for electronic data processing. An example of transaction process-

FIGURE 19-2
Information Systems in Decision Making

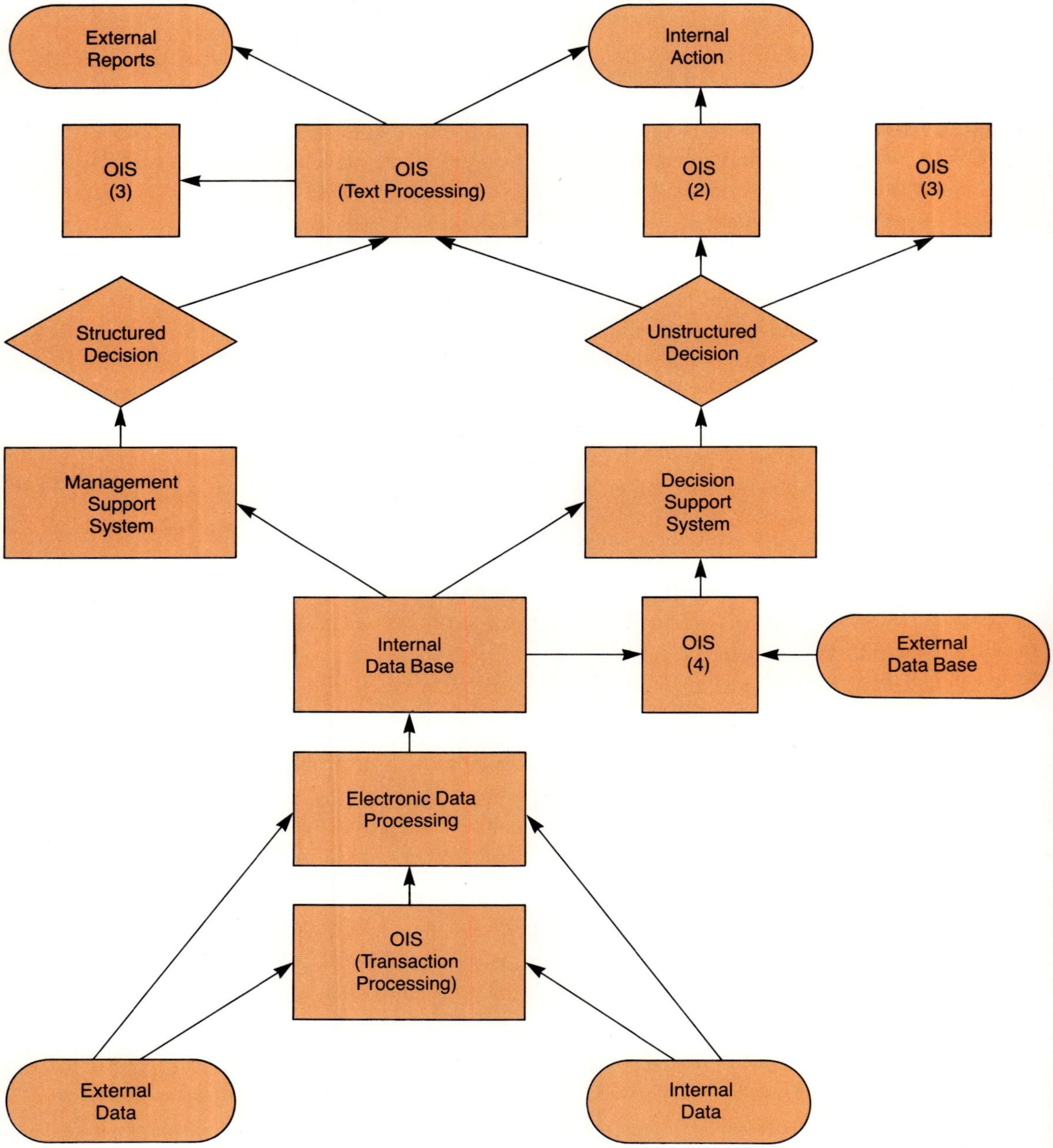

ing is the coding of checks with magnetic ink before they are processed. In other cases, data from computers need not go through a transaction processing stage before entering the data processing operation. After the data processing operation is completed, the resulting information is stored in the appropriate data base, from which it may be retrieved later for use in problem solving or report generation. When the MSS or DSS processes the information and a decision is made, a summary of the decision may be generated by the text processing function of the OIS, or it may be transmitted directly to interested parties via electronic mail. The decision may also be filed electronically by the OIS for future reference. OIS supports the decision-making process at all stages by facilitating the processing of text or transactions, sending information electronically, filing results electronically, and retrieving information from data bases.

Office information systems involve automation of such operations as microfilm access.

Encoding checks with the amount of the check in magnetic ink is the first step in check processing.

RAYOVAC'S INFORMATION CENTER

The increased use of personal computers in organizations has led to the development of the information center, which combines the advantages of personal computers and an MIS Department. An organization's information center is a concept that uses the information processing power of the organization's mainframe, easy-to-use programming languages, and the limited support of the MIS Department. An information center should provide expanded information processing power and avoid the problems of complex information processing and the power struggles that often result from decentralized computing power. The MIS Department guarantees adequate processing power and helps clients within the organization (employees or departments) choose, install, and test software. The client, through his or her personal computer, provides the time and effort to use and manage this particular system.

When Rayovac tested the effectiveness of an information center based on this concept, the company discovered that the following conditions must be met:

Adequate support from senior management must provide the necessary funding.

Available software packages must allow the client to cover a broad spectrum of work.

Individual clients must be willing to do the required work.

The MIS Department must be committed to the information center concept.

A comprehensive plan to develop, install, and maintain the information center must be created.

After a successful pilot test, Rayovac installed a full-scale information center. After 24 months of development, over 100 clients and more than 300 systems were run in the information center environment. Aside from training and ongoing technical support, the MIS Department was involved at a low level—that is, one full-time and one part-time MIS employee. Preparation of a spreadsheet was cut from 12 hours to ½ hour. In general, Rayovac's information center was an unqualified success, because it helped clients solve their own information problems rather than having the MIS Department solve them.

SOURCE: John P. Murray, "How an Information Center Improved Productivity," *Management Accounting,* March 1984, pp. 36–44.

MIS and the Personal Computer

Before the introduction of the personal computer into the work place, the MIS Department manager was only responsible for his or her department and the interaction between computer users and the organization's mainframe. The availability of personal computers has changed this situation. Today, an organization's managers and workers need not wait for the MIS Department to provide their information needs. Instead, these employees can use a personal computer system to satisfy their information needs. As a result, an organization must answer the following set of questions:

What type of personal computer should be purchased?

Should all employees have the same type of personal computer?

How can errors in personal computer data entry be avoided?

How should software be selected?

How can conflicting analyses from different departments be compared?

How can personal computers be hooked into the organization's mainframe? How can they be joined to one another?

If these questions are not answered satisfactorily, personal computers may initially cause more problems than they solve. Today, much discussion involves coordinating the use of personal computers with an MIS Department. Each organization must solve this problem according to its own needs.

MANAGEMENT SUPPORT SYSTEMS

The first objective of management information systems was to generate reports for managers. As the MIS became responsible for more than report generation, the management support system was developed to handle this important task.

Reports for different management levels in an organization can have various forms. Scheduled reports reflect the periodic history of an organization's operations. Exception reports are generated only if a certain condition signals the need for a report. Predictive reports provide forecasts of future conditions to help the manager plan ahead. Finally, demand reports are requested by a manager on a particular subject.

Scheduled reports are the result of the original report generation process, with the addition of needed summary information. These reports help low-level managers make operational decisions that meet objectives set by higher-level managers. For example, if a bank's chief teller wants to know if teller absenteeism is within the 5% limit set by his or her supervisor, a scheduled report of personnel attendance would provide this information.

Exception reports are generated only when an *abnormal* event occurs in the organization. The exception report can help a manager detect problems, and early detection is essential to good management. However, the exception report does not overwhelm the manager with unnecessary information. For example, an MSS might be used to generate an exception report when overtime for a payroll period is greater than 10% of total time worked. When the production manager receives such a report, he or she can investigate the reasons for the excessive overtime—for example, a big production job or poor planning. In the latter case, the production manager's problem would not be immediately evident without an exception report.

A summary report is generated by the management support system that accesses a data base.

A manager uses a **predictive report** to plan for future needs. This type of report is based on historical data and some type of forecasting formula used by the organization. For example, a university wants to predict the number of incoming freshmen to plan dormitory space. As applications arrive before the fall semester, predictions can be made on the number of freshmen that will live on campus. This prediction report is based on the number and quality of applications compared with previous years, the acceptance rate, and the attendance rate for individuals accepted. Although the predicted number of students is increasingly accurate as fall approaches, the earliest predictions can still allow the administration to make plans.

A **demand report** is usually called for when the results of another MSS report or of external information are unexpected. For example, assume that the president of an international soft drink company hears a rumor that a foreign country's leaders may outlaw the use of caffeine in cola drinks sold in that country. As a result of this rumor, the company president requests an MSS report on the percentage of total soft drink sales in that country that would be affected by such a ban. Because this type of information cannot be programmed in advance, special effort is necessary to generate the needed report. A data base must be available to the MIS Department's staff to gather the needed data and produce a report. The MIS Department may simply access the data base to gather the information for the staff to analyze manually, or it may develop a new software system to handle the analysis. Because data bases are important in the preparation of demand reports, we discuss the use of data bases in information systems later in this chapter.

DECISION SUPPORT SYSTEMS

The preparation of various types of reports—such as scheduled reports, exception reports, and so on—is not the answer to every middle- and upper-level manager's decision-making problem. The lack of timely information and the manager's inability to test the effect of a decision using MSS led to the development of decision support systems (DSS). The objective of DSS is to help the manager find answers to questions, thereby contributing to better decisions for unstructured and semistructured problems, through the use of quantitative and graphic models. Decision support systems are used for such diverse activities as ski resort planning, financial planning, and police patrol analysis. The system can be as simple as an electronic spreadsheet on a personal computer or as powerful as a full-scale financial planning package on a mainframe. Most decision support systems are implemented on mainframes because of additional processing power, storage capabilities, and advanced graphics. However, some personal computer DSS packages are available.

Using Models in DSS

To provide the support needed by the decision maker for unstructured and semistructured problems, a system must allow the manager or his or her staff to have on-line interaction with the computer. The system must also allow the decision maker to obtain information from a data base or external sources and simulate from the terminal the effects of changes in the information or the effect of new information. To do this, a model must be developed that represents the physical, economic, or financial situation in question. A **model** is a simplified version of reality that defines the interrelationships

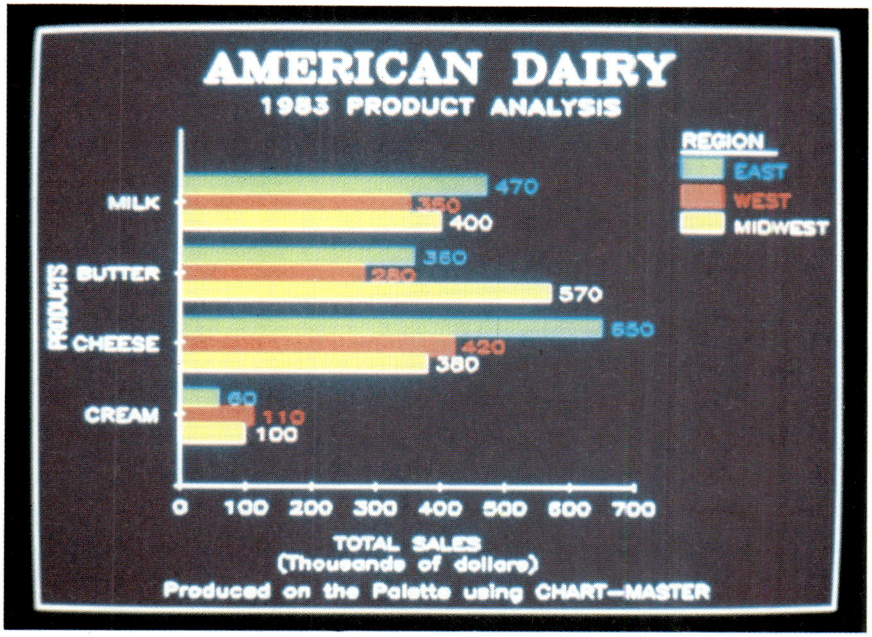

Graphic analyses and modeling are important parts of the decision support system, which aids managers in making better decisions.

among important values in a situation.

For example, to study the effect of total miles driven on the operating cost of a truck, we might use the following formula as a model:

$$\text{Operating Cost} = a + (b \times \text{miles}) + (c \times \text{miles}^2)$$

This formula, which might be developed from past experience, allows the user to find the operating cost for any number of miles. The parameters *a, b,* and *c* distinguish one make or model of truck from another in the formula. Miles driven (in thousands) is the variable in the model, which indicates that the operating cost is not a simple linear function of miles driven. Operating cost also depends on the square of the miles driven, which yields a nonlinear model for the cost.

To simulate this model of the operating cost of a truck, the user changes the miles driven variable, which results in different operating costs. For example, consider Table 19-1, which shows the effects of increasing the miles driven for a certain brand of truck for which $a = 100$, $b = 200$, and $c = 2$. The manager can quickly see that operating costs for a truck that was driven 100,000 miles are more than twice those for a truck driven only 50,000 miles. Other considerations in the model include the initial cost of the truck and the trade-in value after various lengths of time. When solved, this model indicates the best time to trade the truck in for a new one. As with any unstructured problem, the manager in charge makes the final decision, but a simulation of an operating cost model combined with other simulations can be a great help.

In addition to simulating a model to obtain numerical results, a typical decision support system can also represent results graphically. With graphics, the manager can visualize important relationships before making a decision. Often, graphics convey the important relationships in a model better than a

Table 19-1 SIMULATION OF TRUCK OPERATING COSTS

Miles Driven	*Operating Cost*
10,000	$ 2,300
20,000	4,900
30,000	7,900
40,000	11,300
50,000	15,100
60,000	19,300
70,000	23,900
80,000	28,900
90,000	34,300
100,000	40,100

FIGURE 19-3
Graphic Analysis of Truck Operating Costs

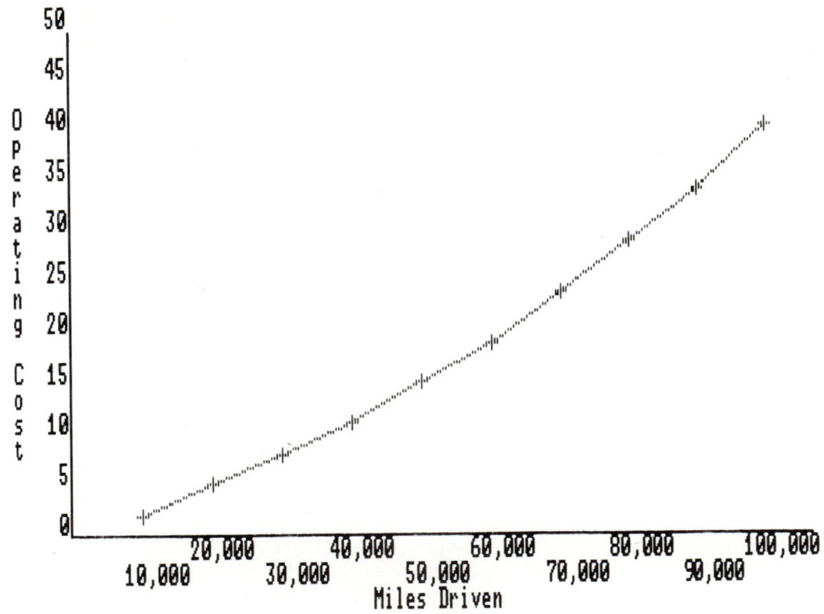

table of numbers. For example, Figure 19-3 is the graphic representation of the truck operating costs listed in Table 19-1.

Parts of a DSS

A decision support system has three major parts—a **data base**, from which information can be retrieved as needed; a **model base**, which has various models that are used and solved as needed to arrive at a solution; and a **dialog base**, which handles the interaction between the manager and the computer. Figure 19-4 shows the relationship between the user and the parts of a DSS.

The data base must be available to the decision maker so that needed information may be retrieved. This information may include internal information, reports from the MIS, and external data from such national data bases as DIALOG or CompuServe. The decision maker combines data with a model selected from the model base to arrive at a simulation. The model base is a

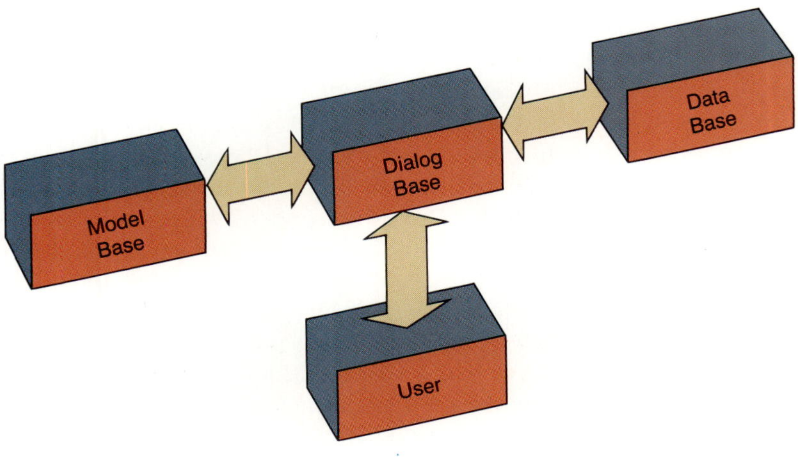

FIGURE 19-4
User in Relation to the DSS

group of computer programs that performs specific operations on the information from the data base. The simulation results can then be portrayed in a tabular or graphic form. The dialog base uses various software procedures that allow the manager to choose data and models as he or she is making a decision. For example, the user may request a plot of the data on the screen from the dialog base. The dialog base combines the correct model with the data to arrive at the requested plot. The dialog base makes the DSS a truly useful tool for the manager because he or she can move about freely in the DSS. Without a user-friendly dialog base, the best DSS would be quickly discarded by managers who had no time to learn the intricacies of working with a data base, models, and simulation.

Types of DSS

Decision support systems are available in three forms—general purpose DSS, specific DSS, and DSS model generators. In the **general purpose DSS**, the user must develop a model and then manipulate variables to simulate results within a general modeling framework. A **specific DSS** is developed for only one type of problem. This program is usually written in a high-level language. Finally, a **DSS model generator** helps the user develop specific models. The dialog base can usually be modified by the user to ask appropriate questions and to output the needed results. The DSS model generator also includes many popular models and a library of commonly used mathematical and graphic operations. Finally, the DSS model generator may include the operations to establish a data base, or it may be easily tied into the organization's data base or an external information source. The DSS model generator is often described as an *electronic workbench* that has all the user's tools within easy reach. The Interactive Financial Planning System (IFPS) is a DSS model generator that is available on many mainframes for helping managers make financial forecasts and decisions.

Comparing DSS with MSS

The relationship between MSS and DSS is often discussed, because both systems "support" managerial decision making. We have already pointed out one difference—the report generation emphasis of MSS versus the modeling emphasis on DSS. We can also link MSS and DSS to different levels of management. For example, MSS is often used by lower and middle management to make the operational and tactical decisions that implement top management's strategic decisions. On the other hand, DSS is often used by upper management to make its decisions. However, this is not always a good way to differentiate between the two information systems.

Another approach to differentiating MSS from DSS involves the type of decisions that each information system supports. In this approach, MSS provides the information to a manager to make **structured decisions**. For example, a structured decision may involve making a short-term sales forecast using a table. Another example is determining the number of spare parts to order using a report of machine usage. The information needed to make a structured decision is often in the form of reports or tables that enable the manager to make decisions using a previously defined procedure. On the other hand, DSS helps managers make **unstructured decisions** in such areas as project management, budget preparation, and research and development planning. For unstructured decisions, the decision maker must use various procedures and information in many forms.

The differentiation between management support systems and decision

The management support system was developed to help managers avoid working with pages of computer output to make their decisions.

support systems from a single viewpoint is not always possible. In general, the difference between MSS and DSS is a combination of the three approaches. MSS is a report-oriented system used primarily by lower and middle management for well-structured decisions. DSS is a model-oriented system used primarily by middle and upper management for semistructured and unstructured decisions.

DATA BASES

Recall from Chapter 12 that a data base is a collection of data usually pertaining to one subject or to one group of individuals or items. Data bases are built to store information that may be retrieved by managers, scientists, researchers, or other interested individuals. The creation of a data base eliminates the need to enter the same data repeatedly for different processing situations. Before data bases, information on the same subject might be stored in several different computer files and therefore not easily cross-referenced for generating a report. Multiple files on a given subject were also difficult to update with new information. In other words, with a data base, repeated occurrences of the same data item are avoided, data are independent of their use, and, because only one file must be updated to reflect a change of information, records are more likely correct.

A data base is commonly stored on some form of secondary storage, and appropriate software is needed to retrieve any information. For example, a college professor's data base includes attendance records and quiz scores for a class of over 400 students. The professor will assign a grade of A to students who have both a perfect attendance record *and* a quiz average greater than 85. Students without a perfect attendance record must have an average of at least 90 to receive an A. With the proper data base software, the professor can access this information quite easily, whereas doing it by hand would be time-consuming.

Data bases and data base software have been available since computers could be programmed in high-level languages. Mainframe data bases and software were used first, followed by data bases for minicomputers. Today, data bases and data base software for personal computers are very common. As with many computer applications, the volume of work is the crucial factor in choosing the type of computer for creating and storing the data base and for retrieving information from the data base. A personal computer is quite adequate for storing attendance and quiz score information for a single college class, but at least a minicomputer is needed to store all student-related information for a small college. A mainframe is necessary to perform the same task at a major university.

The data base is important to the success of management information systems in helping managers make decisions. As an example of a familiar data base that could be used with MSS or DSS, consider the data base that contains the records of the students who are currently enrolled in a certain college. Using this student data base, the college administration can produce reports on the composition of the student body, answer questions from outside agencies, and make decisions using management support systems and decision support systems. For example, combining MSS with a data base could produce periodic reports on the percent of the college student body that is from out of state. MSS could also be combined with data base information to answer questions on the number of students who receive federally supported financial aid. By accessing the data base, the administration could use DSS to make decisions on such things as the effect of a 10% increase in tuition and fees on the size and makeup of the student body.

Storing Information on Data Bases

Recall from previous chapters that the information in a data base is divided into files, records, and fields. For the student information data base mentioned above, one file might include all students' personal information. Each record would contain fields for a student's name, home address, birthday, and Social Security number. Table 19-2 shows three sample records for the student data base.

Data Base Management Systems

A **data base management system (DBMS)** manages a data base and allows users to retrieve needed information. This software is written in a high-level computer language. DBMS software varies according to the type of machine in use (mainframe, minicomputer, or personal computer) and the complexity

Table 19-2 RECORDS ON PERSONAL INFORMATION FILE

Name Field	*Address Field*	*Birthday Field*	*Social Security Number Field*
Chip Monk	250 Fifth Ave., New York, NY 10002	03-15-66	999-13-4321
Eve N. Steven	133 Hilltop Blvd., Chicago, IL 60609	10-22-67	888-43-7890
George P. Burdell	792 Techwood Dr., Atlanta, GA 30622	01-30-65	999-22-6661

of the data base. Easy-to-use DBMS software is available for personal computers for storing records on single files (see Chapter 12). When multiple files must be accessed, more sophisticated DBMS require the user to learn a special query language or to use such high-level languages as COBOL or Pascal.

OFFICE INFORMATION SYSTEMS

An office information system (OIS) supports other information systems by text and transaction processing, document distribution through electronic mail, electronic filing, and accessing internal and external data bases. The movement toward a service and information economy has resulted in a corresponding effort to automate many information processing functions in the office—a process often referred to as *office automation*. Today, the following office tasks are automated to some degree:

- Word processing.
- Reproduction of printed material on programmable copiers.
- Electronic filing on secondary storage devices.
- Information retrieval from internal or external data bases.
- Transmittal of information and pictures via telephone lines.
- Data transcription onto secondary storage devices.
- Conversion of printed material to electronic form through optical character readers.

Processing remittances is an important application of office automation for many companies.

Although the automation of these operations is an important step, the *integration* of these operations is necessary to create a true office information system. The automation of individual operations has improved office procedures, but the real payoff occurs when a series of components are linked together to allow data to flow freely.

Text and Transaction Processing

Because text (word) processing was the first automated office operation, it is considered the most "mature." Word processors, in use for well over a decade, are a well-accepted (and often, expected) part of any office. Early word processing systems used magnetic cards rather than disk or tape for storage and did not have video display terminals. Instead, a typist entered text as if he or she were using a regular typewriter, and the typewriter was used for output. Video display terminals and magnetic disk storage systems greatly speeded up the system because the keyboard was not tied up during output.

Computers that are used primarily for word processing are known as **dedicated word processors**. Such word processing systems are currently available in stand alone or cluster configurations. In a **stand alone configuration**, each word processor has it own storage device and printer, but in a **cluster configuration**, several word processors are tied together by a cable and share storage and printers. Dedicated word processors can sometimes handle other data processing activities—such as arithmetic operations or communications with other computers—but they are generally used solely for word processing.

The future of word processing may lie in the introduction of the personal computer into the office. Personal computers can handle word processing as well as a dedicated word processor and can also combine word processing with such other operations as graphics, spreadsheet analysis, data base access,

Word processing, one of the first applications of office automation, continues to be the most widely used application.

The office information system converts field data to a form that can be entered into the computerized data base.

and telecommunication. With a personal computer, a document can be prepared by one person and edited by a supervisor. This transfer of documents can be handled by physically shifting a floppy disk or by using a telecommunications network.

Transaction processing involves the conversion of handwritten or typed raw data into a form that can be input directly to the data processing system. For example, a handwritten summary of a year-end inventory count must first be converted into a form that the computer can read before the data can be processed by the inventory software. Although many stores and industries use electronic inventory counting systems (either at the checkout counter or by keying the data directly into a magnetic storage device), the need for transaction processing is still huge.

At one time, transaction processing was handled by keypunch operators who transcribed data onto computer cards, which were then fed into the computer for processing. Today, transaction processing is usually accomplished using a VDT and keyboard to enter the data directly into the computer or onto some form of secondary storage (usually disk). The skills needed to perform this processing are the same as with keypunching, but the results are stored in a form that can be accessed by several computers at the same time and that is not susceptible to wear and tear during use.

In the future, both word processing and transaction processing may be accomplished through optical character recognition (OCR) devices that convert written and printed documents into an electronic form without the process of keying in words or data. Currently, machines can read many printed documents, but handwritten documents are often beyond their means. Voice input systems are being studied, but many problems must be resolved before this method can be practical for processing words and data into electronic form.

Electronic Mail

Sending documents, pictures, and messages to one or more persons via the computer is a potentially powerful communications medium. A user simply

The ability of electronic mail to send text and pictures over long distances almost instantaneously has led to its increased use in the office.

turns on his or her terminal, enters the proper commands, types in the document, gives the name of the person(s) to receive it and pushes a button. Instantly, a "mail is waiting" message appears at the proper terminal(s). If the recipient is working at the terminal, the mail can be immediately read; if not, he or she receives the message when the terminal is turned on. Gone is the hassle of typing the document, making copies, addressing envelopes, sending the letters, and then waiting for the recipient to receive, read, and reply. With **electronic mail,** the recipient receives the message and responds immediately by computer.

In the office, the amount of time waiting for a reply to an interoffice memo or a telephone call or waiting to see someone can be decreased significantly. Figure 19-5 shows the use of electronic mail over a **local area network**—that is, a network within one building—using personal computers Electronic mail can also be sent using a mainframe as the "post office" that holds messages until the recipient logs on to the mainframe through a terminal. This process is shown in Figure 19-6.

Combined with word processing, electronic mail can make the preparation of documents more efficient. For example, in Figure 19-7, a secretary prepares the original document and returns it to the executive who initially

FIGURE 19-5
Electronic Mail over Local Area Network

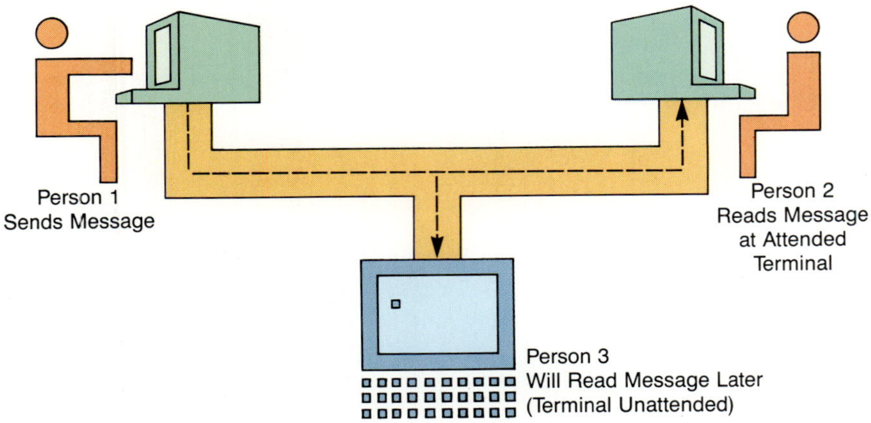

dictated it into an electronic recording device. The executive can print the document on a draft quality (dot-matrix) printer and, if needed, edit the document on his or her word processor. When the executive approves the final product, it is returned to the secretary for printing on a letter quality printer.

Although electronic mail certainly sounds like a good idea, actually implementing trouble-free electronic mail in an office is easier said than done. A large problem involves linking personal computers together in a local area network, especially if they are not the same type of computer or use different operating systems. If a mainframe is used, the entire system is out of order when the central computer is "down."

Electronic Filing

Today's office has a major problem—too much paper. In fact, the U.S. government has a commission whose sole task is to reduce the amount of paper that circulates through the federal bureaucracy. Most organizations face this paperwork problem because many forms, letters, documents, and reports must be filed in preparation for the day (which may, of course, never come) when they must be used for reference. A single document may be filed in numerous places in an organization. For example, the originator has a personal copy, his or her office keeps a copy, the recipient has copies made for his or her staff, and so on. Electronic filing can reduce this paper load.

In **electronic filing**, a document received via electronic mail is read on the screen, and when a reply is prepared, both the original message and the reply are saved in secondary storage, usually magnetic disk. Although this process sounds easy, some problems must be considered. First, a system of

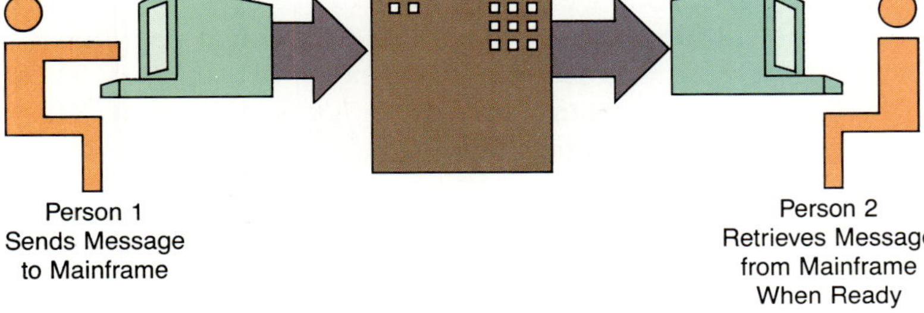

FIGURE 19-6
Electronic Mail Using Mainframe

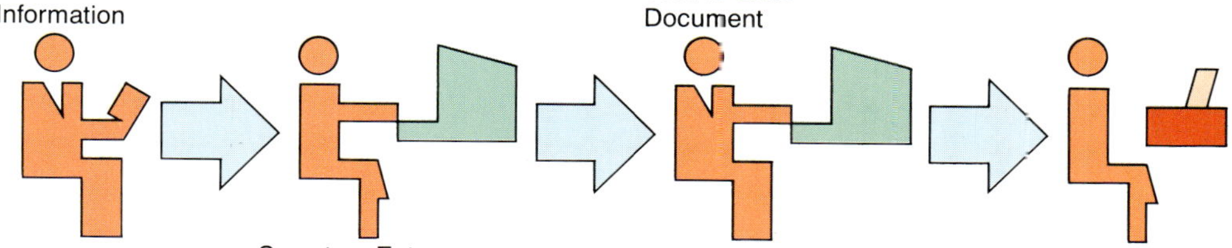

FIGURE 19-7
Combining Word Processing with Electronic Mail

identifying and retrieving a given document must exist. Second, the system must be adequately protected against loss of documents due to problems with the storage medium. Finally, the system must be secure against theft or tampering.

Current operating systems for both personal and mainframe computers are sophisticated enough to have directories and subdirectories. With subdirectories, a user can divide correspondence up into various categories rather than group all letters in one long directory. Subdirectories are not always necessary with floppy disks, but they are indispensable when information is filed on a high-volume hard disk. Current research is aimed at developing electronic files that resemble commonly used manual filing methods. The Macintosh series of computers uses a file cabinet icon (symbol) to represent the function that saves a document. With this approach, electronic files may eventually have "drawers" with "folders" for easier document storage.

To protect documents from loss due to hardware problems, the user must frequently back up secondary storage. Failure to back up a file can lead to its loss. Protection against theft and tampering requires certain security measures, including frequent changes of the passwords for access to the computer. The computer should be programmed not to answer an outside call without ensuring that the caller is a valid user. Computer security is covered in more detail in Chapter 20.

Accessing Internal and External Data Bases

Access to data bases is an important element in a manager's decision-making process. The office information system may allow a user to access any data base—the organization's data base or a national data base—from his or her desk. This access should be available to all knowledge workers within an organization to improve overall output.

COMPUTER NETWORKS

An interesting application of computer technology is how to make the computers "talk to one another." All levels of communications are involved—that is, mainframe to mainframe, mainframe to minicomputer, personal computer to personal computer, and personal computer to mainframe or minicomputer. When only mainframes existed, a "dumb" terminal communicated with the mainframe, so that users could communicate with the mainframe from their homes or offices. The advent of small computers has changed this situation. Now, personal computers must be connected with other personal computers, minicomputers, and mainframes, regardless of the make or model of the computers. With available telecommunications software, the personal computer can be a dumb or "semi-intelligent" terminal tied into a mainframe. However, linking the personal computer and mainframe together so that each works to its fullest potential is more difficult. To make this connection possible, new hardware and software are being rapidly developed.

When computers are tied together, they form a **computer network**. Three basic network configurations exist—the star, ring, and bus networks shown in Figure 19-8. In the **star network**, one "host" computer has several

FIGURE 19-8
Types of Computer Networks

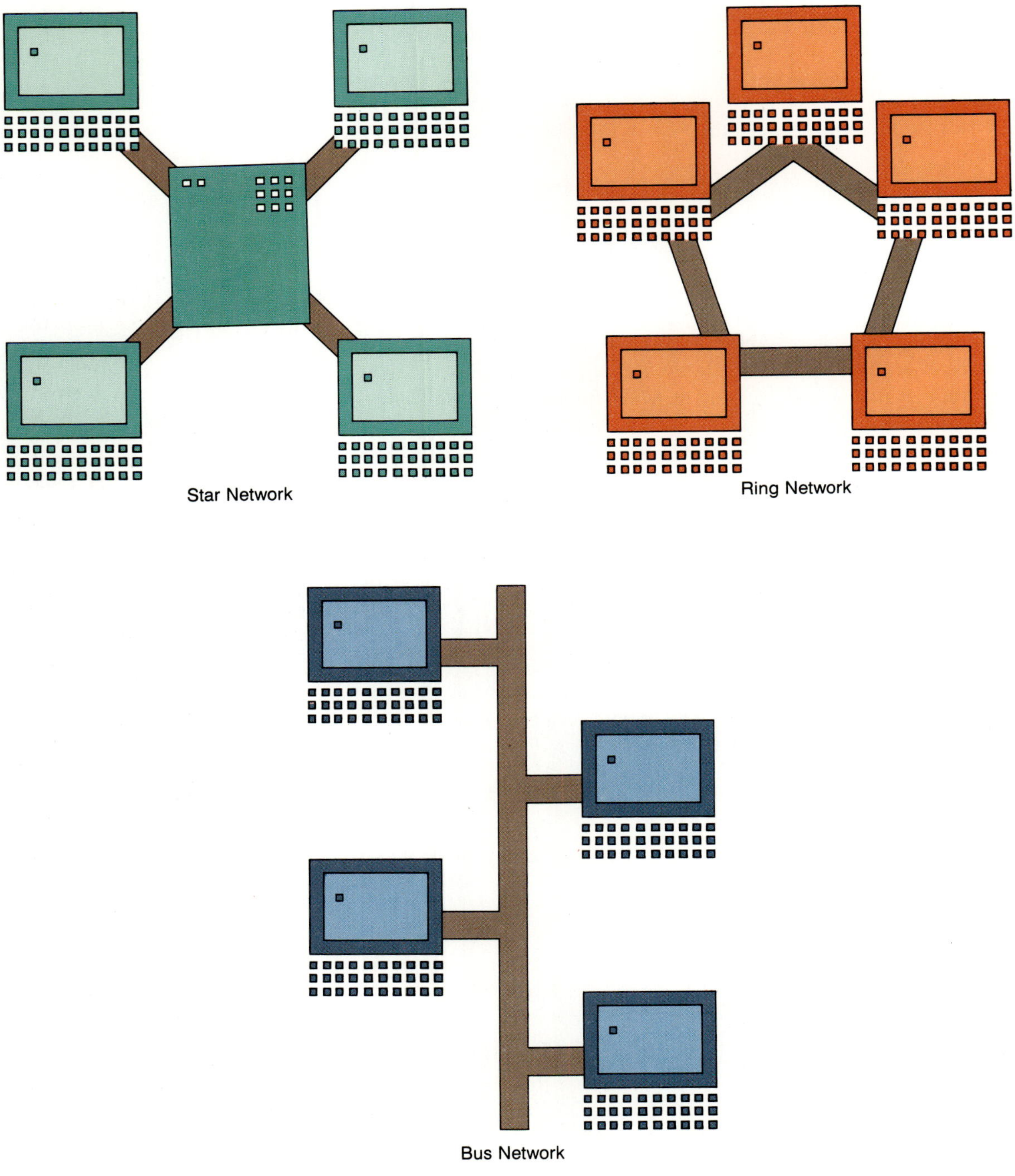

"slave" computers connected to it. Communications between any two computers must be routed through the host computer, which controls all data communications. If the host computer fails, then the entire system goes down. In a **ring network**, all computers are on the same level, and any communications between two computers must be processed by any intervening computer. As a result, if any one computer goes down, the system also goes down. Finally, the **bus network** has computers that tie into a main cable, or bus, without a central computer. The failure of any one computer does not affect the overall performance of the network.

Computer networks are important in the performance of **distributed data processing (DDP)** (see Chapter 13). DDP places computing power as near as possible to the actual location of information processing. In other words, the system decentralizes computer resources. DDP networks can connect mainframes, minicomputers, and personal computers using today's

COMPUTERS AT THE OLYMPICS

At the 1984 Summer Olympics in Los Angeles, California, a hidden electronic mail system really kept things rolling. Because the LA Olympics were held over a 4,500 square mile area, the message system used in prior Olympics was clearly not adequate. At the 1976 Montreal Olympics, messengers on bicycles carried information from venue to venue. The system for the 1984 Olympics, developed by AT&T as part of its Olympics sponsorship, involved over 1,700 video display terminals, 300 printers, hardware to run the network, and 12 AT&T minicomputers. The terminals were located throughout the areas in which the 23 sports events were held, with more terminals concentrated in high traffic areas.

The electronic messenger was a menu-driven system that required no prior computer knowledge for its operation. Its menu choices were displayed in both English and French. It operated 24 hours a day and had a response time of 1–5 seconds. The system had four major parts—a system that allowed reporters to write and send stories directly from a terminal; a data base system that contained information on all of the athletes; an electronic mail system; and a bulletin board system. With the data base and an easy-to-use query system, users could obtain the latest results of events as well as comprehensive results on the games overall.

To address a message on the electronic mail system, a user could look up the recipient's name on the data base using the query system. The bulletin board system continuously displayed results, announcements of press conferences, and individual messages. Like the 1984 Summer Olympics, the AT&T messenger system was judged a resounding success.

SOURCE: Katherine Hafner, "Message Moving," ***Computerworld on Communications,*** **May 2, 1984, pp. 55–59.**

The 1984 Los Angeles Olympics had a computer network that managed the flow of information among the geographically dispersed venues.

One type of computer network has a mainframe host computer monitored by several operators (top). Retailers can speed up deliveries using a computer network of personal computers or terminals (bottom).

THE PRESIDENT'S NETWORK

During President Ronald Reagan's first term, the White House took an important organizational step. On his arrival in 1981, John Rogers, assistant to the president for management and administration, discovered that although 34 different types of word processors were used in the White House, most correspondence was still handled by typewriters. He also discovered that he was expected to keep financial records by hand in a fat general ledger. Rogers decided to automate the White House. After installing 168 new word processors, all of the same type, Rogers set up a network to handle the information processing needs of all persons who report directly to the president. This network would handle electronic mail, access wire services and outside data bases, access the mainframe that processes the federal budget, and perform local processing with individual software packages—all for persons with no computer experience. This network would tie together a series of high-powered personal computers as well as access various mainframes.

The network that Rogers developed is known as EOPNET, for Executive Office of the President's Information Management and Control Network. The system is entirely menu driven, and because a user need only press a particular function key on the keyboard, it is also described as a "Ph.D." network—"press here, dummy." If the user does not press a function key, a picture of the keyboard appears on the screen with a flashing arrow pointing to the function keys. In addition to its ease of use, EOPNET allows users to download information from a news service or a data base into a spreadsheet or word processing package for more analysis. The information can also be sent along as electronic mail with comments. Currently, EOPNET's most pressing duty is to keep up with daily events, so that news stories can be sent to the appropriate people.

Eventually, the EOPNET will have over 40 of the president's top advisors on-line. It is only a matter of time before the Oval Office contains a terminal.

SOURCE: Brad Lemley, "All the President's PCs," *PC Magazine*, May 29, 1984, pp. 139–44.

evolving telecommunications technology. With DDP, an MIS design can match organizational structure, support unique business strategies, and provide a more natural use of information systems. DDP networks can be star, ring, or bus networks, or a combination of those three, depending on the organization's needs.

Local Area Networks

Organizations that use many personal computers have found that sharing information, secondary storage, and printers among the personal computers is more efficient than having them work individually. A user may wish to transmit a document, graph, or analysis to another user. Without a local area network, the user could only transmit the information by physically sharing a floppy disk or converting the information into a data file that could be sent by telephone. The first method is cumbersome and prone to problems if the disk is damaged or unreadable. In the conversion of the original file to a data file, the form of the file is lost and must be reconstructed by the recipient.

A local area network may involve a sharing of peripheral devices. For example, if a single hard disk drive is shared in a network, all users have certain information available to them, and other information may remain specific to a given computer within the network. Similarly, one high-speed letter quality printer or flatbed plotter in a network can serve all the computers in that network. Because both types of peripherals can serve multiple users in the network, unnecessary equipment costs are saved. Figure 19-9 diagrams a local area network with these peripheral devices.

Local area networks can be classified according to the transmission medium used and the way access to the network is controlled. The transmission

One of the questions we should be concentrating on is how we are going to turn personal computers into sophisticated data communicators.

Fred Gibbons, President of Software Publishing Corporation

(As quoted in "Fred Gibbons on Inflated Software Costs and Hardware Incompatibility," *Personal Computing*, March 1983, p. 46.)

FIGURE 19-9
Local Area Network

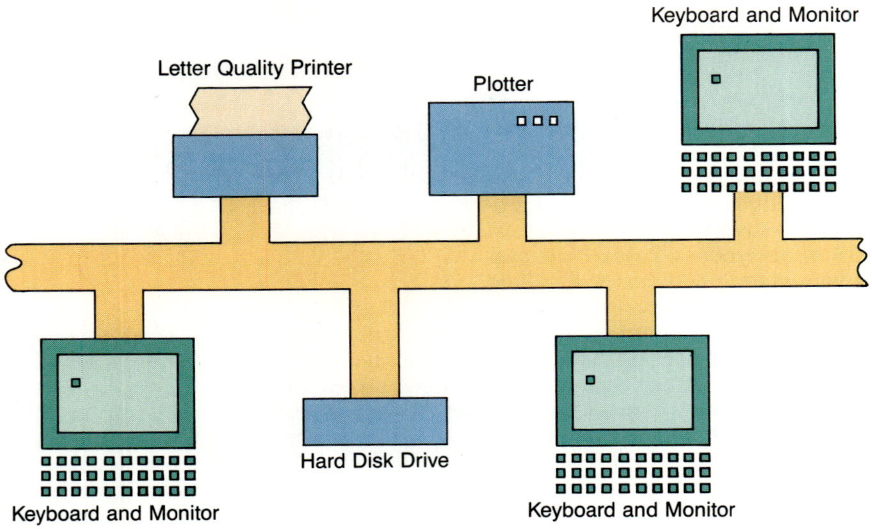

medium used most often is coaxial cable. A **coaxial cable** consists of two or three wires surrounded by a metal shield. This type of cable is used to ensure that the signal is not disrupted by the electrical fields that the cable passes through. Because only two or three wires are used to transmit the information on the network, the signal must be a **serial transmission**—that is, one bit after another. **Parallel transmission**—8 or 16 bits at a time—is used internally in the computer.

The most common form of a local area network is the bus network. Two basic procedures are used to control access to a bus network—the token sharing network and the multiple access network. In a **token sharing network**, a special bit pattern, called a **token**, is sent to each computer sequentially around the network. Only the computer that has the token at a given instance can transmit. Once a transmission is made by a computer in the network, the token is passed to the next computer. In the **multiple access network**, all computers can transmit at any time, but collision detecting software must control the transmissions.

The Future of Local Area Networks

The future of local area networks appears very promising. More personal computers are used in an office environment, and the advantages of tying them together are obvious. However, definite problems must be solved before local area networks are widely used. The most formidable problem is the incompatibility of different types of computers and operating systems. Managers are discovering that connecting an IBM PC, an Apple IIe, and an HP-150 is not as easy as some sales representatives claim it is. The lack of an industry standard for either data transmittal or access control is a second problem that must be solved.

REVIEW OF KEY POINTS

- Management information systems (MIS) help executives manage organizations.
- Three important types of management information systems are management support systems (MSS), decision support systems (DSS), and office information systems (OIS).
- Data bases and networks are important parts of any information system.
- Management support systems and decision support systems help managers make decisions.
- MIS is made up of software and hardware components that work together to provide needed information.
- MSS is helpful for structured decisions, whereas DSS is used for unstructured decisions.
- DSS has a data base, a model base, and a dialog base.
- Important types of DSS are the general purpose DSS, the specific DSS, and the DSS model generator.
- Data bases supply information to various individuals.
- Networks link computers together to take advantage of secondary storage and peripheral devices.
- A local area network links personal computers together within one building.

KEY TERMS

bus network
cluster configuration
coaxial cable
computer network
data base
data base management system (DBMS)
decision support system (DSS)
dedicated word processors
demand report
dialog base
distributed data processing (DDP)
DSS model generator
electronic data processing (EDP)
electronic filing
electronic mail
exception reports
general purpose DSS
information system
local area network
management information system (MIS)
management support system (MSS)
model
model base
multiple access network
office automation
office information system (OIS)
parallel transmission
predictive report
ring network
scheduled reports
serial transmission
specific DSS
stand alone configuration
star network
structured decisions
token
token sharing network
unstructured decisions

REVIEW QUESTIONS

1. Name the types of management information systems that help managers in organizations.
2. Explain the differences between a management support system and a decision support system.
3. How do office information systems and data bases fit into the decision-making process?
4. Name the four types of reports generated by an MSS and explain the purpose of each report.
5. List the parts of a DSS. What does each part do, and how do the parts interact?
6. List the types of DSS commonly used to support managerial decision making.
7. Name the four functions of an office information system. How does each function support MSS and DSS?
8. How does a data base interact with MSS and DSS? What is a DBMS, and what is its purpose?
9. What is DDP? What is a local area network? Which is more important to an office information system?
10. What are three types of local area network configurations? Name two types of access control to a local area network.

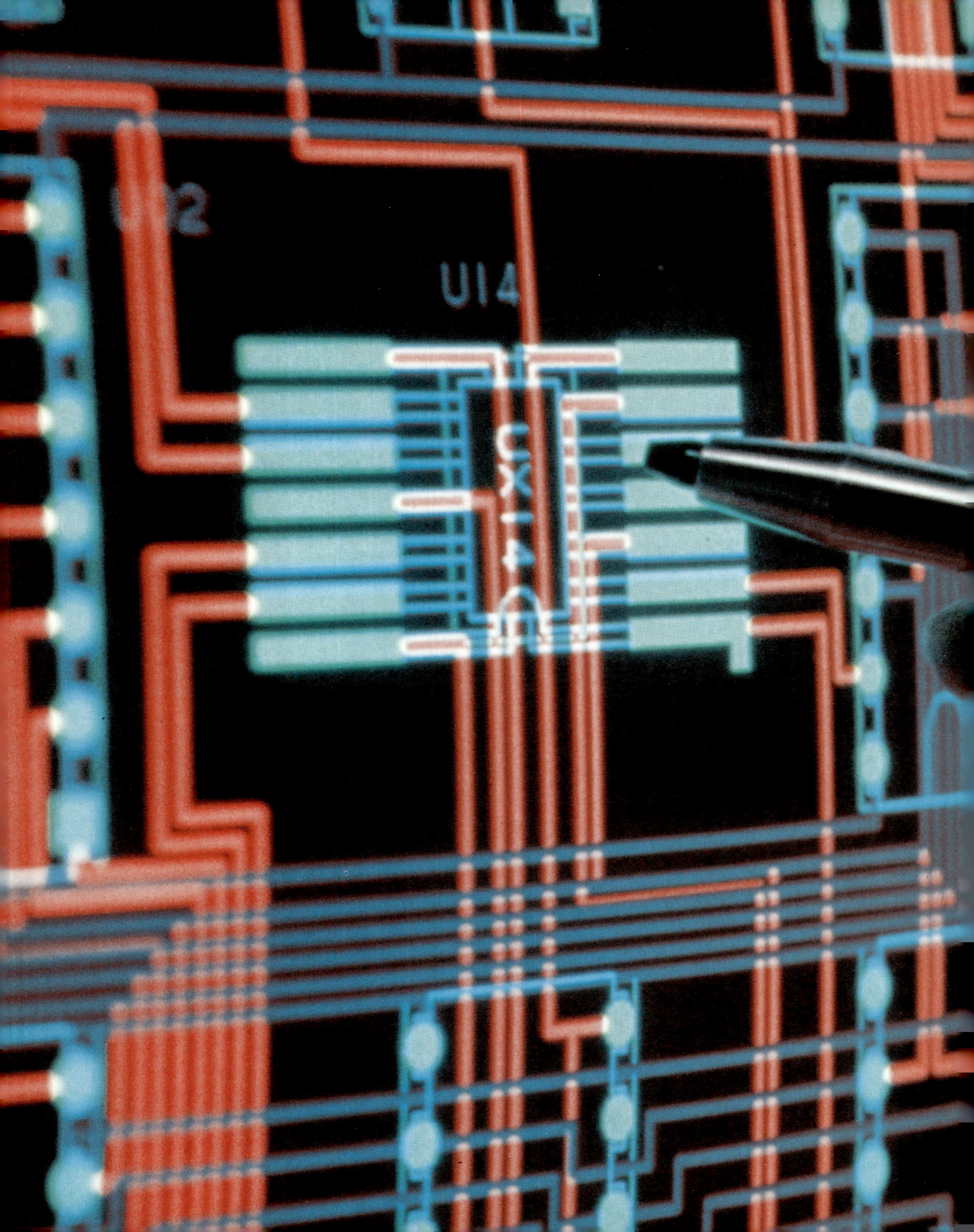
U14

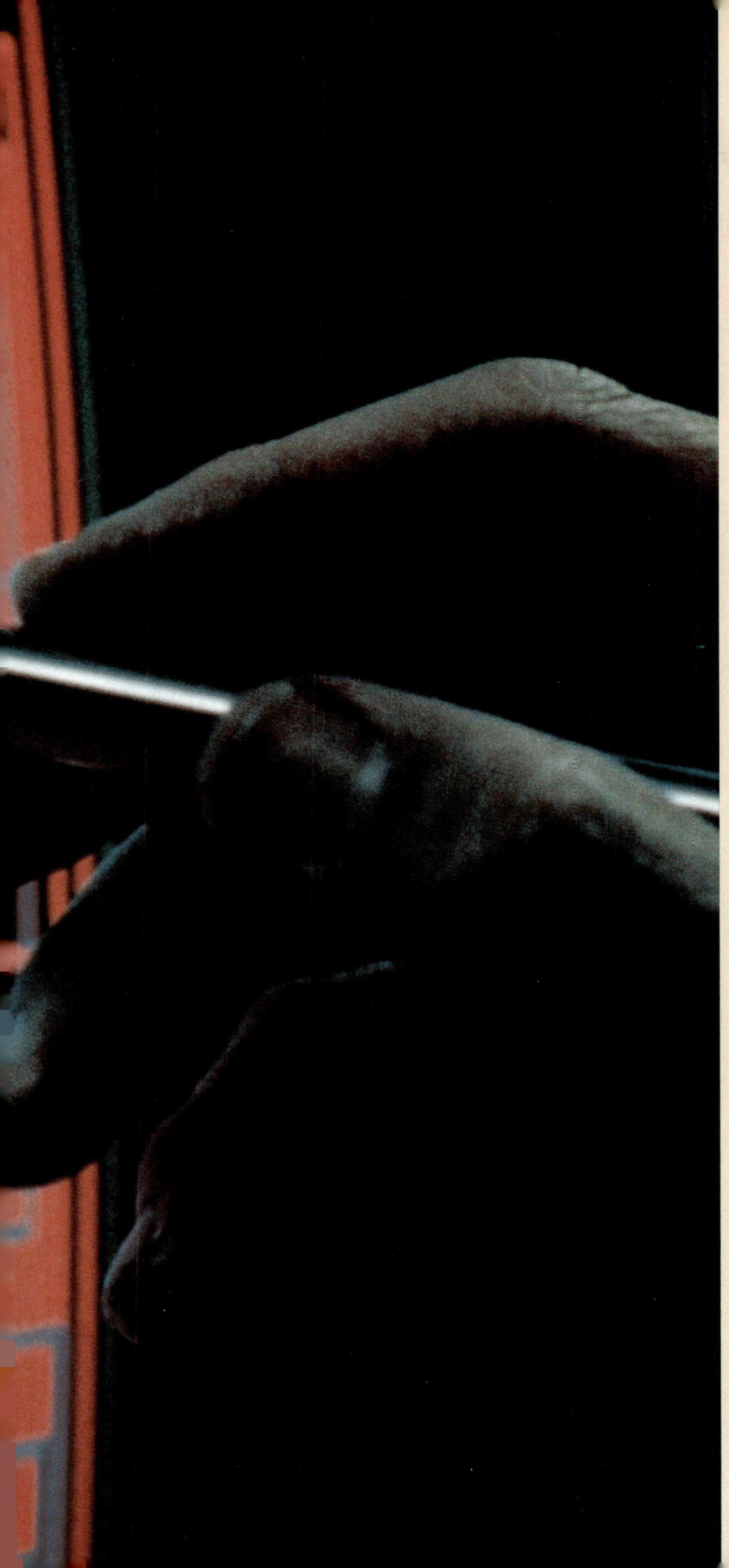

Block 6

HUMAN ASPECTS OF COMPUTER USE

Chapter 5 introduced some of the social issues of computer use, including computer crime and security, personal privacy, health problems. and computer careers. The magnitude of the crime problem and the methods for protecting the computer, the data, and the software are covered in Chapter 20. In Chapter 21, the dangers associated with the invasion of personal privacy by computer are discussed. The chapter also covers the health problems of long-term computer terminal use. Finally, the future of the computer and the many career opportunities available in the computer field are discussed in Chapter 22.

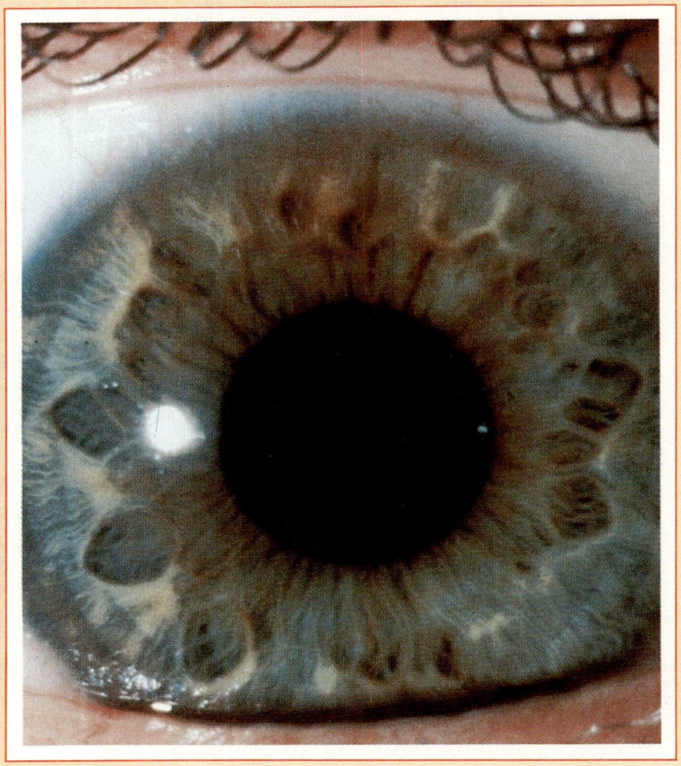

As with almost every human pursuit, people have discovered how to use a computer for illegal or unethical purposes. This chapter considers the two sides of this problem—computer crime and computer security. The first part of the chapter outlines various illegal computer practices, including physical attacks on the computer itself and the use of the computer to steal information or money, to manipulate information, or to deceive others. The second section of the chapter examines computer security, including physical security and data security. Finally, we investigate the impact of the personal computer on both computer crime and security, including software piracy and copy protection.

20

Computer Crime and Security

STUDY OBJECTIVES

After reading this chapter, you should be able to

- Appreciate the magnitude of computer crime and the efforts that are underway to stop it.
- Discuss the various types of computer crime.
- Recognize how computer crimes are committed as well as the type of person who commits these crimes.
- Discuss the legal and insurance aspects of computer crime.
- List security problems encountered at a computer installation.
- Distinguish between physical security and data security.
- Discuss the use of access codes, passwords, port protection devices, and encryption to protect data and software.
- Understand software piracy and protection as well as physical security for personal computers.

THE DARK SIDE OF THE MIND TOOL

Computer crime is sophisticated bank robbery, trespass, and burglary. The losses it creates are already reaching into the pocketbooks of this country's consumers—often unbeknownst to its victims.

Rep. Bill Nelson, D-FL

(As quoted in "Quotelines," *USA Today,* December 6, 1984, p. 12A.)

Throughout this text, we have emphasized how the computer can be used as a mind tool, expanding our mental capabilities and making work easier and recreation more enjoyable. In the majority of cases, the computer is used for ethical and legal purposes. Unfortunately, one class of users has found ways to use the computer unethically or illegally. This group of users has received some notoriety. In the movie *WarGames,* a high school student accidentally breaks into a U.S. Department of Defense computer and almost starts World War III. The "414s," a group named for the Milwaukee telephone area code in which they lived, pooled their knowledge to break into computers across the country. The "414s" were primarily pranksters who broke into computers just to see if it could be done. However, in many cases, large sums of money are stolen or the computer's data are damaged.

The "414s" and the "hero" of *WarGames* are **hackers**, persons who seek unauthorized access to computers. Hackers may be the most notorious of the computer users who engage in unethical or illegal activities, but they are far from the most damaging. The biggest computer crime problem is the individual who uses the computer for personal gain or for revenge against an individual or company. Such computer criminals have caused enormous problems by shifting funds into their personal accounts, stealing merchandise, defrauding innocent people of their savings, or destroying data. Table 20-1 shows the 10 biggest computer crimes in terms of the amount involved.

Table 20-1 demonstrates just how much money computer crimes may involve. In fact, the FBI estimates that the average amount of a computer theft is between $100,000 and $500,000. By comparison, the average armed robbery nets the criminal only $3,000, and the average embezzlement is $19,000. Because of the size of the potential loss, computer security is an important consideration for most computer users. The importance of security is even more evident when we consider that over 100,000 commercial and government computer installations across the country exchange all types of informa-

Table 20-1 COMPUTER CRIME LOSSES

Victim and Year of Loss	*Estimated Loss*
Equity Funding—1973	$ 2.1 billion
O.P.M. Leasing—1980	310 million
Penn Central—1971	110 million
U.S. Army—1974	85 million
Saxon Industries—1982	53 million
Greenman—1981	50 million
Chilcott Portfolio Management—1977	45 million
Cenco—1974	40 million
J. Walter Thompson—1981	31 million
Wells Fargo—1981	21 million

(SOURCE: "White-collar Crime Cuts into Companies' Profits," *USA Today,* August 30, 1984, p. 1B. Copyright 1984 *USA Today.* Reprinted with permission.)

tion every day. Banks and financial institutions in the United States, Europe, and Japan electronically transfer over $800 *billion* each day.

Computer security includes the wide range of methods used to protect the computer, the data, and the computer user from natural and criminal forces. (We include natural forces because fire, water, wind, or earthquake can be as devastating as the criminal who seeks personal gain.) The types of security range from simply locking doors to sophisticated data-coding methods that render the data unreadable to anyone other than designated users.

COMPUTER CRIME

Computer crime is an illegal act that requires special knowledge of computer technology. The extent of computer crime in the United States is unknown because many companies, fearful of losing the public's confidence, are reluctant to prosecute persons involved. Companies also worry that if the details of crimes are publicized, someone might try them again. Annual estimates of computer crime costs range from $100 million to over $2 billion. Because until recently laws against computer crime did not allow adequate prosecution of the computer criminal, individuals received little or no actual jail time, even if large amounts of money were stolen. A person involved in a $500,000 computer crime might be sentenced to only three years *probation*.

Computer crimes may be classified into the following five major categories:

1. Manipulation of data or assets
2. Direct attack on the computer, software, or data
3. Use of a computer for conducting or planning a crime
4. Deception or intimidation of people by computer
5. Unauthorized use of the computer for personal gain

For example, in the first type of computer crime, a personal computer was used to break into a credit bureau computer, from which credit card numbers were stolen. Using these numbers, the hacker then ordered merchandise totaling $75,000. The thief was caught only when delivery personnel questioned making so many deliveries to different people at the same address. In an example of the second type of crime, a disgruntled employee left a "logic bomb" in a computer. The program was executed only when the employee's Social Security number was no longer included on the company's payroll. When executed, the logic bomb erased all the system's files. The Flagler Dog Track case is an example of the third type of computer crime. A computer operator used the dog track's computer to generate bogus winning tickets. The largest computer crime of all, the Equity Funding case, is an example of the use of the computer to carry out a crime by deceiving people. In this case, a group of con artists used a computer to generate over 64,000 fake insurance policyholders who held insurance with face value of over $2 billion. This list was then used to sell over $600 million worth of stock in an imaginary company. The final type of computer crime, unauthorized use of a

It appears there is a "forgive them, they know not what they do" attitude. The honest people get stuck with the bill.

George Minot, Executive Vice-President of CompuServe
(As quoted in "Unauthorized Access," *Online Today*, July 1984, pp. 12–13.)

THE FLAGLER DOG TRACK CASE

A particularly interesting case of computer crime involved the Flagler Dog Track in Florida. The case is referred to as a "pure" computer crime, because it involved only a manipulation of the computer. To understand this case, some background on the concept of racetrack gambling is in order. The *odds* on a given horse or dog winning a race, as determined by the amount of money bet on each participant, are shown on the *tote board* before the race begins. Any attempt to manipulate the outcomes of races for which the odds appear on the tote board would immediately be noticed by knowledgeable race fans. However, one type of bet cannot be reflected in the odds because many possible winning combinations exist. In the *trifecta,* a bettor attempts to pick the exact order of the first three finishers. Therefore, in an eight-dog race, 336 such combinations are possible.

This inability to show the odds on the trifecta races and the need to use a computer to keep track of all the bets led a few track and computer employees to commit a crime. These employees took the main computer off-line for less than 1 minute and input the numbers of winning dogs into losing storage locations. The backup computer continued with the true calculations while the information on the bogus winners was fed into the main computer before control was returned to it. These additional bogus winners diluted the true winners' portions of the betting pool. The portions for the state and the track were not affected, because they came off the top, before any winners' allocations. Because the amounts bet on a trifecta often ran into thousands of dollars, a true winner's portion might be cut from $5,000 to $2,000. However, no one complained, because each winning bettor was overjoyed to win as much as $2,000 on a $2 bet.

Fake tickets that matched the storage locations within the computer were generated and cashed. The criminals were eventually undone by a spouse who talked too much and an accomplice who generated fake winning tickets on a machine that had not sold any trifecta tickets. The scheme lasted for five years, during which the take was an estimated $2 million, although no one is sure of the actual amount.

When caught and convicted, the participants who cooperated with authorities received sentences of 9–18 months. The ringleader refused to cooperate and received the maximum five years in prison.

SOURCE: John Underwood, "Win Place . . . and Sting," *Sports Illustrated,* July 23, 1979, pp. 54–66.

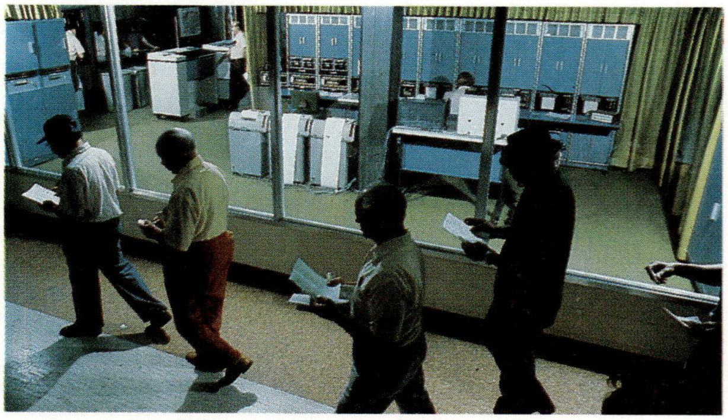

Employees of the Flagler Dog Track in Florida manipulated these computers to generate the bogus winning tickets that they later cashed in.

computer, is very common in many offices and is probably the least reported type of computer crime. Employees may use the computer during work hours, at lunch, or after hours for personal purposes ranging from playing games to setting up a computer service bureau.

The Computer Criminal

Who commits computer crimes? Computer criminals are usually young (19–25 years old), male, college educated, and without a criminal record. Such individuals often view breaking into a computer as a game or a challenge, not a crime.

Computer criminals fall into four major groups—employees, hackers, outside users, and organized crime. Employees form the largest group of computer criminals, usually because they have the easiest access to a computer. Sometimes, a disgruntled employee may wish to get back at the company through attacking the computer physically or using it to steal from the company. Other times, an employee may accidentally find a way to commit a computer crime. The employee may not act on the knowledge immediately, waiting for the perfect accomplice to help carry out the crime.

Hackers are usually interested in unauthorized access for the fun of it, but the potential to damage computer programs and files is very real. Outside users can obtain a computer system's phone number, access code, and password to gain access to the system. This information is often amazingly easy to obtain. For example, a credit bureau may include a user's access code and password on every credit report it sends. When these reports are discarded, a knowledgeable computer criminal can easily recognize this information. A group of electronic bulletin boards across the country display phone numbers and access information for various computer systems. These *cracker boards* are often manned by members of a group called T.H.E.M. (Telecommunications Hackers, Embezzlers, and Manipulators). When any member of the group finds a telephone number and access information, he or she posts it on the bulletin board.

We look around and see new industries, new professions, even new forms of crime—all created or influenced by computers.

Jay Bloombecker, Director of the National Center for Computer Crime Data

(As quoted in "Conscience in Computing," *PC Magazine,* January 24, 1984, p. 99.)

Organized crime has discovered that the computer can be extremely useful in furthering its objectives. In addition to the types of crimes already mentioned, organized crime can use the computer for the following purposes:

Moving prostitutes from city to city and changing their aliases to avoid a large number of convictions for the same name in a single city.

Keeping a list of stolen automobile parts. A computer network is used to check prices nationwide and to send the stolen parts to the place with the highest price and the least chance of detection.

Keeping elaborate gambling records so that debts can be collected regardless of where the debtor has moved.

The Crime Process

To understand fully the problem of computer crime, we should look at the process for committing such a crime. First, we designate a computer crime (except a physical attack on the hardware) as an input crime, a throughput crime, or an output crime.

An **input crime** is committed when a user changes, fabricates, or manipulates data when they are entered into the machine. For example, if a computer criminal can gain access to long distance telephone billing data before bills are mailed, a complete statement of toll calls may be wiped clean. Similarly, a grade may be changed before it is entered on a transcript. On the other hand, an input crime may involve the fabrication of fake suppliers to whom checks are sent or fake customers to whom merchandise is sent.

A **throughput crime** involves modifying software so that data processed by the software are manipulated differently from the original intent. This illegal manipulation of data may involve theft or sabotage of results. For

WHO ARE THESE HACKERS?

We hear a great deal about the hackers who use mainframe terminals and personal computers to break into other computers. Who are these people? The following descriptions may help you identify the hackers around you.

Tron Man is a 17-year-old East Coast prep school student. He has broken into the computer of TRW, a credit bureau company. Tron's first break-in was just for fun, but he can damage TRW's systems if they ever anger him. Tron Man also commented that he had obtained the phone number and password of a national computer retail chain from the top of a computer in a local store.

Matthew was a hacker and proud of it. He started off simply using a program at his local computer center that allowed him to communicate with computer users at other universities. However, Matthew—and probably others—discovered how to steal extra computer time on the network. He also discovered a bug in a telephone company computer that allowed him to make free long distance phone calls. Matthew eventually participated in a million-dollar system for manipulating phones. Matthew's downfall was a romantic relationship with another hacker that went sour—she turned him in.

A street-smart 16-year-old, Rick owns two personal computers and over 200 illegal software programs that he has collected over the last eight months. He estimates the value of these programs at over $9,000, but he has less than $500 invested in his library. Rick builds his software library using electronic bulletin boards, where he trades software with other hackers. He also uses auto-dialers to tap into long distance lines to make free calls.

When the police asked for his help, 15-year-old Peter was only too pleased to aid them in cracking a sex offender's electronic diary. Peter bypassed the offender's secret code in less than one-half hour and printed out some of the more interesting files, leading to the arrest and trial of the individual in question. The police had been trying to do this for over one month!

example, a criminal may plant a **Trojan horse program** to sabotage the original program or modify it to perform illegal activities. Another throughput crime involves using a program to shift small amounts of money to the criminal's account. For example, a program rounded all interest on savings accounts *down* to the nearest penny and accumulated the difference between the rounded amount and the actual interest in the criminal's secret account. This may not sound like a lot of money, but when the program is applied to every depositor over a period of several years, the amount accumulated could be substantial.

An **output crime** involves the theft of processed information for resale, extortion, or the criminal's personal use. A common problem is the theft of an agency's client list, inventory control output, or other information crucial to its successful operation. An employee may start a new agency based on his or her former employer's computerized client list.

Legal and Insurance Aspects of Computer Crime

Although computer criminals reaped large sums from their crimes, they normally did not spend much time behind bars when caught. The theft of information or computer time was not considered a crime under laws enacted prior to the computer age. In some cases, only the mail fraud law could be applied to a computer crime. Even when money was stolen, prosecutors often could not obtain a conviction for several reasons. First, the defendant was often young and clean-cut and had no previous record. Second, the intricacies of the computer, and therefore the crime, were often not easily explained to a judge and jury. Finally, the jury often considered computer crime a "victimless crime," because the injured party was usually a large corporation.

To rectify this problem, the federal government and several states passed laws covering computer crime. The federal statute—the Counterfeit Access Device and Computer Fraud and Abuse Act of 1984 (PL98-473)—applies to federal computers, any computer used in foreign or interstate commerce, or any computer that is connected to an interstate telecommunications network. The statue defines a computer crime involving more than $5,000 as a felony punishable by up to 10 years in prison. Most state laws are similar to this and, when combined with the federal law, should make computer crime a painful vocation.

In 1981, Lloyds of London offered the first coverage for computer crime. Today, at least 12 insurance companies offer some form of coverage for computer crime. Less than 10% of all banks have the coverage, but interest is growing in this type of protection. Most policies cover money stolen by a third party using the computer. They also cover the cost of reproducing stolen or destroyed data and the loss of revenue due to interruption of service. Premiums start at $10,000 per year for an average coverage of $10 million.[1]

If various predictions about computer crime are true, then computer crime insurance may soon be as commonplace as fire and liability insurance. What are these predictions? People feel that computer crime will increase as the computer becomes an integral part of society. Organized crime will use the computer more as a method for controlling activities and as a source of funds. Finally, the size of individual losses will increase.

The capabilities of committing computer crime are increasing faster than the ability of victims to stop it.

Susan Nycum, California computer law expert

(As quoted in "Quotelines," *USA Today,* December 6, 1984, p. 12A.)

COMPUTER SECURITY

If computer crime is the threat to computer hardware, software, data, and output, then with computer security, individuals and organizations can protect those assets. Unauthorized access by outside parties is the most publicized threat to a computer system's security, but it is not the most important for International Business Machines (IBM). Harry DeMaio, director of security for IBM, stated that most damage to computers and data are due to errors and omissions by employees. In fact, outside attack ranks sixth on IBM's following list of threats:[2]

1. Errors and omissions of data
2. Disgruntled employees
3. Dishonest employees
4. Fire
5. Water
6. External attack

Not everyone agrees with IBM's ranking of threats to a computer, but no one argues the fact that these threats exist. The security problem for com-

[1]Susan Spillman, "Latest Insurance: Computer Crimes Covered," *USA Today,* October 4, 1984, p. 3B.
[2]A. Richard Immel, "Data Security," *Popular Computing,* May 1984, pp. 65–68.

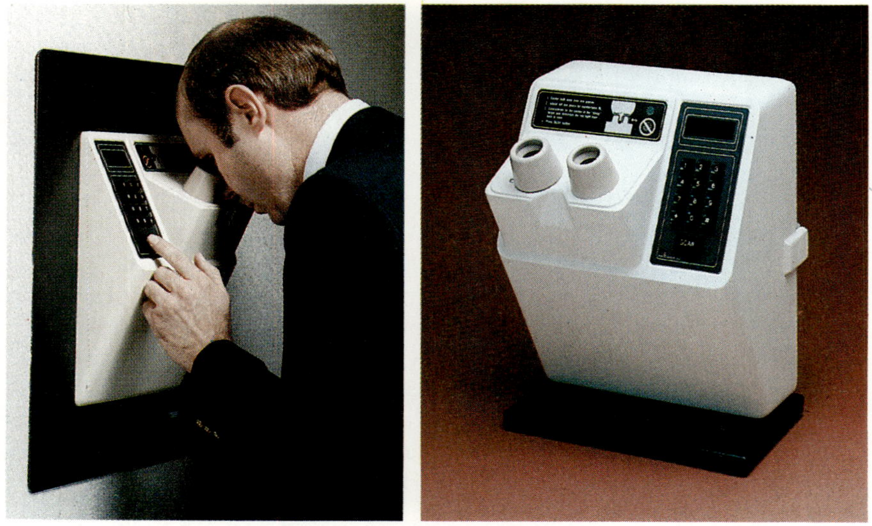

In one method of computer security, a computer compares the pattern in the potential user's retina with the patterns of valid users, which are stored in its memory.

puters must be considered in terms of physical security and data security. **Physical security** involves protecting the computer hardware from natural and man-made damage. **Data security** includes protecting a computer's software and data from unauthorized manipulation, destruction, or theft.

Physical Security

Protecting the computer hardware from outside forces should include the following:

Procedures for excluding unauthorized persons from the computer center.

Design of tamperproof hardware.

Protection of hardware from natural disasters.

Protection of hardware from fire and water damage.

Protection of the tape library.

Methods of physical security include locating the facility where it can be protected from physical attack, controlling entry to the computer facility with a guard, using finger- or voiceprints to identify individuals seeking entry, and, as simple as it may seem, keeping doors locked. In the event of a natural or man-made disaster, back up tape library files should be physically separated from the main computer center. Figure 20-1 is a diagram of some typical security procedures.

Although locking doors may seem like a common sense approach to physical security, a 1984 study of 138 firms by the accounting firm of Price Waterhouse found that 38% were less than enthusiastic about locking their computer rooms. Most firms felt locking doors was impractical.[3] Top management's lax approach to security is often blamed when computer crimes occur.

---

[3]Mark Lewyn, "Computer Security Low Priority," *USA Today,* September 24, 1984, p. 1B.

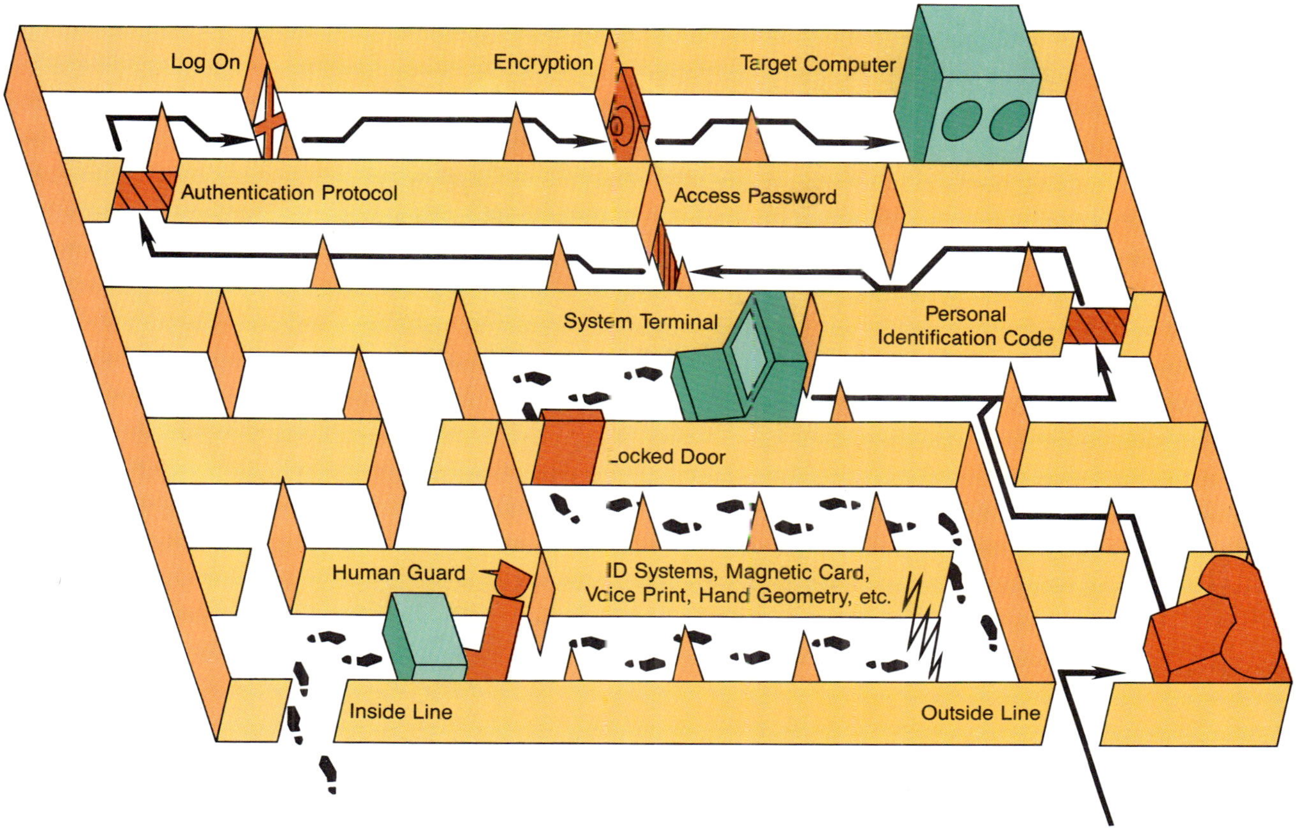

FIGURE 20-1
Security Procedures

Damage from fire and water is on IBM's list of dangers, but this threat is often ignored. Because a computer's circuits can short out, protection against potential electrical fires must be built into the system. Water can damage a computer's delicate circuits, so the danger from water must be considered in the planning of the system. Sprinkler systems are the usual protection against fire in commercial buildings, but they can damage a computer as much as the fire itself.

Data Security

Protecting the software and data is an entirely different problem from the physical protection of a computer. Conflicting objectives exist in the area of data security. The computer should be available and as easy to use as possible. However, the data and software must be protected from unauthorized use. The first objective often takes precedence.

The movement toward easy-to-use systems and the many other changes in computers today create a massive data security problem. These other changes include recent technological and software advancements, the need to access larger amounts of data, and the decentralization of computer systems. The personal computer's popularity has added to the data security problem, because a personal computer may be used to break into computer systems. Many computer systems are connected to telephone lines, which allow access

Computers can be protected from lightning and other electrical surges by anti-surge devices.

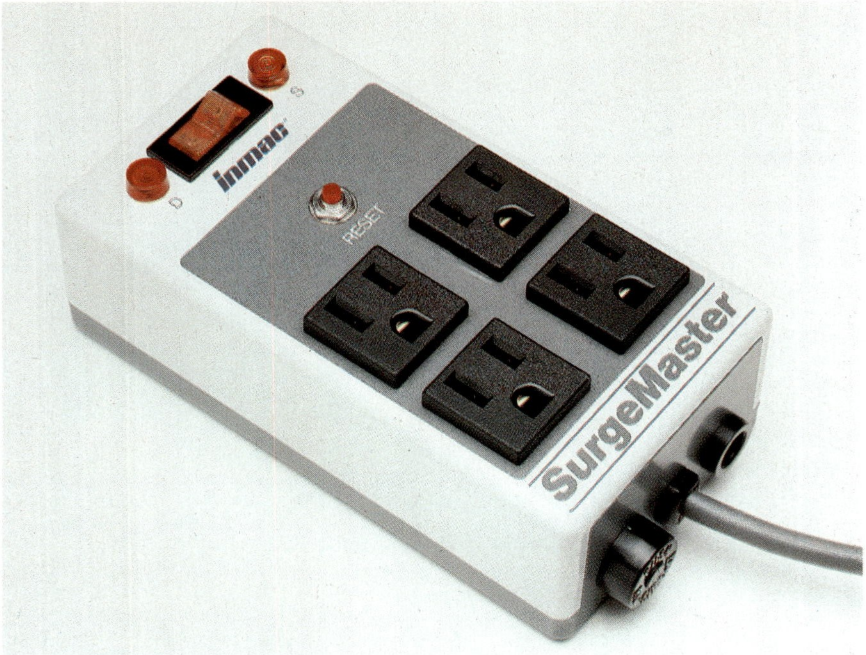

from a user's home or office. The user may have a terminal or personal computer, along with a modem and telecommunications software. The primary method of protecting data on these computer systems is through access codes and passwords. The **access code** is usually an account number that is used for allocating charges for computer time, and the **password** is a sequence of letters and digits supposedly known only to the user. Because a computer uses a high-pitched tone to answer a phone call, it is easily recognizable by phone. This ease of recognition and easily guessed passwords make a computer system with a phone line extremely easy to access. Figure 20-2 shows the methods often used to gain unauthorized access to such **dial-up computer systems**.

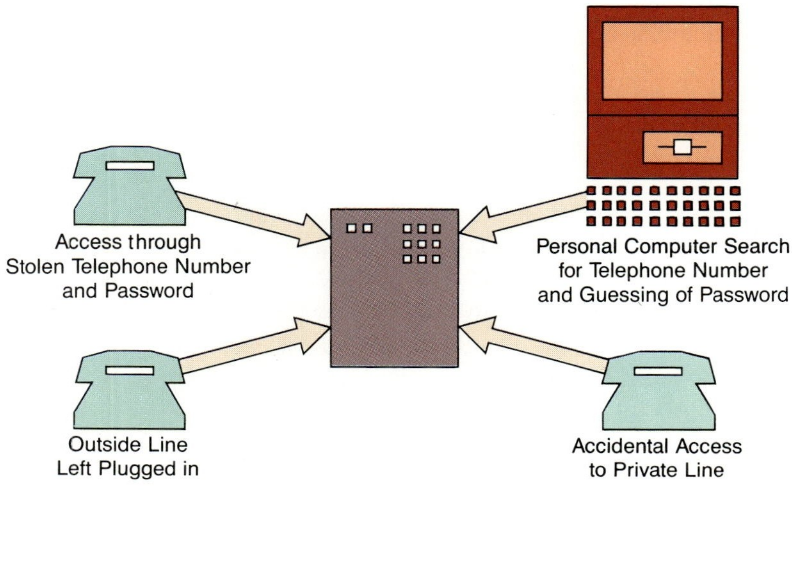

FIGURE 20-2
Unauthorized Access Methods

WARGAMES

Could It Actually Occur?

People who saw the movie *WarGames* probably wondered if those events could ever really happen. The immediate answer from the U.S. Department of Defense and many computer scientists is a resounding no! The scenario of *WarGames* involves a teenage hacker who accidentally gains access to a Defense Department computer through a telephone line. By playing thermonuclear war games with the computer, the hacker almost starts World War III. Most experts feel strongly that this situation could never happen. However, Dr. Donald Williams, the technical consultant for the movie, cites the following three instances which, if combined, could lead to the situation presented in the movie.

1. **In 1981, a private aerospace company suffered a major security breach when a dial-in link to the computer was mistakenly left plugged in. Because this line was unencrypted, the company's computers were open to outside access. Such dial-in links must be unplugged, not just turned off. This link would allow anyone with a terminal and a modem to gain access to the computer.**
2. **In 1979, at a North American Aerospace Defense Command (NORAD) complex, an operator mistakenly loaded an exercise war game tape into the operation computer system. This tape displayed an attack scenario in the command post and transmitted it as real information to other NORAD centers. Although the mistake was determined within seconds and backup systems stopped the launch of a counterattack, the possibility of a serious computer mistake was demonstrated.**
3. **The type of artificial intelligence programs shown in *WarGames* have not yet been developed. However, research in this area could lead to the development of programs that could modify themselves. Programs have, on occasion, modified data mistakenly.**

SOURCE: "Could *WarGames* Happen?" *Personal Computing*, October 1983, pp. 219–40.

Any solution to the computer security problem involves methods of protecting data and information stored on the computer and the prevention of unauthorized release or modification of this data and information. New hardware and software have an important role in solving this problem, but a change in attitude of the people involved is even more important. In the Price Waterhouse study of 138 firms, 47% did not want to use multiple passwords to protect computer access. It is surprisingly easy to find or guess a user's password. Often, a short password chosen by the user includes the name of the user's spouse, children, pet, or other easily guessed words like PASSWORD, SECRET, or TEST! The computer security problem cannot be solved until top management realizes that risking security can be costly and users take more care with passwords.

There is no such thing as absolute safety. You cannot guarantee the security of a computer system if it is not physically or electronically isolated.

Joseph Weizenbaum, Massachusetts Institute of Technology

(As quoted in "Quotelines," *USA Today,* August 19, 1983, p. 10A.)

Some of the methods currently used to protect computer software and data are shown in Figure 20-1 and also include the following:

Not allowing the user to choose his or her own password and requiring that the password be longer than four letters or digits. The user should also have the password changed immediately if any evidence of a security breach exists. All passwords should be changed periodically so that an unauthorized user cannot easily guess them.

Using security software packages that keep track of all attempts to log on the computer, particularly *unsuccessful* attempts. Auditing this log daily would indicate if the system is the target of an unauthorized user.

Using security software that requires a user to wait at least 5 sec-

Modems that incorporate password protection, callback procedures, and key-lock features can protect computers from unauthorized access.

onds between attempts to enter a password. Such software may also require the user to hang the phone up and redial after three such attempts. An unauthorized user cannot use a computer to generate guesses of the password.

Using a system that accepts phone calls and passwords from users, looks up the phone number associated with the password, and then calls the user back at that number. If the password was stolen, the unauthorized user will not be at the correct number.

Using port protection devices. A **port** is an entry line to the computer, and a **port protection device** is an extra level of security to separate the user from the computer. These devices have their own passwords in addition to that used by the software security system. Some devices also camouflage the computer by answering the phone with a voice response rather than a high-pitched signal, thus avoiding recognition of the system by an unauthorized computer search.

IT WAS SO EASY!

The "414s" are a famous set of hackers, named for the telephone area code where they lived. This group of high school students was armed only with small personal computers, modems, and telecommunications software. During the first eight months of 1983, the "414s" obtained access to 60 data banks across the United States, including an unclassified computer at the Los Alamos Nuclear Laboratory, a computer at the Sloan-Kettering Memorial Cancer Center in New York, and a computer at Canada Cement Lafarge Limited of Montreal. Neal Patrick, one of the hackers, explained to a congressional hearing how the access was accomplished. Often, passwords like "test" and "system" that were left by the system developers were still in use. Other passwords and telephone numbers were available on electronic bulletin boards. According to Patrick, the "414s" did not intend to damage any system, " . . . but the potential for damage was enormous . . . If someone with a sinister intent had accessed that computer, the damage could have run into the millions, just in dollar value . . . It's something anybody can do . . . I don't think any members of the group were geniuses. If they had just changed those [passwords], we couldn't have gotten in."

SOURCE: "Computer Trespass: The Whiz Has a Cure," ***The Los Angeles Times,*** **September 23, 1983, part 1, p. 6.**

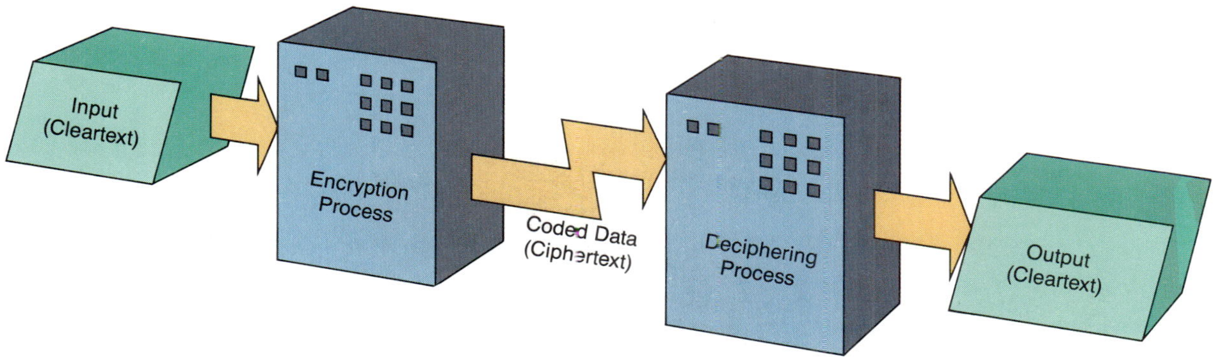

FIGURE 20-3
Encryption Process

Using **encryption** software and hardware to convert the information in the computer into an unreadable form. Encryption is especially important when information is transmitted over networks. In the process, **cleartext** (a readable form) is transformed into **ciphertext** (an unreadable form) at the source computer and then transformed back again at the destination computer. Figure 20-3 shows the encryption process. The American National Standards Institute (ANSI) has developed the **Data Encryption Standard (DES)**, which is a standard method of coding data. Most companies do not use encryption now, but recent decreases in the cost of coding devices should lead to increased use.

Human aspects of computer security are as important as the technological changes previously mentioned. The ethics of computer use will grow in importance as the use of computers increases. People must understand that an unauthorized intrusion, no matter how innocent it appears, is a crime punishable by a fine or imprisonment, or both. Because a system is only as secure as its owners want it to be, users should be involved in the systems design process. Finally, system users must recognize that people, not machines, can give or accept responsibility for computer security.

CRIME, SECURITY, AND THE PERSONAL COMPUTER

The personal computer can be the tool that allows unauthorized users to search for computer systems. However, the personal computer cannot be blamed for the advent of computer crime. In Table 20-1, more than one-half of the ten largest computer crimes occurred *before* the introduction of the personal computer in 1976. The personal computer has just made it easier for the less-than-expert user to break into mainframe computer systems. The personal computer has also led to a new group of ethical, legal, and security problems. Most of these problems involve copying commercial software, but a new security problem has developed with the use of the personal computer in the office.

Software Copying

When mainframes and minicomputers were the only sources of computing power, the user had access to the software that was available at the computer center or that he or she had written. Occasionally, software at other computer centers could be used through a network system, or hackers could access software that was not available to the normal user. This environment seldom fostered the need or the facility to copy commercial software from the computer.

In 1976, the personal computer's popularity grew and users needed one copy of a software package for each machine rather than one copy that served multiple users on a mainframe. The first popular commercial software package, VisiCalc, was released in 1979. Users who bought VisiCalc realized its potential and spread the word. The demand for VisiCalc was high, but the program and the user's manual were easily copied. Numerous copies of VisiCalc were made, not purchased, and the problem of **software piracy** began.

"By putting all our data into code, our competitors can't read it, our unauthorized personnel can't read it, and, I'm afraid, neither can we."

To understand how copying software for personal use differs from software piracy, we should look at the 1980 Software Copyright Act. In this act, copying a piece of software for backup purposes is distinguished from copying it for purposes of resale or for giving it away. Copying a disk for backup purposes is perfectly legal. Any number of copies may be made, as long as all are retained by the user. When a copy is given or sold to anyone else, a federal law is broken. The penalties under this law include monetary damages to the copyright holder—in this case, the software developer—and the loss of any profits made by the person who copied the program. Prison terms can be imposed for willful copying and resale.

Enforcement of the copyright law is generally reserved for the most blatant offenders because of the cost of prosecution. The person who copies a program for a friend will probably not be prosecuted. However, copying and reselling a piece of software in large quantities will bring quick action by the U.S. Department of Justice. Remember, the software developer expects a fair return for the blood and sweat that went into that package. The developer suffers a loss every time someone gives away a copy of the program. If this happened often enough, companies would have no incentive to develop software.

Another part of the copyright act allows a user to modify a program to make it useful. A user may change a program to meet special needs, but he or she *cannot* sell the software as a new product, no matter how much it is changed. The U.S. Department of Justice has tried several cases in which persons have changed a software package and tried to resell the result as their own product.

Despite the laws against software piracy, it occurs among many personal computer users. As a result, some software developers now **copy protect** their programs so that a user can make, at most, one backup copy. Companies often include a second copy of the program in the package or send one for a nominal fee if the software cannot be copied at all. However, copy protecting a piece of software has its drawbacks, because owners may be dissatisfied with the wait of several weeks to receive a new copy or with the inability either to make multiple backups or to copy the program to a hard disk. Micropro, the developer of the popular word processing package, WordStar, tried copy protection for a short time on WordStar 2000 but dropped it because consumers were unhappy.

In response to copy protection, **lockbuster packages** were developed to circumvent the copy protection. The **nybbler**, or bit-by-bit, **packages** (a nybble is one-half of 1 byte, or 4 bits) copy a program 1 bit at a time. Because most operating systems copy an entire sector of a track at one time, the copy

DEC'S REVENGE

Some years ago, Digital Equipment Corporation (DEC) installed several Decmate II personal computers at various test sites across the country. Users were given free use of these machines in exchange for their comments on any technical problems with the system. The word processing package provided with the machines—Decmate II—was then one of the better packages available.

Some of the test users decided to keep a copy to use after the test period ended. The package was used for personal work and was sold to other users. Everything went well for these software pirates until April Fools Day, 1983, when *all* files associated with these bootleg versions of Decmate were purged. DEC had anticipated the software piracy and had included in the test packages a statement that effectively said, If date equals April 1, 1983, then delete all files.

It is not hard to imagine the pain and suffering that the software pirates, their customers, and their friends endured on the day that their word processing documents disappeared. In this case, piracy did not pay off. SOURCE: "DEC Smites April Fools," *Popular Computing*, October 1983, p. 26. Adapted with permission from the November 1983 issue of *Popular Computing* Magazine.

protection usually locks a particular sector. A nybbler avoids this locking mechanism. Another lockbuster package, called a **memory dump program**, copies the program out of the computer's random access memory. All programs must be copiable into RAM to be run. Therefore, the only way to stop this procedure is to make the program too big to fit into memory at one time.

To satisfy users who want multiple backups, some companies have personal computer systems that use a **master disk** along with the normal program disk. The user can make an unlimited number of program disk copies, but they will only run with the master disk, which is copy protected. The response to this latest effort by software developers to protect their investment is not clear. Another protection method allows users to test a program by making small runs on the program, but access to files or other full-scale use is restricted until the dealer provides a special code.

Security for the Personal Computer

Physical security and data security must be considered for personal computers as well as mainframe computers. The personal computer must be carefully protected from environmental harm as well as from theft. In protecting the computer from damage, users should take the normal precautions for protecting any piece of office equipment against fire, water, dust, and other physical damage. The user must also protect the computer and its data against electricity—too much, too little, the wrong kind, or the right kind applied the wrong way can all cause problems. If a computer is hit by a **voltage surge**, or **spike**, due to lightning or other electrical disturbances, the delicate chips and electrical parts can be destroyed. **Surge protectors**, which are available for less than $50, plug into a normal wall outlet. The computer and peripherals are then plugged into outlets in the surge protector. When a surge hits the wall outlet, a circuit breaker in the surge protector is thrown, and the computer and its peripherals are protected.

Too little electricity—such as in a brownout or a blackout—can cause the loss of all data from internal memory. Recall that most RAM is volatile and depends on constant power to retain information. Loss of power means loss of memory. Devices that maintain power in a computer retail for close to $500. Therefore, an individual's best defense against a power outage is fre-

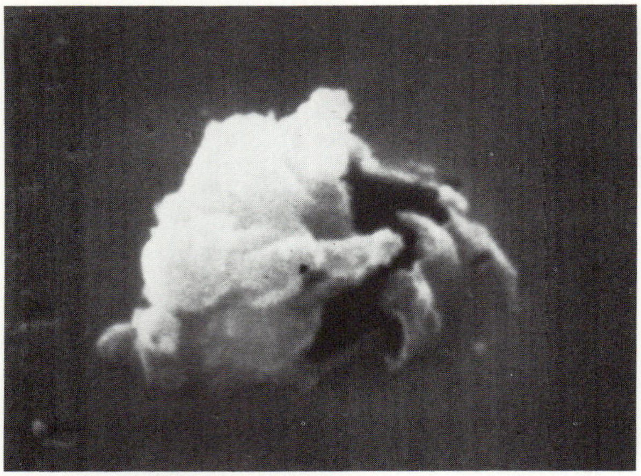

The effect of static electricity on a microchip is shown at left, magnified 10,000 times. This damage was caused by 3,000 volts of static electricity from human contact with the computer. Anti-static rugs (right) can protect computer components from static electricity.

quently saving information in RAM to disk. Static electricity must also be considered in the use of a personal computer. In a dry climate, walking across a rug can generate a charge of static electricity that can significantly damage data or electrical parts. Protection against static electricity can be improved by anti-static spray, touch pads, or special floor covers.

Plugging parts of the system into different outlets can cause explosions in computer equipment. When an outlet with reversed polarity is connected to a system with normal polarity, an explosion results. Obviously, computers are damaged by such events. Users should obtain surge protectors with multiple outlets to connect all computer units to the same outlet. Figure 20-4 demonstrates right and wrong electrical connections.

Protection from theft means locking all the doors that lead to the computer. The computer may be stored in special locked cabinets, or the plug may be connected to an alarm device.

Data Security for the Personal Computer

Data security for a personal computer is similar in many ways to that for a mainframe, except that normally a single user is involved. Disks containing data should be locked up when not in use. Lockup mechanisms on the computer are available for a hard disk system. Passwords can be used with some operating systems to protect files from unauthorized use or damage. Information can be erased from the screen by a single key if an unauthorized person is present.

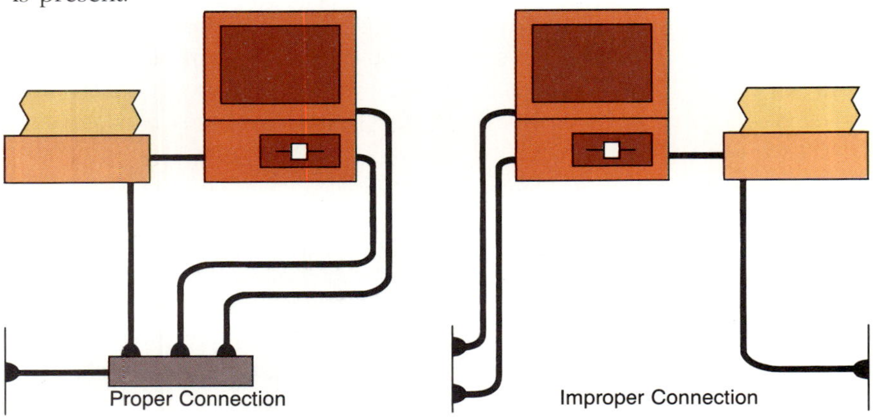

FIGURE 20-4
Proper and Improper Electrical Connections

Encryption for personal computers is available either for use in a network or for stand-alone systems. For example, a software package and the special board necessary to run it have a corresponding number. The software will not run on a computer without that board or with a board that does not have the correct code. Encryption packages for networks protect the data that are sent to another terminal in the network from unauthorized access.

REVIEW OF KEY POINTS

- The computer can be the object of a crime, it can be used to commit a crime, or it can be used to deceive people.
- Computer crimes usually involve a great deal of money, but the penalties have historically not been severe.
- Persons who commit computer crimes fall into four groups—employees, hackers, outside users, and organized crime.
- Access codes and passwords are often used to protect the computer from unauthorized access.
- The three types of computer crime are the input crime, the throughput crime, and the output crime.
- Laws prohibiting computer crime have been strengthened at the state and national levels.
- Computer security includes physical security and data security. Physical security protects the computer itself, and data security protects the data and software.
- Types of data security include frequently changed passwords, software that protects against unauthorized telephone access, and encryption.
- Software piracy is a major problem associated with the use of personal computers.
- Software developers use various copy protection devices to fight software piracy.
- A personal computer must be protected from the same outside threats as mainframe computers. They must also be protected from too much or too little electricity.

KEY TERMS

access code
ciphertext
cleartext
computer crime
computer security
copy protect
Data Encryption Standard (DES)
data security
dial-up computer systems
encryption
hackers
input crime
lockbuster packages
master disk
memory dump program
nybbler packages
output crime
password
physical security
port
port protection device
software piracy
spike
surge protectors
throughput crime
Trojan horse program
voltage surge

REVIEW QUESTIONS

1. Why have computer criminals often stolen large amounts of money but received relatively light punishment?
2. Name and discuss the five types of crime involving a computer.
3. Why are hackers considered computer criminals?
4. How is organized crime using computers for illegal purposes? What other uses might they find for the computer?
5. Discuss the various points in the use of a computer at which a crime can occur.
6. What two types of security are necessary for a computer? Discuss each type, giving examples.
7. Discuss the use of access codes and passwords to discourage unauthorized access. What other devices are used for this purpose?
8. Define *software piracy*. Why is this problem associated with personal computers, but not with mainframes?
9. How are software developers fighting software piracy? Discuss the use of lockbusters.
10. Why must a personal computer be protected from too much, too little, or the wrong type of electricity?

The computer has in general been a mind tool that helps us to do many things that we could otherwise not accomplish. However, problems arise when the computer is not used correctly or ethically. We noted the problems of computer crime in Chapter 20, and in this chapter, we take up personal privacy and health issues. The computer can be used to invade our personal privacy, and the use of video display terminals may cause health problems for users. Both issues are discussed in some detail, including steps for resolving or avoiding the problems.

21 Computer Issues in Privacy and Health

STUDY OBJECTIVES

After reading this chapter, you should be able to

- Recognize the privacy and health issues in the use of computers.
- Understand how the combination of computers and data banks can accelerate the invasion of privacy.
- Discuss past attempts to set up a national data bank and laws that were enacted to protect privacy.
- Explain the current status of data banks and the use of matching to combine data banks to locate various groups of people.
- Discuss the increase in the use of transactional data and the possible unethical uses of this type of data.
- Understand the various health hazards associated with long-term use of video display terminals.
- Apply the meaning of *ergonomics* to computers.
- Discuss the psychological problems associated with computers.

INTRODUCTION

In Chapter 5, we discussed some people-oriented issues common to the use of computers. Two issues have received a great deal of attention in the last few years—the effect of the computer on personal privacy and the effect of long-term use of a video display terminal (VDT) on the user's health. In this chapter, we discuss these two issues in more detail.

Historical Background

Society first regarded the computer as a threat to personal privacy in the mid-1960s. Although the computer could solve many problems faced by society, it could also invade the privacy of individuals. The invasion of personal privacy has always been a concern in the United States. In fact, a primary purpose of the Bill of Rights was to keep the government from looking into our personal lives. Every new technological advance in communications and computers was reviewed in terms of the privacy laws to determine whether new laws were needed. For example, the introduction of both the telegraph and telephone in the latter half of the nineteenth century raised questions. Were telegrams protected like the mails, or were they open to investigation by the authorities? Could the authorities legally listen in on telephone conversations for purposes of protecting the public good? Even the ability to make unposed photographs was a great concern for families in the late nineteenth century.

The personal privacy issue has included the U.S. Bureau of the Census. In 1790, the first census consisted of only four questions. However, by 1890, over 13,000 questions were divided among over 200 different questionnaires. In 1980, these numbers were even larger, as individuals answered either a short form or a long form. The information gathered by the Bureau of the Census is supposedly used only for reporting U.S. population statistics. However, in two major instances, this privacy was abridged. Census Bureau records were used during World War I to track down draft evaders. At the beginning of World War II, Census Bureau records were used to find Americans of Japanese descent, who were moved to detention camps. Ironically, these two instances occurred before the introduction of computers. The privacy issue is

Early keypunch machines (left) were not ergonomically designed. An ergonomically designed data entry center (right) increases the productivity of workers.

not a result of computer use, but computers have made the ability to find or match records much easier.

The increased use of **video display terminals (VDTs)** since the 1970s has raised concerns for the health of VDT users. Before that time, most computer work was handled through **batch access**—that is, computer jobs were prepared on an off-line device, such as a keypunch machine, and then submitted to the computer. The increased sophistication of the computer in the 1970s allowed **interactive access** through VDTs. The use of the keyboard is the same at a VDT as at a keypunch machine, but the number of users has increased exponentially with the introduction of word processing machines and personal computers. The VDT's **cathode ray tube (CRT)** method of display and the concerns of companies and unions for the welfare of office workers has focused attention on the effects of long-term VDT use. The jury is still out on many VDT use concerns; the issue is far from resolved.

PRIVACY AND THE ETHICAL USE OF THE COMPUTER

Concern over the impact of technology on personal privacy did not begin with the introduction of the computer. The use of **data banks**—such as Census Bureau records—for purposes other than those for which they were originally designed is not new. What is new is the ability of modern computers to search multiple data banks in a matter of seconds. The same type of search of a single data bank performed manually would have taken days.

To understand the personal privacy concern, we must define **privacy** as the right to be left alone and to have personal data protected from unauthorized use. Originally, the first half of this definition would have been sufficient, but the increase in the use of computers requires the second half of the definition.

We should remember throughout this discussion that the ability of the computer to process data quickly from one or more data banks has positive effects on our daily lives. For example, without computers and data banks, we could not make airline reservations with any carrier over a toll-free telephone line. We would also not have the large amount of financial credit currently available through credit card companies as the result of credit checks with credit bureaus. The Social Security system and health insurance companies would be unbelievably slow in responding to claims without computers to check records. Clearly, computers and data banks are a necessary part of modern life and, when used appropriately, cause no problems for law-abiding citizens. The problems arise with inappropriate or incorrect use of computers and data banks.

Without the malign intent of any government system or would-be dictator, our privacy is being invaded, and more and more of the experiences which should be solely our own are finding their way into electronic files that the curious can scrutinize at the punch of a button.

Walter Cronkite
[In the Forward to *The Rise of the Computer State* by David Burnham (New York: Vintage Books, 1983).]

If the computer and data banks have such positive implications, then why the growing concern? Computers seldom, if ever, make mistakes, but the combination of humans and computers often make mistakes which can sometimes be difficult to reverse. Often, *computer-generated* results are assumed to be correct when they indeed are not. Consider the following situations:

> An ex-Marine was stopped by police for making an illegal left turn. A check of the national police computer networks indicated that he had been absent without leave (AWOL) from the Marines for five

COMPUTERS AND THE IRS

The U.S. Internal Revenue Service is always looking for ways to use computers to increase U.S. Treasury revenues. For example, the IRS packed information into computers on more than 500,000 tardy taxpayers who owed the government over $1 billion. With this information, the computer generated automated calls to the delinquent accounts, requesting payment. In three months, the system disposed of over $440 million in accounts. The system automatically called the individuals between 8 A.M. and 8 P.M. Monday through Friday and 8 A.M. to noon on Saturday. If a call was not answered, the account was stored in the computer for a later try.

In another effort to collect back taxes, IRS computers matched names on 1982 tax returns with names on a commercial marketing list. The marketing list contained the names of over 2 million heads of households believed to earn $10,000 or more, based on such factors as home ownership. If the name appeared on the marketing list, but no record of that individual's tax return existed, the IRS sent a letter seeking additional information.

SOURCE: William Giese, "High-Tech Helps IRS Catch Tardy Taxpayers," *USA Today,* August 30, 1984, p. 3B; "Mailing Lists Find 5,600 for IRS to Question," *USA Today,* September 26, 1984, p. 2B.

The IRS uses computers in many of its operations, including tracking down overdue tax payments.

years. He was in a Marine stockade for five months before authorities realized that the ex-Marine had been discharged early under a special program.[1]

An individual was picked up for questioning by police in Los Angeles, California, because the computer had determined that he fit at least 61% of the characteristics of a wanted criminal. The fact that he was black and the wanted person was white did not stop the system from designating him as a suspect.[2]

A woman who attempted to rent an apartment was turned down because of a bad rental rating. Her investigation found the cause of the bad rating—an erroneous eviction record from several years in the past.[3]

[1]David Burnham, *The Rise of the Computer State* (New York: Vintage Books, 1983), p. 34.
[2]Curtis Sitomer, "Information Technology and Privacy," *The Christian Science Monitor,* March 1, 1984, p. 21.
[3]David Burnham, p. 35.

The National Data Bank Concept

In the mid-1960s, the Bureau of the Budget recommended that a **national data bank** be established to make the federal statistical system more efficient in its analysis of the U.S. economy. Several independent studies supported this concept, but hearings before the U.S. House of Representatives in July 1966, resulted in the publication of a report entitled "Privacy and the National Data Bank Concept," which was extremely critical of that concept. That report reflected concern for how such a national data bank could affect the average citizen. "The creation of such systems might well make the individual citizen apprehensive about exercising his rights to express controversial views and behave spontaneously."[4] The report further stated:

> Specific units of data might be used to violate the privacy of specific individuals, or cause particular individuals to be unjustly deprived of privileges as American citizens. Malfunction or misuse could occur anywhere in the long process from gathering to utilizing computerized information.[5]

Because of this report and reports of human–computer errors, the concept of the national data bank was dropped. However, the threat of using computers to invade the privacy of individuals did not disappear.

Recent Laws and Reports on Privacy

The proposal for a national data bank and its subsequent rejection opened a period of action on the privacy issue. This action included the following:

- The Fair Credit Reporting Act of 1970
- The 1973 Department of Health, Education, and Welfare (HEW) (now the Departments of Health and Human Services and Education) report titled "Records, Computers, and the Rights of Citizens"
- The Privacy Act of 1974
- The 1977 Report of the Privacy Protection Study Commission titled "Personal Privacy in an Information Society"

The **Fair Credit Reporting Act of 1970** controls the actions of credit bureaus. These private companies collect credit information on every person in the United States who has ever borrowed money and many who have not. When a person wishes to borrow money or engages in various other activities—such as applying for a job—a credit check is requested from a credit bureau. The credit bureau sends a report based on information it has gathered. Note that the credit bureau makes little or no effort to verify the information it gathers and passes on in its reports. The 1970 law attempted to control this industry by regulating to whom such reports can be sent, setting time limits on reporting types of financial data, requiring credit agencies to disclose to consumers the contents of their files, and allowing a consumer to dispute the contents of his or her file by adding a note to it. The credit agency could not use the data for purposes other than the original intent.

---

[4]U.S. House of Representatives, Committee on Governmental Operations, "Privacy and the National Data Bank Concept," August 2, 1968, p. 3.
[5]*Ibid.*

HACKER INVASION

Even when a data bank itself does not invade our privacy, computer criminals can use it to do so. TRW Information Services, the nation's largest credit bureau, discovered that hackers had invaded its computer using a stolen password. The hackers looked at personal data on credit histories, delinquent debts, work histories, bankruptcies, home ownerships, and Social Security numbers. This break-in is regarded as one of the first violations of a personal data system. Although the data in the credit bureau files could not be changed, sufficient data were available in some cases to allow the hackers to commit credit card fraud.

"We're very vulnerable. There is no such thing as 100% security," said Reed Phillips of Advanced Information Management, Inc., a computer security firm. A TRW official said, "We like to feel we can do everything we possibly can and still make products cost-effective; you can put a computer in a lead-lined room, but then you have to charge $100 a report."

SOURCE: Richard Benedetto and Timothy Kenny, "Computer Crooks Spy on Our Credit," *USA Today*, June 22, 1984, p. A1.

The 1973 HEW report studied the effect of computers on personal privacy and the potential for surveillance by the system. The writers of this report formulated the following five principles, which they believed were important to the use of information:

1. Secret data banks containing personal data should not exist. Such secret data banks smack of "Big Brother" from George Orwell's *Nineteen Eighty-Four* and could cause individual citizens to be afraid.
2. Individuals should be able to see the contents of any record containing information on themselves and know how this information is used. This principle would allow a person to examine the contents of his or her credit file and know to whom that file is sent.
3. An individual should be able to prevent having data collected for one purpose used for another purpose without his or her consent. For example, an individual should be able to stop the mailing of financial data to a prospective employer if that was not the original purpose of collecting the financial data.
4. An individual must be able to correct or amend information that is collected or held on him or her. If a credit report contains a reference to a bad check that was actually the bank's mistake, the person should be able to change this information.
5. Organizations that collect data should be responsible for the correctness of the data and take precautions to ensure that it is not misused. For example, long distance telephone call records could not be used to check up on an employee's behavior.

The **Privacy Act of 1974** applied the five principles from the HEW report to most of the record-keeping practices of the federal government. Various law enforcement agencies, the CIA, and the Secret Service were exempted.

As a result of the Privacy Act of 1974, the **Privacy Protection Study**

Commission was established to study the impact of public and private organizations' data banks and to make recommendations regarding their use. The Commission's report made 162 recommendations to minimize intrusiveness, maximize fairness, and create expectations of confidentiality. Many recommendations were impractical from either a time or cost viewpoint, and, at this writing, no new laws have been passed to implement any of them.

Data Banks Today

Although a national data bank does not exist, numerous small data banks do exist, and the number increases almost daily. The computerization of data banks is accelerated by the growth of mainframe power and storage capacity, along with the introduction of personal computers. The personal computer allows small organizations to set up data banks of clients, customers, and so on, and at the same time, communicate with mainframe data banks. Many public data banks exist for federal and state government use, but numerous private data banks are also available. Table 21-1 shows some types of these data banks, divided into various categories.

The data banks in Table 21-1 were set up for legitimate uses, but unfortunately, some of them are also used for other purposes. Often, data banks are combined through a process known as **computer matching** to generate one huge data bank, from which an interested party can derive information. Computer matching takes advantage of the fact that an individual's record on one data bank usually has one or more attributes in common with that indi-

Table 21-1 EXAMPLES OF DATA BANKS

Category	*Data Bank*
Law enforcement	FBI, National Crime Information Center (NCIC) Security clearances Department of Defense surveillance of citizens
Tax and regulatory agencies	IRS State revenue departments Car registration Professional and drivers' licenses Hunting and fishing licenses
Human services	Social Security Aid to Dependent Children Food stamps Veterans' benefits Employment and unemployment registers
Financial	Credit bureaus Credit card companies Financial institutions
Organizational	Personnel files, including intelligence tests, aptitude and personality tests, and appraisals Membership lists Armed forces members
Medical	Hospital and doctors' records Psychiatric and mental-health records
Travel	Airline reservations Lodging reservations Car rentals
Communications	Long distance call records

This group of documents and credit cards demonstrates the variety of data bases in which your name and other information about you could appear.

vidual's record in other data banks. For example, many universities use Social Security numbers to identify students. This number is also required when a student applies for a federally supported loan and when he fills out a draft registration card. Using the Social Security number, the federal government can match male students applying for federally supported loans with individuals who have registered for the draft. If a match cannot be made, the student is not registered for the draft. Either the student is breaking the law (if he is 18 or over) or a legitimate reason exists for failure to register. The student may not be 18 yet, or the student may be female. Figure 21-1 shows some types of matching used to locate various groups of people.

The concept of computer matching is not new, but the areas in which it is applied have expanded since Operation MATCH began in 1978. Operation MATCH is a computer matching system that finds federal employees who also receive federal assistance illegally. Another example of matching is the federal Parent Locater Act. This act requires states that receive Aid to Dependent Children funds to set up a system to track down parents who owe money for child support. This law has resulted in a large-scale telecommunications system that links many state and federal data banks. The system can find these parents and withhold their state and federal tax refunds.

Since 1981, matching has been used for numerous projects, but its use has caused problems. For example, the state of Massachusetts compared the names of people on welfare roles with names on bank accounts. If the bank account exceeded a certain amount, that person was removed from the welfare roles without any type of appeal. In several cases, the data were wrong, and indications that fraud was occurring were incorrect.

"Transactional" Data

The computerization of most travel, credit, and communications services has led to the development of a new type of data. **Transactional data** are collected when a transaction occurs in which the customer must identify himself

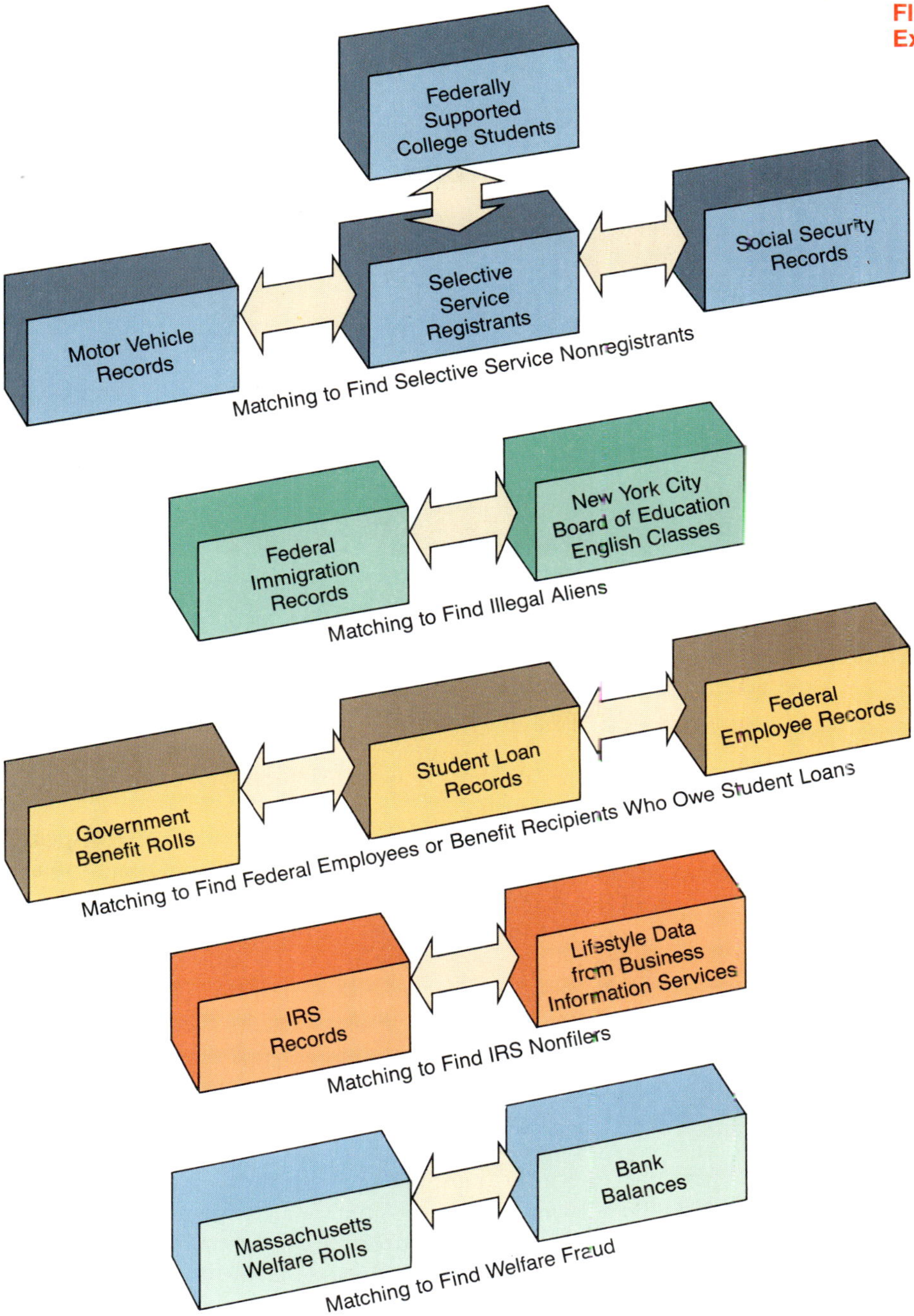

FIGURE 21-1
Examples of Computer Matching

or herself. Examples of transactional data include the credit card receipt signed by a customer, the record of a long distance call, or a rental car contract. Many other types of transactional data exist, but a very complete picture of an individual can be obtained using just these three. The credit card receipts indicate the types of clothes an individual buys, where he or she eats, the hotels he or she uses when out of town, and numerous other lifestyle facts. The telephone call records indicate when calls are made and to whom

Transactional data is created every time you make a purchase or reservation through a computer network.

they are made. Finally, rental car contracts or airline reservations indicate where the customer travels.

Because transactional data are computerized and matching can be used to bring together all of the information on a given person, the statement "you are what you transact" is certainly true! The current technology has outstripped the law, and few regulations control the handling of this type of data.

Computer Ethics

When only mainframe computers were in use, the question of **computer ethics** was concerned with an organization's use of its computer and data or an individual's use of the mainframe. The privacy question fell into the first category, and the actions of the hacker fell into the second. Some ethical questions involving the first category have not been resolved. Using computer matching to find criminals or to find parents who refuse to support their children is apparently ethical, but is removing disabled persons from support rolls solely on the basis of computer results also ethical? In the second category, most people would consider the unauthorized access by a hacker as an unethical use of the computer.

The first important change is that the computer mass-produces what has been called transactional information, a new category of information that automatically documents the daily lives of almost every person in the United States.

David Burnham
[In *The Rise of the Computer State* (New York: Vintage Books, 1983, p. 50).]

The introduction of the personal computer into the home and work place has raised a new set of ethical questions. Management's monitoring of its employees' use of the personal computer is the subject of much debate. From management's viewpoint, **computer monitoring** is necessary to ensure that the appropriate amount of work is performed and that the computer terminal is not used for other than its designed purposes. From an employee's viewpoint, this monitoring is an invasion of privacy. Unions that represent office workers have filed grievances regarding this policy, because they feel that management may use monitoring to determine productivity and pay. One union is seeking legislation to prohibit monitoring.

Other ethical questions involve using the personal computer for purposes other than work, misuse of company data, viewing other users' electronic mail, and copying software. Some companies encourage their employees to use the computer for any purpose they wish, but other companies are strongly against this policy. Misuse of company data is unethical and a security breach, and viewing other users' electronic mail could be considered similar to reading someone's U.S. mail. Finally, copying software is not only unethical, it is usually illegal.

HEALTH HAZARDS

Studies have found some evidence of health problems caused by the prolonged use of a video display terminal. In this section, we discuss the possible health hazards associated with VDT use and the field of study that helps to improve a worker's efficiency in an office with VDTs and other computer-related equipment.

The use of a VDT over a long period of time—whether it is connected to a mainframe, a stand-alone or clustered word processing center, or a personal computer—has brought many complaints from users. In fact, VDT operators have presented more complaints to the National Institute of Occupational Safety and Health (NIOSH) than any other single group of workers. Responsible for monitoring work-related health problems in the United States, NIOSH has collected data on VDT-related problems for some time. Given that over 10 million people work with VDTs every day and that this type of work requires a high level of concentration and manual dexterity, the number of complaints is not surprising. Complaints have included such things as visual difficulties, noise pollution from printers, muscular-skeletal problems, negative psychological effects, and several more subtle problems. In fact, the use of the computer has revealed a whole new dimension in occupational health and safety.

Technology has done more to free people from mundane and unsafe jobs. It is important to understand technology and not be afraid of it.

Ken Steinbruegge, Manager of sensor applications, Westinghouse Corporation

(As quoted in *The Atlanta Journal/Constitution,* November 22, 1984, p. D5.)

Visual Difficulties

Eyestrain is a common complaint associated with prolonged use of a VDT. A study by the Swiss Federal Institute of Technology reported that 55% more VDT operators reported daily episodes of eyestrain than a comparable group of persons working at typewriters.[6] This eyestrain presumably occurs as a result of working for several hours at a VDT that has poor contrast between characters and background, poor resolution, and flickering characters on the screen. Another cause of eyestrain is glare from misplaced light sources and the failure to use a nonglare screen or screen cover. Finally, eyestrain can result from the contrast between the VDT screen and the hard copy from which data are entered. The screen usually has a dark background with light letters, and the hard copy is often white with dark letters. Switching back and forth between the two can lead to eyestrain.

To lessen the eyestrain problem, the user should take frequent breaks from the VDT to rest the eye muscles. A high-quality monitor with a nonglare screen and high-resolution capability should be used. European sources suggest that black and white monitors are more likely to cause eye problems than green and white or green and amber monitors. The screen should be roughly 24 inches away from the user and tilted slightly downward. The VDT should be positioned so that the screen is not near a window and the level of artificial light is somewhat diminished so that contrast is better and glare is reduced. If the user needs more light for hard copy, a light may be attached to

[6]Anita Micossi, "Ergonomics Is Good Business," *PC World,* December 1983, p. 301.

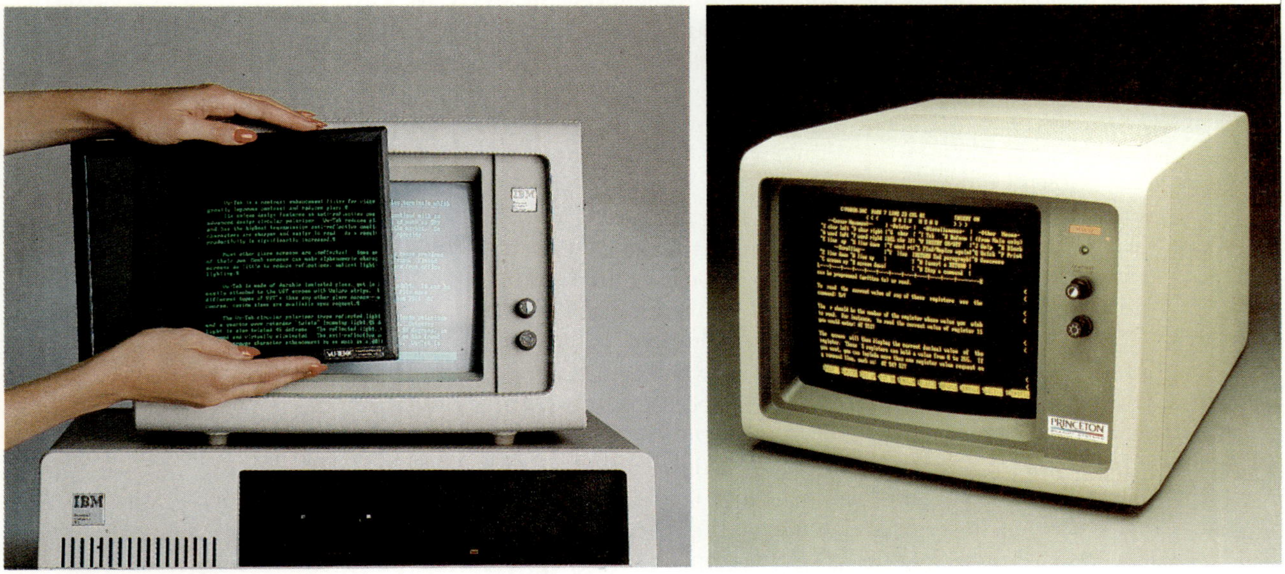

Characters on the monitor are easier to read after a special glare-reducing screen is added (left). Some studies also indicate that amber monitors (right) are less likely to cause eyestrain.

the board that holds the hard copy. Manufacturers are currently offering keyboards and screens with a nonglare surface, which tends to reduce eyestrain. Glare from screens and keyboards may affect eye focus and concentration. A user who wears glasses, especially bifocals or trifocals, may need to obtain a special set of glasses to handle the distance to the screen and keyboard. Routine eye examinations are recommended for VDT users to ensure that problems are found at an early stage.

Radiation Problems

A video display terminal screen is composed of a cathode ray tube (CRT), which emits a stream of electrons that strike phosphors on the screen to form characters. The same principle is used to form pictures on a television screen. This stream of electrons is a form of **radiation** that may be absorbed by the user who works less than 2 feet from the screen. Therefore, certain precautions must be taken, especially by pregnant women. Although radiation effects have not been proved, spontaneous terminations of pregnancies and fetal deformities have occurred among long-term VDT users.

Another problem that may be caused by radiation is cataracts. Two young copy editors for a metropolitan newspaper who worked with VDTs all day long developed radiation-induced cataracts. The cataracts occurred in the back side of the lens capsule, where radiant energy damage would occur. Aging cataracts were ruled out, because of the location of the cataracts and because no other known conditions contributed to their formation.[7]

Other than radiation-induced cataracts, no hard evidence proves that radiation causes problems for VDT users, even in a sizable minority. However, a user should take precautions, especially if she is pregnant or the family history reveals a susceptibility to cataracts. Additional precautions should be taken when a color monitor is used, because the radiation level is higher than that for a monochrome monitor.

People have ignored things that human-factors engineers have known for 30 years. The manufacturers and the employers need to wake up.

Harry L. Snyder, Professor of industrial engineering, Virginia Polytechnic Institute
(As quoted in "No Truce Ahead in War over VDT Safety," *Business Week,* July 25, 1983, pp. 85–86.)

[7]Susan Mark, "The Radiation Question," *PC World,* January 1984, p. 232.

AVOIDING VDT-RELATED PROBLEMS

Not all VDT-related problems can be avoided, but proper use can ensure that problems are minimized. The VDT work station must be properly designed. The keyboard and copy should be at equal distances from the screen to eliminate excessive focus shifting by the operator. (This precaution is especially important for individuals over 40 years of age, because the eye's focus mechanism becomes less flexible with age.) The screen should be slightly below eye level, with the copy holder near the screen to reduce twisting and turning of the neck and eyes. The keyboard should be located so that the wrist and lower arm are parallel to the floor.

The operator's chair must provide proper back support and be easily adjusted by the operator. The operator's feet should be flat on the floor. The VDT operator should be able to move his or her knees and legs without bumping into obstructions.

Work station lighting should provide a 10 : 3 ratio—that is, screen characters (the foreground) should be 10 times brighter than the background, and the room illumination should be three times brighter than the screen background. The best lighting is directed upward and reflected down to the work area.

A short break every two hours is a virtual necessity for VDT users. Some VDT users may need a break every hour or a switch to an alternate, non-VDT task. Such activity allows the user to move about and relieve the stress generated by VDT use.

Screen contrast affects the well-being of the VDT user. Positive contrast means light characters appear on a dark background, and negative contrast means dark characters appear on a light background. The heat generated by a VDT and the quality of the terminal—including less flicker, improved resolution, and reduced screen glare—can affect an operator's work. Negative contrast results in greater legibility, but positive contrast tends to cause less flicker, depending on the type of monitor in use. Besides causing discomfort in a poorly designed room, VDT heat can lower humidity levels in the work place, which in turn causes problems for contact lens wearers. Poor-quality monitors can cause severe eyestrain.

SOURCE: Carl F. Gruning, "VDTs and Vision—New Problems for the '80s," *The Office,* February 1985, pp. 19–22, 34.

Noise Pollution

The use of printers with personal computers has increased the noise level in the work place. If printers are used continually or if multiple printers operate at the same time in a relatively small space, **noise pollution** can result. Although many workers grow accustomed to the noise, it can still cause problems. Constant noise pollution can affect the blood pressure, heart rate, and body musculature, leading to stress on the worker. The stress, in turn, can lead to lower productivity or lost work time. Accoustical covers for printers and office walls that are designed to absorb sound can decrease the intensity of the noise caused by the equipment.

Muscular-Skeletal Problems

The rigid posture required to operate a VDT and the often poorly designed office desk and chair may have caused many muscular and skeletal problems among VDT users. Muscle aches in the neck, shoulders, and back are frequently reported. Back disorders rank with colds and flu as the biggest causes of absenteeism and consume an inordinate amount of medical treatment costs. **Secretary's syndrome** has been treated professionally for years. Its symptoms include tight shoulders, tingling arms, stiff neck, tendinitis, and spinal misalignments—all associated with prolonged sitting at a desk. This position leads to a lack of framework movement and a restricted blood supply to the extremities. Poor circulation to the legs may cause varicosities and blood clots.

Ergonomics

To design an office and work station that solves the physical health problems discussed earlier requires an ergonomic approach to the problems. **Ergo-**

CRT SAFETY
The Controversy Continues

Despite vendors' claims, the issue of CRT (VDT) safety is apparently far from settled. In February 1984, The National Association of Working Women ("9 to 5") released a study implicating CRT use with such widespread health problems as miscarriages, eyestrain, muscle pain, and exhaustion. At the same time, the Koffler Group, an organization of computer consultants, published a report stating that all previous CRT health research had been either poorly conducted or biased.

The "9 to 5" study was a voluntary survey of 6,000 CRT operators, 871 of whom responded. In that study, more than 50% of the respondents reported eyestrain or muscle problems, and 45% suffered problems with pregnancies. The Koffler Group study referred to a 1981 NIOSH study, which reported no evidence of CRT-caused eye problems, and a 1983 Bell Laboratories report, which found no difference between the number of complaints by CRT operators and those by conventional typewriter users.

SOURCE: "CRT Controversy Continues . . . ," *Computerworld OA*, April 11, 1984, p. 9.

nomics deals with the concept of keeping people healthy while they work. The concept, which emerged from Great Britain during World War II, is concerned with the technological demands on a worker that somehow affect his or her well-being. An office that is ergonomically designed increases the worker's productivity by allowing him or her to remain comfortable and healthy while pursuing work objectives. Ergonomics is described as follows:

> Today, ergonomics, or human factors engineering as it is called in the United States, emerges in the talents of engineers, architects, physiologists, behavioral scientists, physicians, and designers. These diverse professionals investigate the capacities and limitations of the human and apply their findings to the design of tools, tasks and environments. The goal of the discipline is an optimum balance between productivity and well-being.[8]

Detachable keyboards (left) and tilt screens (right) are two examples of ergonomic design incorporated into computers.

[8]Anita Micossi, p. 302.

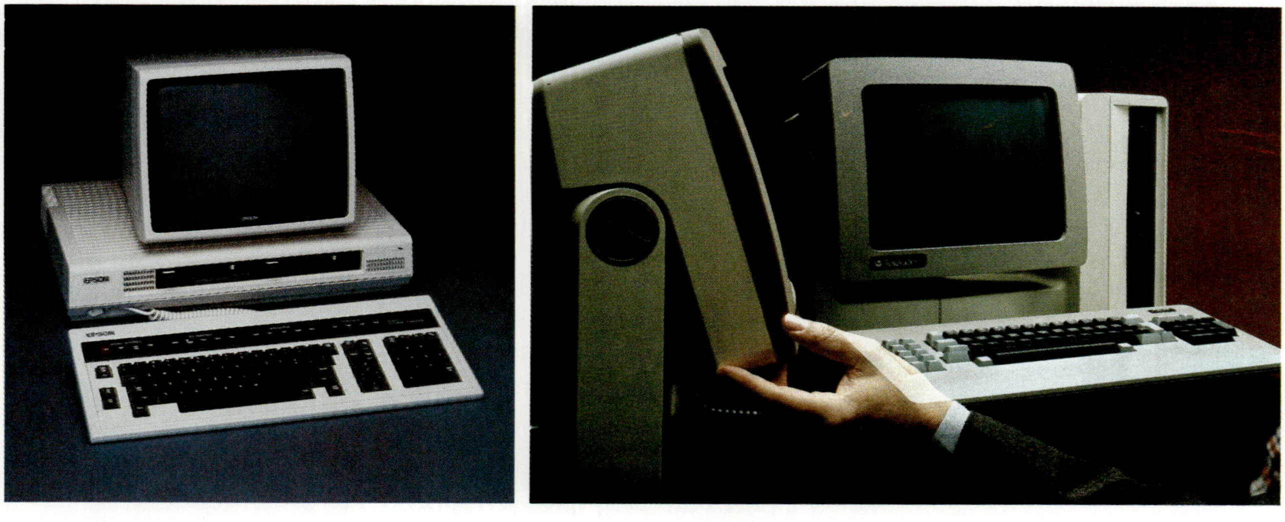

THE JEFFERSON CHAIR

Most ergonomically designed chairs for VDT users assume that workers produce best while sitting with backs upright and feet on the floor. One chair designer has gone back in time for a different design. The Jefferson Chair was originally designed by Thomas Jefferson, the third president of the United States, for his "manual" word processing. This reclining chair raised the feet off the floor slightly. To adapt this design for a VDT user, industrial designer Neils Diffrient updated Jefferson's idea by combining a recliner and ottoman with an adjustable lamp and three separate pivoting tables. The three tables can support the keyboard, the CPU, the monitor, and even a telephone.

Diffrient believes in Jefferson's original premise that this unorthodox working position is better because it makes work more comfortable. The comfortable VDT user can concentrate on the task at hand rather than on his or her aching back. In addition to the reclining position with footrest, Diffrient includes a headrest that duplicates the natural pivotal motions of the head as it rests on the neck. According to Diffrient, "The chair's actions are designed to parallel natural body actions." The Jefferson Chair is available from Sunar-Hauserman Company for $2,500.

SOURCE: Martin Porter, "A Diffrient Design," *PC Magazine,* October 2, 1984, pp. 145–46.

The Jefferson Chair may be the ultimate ergonomic chair design for personal computer users.

When applied to the VDT work station, ergonomics plays a role in the positioning of the screen, the height of the keyboard, the distance of the worker from the screen, the chair the worker sits in, and any other environmental factors affecting the worker—such as air quality and temperature, noise, and so on. Ergonomic designs for VDTs have resulted in the detachable keyboard and a tilting, swiveling monitor. The worker's chair is an important, but often the least considered, ergonomic factor at the VDT work station. Adjustability is a key factor in selecting a chair. Besides adjusting the height and the back support, other chair considerations include backrests that may be raised or lowered, armrests that reduce upper body fatigue, seat edges that avoid constriction of blood supply, and chair surfaces that provide good ventilation.

Psychological Problems

The increased use of the personal computer has resulted in a whole new field of study in behavioral science. Initially, computers were used by a very small segment of the population and, therefore, had little or no effect on the general population. However, with businesses and schools using computers for

The hacker loves the machine for itself—not just for what it can do, but for how it makes him feel. He can spend 18 hours a day on it.

***Sherry Turkle, author of* The Second Self: Computers and the Human Spirit**

(As quoted in "Kids Love Computers, But Adults Fear Them," *USA Today,* April 30, 1985, p. 11A.)

word processing, electronic mail, accounting, and other numerous applications, the emotional effects of confronting the computer are widespread. **Computerphobia**, or **cyberphobia**, is a clinically recognized behavioral condition that is characterized by fear of the computer. Age, race, sex, education, or economic circumstances do not deter computerphobia.

Several factors apparently contribute to the occurrence of computerphobia. Simple fear of the unknown is probably the primary cause. This fear creates an anxiety that can precipitate emotional and physical stress and tension. This anxiety produces such physical symptoms as increased blood pressure and pulse rate, headaches, and nausea.

This fear of the computer has more dimensions than just a simple apprehension over learning to use a new machine. Many people view the computer as a threat to personal identity. Suddenly, a task that previously required a personal touch with a particular individual's expertise can now be performed much more quickly by an electronic box. The individual may feel powerless and depersonalized. Some workers even change jobs to avoid the confrontation with the computer.

Milder forms of fear and anxiety exist. This anxiety may be related to such issues as finding the time to learn to use the computer and worrying about how the job will change after the introduction of the computer.

The **computerphylliac** is totally involved with the computer, to the exclusion of all other concerns. This person is obsessed with the computer the way some people are obsessed with gambling. This personality type tends to be introverted and more detached. He or she usually has fewer communication skills than the average person and often cannot recognize the compulsiveness in the behavior. Some people view this behavior as an escape from unpleasant circumstances. Others have suggested that because this type of personality is less social, such individuals can more easily relate to the computer than to other humans.

Computerphylliac behavior has legal, social, and psychological consequences. Hackers who find ways to obtain unauthorized access to computers are breaking the law and are subject to the new laws on computer crime. They also tend to alienate themselves from their family and friends in their involvement with the computer. The Silicon Syndrome, a type of computerphyllia, is a recognized psychological problem in high-tech areas of the country.

The Future

We have just examined some health hazards associated with the use of VDTs. Some alarming conditions are receiving attention. Other subtle conditions will take longer to be resolved. Action by the U.S. government is slow, but several European governments have issued standards for VDT design and use. In the United States, the National Institute of Occupational Safety and Health is monitoring and documenting the problems previously discussed. Several states are developing legislation to stipulate guidelines for both design and use of VDTs. Labor advocates are lobbying for worker protection and education.

REVIEW OF KEY POINTS

- Each new technological advance in communications has brought the threat of invasion of privacy.
- The computer enables us to perform many tasks, but it can also be used to invade our privacy.
- A national data bank proposal in the mid-1960s was never implemented.
- Two important laws enacted in the 1970s help protect citizens from invasion of their privacy by computers.
- A 1973 HEW report lists five important principles that should be followed in the use of computers and data banks.
- The numerous governmental and private data banks that are in use today can effectively be combined into a national data bank.
- Because a parent locater law was passed, the computer is now used to track down parents who have not made child support payments.
- Transactional data can be used for unethical surveillance.
- Unethical use of computers and data is an issue that must be addressed by organizations.
- Long-term use of video display terminals has resulted in reports of health problems—such as eyestrain, radiation problems, noise pollution from printers, and muscular-skeletal problems.
- An ergonomically designed work place is more comfortable and productive.
- The impact of the computer on the home and work place is causing such psychological problems as computerphobia and computerphyllia.

KEY TERMS

batch access
cathode ray tube (CRT)
computer ethics
computer matching
computer monitoring
computerphobia
computerphylliac
cyberphobia
data banks
ergonomics
eyestrain
Fair Credit Reporting Act of 1970
interactive access
national data bank
noise pollution
privacy
Privacy Act of 1974
Privacy Protection Study Commission
radiation
secretary's syndrome
transactional data
video display terminals (VDTs)

REVIEW QUESTIONS

1. Why do technological advances in communications always bring the threat of invasion of privacy? Why do we include computers among these technological advances?
2. List three uses of computers and data banks other than those mentioned in the chapter.
3. Why has the introduction of the computer increased the fear that data banks are used to invade personal privacy?
4. Why do we say that individual data banks can be effectively combined to form a national data bank?
5. Using newspapers or magazines, find and discuss a possible case of invasion of personal privacy using computers.
6. Why are transactional data different from other types of historical data? Give examples of transactional data other than those listed in the chapter.
7. Discuss the advantages and disadvantages of management's monitoring of terminal and personal computer use by employees. How do you feel about this practice?
8. What health hazards are reported from the long-term use of video display terminals? Have you ever experienced any of these problems while using a VDT?
9. Discuss the use of ergonomics in the computer-oriented work place. Why is this an important concern for management?
10. Discuss the difference between a computerphobe and a computerphylliac. If you have ever known a person who demonstrated either type of behavior, write a case history of your observations of that person.

Computers at Work in the Arts

Computers are used extensively to generate graphics for advertising. A Canned Food Information Council commercial (1a) stars the Sexy Robot—the first computer-generated figure to have authentic human motion. Computer-generated artwork lent a magical quality to a commercial introducing a new Hoover vacuum cleaner (1b). Computer graphics (1c) dominate TRW's award-winning commercials.

1a

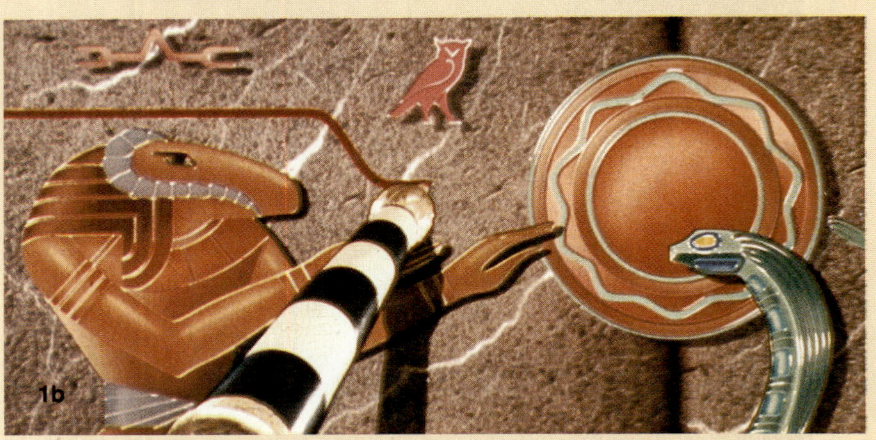

1b

1c

A Gunstar chases a Xurion Cargoship in the motion picture *The Last Starfighter*. The movie contains 25 minutes of such images, created entirely by a supercomputer rather than by the filming of models. (Digital Scene Simulation by Digital Productions, Los Angeles, CA U.S.A. © Copyright 1984. All rights reserved.)

The ABC logo introduced during the telecasts of the 1984 Summer Olympics was developed using a combination of computer-generated imagery (CGI) and multiple passes of the film through a computer-controlled camera.

The flowering plants were "grown" by a computer using an algorithm that defines a plant's growth patterns. After the computer was given a range for the height and angle of a blade of grass, it created the different blades.

4

Using a supercomputer to produce artwork results in the smooth, bright, and intense shapes demonstrated in these two examples (5a and 5b).

5a

5b

6a

Designers called *console artists* custom-design computer art like this (6a and 6b) to suit clients' individual needs.

6b

7a

Using the geometry of fractals—that is, the geometry of fractured or broken shapes—a computer can generate such realistic images as this earthrise seen from the moon (7a). By combining fractal geometry with a random element and other algorithms, a computer can generate the landscape (7b). Changing a few parameters alters the size and texture of the mountains.

7b

The new bells at Mission San Juan Capistrano in California are controlled by a computer. An operator enters individual notes or calls up preprogrammed pieces of music at a special console (8a), which controls the mechanism that rings the bells (8b).

8a

8b

A dancer's position is compared with that generated by the computer. The computer can record and play back a dance as needed to help the choreographer and the dancer improve their work.

9

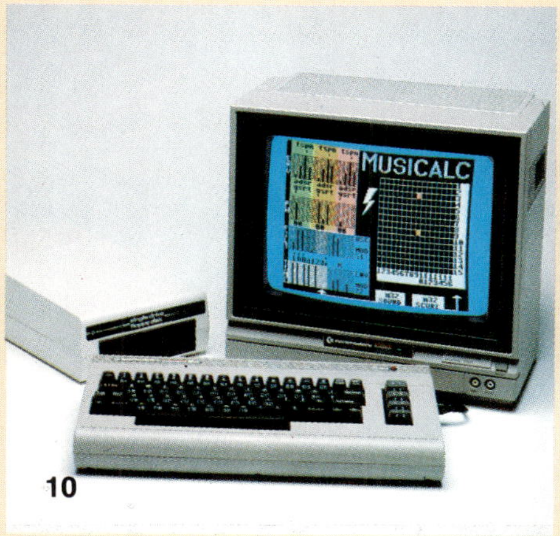

With Musicalc applications software and a personal computer (left), a user can create quite sophisticated music.

Special purpose software (right) can help set designers find the optimal theater configuration and stage sets for a specific play.

At Stanford University's Center for Computer Research in Music and Acoustics, musical instruments are connected to computers to aid composers in their work.

22

Computers: The Future and You

The future of computers in our society is a multifaceted one, with many exciting developments and opportunities. In this chapter, we consider the future technology of computer hardware and software and the future of the related field of telecommunications. We also discuss employment prospects in the computer field. Computers will get smaller and faster, and software must become easier to use to attract new users. Expect advances in the areas of voice input, natural language, and expert systems. In telecommunications, electronic funds transfer and videotex combined with new satellite systems appear to be fields with tremendous potential for growth. The number of careers in computers will grow dramatically, with opportunities in operations, analysis and programming, information management, repair and servicing, sales and marketing, instruction, and engineering.

STUDY OBJECTIVES

After reading this chapter, you should be able to

- Recognize the movement toward an information society.
- Discuss the trends in hardware development that lead to increases in speed and decreases in size.
- Explain how parallel processing and pipelining increase the speed of computers.
- Understand the possible reorganization of computer use over the next 10 years.
- Recognize the potential effect of robotics on employment.
- Understand the need for "softer" software to make the computer easier to use.
- Understand the potential effect of telecommunications on our daily lives.
- Discuss various computer related careers.

TOMORROW IS HERE

This [computer] industry is over 30 years old, and it has not even reached its infancy.

John Imlay, Chairman of the board of Management Science America

The recent progress in the field of computers and several related fields has been almost unbelievable. Who would have believed 10 years ago that the computer would be so important in our daily lives? Personal computer applications have moved from the hobby to the work place and the home. A computer store was virtually unheard of 10 years ago. Today, a town of any size has at least one computer store. The increase in the use of personal computers has resulted in a corresponding increase in the use of mainframes to hold the tremendous amounts of information that our computerized society is generating. The supercomputer allows us to research weather, energy, and other areas that would be impossible without the amazing power and speed of these monster computers. The price of computer hardware has dropped dramatically, and computer speed has doubled roughly every two years. Personal computers with over 64,000 characters of memory and more computing power than many of the early mainframes sell for approximately $200. We can now access our money on a 24-hour basis through electronic funds transfer (EFT) or make purchases using videotex over a telephone line with a personal computer.

The mind-boggling advances that have occurred in the last decade are only the beginning. **Futurists** are people who research the future, and they predict that we are on the threshold of even more dramatic advances through computers. In the next 5–10 years, computers will be smaller, faster, less expensive, and easier to use. Robots will perform more and more work in manufacturing. The transfer of information and money via telecommunications will grow at an even faster rate than the rapidly expanding computer industry. At the same time, the job market for persons with computer interests and skills will grow faster than all other occupational fields.

In his very popular book, *Megatrends,* John Naisbitt talks about the evolution of the U.S. economy from an agricultural society 100 years ago to an

With today's computer technology, we can see other worlds. Using a special silicon chip in a charge-coupled device to record images digitally, astronomers have found a solar system outside of our own (left). The image of Jupiter and its moons at right was computer-analyzed by Voyager 1, transmitted to earth, and then reconstructed as this photograph.

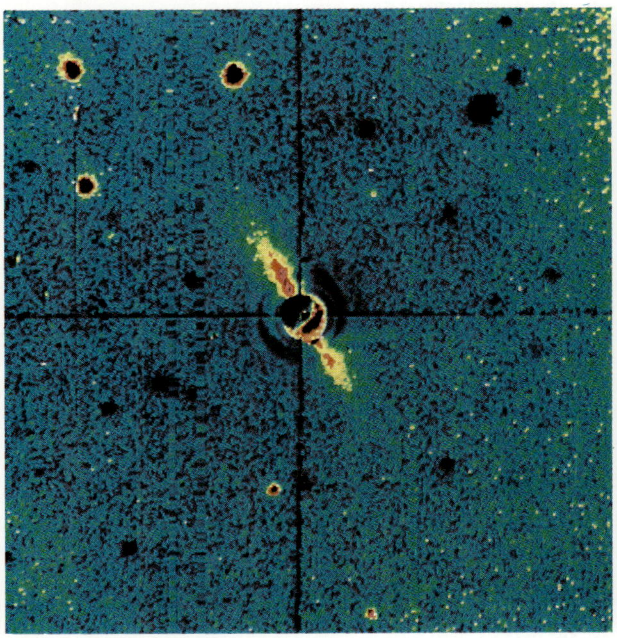

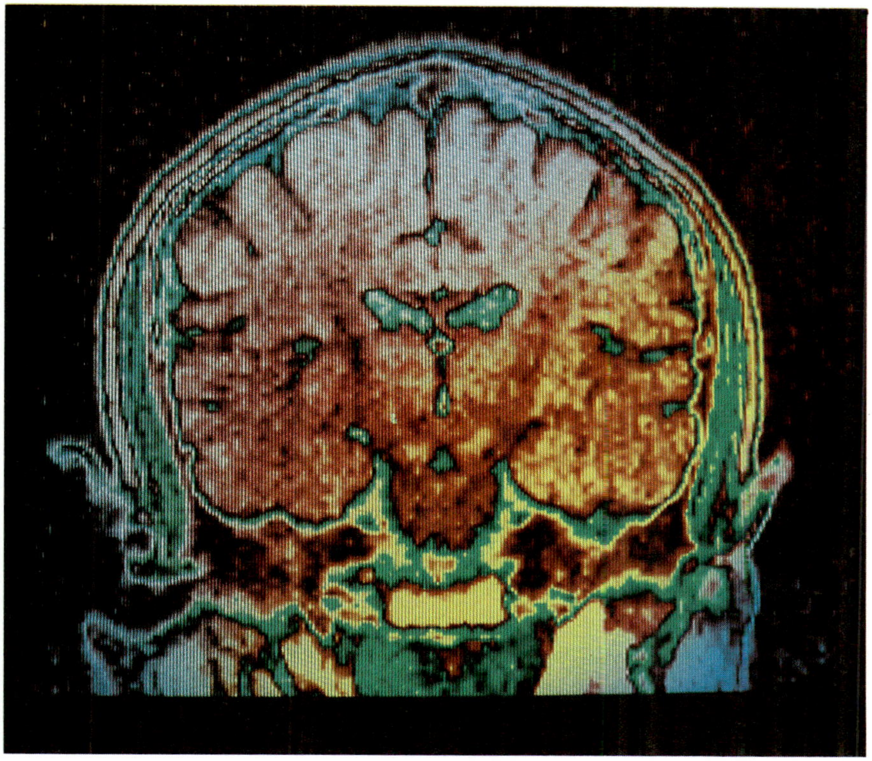

This photograph of the soft tissues of the brain was obtained through nuclear magnetic resonance (NMR), in which the computer generates the final picture.

industrial society in the first two-thirds of this century to what he calls an information society. He defines an **information society** as an economy and society built on the transfer of information. Naisbitt cited some interesting statistics concerning the evolution of U.S. society. In 1950, only 17% of all Americans were involved in information jobs—for example, teachers, programmers, analysts, clerks, bureaucrats, and accountants. By 1983, this number had risen to over 65%. In May 1983, only 12% of us were employed in traditional manufacturing jobs. Naisbitt lists five points to remember about the movement from the industrial society to the information society, two of which are pertinent to the future of computers.

> Innovations in communications and computer technology will push the movement forward at an increasing rate by reducing the **information float**—that is, the time between the occurrence of an event and the point at which it is general knowledge.
>
> The new information technology of communications and computers will be applied first to existing industrial activities, then it will give birth to new activities.

Obviously, Naisbitt feels that communications and computers will be in the forefront of the technology needed to develop the information society.[1]

Operating a computer will be like driving a car. You won't be able to get to work without one.

***Marvin Cetron, author of* Jobs of the Future**

(As quoted in *USA Today*, "Will USA Be Prepared to Fill Openings?" August 21, 1984, pp. 1B–2B.)

---

[1]John Naisbitt, *Megatrends* (New York: Warner Books, 1984), pp. 1–33.

Computer-aided engineering (CAE) systems allow engineers to simulate the performance of circuit elements as they are drawn on the screen. This procedure cuts months off the time needed to design a new chip.

MAKING THE COMPUTER FASTER

Of the four areas that we consider in the future of the computers—that is, hardware, software, telecommunications, and careers—hardware is the easiest to discuss in concrete terms. Recall that modern computer technology began in 1947 with the invention of the **transistor**. Ten years ago, a chip could hold at the most several thousand transistors. Today, the transistors are so small that over 250,000 transistors can be squeezed onto a single **silicon chip**. With chip density increasing at the rate of 20% per year, by 1990, chips will hold over 1 million transistors. This increase in the number of transistors on a chip results in an associated increase in speed, because the information will not move as far as in current computers.

Production of semiconductor devices using gallium arsenide technology is being pioneered in prototype production facilities.

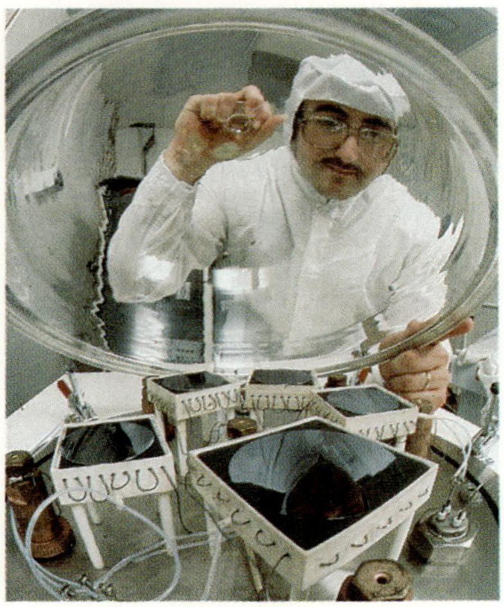

The cost of chips has decreased dramatically over the years. In 1960, a two-transistor, five-part circuit cost approximately $10. By 1978, the same device cost 10 cents. By 1990, the chip will probably sell for about one-tenth of a cent.

The theoretical limit of miniaturization of silicon chips will probably be reached in 5–10 years, and researchers are already working on new substances that are better than silicon for chips. One of these substances is **gallium arsenide**, another semiconductor material. Gallium arsenide will increase computing speed because it is five times faster than silicon in transmitting electrons. Another approach to faster computers is the **Josephson Junction**, a super-fast electronic switch that could replace the transistor in computers. This switch works at temperatures close to absolute zero. At these temperatures, virtually no resistance to electricity exists, and switching operations can take place at very high speeds. Unfortunately, the technology necessary to work at these low temperatures is not available, so the use of the Josephson Junction must be delayed.

The computer's data storage capacity will increase in the near future. RAM capacity of over 500,000 characters is already available on several computers,

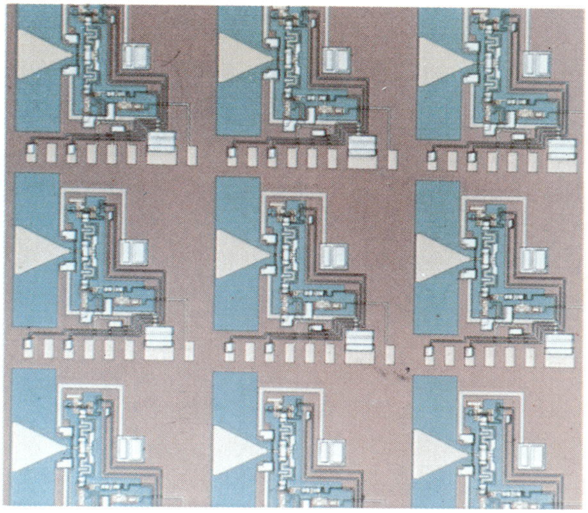

A dense array of superconducting sampling oscilloscope circuits, or Josephson Junctions, is on a single chip (left). Cryogenic testing of a superconducting chip is carried out in liquid helium at temperatures close to absolute zero (right).

and 1 Mbyte (one million characters) of RAM capacity is just around the corner. (In fact, it may be available by the time you read this.) Floppy disks that can hold over one million characters are already used on the IBM AT personal computer; microfloppies with the same capacity are also available. The **optical disk** will almost certainly be used for external storage. A big market already exists for optical disks for audio purposes. Optical disks are currently available only as *read only* storage devices, so a user cannot store data on one. When the technology is available for writing data on the optical disk, we will see gigabytes (one billion characters) of external memory. **Bubble memory** is another promising form of memory. When the technology can finally reduce the cost of bubble memory, it will provide internal memory that does not disappear when the power to the computer is turned off.

The Effect on Computers

What do these technological advances mean for computers? For the personal computer user, it means that in the not too distant future, a personal com-

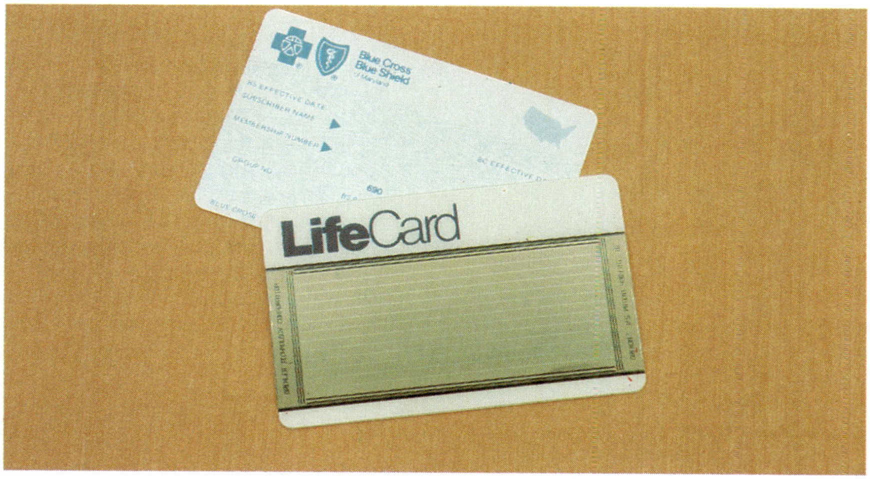

On the Blue Cross and Blue Shield "Lifecard," a wide laser optic memory strip carries a complete description of a member's benefits and medical history, including a digitized photograph and signature.

The easy-to-use, highly interactive training system at left utilizes advanced laser disk technology.

The future of secondary storage depends largely on the development of laser disk storage (right).

puter with over 1 Mbyte of RAM and 1 Gbyte of optical disk storage will be available. This computer will use a true 32-bit CPU chip, which will manipulate 32 bits at a time rather than the 8 or 16 bits manipulated by current machines. Mainframes should be more powerful and store more information, and the supercomputers will have faster and faster computing times. This increased power and speed will be the result of two new approaches to computing—parallel processing and pipelining.

To understand how parallel processing and pipelining can dramatically change the way most current computers work, we must return to the concepts behind a computer. Recall that since Von Neumann developed the stored program, computers have all been **serial machines**—that is, they work on only one instruction at a time. A new instruction or piece of data is fetched from memory when needed. With **parallel processing**, several instructions could be executed simultaneously by multiple CPUs. In other words, four or five instructions could be executed in the time that one instruction is executed today. Figure 22-1 shows the difference between serial processing and parallel processing.

THE CONNECTION MACHINE

Two large companies—Cray and Control Data—are working on parallel processing for their supercomputers to avoid the "Von Neumann bottleneck" that faces serial processors. A small artificial intelligence company is working on the same idea from a different viewpoint. Led by MIT graduate Danny Hillis, the Thinking Machines Corporation is working on a prototype of the Connection Machine. Hillis is trying to develop a computer that operates like the human brain. The machine uses many processors, each of which communicates with the others much like a telephone network. Hillis is using 64,000 individual custom designed silicon chip processors and specially designed software to ensure that the processors can communicate with one another, sending billions of messages back and forth. If a working prototype of the Connection Machine can be developed, Hillis hopes to build a computer with millions of processors that will truly emulate the brain.

SOURCE: William D. Marbach, "Big Things on the Way," *Access* (by *Newsweek*), Fall 1984, p. 52.

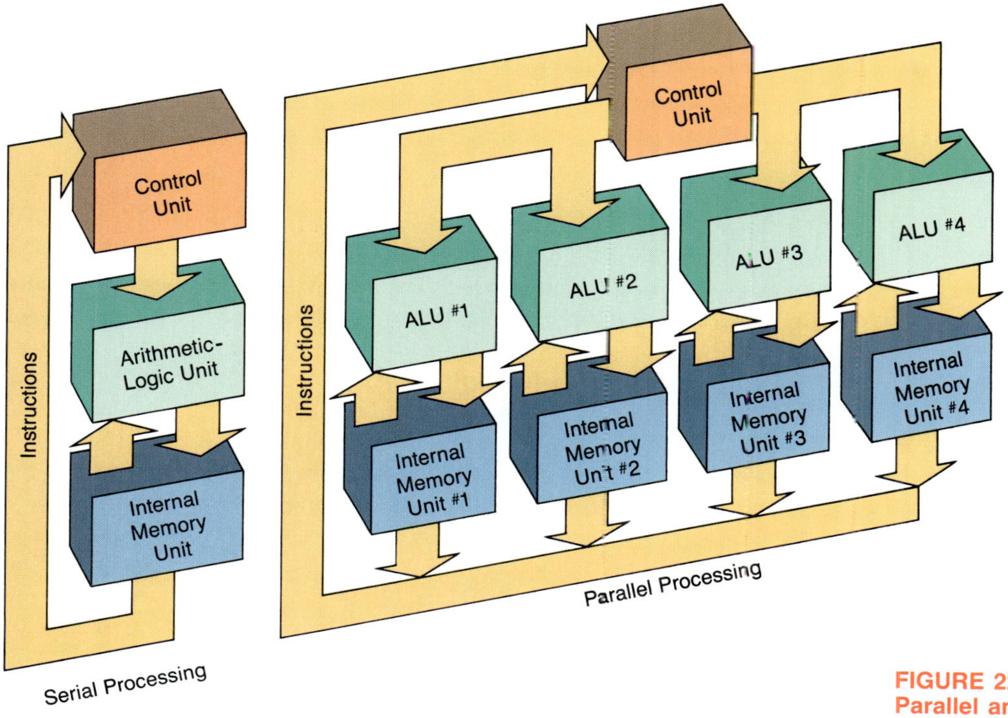

FIGURE 22-1
Parallel and Serial Processing

Current supercomputers use a type of parallel processing known as **array processing**, which allows them to perform the same operation on a list of values. For example, instead of adding two lists of numbers together one pair at a time to arrive at a third list, one array processing instruction would cause all pairs on the two lists to be summed at one time. Parallel processing requires special software and hardware to ensure that all communications take place between the various operations.

Pipelining speeds up processing by eliminating the time lost when the CPU decides it needs another piece of data and sends an instruction to retrieve it. Data are constantly in the "pipeline" to the CPU rather than waiting in storage for a request from the CPU.

The Reorganization of Computer Use

The introduction of personal computers into the work place has started a reorganization of the way computers are used. Recall that originally mainframes and then minicomputers—essentially scaled-down mainframes—were used in the work place. The development of personal computers changed attitudes toward working with computers. Now, instead of using the company computer, employees perform needed analyses on individual "users' " computers. A mainframe is needed primarily to hold the information that is required by all individual users. Sales figures show that the level of mainframe sales is increasing at approximately the same rate as personal computer sales. The big machines handle the demand for information generated by the use of personal computers. When information sharing among personal computers is needed, a local area network is established.

The increasing speed, power, and storage capacity of personal computers and the access to virtually unlimited amounts of information from the company mainframe may eventually squeeze out the minicomputer. Many operations performed by a $120,000 minicomputer may soon be performed just as well by a $10,000 "supermicro" computer.

Other Advances

Advances in chip technology will certainly increase the speed of general purpose computers, and they also hold the promise for other uses. Custom microprocessors will probably be used in household appliances to improve the efficiency of their energy consumption the same way that chips are used in automobiles to improve gas mileage. Special purpose chips will be used in computers to provide high-quality, three-dimensional graphics and sound.

With on-going developments in liquid crystal displays similar to those used in watches, flat screens may soon replace the current bulky monitors. Someday, we may have **holographic displays** that project three-dimensional images. Holographic images could be useful in teleconferencing to make each party at the conference feel the others are really present.

The time will come when every home will have some personal computer device which will probably merge the telephone and personal computer into a single product—which is yet to be defined by anybody.

John Sculley, President and chief executive officer of Apple Computer, Inc.

(As quoted in "Someday All Homes Will Have Computers," *USA Today*, May 14, 1984, p. 11A.)

The field of **robotics** will expand dramatically. Currently, over 3,000 robots are used in the United States for manufacturing, whereas Japan uses over 10,000. This number will grow rapidly between now and the end of the century, sharply reducing the need for human labor in many assembly line operations. The robotics industry is expected to grow by a factor of three between now and 1990—to $1.5 billion annually—as more and more industries purchase robots to automate their operation.

The increase in automation will not be accomplished without pain. The use of robots in factories is a controversial issue, because workers worry about the loss of their jobs and labor unions know that robots don't pay union dues. Robots in the work force may someday cause the loss of 50–75% of all factory jobs. Robotics experts readily admit that unskilled and semiskilled

High-quality three-dimensional graphics enable designers to see immediately the effect of a design and to make necessary changes.

Future computers will be smaller and more powerful with increasing memory capacities and liquid crystal display monitors.

jobs will definitely be lost to robots over the next 20 years. How many jobs will be lost? How will displaced workers be retrained? For now, the answers to these questions are unknown.

Although robots will replace humans in many dirty, dangerous, or repetitive jobs, skilled individuals will always be needed to work with and around robots. For example, people must design and build the robots, write the programs that control the robots' actions, repair the robots, and interface with the robots on tasks that require a human's touch, sight, hearing, and, most important, reasoning ability.

CAN SOFTWARE BECOME SOFTER?

The fact that faster computers are built every day does not mean that the general public will use them more. The key to increasing computer use depends on how easy it is to use the computer. Truly "user-friendly" operating systems and applications programs must be introduced, and computer applications must include more problems in the home and the work place. The more people use computers, the more they expect from them, especially from the software.

The future of **softer software** lies in three interrelated areas—voice input, natural languages, and expert systems. Research in each area is aimed at a computer that acts and responds in a way that implies a certain amount of intelligence on its part.

In 1982, the Stanford Research Institute (SRI) prepared a list of software that may be available in the 1990s. This list includes the following types of software, all of which fall into at least one of the three categories mentioned above or into the broader category of **artificial intelligence**:[2]

---

[2]David Kolbus and Claudia Mazzetti, "Artificial Intelligence Emerges," SRI, Inc. Business Intelligence Report No. 673, 1982.

There will be a little guide in the computer which will anticipate what you might want or suggest things you might do or watch your patterns.

Steven Jobs, co-founder of Apple Computer, Inc.
(As quoted in "Sales Soften; Firms Seek New Uses," *USA Today,* March 21, 1985, pp. 1A–2A.)

Expert parenting systems that monitor children's activities and alert parents when problems are brewing.

Intelligent games that automatically adjust to a player's skill level and that change over time to avoid boredom.

Story generators and animation packages that create personalized forms of entertainment.

Expert systems that help do-it-yourselfers.

Intelligent control of appliances that responds to voice commands.

Programmed advice on issues ranging from nutrition to taxes.

Improved systems for working with disabled individuals.

Expert information request systems.

Voice Input

Voice input is a key breakthrough in computers that would create a friendlier environment for the novice user. Many people are put off by having to communicate using a keyboard. This *keyboardphobia* may be part of the reason for the success of the Apple Macintosh, which has mouse-driven pull-down menus.

In Chapter 7, we discussed the problems that are involved in building a computer capable of accepting voice input, including words that are run together, similar sounding words that mean different things (to, too, and two), and different voices from different speakers. Some strides have been made to solve these problems. In 1985, Kurzweil Applied Intelligence, Inc.

Voice recognition systems have been developed for use in the high-noise environment of fighter aircraft.

announced a voice input system that understands up to 1,000 words of vocabulary as long as each word is spoken with a clear break after it. The system can be attached to a personal computer for use in filling out forms or writing simple reports. The same company stated it would deliver a 10,000-word dictation system in 1986 that could distinguish between similar words or phrases.

Natural Language Systems

Unlike high-level computer languages, a **natural language system** does not require a special vocabulary and syntax to give the computer instructions. The problems of using a natural language system include teaching the computer to make inferences and to understand a wide range of words and sentence structures. Regardless of the difficulty involved in building a natural language system, this system is as important to the future acceptance of computers by the general public as voice input is, but for a different reason. Whereas many would-be users are put off by the keyboard, another group is put off by the notion that programming is necessary to use a computer. They are uncomfortable with learning a new vocabulary and a new way of thinking regardless of whether this involves writing a program or learning the intricacies of MS-DOS or WordStar.

A second advantage to natural language systems exists, even for persons who are not bothered by computer languages—a natural language command is usually shorter and more concise than the high-level language specification of the command. For example, the following command

Show me all employees making more than $30,000 per year who have worked here less than 2 years.

would be much longer in the vocabulary and syntax of a data base management language.

If voice input and natural languages can be combined, then we can develop the type of computer system that even the most computerphobic person could use comfortably. In this system, the user could speak to the computer in common English, giving commands or asking questions. Such a system may be in use before the end of this decade.

Expert Systems

Many of us would like advice from experts on any number of issues. However, we may not know where to ask or what questions to ask. **Expert systems** (discussed in Chapter 15) make the collective knowledge of various experts in a field available to the user through a computer. When combined with the increased internal and external memory predicted for future computers, such expert systems may make each of us an instant "expert" on any topic of interest!

TELECOMMUNICATIONS

The ability to transfer data from one user to another or from a mainframe to another mainframe or to a personal computer is one of the most important computer capabilities today. The relationship of computers and communications is easily seen at the industrial level. For example, two giants in the telephone industry—AT&T and ITT—have both moved into the computer market, and a giant in the computer industry—

What networks of railroads, highways, and canals were in another age, networks of telecommunications, information, and computerization . . . are today.

Bruno Kreisky, Chancellor of the Federal Republic of Austria
(As quoted in "The Computer Moves In," *Time,* January 3, 1983, p. 14.)

IBM—has purchased a controlling interest in a leading communications company—Rolm. A leading computer publication, *Computerworld,* now publishes a version called *Computerworld on Communications.*

Currently, **telecommunications** is widely used for accessing data banks, using **electronic funds transfer (EFT)**, accessing electronic bulletin boards, and communicating with other users. In the future, telecommunications uses will likely include a tremendous increase in the use of **videotex**—that is, the use of a computer and telephone to order goods and services without leaving the home or office. Currently, this service is only available on a limited basis in the United States, but its availability may soon be expanded, as it has in several European countries.

Large increases in use are predicted in EFT. Figure 22-2 shows one prediction of future EFT use. In the figure, EFT use is divided into four types of use—electronic clearing houses that clear checks between banks; automated teller machines that allow 24-hour banking; point-of-sale terminals that record daily transactions; and home banking terminals that allow a user to move money from the comfort of his or her home or office.

EFT and videotex allow buyers to transfer even small amounts of money between financial institutions or to various merchants. The increasing use of these two services may help develop a cashless society. Such a society must deal with the problems of crime and invasion of privacy.

Other telecommunications applications involve transferring information via satellite. One such use involves a new type of satellite called a **direct broadcast satellite (DBS)**, which allows the use of inexpensive home reception disks (less than $300) to receive high-power signals. These transmis-

FIGURE 22-2
Growth of EFT
(Source: John Vacca, "Money on the Move: Electronic Funds Transfer," *Computerworld on Communications,* May 2, 1984, p. 85.)

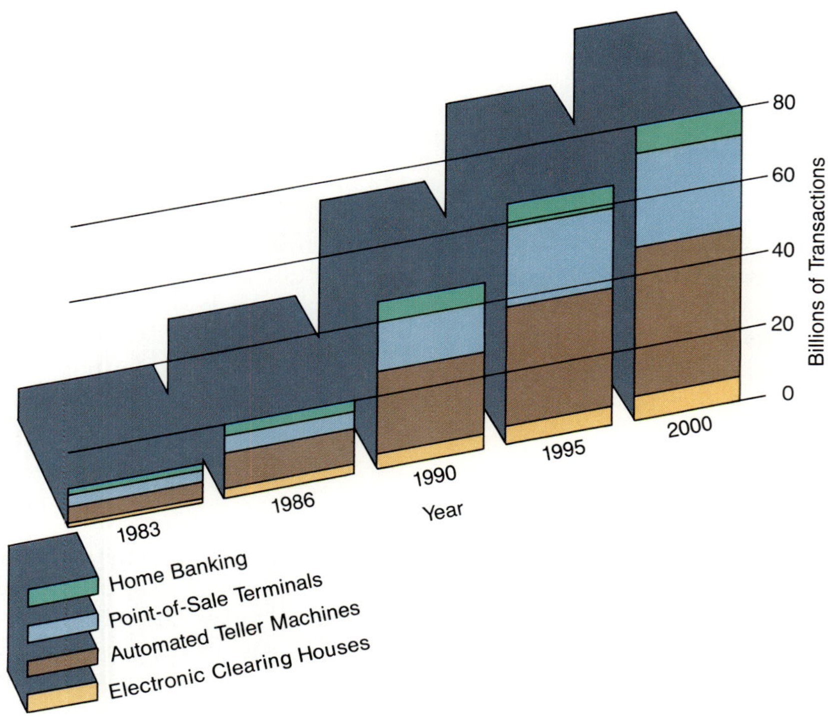

VIEWS OF THE FUTURE

In a series of interviews, five computer industry executives were asked the following question: How do you view the computer in 1990? These five men—Ben Dyer, chairman of Comsell, Inc. (and founder of Peachtree Software); Dennis Hayes, chairman of Hayes Communications, Inc.; Bertil Nordin, president of Digital Communications Associates; John Imlay, chairman of Management Science America; and Leland Strange, president of Intelligent Systems, Inc. (which includes Quadram and Princeton Graphics)—answered the question as follows:

DYER: I would say that is going to be a situation where computers are going to be more embedded in the things we do or use on a day-to-day basis and less recognizable as computers. We will think of them less as computers and more as just machines that are used in the normal course of business or everyday life. In particular, I would say that the video or laser disk is going to be an important facet in computers very soon.

HAYES: The computer marketplace is going to be much expanded from what it is now. Computers are going to get bigger and smaller at the same time. I think we will learn a lot about managing the interface between different computers. We will also learn a great deal managing distributive data bases and accessing information in centralized data bases.

IMLAY: One thing I think we will see very soon is the "smart building," where microprocessors will control everything from the temperature to the security to the communications. On a different level, I think the micro-to-mainframe link will become extremely important with the micro acting as a work station and the mainframe acting as a hugh repository of information. I think we will see 90% of the computing done at the work station level and 10% at the mainframe.

NORDIN: First of all, it's going to be a lot more widespread. Second, I think there will be a lot more distributive processing—processing at the person's fingertips—which is what the personal computer has begun to make available. All small-scale processing will be handled at the terminal, with the mainframe handling the large-scale processing and storage of the central data base. I think that by 1990, we will see terminals on virtually every desk in most offices.

STRANGE: In general, I think that we will see computers becoming smaller and faster at the same time. In the process, the mainframes and microcomputers will squeeze the minicomputers, possibly leaving no market for them. A specific improvement that we will see is array processing. This has the potential to speed up the personal computer by a factor of 50, and I believe we will see it incorporated by the end of the decade.

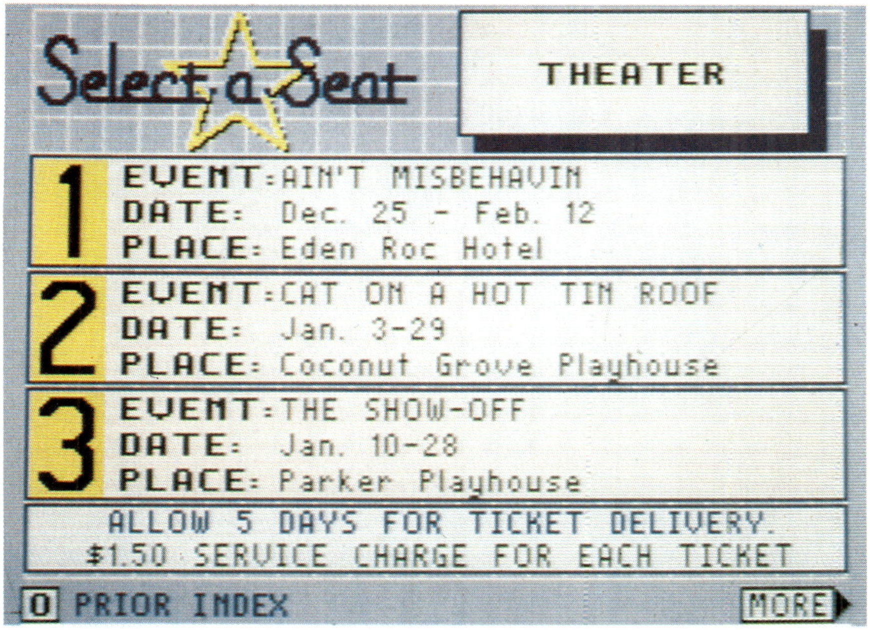

Using videotex systems, a user can purchase tickets to various entertainment events from the comfort of home.

sions could include software that is sent to prospective users, teleconferencing that allows live conferences among widely dispersed parties, and improved videotex. The high cost of teleconferencing has so far restricted its use to very special needs.

From a technological viewpoint, the use of glass-fiber cables promises a great increase in the amount of information transferred in a telecommunications network. A glass-fiber cable can carry the same volume of information in 1 second that copper cables would need 21 hours to send.

CAREERS IN COMPUTERS

As the United States evolves into an information-oriented society, the job market in the computer and communications industry grows by leaps and bounds. Employment in computer and computer-related fields should increase dramatically from its current levels between now and 1990. Specifically, the four fastest growing computer-related occupations should be computer repair technician, machine operator, applications programmer, and systems analyst. Figure 22-3 shows the projected growth in levels of employment in each field.

Seven major career fields are available in computer and computer-related fields (including telecommunications). Each major field requires a different

FIGURE 22-3
Computer Career Employment
(U.S. Bureau of Labor Statistics)

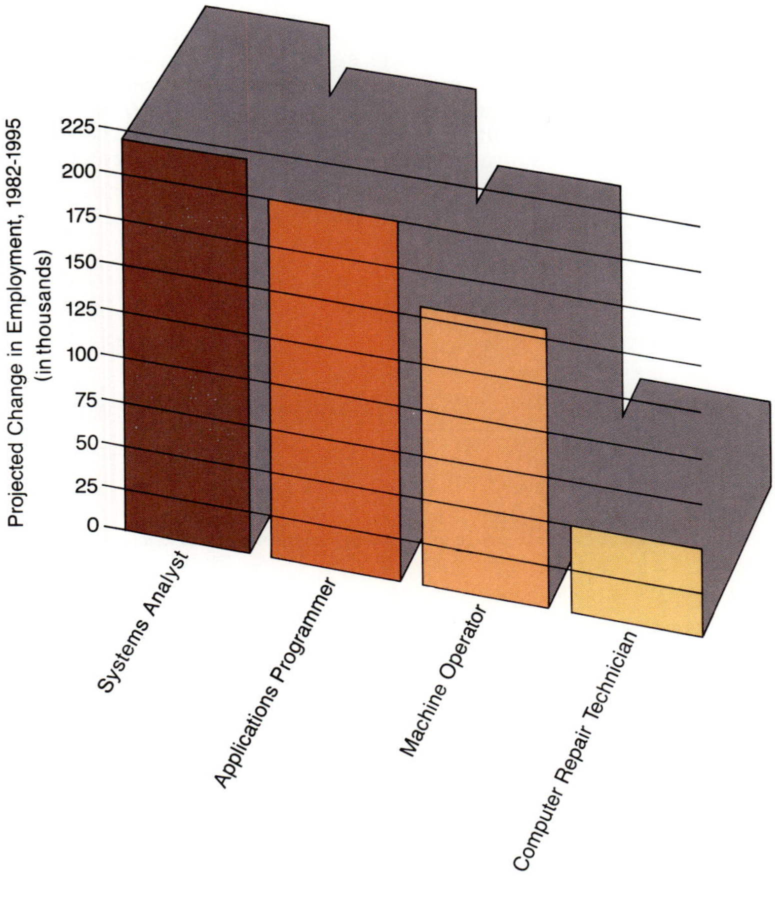

level of education and experience. These seven career fields are operations, analysis and programming, information management, repair and servicing, sales and marketing, instruction, and engineering. Operations involves the direct operation of the computer and data preparation. Analysts and programmers design and write the software that is used with the computer system, and information managers oversee the operation of various parts of the computer and the information system. Repair and service personnel provide either maintenance or repair of the computer. This work is usually performed on-site for mainframes and large groups of personal computers, but walk-in service is common now for small computers. Sales and marketing is a fast-growing area—especially in the personal computer field—that does not require a highly technical background. Instruction is an important career area. People are needed at all educational levels to teach about the computer. Engineering, the most technical field, involves the design, production, and maintenance of computers. Table 22-1 shows these career fields, along with the average educational level required and the approximate salary range. Table 22-2 shows a survey of computer-related occupations, giving the top 10 jobs in terms of growth in the number of openings from 1983 to 1984.

Lawyers can now access huge amounts of information through computers. They're going to depend even more on computers. There will be a lot of people finding jobs in the computer field, but the big impact of the computer will be that it will revolutionize all kinds of other jobs.

***Edward Cornish, President of the World Future Society and author of* The Study of the Future**

(As quoted in "Computers Will Alter Nearly Everyone's Job," *USA Today,* December 31, 1984, p. 11A.)

Table 22-1 COMPUTER OCCUPATIONS

Career Field	*Educational Level*	*Salary Range*
Operations	High school	$12,000–$18,000
Analysis and programming	College	$15,000–$40,000
Information management	Masters degree	$20,000–$100,000
Repair and servicing	High school	$13,000–$35,000
Sales and marketing	College	$15,000–unlimited
Instruction	College to Ph.D.	$15,000–$60,000
Engineering	Engineering degree	$30,000–$70,000

Table 22-2 FASTEST GROWING COMPUTER JOBS, 1983–1984

1984 Ranking	*Job Title*	*Percent Rise over 1983*
1	Software engineer	20.1
2	Systems/software programmers	18.9
3	Telecommunications specialists	18.1
4	Data base managers	18.1
5	Applications programmers	17.1
6	EDP auditors	16.3
7	Software systems managers	15.6
8	Software programming managers	14.1
9	Systems analysts	13.5
10	Applications programming managers	11.9

(SOURCE: Fox-Morris 1984 U.S. Computer Market Job-Salary Review)

Computer careers include data entry and operations positions.

Operations

The increasing use of mainframe computers has meant an increased demand for on-site personnel to operate the computer or prepare data for entry into the computer. Sample job titles in this classification include computer operator, data entry clerk, EDP (electronic data processing) clerk, keypunch operator, tape or media librarian, and EDP specialist. These entry-level positions usually require a high school education. (Often, these positions have flexible work hours, which allow a student to obtain valuable practical experience while going to school.) Persons with experience in computer operations are often in great demand, because they can usually step right into any operation and take charge.

Operators should be able to initialize (start up) the computer system, monitor its operations, load tapes when requested by users, and take any necessary preventive or remedial actions. Data entry clerks and keypunch operators prepare or enter data into the computer, and the tape or media librarian maintains the tapes or written documentation.

Analysis and Programming

The systems analyst's job was discussed in detail in Chapters 4 and 18. Recall that systems analysts evaluate and generate problem solutions, which are then converted into software by the programmer. Ideally, these two positions are separate, but in many small organizations, the title "programmer/analyst" designates a person who performs both operations. Job titles in this group include programmer (I, II, and so on), information analyst, systems designer, and systems support specialist.

People interested in programming often wonder what computer language they should learn to improve their chances of being hired. As expected, this is not an easy question to answer. Many entry-level positions are open to individuals who are familiar with any language. Generally, for a mainframe position, a majority of help-wanted ads ask for one language—COBOL. RPG (Report Program Generator) is another language that is often encountered in a mainframe environment. For a personal computer programming position,

Systems analysis and programming positions are growing both in number and in salary level.

BASIC is the number one language, with C and Pascal programmers also in demand.

Experience is very important in programming. Entry-level positions for persons with no experience in programming may sometimes be difficult to find in a desirable geographic region, but experienced individuals are in great demand everywhere. A person interested in programming might consider either working part-time at some programming position while still in school or obtaining an internship for the needed experience.

Information Management

As with any organization, managers are necessary to ensure that objectives are met and that the operation stays within budget or makes a profit. These persons do not need a technical computer background, but they should understand the goals and objectives of their organization or business. This person usually has some training in management and experience in the computer field. Job titles common in this field include systems programming manager, applications programming manager, and data base manager. In the first two cases, the manager has a "people-related" position, supervising analysts and programmers. The data base manager oversees the organization's data base operations.

Repair and Servicing

This career area should grow dramatically over the next few years. Two types of repair and servicing career fields exist—mainframe and minicomputer

SALARIES

The market for computer jobs is one of the fastest growing areas in the economy, and these jobs pay well. To determine just how well computer-related jobs pay, Abbott, Langer & Associates surveyed more than 1,000 organizations that employ workers in the management information systems/data processing (MIS/dp) field. According to the report, the highest paid professionals in MIS/dp are individuals who manage at least 25 other MIS/dp professionals and who control a budget of $10 million or more. An individual in this group tends to earn more than $100,000 per year in salary plus a cash bonus and/or profit sharing. Median salaries for other positions in the MIS/dp field are as follows:

Position	*Annual Salary*
Top MIS/dp officer	$40,675
Top dp manager	37,800
Data base manager	36,000
Computer operations manager/supervisor	34,140
Senior systems analyst	33,773
Communications manager	33,500
Senior systems analyst/programmer	31,750
Senior systems programmer	31,500
Senior applications programmer	27,000
User support coordinator	24,575
Senior computer operator	17,760
Senior key entry operator	13,586
Junior key entry operator	12,000

SOURCE: Abbott, Langer & Associates Report, as quoted in *Changing Times,* March 1985, pp. 18–19.

I think the growth in the microcomputer service industry will be between 50 and 60% a year for the next decade.

George Harmon, owner of Serviceland microcomputer service centers

(As quoted in "Computer Doctors Are On Call," *USA Today,* August 27, 1984, pp. 1B–2B.)

service and repair and personal computer service and repair. Mainframe and minicomputer maintenance personnel usually work for the mainframe or minicomputer supplier, which has a maintenance contract with the owner or lessor of the computer. These people are specially trained by their company to work on that particular variety of computer.

On the other hand, personal computer repair persons are often entrepreneurs who set up a business to work on the small computers. Personal computers are not particularly prone to breakdowns, but they do have problems periodically, especially with disk drives and printers. Until recently, such big companies as IBM did not repair personal computers. Such repairs were arranged by the stores that sold them. Today, however, IBM has decided to enter this lucrative field. The repair and servicing field has no special educational requirement for work on the smaller machines. Some persons who at one time were hobbyists in personal computers now find their practical knowledge of computers handy, and they are starting service companies to handle the demand from personal computer owners.

Sales and Marketing

Anyone with an interest in computers, some knowledge of how they work, and an ability to meet the public or to express ideas in an understandable fashion can enter the computer sales and marketing field. A growing need exists for salespeople who can present their product in an understandable fashion without threatening the customer. These people need not be techni-

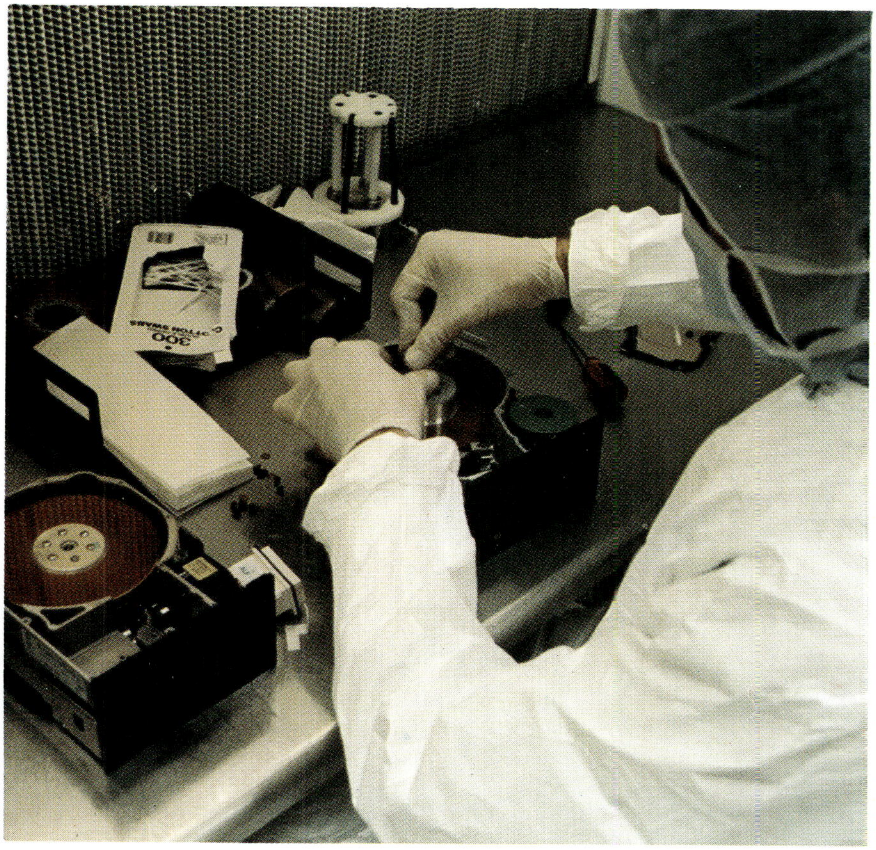

Service technicians often repair or align disk drives for personal computers.

Mainframe computer manufacturers train support technicians to handle customers' hardware and software problems.

For persons who enjoy meeting the public, computer sales offers an opportunity to combine computer training with "people" skills.

cal experts on computers, but they must have a knowledge of computers at the level covered in this text.

Marketing personnel present the product in written and illustrated material and write documentation. In fact, individuals with a liberal arts background and some knowledge of computers may be the best people to write documentation. Often, documentation is written by someone who is close to the product, and the explanations are either difficult to follow or poorly written. The intense competition in the software market demands good documentation—it can be the difference between a big seller and a mediocre seller.

Instruction

The growing interest in computers and the demand for computer science courses at all education levels has resulted in a corresponding need for people to provide instruction. The demand far outstrips the supply, and a teaching candidate with a knowledge of computers should have little or no difficulty finding a suitable job. At the elementary and high school level, a degree in education and some coursework in computer science is usually satisfactory. For technical school and college teaching, at least a master's degree in computer science or a related field is necessary. The Ph.D. is usually required at the university level, where the greatest demand exists. University professors are being lured into the industry, and the supply of Ph.D.'s is not increasing fast enough to take up the slack.

As the use of computers increases, so too does the need for individuals who can teach others to use computers.

COMPUTER DOCTORS

Dave Green always liked to tinker with electrical devices as a kid. He has turned this childhood avocation into a lucrative business repairing personal computers. Green and his partners started a business called Microcomputer Doctors, which netted $50,000 in 1983 and has a projected 1984–1985 income of $400,000. The doctors would do more business, but qualified technicians who can walk into a business and diagnose and repair an ailing computer are hard to find.

Many of these repair people are recent college or technical school graduates who want to use their academic tools, and others are former television repair people or auto mechanics. Some are even former employees of large companies like TRW or RCA who hope to get in on the ground floor of a growing business. Personal computer repair is definitely growing; analysts predict that revenues from personal computer repair will more than double in the next five years.

Versions of Microcomputer Doctors are springing up all over the country. For example, Serviceland Corporation, which opened in August 1983, now has 11 franchises in 8 states and hopes to sell 89 more. Computer Doctor, Inc., a repair operation that opened in 1983, hopes to grow to 500 outlets by 1989.

SOURCE: Mark Lewyn, "Computer Doctors Are on Call," *USA Today*, August 27, 1984, p. 1B.

Serviceland technicians are experts at repairing today's personal computers.

Positions are available in computer manufacturing companies at both technician and engineer levels.

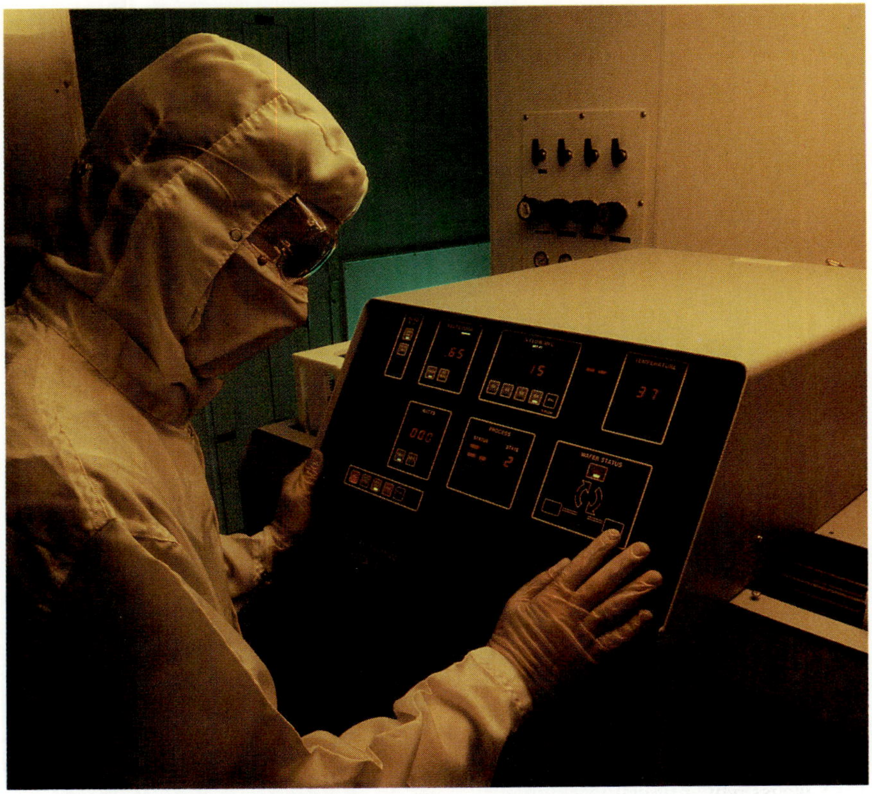

Engineering

Designing and building computers requires the technical background usually provided by an engineering program. Sometimes, an individual with a degree in mathematics or physics can find a position in this field, especially if he or she also has an interest and some background in computers.

REVIEW OF KEY POINTS

- Our society is becoming an information-based society rather than an agricultural or industrial society; the reduction in information float will accelerate this movement.
- Computers will be smaller and faster as the number of transistors on each chip increases.
- Internal and external storage capacities will grow.
- The use of video disks for external storage is apparently a strong possibility in the near future.
- Supercomputers will grow more powerful through the use of parallel processing and pipelining.
- The markets for mainframes and personal computers are growing at about the same rate, but the use of minicomputers may decline in the future.
- The use of robots in assembly line operations should grow dramatically in the future, but it will affect some human workers negatively.
- Software must be easier to use so that new users are enticed into the computer market.
- This "softer" software will include voice input, natural language systems, expert systems, and other forms of artificial intelligence.
- Telecommunications may be the most rapidly expanding computer-related field.
- Electronic funds transfer and videotex may eliminate the need to leave the home or office to shop or handle financial matters.
- Opportunities for careers in computer-related fields are expanding.
- The seven major areas in computer careers are: operations, analysis and programming, information management, repair and servicing, sales and marketing, instruction, and engineering.

KEY TERMS

array processing
artificial intelligence
bubble memory
direct broadcast satellite (DBS)
electronic funds transfer (EFT)
expert systems
futurists
gallium arsenide
holographic displays
information float
information society
Josephson Junction
natural language system
optical disk
parallel processing
pipelining
robotics
serial machines
silicon chip
softer software
telecommunications
transistor
videotex
voice input

REVIEW QUESTIONS

1. Why is predicting the future of hardware easier than predicting the future of other computer areas?
2. Why is gallium arsenide a possible replacement for silicon in chip manufacturing?
3. What problem is hindering the use of optical disks for external storage?
4. For what jobs will robots most likely be used? What new jobs might be created by the use of robots?
5. Why is "softer software" necessary to attract new computer users? Why is new software needed rather than new hardware?
6. Discuss why artificial intelligence is a hot topic in computers today.
7. Why have communications companies moved into computers and computer companies moved into communications?
8. Why do we say that EFT and videotex may reduce the need to leave home to shop? What do direct broadcast satellites have to do with this?
9. Research the demand and salary possibilities in your area for one of the seven major computer career fields.
10. Discuss the difference between mainframe and personal computer repair and servicing. If possible, discuss the differences with the personnel at a mainframe computer center and a personal computer repair facility.

APPENDIX

American Standard Code for Information Interchange (ASCII) Ordering of Symbols

ASCII Order	HEX Symbol	Control	Character	ASCII Order	HEX Symbol	Character
000	00H	NUL	(null)	032	20H	(space)
001	01H	SOH		033	21H	!
002	02H	STX		034	22H	”
003	03H	ETX	♥	035	23H	#
004	04H	EOT	♦	036	24H	$
005	05H	ENQ	♣	037	25H	%
006	06H	ACK	♠	038	26H	&
007	07H	BEL	(beep)	039	27H	’
008	08H	BS	(backspace)	040	28H	(
009	09H	HT	(tab)	041	29H	)
010	0AH	LF	(line feed)	042	2AH	*
011	0BH	VT	(home)	043	2BH	+
012	0CH	FF	(form feed)	044	2CH	,
013	0DH	CR	(carriage return)	045	2DH	-
014	0EH	SO		046	2EH	.
015	0FH	SI		047	2FH	/
016	10H	DLE	▶	048	30H	Ø
017	11H	DC1	◀	049	31H	1
018	12H	DC2		050	32H	2
019	13H	DC3	!!	051	33H	3
020	14H	DC4	¶	052	34H	4
021	15H	NAK	§	053	35H	5
022	16H	SYN	■	054	36H	6
023	17H	ETB		055	37H	7
024	18H	CAN		056	38H	8
025	19H	EM		057	39H	9
026	1AH	SUB	→	058	3AH	:
027	1BH	ESC	←	059	3BH	;
028	1CH	FS	(cursor right)	060	3CH	<
029	1DH	GS	(cursor left)	061	3DH	=
030	1EH	RS	(cursor up)	062	2EH	>
031	1FH	US	(cursor down)	063	3FH	?

ASCII Order	HEX Symbol	Character	ASCII Order	HEX Symbol	Character
064	40H	@	096	60H	‘
065	41H	A	097	61H	a
066	42H	B	098	62H	b
067	43H	C	099	63H	c
068	44H	D	100	64H	d
069	45H	E	101	65H	e
070	46H	F	102	66H	f
071	47H	G	103	67H	g
072	48H	H	104	68H	h
073	49H	I	105	69H	i
074	4AH	J	106	6AH	j
075	4BH	K	107	6BH	k
076	4CH	L	108	6CH	l
077	4DH	M	109	6DH	m
078	4EH	N	110	6EH	n
079	4FH	O	111	6FH	o
080	50H	P	112	70H	p
081	51H	Q	113	71H	q
082	52H	R	114	72H	r
083	53H	S	115	73H	s
084	54H	T	116	74H	t
085	55H	U	117	75H	u
086	56H	V	118	76H	v
087	57H	W	119	77H	w
088	58H	X	120	78H	x
089	59H	Y	121	79H	y
090	5AH	Z	122	7AH	z
091	5BH	[	123	7BH	{
092	5CH	\	124	7CH	|
093	5DH	]	125	7DH	}
094	5EH	ˆ	126	7EH	~
095	5FH	—	127	7FH	

GLOSSARY

A

absolute address The actual location of a record in secondary storage. (Chapter 12)

access code *See* user number.

accounting A process that tracks the financial health of a company or individual. (Chapter 11)

accounting information system (AIS) A subsystem of the management information system that processes primarily economic and financial data. (Chapter 4)

accounting (software) package A group of programs that allows a business to keep track of its financial affairs. (Chapters 1, 3, and 11)

accounts payable A module of a business accounting software package that monitors the money owed by a firm to its suppliers. (Chapter 11)

accounts receivable A module of a business accounting software package that keeps track of money owed to a firm and of when payments are due. (Chapter 11)

acoustical (coupler) modem A type of modem with a pair of rubber cups into which a telephone handset can be plugged. (Chapter 13)

address The location of data or instructions in internal memory; the location of a record in direct access secondary storage. (Chapters 6 and 12)

address bus The communications line over which the address of a data item or instruction is transferred to the control unit. (Chapter 6)

algorithm A step-by-step procedure used to solve a problem. (Chapters 4 and 14)

American Standard Code for Information Interchange (ASCII) A code for the binary representation of characters within the computer. (Chapter 2)

analog A physical relationship that represents data. (Chapter 13)

analog computer A machine that uses physical relationships to make its calculations; a measuring machine. (Chapter 1)

analysis The third step in the systems analysis and design process, in which the analyst determines the details of the system under study. (Chapter 18)

analysis graphics A graphics software package that analyzes data to gain a better understanding of it or to determine whether patterns exist. (Chapter 10)

Analytical Engine A prototype computer designed by Charles Babbage in the early nineteenth century. (Chapter 1)

androids Robots that have built-in microprocessors and can move around. (Chapter 6)

answer mode In full-duplex communications, one of two audio frequencies that can be used by a computer to send information (the other frequency is the originate mode). (Chapter 13)

applications software Software that performs specialized tasks and constitutes the greatest proportion of software used on computers. (Chapter 3)

argument A variable or constant that gives a function the information it needs to perform an operation. (Chapter 17)

arithmetic-logic unit (ALU) The part of the central processing unit that handles the actual manipulation of data. (Chapters 2 and 6)

array A list or table of numbers or strings. (Chapter 17)

array processing A type of parallel processing that allows supercomputers to perform the same operation on a list of values simultaneously. (Chapter 22)

artificial intelligence (AI) Hardware and software systems that exhibit human intelligence-related activities—for example, listening, reading, speaking, solving problems, and drawing inferences. (Chapters 1, 15, and 22)

assembler A translation program that converts assembly language mnemonic commands to machine language. (Chapter 15)

assembly language A machine-specific language that uses words and letters for commands. (Chapters 3 and 15)

assignment statement A BASIC statement that assigns a value to a memory cell. (Chapter 16)

asynchronous communication A form of communication between computers that does not require their rates of processing data to be synchronized. (Chapter 13)

auto-answer capability The capability of a modem to receive outside telephone calls under the direction of the computer. (Chapter 13)

auto-dial capability The capability of a modem to dial a telephone number under the direction of the computer. (Chapter 13)

B

backup A copy of software or data that is made by the user to guard against accidental loss of software or data. (Chapters 5 and 8)

backup hierarchy A policy of backing up information on floppy disks that rotates three or four disks to generate the most recent backup copy. (Chapter 8)

band printer An impact printer used with mainframe computers that prints an entire line of text using a band of letters. (Chapter 7)

bar chart A type of analysis graphics that shows relative differences among categories of data using vertical or horizontal bars. (Chapter 10)

bar code Combinations of light and dark bars that are coded to contain information. (Chapters 1 and 7)

batch access *See* batch mode.

batch language A language that is entered into the computer and executed as a whole, with no interaction between user and computer. (Chapter 15)

batch mode A job entry mode in which the entire job is entered at one time from a card reader, disk drive, or tape drive. (Chapters 9, 20, and 21)

batch package A software package that has all data submitted at one time in a batch. (Chapter 9)

batch processing Combining data from multiple users or time periods and then submitting the combined data to the computer for processing in a batch. (Chapter 4)

baud rate The number of bits per second that can be transmitted and received by a modem. (Chapter 13)

bidirectional printer A printer that can operate with the print head moving in either direction. (Chapter 7)

binary number system Base 2 number system, which uses the digits zero and one. (Chapters 2 and 6)

bit The basic unit of measure in a computer; contraction of BInary and digiT. (Chapters 2 and 6)

bit-mapped graphics A type of graphics in which each pixel on the screen can be controlled individually. (Chapter 10)

block-action command In word processing, the definition and subsequent movement, deletion, or other action on a block of text. (Chapter 10)

block graphics A form of graphics in which the pixels on the screen can be controlled only as groups, and each group, or block, corresponds to an ASCII character. (Chapter 10)

blocked records A combination of logical records into a physical record that is read by the tape drive. (Chapter 8)

body of loop The part of a loop that is repeated. (Chapter 14)

boiler plate material In word processing, a block of text that is defined and then copied to different points in a document or to different documents. (Chapter 10)

booting The process of starting up a computer. (Chapter 6)

boundary The delineation between a system and its environment. (Chapter 4)

break-even analysis A process that calculates the number of units of a given product that must be produced and sold before a profit is realized. (Chapter 11)

bubble memory A nonvolatile form of random access memory that uses bubbles in a magnetic field to store information. (Chapters 6 and 22)

budgeting A process that compares anticipated expenses with anticipated income. (Chapter 11)

buffer A temporary storage area; during the input/output process, it keeps the CPU from being slowed down. (Chapters 2, 7, and 9)

bug An error in the execution of a program. (Chapters 3 and 14)

burning in the circuits Programming a read only memory chip. (Chapter 6)

bus network A computer network in which computers are tied into a main cable, or bus, without a central computer. (Chapter 19)

byte A group of 8 bits. (Chapters 2 and 6)

bytes per inch (bpi) A measurement of the storage density on magnetic tape. (Chapter 8)

C

card reader A machine that converts the holes in a punched card into electronic signals to the computer. (Chapters 2 and 7)

carrier tone An audio tone that is modulated to send signals between computers. (Chapter 13)

cartridge A form of read only secondary storage used mainly for computer games. (Chapters 2 and 7)

cartridge tape A form of magnetic tape that is stored in a cartridge; cartridge tape stores data using a magnetic bit pattern. (Chapter 8)

cassette tape An inexpensive form of secondary storage for personal computers that uses audio tones to store information. (Chapter 8)

cathode ray tube (CRT) The picture tube in a monitor or video display terminal. (Chapter 21)

cell The intersection of a row and a column in a spreadsheet. (Chapter 11)

cell pointer A special cursor that designates the cells into which information is entered in a spreadsheet. (Chapter 11)

centering The word processing function that centers material between the margins. (Chapter 10)

central processing unit (CPU) The part of the computer that handles the actual processing of data into information. (Chapters 2 and 6)

chain printer An impact printer that uses a chain of letters to print lines of text; used with mainframe computers. (Chapter 7)

channel A hardware unit that controls the input/output process without direction from the central processing unit. (Chapter 9)

chip *See* microchip.

ciphertext A coded (unreadable) form of information. (Chapter 20)

cleartext A readable form of information. (Chapter 20)

clock A device in the CPU that sends out electrical pulses at a set rate; the control unit uses the pulses to synchronize its operations. (Chapter 6)

cluster configuration A dedicated word processing system in which several word processors are tied together by cable and share storage and printers. (Chapter 19)

coaxial cable A large number of copper wires surrounded by a metallic shield; often used to send data at high speeds with little outside interference. (Chapters 13 and 19)

color monitor A monitor that displays material in more than one color. (Chapters 2 and 7)

column A series of values placed vertically in a spreadsheet. (Chapter 11)

command-driven package A software package that requires the user to know and enter the needed commands and data. (Chapter 9)

command interpreter Part of the operating system that interprets the user's keystrokes and sends a message to the appropriate utility or applications program to execute the command. (Chapter 9)

command mode A word processing mode that allows the user to enter commands. (Chapter 10)

comment statements Program statements explaining the statements that actually execute program logic. (Chapter 15)

communications software A type of software package that enables the computer and modem to communicate with other computers, sometimes uploading and downloading files. (Chapter 13)

compilation The process of converting an entire source program into machine language before executing any of the program. (Chapter 14)

compiled language A high-level computer language in which an entire source program is converted to object code before the program is executed. (Chapter 15)

compiler A translator program that converts a high-level language into machine language by compilation. (Chapters 3, 9, and 15)

completion screen A screen that requests information and data from the user. (Chapter 11)

composite signal A single signal that includes all the information needed for a monitor to produce a video image. (Chapter 7)

computer An electronic, automatic machine that manipulates and stores symbols based on instructions from the user. (Chapter 1)

computer-aided design (CAD) A graphics software package that assists the user in developing engineering and architectural designs. (Chapter 10)

computer-aided instruction (CAI) Using a computer like a tutor in the instructional process. (Chapter 3)

computer board A plastic board with chips and circuits that can increase the memory or functions of a computer. (Chapter 10)

computer card *See* punched card.

computer competence The level of computer knowledge reached by an individual who can solve sophisticated problems in his or her field of expertise using a computer. (Chapter 1)

computer crime The unauthorized invasion of a computer data file or theft of money, merchandise, data, or computer time using a computer. (Chapters 5 and 20)

computer error A misnomer—actually, a human error. (Chapter 1)

computer ethics The ethics of organizational or personal use of the computer. (Chapter 21)

computer language A language used by humans to give instructions to computers. (Chapter 3)

computer literacy An understanding of what a computer can and cannot do, and an ability to make the computer do what is desired. (Chapter 1)

computer mastery The level of knowledge required of an individual who wants to be a success in the computer field. (Chapter 1)

computer matching The process of matching records in two data banks to determine which records exist in both data banks. (Chapter 21)

computer monitoring Management's monitoring of an employee's use of a personal computer. (Chapter 21)

computer network *See* network.

computer package Commercially available software. (Chapter 1)

computerphobia Fear of the computer, especially among first-time users; also called cyberphobia. (Chapters 1 and 21)

computerphylliac A person who is totally involved with the computer, to the exclusion of all other concerns. (Chapter 21)

computer program A set of specific instructions for controlling the computer. (Chapter 3)

computer security A wide range of methods used to protect the computer, the data, and the user from natural and criminal forces. (Chapter 20)

computer system All parts of a computer that make a working entity—CPU, keyboard, monitor, secondary storage devices, and other peripherals. (Chapter 4)

computer terminal A keyboard and monitor without a CPU or any secondary storage devices. (Chapter 13)

computer word The number of bits that are processed by the registers in the ALU at one time. (Chapter 6)

conceptual computer A simplified computer that can demonstrate the major functions of a computer without involving the machine's operational details. (Chapters 2 and 6)

connector symbol In flowcharting, a circle that is used to show a connection between two parts of a flowchart. (Chapter 14)

constants The data that are stored in the computer's memory cells. (Chapter 16)

control bus The communications line over which an instruction is transferred to the ALU from the internal memory unit. (Chapter 6)

control key A key on the personal computer keyboard that is used in conjunction with other keys to enter commands. (Chapter 10)

control unit Part of the CPU that manages the symbol manipulation process. (Chapters 2 and 6)

co-processor A type of chip that enables the computer to handle special operations. (Chapter 6)

copy protection The process whereby software manufacturers guard against software piracy by making personal computer software impossible to copy. (Chapters 5 and 20)

core A form of random access memory that utilizes tiny ferrite donuts or wires; its use preceded the use of RAM chips. (Chapter 6)

counter In programming, a variable that is used to count the number of repetitions of a program. (Chapter 16)

credit An accounting term used in double-entry bookkeeping. (Chapter 11)

cursor A blinking rectangle of light on the monitor that designates the user's current position on the screen. (Chapters 2 and 10)

cursor control The movement of the cursor to any point on the screen. (Chapter 10)

cursor movement keys Keys on a personal computer keyboard that control the cursor's movement on the screen. (Chapter 10)

cut-and-paste In word processing, a block-action command that defines a block of text and then moves it to another spot in a document or to another document. (Chapter 10)

cyberphobia *See* computerphobia.

cylinder A disk pack storage scheme in which all tracks with the same track number make up a vertical cylinder. (Chapter 8)

D

daisy wheel printer A personal computer printer that uses a wheel of symbols to produce high-quality print. (Chapter 7)

data Raw facts that are fed into the computer for processing. (Chapters 1 and 2)

data bank A store of information on people or organizations. (Chapters 5 and 21)

data base A collection of information organized so that needed information is easily found. (Chapters 1, 3, 12, and 19)

data base management (software) package A package that manages an electronic data base, allowing the user to find data base elements that fit some criterion; also called a **data base management system (DBMS)**. (Chapters 1, 3, 12, and 19)

data bus The communications line over which data flow to the ALU from the internal memory unit. (Chapter 6)

data deck A deck of computer cards that contain instructions or data. (Chapter 7)

data dependence The interdependence of software and data storage. (Chapter 12)

data dictionary A list of data elements, including information regarding name, source, description, and use. (Chapters 4 and 18)

Data Encryption Standard (DES) A standard method of coding information into ciphertext. (Chapter 20)

data entry problem The problem caused by slow and/or incorrect data entry to the computer. (Chapter 7)

data entry screen A set of requests to the user for data that are displayed on a monitor screen. (Chapter 12)

data file A file containing any type of information, including data, text, or programs. (Chapter 8)

data flow diagram A pictorial representation of the flow of data into and out of a system. (Chapters 4 and 18)

data integrity The correctness of data in a data base. (Chapter 12)

data manipulation and reporting system A subsystem of the management information system that allows an individual to use a personal computer to manage efficiently the information at his or her disposal. (Chapter 4)

data processing The mechanical process of converting raw data into meaningful information; usually refers to the processing of numeric data. (Chapters 1, 4, 10, and 19)

data redundancy The repetition of data on multiple data bases. (Chapter 12)

data security The protection of a computer's software and data from unauthorized manipulation, destruction, or theft. (Chapter 20)

debit An accounting term used in double-entry bookkeeping. (Chapter 11)

debugging process The process of tracking down and correcting execution errors in a program. (Chapter 14)

decision block One or more program statements that handle the choice between alternative program sections based on whether a condition is true or false. (Chapter 16)

decision support system (DSS) A subsystem of the management information system that combines data with models and graphics to answer a decision maker's questions about the data. (Chapters 4 and 19)

decision symbol In flowcharting, a diamond that designates a decision among two or three alternatives. (Chapter 14)

dedicated word processors Minicomputers that are used solely for word processing. (Chapters 10 and 19)

delayed conference A form of teleconferencing in which participants' comments are stored sequentially as they are entered; the responses to comments may be recorded over a long period of time. (Chapter 13)

demand report A report that is generated by the management support system after a request by a manager. (Chapter 19)

demonstration disk A floppy disk provided with personal computer software that demonstrates the use of the software. (Chapter 9)

density A measure of the amount of information that can be stored on a floppy disk. (Chapter 8)

desk check The process of checking every step of a program to find errors. (Chapter 14)

desk-top computers *See* personal computers.

desk-top metaphor A view of the computer as a desk equipped with a file cabinet, telephone, wastebasket, scratch pad, and so on. (Chapter 7)

destructive replacement The process of replacing the contents of a computer memory location with a new value; the old value is lost. (Chapters 6 and 16)

dialog base Part of the decision support system that handles the interaction between the user-manager and the computer. (Chapter 19)

dial-up computer system A computer system that can be reached from a personal telephone. (Chapter 20)

digital computer A machine that uses numbers to make its calculations; a counting machine. (Chapter 1)

direct access A form of access that allows a record to be accessed regardless of its physical storage location. (Chapters 2, 8, and 12)

direct access file A file in which each record may be accessed directly, regardless of its relative position on the file or the order that records were placed on the file. (Chapter 8)

direct access storage device (DASD) A secondary storage device on which information can be accessed in any order. (Chapter 8)

direct broadcast satellite (DBS) A satellite that allows the use of inexpensive home reception disks to receive its high-power signals, including software and data. (Chapter 22)

direct-connect modem A type of modem that is connected directly to a telephone line and to a computer. (Chapter 13)

direct conversion A conversion process in which the current system is discarded when a new system is installed. (Chapter 4)

disk A thin, record-like piece of metal or plastic that is covered with iron oxide particles; the magnetic direction of the particles can be arranged to represent symbols. (Chapter 2)

disk commands DOS commands that must be accessed from the DOS disk; they are not stored in internal memory. (Chapter 9)

disk directory A list of the files that are stored on a disk. (Chapter 9)

disk drive A device that writes information onto or reads information from a magnetic disk. (Chapters 2 and 7)

diskette *See* floppy disk.

disk operating system (DOS) A personal computer operating system that depends on a disk for secondary storage. (Chapters 3, 8, and 9)

disk pack A collection of magnetic disks used on a mainframe computer. (Chapters 2, 7, and 8)

distributed data bases Small, specialized data bases that are separate from a primary data base; usually associated with minicomputers in a distributed data processing system. (Chapter 13)

distributed data processing system (DDP) A processing system that uses a mainframe computer for data base storage and for large-scale processing, combined with minicomputers or personal computers for local processing. (Chapters 4, 13, and 19)

division/remainder procedure A hashing procedure that uses the remainder from division as a relative address of a record in secondary storage. (Chapter 12)

documentation A written description of a software package and the tasks it can perform; in a program, the explanation of the logic and program statements. (Chapters 9 and 15)

dot matrix printer A personal computer printer that uses a matrix of wires to form symbols on paper. (Chapter 7)

double-entry bookkeeping An accounting system in which each transaction recorded changes a credit account and a debit account (Chapter 11)

download The process of shifting software or data from a central computer to a personal computer and saving it on disk. (Chapter 13)

drum printer An impact printer made up of 132 cylinders, each of which contains all of the letters, digits, and symbols needed to print documents. (Chapter 7)

DSS model generator A general purpose decision support package that contains many models which, when combined, can help a user solve his or her problems. (Chapter 19)

dual in-line package (DIP) A plastic carrier that protects the tiny chip and is the means by which the chip is connected to a circuit board. (Chapter 6)

dummy values Data values that are included solely to meet the requirements of the INPUT statement. (Chapter 17)

E

edit line The line above or below a spreadsheet on which the information being entered actually appears. (Chapter 11)

electronic bulletin board A computerized version of a bulletin board that allows users to post messages for other users. (Chapter 13)

electronic data processing (EDP) *See* data processing.

electronic filing Storage of a document on some form of secondary storage for later retrieval. (Chapter 19)

electronic funds transfer (EFT) The payment of bills and other forms of funds transfer via computer. (Chapters 1, 13, and 22)

electronic mail The process of sending letters, documents, and messages between computers. (Chapters 13 and 19)

electronic spreadsheet A spreadsheet on a computer that allows the easy recalculation of values based on changes within the spreadsheet (Chapter 11)

encryption The process of converting information into a coded (unreadable) form. (Chapter 20)

environment The elements outside of a system that affect the system. (Chapter 4)

erasable programmable read only memory (EPROM) A PROM chip that can be erased and reprogrammed. (Chapter 6)

ergonomics The study of the relationship between efficiency and comfort in a worker's use of machines. (Chapters 5 and 21)

error trapping A mechanism in a software package that prevents a user from entering the incorrect type of data. (Chapter 11)

exception report A report that is generated by the management support system only when an abnormal event occurs. (Chapter 19)

execution The implementation of the object code form of a program to solve a specific problem. (Chapter 3)

Execution-time (E-time) The period in the execution process during which an instruction is carried out by the ALU and the results are sent to internal memory. (Chapter 6)

expert system A computer system that makes the collective knowledge of various experts in a field available to the user. (Chapter 22)

Extended Binary Coded Decimal Interchange Code (EBCDIC) A code for the binary representation of characters within the computer. (Chapter 2)

eyestrain Eye discomfort sometimes associated with long-term use of a video display terminal. (Chapter 21)

F

Fair Credit Reporting Act of 1970 A federal law that controls the actions of credit bureaus, allowing consumers to view and make additions to their files. (Chapter 21)

feasibility study The second step in the systems analysis and design process in which the analyst determines whether an acceptable solution to a problem exists. (Chapter 18)

feedback A form of output that is sent back to a system's input or processing function, enabling the system to change its operation, if necessary. (Chapter 4)

fetch, decode, and execute process A process in which a computer fetches an instruction, decodes that instruction, and then executes it. (Chapter 6)

fiber optics The use of thin, glass cables to transmit voice and data. (Chapter 13)

field A single piece of information—such as a name, Social Security number, or profit value. (Chapters 8 and 12)

field width The number of positions set aside for data in a particular field. (Chapter 12)

file A collection of records that have the same fields, to which the user can attach a name. (Chapters 3, 8, 12, and 17)

file manager Part of a data base management package that controls the actual creation of a file and the various utility functions associated with the use of the file. (Chapter 12)

file processing package A data base management package that can only work with one file at a time to produce various types of reports. (Chapter 12)

financial analysis *See* spreadsheet analysis.

financial analysis software *See* spreadsheet analysis.

financial reporting Internal reports to management and external reports to stockholders and other interested parties on an organization's financial status. (Chapter 4)

firmware Instructions on a ROM chip. (Chapter 6)

fixed expenses Expenses that do not change from month to month. (Chapter 11)

fixed length record A record with a specified number of spaces set aside for each field. (Chapter 8)

fixed length word A word that consists of a specific number of bytes. (Chapter 6)

floppy disk A disk made of Mylar plastic and covered with iron oxide particles for use with a personal computer. (Chapters 2 and 8).

flowchart A pictorial form of an algorithm that can easily be converted into a computer program. (Chapter 14)

forecasting A process that uses currently available information to predict future occurrences. (Chapter 11)

FOR loop A pre-test loop in BASIC that is controlled by a counter variable. (Chapter 16)

formal documentation For the systems analysis and design process, the data dictionary and list of data elements; for a software package, the user's manual and other written descriptions. (Chapter 18)

formatting Organizing the sectors and tracks on a floppy disk; in word processing, setting up a document in a particular form. (Chapters 8 and 10)

formulas Combinations of spreadsheet values with other constants that define the relationships among the spreadsheet values. (Chapter 11)

freeware Software packages that can be obtained free or for a small fee. (Chapter 11)

full color monitor *See* color monitor.

full-duplex mode A mode of communications between computers in which both computers can transmit at the same time. (Chapter 13)

full-screen editing The ability to move to any point on the screen to make changes. (Chapter 10)

function In a spreadsheet, a specific operation; in programming, a short program stored in computer memory that can be accessed by the main program as needed. (Chapters 11, 15, 16, and 17)

function (built-in) A specific numeric or string operation in BASIC that is accessed by the programmer as needed. (Chapter 17)

function keys A set of keys on some personal computer keyboards that perform special functions. (Chapter 10)

futurists People who research the present to make predictions about future conditions. (Chapter 22)

G

gallium arsenide A semiconductor material that may soon replace silicon in microchips; gallium arsenide may increase the speed of the computer. (Chapter 22)

general ledger The record that contains all of a firm's financial transactions. (Chapter 11)

general purpose DSS A decision support system that can be used to solve various types of problems; the user develops a model and then manipulates variables to simulate results. (Chapter 19)

general purpose computer A computer that can be used for many purposes. (Chapter 1)

general purpose language A computer language that is used to solve almost any type of problem. (Chapter 15)

generic operating systems Personal computer operating systems that run on many different makes of computers. (Chapter 9)

global change In a spreadsheet, a user instruction to change all cell widths. (Chapter 11)

GO TO statement A transfer statement that should be avoided in structured programming. (Chapter 15)

graphics editors *See* paint packages.

graphics (software) package A group of programs for visual presentation of information or for creation of new and different art forms. (Chapters 1, 3, and 10)

H

hackers Individuals who gain unauthorized access to a computer for fun or challenge. (Chapters 5 and 20)

half-duplex mode Communications between computers in which both computers can send and receive information but only one computer can send at a time. (Chapter 13)

hard copy A printed version of the material on a video screen. (Chapters 2 and 7)

hard disk A scaled-down version of a mainframe disk pack that is used for storing information from a personal computer. (Chapters 2 and 8)

hard sectored A disk sectoring plan that is defined by the use of additional index holes in a disk. (Chapter 8)

hardware The electronic part of the computer that stores and manipulates symbols under the direction of the computer software. (Chapters 1, 2, 6, 7, and 8)

hashing Converting the primary key on a record into a relative address. (Chapter 12)

head crash The destruction of a magnetic disk and its data when the read/write head makes contact with the disk. (Chapter 8)

head window The area of a floppy disk that is in contact with the read/write head. (Chapter 8)

hexadecimal (hex) number system A number system that uses digits 0–9 and the letters A–F to represent the numbers 0–16. (Chapter 6)

Hierarchical Input/Process/Output (HIPO) technique In the system design stage, a method for developing a high-level design of the recommended software system. (Chapter 18)

hierarchy chart A chart that divides the software package into small pieces until a program can be written to implement each piece. (Chapter 18)

hierarchy of operations The order in which arithmetic operations are executed. (Chapter 16)

high-level languages Computer languages that combine English words with a specific grammar to generate computer instructions. (Chapters 3, 14, and 15)

holographic displays A three-dimensional display using lasers. (Chapter 22)

horizontal scrolling In a spreadsheet, the horizontal movement of the columns across the screen. (Chapter 11)

host computer A main, or central, computer which is linked to other, smaller computers. (Chapter 13)

hub ring The part of a floppy disk that the disk drive clamps onto to rotate the disk. (Chapter 8)

I

icon Pictures that represent various computer operations. (Chapters 7 and 9)

IF–THEN statement In BASIC, a statement that implements a one-alternative decision. (Chapter 16)

IF–THEN–ELSE statement In BASIC, a statement that implements a two-alternative decision. (Chapter 17)

imbedded print codes Codes placed in a word processing document to print boldface type, underlining, subscripts, superscripts, and so on. (Chapter 10)

impact printer A type of printer that uses some form of hammer to press ink onto a page. (Chapter 7)

importing files A word processing function that converts a non-word processing file into word processing format. (Chapter 10)

index The position of each element in a one-dimensional array. (Chapter 17)

indexed sequential access method (ISAM) A method of storing and retrieving records from secondary storage. (Chapter 12)

index hole A hole in the vinyl cover of a floppy disk that indicates to the computer the current position of the disk in its rotation. (Chapter 8)

indexing A system of keeping track of the physical location of records in a data base using record numbers. (Chapter 12)

information Data that have been processed into a form that is useful to the user. (Chapter 1)

information float The time between the occurrence of an event and the point at which it is general knowledge. (Chapter 22)

information society A society in which the majority of the workers are involved in the transmittal of information. (Chapters 1 and 22)

information system A system within an organization that converts raw data into useful information for managers and other interested parties. (Chapters 4, 18, and 19)

initialize The process of setting one or more values to some beginning value. (Chapters 14 and 16)

ink jet printer A nonimpact printer that forms symbols by spraying dots on paper. (Chapter 7)

input Receiving the symbols to be manipulated and the instructions for performing that manipulation. (Chapters 2 and 4)

input crime A computer crime in which the user changes, fabricates, or manipulates data when they are entered into the computer. (Chapter 20)

INPUT loop In BASIC, a pre-test loop that inputs data as long as valid data are received. (Chapter 17)

input/output (I/O) The process of instructing the computer, feeding it data, and receiving processed information from it. (Chapter 7)

input/output symbol In flowcharting, a parallelogram that designates input or output operations. (Chapter 14)

Input/Process/Output (IPO) chart A chart for each module of a software package showing the input to that module, the processing that takes place in the module, and the output from the module. (Chapter 18)

insert mode A word processing mode in which new symbols are inserted to the left of existing symbols, pushing the existing material to the right. (Chapter 10)

Instruction-time (I-time) The period in the execution process during which an instruction is fetched and decoded. (Chapter 6)

integrated circuit (IC) The combination of transistors and circuits on a chip. (Chapters 2 and 6)

integrated data base A data base that contains all needed information for use by different groups of users. (Chapter 12)

integrated (software) package A software package that contains two or more commonly used packages and a procedure to access them. (Chapters 3 and 9)

integrated system A processing system with a single data base that users access from terminals. (Chapter 4)

interactive input The user interacts directly with the computer during input; also called **interactive access**. (Chapters 7, 20, and 21)

interactive language A language in which a user interacts with the computer during data entry and execution. (Chapter 15)

interactive link The link for interaction between a user and a mainframe computer. (Chapter 7)

interactive package A software package that allows the user to interact with the computer during data entry and execution. (Chapter 9)

interblock gap (IBG) The space between blocks on magnetic tape at which the tape starts and stops. (Chapter 8)

internal memory The part of the computer that stores instructions and data internally. (Chapters 2 and 6)

interpretation The conversion of each program statement into machine language as the statement is encountered during program execution. (Chapter 14)

interpreted language A high-level computer language which must be converted into machine language as each statement is encountered during program execution. (Chapter 15)

interpreter A translator program that converts high-level language statements into machine language statements. (Chapters 3 and 15)

inventory control A process that keeps track of a company's raw materials, goods in process, finished goods, and other supplies. (Chapter 11)

investment analysis A process that determines the best use for available cash. (Chapter 11)

investment analysis packages Software packages that help a user choose the best investments and keep track of them. (Chapter 11)

I/O bound The computer's condition when it must wait for input or output before it processes the data into information. (Chapter 7)

J

job control language (JCL) An English-like computer language that allows the user to communicate with the computer's operating system. (Chapter 9)

Josephson Junction A super-fast electronic switch that works at temperatures close to absolute zero. (Chapter 22)

joystick An input device that utilizes a handle and buttons to control movement on the screen. (Chapters 2 and 7)

justification The word processing function that lines material up at the right margin. (Chapter 10)

K

Kbit 1 Kbit = 1,024 bits. (Chapter 6)

Kbyte 1 Kbyte = 1,024 bytes. (Chapters 2 and 6)

keyboard An input device made up of keys that allow the input of alphanumeric and punctuation characters. (Chapters 2 and 7)

keypunch machine A machine used to punch holes in a computer card. (Chapter 7)

keypunching The process of placing holes in a punched card. (Chapters 2 and 7)

key-to-disk The process of entering data directly to magnetic disk (Chapter 7)

key-to-tape The process of entering information directly to tape. (Chapter 7)

keyword Words that are part of a computer language's syntax. (Chapter 15)

L

label In a spreadsheet, a combination of letters and

numbers that defines a cell; in programming, a number that refers to a statement in the program; in BASIC, any string constant enclosed in quotation marks. (Chapters 11, 15, and 16)

laser printer A nonimpact printer that uses a laser beam to write dots on a drum coated with light-sensitive material, which transfers ink to paper. (Chapter 7)

leased lines Special high-speed telephone lines that are leased from a telephone company to transmit data between computers. (Chapter 13)

left-justified Text that is lined up with the left margin. (Chapter 10)

letter-quality printer A type of printer that produces output of typewriter quality. (Chapter 7)

light pen An input device that allows the user to select a command by pointing it to a portion of the screen. (Chapters 2 and 7)

line chart A type of analysis graphics that shows relationships by connecting points on the screen. (Chapter 10)

line editor A type of software editor that allows the user to make changes in a document on a line-by-line basis. (Chapter 10)

line numbers Numbers between 1 and 99999 that identify the lines in a BASIC program. (Chapters 15 and 16)

line printer A high-speed printer that can print an entire 132-character line in one motion. (Chapters 2 and 7)

link editor Part of the operating system that links the object code with any necessary library routines. (Chapter 9)

list A column of numbers or strings of characters. (Chapter 17)

local area network (LAN) A network of personal computers within one building. (Chapter 19)

local change A change in a spreadsheet that alters the width of only a designated group of cells. (Chapter 11)

lockbuster package A software package that circumvents the copy protection devices on a disk. (Chapter 20)

logic Step-by-step solution in computer programming. (Chapters 3 and 14)

logical record A piece of information in a block of records stored on tape. (Chapter 8)

loop The repetition of one or more actions in a program. (Chapter 14)

loop termination decision A decision that determines when a program loop ends. (Chapter 14)

low-level languages Languages at the computer's level—such as machine and assembly languages. (Chapters 3 and 15)

M

machine language A computer's machine-specific binary language, which details every computer operation as a series of zeros and ones. (Chapters 3, 14, and 15)

magnetic core *See* core.

magnetic disk A metal or plastic disk coated with ferrous oxide particles onto which information can be stored using a magnetic bit pattern. (Chapters 2, 7, and 8)

magnetic drum storage An early form of secondary storage that used magnetized spots on a rotating drum. (Chapter 6)

magnetic ink character recognition (MICR) An input procedure often used to process checks; a machine reads the characters printed in magnetic ink and processes the check. (Chapter 7)

magnetic (mag) tape Thin Mylar tape coated with ferrous oxide particles; information is recorded in binary form by selective magnetization of the particles. (Chapters 2, 7, and 8)

mail-merge A word processing function that prepares form letters by combining one letter with different names and addresses. (Chapter 10)

mainframe A large, fast computer that requires a special support staff and physical environment. (Chapter 1)

main memory *See* internal memory.

main program In a top-down designed program, the top-level program that manages the modules performing the actual work. (Chapter 15)

maintenance For an existing program, the process of fixing bugs, adding features, altering parts of the program, and performing other activities to keep the program current. (Chapter 15)

management information system (MIS) An integrated user–machine system that provides information to support operations, management, and decision-making functions in an organization. (Chapters 4 and 19)

management support system (MSS) A subsystem of the management information system that provides reports to managers on a scheduled or demand basis. (Chapters 4 and 19)

management system A system in an organization that has as its goal the management of the organization through planning, organizing, and controlling functions. (Chapter 4)

mass storage A form of secondary storage that combines the high-volume capabilities of tape with the speed of disk. (Chapter 8)

master disk A disk that must be used to operate a software package. (Chapter 20)

megabyte (Mbyte) 1,048,576 bytes of storage. (Chapter 2)

memory board A hard plastic board with memory chips that increases the computer's memory. (Chapter 10)

memory card A plastic card or key on which information is stored either magnetically or optically. (Chapter 8)

memory cells Storage locations in a computer's memory. (Chapter 16)

memory dump program A program that circumvents copy protection by dumping the program out of RAM onto a disk. (Chapter 20)

menu A list of commands or requests for data. (Chapter 9)

menu-driven package A software package in which command selection or data entry are accomplished through a menu. (Chapter 9)

microchip A tiny piece of silicon that consists of thousands of electronic elements packed onto an area the size of a pea. (Chapters 2, 6, and 22)

microcomputers *See* personal computers.

micro-floppy A floppy disk that is less than 4 inches in diameter and usually contained in a hard plastic cartridge. (Chapter 8)

microprocessor A CPU on a microchip. (Chapters 2 and 6)

microwave relays Towers that allow the transmission of voice and data over line-of-sight distances using microwaves. (Chapter 13)

mind tool Another name for a computer. (Chapter 1)

minicomputer Computer size between a mainframe and a personal computer. (Chapter 1)

mini-floppy A floppy disk that is $5\frac{1}{4}$ inches in diameter. (Chapter 8)

mnemonics Words that imply their action; often used in assembly language programming. (Chapter 15)

model A simplified version of a system that allows a systems analyst to understand the system's important parts. (Chapters 18 and 19)

model base In a decision support system, a collection of models that are used and solved as needed to arrive at a solution. (Chapter 19)

modem A communications device that modulates computer signals into outgoing audio signals and demodulates incoming audio signals into computer signals. (Chapters 2 and 13)

module A separate program that performs a specific task and shares data with other modules in an integrated software package. (Chapters 11, 15, and 18)

monitor A cathode ray tube output device that shows computer output on a video screen. (Chapters 2 and 7)

monochrome monitor A monitor that displays material in only one color. (Chapters 2 and 7)

mother board The board in the computer that contains the CPU chip and related circuitry. (Chapter 10)

mouse An input device that is about the size of a mouse and is connected to the computer by a long cord; to control the cursor and make selections, the user moves the mouse over a flat surface. (Chapters 2 and 7)

multiple access network A local area network in which all users can transmit at any time, but collision detecting software is necessary to control the transmissions. (Chapter 19)

N

national data bank A data bank that would contain detailed information on everyone in the United States; the concept was proposed but never implemented. (Chapter 21)

natural languages Languages that implement everyday terminology and grammar in communication with a computer. (Chapters 15 and 22)

nested FOR loops A FOR loop within a FOR loop. (Chapter 17)

network Two or more computers connected by a communications system that allows exchange of information between them. (Chapters 4, 13, and 19)

network/hierarchical data base package A data base management package that allows mainframe computers to work with multiple files and users. (Chapter 12)

noise pollution A condition caused by continuous noise; sometimes associated with constant use of computer printers in a small area. (Chapter 21)

nondestructive fetch A process in which data can be retrieved from any memory cell but not destroyed. (Chapters 6 and 16)

nondocument A file that is not a word processing document. (Chapter 10)

nonimpact printer A printer that uses some device other than a hammer to form symbols on paper. (Chapter 7)

nonprocedural language A computer language that does not require the user to develop a logical procedure; a user need only answer questions or make choices from a menu. (Chapters 12 and 15)

nonvolatile memory Memory that does not disappear when computer power is turned off. (Chapter 6)

numerical constant A positive or negative number that is placed in a memory cell. (Chapter 16)

nybbler package A lockbuster package that circumvents copy protection by copying a program 1 bit at a time. (Chapter 20)

O

object-oriented language A language based on the concept of sending messages using icons. (Chapter 15)

object program A machine language program that is actually executed by the computer; also called **object code**. (Chapters 3, 9, and 14)

office information system (OIS) A machine (or machines) and a communications system that help users efficiently handle the job of obtaining, organizing, storing, retrieving, and preparing needed information; also called **office automation**. (Chapters 4 and 19)

off-line Having an input or output device not tied directly into the computer. (Chapter 7)

one-alternative decision In programming, a decision that results in only one action; for example, if a condition is true, action is taken by the program, but if the condition is false, no special action is taken. (Chapter 16)

one-dimensional array A list of numbers or strings. (Chapter 17)

on-line Having an input or output device linked directly to a computer. (Chapters 7 and 13)

on-line processing A user interacting with a mainframe computer to input data. (Chapter 4)

operating system The primary component of systems software; manages the tasks that are accomplished concurrently within a computer. (Chapters 3 and 9)

operator In BASIC, a symbol for one of the five arithmetic operations. (Chapter 16)

optical character recognition (OCR) A process that reads characters in a special font into the computer. (Chapter 7)

optical disk A form of secondary storage that uses lasers; pits in a disk's reflective surface store information. (Chapters 8 and 22)

order processing A business accounting software module that a retail or wholesale operation uses to ensure that customers' orders are filled in a timely manner. (Chapter 11)

originate mode In full-duplex communications, one of two audio frequencies that a computer uses to send information. (Chapter 13)

output The results of data processing displayed or printed for the user. (Chapters 2, 4, and 7)

output crime The theft of processed information for resale, extortion, or the criminal's personal use. (Chapter 20)

overflow area In the indexed sequential access method (ISAM), an area of storage to which new records are added when the original storage area is filled. (Chapter 12)

overlaid window On a monitor screen, the current task is shown in a window that appears on top of the other windows. (Chapter 9)

P

pages Sections of computer memory in secondary storage that are transferred into internal memory as needed. (Chapter 8)

paint packages Graphics packages that are used to develop artistic creations on computer. (Chapter 10)

paper tape A roll of paper with holes punched in it that communicate characters to the computer. (Chapters 2 and 7)

parallel conversion The conversion of one system to another, during which both systems run in parallel before the conversion is completed. (Chapter 4)

parallel form The processing of data 8, 16, or 32 bits at a time. (Chapter 13)

parallel interface An interface that sends all necessary information for a character to the printer at one time. (Chapter 7)

parallel processing A form of computer processing that allows multiple instructions to be processed simultaneously. (Chapter 22)

parallel storage device A secondary storage device on which an entire byte is encoded in one operation. (Chapter 8)

parallel transmission The transmission of data 8, 16, or 32 bits at a time. (Chapter 19)

parity bit An extra bit on magnetic storage devices and in communications that is used for error checking. (Chapter 8)

password A secret combination of letters, numbers, or symbols that, when used with a given user number, ensures that only the user can access a computer. (Chapters 13 and 20)

patch A correction or update to an operating system, usually for personal computers. (Chapter 4)

payroll A list of employees and the amount each is paid by an organization. (Chapter 11)

p-code In the UCSD p-system, an intermediate translation of a source program that is then translated into machine language. (Chapter 9)

peripheral devices Any computer device other than the CPU, the keyboard, or the monitor. (Chapter 2)

personal budgeting (software) package A group of computer programs that includes checkbook accounting and home budget planning. (Chapters 1, 3, and 11)

personal computers Small, one-user computers that are relatively inexpensive to own and do not require a special environment or special knowledge to use them. (Chapter 1)

photomask A procedure similar to the production of a photographic negative used to imprint an electronic circuit on a microchip. (Chapter 6)

physical record The actual amount of magnetic tape that is read by a tape drive before it stops at an interblock gap; made up of one or more logical records. (Chapter 8)

physical security The protection of computer hardware from natural and man-made damage. (Chapter 20)

pie chart A type of analysis graphics that demonstrates how some quantity is proportionally divided; divisions are shown as pieces of a pie. (Chapter 10)

pipelining A process that speeds up computer processing by keeping data and instructions in a pipeline ready to be used, rather than in internal storage. (Chapter 22)

pixel A picture element made up of a dot of light on the monitor screen. (Chapters 7 and 10)

pixel resolution A measure of the number of dots of light on a monitor screen. (Chapter 7)

plotter A nonimpact, hard copy output device with moving pens that draw charts and graphs on various types of paper, vellum, or transparencies. (Chapter 7)

p-machine emulator Machine-specific software that converts p-code into machine language. (Chapter 9)

port An entry line to the computer. (Chapter 20)

port protection device An extra level of computer security that requires a user to have an additional password; it can also camouflage the computer's answering device. (Chapter 20)

post-test loop A program loop in which the loop termination decision comes after the body of the loop. (Chapter 14)

predictive report A report generated by the management support system to predict future needs and occurrences; it is generated using historical data and a forecasting formula. (Chapter 19)

preprocessor A small computer that controls terminals and remote job entry sites, relieving the CPU from this responsibility. (Chapter 9)

presentation graphics Graphics software packages that present data and information in a more understandable or dramatic form than analysis graphics. (Chapter 10)

pre-test loop A program loop in which the loop termination decision comes before the body of the loop. (Chapter 14)

primary key The field or combination of fields that uniquely identifies a particular record among all records on a data base. (Chapter 12)

printer An output device that places words and symbols on paper. (Chapters 2 and 7)

printer driver In word processing, a software package that converts a document's special characters into symbols the printer can use. (Chapter 10)

print spooler A word processing function that allows the printing of text while more text is entered or edited. (Chapter 10)

PRINT zones In BASIC, zones that are 14 spaces wide and control the exact spacing between labels and variables in output. (Chapter 16)

privacy A person's control of personal information about himself or herself. (Chapters 5 and 21)

Privacy Act of 1974 A law that applied principles of privacy to the federal government's record-keeping practices. (Chapter 21)

Privacy Protection Study Commission A federal commission established to study the impact of public and private organizations' data banks and make recommendations regarding their use. (Chapter 21)

problem definition The first step in the systems analysis and design process; both the problem to be analyzed and the system to be designed are defined. (Chapter 18)

procedural language A computer language that requires the programmer to use a logical procedure to perform some task. (Chapters 12 and 15)

procedure Another name for a module in top-down design. (Chapter 15)

procedure symbol In flowcharting, a rectangle containing double vertical lines that designates a procedure that is flowcharted separately. (Chapter 14)

processing The conversion of raw data into usable information. (Chapters 1 and 4)

processing block One or more program statements that handle input, output, and calculation functions. (Chapter 16)

processing/internal memory unit Part of the computer in which data are stored and manipulated. (Chapters 2 and 6)

processing symbol In flowcharting, a rectangle that designates any type of processing operation. (Chapter 14)

program A series of instructions to the computer. (Chapters 1 and 14)

program file A computer file that contains a list of program statements. (Chapter 8)

programmable read only memory (PROM) A read only memory chip that can be programmed by the user. (Chapter 6)

programming The process of writing a series of instructions for the computer to follow in performing a specific task. (Chapters 1, 3, 9, and 14)

proofreading A word processing function that checks a document for spelling errors. (Chapter 10)

proprietary operating systems Personal computer operating systems that run on only one type of computer. (Chapter 9)

protocol The set of rules two computers follow when

communicating with each other. (Chapter 13)

pseudocode A written form of an algorithm that can be easily converted into a computer program. (Chapters 14 and 18)

puck A stylus on a digitizer tablet used in computer-aided design. (Chapter 10)

pull-down menu A menu that uses icons to represent various commands or operations; it appears on the screen as needed. (Chapter 9)

punched card A stiff paper card into which holes are punched to represent symbols. (Chapters 2 and 7)

Q

query language A computer language associated with data base management packages that allows a user to request information. (Chapter 12)

R

radiation Another name for the stream of electrons that generates the picture on a video display terminal. (Chapter 21)

random access memory (RAM) The section of memory that can store the instructions to the computer and the symbols to be manipulated. (Chapters 2 and 6)

read only memory (ROM) The section of memory that is placed in the computer during the manufacturing process; ROM remains intact even after the computer is turned off. (Chapters 2 and 6)

read/write head The part of a disk or tape drive that handles the actual transfer of information to or from the disk or tape. (Chapters 2 and 8)

real time conference A form of teleconferencing in which all participants are logged onto the system at the same time. (Chapter 13)

record A collection of information fields that usually pertains only to one subject (person, place, event, and so on). (Chapters 8 and 12)

record number The physical position of a record in a list. (Chapter 12)

reel-to-reel magnetic tape A form of magnetic tape that runs between two reels; used for secondary storage in minicomputers and mainframes. (Chapter 8)

register A temporary holding place in a computer for a particular instruction, data item, or piece of information. (Chapters 2 and 6)

relational data base package A data base management package that can work with multiple files simultaneously. (Chapter 12)

relational operator In BASIC, one of six arithmetic operators that handle comparisons between constants and variables or between variables. (Chapter 16)

relative address The location of a record in secondary storage relative to all other records. (Chapter 12)

relative copy A copy of a spreadsheet formula that is entered into another cell; the original formula structure is retained, but the formula copy matches the new cell location. (Chapter 11)

remark In BASIC, a program statement that explains a program and its logic to other users. (Chapter 16)

remote job entry (RJE) site A batch job entry site that is separate from the main computer center. (Chapter 9)

repetition block A block of program statements that handles the repetition of one or more actions. (Chapter 16)

replace mode The word processing mode in which current symbols are replaced by new symbols. (Chapter 10)

report generator Part of a data base management package that handles the reporting of information in the order desired by the user. (Chapter 12)

reserved word In BASIC, one of almost 160 words that cannot be used as variable names. (Chapter 16)

resident commands Disk operating system (DOS) commands that reside in internal memory when the computer is in use. (Chapter 9)

resist A chemical that is used to build up each layer of a chip. (Chapter 6)

resolution The quality of the picture on a monitor, as defined by the number of pixels on the screen. (Chapter 10)

reverse Polish notation (RPN) A method of organizing arithmetic operations that places the operators before the values. (Chapter 15)

reverse video Dark letters appearing on a light background on a monitor instead of vice versa. (Chapter 11)

ring network A computer network that links multiple computers in a circle, or ring, with no host computer. (Chapters 13 and 19)

robotics The use of machines rather than humans to perform physical tasks. (Chapters 6, 15, and 22)

robots automated machines. (Chapter 1) (*See also* robotics.)

rotational delay time The time needed for the appropriate sector of a disk to come under the read/write head. (Chapter 8)

rows A series of values placed horizontally in a spreadsheet. (Chapter 11)

RS-232C card A computer device that converts data from parallel form to serial form, and vice versa. (Chapter 13)

RS-232 port The hardware connection on most personal

computers into which the cable from a modem or serial printer is inserted. (Chapter 3)

ruler line The line at the top or bottom of a word processing document that defines the margins and tab stops. (Chapter 10)

S

satellite links The transmission of voice and data over great distances using satellites. (Chapter 13)

scatter diagram A type of analysis graphics that plots the relationships between values on horizontal and vertical axes. (Chapter 10)

scheduled report A regular report generated by the management support system that contains summary results of the data processing operation. (Chapter 19)

schema A plan that shows the relationships among various data base elements. (Chapter 12)

scrolling In word processing and spreadsheets, the up, down, and sideways movements of material on the screen. (Chapter 10)

search and replace In word processing, searching for and replacing a particular character string with another string. (Chapter 10)

secondary keys Fields or combinations of fields that are not necessarily unique to a record but that can be used to find a group of records. (Chapter 12)

secondary storage Storage area outside of the computer; used to hold an overflow of information or to save information when the computer is turned off. (Chapters 2 and 8)

secretary's syndrome A set of symptoms associated with prolonged sitting at a desk, including tight shoulders, tingling arms, stiff neck, tendinitis, and spinal misalignment. (Chapter 21)

sector A pie-shaped division of the tracks on a floppy disk. (Chapter 8)

seek time The time needed for the read/write head to move to the correct track on a disk. (Chapter 8)

self-documenting language A computer language that does not need comments or other documentation. (Chapter 15)

semiconductor A mineral that conducts electricity only under certain conditions. (Chapter 6)

sequential access A form of access in which records are accessed in the order that they were physically stored. (Chapters 2, 8, and 12)

sequential access file A computer file in which the records are accessed in the order that they were entered. (Chapter 8)

sequential access storage device A secondary storage device from which information is read in the order that it was written onto the device. (Chapter 8)

serial form The processing of data 1 bit at a time. (Chapter 13)

serial interface An interface that sends information to a printer 1 bit at a time. (Chapter 7)

serial machines Computers that can process only one instruction at a time. (Chapter 22)

serial port The connection between the RS-232C card in the computer and the modem cable. (Chapter 13)

serial storage device A secondary storage device on which data are stored 1 bit at a time. (Chapter 8)

serial transmission Transmission of data 1 bit at a time. (Chapter 19)

silicon chip *See* microchip.

simplex mode Communications between computers that can only be in one direction. (Chapter 13)

softer software Software that is very easy to use. (Chapter 22)

soft sectoring A disk sectoring plan that depends on the personal computer and the disk operating system in use. (Chapter 8)

software Programs that direct the activity of the computer. (Chapters 1, 2, and 3)

software gap The relative difference between the costs of hardware and software. (Chapter 3)

software package A combination of one or more computer programs and the related documentation. (Chapters 3 and 9)

software piracy The unauthorized copying of software for personal use or financial gain. (Chapters 5 and 20)

sort The process of arranging records in ascending or descending order. (Chapter 12)

sorting an array The process of arranging an array from smallest to largest, or vice versa. (Chapter 17)

source program The original high-level language program written by the computer user; also called **source code**. (Chapters 3, 9, and 14)

special purpose computer A computer designed for only one purpose. (Chapter 1)

special purpose language A computer language that is designed to handle a specific type of task. (Chapter 15)

specific DSS A decision support system that solves a specific problem; usually written in a high-level language. (Chapter 19)

spike *See* voltage surge.

spreadsheet A table with rows and columns of values, labels, and formulas that can be used to make calculations, plan budgets, make forecasts, and ask "what if?" questions about data. (Chapters 3 and 11)

spreadsheet analysis An analysis of data that uses a spreadsheet of values. (Chapters 1, 3, and 11)

stand alone configuration A dedicated word processor with its own storage device and printer. (Chapter 19)

standard floppy A floppy disk that is 8 inches in diameter. (Chapter 8)

star network A computer network with one host computer linked to many smaller computers or terminals. (Chapters 13 and 19)

start bit A bit at the beginning of a character in asynchronous communication that signals the transmission of a character to the computer. (Chapter 13)

stop bit A bit at the end of a character in asynchronous communication that signals the end of the transmission of a character to the computer. (Chapter 13)

stored program The concept suggested by John Von Neumann of storing a program in the computer's internal memory. (Chapter 6)

streaming tape A special, high-density recording tape that streams by the tape head at high speeds; used to backup a hard disk. (Chapter 8)

string constant In BASIC, a string of ASCII symbols or characters that are enclosed in quotation marks. (Chapter 16)

strongly typed language A computer language that requires the declaration of all variables as to their type. (Chapter 15)

structure chart A chart that demonstrates the top-down design of a program, showing the input to each module. (Chapter 18)

structured approach In systems analysis, a set pattern of steps from a logical design of a system to a physical design. (Chapters 4 and 18)

structured decisions Decisions for which policy can be set in advance. (Chapter 19)

structured programming Programming using the processing block, the repetition block, and the decision block, with no transfers into, out of, or between blocks. (Chapter 15)

structured walk-through In the systems analysis and design process, the analyst's presentation to his or her peers of the current status of the project. (Chapter 18)

suboptimized system A system in which at least one subsystem is not integrated with other subsystems, resulting in a less than optimal performance by the overall system. (Chapter 4)

subroutine A section of a program that carries out a specific operation; another name for a module in a top-down designed program. (Chapters 15 and 17)

subscript *See* index.

subsystem A system that is part of a larger system. (Chapter 4)

supervisor program The major unit of the operating system that resides in internal memory to manage the loading of applications programs and other parts of the operating system. (Chapter 9)

support staff A group of persons in a mainframe computer center who answer users' questions about the available software. (Chapter 9)

surge protector A device that protects a computer's hardware and memory from a voltage surge. (Chapter 20)

symbol processor A computer that manipulates symbols as well as numbers; another name for a computer. (Chapter 10)

synchronous communication A form of communication between two computers that requires them to process data at the same rate. (Chapter 13)

syntactical (grammatical) form In programming, the syntax that must be followed in the writing of a program. (Chapter 14)

syntax error In a computer program, an error in the syntax or vocabulary of a program. (Chapter 16)

system A group of elements organized for the purpose of achieving a particular goal. (Chapters 2, 4, and 18)

system bus A communications system that allows the transfer of instructions, data, and control commands among the control unit, the arithmetic-logic unit, and the internal memory unit. (Chapter 6)

system command In BASIC, a command that results in some action by a program. (Chapter 16)

system design The fourth step in the systems analysis and design process in which the analyst develops a high-level design of the new system that includes its actual parts. (Chapter 18)

system interrupt An operating system command that temporarily interrupts the current job so that another job can be executed. (Chapter 9)

system operator (sysop) A person who runs an electronic bulletin board. (Chapter 13)

systems analysis and design The process of developing a system design to meet a new need or to solve a problem in an existing system. (Chapters 4 and 18)

systems analyst A person who carries out the systems analysis and design process. (Chapters 4 and 18)

systems approach An approach to problem solving that views problems or activities as systems that must be managed. (Chapter 4)

systems flowchart A special flowchart that demonstrates the flows of information and control in an existing system. (Chapter 18)

systems programmers Programmers who maintain and update mainframe operating systems. (Chapter 4)

systems software The computer programming that controls the operations of utility software and applications software. (Chapter 3)

T

table A group of elements organized into rows and columns. (Chapter 17)

tape *See* magnetic tape.

tape drive An electronic device with a read/write head that transfers information to and from magnetic tape. (Chapters 2, 7, and 8)

tax planning and preparation package A software package that keeps track of tax records throughout the year and determines the effects of different financial decisions. (Chapter 11)

telecommunications The combination of a computer with a communications link, a modem, and appropriate communications software to communicate with others. (Chapters 13 and 22)

telecommunications (software) package A group of programs that allows a personal computer user to communicate with other users, computers, and data bases. (Chapters 1, 3, and 13)

telecommuting Working at home using either a personal computer or a terminal linked to a mainframe. (Chapters 5 and 13)

teleconferencing Live conferences between widely dispersed parties using direct broadcast satellites. (Chapter 22)

teletype (TTY) An early form of computer terminal that used paper output. (Chapter 13)

template A skeleton spreadsheet for a particular application that does not include the data. (Chapter 11)

temporary variable A variable that is used to store a value temporarily. (Chapter 17)

terminal The combination of keyboard and video screen. (Chapter 1)

terminal symbol In flowcharting, an oval that starts and ends all flowcharts. (Chapter 14)

test data Data that are used in hand calculations to determine in advance the results expected from a program. (Chapter 14)

text editing The word processing function that allows the change, insertion, or deletion of existing text. (Chapter 10)

thermal printer A nonimpact printer that uses a matrix of heated wires to form symbols on special paper. (Chapter 7)

throughput crime A computer crime that involves modifying software so that the data it processes are manipulated differently from the original intent. (Chapter 20)

tiled window A form of windowing that shows each window completely. (Chapter 9)

time-sharing system A computer system that gives many terminals equal slices of CPU time to execute their programs. (Chapter 9)

time-slice A small fraction of a computer's total execution time that is allocated to a terminal in a time-sharing system. (Chapter 9)

token A special bit pattern used in a token sharing local area network to determine the user that can transmit information. (Chapter 19)

token sharing network A local area network in which a bit pattern, called a token, determines which user on the network can send information. (Chapter 19)

top-down approach *See* structured approach.

top-down design An approach to writing a structured program in which the program is divided into blocks or modules that are written individually and then combined into the final program. (Chapter 15)

touch pad An input device with which the user may enter information through a pad that is sensitive to pressure. (Chapters 2 and 7)

touch screen An input device; the user simply touches part of the monitor screen to make selections. (Chapters 2 and 7)

tracks Parallel magnetic lines that run the length of magnetic tape on which information is stored; also, concentric regions on a magnetic disk. (Chapters 2 and 8)

trailer record A special data record that signals the end of data to an INPUT loop. (Chapter 17)

transactional data Data that are created in a transaction that requires a consumer to reveal his or her identity. (Chapter 21)

transaction screen A screen in a personal budgeting package that prompts the user to enter actual income and expenses. (Chapter 11)

transactions processing The conversion of monetary transactions into an understandable summary form. (Chapter 4)

transfer The return to the beginning of a loop that repeats an action. (Chapter 14)

transistors Solid state elements on a microchip that carry out the computer's control and logic operations. (Chapters 2, 6, and 22)

transmission time The actual time needed to transfer data to or from a disk. (Chapter 8)

Trojan horse program A computer program that sabotages another program or modifies it to perform illegal activities. (Chapter 20)

turtle A graphics character used in the LOGO computer language. (Chapters 3 and 15)

tutorial disk A floppy disk provided with personal computer software that demonstrates the use of the software. (Chapter 9)

two-alternative decision In programming, a decision that results in one of two possible actions; one action is taken by the program if a certain condition is true, and another action is taken if that condition is false. (Chapter 16)

two-dimensional array A table of numbers or strings. (Chapter 17)

U

unblocked record A physical record that corresponds to one logical record. (Chapter 8)

unstructured decisions Decisions for which policy cannot be set in advance. (Chapter 19)

upload Shifting software or data from a personal computer to a central mainframe computer or minicomputer. (Chapter 13)

user-defined function A specific numerical or string operation in BASIC that is defined by the user. (Chapter 17)

user friendly Easy to use. (Chapter 9)

user number A number or combination of letters and numbers that identifies a computer user for accounting purposes. (Chapters 13 and 20)

user prompt In BASIC, a string constant that is included in the INPUT statement to prompt the user to enter needed data. (Chapter 16)

user's manual A set of directions for the use of software packages. (Chapter 3)

utility software Software that controls a computer's daily housekeeping operations. (Chapters 3 and 9)

V

value A positive or negative number that may have a decimal. (Chapter 11)

variable In programming, the name for a memory cell. (Chapters 15 and 16)

variable expenses Expenses that fluctuate from month to month. (Chapter 11)

variable length records Records that have only the number of positions actually needed in each field. (Chapter 8)

variable length word A computer word that combines as many bytes as necessary to represent a symbol. (Chapter 6)

verification The process of comparing information on a punched card, tape, or disk with the correct information. (Chapter 7)

video disk A read only form of secondary storage, usually a laser or optical disk. (Chapters 2 and 8)

video display terminal (VDT) Any personal computer or terminal tied into a mainframe that uses a cathode ray tube (CRT) to input data and display output. (Chapters 5 and 21)

video page The amount of word processing text that can actually be seen on the screen at one time. (Chapter 10)

videotex The process of shopping, banking, or managing stocks and bonds from home using a computer and a communications link. (Chapters 13 and 22)

virtual memory The use of disk drives to give the appearance of increased internal memory. (Chapters 8 and 9)

virtual memory controller (VMC) Software that determines if needed information is in internal memory or on secondary storage. (Chapter 8)

voice input A form of input to computers that uses the spoken word to enter data and instructions; also called **voice recognition**. (Chapters 3, 7, and 22)

volatile memory Computer memory that only exists while the computer has power or the user is connected to a mainframe. (Chapters 2 and 6)

voltage surge A surge in electricity that can destroy a computer's hardware or memory. (Chapter 20)

W

wand An input device that reads bar codes. (Chapter 7)

weakly typed language A computer language that does not require the declaration of variables as to their type. (Chapter 15)

WHILE loop In BASIC, a pre-test loop that continues as long as (while) some condition is true. (Chapter 17)

wildcard search In word processing, a search for a word when only part of the word is known. (Chapter 10)

window A section of the monitor screen that is set aside by the software package to display a specific portion of output. (Chapters 9 and 11)

word processing Ability to manipulate letters, digits, and punctuation marks to compose letters, papers, and documents on a personal computer. (Chapters 1, 3, and 10)

word processing software (package) A program designed to enter and edit text, which is then formatted and printed. (Chapters 3 and 10)

word wrap The word processing function that moves to the next line words that fall outside the right margin. (Chapter 10)

work station A terminal linked to a mainframe or minicomputer or a personal computer that allows a worker to process information. (Chapter 4)

write-protect notch A notch in the vinyl cover of a floppy disk that, when covered, prevents the user from writing on the disk. (Chapter 8)

Photo and Illustration Credits

Cover: *(top left)* HBJ Collection; *(top right)* Genealogical Library, Church of Jesus Christ of Latter-Day Saints; *(bottom left)* M.I.T. LOGO Laboratory; *(bottom right)* Courtesy of International Business Machines Corporation.

Block 1

2 HBJ Collection

Chapter 1

4 Photophile. **6** Evans and Sutherland. **8** *(both)* Courtesy of International Business Machines Corporation. **9** *(top left, bottom)* Sperry-Univac, a division of Sperry Corporation; *(top right)* Courtesy of Wang Laboratories, Inc. **10** *(left)* Atlantic Richfield Company; *(right)* National Medical Enterprises. **11** From the MGM release "2001: A Space Odyssey" © 1968 Metro-Goldwyn-Mayer Inc. **12** Copyright 1982 Time Inc. All rights reserved. Reprinted by permission from TIME. **13** *(top left)* Burlington Industries; *(top right)* General Motors; *(bottom left)* Ford Motor Co.; *(bottom right)* National Center for Atmospheric Research/National Science Foundation. **14** *(top left)* Standard Oil of Indiana; *(top right)* Photo courtesy of Hewlett-Packard Co.; *(bottom)* Wright State University, Dayton, Ohio. **15** *(left)* Atari, Inc.; *(right)* AT&T, Bell Laboratories. **16** *(left)* Control Data Corporation; *(right)* Courtesy of International Business Machines Corporation. **19** *(left)* FBS; *(right)* Courtesy of Apple Computer, Inc.

Chapter 2

22 HBJ Collection. **25** *(top left)* Iowa State University; *(top right, bottom)* Courtesy of International Business Machines Corporation. **26** Reprinted by permission of Intel Corporation © 1985. **27** *(top)* Control Data Corporation; *(bottom left, right)* Atari, Inc. **28** Courtesy of International Business Machines Corporation. **29** Photo reproduced by permission of Zilog © 1981. **30** *(left, right)* Courtesy of International Business Machines Corporation; *(center)* Sperry Corporation, Computer Systems. **32** Control Data Corporation. **33** *(top left)* Sperry Corporation, Computer Systems; *(top right)* Tallgrass Technologies; *(bottom)* Photo courtesy of 3M. **34** Radio Shack, a division of Tandy Corporation. **35** *(top)* Courtesy of International Business Machines Corporation; *(bottom)* Hayes Microcomputer Products, Inc. **36** CyberLYNX. **41** Patrick G. McKeown.

Chapter 3

44 Photophile. **48** Lotus Development Corporation. **49** M.I.T. **51** Sperry Corporation, Computer Systems. **52** Farmplan. **53** *(left)* ISSCO; *(right)* Courtesy of Wang Laboratories, Inc. **55** *(left, right)* Billy Dunbar; *(center)* Atari, Inc. **56** Control Data Corporation. **57** Sallie E. Dashiell. **58** *(left)* Atari, Inc.; *(right)* Spinnaker. **59** Courtesy of Lotus Development Corporation. **60** *(left)* Courtesy of Apple Computer, Inc.; *(right)* Pelham and Friends Photography, Inc. **62** *(left)* CompuServe; *(right)* Computerland, Inc. **63** U.S. Navy.

Chapter 4

68 Photophile. **70** Sperry Corporation, Computer Systems. **71** Clarkson University. **73** Motorola Semiconductor Product Sector. **75** Charlene Gaygan, Photographer. **77** *(top left)* NCR Corporation; *(top right)* Courtesy of Bell & Howell Company; *(bottom)* AT&T. **78** *(both)* University of Georgia. **80** *(left)* NCR

Corporation; *(right)* Sperry Corporation, Computer Systems. **81** Sperry Corporation, Computer Systems. **85** *(both)* Sperry Corporation, Computer Systems. **86** *(both)* Merck & Co. **88** *(top)* Northrop Corporation; *(bottom)* Courtesy of International Business Machines Corporation. **89** Photo courtesy of Hewlett-Packard Co.

Chapter 5

92 HBJ Collection. **95** *(both)* Atari, Inc. **96** *(left)* NCR Corporation; *(right)* Bloodstock Research Information Services, Inc. **97** Ford Motor Co. **98** Dartmouth College News Service. **99** *(left)* National Semiconductor; *(right)* Bank of America. **100** FBI **103** *(top)* Microframe, Inc.; *(bottom)* From the UA release "WarGames" © 1983 United Artists Corporation. **104** Flagler Greyhound Track. **105** Courtesy of International Business Machines Corporation. **106** Comsell. **107** *(top)* Control Data Corporation; *(bottom)* Computerland, Inc. **108** Interface Group, Inc.

Block 2

110 AT&T

Chapter 6

112 AT&T. **115** Photo courtesy of Hewlett-Packard Co. **116** Photo reproduced by permission of Zilog. **117** Courtesy of Apple Computer, Inc. **120** John Von Neumann Institute for Advanced Studies, Princeton, NJ. **121** Quadram Corporation. **122** Amdahl. **124** Courtesy of Texas Instruments, Inc. **125** Reprinted by permission of Intel Corporation © 1985. **128** *(all)* J.M. Waltz. **129** *(left)* Fidelity International, Inc.; *(right)* Ford Motor Co. **130** Courtesy of Motorola Semiconductor Products. **131** Courtesy of Motorola Semiconductor Products. **132** National Semiconductor. **133** *(all)* Reprinted by permission of Intel Corporation © 1985. **134** *(top, left center, right center)* National Semiconductor; *(bottom)* Sperry Corporation, Computer Systems. **135** Courtesy of Texas Instruments, Inc. **136** Sperry Corporation, Computer Systems. **138** Lucasfilm Ltd. © 1985. All rights reserved.

Chapter 7

140 Photophile. **143** Control Data Corporation. **144** I.R.S. **146** *(left)* MSI Data Corporation; *(right)* Courtesy of Burroughs Corporation. **148** *(left)* Courtesy of Apple Computer, Inc.; *(right)* © Susan Holtz. **151** Tymshare. **152** Photo courtesy of Hewlett-Packard Co. **153** *(left)* Houston Instruments; *(right)* FMC Corporation. **154** Speech Command System. **155** NASA **156** TeleVideo Systems, Inc. **157** Princeton Graphics System. **158** *(left)* Sperry Corporation, Computer Systems; *(right)* Photo supplied courtesy of Epson America. **162** *(left)* Brother International; *(right)* Microframe, Inc. **163** *(both)* Houston Instruments.

Chapter 8

166 © Tom Tracy, Photophile. **169** Verbatim Corporation. **170** *(both)* Genealogical Library, Church of Jesus Christ of Latter-Day Saints. **173** *(both)* Photo courtesy of Hewlett-Packard Co. **176** *(left)* Micro-Design; *(right)* Photo courtesy Seagate Technology. **178** *(top)* Photo courtesy of Memorex, a Burroughs Corporation; *(bottom)* Photo courtesy of Inmac. **182** Verbatim Corporation. **185** *(left)* Courtesy of Apple Computer, Inc.; *(right)* Photo courtesy of Seagate Technology. **186** Photo courtesy of 3M. **189** *(top)* Photo courtesy of 3M; *(bottom)* Videodisc Publishing, Inc. Photo: L.M. Wasserstein.

Block 3

192 Sperry-Univac, a division of Sperry Corporation

Chapter 9

194 © Arthur Meyerson, Monsanto. **196** Courtesy of Apple Computer, Inc. **197** Informatics. **198** *(left)* Sperry Corporation, Computer Systems; *(right)* Patrick G. McKeown. **201** MSA. **202** Pelham and Friends Photography, Inc. **203** Paladin Software Corporation. **205** Courtesy of Burroughs Corporation. **212** Digital Research. **213** Reprinted by permission of Intel Corporation © 1985. **216** *(top)* Radio Shack, a division of Tandy Corporation; *(bottom)* Courtesy of Apple Computer, Inc. **218** *(left)* Courtesy of Ashton-Tate; *(right)* Courtesy of Apple Computer, Inc.

Chapter 10

220 Robert Abel & Associates. **222** *(left)* SSI Software; *(right)* MicroPro International Corporation. **224** HBJ Collection. **226** Gannett Co., Inc. **228** Photo courtesy of Hewlett-Packard Co. **230** Radio Shack, a division of Tandy Corporation. **234** *(left)* Genigraphics; *(right)* National Semiconductor. **236** Graphic Communications Inc. **237** *(top, center)* Ford Motor Co.; *(bottom)* Mindset Corporation. **238** Courtesy of Lotus Development Corporation. **239** *(top)* Genigraphics; *(bottom left)* HBJ Collection; *(bottom right)* ISSCO. **240** *(top)* Polaroid; *(bottom)* Houston Instruments. **241** Evans and Sutherland. **244** Courtesy of Apple Computer, Inc.

Chapter 11

260 © Tom Tracy, Photophile. **262** Genealogical Library, Church of Jesus Christ of Latter-Day Saints. **263** Egghead Software. **264** Photo courtesy of Hewlett-Packard Co. **268** Courtesy of Apple Computer, Inc. **269** *(both)* Decision Resources. **270** *(both)* Ashton-Tate. **272** Courtesy of Lotus Development Corporation. **273** Paladin Software. **274** Informatics. **276** Microsoft Corporation. **278** Farm Industry News.

Chapter 12

294 American Airlines. **296** Logicon. **297** Courtesy of Apple Computer, Inc. **300** Bloodstock Research Information Services, Inc. **303** *(both)* Courtesy of Apple Computer, Inc. **306** International Aviation Development Corporation. **307** Atlantic Richfield Co. **308** *(left, center)* Genealogical Library, Church of Jesus Christ of Latter-Day Saints; *(right)* Courtesy of International Business Machines Corporation. **309** Bloodstock Research Information Services, Inc. **310** *(both)* National Medical Enterprises. **311** Photo courtesy of Hewlett-Packard Co. **313** New York Stock Exchange. **315** New York Mets. **320** Photo courtesy of Intelligent Systems Corporation. Photo by Rob Wheless Studio, Inc.

Chapter 13

324 AT&T. **326** *(both)* AT&T, Bell Laboratories. **328** *(left)* Photo courtesy of 3M; *(right)* CompuServe. **330** Bank of America. **331** CompUcard. **332** CompuServe. **333** Hayes Microcomputer Products, Inc. **335** AT&T, Bell Laboratories. **336** *(all)* Dialog Information Services. **337** The photographs are the property of the Federal Express Corporation and are reprinted with its permission. All rights reserved. **339** *(all)* Viewdata Corporation of America, Inc. **340** Courtesy of Zenith Electronics Corporation. **345** Bloodstock Research Information Services, Inc. **346** M/A-Com, Inc., © 1982.

Block 4

354 Zenith Electronics

Chapter 14

356 Courtesy of Apple Computer, Inc. **358** U.S. Department of Education, David C. Snyder. **363** Radio Shack, a division of Tandy Corporation. **372** © Sidney Harris. **377** Courtesy of Apple Computer, Inc.

Chapter 15

387 Heath Company. **393** Atlantic Richfield Company. **395** Courtesy of International Business Machines Corporation. **399** Dartmouth College News Service. **401** Patrick G. McKeown. **402** Courtesy of Apple Computer, Inc. **404** M.I.T. **406** General Instrument Corporation. **408** *(top)* Courtesy of Ametek-Straza; *(bottom)* Heath Company. **409** *(top)* Veterans Administration; *(bottom left)* Memorial Medical Center of Long Beach, CA: *(bottom right)* Visions Research Group. **410** *(top)* Hitachi; *(bottom)* Hayes Microcomputer Products, Inc. **411** *(top)* Martin Marietta; *(bottom)* NASA. **413** Human Edge Software Corporation.

Chapter 16

416 M.I.T. LOGO Laboratory. **419** Microsoft Corporation. **425** © 1984 Stuart Bratesman. **438** Patrick G. McKeown.

Chapter 17

440 © Susan Holtz. **444** © Susan Holtz. **448** Patrick G. McKeown. **456** John Chase. **458** Hayes Microcomputer Products, Inc. **459** By permission © News America Syndicate, 1985. **463** Courtesy of International Business Machines Corporation. **464** Commodore International, Ltd. **465** *(both)* HBJ Collection. **467** Kaypro Corporation. **469** Courtesy of Apple Computer, Inc. **470** Courtesy of Tandy Corporation. **471** *(left)* Courtesy Texas Instruments, Inc.; *(right)* ITT Corporation. **472** *(left)* Compaq; *(right)* Courtesy of Tandy Corporation.

Block 5

476 Courtesy of International Business Machines Corporation.

Chapter 18

478 © Tom Tracy, Photophile. **482** © Sidney Harris. **485** Avon Products Inc. **495** Merck & Co. **498** Northrop Corporation. **501** Armstrong Rubber. **502** *(left)* Courtesy of International Business Machines Corporation; *(right)* Photo courtesy of Hewlett-Packard Co. **505** Courtesy of Apple Computer, Inc.

Chapter 19

508 Perkin-Elmer. **513** *(top)* Courtesy of Bell & Howell Company; *(bottom)* Courtesy of Burroughs Corporation. **515** International Aviation Development Corporation. **517** Decision Resources. **520** Courtesy of Bell & Howell Company. **522** Courtesy of Bell & Howell Company. **523** Courtesy of Wang Laboratories, Inc. **524** Sperry Corporation, Computer Systems. **525** Photo courtesy of 3M. **529** AT&T. **530** *(top)* Tymnet, Inc.; *(bottom)* General Electric Information Services.

Block 6

534 HBJ Collection

Chapter 20

536 Photo Researchers, Inc. **540** Lane Stewart/*Sports Illustrated.* **544** Eyedentify, Inc. **546** Photo courtesy of Inmac. **548** Photo courtesy of Inmac. **550** © Sidney Harris. **552** Photo courtesy of Inmac.

Chapter 21

554 Photo courtesy of Sunar-Hauserman, Inc. **556** *(left)* Courtesy of International Business Machines Corporation; *(right)* Courtesy of Bell & Howell Company. **558** I.R.S. **562** © Susan Holtz. **564** *(left)* NCR Corporation; *(right)* United Airlines. **566** *(left)* American Hoechst Corporation © Dave Hawkins; *(right)* Intelligent Systems Corporation. **568** *(left)* Photo supplied courtesy of Epson America; *(right)* TeleVideo Systems, Inc. **569** Photo courtesy of Sunar-Hauserman, Inc. **572** Robert Abel & Associates. **573** *(top)* Digital Scene Simulation by Digital Productions, Los Angeles, CA, USA. © 1984. All rights reserved.; *(bottom)* Bo Gehring Associates. **574** *(top)* Lucasfilm, Ltd. © 1983; *(center, bottom)* Los Alamos National Laboratory. **575** *(top, left center)* Genigraphics; *(right center, bottom)* Courtesy of International Business Machines Corporation. **576** *(top)* Photos by Harry Monahan. Courtesy of Mission San Juan Capistrano; *(bottom)* Mark Richards. **577** *(top left)* Castleton State College; *(top right)* Waveform Corporation; *(bottom)* Patte Wood, Center for Computer Research in Music and Acoustics, Stanford University.

Chapter 22

578 © Tom Tracy, Photophile. **580** *(left)* Jet Propulsion Laboratory, California Institute of Technology; *(right)* NASA. **581** Huntington Medical Research Institute. **582** *(top)* Photo courtesy of Mentor Graphics; *(bottom)* ITT Corporation. **583** *(top)* Hypres, Inc.; *(bottom)* Blue Cross and Blue Shield of Maryland. **584** *(both)* National Education Corporation. **586** Courtesy of Spectragraphics Corporation, San Diego. **587** Radio Shack, a division of Tandy Corporation. **588** Lear Siegler Corporation. **591** Viewdata Corporation of America, Inc. **594** Bank of America Managistics. **595** Intelligent Systems Corporation. **597** *(top)* Serviceland; *(bottom)* Amdahl. **599** *(top)* Bloodstock Research Information Services, Inc.; *(bottom)* Serviceland. **598** Egghead Software. **600** National Semiconductor.

INDEX

D

E

F

J

K

L

M

T

U

V

W

B6
C7
D8
E9
F0
G1
H2
I3
J4

BASIC Reserved Words

Reserved words include all BASIC commands, statements, function names, and operator names. Reserved words cannot be used as variable names in BASIC statements.

ABS
AND
ASC
ATN
AUTO
BEEP
BLOAD
BSAVE
CALL
CDBL
CHAIN
CHR$
CINT
CIRCLE
CLEAR
CLOSE
CLS
COLOR
COM
COMMON
CONT
COS
CSNG
CSRLIN
CVD
CVI
CVS
DATA
DATE$
DEF
DEFDBL
DEFINT
DEFSNG
DEFSTR
DELETE
DIM
DRAW
EDIT
ELSE
END
EOF
EQV
ERASE
ERL
ERR
ERROR
EXP
FIELD
FILES
FIX
FNxxxxxx
FOR
FRE
GET
GOSUB
GOTO
HEX$
IF
IMP
INKEY$
INP
INPUT
INPUT#
INPUT$
INSTR
INT
KEY
KILL
LCOPY
LEFT$
LEN
LET
LINE
LIST
LLIST
LOAD
LOC
LOCATE
LOF
LOG
LPOS
LPRINT
LSET
MERGE
MID$
MKI$
MKD$
MKS$
MOD
MOTOR
NAME
NEW
NEXT
NOT
OCT$
OFF
ON
OPEN
OPTION
OR
OUT
PAINT
PEEK
PEN
PLAY
POINT
POKE
POS
PRESET
PRINT
PRINT#
PSET
PUT
RANDOMIZE
READ
REM
RENUM
RESET
RESTORE
RESUME
RETURN
RIGHT$
RND
RSET
RUN
SAVE
SCREEN
SGN
SIN
SOUND
SPACE$
SPC(
SQR
STEP
STICK
STOP
STR$
STRIG
STRING$
SWAP
SYSTEM
TAB(
TAN
THEN
TIME$
TO
TROFF
TRON
USING
USR
VAL
VARPTR
WAIT
WEND
WHILE
WIDTH
WRITE
WRITE#
XOR

Conversion of IBM PC Keys to Apple Keys

IBM Key	Corresponding Apple Key(s)
Ins	Control-o
Del	Delete
Home	Control-t
End	Control-e
F1	Control-f
F3	Control-v
F4	Control-p
F5	Control-s
F10	Control-h